D1453966

A Reader
in Cultural
Anthropology

A Reader in Cultural Anthropology

CARLETON S. COON

Professor of Anthropology
Harvard University

ROBERT E. KRIEGER PUBLISHING COMPANY
HUNTINGTON, NEW YORK
1977

Original Edition 1967
Reprint 1977, with corrections, deletions, and new material

Printed and Published by
ROBERT E. KRIEGER PUBLISHING CO., INC.
645 NEW YORK AVENUE
HUNTINGTON, NEW YORK 11743

Printed in the United States of America

Library of Congress Cataloging in Publication Data

Coon, Carleton Stevens, 1904- ed.
  A reader in cultural anthropology.

  Reprint of the 1967 ed. published by H. Holt, New York.
  Includes bibliographical references and index.
  1. Anthropology—Addresses, essays, lectures.   I. Title.
GN8.C6   1976   301.2   76-78
ISBN 0-88275-394-0

Contents

Preface

1. Why a New Reader?

A half century ago, when I was a student, about fifty Harvard undergraduates and twenty-odd Radcliffe girls took Anthropology I, in separate classes. Between two and twenty undergraduates and graduate students signed on for middle group and advanced courses. We were taught by lectures, demonstrations, and individual conferences, as well as by reading assignments.

The latter presented no problem. Our Museum library shelved enough copies of whatever books and professional journals our professors chose to assign, with at least three or four copies each, and no one stole the books, defaced them with ink, or cut out pages, as they do today. What we read represented many different schools of interpretation and points of view, as well as simple description; we were not indoctrinated or slanted in any way.

Even thirty years ago, so popular had Anthropology become in many colleges, and courses so crowded, that it had become impossible to assign original sources. In an attempt to fill this gap, I produced *A Reader in General Anthropology*, a sourcebook rather than a text. As far as I know it was the first of its kind, except for one reader in Physical Anthropology, a subject which would be out of place here. To correct a technical inaccuracy implied in the original title, I am calling the present edition *A Reader in Cultural Anthropology*, which it has always been.

What was once the Appendix is now the Introduction, considerably rewritten to include more recent ideas. The body of the text remains much the same because new eye-witness accounts are becoming scarcer each decade, and few old ones previously overlooked are being rescued from mildewed diaries. Anything that is both new and pertinent has been added when possible, in order to continue to allow students a freedom of choice and the precious privilege of keeping open minds.

2. The Study of Whole Cultures.

The subject matter of anthropology is enormous. It includes the study of man and all his works, in time and space. Until recently, however, few anthropologists aspired to claim so vast a territory. Most were content, in time, to deal with the remains of peoples who had left no written records, and in space, to concern themselves with the peoples outside the pale of Western European and American society. That pale, however, was very mobile. Its exact location depended on the interests of the individual scholar.

This concentration on primitive* cultures, whatever its motivation, had one important effect. Whereas no one person could hope to learn all the essentials of modern European or American law, medicine, economics, government, manufacturing techniques, etc., in a lifetime, it was possible for him to obtain a reasonable grasp of all departments of a simpler system. He could study a given culture as a whole. Once he could see a primitive culture from this point of view, he

---

*The adjective "Primitive," when applied to peoples, refers specifically to technology and literacy, rather than to sophistication. It is not a pejorative label. Its place in the vocabulary of Anthropology should be restored and maintained, if only for the sake of clarity.

might understand the interrelation of its component elements, and be able to predict events.

This special point of view, this preoccupation with whole societies, has given workers in other fields who had tried to study the complexities of modern societies piecemeal the tools with which to treat them as entire units, comparable to primitive communities. The results of these pioneers' efforts may already be seen in city planning, and in efforts at conservation.

3. Eyewitness Accounts.

The decision to study whole cultures rather than such topics as "primitive economics" or "primitive religion"—ethnography rather than ethnology—gives us a great advantage in our choice of material. Much more has been written about the peoples of the world in terms of whole cultures than by topics. This is particularly true of the raw material of ethnography, the stuff from which the arm-chair writers derive their principles. I propose to give the beginning student this raw material, filtered through as few eyes and as few "conceptual schemes" as possible. I believe that direct, personal observation and reporting of fact, who did what to whom, when, where, and in what fashion, as written down by the man who was there and saw and heard and smelled it happen (e.g., Egan's Indian Grasshopper hunt in Chapter 2 and Ibn Fadhlan in Chapter 8), is many times as valuable as a general statement in Y's book, when Y got his material from the work of Z. In choosing selections, I followed two guiding principles—to give preference to the passages based on eye-witness testimony, and to keep my comments to a minimum, leaving as much as possible of the interpretation to the student himself.

The reader will see that many of the passages selected were not written by professional anthropologists. Had we relied entirely on their product, our material would have been drawn only from works written in the last century. Luckily good observers have existed at all times and in many countries. Aristotle, Ibn Fadhlan, Huien Tsiang, and Bernal Diaz could hardly have given better eyewitness accounts had they been trained by any great teacher of modern times. The inclusion of such sources has the additional advantage that through them we see the reactions of men reared not only in different periods, but in civilizations wholly separate from our own. To see how a learned and intelligent Arab or Chinese reacted to peoples of other cultures is an interesting exercise, and one which adds depth and perspective to our viewpoint.

4. Concerning Levels of Complexity

This use of alien sources serves further to remind us that we professional anthropologists are supposed to be scientists, and thereby objective. Objective scientists follow the quantitative method, working from relatively simple to relatively complex. It has worked in other fields, and is well adapted to our own. The essence of the quantitative approach to cultural anthropology lies in the thesis that the main streams of human culture must have proceeded from simpler to more complex. The evidence of archaeology and of history support what we know of life in general. It must be equally apparent that the living cultures of the world vary in degrees of complexity, and that whole cultures can be listed and studied with greatest profit on the basis of such a progressive scheme.

This scheme is the normal order of presentation employed by teachers in all other subjects which follow the scientific method. Every teacher of mathematics, physics, chemistry, and biology knows that it is easier to make students understand a complex system if they have been led to it gradually through the study of simpler related forms. In order to give students of anthropology the benefits of this same pedagogical method I have arranged the text which follows in a progressive scheme, of six levels of increasing cultural complexity. In order to explain this scheme I have written an introduction, which is offered to the attention of both teacher and students to use as they may see fit. It is in effect a condensed and simplified account of the dynamics of human relations, as exemplified by the selections which follow it.

The choice of these passages was limited by two factors—the size of the book and my desire to represent each cultural level adequately. I had to sacrifice a complete geographical coverage—some favorite anthropological areas are not represented. I had to sacrifice an equal treatment of hunters, fishermen, farmers, herdsmen, etc., and I even had to omit some of the best available authors. The trouble was that much of the best material in anthropological literature is lumped around a middle zone of cultural complexity. I made these sacrifices in order to proceed from the simple to the complex, in the perhaps mistaken belief that in this way I could help students to get some idea of the essential unity of mankind, and of *what makes things tick*.

5. Acknowledgements

No names need be added to those listed in the first edition, except for that of my patient publisher, David Boynton. Of the previous roster, at least seven are now dead.

West Gloucester, Mass.   Carleton S. Coon
August 25, 1974.

Introduction

1. Whole Cultures, Natural Groups, and Scientific Procedure.

In the preface I promised to explain what is meant by levels of cultural complexity. This is no simple task. One can no more explain such a concept without stating the premises on which it is based than a railroad man can talk about a caboose without reference to the rest of the train and the tracks.

One of these premises is, that the units of human society which can be studied with greatest profit are the groups of individuals who participate in whole cultures, whether these cultures constitute the way of life of a few hundred chilly hunters, or that of millions of comfortable Roman citizens. In any one of the simpler societies which have been described, a band may consist of let us say ten families of, on the average, five persons each, thus making a total of fifty persons. If fifty persons make up the total number of individuals who normally see one another, everyone knows everyone else. The group has a stability of its own, depending on the mutual relations of the human units in it. From time to time the group will be shaken by a crisis, as when the best hunter dies, but it recovers. Another man becomes best hunter in his place. Such an aggregation of human beings is what some anthropologists and other social scientists call a face-to-face, or *natural,* group.

Among people whose lives are made more complicated by the possession of a surplus of food, better tools, or other advantages, the "whole culture" group will contain more persons, perhaps as many as three hundred. Here, although everyone may still know everyone else, subdivisions arise by the nature of the things that the persons have to do, and by the nearness or distance of the persons from one another. The villages may have a single superior chief, because only through united effort in the springtime can they handle the big nets needed to catch the fish on which they all live through the winter. Other activities, such as the collection of acorns in the fall, make it necessary for the villagers to stay in their own territories part of the year. Thus you will find these natural groups combined into larger units.

If we carry this method over into more complicated societies we reach, before long, a frontier. It is the borderline between the situation in which everyone knows nearly everyone else whom he is likely to see, and must take special steps when a stranger appears—and that in which a person may go about his business every day, passing strangers on the street without greeting and without fear.

Here one may say that the concept of natural groups breaks down. To a certain extent this is true. Everyone you meet, everyone with whom you have any dealings at all, may not be a fellow member of any natural group to which you are aware that you belong. You have learned to pass people coldly, people to whom you have made no specific personal adjustments. Perhaps in this sense you are a "civilized" human being.

Besides these people whom you pass by, there are others whom you deal with when you arrive at your destination. If you are going to work, you will join others in your office or shop or classroom to whom you may have made some adjustment. If they are few enough you know them, and with them you form a natural group. If you are on your way home, you will join your family, a natural group in any society or civilization.

In cities and in large nations we forget to think in terms of natural groups and lump people together on the basis of single criteria. Thus a man may write a book about the unity of the "Aryan" race, when the word refers to a family of languages better known as Indo-European or someone else will talk glibly about France as if it were a person and not a unit of landscape whose multilingual inhabitants fall under a single government.

This vague habit of lumping persons in categories which have no structure, of throwing together individuals who have had no chance to adjust themselves to each other, is a result of the complexity of modern life and one of its greatest dangers.

It comes from the fact that our ability to tie together the units of society as it is officially conceived has not kept pace with the modern increase in the division of labor. Still, in our society as in all others however simple or complex, natural groups exist, and continue to form the units of organization, official or undercover, since the formation of social structure is both natural and automatic.

The street-corner gang is a natural group if it has a leader and its members meet with sufficient frequency. So is the ward organization with its boss, no matter how much the good-government people may frown on it. The college board of overseers is really run by a group of old cronies who went to school together, or who became friends later on the golf links.

Natural groups are the stuff of which whole cultures are built; it is, however, only in the simpler societies that natural groups as we have defined them are coterminous with nations and cultural units. In the more complex societies, even at the preliterate level, one finds people organized into institutions which are composed of multiples of natural groups, either similar or differentiated. If we are to study them, as objectively and as systematically as we can, working from most simple to most complex, we must do what scholars in other disciplines have long since learned to do, to *follow scientific procedure*.

Scientific procedure consists of four steps: description, theorizing, experimentation, and the derivation of principles. In anthropology, description requires field work. The observer in the field describes who does what when, where, with what material objects, with whom, and with what results, over a period of time, in the community which he his studying. The classes of things that he should observe are the facts and events covered in the rest of this Introduction.

In order to do this he should develop enough linguistic competence to understand what his subjects are saying in their own language, and he should learn how to watch and question them without disturbing the very events in which he is interested. It is usually best to start with overt, noncontroversial matters such as the landscape, flora and fauna, and work techniques, and to leave the more emotionally charged subjects such as familial behavior and ritual until later. This order is based on two considerations: language and intimacy. As time goes on our field man, if he is doing a good job, learns to handle increasingly subtle topics of conversation, and at the same time gradually breaks down the reserve of his informants on subjects which they are loath to air with an outsider.

The height of objectivity is probably reached by students of animal behavior in the wild, for there interaction between the observer and his subjects can be virtually eliminated. These scientists watch their subjects day after day, with field glasses and stop watches. In some cases they even paint numbers on the animals and then release them. They record all movements, all advances made by one animal to another, and measure these in seconds. With special devices they make records of all sounds made by the animals. When the study is over, they shoot the animals and examine their bodies for food eaten, pregnancy, etc. They thus obtain data which they can analyze mathematically, and from which they can make truly objective deductions.

It is not feasible to place numbers on human beings or to shoot them for this purpose, and it is not easy to keep an objective record of what each one does at each moment in relation to all other individuals. There are too many people in every natural group, and their actions are too complicated. We can, however, take samples. We can record on the scale of time the sequence of actions that habitually go into any specific mechanical operation. This method, which has been highly developed in the field of modern industry, can be employed with equal profit in studying the technique of an Australian aborigine chipping a flint blade, a Polynesian making fire with a fire plow, or a pair of Eskimos building an igloo.

It is unlikely that any race or group of people has a monopoly on the capacity for manual skill. The difference lies in the amount of time individuals have to spend on given operations. If you are a professional shoemaker and work at your last all day every day, you will probably make better shoes than if you spend an hour a week at it. In those societies in which specialists can be supported, manual skills are always highly developed. The skilled motions which people use repetitively are learned, and once learned become habits. Motor habits of different peoples differ markedly and are well worth observation.

Special studies of this kind are all very well, but the field worker cannot observe every single act that every person does every day. If he did he would have a vast body of information that he would never be able to work up statistically. He can, however, observe frequencies of events. It is not difficult to record how often a given man visits the men's clubhouse in the village, or how often he quarrels noisily with his wife, and the relationship between these events will be clear. After the observer has been in residence for a while, he can also begin to observe habit patterns. The reader has, no doubt, at one time or another, been in the habit of catching a certain train, or going to lunch at a given place at the same time each day. He has probably noticed that the same people tend to sit in the same seat on the same car of the train each day, that he sees the same faces if he walks down the street at a given time each morning, etc.

Human beings develop habits of actions and sequences of action on a daily, weekly, seasonal, or other time-scale basis. This is very useful in wartime for intelligence agents to know, for they can learn to anticipate the actions of the people in whom they are interested. It is equally useful for anthropologists.

Just as people develop habits of sitting in a given seat, of eating at a given time, so they also develop conditioned ways of performing their daily tasks. A shoemaker always holds his shoe in one hand, and his knife in the other; he does not change hands. A blacksmith shoeing a horse on Monday will follow exactly the same procedure on Friday unless something unusual has come up to disturb him. The anthropologist must know the meaning of uniformities, and how to observe and describe them. He must know them so well that if he sees someone do something out of the ordinary he will seek the reason.

This is true not only of sequences of actions in work processes, but also in human relations. Husbands and wives develop standard ways of behavior toward one another, and in a given society there will be accepted forms of behavior in every kind of relationship. Most of the people will, by and large and on the average, behave in some such way. Thus it is possible to say that among the Iroquois the women own the houses and the men go to live with their wives' families, while among the Pathans of Afghanistan the men own their houses and and the wives go to live with their husbands' families. There are exceptions to these rules, but still the rules are descriptions of habitual behavior, and it is only through the maintenance of such norms that societies function. The anthropologist should learn to record the habitual action or uniformity. He should also record the exceptions, because it is through the exceptions, and the situations which arise when exceptions are made, that one can discover the structural pattern of the society. This is a substitute for experimentation.

Besides a record of sequences of action, habitual and exceptional, the field anthropologist should obtain or make a good map of the region, and plot, on a large scale, the territories that belong to different tribes or villages, and even individuals; the gardens, houses, the ritual edifices, or sacred springs or trees. He should make an exact census of the group he is studying, noting how many persons it includes of each sex and age group, and if possible this census should be carried on over a number of years to yield evidence of change.

By techniques such as these anthropologists describe societies and learn what forces make them operate. But the very study of operations, the physiology of a society, as contrasted to its gross anatomy, can only be made on the time scale, and the anthropologist has seldom much time. He should, however, plan to stay a year, or to make several visits at different times of year, for unless he is in a climate where the weather is constant day after day throughout the year, the people whom he is studying are bound to do different things as the weather changes.

The greater the change in seasons, the greater, as a rule, the change in human activities. Before the coming of the whites the Maidu of the Sacramento Valley spent the summer collecting acorns, pine nuts, and grass seeds; hunting antelope; and spearing salmon. For the long eight months of winter and spring they ate the food so obtained, and kept themselves busy dancing and putting on dramatic spectacles. A man who visited them in January and one who was there in August would tell two entirely different stories about these people.

Societies, however, go through other changes than those of the annual cycle. From time to time they undergo permanent change. This is history, and the anthropologist is seldom able to sit out an entire historical event in a community which he is studying. However, there is one kind of historical event which he can hardly avoid, and that is the adjustment of the people he is studying (if they are not Europeans or Americans) to the presence of the white man and all he has brought with him. This side of anthropology is called acculturation. It is useful not only because it records history but also because it serves in lieu of experimentation, although it is often tragic in its consequences.

Our second stage in scientific procedure, as previously mentioned, is making theories. This means simply that the field man should figure out as accurately as he can, usually intuitively, the cause-and-effect relationship between different classes of events. Having figured these out in certain categories of behavior, he can let someone else do the third step, the experimenting, for him. For example, if in an East African tribe the government forbids the purchase of wives with cattle, the young people will stop getting married, and the whole tribe will be thrown into a state of confusion. The observer can thus test his theory of the functional value of cattle purchase as a symbolic procedure in matrimony. If he had no theory before, the unusual event will give it to him.

The fourth step, deriving principles, comes when you can reproduce an experiment in spatially separate and non-intercommunicating areas and obtain the same results. For example, in Tierra del Fuego when a whale washes ashore people come from far and near to eat it while the meat lasts, in complete disregard of tribal boundaries which they otherwise strictly observe. In Australia the same thing happens when once in several years a certain kind of fruit ripens in a certain place in great abundance. The principle is that when a windfall comes to simple food-gathering peoples, they forget their territorial rules for the duration. This can be tested over and over and will always be found to work out the same way.

2. Background to Behavior—the Four Components.

Few principles which anthropologists have propounded during the last hundred years have been based on experimentation, or have even passed beyond the idea stage. That is why there is so much disagreement, and why so many schools have arisen around the personalities of powerful teachers. All will agree, however, that principles exist. No one seriously challenges the laws of physics which govern the movement of organisms, human and otherwise, just as they govern inanimate nature. No one doubts that if a man jumps out of an airplane without a parachute he will fall in the same manner as any other object of the same weight, volume, and shape.

Most of the things which human beings do are also done in a simpler fashion by other animals. All are governed by the same rules. Overexertion produces fatigue, and fright changes the balance of hormone secretion in men and horses and dogs. In the so-called higher processes, of "thinking," associating ideas, and the like, which are quantitatively limited to human beings, other rules must be in force. We are still segments of the universe. In the rest of this introduction I shall list, and explain briefly, the various things that people do, and the kinds of natural groups which form as a result. As in any other problem of science, the "breakdown" is of supreme importance. If the various elements in a theorem are clearly separated and defined, their interrelation in time and space will be easier to understand than if they are left in solution.

Our breakdown begins by segregating the individual from his external environment. This environment may be further divided into two categories: other people (the social environment), and the rest of the world (the natural environment). The individual, however, perceives the world around him, including human and non-human, animate and inanimate, beings and objects, through his senses. When he sees another man what happens is that an image of the second person's body is cast on his retina and picked up by the rods and cones of the retina. When he hears a lion roar, sound waves of a certain sequence of frequencies produce vibrations on the organs of his inner ear. He does not respond to the image of a man, or the sound of a lion's roar, until he has learned what these things mean. And these things are symbols. The symbol, which must be learned to be appreciated, is the fourth element in the universe of which man is a part. It has no separate existence apart from the other three, out of elements from all of which it is composed.

Our four elements, then, are (1) the individual; (2) other people; (3) the rest of the world; (4) symbols.

3. The Individual.

The individual is a bipedal primate; a he or a she. For purposes of simplification (since the writer is a male) it will be referred to here, unless otherwise specified, as he. This primate stands or walks erect on the ground, or sits erect in a chair, during most of his waking hours. He has two legs, with which he can walk up to four miles per hour or run for a short distance at the rate of 100 yards in 10 to 20 seconds, depending on his age, build, and state of physiological efficiency. He also has two arms, terminating in hands. These arms are so attached to his torso that they may be rotated in nearly a complete ball. With his hands he can pick up objects and perform delicate operations such as chipping pieces of flint, writing, operating lathes, and feeding himself. Since his forelimbs are not used for locomotion he can develop elaborate manual skills, with different operations for each hand.

The individual possesses a primitive kind of reproductive apparatus which can function at all times; whether the individual is a he or a she, and in good health, the sexual urge is fairly constant, without marked periodicity. The individual also possesses a relatively hairless body, but a hairy scalp (there is considerable variation in both these matters). In many regions at various times he covers much of this body with material derived from the environment.

He has a head and a face; this top part of his body contains the principal organs by which he perceives what is going on and communicates with his fellows. These organs include his ears, and his hearing is acute; and his eyes, which with a combination of stereoscopic color vision and the fine perception made possible by a macular area, are the best in the animal kingdom. He is not noted as a smeller, but his olfactory apparatus has greater potentialities than many people realize. Can you not recognize the place in which you grew up by some particular smell?

The part of the head which takes care of smell has a number of other functions. The nasal passages, maxillary sinuses, and ethmoid air chambers, like the hollow part of a violin or harp, act together as a sounding box to the palate. By moving your tongue, lips, and soft palate about, you can produce as many as thirty consonants, which your nasal sounding box will accentuate. If you doubt this, listen to someone with a bad cold, whose nasal passages are filled.

Below the sounding box lies the primary apparatus of speech: the tongue, soft-palate, lips, teeth, and vocal cords. These organs retain their early duty of passing food into the stomach, but much more time is spent each day in talking than in eating. Like the nose, they are all-purpose organs. Above the sounding-box is the brain, the pilot of the body, the soft and spongy edifice that by its size, proportions, and capabilities distinguishes man from the rest of the animal kingdom, except for giants, e.g. the whales.

The brain is the focal center of the nervous system. By means of the nervous system the human being not only keeps himself informed about what is going on around him,—and this is, in the Darwinian sense, essential for survival—but he also maintains his body in a state of adjustment or "equilibrium." This means simply that his temperature remains within a narrow band, that he breathes no faster or more slowly than his heart can accommodate, that he expels no more than a certain amount of heat each twenty-four hours; that, in short, his various bodily activities remain within normal limits.

The individual does not regulate these things consciously. Continuous, rhythmic bodily activities are automatically regulated by a portion of the nervous system called the autonomic, in cooperation with a number of endocrine glands. Another part, the somatic, operates the muscles of the arms, legs, jaw, etc. A third, the central nervous system, is what the individual "thinks" and "remembers" with. Thought and memory are composite end results of many different processes which psychologists, neurologists, and biochemists are just beginning to understand.

For present purposes it may not be too inaccurate to describe the brain (for that is the seat of the central nervous system) as an automatic, highly complex, chemical (rather than mechanical) switchboard and clearinghouse for nervous impulses, which arrive over the nerve channels in response to changes in the external environment. The brain is gradually and progressively trained throughout the life of the individual to receive these messages, sort them, store them for future reference, and initiate action to the appropriate somatic organs. By the time senile decay sets in, an efficient neural system has usually been developed.

When the sensory nerves have warned the cerebral cortex of a crisis, such as an avalanche approaching at high speed, the latter sends an impulse down to the autonomic, which in turn diverts the blood from its peacetime task of digesting food to its wartime job of reinforcing the muscles of the legs to give the body a chance to run quickly out of danger. It is the same when two people are having a conversation, although the crisis may be less acute. However, if the conversation consists of an employer firing an employee, or a judge sentencing a criminal to be hanged, the emotions may be just as fully aroused as in the case of the onrushing avalanche, the excitement just as great. Whatever the stimulus received from the outside environment, or the succession of stimuli, it is the autonomic which has the task of maintaining equilibrium, in all the dealings that the individual has with other people and with the nonhuman environment.

The business of filing messages in the gray matter (cortex) of the brain is known as learning. No one knows in complete detail just how the filing system works. It is known, however, that the nervous control over actions which are repeated time after time tends to move down into the more ancient part of the brain. A shoemaker has to keep his mind on his work until he has learned his trade, but as he grows older he can carry on an animated conversation with the man at the next bench while his hands are performing nearly automatic actions.

Our individual passes through a life cycle like that of any of the other higher mammals. He is born, grows gradually, learns how to behave, arrives at maturity, lives as an able-bodied adult for a term of years, and, unless he is killed or acquires a fatal malady, will age and die. Now and then he will probably be ill. His internal adjustment will be disturbed periodically, not only by illness, but also by physiological changes which the passage of time brings on. When his sex organs first become active this will cause a change in his metabolism, requiring a corresponding change in his human relations, and will disturb him. If the individual is a woman, menopause will bring about a second disturbance.

4. Other people.

The individual is never alone for long periods, unless by accident or through some special circumstance. He starts life in his mother's womb, and after he is born is constantly with her, an older sister, or a nurse until he has been weaned, and has learned to walk and talk. From that moment on he spends part of his time with his elders, and part of it with other children of roughly his own age, with whom he plays. As time goes on the number of persons whom he habitually sees and with whom he does things usually increases. At some point he will enter into a high-frequency relationship with a member of the opposite sex, known as marriage, and soon, if all goes well, the cycle will begin again.

The various parts of the human organism are adapted to interaction* as much as to requirements of the external environment. The hands, vital for working, are essential for grooming and caressing, massaging, gesticulating and shaking hands. The touch of another person's hand is often more comforting than any amount of conversation. Further, the hands are used in fighting, with or without weapons, and no interpersonal conflict beyond a verbal battle is conceivable without them.

The mouth serves for talking as much as for eating or drinking; the nose while constantly engaged in breathing is also essential for speech. One could go on with this list at some length, but it is not necessary.

With an organism built for interaction, the average individual spends a larger part of his waking hours in doing things with other people than in doing things alone. I suggest that the student reading this chapter make out a time schedule of all his activities from the moment he wakes up to the time he falls asleep, for each day of a typical week. Then let him divide his activities into two categories, solitary and with other people. The latter will include talking, walking together, etc., as well as work activities. Then let him see which takes up the greater part of his time. Unless he is engaged in a very unusual curriculum he will find that the statement at the head of this paragraph applies to him as to most other people.

5. The Rest of the World.

Whether he is engaged in solitary actions or interacting with others, the individual is always dealing with the non-human environment, for he has to stand,

---

*It is now fashionable to call interaction "communication", but interaction is still the better word for our purpose, because it includes doing things together, instead of just talking about it, as on television.

sit, or lie on something, and he has to breathe. The non-human environment furnishes the individual with the very substance out of which his body is made; air, food, water, radiation, and with the tools and raw materials with which he works. He is a part of the physical world, from which he can escape only by death, however this may be defined.

This physical world in which he lives is the surface of the earth, of which 72 percent is water. The other 28 percent is the landscape, part of which has been altered by human agency. Geographers classify the unaltered landscape in a number of ways, using as their chief criteria such variables as mean annual temperature, annual temperature range, variations of rainfall by month and by year, water vapor pressure, altitude, and surface configuration. Vegetation furnishes a general summary, since the combination of plants which will grow in any given place at any time reflects the balance between the other features mentioned. Furthermore, the plants provide food for animals, and animals provide food, skins, and other substances useful to man. The flora and fauna, along with the abundance of water and the surface configuration, are the most important factors in the environment to man, at least in his simpler cultural stages. When his life grows more complicated, he may think about coal and oil, streams that can be dammed, and deposits of uranium ore.

Following Preston James,* we recognize eight principal types of landscape. These are the Dry Lands or Deserts, Tropical Forests, Mediterranean Scrub Forests (or more simply, Mediterranean Lands), Mid-Latitude Mixed Forests (people are beginning to call these Hardwood Forests), Grasslands, Boreal Forests, Polar Lands, and Mountain Lands. Each of these offers different opportunities and imposes different limitations to human beings for their exploitation. Each of them has a different sequence of seasons, which have meaning for human occupancy.

The tropical forests, for example, are divided into two types,—the rain forest and the monsoon forest. In the rain forest every day is like the next and there is no seasonal change, no need to look ahead and plan for the future. The monsoon forest has a wet and a dry season, which set definite dates for changes in human activity. The Mediterranean climate has a chilly wet winter, a long, beautiful spring, and a hot summer. Much of our ceremonial calendar associated with the springtime is derived from the Mediterranean. Boreal forests, which have short, warm summers, and deadly cold winters, so that no people can survive their winters who have not invented or learned efficient methods of preserving body heat.

Tropical forests are admirable homes for subhuman primates, and in fact all of them still live there except for certain macaques, which range north of the snow line in Japan, and some of the baboons, which run about on the grasslands on all fours like dogs. Grasslands are fine for hunters and pastoralists. For farmers with tractors and deep plows they are excellent for growing grain. They are of no use at all to slash-and-burn agriculturists.

Each of these environments is at its best for peoples who practice certain techniques, and at its worst for others who live by different methods. For the most

* Preston James, *An Outline of Geography.* Boston: Ginn and Co., 1935. This material is also summarized in Chapter 5 of Chapple and Coon, *Principles of Anthropology.* The student is advised if possible to read the original.

primitive of men, the warmer grasslands and Mediterranean scrub forests are most favorable, for they offer the greatest abundance of food in return for the least skill. Exotic river valleys, like the Nile, Tigris-Euphrates, and Indus, are better still for people who have learned some simple form of agriculture, while midlatitude forests, with ample feed for cattle and horses and ample underground resources, such as coal and iron, are best for those living in the industrial civilization.

Some lands are poor for anybody, no matter how many tricks they have learned, or how clever they are. Whatever they do, the population will be small and scattered. This is true of the Polar Lands, inhabited by the well-known Eskimo, and of most deserts.

6. Signs and Symbols.

When a child is born and his eyes have opened, light floods through the pupillary opening and into the lens, and past the lens to the retina. At this point he does not really "see" anything. In the same way all sorts of sounds ring in his ears. By squirming and moving around various parts of his body come into contact with other substances, such as his bed or cradle, his diapers, a safety pin, and his mother's body. If the light is too strong it will upset him and he will cry and scream. If he touches anything too hot or too cold, or if an open pin pricks him, he will react in the same way.

As he grows older, identical events happen to him again and again at regular intervals. The baby begins to learn, by the process of repetition. This learning involves association. When he hears bottles rattle in a tray, this particular sound conveys to him the meaning that he is about to be fed. The sound of bottles rattling is what psychologists call a sign. As he keeps on growing older, the number of signs which the baby recognizes, through his various senses, increases. Among these are vocal sounds produced by the older people who take care of him. At first these sounds may serve merely to identify individuals, by their different tones, or to indicate whether they are pleasant or unpleasant. Later on, as the older people make a conscious effort to teach the baby how to speak, individual sounds take on special associations.

I have used the word "signs" for these examples in order to follow psychological fashion. Most psychologists nowadays reserve the word "symbol" for something else. While a "sign" is considered to be the trigger that sets off a Pavlovian conditioned reflex, a "symbol" is a kind of supersign, which may crop up within a person's brain. If a man is "thinking," reminding himself of something, or making an internal association, rather than responding to a direct, overt stimulus, the units which he employs in this process are called "symbols." If we make this distinction, then "signs" are common to all animal life, while "symbols" are largely if not wholly limited to man who alone has language. Configurations of signs are species-specific. Configurations of symbols (languages) are myriad within a single species, and many individuals can speak several languages at will.

For present purposes I am chiefly interested in symbols, and a few pertinent signs. Edward T. Hall considers the totality of culture, and not just language alone, as "the link between human beings and the means they have of interacting with others."*

*Edward T. Hall, *The Silent Language,* New York, Doubleday, 1959, p. 213. See also his *The Hidden Dimension,* ibid. 1966.

7. Clusters or Configurations of Symbols.

Psychologists generally agree that we do not store up our repertoire of signs and symbols as single units, but that we remember them by classes of things that fall into natural categories. If one unit of a certain group is evoked, others to which it is linked arise with it. For example, if a man who traveled widely in his youth smells a certain spice, it may instantly make him think of Egypt, and of some young lady with whom he once had a romantic attachment in that country.

The spice, Egypt, and the girl are all part of a private cluster of symbols which has meaning to one individual only, the man in question. There are other clusters or collections of symbols which belong to groups of people. These are known as *symbolic configurations*. The easiest example of a symbolic configuration is a language. People who speak the same language use the same collection of symbols. Someone who does not know that language cannot understand them. If you listen to a group of foreigners conversing in some strange form of speech, you will soon lose interest.

Another example of a configuration in symbols is the totality of ritual objects which the members of a Christian community uses in its services, such as the cross, Bible, and altar; this includes the music and the special ritual vocabulary, and even the tone of voice in which the preacher delivers his sermon. The corresponding objects, postures, tones, etc., used by a Moslem community form another.

A configuration of symbols has all of the properties of a natural group, although it is composed not of people but of semantic units. It has its own system of adjustment, equilibrium, or whatever you wish to call it; it too is governed by the principle of the conservation of energy. As George Zipf has shown,* in any language the shortest words are those most commonly used, the longest the most rarely. The natural cohesion which exists within a body or configuration of symbols makes it resistant to impact with another configuration which fulfills the same purpose. At a given moment you either speak English or some other language. You are a Christian or a Moslem; you cannot be both at once.

Thus is should not be hard to understand that when people are used to one set of symbols, the appearance of another set which fills the same purpose for another group of people may upset and annoy them. To a Moslem the sound of church bells symbolizes Christians, people whose religion he does not like. In Libya, during the Italian occupation, the Arabs were deeply chagrined when the Italian government officials insisted on posting the Italian coat of arms beside the door of each mosque. The coat of arms contains a cross. Although to the Arabs the sound of bells and the sight of the cross directly means Christians, what it basically refers to is the discomfort, shame, and nervous upset which the presence of Christians in their country caused them. The final referent of any symbol is the psychological condition with which it is associated.

Conflicts between symbolic configurations are just as real as any other kind of conflict. Very often when wars are fought it is the symbols that are given as the reason. Anyone who doubts the power of symbols need only imagine himself in the following situation. You will go to a foreign city where no one speaks any language which you understand. In this city the inhabitants wear clothing entirely different from yours, and they worship gods you have never heard of with

* G. K. Zipf, *The Psychobiology of Language.* Boston: Houghton Mifflin Co., 1935.

rituals unknown to you. They expose parts of the body which you cover, and vice versa. Actions which you consider proper are to them highly reprehensible, and vice versa. How long would you last in such a city? For real instances of this type of situation, read Bernal Diaz's account of the conquest of Mexico by Cortez, not only the sections quoted in this book, but the rest. Even if you know the customs of the strange people, you may find it difficult to get along with them; if you doubt this, read Sir Richard Burton's *Pilgrimage to Al-Madinah and Meccah.**

8. Of Energy.

Now that we have described the individual and placed him in the company of other people on the landscape, and equipped him with a set of symbols with which to deal with the outside world, it is time to set the whole scene in action. Action implies, in human affairs as in all other departements of the physical world, the expenditure of energy on the scale of time.

Energy is found in all of the first three categories, and makes the fourth operate. The individual eats and drinks, thereby obtaining calories to maintain bodily heat and keep the blood stream flowing. He uses some of this energy for breathing, thereby obtaining oxygen, a source of further energy. From the rays of the sun still more energy reaches him. The individual thus obtains energy from the nonhuman elements of the landscape. A suckling child obtains energy from another person.

All human beings not only receive, but also expend energy, through heat loss, through muscular movements, and through the action of the nervous system. It takes far less caloric energy to spend a morning in deep thought than to hoe a garden for the same length of time, but the former action may be of much greater moment to the world than the latter. If we had some simple means of measuring the expenditure of energy by human beings, hour by hour, day by day, and could break this down into the amount used for body heat, muscular action, and nervous energy, we could compare these figures with the total intake, and plot both against production. This can be done only roughly by comparing the caloric needs of office workers and laborers. Even without an exact measure of this kind, we know that individuals, whatever their occupations, vary enormously in the amount of energy expended, and in its results.

The individual has at his command not only his own bodily energy, but that from two outside sources. If he can persuade a group of other people to work for him or with him, all of them together can lift heavy stones, tow large barges up swift streams, and defeat powerful enemies. If he can harness the energy of the outside world, there is no limit to what he may accomplish. He can use fire to cook his food, bake his pottery, smelt his metal, and run his engines. He can use the muscular force of domestic animals to haul his carts and turn his wheels. He can divert streams through his mill, and utilize gravity. He can detonate unstable inorganic compounds such as gunpowder, and conquer nations, and he can split atoms, and is beginning to harness the power of the sun.

9. Of Time.

All of this enery is expended on the linear scale of time. Every man, woman,

* London, 1893.

and child on earth, rich or poor, civilized or otherwise, lives subject to the rotation of the earth on its axis, through the same succession of 24-hour cycles of light and darkness, waking and sleep. The one universal dimension in which the expenditure of energy can be measured is time. The college gives you credit for so many hours of Anthropology, and the electric power company bills you in terms of kilowatt hours.

It is easier to plot the energy of fire, of gunpowder, of water-power, etc., against time than it is that of human energy. Physicists and engineers have worked out exact constants for these. Since in running machines which utilize such sources of power men are seldom called on to expend more than a portion of their muscular energy, the factor of human energy may be taken as a constant and left out of the calculation. This applies. however, only to the more advanced civilizations, the ones with which anthropologists seldom deal. For food gatherers and for slash-and-burn farmers, success in obtaining food and other necessities depends in a large measure on the direct outlay of muscular energy, and at present we can measure these actions most accurately and significantly in terms of time.

Time is the scale on which we measure the life history of the individual, from birth to death, through all of the usual and unusual crises which he passes. Time is the scale on which we measure the daily cycle of human activities, from waking to falling asleep; the weekly and monthly cycles, if any, and the yearly cycle, in all environments in which there are seasons. If we are to develop a useful statistical method in the study of cultural anthropology, our chief dimension will be that of time, as expressed in the first chapter of Ecclesiastes II.

10. Action and Interaction.

What is the unit of the expenditure of human muscular energy on the scale of time? This question can be answered only in an arbitrary manner. For convenience we may say that when a man starts a sequence of actions, continues with it, and completes it without repeating, that is what we are looking for. That is an event. A potter puts a lump of clay on his wheel, spins it, and shapes the pot. He takes the product off and reaches for another lump. He has been through one cycle of his daily activity.

Supposing, however, that the potter is not working alone. A boy hands him the unshaped lump of clay, and later takes the blank pot away, handing it to another man to paint. When the painter has finished decorating it, the boy sets it out in the sun to dry before it is baked. Here we have two men and a boy working together. Their actions are so timed that their efforts are complementary. This in interaction. The boy in particular watches the other two in order to serve them when they are ready. Here three persons are working together, and accommodating themselves to each other's time schedules.

When a person is doing something alone, his actions form *solitary events.* When two persons are doing something together, we speak of *paired events,* and when several people (three or more) are involved, *group events.* The differences between these three kinds of events are marked and are basic for the structure of human societies. In a solitary event the individual keeps on working uninterruptedly and pauses only as the work requires, or as he becomes fatigued. In a paired event two people have to accommodate themselves to each other. This may

be seen most easily in the give and take of a two-person conversation. Chapple
has made exhaustive studies of the mathematical properties of this kind of paired
interaction, from which he has devised a practical method of analyzing the personalities of individuals.*

In a paired event one individual is more likely to start things off than the other.
Human beings show just as much variation in dominance as do hens or mice or
monkeys, whose behavior patterns have been exhaustively studied by biologists
and psychologists. But the nature of paired events is such that each person
initiates in some actions and responds in others. If one does all the work and
makes the other watch, or if one does all the talking and the other never gets a
chance to say anything, it is not a paired event. The relationship will probably
soon break up.

But when several persons are doing something together, an entirely
different situation arises. The group must have a leader, who must make sure
that each person does his part of the activity at the right time, or disorder will
result and nothing will be accomplished. Sometimes a leader is appointed from
above; at other times a leader emerges through his possession of the necessary
qualities of personality. A successful leader is a person who can initiate action
to several other persons at once, and they will respond in concert.

The conductor of a symphony orchestra is one of the most obvious examples.
If he is a good conductor and wants to keep his artists together, he will not only
be able to lead them as a group in rehearsals and concerts, but he will have the
power to deal with each one of them privately in paired events, in which each
musician can talk directly with him, man to man. The ability to do both these
things, combined with the exercise of good judgment, are the characteristics of a
successful leader. It is easy to see that a high survival value is attached to a
group in which one man at least has the personality of a leader and the others of
followers. If all or none were capable of leadership, confusion would result.

11. The Components of Events.

Every event in which human beings participate may consist of a number of
different component elements, as follows: (1) *personnel,* (2) *materials,* (3) *instruments,* (4) *energy consumed,* (5) *actions,* (6) *interaction.* These elements,
in motion, are measured on the scale of time.

Let us illustrate this with examples. Three men who live in a middle eastern
country decide one November morning to make olive oil. They lead a mule
loaded with baskets of olives to the grinding platform. This is a raised stone
disk which acts as nether stone. Another disk, set on edge, is pivoted to a vertical
post set in a hole in the middle of the first stone. The pivot is a horizontal bar
extending out beyond the platform. The men unload the mule, dump some of the
olives onto the nether stone, and hitch the mule to the bar. One of the men
drives the mule around and around, crushing the olives, while a second moves the
mash into place with a stick. The third man prepares squeezing baskets for the
next operation, and gets the wooden screw-press ready. About forty minutes
later, when they have crushed one load, the men remove the mash from the platform and pack it into baskets. Then they dump more olives on the platform.

*See Eliot D. Chapple, *Culture and Behavioral Man,* New York, 1970, Holt, Rinehart, & Winston,
and his pertinent monographs listed in that book's bibliography.

One man again drives the mule, another again pushes the mash under the wheel, while the third starts turning the screw. When he gets the oil flowing out of the baskets, he needs help, and the other men stop work to lend their muscles to the screw-bar. They do this as long as their olives last, until about noon. They collect the oil in jars and go home.

(1) *personnel*. Three men, Mohammed, Hamid, and Ali.

(2) *materials*. Olives.

(3) *instruments*. An olive masher and a screw press, panniers, pressing baskets, pots, a stick.

(4) *energy consumed*. The muscular energy of three men, singly and combined. The energy of one mule.

(5) *actions*. Unloading the mule, dumping the panniers, hitching the mule to the bar, driving it around, unhitching it, stirring the mash, putting it in baskets, putting the baskets under the screw-block, placing the pots, turning the screw, changing the pots, loosening the screw, emptying the baskets.

(6) *interaction*. Most of the time the three men are doing different tasks. However, these are all interrelated, and the men must time their actions to each other. In one action, turning the screw at the hard spot, the three worked together. In this Mohammed, the man who had been at the screw from the start, took the lead, and emitted a rhythmic sequence of grunts, a signal to apply pressure.

The next day is Friday. Mohammed, Hamid, Ali, and a dozen other men like them wash, put on clean clothing, and walk to the mosque. It is a bright, clear day and the congregation meets out of doors. The leader of the mosque, Si Abd el Kadher, a fine old man with a white beard, is there to greet them. He shakes hands with each of the men, one by one, kissing his finger and touching his forehead in each case. While they are waiting for all to arrive, the men chat with each other informally, mostly in pairs, although a group of five listens for a short while to the narrative of one man.

Si Abd el Kadher now takes his place at one end of the little terrace in front of the mosque, and the others face him. In a fine, well-modulated voice Si Abd el Kadher begins to pray, and the others pray after him. He kneels, prostrates himself, and comes back on his haunches, then arises. Each part of this sequence of actions is accompanied by elements of his prayer. He does this several times, and so do the men who face him. When they are through he delivers a sermon, to which they listen attentively. When he has finished some of them stop to speak to him briefly, and all go home.

(1) *personnel*. Si Abd el Kadher and his communicants. About twenty men.

(2) *materials*. No tangible materials are needed. Si Abd el Kadher is not processing goods; he is working with the nervous systems of men.

(3) *instruments*. These are equally intangible. His tools are symbols—words and gestures, of high emotional content.

(4) *energy consumed*. Only that needed in praying, kneeling, and prostration. But a great deal of emotional, nervous energy is on hand.

(5) *actions*. The ritual words spoken, the movements performed.

(6) *interaction*. The paired conversations of the men before the service, and with Si Abd el Kadher briefly afterward. The brief group conversation on the steps before the ceremony. The key event, however, is the group interaction in the ceremony, when Si Abd el Kadher leads, and the others

respond. That is what the ceremony is for. From what they did on Thursday our men got oil, but from what they did on Friday they got a restoration of the fine balance of their nervous systems, somewhat frayed by the events of the week, and a feeling of brotherhood and "belonging" to a group.

12. Symbols Which Serve as Tools.

In the last example, as we saw, Si Abd el Kadher, the holy man, used certain symbols as tools. He did this so effectively that the point was obvious. All of us, however, use symbols as tools every day. Tools of this kind work just as directly as hammers, saws, and chisels. They are just as real, just as finite, as these solid artifacts, because with them we work on something as finite as wood, meat, and skin—the human nervous system and those endocrines with which it has a mutually reenforcing feedback relationship. Six classes of such tools are noteworthy: language, gods, art, mathematical symbols, and the representation of natural laws, each singly or in combination.

Words are the symbols of persons and all their recognized attributes, of the external, nonhuman world in all its aspects which concern the people speaking the language, and of the symbols of other kinds which the speakers recognize or employ. Languages change as the personnel, environment, symbols, and actions of people change. A language is the true mirror of those who speak it, since it is the vehicle for interaction of every category.

Gods, spirits, souls of the dead—these are the symbolic counterparts of areas of disturbance. Once a person has died, it is much easier for those most upset by the void of his passing to believe that although his body is destined for disintegration, his personality and vital energy have left it to live on elsewhere. Since no one has yet been able to prove that this is not so, since the belief is so essential for the well-being of the bereaved, and since no one has discovered a better way to comfort them, this belief persists in our own society. Some gods have arisen through the extension of a belief in the soul of a dead man from his immediate kin to an entire group of people. Others personify forces of nature which create change. Almost everywhere one can discover gods of the weather, storm gods, rain gods, Zeus with his thunderbolt, Thor with his hammer. Other gods may symbolize special activities: Athene the goddess of weaving, Hephaistos the smith. When a society is so segmented through the division of labor that it consists of a number of interlocking occupational castes, the chances are that each will have its own special god, or patron saint, while a high god will represent the relations of the group as a whole in reference to the known universe.

In the most highly evolved ethical religions as in many others at all levels, the concept of God as a universal source of power and harmony simply represents the forces and natural laws of the universe which we understand a little more than we did a century ago, but which reveal further mysteries the more deeply we penetrate. Any god is real to the people who believe in him. The referent of the symbol, the disturbance or activity which the god represents, is, of course, real to everyone. The God of ethical religions, which symbolizes the forces of the universe, is real to everyone who spends much time thinking about these forces and about man's role in the universe. Whether or not any human being believes in these forces or symbolizes them, they are just as real as man himself, and have been in existence much longer.

Any artist, whatever his medium, follows a regular set of conventions in his choice of symbols; otherwise they would not stimulate his audience esthetically. In Western European music a standard scale of sound intervals has been worked out which everyone recognizes and which people like to hear. Most of the people who flock to the Symphony on Friday afternoons would get little thrill out of the song of a Paiute Indian, who in turn would probably not appreciate the concert. "Modern" paintings, and sculptures intended as abstractions arouse uncomplimentary remarks from people who like to see their art represent something concrete which they can recognize. These conventions change with changes in their referents, the internal relations of peoples. So sensitive are these mirrors of fashion that it is easier to define them than to discover what causes them. The rate of change differs greatly in different media; church music remains the same for centuries, because its referents remain the same, while dance music goes through rapid cycles.

The activity of trading is made much easier if people are able to develop standards of value, as represented by fixed units. These will of course be things that come in convenient shapes and sizes, can be transported without difficulty, and are relatively uniform. The head of cattle is a standard wherever people breed them in numbers. They are not only fairly uniform, but they transport themselves. In the south seas, coconuts are often standards. Cattle die, coconuts decay, and both are edible. The trader who wishes to carry on commerce methodically and on a large scale will do better with something more concentrated and less perishable. To people who have precious metals, these are obviously better. Weighing out the metal, however, takes time; if they can be stamped in standard sizes and weights business is made that much easier.

If people can trust each other enough, they can use paper money, for which a banking house or government holds itself responsible, and they can transfer funds through checking accounts or over the telegraph system. Money, whatever form it takes, is a symbol of the confidence of people in each other, and particularly in their governments. The simpler peoples of the world have none, and hence no reason to worry about it. If they find a coin, they will make it into a piece of jewelry.

It is commonly said that mathematics is the language of science, and so it undoubtedly is, but it is also the language of commerce and of ritual. Many of the world's inhabitants cannot count beyond three, for there is nothing in their way of living that makes the use of higher figures necessary. Two special circumstances have fostered mathematics historically. The first is the need of farmers to know when the rainy season will begin, so that they can plant at just the right moment in advance. The second is the need of merchants and stewards to keep accurate accounts. The need of accurate prediction has led priests in several ancient civilizations to study the behavior of the sun and moon and Venus in relation to the earth; this was the beginning of astronomy, and of attempts to predict the future, and to pick lucky and unlucky days, by astrology.

The discovery of natural laws by actual experimentation rather than by trial and error is a privilege of peoples living in complex civilizations, where there is enough surplus food and enough realization of the advantages of change, and enough tools to work with, to make the life of a scientist possible. There is a world of difference between a man who sees a certain kind of tree, discovers that its limbs are very flexible, makes a bow of its wood, and tests it, and the man who measures the reaction of a certain kind of protozoa to light at different intensities. The first man wants a bow, and his testing is for that purpose only. The second wants nothing except his salary and the chance to work as he pleases. He is interested in general, not specific problems. Whether or not his discoveries will have practical applications is of little interest to him.

The discoveries of both men, however, will be of use to those to whom they communicate them. Standards of measurements, the properties of metals or of organisms, these are the pieces of knowledge which the craftsman needs if he is to manufacture his products, and particularly if he is to plan ahead. The findings of scientific research in human relations will also permit successful planning if a true scientific procedure is followed.

13. The Division of Labor.

While they are grinding and pressing olives to make oil, our friends Moham-med, Hamid, and Ali are performing different operations most of the time. The reason for this is that they have an efficient set of machinery, and a mule to supply energy. If they had no mule, all three would have to push on the bar which turns the crushing wheel. With a mule, one can drive while the other two do other things. The three of them have to strain together on the screw, but if they had some device for turning it by water power or even electricity, one man could operate it alone, and the others could be doing other things at the same time. It is easy to see how an increase in component number 4, the amount of energy, speeds up the whole operation and how it also brings about an increase in the division of labor.

These three men are performing different aspects of a single process on Thursday. But they are not full-time specialists at oil pressing. The machinery belongs to the village, and the men take turns using it in teams; the time allotted these men is half a day. On Friday, a recurrent point in time, they will all go to the mosque, and on Saturday they may all be helping a neighbor build and roof a house before the rains become severe. In the winter they will all be seen ploughing and sowing their fields, and in the late spring reaping. If you measure the duration of their different activities on the scale of time, you will see that they are not specialists at all but jacks-of-all-trades. Si Abd el Kadher, however, up at the mosque, is a specialist, because he does not plow or reap or press oil. He leads the prayer, comforts the sick, and instructs the young. A division of labor exists between him and the other men.

A true division of labor in the accepted sense implies that individuals of the same sex and age who provide each other with commodities or services do different things at the same time. Several other kinds of division of labor exist. One is seasonal, as noted above. Another distinguishes between the activities of children, adults, and senile individuals, who obviously cannot all do the same things except when they are in their prime; still another designates the different and complementary activities of men and of women, found in all human and some animal societies.

In some parts of the world a division of labor may also been seen between different kinds of people with separate cultures. Examples are the outcaste bands of hunters and gatherers who trade their products with villagers in India, and the relationship between Pygmies and their Negro trading partners in Central Africa.

This kind of relationship is symbiotic, comparable to the symbiosis between different species in plants and other animals.

Finally, a sharp division of labor may stem from differences between symbols. In an otherwise simply organized society with little or no division of human labor, gods may be worshipped as departmental specialists. One will be held responsible for the weather, another for success at hunting, another for the visitations of epidemic diseases, and each must be appeased just as, in the Iliad, Apollo had to be given a sacrifice of a hecatomb of cattle to induce him to lift the plague that he had cast over the Achaeans besieging Troy.

14. Activities: the Catalogue of Events.

We have now reached the point where people are expending energy from various sources at given speeds in solitary, paired, and group events, with and without a division of labor. But what are these things that they are doing? Hunting, fishing, making love, spanking children—how can we classify all of the thousands of different things that people do? We need such a classification in order to find out how any given society works, and also to make comparisons between two different peoples. Since all societies work on the same principles, we must be able to know what are the corresponding activities. With great differences in environment and in complexity of civilizations, these relationships are not self-evident. If one looks for the opposite number of the American Indian shaman in our society, where is one to find him? Who, among the Indians, corresponds to our Registrar of Motor Vehicles?

All human beings have certain basic needs. Our bodies must be kept warm, but not too hot. Our stomachs must be kept reasonably full of food and drink. We must get enough sleep. When we are sick, someone must do his best to restore us to health. When one of our parents or children dies, we can get over the shock more easily if someone outside the immediate family comforts us. With the people whom we see most frequently and with whom we stand in a relationship of mutual dependence, we must get along. With outsiders, particularly if they are our rivals, we often have to fight.

What this really amounts to is that our basic needs consist of caring for the equilibrium of the individual, and of the group or groups of which he is a part. Some of our activities, like providing food and clothing and warm houses, work directly to keep up his body temperature and supply of energy. Others, like the orderly process of government in the community, serve to maintain the equilibrium of the group. Still others, ritual and ceremony, restore equilibrium to individuals and to groups after shocks, while warfare may prevent destruction by outside agencies.

Within this framework of maintaining equilibrium, restoring it, and preventing its destruction, single activities often play more than one role. The Aztecs might fight a battle, for example, not to prevent attack, for they feared none, but to protect trade routes, to obtain victims for sacrifice, or both. Warfare was also necessary to keep their citizens busy and in order. The concept of equilibrium is a necessary one for our purpose, but it is not the only one we need. We still must classify the activities themselves.

The only way left to do this which I can devise is to follow the historical approach. That means, to see and to list those activities which human beings in all known societies have in common with lower animals, for these must have been the very ones with which our ancestors, a million or more years ago, started their unique career, and out of which more elaborate behavior patterns have developed. This list is the common denominator of human behavior.

15. Eating, Drinking, and Feeding.

One of the first things that an individual does after birth is to take food from its mother, and eating and drinking take up a certain amount of each person's time every day. Whereas we sometimes eat and drink alone, human beings everywhere form the habit of eating at least one meal a day together. This is because it is simpler to cook for several people at once than for each person separately. The standard human practice is for people to get together at the end of a day, prepare their food, and consume it. When the same persons do this day after day a bond arises between them. Eating is a pleasurable action, and hence the association becomes agreeable. Among many peoples of the world it is the custom that those who have eaten together cannot be enemies; hence eating something or drinking something together serves as a symbol of a close relationship.

The reader has no doubt observed that when people sit to a common meal it is considered poor manners for each to pitch in at once. Someone sits at the head of the table, and whether or not he says grace, the others will wait for him to begin. The group that eats together has a tendency to take on structure, with one person in the lead, and that structure is most commonly a family.

There are not many ways to eat and drink. Whether you use a fork, chopsticks, or your fingers, you have to convey food to your mouth. Hence this is one of the least variable of human activities, and everywhere the rules that govern it tend to be similar.

16. Grooming and Healing.

Grooming is a semitechnical term used by specialists in animal behavior to describe the care of the body. When a cat sits down and washes itself, cleaning and smoothing its fur by licking and manipulation, that is grooming. Sometimes one cat will groom another. Monkeys and apes spend much more time than cats in interpersonal grooming, as explained in Chapter 1. Everyone who reads this page has probably seen monkeys doing this in zoos. Monkey A lies down and relaxes. Monkey B searches through A's fur, picking out small particles of dead skin, examines these, and puts them in his (B's) mouth. Monkey A obviously enjoys this. Before long B may lie down and A will groom him (or her) in return.

Aside from keeping the animals' bodies clean, grooming helps build up habitual relationships between individuals. This is just as true of human beings, whose autonomic nervous systems work in the same way as those of other mammals. As one might expect, human beings at all cultural levels and in all regions groom each other. This may consist in two women combing each others' hair, or painting each others' bodies; or it may be that a mother will stroke and massage her child to calm it.

All of these activities help preserve or restore the equilibrium of the body, but they become most critical when done in cases of illness. This involves the professional act of "laying on of hands" by a shaman, nurse, or masseur.

In almost any primitive group the anthropologist will find one man at least who is an expert in this, who is a healer. When a person is ill his relatives will send for the shaman, as this expert is called. The shaman will go through an emotional ritual, in which he may simulate the actions of calling on supernatural beings, and in the course of which he will rub the patient and probably suck the sore spot. What he actually succeeds in doing is to conduct a religious ceremony which relieves the feelings of everyone present, patient and family included, and what healing can be done by faith and suggestion alone will be accomplished. The physiotherapy which forms part of his treatment may also have a mechanical effect on the patient's nervous system and circulation.

Aside from illness, the patient needs the holy man's help at times of personal crisis, when he is changing from boyhood to manhood, in many cases when he is getting married. At such times the shaman will conduct *rites of passage,* symbolizing the *removal* of the individual from his earlier state, his *transition* to the next, and his *incorporation* into the company of initiates, married men, or whatever.

From time to time crises arise which disturb everyone equally because they come from forces outside the group concerned; these may be the sudden descent of an enemy band, or a severe storm or violent wind. Here the holy man again shows his versatility, for he conducts mass ceremonies to allay these dangers by magical means, and actually succeeds in uniting the people into a common effort with zeal replacing fear and confusion. In a country where the seasons differ greatly and the annual cycle involves changes of human activity, such ceremonies become annual. Performances of this second category are called *rites of intensification.*

Even beside all these duties, the shaman may be a sorcerer as well. This means that by his magical efforts he undertakes to send illness, death, or other misfortune against an enemy of his client. If the enemy learns of this, a belief in his fate may well cause him discomfort, and in any case the belief that the magic works does much to restore the spirits and good health of the client. Naturally a shaman must not openly accept commissions of this kind when directed against members of the same camp or he will start more trouble than he allays.

Anthropologists have long known that out of the generalized all-inclusive healing operations of the shaman have developed two special professions in more complicated societies, those of the physician and of the priest. The physician has taken over the physical aspects of healing, which include the use of medicine, as well as surgery; these work on the body as a whole, and all its parts. The priest has taken as his share the aspects of healing which make use of ritual symbols, and his ministrations have their effect through one part of the body only, the higher nerve centers which respond emotionally to his symbolic procedures and thus restore equilibrium in the organism as a whole.

A surgeon, however, has to deal with his patients one by one, and normally everyone does not have appendicitis at the same time. Even if they did he could only operate on one at a time. His relations with his patients are therefore *paired* relations. The priest may perform his rites for the individual, and often does, but his principal task is to take the lead in ceremonies in which he restores equilibrium to a group as a whole. For example, a Greek Orthodox priest praying to St. Elias in the fields during a summer drought, with his flock kneeling about him, while he asks for rain, calms them and keeps them in order during the upset caused by the natural crisis which disturbs them all in concert. Whether or not rain falls, he has performed a real and necessary therapeutic task which has survival value for the society, something which those who try to "debunk" religion fail to realize. He has, however, done something else; he has headed up a number of people in a group event, something which the surgeon, by the limitations of his task, does not do. He and his fellow priests form, in consequence, a complex hierarchy, challenging kings and dictators. The physicians and surgeons have only their medical association, for their patients are usually individuals, not groups.

17. Learning and Teaching.

It is generally agreed that the widest difference between human beings and other animals lies in the far greater capacity of the former to learn things. The mother gives the child its first training, and the mother or helpers, an older sister or nurse, teach the baby how to eat, how to regulate its elimination, and how to walk and talk. Once a child has learned to speak and understand spoken words, teaching is easier than it was before, because communication is greatly facilitated. In nearly all human societies the earliest teaching that a child receives is from its parents and other close kin such as its brothers and sisters. This is usually informal. When the child is old enough to walk about without close supervision, it spends part of its day in a play group with other children its own age, and these children learn from those a little older than themselves. It is only in cases of extraordinary isolation that such play groups are not found.

Children learn by imitating the actions of older people. They use dolls to represent babies, they make toy houses out of whatever materials are available, they fight with toy weapons, and they repeat their play activities over and over again. Everyone knows that a child will reread the same book many times if the book is agreeable to him. Dolls, make-believe houses, and wooden swords are symbols, whose significance is enhanced by repetition. Words, the commonest and most easily recognized form of symbol, also have to be learned by repetition.

Other than repetition, what is learning? To answer this question is the job of psychologists, and they are divided into many schools. All I can do here is to try to summarize the points on which most of them agree. These include a division of the learning process into three main components:

1. *Sign learning*. An animal learns through repetition to respond to the same sign. This is learning in the sense of Pavlov and of B. F. Skinner.

2. *Solution learning*. A chimpanzee is left in a cage with a dismounted two-piece stick. Outside the cage is a banana. Will the chimp put the two pieces of the stick together and with it poke the banana within reach? If he finds out how to do this, the next time this situation arises he will know what to do. Some psychologists subdivide solution learning into *trial-and-error learning* and *insight*. If he experiments with each section of the stick in turn, finding that neither is long enough to reach the banana, and then, discovering the socket, puts the two together, this is *trial and error*. If he just sits there and looks at the banana and the two pieces of stick, then joins them without experiment, and completes the action, it is *insight*, or *visualization*, done without language.*

3. *The rational process*. You are eighteen years old, sitting alone in your room, and thinking about how you will persuade your mother to let you take out the

*See John Paul Scott, *Animal Behavior*, Chicago, Chicago University Press, 1958, pp. 152-4.

family car on Saturday night. This is a rational process, confined to man, combining insight with unspoken language. Words and the rational process go together.

There comes a time in the life of every male child, and in some societies of girls as well, that his education is no longer the concern of his family and his playmates, but of the larger group in which he lives. The boy is about to become a man, and he must be taught how to act like a man. Time and again the student discovers, in reading an account of native life in widely distant countries, that we old men take the boys away from their mothers, isolate them in the wilderness, put them on short rations, subject them to ordeals, frighten them, reveal to them tribal mysteries, and instruct them. This is the "bush school", that teaches quickly and indelibly by shock treatment. It is also a puberty rite, in which the sequence of events serves both as a formal education in the fundamentals of adult behavior and as a rite of passage.

Whether the society is simple or complex, and whether the boys are put through puberty rites or sent to the kinds of school we have, matters little, for the technique of good teaching rests on the same principles. Chief among these is the necessity that a good teacher has to be an artist, as you will see if you examine the procedure of bush schools and initiation rites in detail. We can afford a few failures, but peoples living from hand to mouth cannot.

The details of teaching curricula fit the patterns of the adult cultures concerned. In some Hindu families, babies and young children are allowed to sit on their fathers' laps, it being the older persons' intention to train the young to feel an equal attachment to all senior members of the joint family group. Another example: in the Riffian households in Morocco, boys used to be brought up amidst scenes of bloodshed, and were constantly reminded by their fathers and uncles and elder brothers of their grisly obligations. The same used to be true in Albania. A native of that country once told me that he had emigrated to the United States at nineteen; he could not have come earlier because he had had to wait until he had avenged his father's murder. Here he eventually became a clerk, and no more blood-thirsty than any of the hundreds of other clerks whom he passed on the streets daily on his way to work.

18. Talking.

All free moving animals have some means of communicating with one another, because these are necessary for survival and reproduction. It seems safe to say that no land-based mammal spends more of its time communicating than man does. This communication is based on a blend of signs and symbols. Among other primates these consist mostly of vocal calls, facial gestures, and movements of the trunk and limbs. We also gesture, make faces, and touch each other, in various degrees depending on the culture concerned, but the major part of our communication is through words.

The repertoire of words which the members of a group of people use in communicating with each other is a language. A language is a configuration of symbols. As such it mirrors the habitual activities and processes of rationalization of the people who speak it. As the prime means of communication speech is an essential part of all other forms of interaction. Only in a Trappist monastery and in a few other unusual institutions do people find it possible to get along together without conversation. Furthermore people often talk for the sake of interacting alone, rather than through any need of communicating specific thoughts. They also use language as a medium of art, as we shall see later.

19. Mating.

Man is descended from a long line of tropical ancestors. In tropical rain forests there is no optimum time of year for births, for there are no seasons, and hence there is no need for a special breeding period. In many tropical species, however, the female goes through a lunar cycle during which she is alternately eager and loath to receive masculine attentions. Although the human female also passes through a 28-day cycle of ovulation and menstruation, the changes in her desire or ability to have sexual relations are much less marked.

The upshot of all this is that organically and physiologically human beings are so constituted that mating interests them frequently and at all times of the year, and that it is a primary mechanism by which an individual man and an individual woman build up close and intimate relationships with one another. Since the sexual act is also the means of fertilization, the children which result will make this bond even stronger, for once they are born the parents need to care for them. Local customs of positions of intercourse, time of day or night, place, etc., are of special interest to ethnographers, but are always secondary to the fact that everywhere one studies human societies the physiology of reproduction is much the same, and the results, in the formation of families, similar.

20. Sharing.

It is a part of the primeval division of labor between old and young, men and women, that the individuals who live together should share the food and warmth produced by their separate and collective efforts. In your own family you can doubtless recall many occasions on which your father, grasping a knife firmly in one hand and a fork in the other, carved a roast and laid the slices on your plates to be handed around the table for distribution. This practice goes back as far as that of eating meat, or any other food which comes in large pieces or is cooked as a unit of more than one portion.

People who live off the land do not always bring home an equal amount of food every day. If a number of families are living together, and the men are hunters, one man may bring in an antelope one day, but following that he may have no further luck for a week. It is much more economical, much more likely to permit their survival, for several families living under these circumstances to camp together, and to share their food. Four men setting out each morning in different directions are more likely to kill an animal than one man alone, and one animal is enough for all of their families for one day. Whoever brings in the meat, everyone can eat. The food will not spoil or be wasted.

This is a business in which disputes could easily occur, especially when people are hungry, and could disturb the relations of the members of the group. Hence rigid rules have always been established by custom, and some man of authority cuts the meat and hands it out. He is usually an older man, and a man whom the others respect. If we look at the process of government in other societies, up to and including our own, we will see the same thing going on. The people earn their livings. They pay a portion of their returns to the government, be the returns in grain or in cattle or in money, or even in work. The government stores these taxes, and spends them in public works. The chief, the king, the president, is essentially the man who divides the meat.

21. Leading and Deciding.

The man who divides the meat is also the man who decides when that particular section of the country has been hunted out, or when the berries or acorns will be ripe in another valley. People talk about it a lot, but he is the man who says, "Now is the time to move. Let's go." He is the leader. His leadership may not be due to any superior knowledge on his part, but simply to his ability to weigh things calmly, make decisions, and get people to follow him. He is also the man who settles disputes in the camp, and who sees to it that so-and-so is killed after he has disturbed the peace too many times. He is the man whom you see, in our society, sitting in a judge's chair, or acting as the chairman of the board of a big corporation.

22. Fighting.

Quarreling in the camp is poor business and bad for the survival of the people who live in it. Fighting with outsiders, however, may be necessary to permit the survival of the group as a whole, and the group which has the best warriors will be the one to keep alive when there is hunger everywhere and not enough food to go around.

Hunger and population pressure are not the only reasons for warfare. In some countries the men have nothing to do during the off season; this happens in areas of slash-and-burn agriculture, as in Borneo and parts of South America, between the harvest and the preparation of the land for the next growing period. At this time the men of a village or group of villages will get together under a war chief, go through elaborate rituals, and set off on an expedition to lift heads, capture sacrificial victims, or obtain other visible tokens of their prowess. When they come home they hold further ceremonies and eventually resume their peacetime occupations. This seasonal warfare gives them an activity to take up their spare time; it also provides a mechanism for initiating young men, inuring them to hardships, and stabilizing the government. Even modern European nations have been known to resort to war outside to keep the peace at home.

The man who leads the warriors, however, is not always the man who divides the meat and decides where to go. Good judgment and leadership are not always lodged in the most muscular and vigorous bodies or associated with bravery in combat. Among many peoples we find a division of leadership, between the civil and military chiefs, between the professions of politician and soldier. Although one gifted man may combine the two types of personality, they are much more frequently separated.

23. Playing.

Warfare is essentially an affair of two individuals, or two teams of individuals, acting simultaneously against each other. Each is trying to take the lead; neither is following. When two women have a verbal battle, both talk at once, and each incites the other to greater effort. This type of behavior can be observed in almost any species of lower mammal. Among human beings one other kind of competitive effort is universal, that of playing games. Large books have been written describing the games of different peoples, from board games to college football and Olympic contests. Some games require little effort; others are so rough that contestants may become maimed or killed. Sometimes they end in fights.

Games serve a number of purposes. They take up slack time, like off-season warfare, and give people a routine to follow when they have come together for a ceremony. That is why in non-Christian societies games are so often played at funerals. They give rival institutions a chance to work off steam, and furnish the routine, the context, of many ceremonial occasions. When people get together and don't know what else to do, someone will say, "Let's play a game."

24. Entertaining.

No single, simple English word presents itself to express the type of activity meant in this paragraph. I refer to the entire body of esthetic actions which human beings perform—singing, dancing, reciting poetry, playing instruments, acting out episodes or plays, painting, carving, embellishing the body—everything that gives esthetic pleasure to people, the whole field of art in its widest sense. Artistic expression is common to all peoples and goes far back in the past. Many other animals, such as birds, produce and respond to artistic efforts. Even the monkeys and apes seem to have their moments of rhythmic chest thumping, jumping about for no other possible purpose than entertainment and esthetic vocalization.

Art stimulates emotions and lowers the threshold of resistance to belief and persuasion. A good teacher uses language with an emotional content, as does a successful preacher. A tribal chief urging his men to battle will evoke a wider response if he uses words of emotional content to his followers than otherwise. The literature of anthropology is full of references to fine orators, among the Maori, Iroquois, and others.

One thing that is important to remember is that the esthetic needs of people everywhere may be equal in quantity. A band of pygmies in the forest dance every moonlit night; through the long winter of the northern forest, the Finnish farmers play games and listen to their bards recite epics to the accompaniment of zithers. Art is an all-purpose activity which may be blended with profit in any kind of enterprise. It may take many forms, and it is often present when people do not realize that it is there. Like the leader, like the healer, the artist has a special kind of personality of his own. So has the joker.

Artistic performances, whatever the medium, vary greatly in this last respect—the amount of humor which they contain. Some depend almost entirely on this element for their appeal; in others it is a pleasant, lightening factor. In still other performances where a number of actors are creating great tension, a clown will introduce comic relief. Humor depends essentially on the juxtaposition of symbols from separate and even conflicting configurations. A man wearing a silk hat and diapers will amuse many people, but he may shock others. There is often a thin line between laughter and anger. Neurologically they are closely related emotions. Both are essentially human, and all peoples ever studied joke and lose their tempers.

25. Getting Raw Materials.

So far we have been dealing entirely with interpersonal relations—between the individual and other people. In his dealings with others, however, the individual makes use of materials derived from the rest of the world, such as food, clothing, weapons, ceremonial paraphernalia, and musical instruments. Handling materials is called *technology*. There is a simpler word for technological activities, and that is *work*.

One kind of work is to go out and get the things that you need, the things that can be made into food, clothing, weapons, etc. Every single group of people has to do this. So do the lower animals. But the lower animals—at least those most closely resembling man, the other primates—do not bring things home. They consume them on the spot. One of the first essentials of human behavior is bringing in the results of the day's hunting or gathering expedition, processing it, and sharing it, as we have seen above.

For the first million years of human existence, all men were hunters and gatherers. Some of us still are. It is probably a long time, however, since any people relied exclusively on their hands for obtaining their raw materials. Hunters make use of spears thrown by hand, spears thrown with the wommera (spear thrower), bows and arrows, slings, throwing sticks, and other projectiles. By these means they can hit the animal from a distance. In order to get close enough for this, hunters learn how to glide through the forest silently, or to creep through the grass of an open plain, with or without disguise.

Some forms of hunting require the synchronized efforts of several people, each with his special role; others, such as the surround or net hunting, need the organized efforts of the whole camp or village. Trapping does not take many people, but it takes much skill. Hunting is fine exercise for body and brain. It stimulates and may have "selected for" the qualities of self-control, cooperation, tempered aggressiveness, ingenuity, inventiveness, and a high degree of manual dexterity. Mankind could have gone through no better school in its formative period.

Gathering and collecting are the words usually employed to designate the chief daily activities of women among people who live off the land. While men are off hunting, women may walk about with string bags over their shoulders, and digging sticks in their hands, on the lookout for wild plants with succulent roots, for berries, mushrooms, snails, edible insects, and small animals that move slowly or can be dug out of their burrows, known to the trade as "slow game."*

Foodstuffs, with accompanying skins, sinews, and bone, are not all the raw materials that people need, however. Nor do saplings for spearshafts, withes for baskets and hut frames, grass and leaves for roofing and beds, complete the list. All human beings require at least a minimum of raw minerals. They must have friable stone to knap into cutting tools, to shape their weapons and cut their meat, and they must have clay and ochre to rub on their bodies and to paint their sacred emblems on cliff or wood or stone. Ritual life is just as necessary for the survival of the small, natural group of people living off the land as the food they eat. Esthetic materials cannot be neglected. And in all societies you will find that people spend much more time, care, and skill on objects intended for ritual or

---

*In tropical Africa and India, wild honey is a staple. Gathering it from high trees or the faces of overhanging cliffs can be dangerous work, like hunting, and is done only by men.

symbolic than for utilitarian or nonsymbolic use, if the two can be separated. Probably the distinction is purely quantitative.

Another means of acquiring raw materials is by breeding and growing them. During the last ten thousand years some of the peoples of the world have been engaged in propagating plants and animals in captivity. The farmer and animal breeder can select and alter the form or habits of plants and animals to suit their needs, whereas the wild forms of each are subject to natural selection. In a state of nature a cow with a large udder, capable of yielding ten to twelve times the animal's weight in milk a year, would be at a disadvantage, as would a sheep with a long coat of wool; a variety of potatoes yielding tubers of two pounds' weight would not have much chance of surviving in the struggle with smaller fruited wild species and weeds. The artificial propagation of these freaks of nature increases the amount of food that people can derive from landscapes in which agriculture and animal husbandry are possible.

The farmer with plants alone is not much better off than the hunters and gatherers in rich regions, for there is a limit to the amount of muscular effort he can expend. When he has domestic animals to haul his plough and grind his olives, he can produce much more food per unit of effort. However remarkable the advances of modern science, increasing the yield of the land, speeding up the farmer's work, releasing more and more people for industry and the professions, we all have to eat, and some of us still have to raise the raw materials from which our food is made.

26. Processing.

Processing materials is no monopoly of man. If you watch the apes at feeding time in any zoo you will see how carefully they peel the bananas and sweet potatoes which are given them. There is one thing, however, that *is* a monopoly of man—*the use of fire*. Everyone in the world uses it—to keep warm, to keep dry, and to cook food. Keeping warm and dry permits people to live in climates otherwise lethal to furless mammals. Cooking food is one of the prime causative factors in human evolution. Cooking meat breaks down the cell structure, reduces some of the complex protein molecules into smaller molecules, causes the tendons and less digestible tissues to swell, soften, and be easily pulled apart from the more edible tissues, and reduces the dangers of food poisoning, particularly from organisms of the salmonella group. Cooking vegetables converts some of the cellulose into sugar as in baking potatoes; it also converts some of the starches to sugars. It breaks down woody cell structures mechanically, by the explosion of trapped steam.

Cooking increases the efficiency of foodstuffs available to human beings, particularly to those who live off the land. It makes them more easily digestible. It reduces the amount of time which must be spent eating—witness the length of time each day it takes a gibbon, who lives on watery fruits, to eat (see Chapter 1). Most important of all, it reduces the work of the teeth and jaws, making possible the evolution of the human face and skull to their present form. Our face is built for talking, not for biting. Just as the habit of standing erect and walking on two legs alone freed the hands for all their delicate skills, so the use of fire freed the face for its intricate task of communication. With skill and cleverness at a premium, the brain grew.

This diversion into physical anthropology serves only to emphasize the controlling character of work activities in human history. Aside from using fire, of course, the most important activity is tool making. In nature there are not many substances which will take and hold an edge with which one can cut skin, meat, bones, and wood. The best of these which can be handled without other tools is flint. A man can pick up a flint nodule which has eroded out of a bank of chalk or clay, smash it with a stone, and find among the fragments some pieces with long enough, straight enough fracture edges to serve as knives and scrapers. Or he can throw the nodule into his fire and pick up the pieces after it has burst.

Further work, trimming and flaking, may improve the tool. If the man knows how to handle flint well, he can prepare a striking platform from which he can tap off many blades of the size and shape most useful to him. Flint will cut meat and skins as well as any other tool material, but it is poor with wood, for the tough fibres shatter its edge. Some peoples have never learned to make efficient wood-cutting tools and hence manufacture few and simple articles of wood. Others have learned—and this is a relatively recent skill less than ten thousand years old—to grind the surfaces of a hard-grained pebble to a cutting edge, which will not shatter in contact with wood, and can be hafted as an axe. With such an axe it takes a long time to fell a tree of any size, but it can be felled. With the tree a good carpenter can make a canoe, even a ship, or a warm, weatherproof house, very little different in appearance from those some of us live in.

A still more recent skill is the reduction of raw minerals to the state of commercial metals. People who mine and smelt and cast and forge copper, bronze, and iron must be professionals, for these work tasks take much dexterity, and this craft requires a long period of full-time apprenticeship. The use of metal not only increases the speed and efficiency of cutting and processing wood. It also permits the manufacture and use of special tools, like saws and drills and planes and files. With metal for bolts and tire rims, one can make far better wheeled vehicles than with flint and stone the only available mineral materials. The shipwright can work much better too with metal tools and metal bolts and fittings.

If people are to handle much in the way of materials, raw or processed, they need containers. The easiest containers to make are those which one person can fashion without special tools—a basket, a piece of folded bark, or even an empty mollusc shell or turtle carapace. A little more work will produce a wooden bowl. It takes more skill to dry a basketful of clay, pulverize it, mix in a tempering material such as sand or ground shell, wet it, shape it into the form of a pot, and bake it at a hot enough temperature. Pottery repays all this work, because the material is cheap, the work is rapid, and the shapes and sizes made depend largely on the potter's own skill. Another great advantage is that pots can be placed over the fire. You can boil food in them. Pots break but are easily replaced. Metal vessels are better for people who move about frequently, for if they are dented they can be hammered back into shape.

One of the simplest operations known to man is handling vegetable fibers; it is possible for one person working alone to make excellent baskets without tools. Another use of these fibers is in matting, from which textiles is the next logical step. In order to produce textiles in any quantity, one needs an abundance of raw materials, and this can only be obtained through agriculture (flax, cotton) animal husbandry (wool, hair) or both.* Independently in at least two parts of the

*The Northwest Coast Indians, who had no agriculture, bred special wooly-haired dogs for this purpose.

world, the Andean Highlands and the Middle East, textile methods were invented and developed by people who had ample supplies of both vegetable and animal fibers, and in both areas the methods of spinning and weaving and of decoration are the same. When there is only one good way to do something, more than one person will think of it.

Another class of fiber processing is paper-making. In its simplest form this involves beating out the moist bark of certain trees, such as paper mulberry, into fine sheets. Polynesians, African pygmies, and many South American Indians, to mention but a few, make bark cloth and use it for clothing. The manufacture of paper for printing is but a refinement of the same process of felting vegetable fibers together and is one of the essentials of our civilization. How many sheets of paper are used in your college or business every week?

Cloth, leather, and felt, which is technically akin to bark-cloth and paper, form the materials of our clothing. Some of us who are rich or who live in very cold climates, or both, also wear furs. If one surveys rapidly the different styles of clothing worn by human beings one sees every range and variation from the complete nudity of some of the inhabitants of warm countries to the very efficient fur garments of the Siberian natives and Eskimo. Many factors affect the style of clothing which people wear. The need for circulation of air and free perspiration is paramount in the tropics, and the need for body heat retention vital in the far North. Peoples long resident in regions of extreme climatic conditions have in most cases adopted appropriate costumes, yet this is not always the case. Clothes are also symbols. They represent a person's sex, age, social status, wealth, religion, and prowess at arms. In countries where the requirements of the environment are not so strong that to wear the wrong kind of clothes would be lethal, the symbolic value of a costume is often more important than comfort or convenience in determining its cut and form. Yet we must remember that it was the invention of warm tailored clothing as much as anything else that finally, in the time of the last ice sheet, permitted human beings to occupy those extensive portions of the earth's surface where winter cold would kill off naked people or people clad only in the simplest and most widespread of garments—the sleeveless and legless robe.

27. Carrying.

The lower primates and other kinds of mammals, such as cats and skunks, carry their helpless offspring from tree to tree or lair to lair. Few of them carry food. None of them carry fire or tools. Among the most simply living peoples known, as among the most advanced, there is always a "bottleneck" in transportation. No one can carry as much as he would like. The quantity and nature of one's possessions depend on what can and cannot be moved.

Travelers in lands strange to them have often remarked, "Look at the lazy so-and-so, his wife is loaded like a donkey, and he walks empty-handed!" If the traveler looks a little more closely, he will discover that the "lazy" man is not quite empty handed. He carries his own personal belongings in a pouch at his waist, and is probably armed with a gun or a bow. He is very much on the alert. He may spy an animal which he can kill for the pot, or an enemy, and he cannot afford to be caught napping. Transport by land in large parts of the world depends on the muscle, bone, and sinew of human beings. Some, as in Negro Africa, carry their burdens on their heads; others, as in Tibet, on their backs. Peoples so fortunate as to have domestic animals can either pack them, hitch them to sleds or wheeled vehicles, or ride them. Sleds, of course, are more efficient on snow or ice; vehicles on flat land surfaces. Some surfaces suitable for vehicular traffic are natural, as the plains of Central Asia; others have to be built, like our roads, and those of the Romans.

A measure of the importance of land transport in our civilization may be obtained by finding the portion of our national budget spent on the building and maintenance of roads and railroads, on the purchase and upkeep of rolling stock and motor vehicles, the amount spent on fuel, tickets on trains and busses, salaries to the employees of transport companies, etc. If you add to this similar figures for air traffic and shipping, you will find that transportation looms in the same category as food in importance. So it does throughout the world. To reckon this for peoples without cash or budgets, calculate the amount of time which they spend carrying things around.

There is no space here to consider the history of shipping, which can be read elsewhere. We may, however, discuss its importance. Seagoing craft could not be made before people had tools of polished stone. With these all the huge sailing vessels of Polynesians were built, the double hulls which carried them across the Pacific from Southeast Asia and Indonesia to such distant islands and groups of islands as Easter, Hawaii, and New Zealand. With polished stone and a little copper were made the ships which men in earlier times sailed from the Eastern Mediterranean through the Pillars of Hercules and up the coast of Europe to Scotland and Scandinavia. Sea travel connects far distant regions. The people of an island may have more frequent relations and a greater cultural affinity with other maritime people a thousand miles away than with land-locked neighbors over the next range of mountains.

28. Trading.

One of the principal reasons why people carry things is so that they can trade, or exchange them. Even in the simplest of societies this is necessary. The reason is of course that nature's favors are unevenly distributed over the landscape. The student must be sure to distinguish clearly between the two quite different acts of *sharing* and *trading*. People who share give each other the same kinds of goods. They throw their day's catch into a common pool, and then distribute it. People who trade give each other different kinds of goods, each to make up for the other's lack. Trading implies some degree of specialization; sharing does not.

Among peoples who make their cutting tools of flint, some bands or tribes may live in a rich flinty area; others in completely flintless territory. The flintless ones may, however, live where there is iron ore, useful as red paint material. So the two will meet from time to time and exchange products. Now these meetings, whether people are trading flint for ochre or coal for iron or crude rubber for "cheap tin trays," must take one of several forms. Sometimes people come together and hold an elaborate ceremony, which serves to build up and intensify their adjustment to each other, and then trade, as if wholly incidentally. Several examples of this have already been given. Or the traders may be protected by political authority; witness the military aspect of Aztec trade. Or they may be considered out-castes or noncombatants and permitted free circulation, as in Arabia.

Still another way of trading is silent trade, conducted by jungle nomads in many parts of the world. The forest people creep through the lianas to the trading place, and leave a neat pile of jungle products, such as wax, camphor, monkey's gall bladders, birds' nests for Chinese soup. They creep back a certain distance, and wait in a safe place. The partners to the exchange, who are usually agriculturalists with a more elaborate and extensive set of material possessions but who cannot be bothered stumbling through the jungle after wax when they have someone else to do it for them, discover the little pile, and lay down beside it what they consider its equivalent in metal cutting tools, cheap cloth, bananas, and the like. They too discreetly retire. The shy folk then reappear, inspect the two piles, and if they are satisfied, take the second one away. Then the opposite group comes back and takes pile number one, and the exchange is completed. If the forest people are dissatisfied, they can retire once more, and if the other people want to increase their offering they may, time and again, until everyone is happy. The first record of this kind of transaction in history is in the *Periplus* of Hanno, the account of a Phoenician trading and exploring voyage around Africa, made about 1000 B.C. In one sense it is like our mail-order business, in that the participants never see each other and have to have faith in each other if they wish the relationship to continue. What I would like to point out here is that the trading relationship need not be a very emotional one, like sex or religion. Unless he is a slaver, the trader deals in goods and not in human relations.

29. Testing and Experimenting.

Animal psychologists have conducted many experiments with apes to test their powers of reason and imagination. One favorite is the "chimpanzee plus jointed stick and banana" test mentioned in section 17. In this experiment, the psychologists tested the chimpanzee. The ape tested something, too.

This is what human beings do in problems of equal or greater complication. Some people are more inventive than others. The inventor, a familiar type in our civilization, has just as marked a personality as the other kinds of specialists who have been mentioned. The inventor works by experimenting. He gets an idea and tests it. His experiments are symbolic actions, for he is not trying to make something, but to discover something. If he succeeds, manufacture can come later. His own satisfaction is his greatest reward.

All the progress of man from the level of a big-toothed bipedal animal has depended on the cumulative success of men interested in scientific problems, however they themselves would have interpreted their interests and actions. These men have had a hard time throughout history, because they have initiated changes. Change disturbs the equilibrium of the group, and when people are disturbed they turn on the individual who has caused the upset. They drive out the scientist, accuse him of heresy, try him for witchcraft. But now and then they need his inventions and use them. This occurs only, as a rule, when their relations have been disturbed already by some change which they could not avert, and when the adoption of the new technique actually restores equilibrium. A man who produces a new weapon just when his fellows are hardest pressed by an enemy attack is always popular. During and after World War II the physicists and chemists were no longer absent-minded crackpots, the underpaid butts of cartoonists and movie comedians. They were mysterious geniuses in whose hands lay the destiny of mankind.

Science, however, is not merely an affair of retorts and bunsen burners and atomic bombs. Scientists concern themselves with the individual and with groups of people as well as with the world outside. The task of the social scientist is harder than that of the physical or natural scientists, because his subjects are men like himself. They will not hold still; they interact as they are studied; and their nervous systems constitute the most complicated physicochemical fact in the world.

30. The Expenditure of Energy and the Interchangeability of Activities.

I have just listed (sections 15 through 29) fifteen kinds of activity in which human beings ordinarily take part, either alone, in pairs, or in groups. The number fifteen is what I arrived at after many attempts, but I do not consider it final. Some of you may discover others or decide to combine some of those on my list. Any classification of phenomena into mutually exclusive categories is artificial, because all differences are quantitative. A category is a locus on one or more scales at which units tend to congregate.

To demonstrate this, we need only consider the physiological differences which certain activities generate. Probably the two most intense activities in which people participate are fighting and copulating. When two men are standing face to face within arms' length, slashing at each other with swords, no matter how used they are to combat, if they are fighting for keeps and not just sparring, each is keyed up to a high pitch. His organs of perception are on the alert to detect each motion, each flick of the wrist, of his opponent as soon as it has begun. Most of his blood has left his internal organs and is coursing through the vessels of his limbs, supplying emergency sugar to tense muscles. His adrenal glands are secreting swiftly; the pupils of his eyes may be dilated, and his hair erect. When the fight is over, if he is still alive, he will be exhausted. The sexual act creates almost equal physiological changes. That is why elderly men often die of heart failure after marrying young women.

A preacher at the height of his sermon may be seen to show evidences of emotion. His voice will tremble, his brow perspire. A good lecturer is nervous before he steps on the platform, and then "warms" to his audience. At the end of his discourse he needs some time to cool off before he can set his mind to other matters. A friend of mine who is a distinguished actor told me that performing on the stage takes less out of him than lecturing. In lecturing you are addressing the audience directly and can see their reaction. On the stage you address the other actors, and behind the footlights the audience is so nearly invisible that you do not notice them.

All things are not the same to all people, but ordinarily a man who works at a solitary task puts little emotion into it, and the whole category of work activities contains less emotional context than out-and-out human relations. Only in bargaining, haggling in the market, bidding and raising, the more complicated facets of exchange, is much emotion aroused. Each person is endowed with a certain daily quota of energy, a certain amount of which must be worked off in interaction with his family, friends, customers, or enemies if he is to remain happy.

That is why the solitary worker may want to talk a lot in the evening, or to be entertained; why miners who work apart in their underground tunnels for hours at a time like to organize and hold meetings—they will never get what they really want, which is a job with more interaction and less danger, until the whole technique of mineral extraction is changed. That is why the professor, who has been lecturing all day, wants solitude, a book, and bed.

If we examine even more closely the quantitative aspects of interaction we will see why warriors, before going out to fight, are always separated from women for a certain period of anticipation and training, and are rarely allowed sexual relations while on a mission. Fighting and copulating are too much alike, and ordinarily the warrior needs all his emotional energy and attention for combat. The man whose specialty it is to heal and comfort others is another case in point. People have a habit of falling ill and of dying in the middle of the night. The shaman, doctor, or priest cannot live a normal family life and attend to his job as well. He must neglect one or the other. Furthermore, if he uses ritual that requires a high emotional output, this reduces the amount left for his family below the critical level. And his subjects include persons of both sexes and all ages. For the purposes of his job, he must appear sexless and ageless. These are the perfectly valid reasons why so many societies demand that the shaman, the healer, the priest be celibate. The principle is that one man cannot serve a family and mankind as well, and in order to enforce it societies surround this restriction with sanctions and tabus.

31. Relationships which These Activities Create—Role and Status.

In most of the fifteen activities listed in sections 15 through 29, solitary efforts are possible, but in none are they typical. As a rule, people do not choose to work alone, and hence the only solitary actions that occur with any frequency are those that require individual concentration without interruption. Hunting a seal at a blow-hole is one of these. A second person is unnecessary and might make a noise and frighten the seal. Painting pictures is another. The artist can work best if he is alone with his thoughts and the scenery.

In some other kinds of work, paired events are best: a man dictating a long list of letters to his secretary, two men sawing logs, or two men paddling a canoe. It is the third kind, the group event, that concerns us most here, since it is events of this kind that build up natural groups and institutions. But in any group or institution there must be paired events as well as group events or the structure will not achieve stability.

Whenever an individual does something with or to another person, or with or to several other persons, and repeats this time after time, he gradually creates habitual relationships between himself and the other or others. Before long he knows which end of the canoe he will sit in, and whether he will give orders or obey them. If it appears after a while that he is the best cook in the party, he will be the one to do the cooking, unless he is also the boss and can order someone else to cook for him. The relative positions and special duties of individuals shake down after a while, and before long each person has learned his or her station.

All the relationships which people develop can be divided into two convenient classes, (a) those that are common to all kinds of activities, since they form in themselves the mechanism of interaction; and (*b*) those that arise from each separate activity through the special requirements of the business at hand. Let us carry this a little further.

    a. Common Activities. Three of these are self-evident.

    (1) *Supervisory.* Every group of three or more persons who are working at the same job must have a leader if it is to accomplish its task, and the leader is the man who starts the ball rolling. In every activity which takes three or more persons to complete it, this *supervisory* relationship is always found. It is the relationship between leader and followed, supervisor and supervised, superior and subordinate, boss and hand. In the more complex societies a derivative relationship, the *staff line*, may also arise. This represents the activities of inspectors toward all branches of an organization. Police and M.P.s who can arrest any civilian or military personnel regardless of rank, are the political and military equivalents of industrial inspectors.

    (2) *Interactional.* When people do things together, and this includes talking, they make adjustments to fit each other's personalities. One person will habitually start things off; another is a follower. A third person gets along by joking frequently. These patterns of adjustment create habitual relationships, repetitive sequences of events which form part of the behavior pattern of individuals in all kinds of activities.

    (3) *Classmate.* This relationship is created among people who are members of the same terminal class in a group, people whose position in a given event is habitually the same. The children in a family, the pupils in a classroom, the audience in a theater, the employees in a factory, as contrasted to parents, teachers, actors, and employers, form mutual relationships if they meet together with sufficient frequency and regularity.

    b. Special Activities.

    The only way that these can be described is by going down the line of the fifteen activities described earlier. The act of feeding is most frequently carried on in families, and ordinarily it is a parent who feeds the young. In such cases, feeding produces a *parent-child* relationship, which is a warm and close one. Eating is a pleasant thing, and the pleasure it gives is extended to the relationship between the giver of the food, and the receiver. When people who are not members of a single family habitually eat together they too may begin to feel a bond, and it may not be long before they begin to call each other "aunt" and "uncle," "dad" and "son," symbolizing the sentiments that this intimacy has induced. If however the food is poor, the displeasure felt in eating it may extend to one's messmates. If the latter are numerous and chosen at random, no such relationship results.

    Grooming again is commonly a familial exchange. In the relaxed condition which it produces it resembles sex, and indeed it often though by no means always forms part of sexual play. It also resembles the soothing actions of parents toward children. The relationship between the doctor and his patient, and that between the priest and his client, are very close ones in all societies, not only because of these resemblances, but also because the stakes are high. The doctor is toying with life and death, and the priest the same thing on a symbolic level, which is equally critical. In both cases we may speak of a *healing* relationship.

    A good teacher builds up a close and warm relationship between himself and his pupils, which often lasts throughout life. Few things give a conscientious instructor more pleasure than to have his old students come back and visit him after graduation. Since the teacher instructs by having his students repeat and imitate, it is only natural to expect that they should imitate him outside the classroom as well as in it, and that is why teachers are supposed to lead worthy and circumspect lives. In this way the teacher in many societies resembles the healer or priest; he often *is* the same person. Like the priest or healer, there are some tasks which he can do best with one student, others with a whole class. Teaching a language or a musical instrument is done best in single conferences. General lectures are best when delivered to a group, for it is hard to work up the same emotional pitch in front of a single listener. The *teaching* relationship results.

By the physical limitations of the act itself, mating is a paired activity. When a man has two wives or a woman two husbands, one of the plural spouses has to wait, and a conflict situation is the natural result. The relationship which arises from this act is of course that between husband and wife, the *conjugal* relationship, common to all mankind and to many of the lower animals.

Sharing, in contrast, is essentially a group affair, and produces no clearly marked relationship other than the supervisory. In it, however, the status of the distributor need not be clearly marked; he may be simply one man chosen or emerging from a group or equals, usually a top age grade in the simpler societies. Where he has greater authority it is because this activity is merged with that of general leadership. General leadership over a sovereign group, varying anywhere from a collection of three or four families owning its own hunting and gathering territory to a modern nation of over a hundred million people, distinguishes itself in one special way. The leader of a sovereign group has the final authority. If a conflict arises between his power and that of the leader of some overlapping or subsidiary group—for example a trader and his clients or a shaman and his devotees—the political leader will have the final say. Hence his relationship to his followers is not merely supervisory but *political*.

In armies, the chain of command works in standard supervisory or leader-follower fashion. It requires greater discipline than most, an emphasis on command and obedience, because the leader is ordering his men into action in which some will be killed. Another relationship comes out of this however, that from fighter to fighter, a reciprocal of great intensity in which each initiates action to the other at once. This is a *conflict* relationship. Exactly the same, but usually with less intensity, is the *sporting* relationship, found in games. That is why games and warfare are so much alike and so often substituted for one another, and why the threshold between them is so hard to define.

In the field of entertainment, artists create their own publics and draw their own groups of "fans" or *aficionados;* that this relationship may become an intense one is demonstrated by the violence with which youthful devotees surround and mob their favorite movie stars. The fan mail of a top performer, including offers of marriage, also shows this clearly. In this relationship, which we may tentatively label the *esthetic,* the artist performs at random, since to him the audience is not a collection of individuals but a unified body; the response is what is often personal.

Turning to the field of material culture, we find that the activities of *acquiring* raw materials need not require any relationship at all, since solitary work is possible; if two people work together, ordinary paired interaction usually results, unless one is a teacher, the other an apprentice; when group events are involved the ordinary supervisory relationship is found. The same is true of the occupants of workshops and factories and any other place where processing is carried on.

Carrying and trading both involve the usual supervisory and staff-line relationships if their business is great and complex enough. But they also have special characteristics of their own. If the object transported is a person, the situation is a little different than with goods or livestock. Passengers have to be fed and allowed to sleep, and provisions for these necessities often require extra staff and subordinates such as stewards and waiters. For the duration of the voyage the steward becomes the passenger's servant. But in a question where decisions are involved, it is not the passenger but the carrier who makes them. If a passenger does not come aboard at sailing time, the captain will not hold the ship. If two men come to blows on a train, the conductor stops them. Only the conductor can decide when and where a train is to stop. These things are necessary for two reasons: because many persons are involved, and because transportation is a dangerous business. The decisions must be left to the experts.

In trading again, we find something like sex, warfare, and games, with two parties originating action to each other with equal force. Whether two persons or two teams are involved the action is essentially paired. Even in an ordinary grocery store, the clerks must wait on the customers one at a time. It is paired interaction throughout. None of the elements are present from which strong relationships arise. Under ordinary circumstances a merchant will sell to anyone who can pay and who behaves himself. There are even antidiscrimination laws to enforce this.

Out of these various activities and probably others are derived the special positions which individuals acquire in societies. The job which a person is supposed to do, such as caring for the young, healing the sick, providing food, or carrying persons or things from place to place, is what Linton and others call his *role*. The position which he occupies on the social ladder, as a result of his general practice of leading or following, supervising or being supervised, in the totality of his activities, is his *status*. These words are brief, clear, and useful labels to describe the habitual activities and position of a person in a society.

32. Rules, Regulations, Ethics, Standards.

If you want to learn how to shoe a horse, skin a mule, say a prayer, or do anything at all that people customarily do, you must be taught by someone who knows. That someone has learned through earlier training and later experience that there is a *right* way and many *wrong* ways to do a thing. Putting it on purely physiological terms, doing it the right way preserves group equilibrium, doing it the wrong way disturbs it. If you grasp the pommel firmly, place your left toe in the left stirrup, and leap gracefully into the saddle from the left side, the cowboy may consider you at least in part a human being, but if you fumble about, approach the horse from the right, and crawl into the saddle by some unconventional means he will reckon you lower than the insects. What goes for mounting a horse also applies to the handling of teacups and conversation at diplomatic parties.

The statement in words, whether oral or written, of what are the right ways of doing things comprises a special symbolic configuration in the case of each human activity. In these statements the exact sequence of events may be detailed. For example, the Gallas in Ethiopia have a long list of rules, all in verse, detailing the duties of a nobleman toward blacksmiths, tanners, hunters, women, and each other. Each nobleman has to learn this anthology as part of his initiation ceremony, and he must be prepared to recite appropriate verses on suitable occasions. The ten commandments cannot be paraphrased; they must be written exactly as they have been handed down over generations.

What we are talking about is *rules and regulations*. If everyone follows the rules, life proceeds smoothly, but if some blunderer or innovator does things the wrong way or tries to change the system, everyone concerned is upset. From the standpoint of practical mathematics, it would be better if we counted from one to a dozen instead of from one to ten, and devised two special symbols for ten and eleven, so that twelve would be written 10. A gross, now 144, would be written 100. The advantages of this duodecimal system are clear; one-sixth would be written .2, one-fourth .3, one-third .4, and one-half .6. We would have no more trouble with infinity at the important fraction places of one third and two thirds. We would be using a unit of handy size divisible by four components rather than by two. Twelve eggs fit into a box better than ten. Why don't we shift to a duodecimal system?

We cannot shift because all the typewriters and calculating machines and fonts of type in the civilized world are set up in units of ten; because from kindergarten on we have all been trained to calculate in tens, except for some "survivals" like the twelve-inch foot, the twenty-four hour day, and the twelve-penny shilling which the British so stubbornly retained until a few years ago; because we would all have to learn over again, and some people are too old to learn; because it would create complete confusion over most of the world; because, and this is the key to all, we are mammals with ten fingers each, and from time immemorial men have counted on their fingers. The reason for the retention of the decimal system is fundamentally historical, taking us back to the time when our fingers were all we had to count with. No explanation of any phenomenon in human behavior is complete without historical depth, a knowledge of how that particular thing has operated in the dimension of time.

However remote the beginning of any set of rules and regulations, they all must have had a simple survival value at one time or they would not have been adopted. Let us consider the examples of the Moslem tabus against pork and wine. Pigs in a Mediterranean environment can be herded in scrub forests, where they live on acorns, beech nuts, and roots and tubers. These are foods that human beings do not touch except in times of famine. People eat the pigs, and that much food is gained. In Arabia, however, there are no acorns or beech nuts. Pigs would have to be fed the same staples as humans, and a pig eats more than a man. Economically, keeping pigs would be luxurious and wasteful. Pork is fatty meat. It generates many calories, and gives little protein. Arabs do not need fat; their problem is to dispose of excess body heat, not to generate it. Pork in tropical countries is full of fluke worms. To keep pigs in Arabia would make very little sense. Furthermore, in a country where food is scarce, it would be an antisocial act. It would emphasize the difference between rich and poor, and it would reduce the total amount of food and hence the potential population. In a country such as Arabia, to forbid pork is to prevent disturbances of the relations of people in groups.

As to wine: vineyards in the Mediterranean occupy hill slopes too steep for sowing. The grapes and the wine are an extra agricultural dividend. In Arabia vineyards would take up land needed for grain. The part of Arabia in which Islam arose is not a wine country. If people drank wine frequently, most of it would have to be imported, and it would take up much valuable cargo space on camels and in ships. The Arabs of Mohammed's day were not so much interested in consuming imported goods as in passing them on for profit. Then again, if you drink more than a little of any alcoholic beverage in the heat of Jidda and the Mekka region, you will regret it. Hangovers last for days; it is very difficult there to eliminate the body heat generated by wine. This is true at all seasons of the year. Some of the pre-Islamic literature dwells at length on the drunken habits of the early Arabs. That Mohammed sought to eliminate this cause of inefficiency through ritual sanctions is not surprising.

The question now arises, why is it that after the Moslem religion had been introduced to countries where pork and wine are not disturbing factors, these tabus did not disappear? The answer is that these regulations grew to serve a second purpose—to emphasize the differences between the Moslems and the other peoples with whom they came in contact as they spread. The Christians became scandalous, unclean pig eaters; the Jews frightful wine bibbers. Prohibitions against pork and wine now became a much stronger set of symbols than before, since in conflict situations they reinforced the internal solidarity of the Moslem groups. The Moslems could still live perfectly well without pork, grazing goats in the scrub forest instead of pigs. The grape crop could be turned into raisins.

Every kind of activity known to human beings has its rules, the right way and the wrong way. Some of the rules tell you the exact sequence of actions in a technical procedure. Others tell you how to behave while following these sequences. The latter class of rules is known as *ethics*. There is no need to detail the kinds of procedures employed in each class of activity we have listed. Three in particular, however, merit special attention, because those three are concerned with critical actions in reference to the equilibrium of groups. These three fields are relations between the sexes, government, and ritual.

a. Rules which govern sexual relations are everywhere carefully defined, for they are needed to prevent the most fundamental kind of conflict between individuals. Essentially these rules state who shall marry whom. The choice of spouses in any given social system follows one universal principle: the ideal or preferred mating is one which under normal circumstances will produce the minimum of disturbance to all persons in any way concerned. All marital codes forbid marriage of a man with his daughter or a mother with her son. Such unions would obviously produce conflicts within the family. Were a widower to marry his daughter she would be placed in the position of mother to her brothers and sisters and to herself, and grandmother to her own child; the whole system of relations in the family would be confused. It is a characteristic of codes and systems of law that there be no exceptions, no extenuating circumstances. This must be so or they would not work.

Brother-sister marriages are disadvantageous for another reason. Wholly aside from the biological results of such close inbreeding, human beings need to establish working relationships with people outside the immediate family, for purposes of sharing, and to have friends over the hill in case of famine. Then again, if a half dozen families are living together in a band and sharing food, the young people see each other every day and establish close personal adjustments. The boys and girls are all good friends and playmates. If suddenly the boys of a certain age grade go through a puberty ceremony, and then one of the boys marries one of the girls, her relationship to all of the other boys undergoes an abrupt change. She cannot be as friendly with all of the boys as she was before. Such habits are hard to break. It is far less likely to cause trouble in the camp if she marries someone in another camp whom she has seen but a few times at ceremonies, rather than every day, and if each boy in her camp brings in a girl who is a comparative stranger from outside. Then the girl builds up her adjustment to her new husband and has none with his classmates to break. But one must not go too far afield for a wife; she must if possible have been brought up with the same language, the same general set of customs as the groom's sisters, or she will cause too much disturbance among the other women and perhaps among the men with her outlandish ways. If you find that among one tribe of people it is the custom to marry the mother's brother's daughter and in another the daughter of the father's brother, study the whole picture of how these people live, how they get their food, what is the seasonal work calendar of the men and of the women, who stays together at what time of year, and for how long—and you will see that the rules which regulate marriage make sense. But remember, if there is a choice between two or more equally efficient sets of rules, the one selected may be simply a historically governed choice, like that of driving on the right or the left. It matters less which side you choose than that all do it the same way.

b. Sharing, leading, deciding are all political actions, and the rules governing them are *laws*. Study the laws of any people whose lives are simple or complex, and whether the laws are codified or uncodified, oral or written, they constitute a statement of what not to do. What not to do means what actions, if followed, will upset the equilibrium of individuals and of groups. Laws exist to prevent disturbance. Find out who enforces the law, who delivers the punishment, and you will see that it is always the person or group disturbed by the lawless act that takes action. In any society containing many locally independent units, laws, like leadership, may be informal and nascent, but both emerge when needed. In them murder is the concern of the victim's kin only, and it is up to them to take vengeance. In our society our lives are so closely integrated that murder upsets many people and private vengeance is forbidden; enforcement of the law, trial, and punishment are the duty of the state. But even in the simplest societies where private vengeance is sanctioned, the murder of a guest, or that of an honored stranger, is the affair of the group, because their relations as a whole with people outside have been imperiled.

c. The whole effect of ritual on people is to restore equilibrium after they have been disturbed or threatened, and it is just as essential for survival of groups as proper marriage regulations or law. If ritual is to have its full restorative effect on people, they must believe in the efficacy of its symbols. As part of the same process they will believe in ritual sanctions against breaches of marital rules, political laws, and ethical standards in all classes of behavior. "If you pour the dishwater out the front door you may wet one of the Little People, and they will be angry." The story of Oedipus, almost as widely known now as it was in the time of the ancient Greeks, illustrates how those people believed incest to be subject to divine punishment. Fear of supernatural wrath is as potent a mechanism for keeping people within bounds as the threat of any human agency.

33. Institutions: How Stable Groups Are Formed.

I have left the study of institutions to the end, for they are the end products of all the things we have been talking about. In ordinary English the word *institution* has many meanings, but in sociology and social anthropology it is a technical term which can be closely defined. In its simplest form an institution is a group of people who meet together in isolation often enough, regularly enough, and long enough each time, to do something together intensely enough and emotionally enough so that as a separate entity the group builds up its own set of rules, its own internal equilibrium, and its own structure.

So far, an institution is nothing more nor less than a natural group, as defined on pp. 563–564. A *simple institution is* a natural group, but in the more complicated societies we also find groups of groups, some merely clusters of similar groups, others differentiated by a division of labor between sub-groups. These constitute respectively *compound* and *complex institutions*. The army is a large, complex institution. Only the platoon and the company are small enough, and sufficiently undifferentiated, to retain habitual face-to-face relationships between members. It is by platoons and companies that soldiers go into combat.

Returning to our definition of an institution, we find that it includes ten points which seem self-evident, or at least they do to me. Perhaps you can discover more. Of these ten points seven are conditions and three are results. (1) *Isolation,* (2) *frequency,* (3) *regularity,* (4) *duration* of meetings; (5) *repetition,* (6) *intensity,* and (7) *emotional content* of interaction in the meetings—these are the conditions. (8) *Rules of procedure,* (9) *equilibrium,* and (10) *structure* of the institution—are the results. If the combination of the first seven of these points reaches a high enough quantitative level, an institution is created. If not, the group is a chance one. Let us study these points separately.

1. *Isolation.* Members of a certain family disperse during the daytime to do solitary tasks, to work in pairs, or to work in other institutions. The only time at which they meet as a group is at dinner. At this time every evening father, mother, and children are present, and single individuals will address the others in group events. During dinner time outsiders will hesitate to come in unless invited. The family needs privacy while it is meeting as a whole. In the same way while the father is in his shop working with his partners and apprentices, he does not encourage others, even family members, to drop in unless on business. His work institution also needs privacy while its members are busy.

2. *Frequency of meeting.* If a number of people who happen to be traveling along a road join together to push a car out of a ditch, and then separate to go about their own affairs, this is a group which meets but once. It is not an institution. If all the dairymen in a certain county get together once a month to talk over their problems and take collective action about price controls, inspection, etc., the chances are that they will elect a president, a secretary, and a treasurer, and will write out a regular membership roll. These people meet often enough, all else equal, to fulfill the requirements of an institution, which are rules, stability, and structure.

3. *Regularity of meetings.* However often they meet, members of a stable group usually come together at fixed intervals. The members of an ordinary Christian, Moslem, or Jewish congregation skip six days and meet on the seventh, year in and year out, over and over again. The county fair meets once a year, as do Australian aborigines who come together at the season when food is most plentiful to dance and initiate their young men and perform their ancient rituals. It is rarely that groups which possess any constancy meet at irregular intervals; for this to be true other factors must be very high in frequency. The human organism operates rhythmically, and so do the seasons; the rhythm produced by the regular alternation of meeting and separation aids greatly in building up automatic habit patterns.

4. *Duration of meetings.* Meetings which take place every day need not be long; with this high a frequency habitual relations are easily established. Annual meetings, however, often last for days, weeks, or months at a time, since the periods of isolation between them are so great. This is the case with many of the simpler hunting and gathering peoples whose environment provides an annual cycle of scarcity and abundance of food. These people will stay together as long as the food supply permits; when they begin to grow hungry they will scatter.

5. *Repetition of activities.* People who meet together must also do something together if they are to build up stable mutual relations. A number of people sleeping in the waiting room of a railroad station will never form an institution. Whatever they do, whether it is the routine of daily life within a family, or some single kind of activity like making hats, they must do it more than a minimum number of times if their relationship is to become habitual.

6. *Intensity of interaction.* When members of a group meet, they may either sit around lethargically, like professors at a faculty meeting watching the clock, or they may engage in violent and heated interaction; or anything in between. All else equal, if members of a group interact rapidly and extensively in a meeting, their group is more likely to persist than if they are sluggish.

7. *The emotional content.* One of the most powerful elements of all in producing group cohesion is the emotional content of the procedure in the meetings. In a church this is always high, and is produced by the use of ritual language, gestures, music, etc. At a college football game it is built up by songs, marching, and cheers, as well as by alcohol. In a primitive get-together, such as an Australian coroborree, the whole sequence of ritual action, with recitations, the formal movements of costumed actors, etc., has a tremendous emotional content for the persons meeting together. Many a group which meets rarely and for a short time is held together mainly through a high incidence of the emotional factor.

8. *Rules governing procedure.* If the combination of these seven—or more, for I may have missed some—factors totals up high enough, then the fact that the members of the group repeat their actions requires them to work out a code of rules governing procedure, if such a code has not already been formed for similar institutions.

9. *Equilibrium.* In section 8 I pointed out that the individual is in a state of physiological equilibrium as long as he remains alive. As Chapple and I stated on page 704 of *Principles of Anthropology,* a system is in equilibrium if, when a small force is impressed upon it, a change takes place within it, and once this force is removed, the system returns to approximately its previous state. This definition is exact enough for the requirements of anthropology in its present condition as a social science. Physicists and chemists can measure the equilibria of in-

organic substances very exactly, and to them our definition may seem crude. Some day we hope to be able to measure the equilibrium of organisms with equal precision on our own scale. When that day comes we too can hope to establish exact formulas. For the present, when we use the word *equilibrium,* we are using it in terms of our own definition. The analogy between biological and physicochemical equilibrium is still imperfectly known.

Just as the individual human being has his own kind of equilibrium, which ceases when he dies, so each institution has a cohesion of its own to which social scientists have ventured to apply the same word. If a group of people fulfills the seven requirements listed above, then that group may be said to be in a state of equilibrium in which it remains until the balance of frequency, duration, etc. falls below a critical threshold and the group disintegrates. Just as the equilibrium of an individual differs from that of a chemical substance, so does group equilibrium differ from that of an individual. A normal, healthy individual remains in equilibrium from birth to death, except for short periods of disturbance. Apart from contributing single cells to the production of new individuals in procreation, the cells of his body, although constantly sloughed off and replaced, remain in formal association. Our man usually stays in one piece until he dies. But groups can be segmented and reassembled. An individual may belong to several groups simultaneously, and he will probably change his memberships several times during his life. The group can perish, while its component parts live on and join new groups. If, as we maintain, these three different states may all be called equilibrium, then they are varieties of equilibrium placed on progressive levels of complexity. Needless to say, this whole subject is barely in its infancy. Ask your friends in mathematics, physics, and chemistry what they think.

Little as we know about it, however, we may venture a few generalizations. One is that the equilibrium of an institution is always in a state of motion, if for no other reason, because of the fact that human beings grow old and die, while others are born and reach maturity. No matter how stable an institution is in other respects, it is intermittently, if small, and constantly, if large, faced with repeated changes of personnel. In a small, tightly knit institution such as a family, the loss of a member may be a blow serious enough to cause disintegration; on the other hand, in some very large institutions, such as certain modern fraternal organizations, the main activity of the members seems to be burying each other. The funeral rites, in addition to those of initiation, provide the chief routines of their mutual relations.

The equilibrium of some institutions may be more important for the survival of human beings than the lives of the component individuals. No man can live alone. Many men, from the beginning of human history, have volunteered to die in order to preserve the institutions to which they belonged.

10. *The structure of institutions.* This capacity far exceeds that demonstrated for any other organism, the social insects not excepted. At the present moment over two hundred million people live together in the United States, subject to one government, using one language with various degrees of efficiency, trading in a single currency, and engaging in hundreds of different trades and occupations. The institution known as the United States is an extremely complex one, and we can understand how it is organized only if we begin with the simplest forms of institutions and proceed in the direction of increasing complexity.

The simplest institutions may be exemplified by families and small clubs. In a family of five persons, father, mother, and three children, each person may and often does address the others as a group. But no matter who takes the initiative in individual events, one person, usually either the father or mother, will make the decisions and silence the others if necessary. In a small club the president may open the meeting, ask the secretary to read his report, and call for speeches from the floor. In family or club it does not matter that individuals may address segments of the institution at times; what is important is that when the group is together one person takes the lead, if only to act as moderator and call for votes, and that whoever is speaking, he or she addresses the others directly, without intermediary.

Most families are *simple* institutions, which we will define as those in which one person initiates action in group events to the others directly. Even if three generations are living together, and the grandfather may say to his son, "See that your boy stops quarreling with his cousin," still the grandfather may also speak directly to the boy on most occasions. What is important here is not a present or absent, open or shut distinction, but one of relative frequency. It is quantitative rather than qualitative, like most distinctions that work. Some families may be so large, so formally organized, that a chain of command is actually built up, so that the person at the top will initiate action to those at the bottom through regular, habitual intermediaries. Such a family is not a simple but a compound institution. The reason why such families are rare is that the family depends on individuals of different generations for its personnel, and life is short; furthermore, living together is ordinarily so intimate a process that all individuals are brought together frequently.

A compound institution is therefore one with a chain of command, from speaker to lieutenant to the individuals at the end of the chain. By nature it is a more numerous aggregation than a simple institution where such structure is under most circumstances unnecessary. A compound institution also is more rigidly organized than a simple one need be, for anyone cannot speak up, choose his intermediaries, and pass the word through them. Leadership is more fixed and more formal; *classes* of individuals begin to appear. A typical compound institution is a small kingdom in Africa, where one man rules several villages. Each village has a chief, and the chiefs report to the king. Within the village the chief deals directly with his fellows, but it is only rarely, during severe crises and on great ceremonial occasions, that the king will summon all his subjects together and address them as a group.

Some compound institutions may grow so large that several grades of intermediaries may be needed. When this happens, however, a division of labor usually arises between sub-institutions. Take, for example, an army. Among the simpler peoples every warrior is armed alike, and when they prepare for battle one man is chief, the others followers. If the army is large, and men from different villages participate, probably several chiefs and one supreme commander will be elected for the purpose. The army has become a compound institution.

In such an army each man can carry his own food, or forage for himself. But when the army grows larger, it cannot ordinarily plan to live off the land because in a few days in any one spot it will have eaten everything within reach, and it will have to move on. The enemy can simply wait until this has happened. So a large army needs a commissary. A special group of men must be selected, to find food and bring it to the army, so that the soldiers will not have to spend their time foraging. It will be more efficient to have some men provide the food, others transport it, and still others cook it and feed the soldiers. We are now dealing with a complex institution.

A complex institution is one which consists of a number of smaller groups, some of which perform different activities from others. This does not mean, for example, that one man runs two businesses, one to make shoes and the other matches; it means that within the departmentalized institution some groups service others, and that all work together to produce a single end result. A government of any complexity has a secretariat, a department of public works, a treasury, a police force, and an army. Together these various departments keep the state running and secure.

Once a situation has been reached in which complex institutions have arisen, still further complexities are possible. These consist in all kinds of mergers and combinations, further divisions and subdivisions and sub-subdivisions, with all sorts of interlocking relationships producing a structure of fiendish complexity, such as that in which we live today. In any complex institution interlocking relationships are necessary to keep the whole together. These are the exact counterparts of the ability, in a simple institution, of any member to address the group as a whole. Inspecting and police departments partly fill that need. The inspectors can examine anyone's books, and investigate the behavior of any individual, however highly placed, insofar as that behavior concerns the institution. A policeman can arrest anyone whom he finds breaking a law. Since distinction of rank and class are bound to arise in any complex institution the individual grades are bound to organize into such face-to-face groups as employees' clubs, foremen's groups, and locals of unions, to see that their rights and material needs are cared for.

34. Special Activities and Kinds of Institutions.

Anthropologists commonly distinguish between several different kinds of institutions. The first to be mentioned is always the family. That is because the family, being founded on the universal activities of procreation and rearing the young, is present in all societies. In all societies, likewise, one discovers a division of labor based on sex, and another on age. The family is everywhere the smallest natural group, the least common denominator of social organization.

Members of a family commonly address each other by kinship names, such as *mother, father, brother, sister*, etc. As time goes on and brothers and sisters produce their respective young and then die, the roster of individuals to whom a person may feel himself akin will change. We have cousins of various degree, aunts and uncles, and other relatives which the English language is not equipped to describe by separate words, although in other languages it may be possible to keep many different kinds and degree of kin clear.

Briefly, there are two kinds of kinship, bilateral and unilateral. Our system is bilateral, in which both father's and mother's kin are equated. For example, we use the word "uncle" to designate the brothers of both parents. In a unilateral system, as in Arabic, the father's brother is called *'amm* and the mother's brother *khal*. In a bilateral system it is easy to forget who's who beyond the third generation, but a unilateral system may turn into a set of marriage classes, as in parts of Australia, or a clan, as among Albanian mountaineers and Gaels. In these examples, an individual may not know a classmate or kinsman personally, but will recognize him by his name and regalia alone.

When the social fabric of a people needs a king, one will arise. The royal family will thus occupy the peak of the political institution, and its new role will overshadow its original status as a purely familial institution.

Where people who are not members of the same family are in the habit of working together, their work activities determine the nature of the resulting institution, which is called *economic*. In the same way the members of a church form a *religious* institution, and fellow members of a nation, however small or great, who share their possessions as needed for public works, and who accept the leadership of a civil or war leader in internal and external relations, constitute a *political* institution. The clubs, secret societies, fraternal orders, and the like which people create to piece out their needs, because their other relationships are inadequate, serve to act as cross channels in the more complicated societies and make the whole structure move more smoothly. These are called *associations*.

Beyond the family, beyond the simple political, economic, religious, and associational groups which are found in many preliterate societies, other kinds of institutions emerge as the special activities on which they are based separate and differentiate. Thus a hospital is different from a religious congregation, though both are concerned with healing. Although money passes hands in both, neither the church nor the hospital has money-making as its primary objective. The school is often an adjunct of the church, or of the workshop, but separate universities may be found in various countries, and they are institutions in their own right. They too use money, but they are not commercial. Just as the hospital has free beds, so does the university have scholarships and an endowment fund.

If we review the interaction component of the special activity on which any given institution is based, and then estimate the quantitative values of this interaction in terms of each of the seven components listed in section 33, we may find that each kind of institution has a special balance of its own. The religious institution is long on number 7, *emotional content;* a secret society may emphasize number 1, *isolation;* while in the ordinary family, all seven may be quantitatively high. I suggest that you try this for the institutions of which you are a member, grading each of the seven components on a scale of 1 to 10. See how you come out. Then do the same for some other culture described in this book. An institution such as the family will vary in many respects between different cultures. Someday someone may devise a more accurate method of handling this kind of material.

35. Why Are Some Institutions More Elaborate Than Others?

The answer to this simple question has been known for a long time, but few anthropologists have discussed it. They have been more concerned with learning what people do in the simpler societies than in studying the mechanism of institutional growth. It is necessary to know it if we are to study the dynamics of societies, or more simply, to find out what makes them move forward on the time scale.

What makes them move is, of course, energy. And the degree of complexity which their institutional structures attain is a function of the relative amounts of energy consumed, subject, of course, to various qualifications and controls.

For present purposes it matters less whence this energy is derived, than how it is used. The important variable is how much energy can be expended per time unit in a single operation and for how long. If a man makes tools of flint or stone, he chips or grinds his material with his hands. No division of labor is necessary, although trade may be involved on account of the unequal geographical distribution of the raw materials. If he makes them out of bronze, his consumption of energy is greatly increased. It takes a hot fire to smelt the ores, and another one to melt the ingots for alloying and casting. Prospectors have to travel long distances to find the deposits of copper and tin, which are much scarcer than supplies of flint and fine-grained stone. Miners have to do a lot of digging to produce the ore; to make the fire to smelt it, men have to cut wood, dry it, and burn charcoal. Once the ingots have been made, other men carry them to the place where the bronzesmith melts, alloys, and casts them. Still others may carry the finished products around to trade.

Many persons have been employed in many different tasks. Most of them are specialists. They have to be for their work requires skill, and skill requires a long learning period without interruption. When people begin to use iron instead of bronze, the amount of metal available increases, but the amount of energy used per ton of metal does not, as long as the smelters and smiths keep on burning charcoal. The discovery that coke could be made from coal opened a new source of abundant fuel, and greatly increased the output of the iron industry. It also created a coal industry. The result was the employment of vast numbers of persons in huge, complex institutions, and through the experimental work which was made available by the invention of new kinds of instruments, new methods of producing steel and steel products, and coal by-products, were discovered. With the new blast furnaces and rolling mills, much more energy was expended than ever before, and the social as well as the industrial machinery increased in complexity.

Tool-making is of course at the root of all this change. But the change extends to all other fields of human activity, some of which in turn affect tool-making. It takes better tools to make a composite, reflex bow than a simple one-piece spear. Flint arrow points penetrate as far as iron ones, but the flint breaks off when it hits bone and has to be replaced. Once the hunter has a gun, he is in danger of killing off the game. The fisherman can do better with a sailing vessel and nets than he can out in a flimsy canoe with a fish spear, and with a power trawler he can bring in an even greater haul. In mining, we move from men with hammers and horn wedges carrying the ore out by hand, to mule cars in the tunnels and power hoists, to explosives and conveyor belts; in manufacturing, the use of animal power historically replaced much of the drudgery of hand work, and water power and windmills replaced much of the animal power. In transportation the sequence on both land and sea is too well known to require repetition.

In the part of the list devoted to purely interpersonal activities, the effect of this increase in energy consumption is also visible. Techniques of processing food, preserving, milling, canning, preparation of "quick" dishes, the development of bakeries and restaurants, have reduced the amount of time needed for a family to spend getting their meals ready, and have made it easier at times to "eat out" than to have a private meal together. The reduction of the element of privacy reduces the effectiveness of the family as an institution.

In healing, of course, great changes have resulted. Advances in metallurgy have given the surgeons better instruments, and better equipment in general. The oil industry has given him ether. Time for study and specialization have helped him improve his technique, and the supply of corpses from the lower classes of a stratified society have given him laboratory material to improve his knowledge of anatomy. The great wars which only complicated societies can wage have given him numbers of grotesquely mutilated persons on whom to practice plastic surgery.

The preacher, too, has been able to expand. Automobiles bring his congregation members from considerable distances to his vast, steam-heated cathedral, and the radio carries his prayers over a continent. The teacher has movies to instruct with and, in every technical discipline, the tools of that craft or profession. He also has books. Probably next to tools in importance has been the development of extensions of speech; picture writing, syllabaries, alphabets, on clay, stone, and paper; then the great spurt brought about by printing, then the telegraph, telephone, radio, the photograph, and the ordinary typewriter which while using only human muscular energy, speeds up the process of writing legibly by its clever use of levers.

36. Concerning Levels of Complexity.

In any civilization, any country, any locus in space and time within human history, the people living in that particular spot are characterized by a given degree of social complexity which can be determined by a study of the interrelated institutions to which they belong. That this has been historically determined is clear from what we know of history. Since the beginning of written records, the complexity of human institutions and hence of societies has increased several times. What happened before that is subject to our interpretation of the archaeological record. This record shows a change through time in key areas, from the simplest tools of flint to better and more varied ones to the addition of polished stone to the beginnings of metal, all in the prehistoric period. It is logical to assume that each stage of social complexity must also at some time have made its first appearance, but for several reasons we cannot determine exactly when or where these changes took place. The archaeological record is far from complete. The cause-and-effect relationship between tools and social structure, while known in general, cannot be pinned down to an absolute formula. The Aztecs, Neolithic from the standpoint of cutting tools, were institutionally on a level with the Hindus, who make excellent steel. Still we do not know that the Neolithic inhabitants of Egypt, Palestine, Turkey, and Iraq were not on the same level. They probably were. The Lapps and Pygmies use iron, as did the Andamanese; none of them produced it. An attempt to classify societies on the basis of tool materials leads us astray.

What makes societies simple or complex is not any single trait or group of traits but the whole combination of technology and environment, including trade, as influenced by history. On this basis I have postulated, *very tentatively* (reviewers note), what appear to be six levels in contemporary and historically documented societies, which have existed without the benefit of gunpowder, coal, and steam engines. I have based my judgment on combinations of four criteria: (*a*) The specialization of individuals, (*b*) Amount of consumer goods obtained by trade, (*c*) Number of institutions to which an individual may belong, (*d*) Complexity of institutions.

(*a*) THE SPECIALIZATION OF INDIVIDUALS

Level   I. Peoples living on the simplest institutional level have no full-time specialists. A number of men are part-time specialists in *healing;* i.e., shamans. Peoples whose institutional simplicity is clearly environmental in cause, as the Lapps, may be all specialists, as in reindeer herding, and conduct stable if irregular trade relationships with other ethnic groups.

II. Shamans are specialists, usually part-time only. Older men may specialize in teaching and conducting ritual. A few men may be part-time specialists in work activities.

III. Shamans may become full-time, and specialists in the esthetic arts may arise. There may also be some specialization in processing and in trade. The political leader may be a full or part-time specialist.

IV. Specialists become relatively numerous, in government, healing and ritual, the arts, processing, and trading. In some cultures specialization goes by hereditary castes.

V. Probably half of the population is engaged in some non-food-producing specialty, at least half of the time. Many traders, skilled craftsmen, boatmen, caravan men, soldiers, priests, diviners, etc.

VI. Nearly everyone is a specialist in some kind of activity, including farming.

(*b*) AMOUNT OF TRADE

Level   I. Usually very slight. People make their own tools, as a rule. In cases of environmentally enforced simplicity, trade may be great—Eskimos get soapstone for lamps from great distances, Lapps obtain all metal tools by trade. Among technologically primitive peoples at low levels the chief objects of trade are body-paint materials and other ritual or esthetic objects.

II. Moderate amount of trading, usually once or twice a year only, with paint, drugs, luxury objects predominant.

III. Trade increases; tool materials commonly exchanged as well as luxuries; some food may be exchanged.

IV. Probably one half of all consumer goods other than food are obtained by trade. Tool materials move long distances, through many hands.

Level   V. More than half the goods consumed, other than food, is obtained through trade. Special foods traded as well.

VI. An almost complete exchange of products, with only rural communities producing majority of own food.

(*c*) NUMBER OF INSTITUTIONS TO WHICH AN INDIVIDUAL MAY BELONG

Level   I. One. His family band.

II. Two. His family and the band or village. Membership in an age-grade, totemic association, etc. may take on characteristics of an institution and thus increase the number to perhaps a half dozen.

III. Anywhere from two to a dozen. These include family, band, or village, shaman's clientele, ritual group, and trader's clientele.
IV. About twice as many as on Level III.
V. In extreme cases, as in India, between 60 and 100.
VI. May go into the hundreds.

(d) Complexity of Institutions

Level   I. A simple institution consisting of a biological family, often with a few extra-familial dependents. Meetings with other families, even kin, are too infrequent or casual to establish stable relations or institutional structure as part of a larger group.
II. An institution consisting of a number of biological families grouped into a band or village, often with age grading. Authority usually rests in a number of older men. Relations with other bands or villages may approach but not attain institutional status.
III. Groups of bands or villages attain stability under a combined leadership, forming a compound institution. Individual leaders, with simple staffs, tend to take command as amount of political business increases. Religious institutions and associations may coexist with the political, and simple economic institutions as well.
IV. Stable hierarchies appear in political or religious institutions, or both. Regional confederations may take on structure. Economic institutions increase in number, and regular markets may appear.
V. One or two institutions, political or religious, become departmentally complex. Economic institutions remain simple.
VI. The state is a complex institution with hierarchies and many interlocking departments, including religious and economic. Equilibrium is maintained by an elaborate system of interdepartmental control. Economic institutions are still simple owing to persistence of hand techniques in industry.

I have placed the Lapps tentatively on the first level, to illustrate the principle that no matter how skilled people may be technologically, or how complex a society their ancestors may have lived in, the environment can reduce the amount of interaction between individuals to such an extent that the most highly skilled peoples in the world may be reduced to any institutional level.

This example will also serve as a warning to the student of cultural history. Cultural evolution has been a very complicated business. If we are to proceed from simple to complex in an historical as well as a contemporary sense, then we must pay great attention to the environment, which is itself a variable. Over much of the earth's surface the climate has changed profoundly several times since human beings first obtained the use of fire and tools.

Differences in environment along with the effect of environmental barriers, such as oceans, mountains, and deserts are the chief if not the only reason why historical changes have proceeded at different rates in different places, and why more complicated systems have not diffused more rapidly from centers of development. Among some of the peoples living very simple lives the evolutionary procedure may have been reversed; these are the inhabitants of some of our most barren deserts, whose ancestors must once have lived on richer lands—else the desert refuge could not have been reached.

Whatever the historical sequence, whatever the reason, peoples still surviving in the middle of the twentieth century live at every stage of technological competence known to archaeologists and historians and at every level of institutional complexity from that of subhuman primates to that of the United Nations, as originally, and hopefully, conceived. After having mulled this over for a quarter of a century, I have found no more useful framework for intercultural studies in an overall sense, than the concept of levels of complexity, which will be illustrated in the pages to follow.

Level Zero

Subhuman Society

1

Life in the Trees: The Behavior and Social Relations

of Man's Closest Kin

L ET us imagine that we are sitting in front of an H. G. Wellsian television set, rigged to project images through time. The operator sets it back to one million years before Christ and then gives us glimpses of the lives of our ancestors at ten-thousand-year intervals. At the beginning we should probably see creatures much like ourselves from the neck down, but in better physical condition than most of the audience. From the neck up we would notice startling differences. The teeth would be large, the jaws protruding, the brow sloping, and the brain case small. These creatures would be moving about during the day in search of food, killing small animals, digging up roots, picking berries and seeds, and eating some at least on the spot.

A little later (little in terms of projection time only) changes would appear. Our ancestors would be carrying smouldering embers about with them, and making fires at night for warmth and protection. They would be chipping out tools of flint, and whittling and scraping sticks of wood. These sticks would take the shape of clubs and spears, with which they could kill other animals at a convenient distance. Instead of eating on the spot, they would bring their raw foodstuffs home and cook them. While doing all these things they would talk to each other. And if you looked closely, you would see that their teeth were smaller than before, their jaws less protruding, their foreheads less sloping, and their brain cases larger. Flint and fire had reduced the work of the jaws. The mouth was now used as much for talking as for eating. Flint, fire, and speech mark the threshold between subhuman and human. It is at this critical point that man may be said to have come into being, to have replaced pre-man.

We have a fair idea that the events described above were true, on the basis of archaeological evidence. The archaeological sites, however, give us no indication of how the earliest men behaved with each other, what kind of groups they formed, or how these groups were organized. It is probable, but by no means necessary, that human beings lived under social conditions of the utmost simplicity at that time. In order to find out what the simplest level of social organization attributable to man may be or have been, we can use two methods of approach—to study the most simply organized living peoples, as we shall presently, and to find out what is known about the behavior of the subhuman primates, man's closest living relatives, who still get along without flint, fire, or speech in the human sense.

Among all free-living, sexually reproducing animals, some forms of social relations inevitably take place between members of the same species. Such relations provide mechanisms for reproduction, for training the young, and even for survival. As a rule the more highly organized the animals are in a physical sense, the more complex their systems of relations. Physical organization reaches its highest point in the development of the nervous system, and the animals with the most complex social structures are, all else equal, those highest on the neurological scale.

The reader is probably familiar with some aspects at least of the social relations of fish, which swim in schools; ducks and geese, migrating in flocks; and deer, bison, caribou, and other animals, which live in large herds. The social organizations of bees and termites are even more complex, and in fact, considering for the moment only results and leaving causes and methods of transmission aside, they are more complex than the simplest societies of man.

The animals closest to man zoologically are the lower primates, including the higher monkeys and apes. These animals resemble man in the general balance of the senses—visual, auditory, olfactory, and tactile; in the form of the brain; in the general organization of the nervous system; and in many physiological processes. Like man they have no annual breeding season, produce helpless young, and protect their offspring during a conditioning period lasting a number of years.

Whatever the exact historical or genetic relationship between man and the different genera of lower primates may be is not important here. We are concerned with the behavior of animals resembling in a general way our own ancestors at that remote period before they acquired true speech and the ability to use fire and make tools. The subhuman primates come closest to our needs. Of these the most profitable to study is not the chimpanzee or the gibbon, which, wholly regardless of anatomical features, is nearest to man in its behavior, including sexual habits, in its family composition, and in its use of vocal symbols for communication.

A detailed, objective study of gibbon society is presented in the following extract from a monograph * by Clarence R. Carpenter.

CHAPTER I—THE ASIATIC PRIMATE EXPEDITION, EQUIPMENT AND PROCEDURES

The wide geographical range of the *Hylobatidae* in Southern Asia and the East Indies as well as rather extended altitudinal range from sea level to approximately 7000 feet, where temperatures may drop to the frosting point, would indicate that gibbons have a considerable adaptability to climatic differences and to variations in foods. Furthermore, this widespread distribution and the density of population in regions where I have worked would suggest that the world population of gibbons may be counted by the tens if not hundreds of thousands.

Camp Dao.—Buddhists from as far south as Bangkok, from as far north as Chiengrai and from as far west as the Burmese border visit Doi Dao. It is located about forty miles from Chiengmai near the village of Chieng Dao. The mountain has great caves, an un-

* "Field Study in Siam of the Behavior and Social Relations of the Gibbon (*Hylobates Lar*)" *Comparative Psychology Monographs*, vol. 16, No. 5, December 1940. Reprinted by permission of the author and the publisher.

derground stream, and a clear spring at its base which are sacred to Buddhists. A succession of temples have sprung up around the mouth of the caves and near the spring. It was in the temple grounds with an open-shed guest house for cover, that a second camp, Camp Dao No. 1, was established.

From the camp at about 1400 feet above sea level, the rugged limestone mountain rose in a series of peaks to a height of about 7000 feet. During the dry season (December until April) the mountain range was obscured by smoke from forest fires in the territory, but after the first rains in April, clouds flowed up or down the steep slopes and cliffs. The physical requirements of a camp were abundantly provided but the all-important question remained to be answered: Were gibbons present in the surrounding forests and could they be observed repeatedly in sufficient numbers and for long periods of time so that I could get a relatively complete story of their behavior and social relations? On the answer to this question depended the success or failure of the Behavior Research Division of the Asiatic Primate Expedition.

The territory around the Buddhist temple located at the base of Doi Dao proved to be almost ideal for observations of gibbons because of the following conditions: 1. Gibbons were plentiful in the area. 2. The natives were prevented from shooting or frightening the animals because of the fact that the surrounding territory was a protected area where, within certain limits around the temple, shooting was not permitted. In addition, the natives considered the gibbons to be quasi-sacred, especially the buff-colored ones. The attitude of the natives toward gibbons can be traced to the fact that Buddhist teachings prohibit the taking of life except when that is made necessary in order to

obtain food. 3. The topography of the area was uneven; the valleys were narrow, and from their floors precipitous cliffs rose to heights well above the trees. This made possible the observation of gibbons from cliffsides and from tops of rocky peaks as the animals ranged in the thin, irregular, open forests in the valley below. 4. Parts of the valleys and foothills were cultivated; hence the jungle of false teak, fruit-bearing trees, and bamboo was broken by clearings which opened up large vertical walls of forest where animals might be seen traveling, feeding, and playing. 5. During the months of March, April, and May many of the trees shed their leaves. This also served to open up the vegetation and thus facilitate observational work. Even though many trees lost their leaves, in the valleys where there was sufficient moisture, islands of evergreen and fruit-bearing trees fed the gibbons during the dryest periods. 6. The forests were crisscrossed with a network of trails made by the natives in their search for bark, fruits, roots, orchids, and choice teak trees. These paths, as well as the occasional trails made by elephants used in logging operations, greatly simplified my work. In addition, the frequent contact with natives passing through the forest somewhat conditioned the gibbons to the presence of human beings and made them more approachable. 7. The fact that the gibbon foods were concentrated in particular areas and not too widely scattered, made the prediction of group movements more reliable, the location of blinds easier, and thus increased the observational possibilities.

. . . in these primates one may observe *anlagen* of human motivation and behavior, free from cultural veneers and far enough removed to avoid the well-known errors involved in man's study of himself. Man must be studied in the zoological context from which he came and of which he is a part, proper precautions being taken to avoid describing homologous functions as being identical. Both theriomorphism (falsely attributing animal characteristics to man) and anthropomorphism (projecting human characteristics to animals) should be avoided.

Methods of work in making this field study on gibbons were refinements and improvements of the time-honored methods used by naturalist-scientists for centuries. The methodological problem was that of directly observing a representative sampling of individuals and groups for long periods of time in their undisturbed natural habitat and of accurately recording and reporting the observations. All possible precautions were taken to avoid disturbing the gibbons while they were being observed. Everything possible was done to secure records of the gibbons' free, natural, undisturbed behavior and of their social responses and relationships.

As much as was necessary in order to plot changes, observations were made throughout the day and occasionally near camp at night.

Extensive and prolonged observations were necessary in order to get some general ideas of variations in the behavior of individuals. Most important in this connection were notes on sex and age differences, but also data were obtained on behavior variations of like-sexed and like-aged individuals. Similarly, having become intimately familiar after weeks of study with one group which served as a kind of norm, I studied twenty one groups in order to understand group interactions. The task of describing a behavior pattern is considered incomplete without indicating its normal variations.

No observations were accepted unless they were adequately checked. Sometimes this checking involved days of work and laboriously repeated observations. For example, group counts were all carefully checked. The reliability and completeness of the first observation of any given activity can always be increased by repeated checking. Every effort was made to avoid the error of "dramatic incident," which is so frequently made in the writings of naturalists, hunters, and travelers. The original observation of nest building, in which it seemed that gibbons might build nests because they were seen in them, later turned out to be false when further observations showed that the gibbons were playing in nests built by bears. In this case, a hunter might have concluded on the basis of his first observation that gibbons build nests. Only careful checks could prevent this error. One must become sufficiently familiar with the normal behavior of animals so that he won't become excited by unusual behavior and form unwarranted generalizations. This is the pitfall of the "dramatic incident."

Visual and auditory observations with written descriptions were supplemented and checked by photographic recordings, using both still and moving pictures, and by sound recordings. The recording method of studying vocalizations introduced a new technique into naturalistic research on primates and should in the future elucidate the interesting and important field of naturalistic non-human primate communication.

The documented notes as they appear in this report have the following history: Observations were first briefly jotted down during work in the field. Every night the notes made in the field were written up chronologically and fully in a bound, indexed notebook.

These notes were then rewritten, classified as to subject, and typed on 5 x 8 cards which were filed under subject headings. From these cards have been taken the observational descriptions which supply the basis data of this monograph. Under each heading, only selected notes appear. Since the types of activity observed varied from day to day, I have not included the actual notes for any full day. However, the section on diurnal activity has been summarized from many daily observations and represents the typical day for a gibbon group.

A daily routine of observations usually began about six o'clock in the morning while the gibbons were still giving their morning calls and while one group or more could be located by these calls. Since the camp was located in the midst of the ranges of several groups, the early calls and their frequencies as well as their special characteristics could be noted from camp. When a group was located, unless the program for the day was checking a number of groups, the animals of the group were observed for as long a time as possible while notes were taken on their behavior. Sometimes a group could be followed for an entire day without disturbing it, but usually, if a group was followed for half a day, another group would be observed in the afternoon. Occasionally when several groups came together, they could all be observed simultaneously. With the wilder groups and those whose ranges were located at a considerable distance from camp, it often required several hours of travel and cautious stalking before the groups could even be located. In these instances it would take an entire day to get a few observations.

In addition to observations made on wild animals at Doi Dao, some facts given in this monograph were obtained from captive gibbons.

CHAPTER II—DIURNAL CYCLE, CROSS-SECTION OBSERVATIONS AND RELATIONS OF GIBBONS TO OTHER ANIMALS AND HUMAN POPULATION

The Diurnal Cycle of Behavior. —At dawn, about 5:30 on a clear April morning in Northern Siam, the field worker may observe the first random, undirected movements of a gibbon family as it breaks up the grouping in which it has passed the night. If there is an infant in the group, it nurses; juveniles begin mild play and occasionally pluck bits of food; the adults soon begin their early morning calls. These calls stimulate groups in adjacent territories, which give a series of similar notes and the contagion of sound spreads from one group to another until each has called repeatedly during the next hour. Often one first becomes aware of the location of groups of gibbons through their early morning calls, which may be produced at intervals for the next hour or hour and a half. The various animals of the group feed in a desultory fashion, play gently and begin their first progression of the day toward trees with ripe fruit, a vine filled with grapes, or perhaps a tree with succulent buds or young leaves.

Temperature and light affect the time of the early morning calls and also the time when the groups begin to travel. During foggy, dark, and cool (45° F.) mornings on Doi Intanon, the morning calls were not heard until about 7:00 o'clock and the groups started moving about 8:00 o'clock. On clear mornings with temperatures around 65° F. at Doi Dao, the animals would start their morning calls near 5:30 and begin progression between 6:00 and 7:30 o'clock.

Having exchanged calls with neighboring groups and engaged mildly in a variety of activities, a group of gibbons sets out on its regular day's journey. First it moves away from the place where it has spent the night and each animal follows the temporary leader rather swiftly and directly to some source of food. If the distance is 800 to 1000 yards, the apes swing lightly and swiftly for a few minutes over an arboreal pathway to which they have become accustomed and then they stop and loiter. Perhaps they may come near another group which is on the move and if so, calling begins of a different type from that heard earlier in the morning. These vocalizations consist of a rather long-drawn-out series of sounds which, after a number of repetitions, rise in pitch and power until the crescendo breaks off suddenly with a few notes forming the diminuendo and closing the series. If each group stands its ground and there is competition either for a passageway or perhaps for a food tree, then a veritable vocal battle ensues during which each group calls loudly and frequently until one group gives ground and retreats.

With the periods of loitering and with all the possible interruptions, the chances are that active feeding will begin on an average about 8:30 or 9 o'clock. Gibbons eat slowly, chewing their food rather thoroughly, so feeding continues for about two hours. Since gibbons have no cheek pouches for storing food, they eat it as soon as it is plucked. Usually they prepare the food by peeling it, shelling it, or removing seeds before it is eaten. Gradually, as each individual becomes satiated, the group's behavior changes. The late infants and juveniles begin playing and grooming, the mother cares for her infant or becomes quiet and rests, and the adult male rests or remains watchfully observant for possible disturbances and approaches of strange gibbons.

As feeding ceases, the group moves to a place well protected from the hot sun or strong winds so characteristic of the climate during certain seasons in Siam, and there it settles down for a few hours of relatively stationary activity. Grooming, play and rest characterize this rather quiet "siesta" period in the gibbon's day. It is the depressed period found in the behavior of many tropical wild animals.

The group gradually arouses itself after about three hours and travels slowly, less directly than during the early morning, and feeds randomly in some other fruit-bearing tree, probably a fig or "bamboo." If a shower of rain falls, the group stops moving and each animal sits quietly hunched over into a ball of fur until the rain stops. Then very active grooming will precede the next period of travel.

With their hunger satisfied after a second period of feeding, the group orients its direction of travel back over some pathway with which each individual seems to be familiar and slowly they swing back to a suitable abode tree, where a period of mild activity precedes settling down for the night just about sunset or a little before.

. . . .

During the day, the group will probably have traveled on the average between 1800 and 2000 yards, all within its own territory or occasionally in regions immediately adjacent to its range. The area occupied by the average group would include about 35 or 40 acres.

. . . .

Cross-section Observations.—
. . . *March 27, 1937, Group 2, Doi Dao.*—I had climbed into Observation Post No. 5 . . . anticipating the approach of Group 1, which I had just seen in the valley. To my left I heard the clank of bamboo, a sound produced by animals jumping from one stalk to another and making the swaying stalks

strike together. Turning, I saw a buff-colored gibbon of adult size. A few minutes later, the whole of the group, later known as Group 2, came into view in the following order: buff male, buff female, buff young juvenile, and black young juvenile. I could see them all very clearly.

The two young animals played for 45 minutes. The patterns of play behavior observed were the following: 1. Chasing, consisting of either of the juveniles trying to catch the other, which attempted playfully to escape but when it was followed no longer it would return to stimulate play further. 2. Repetitive behavior, involving the movement of each animal over the same pathway again and again. When such activity was shown, there were usually rather difficult climbs or jumps in the chosen pathway. This was essentially a play with supports with each animal stimulating the other. 3. Wrestling. This was done while each gibbon swung by one arm and used its other three appendages vigorously. Biting supplemented the patterns of clutching and grasping. 4. Attacks, involving surprise when one animal would attempt to approach the other stealthily and then would spring upon it. This activity was usually followed by wrestling or chasing.

There was no doubt that the small buff animal was more strongly motivated for play than the larger black one. The first was extremely active, played alone when the other would not cooperate and would persistently attempt to engage the black one in play when the latter became inactive or showed avoidance behavior.

Throughout the 45 minutes of observations, the group of animals was coming nearer to my blind, which was located on a sheer cliffside. The adult buff female came within 20 feet of me. At this close range, she filled completely the field of my 7-power binoculars. (What a thrill after my experiences on Doi Intanon.) Her pendulous nipples could be seen distinctly. One was longer that the other and the mammae were close together.

The juveniles had fallen behind the other two gibbons while they were playing. Apparently the younger one suddenly saw that it was being left behind and began a little whimpering cry. Then it hurried along through the trees and caught up with the female, which had just passed my blind.

At this time the other adult buff gibbon approached within 40 feet of the blind. He came over leisurely, searching through bamboo leaves and under bits of husks on the stalks. Several times he apparently caught insects and ate them. The gibbon sat with his back to me on a large stalk of bamboo grooming himself. As he turned, I could see his face clearly and, when he yawned, his long canine teeth. The nipples showed as small black spots in the dense grayish-brown fur of his chest. A very dark tuft of hair covered the area of the scrotum and penis but I was certain that this animal was a male.

The older of the two juveniles, the black one, came closer, to within 25 feet of my blind. I was lying flat on my stomach looking through the 7-power binoculars at the gibbon which was in a tree at the same height. For 15 minutes I watched this animal as it sat grooming itself. In vain I attempted a sexual diagnosis. The animal was noticeably smaller than the two adults.

Several times this juvenile looked in my direction but seemed not to differentiate me from the surrounding boulders. Then finally, with a quick glance in my direction and a cry of alarm, its speedy flight began. Down and out of the tree, down through a clump of tall bamboo and on down into the trees a hundred yards beyond, it fled in a manner typical of gibbons alone of all arboreal primates, by brachiation or swinging with its arms. Its alarm calls set the adult female calling and provoked exclamatory behavior on the part of the male which sat 40 feet away, until that moment contentedly grooming himself. One lunge and he had disappeared.

The family continued giving alarm calls for 15 or 20 minutes and then with the coming of dusk, they settled down for the night. I had observed the animals from 3:30 to shortly after 5:00 o'clock.

. . . .

April 13, 1937, Group 3, Doi Dao.— The episode began with the buff adult male and female of Group 3 in a fig tree while I was in a blind 50 feet below them, almost under the tree. A black young adult, possibly the black young adult of Group 11 or perhaps the solitary animal that I had previously observed near the spring, came into the perspective of my blind. He was attempting to enter the fig tree in which the buff female was feeding while the buff male was feeding intermittently between sallies away from the tree and back again. The black young adult, which I judged to be a young male, took every advantage of the absence of the buff male to approach the female, but when he did so, the buff male would rush back toward the young black male, who would immediately leave the tree, only to return a few minutes later when the buff male was off guard. This unusual approach and fleeing alternated between the young black male and the buff male, with the female as the focus of their activity. At least four times the young male was driven from the tree only to return.

The female (the buff female of Group 3) reacted more positively to the buff male (also of Group 3) than she did to the young adult animal, but she didn't show any avoidance or antagonistic reactions toward him. She seemed relatively indifferent to him and after having eaten, she swung from the tree and disappeared with the buff male following her closely. The young adult trailed along at some distance behind.

That keen rivalry existed between the black young adult and the buff male was very evident but as long as the female was in the fig tree I couldn't be absolutely certain of the incentive for which these two gibbons were competing. There were two possibilities— the food or the female, which I suspected of being receptive. However, when the female left the tree and both males followed her, it became clear that she was the incentive.

The activity was especially interesting because it presented the following qualities of behavior:

1. Competition between two males for a female, with one of the males dominant.
2. Competition between an animal within and another outside the closed group, with the latter trying to break into the group.
3. Effective repulsion of an animal without actual overt pugnacity, at least not during the observations.
4. Guarding behavior, in this instance a male guarding a female.

May 12, 1937, Groups 1 and 6, Doi Dao.—At noon today Group 1 was in the trees on the cliffside above my camp. Two of the gibbons were calling repeatedly as they swung to and fro, up and down through treetops and clumps of bamboo.

The behavior of the animals was directed first toward Group 6, which was located 200 yards further south on a ledge of the mountain and, second, toward the captive gibbons which were tethered around camp. The captive animals did not respond to the vocalizations of the other animals.

For more than an hour the gibbons of Group 1 swung randomly through trees of the steep mountain side; then, with a flash of speed not hitherto shown, three of the animals plunged downward with a series of long leaps and superb brachiation through bamboo clumps and into a fruit-filled grapevine. Immediately Group 6, in whose territory the grapevine was located, became active.

At least two apes of Group 6 began to call excitedly and also dashed into the vine-covered tree. When the gibbons of Group 6 approached the tree rapidly, Group 1 fled with but a few grapes as a reward for their efforts. They were followed by the buff female of Group 6 until they had returned well into Group 1's territory opposite my camp.

The behavior of Group 1 was obviously motivated by hunger, and the grapes were strong incentives. These were located near the border of Group 1's territory but at a place where I had never previously seen Group 1 but had repeatedly seen Group 6. Group 6 had fed heavily on grapes during the morning and was, as I interpreted the observations, guarding the grapes and reacting defensively against Group 1. Again, this observation is an example of the dominance of a group within its own territory, even though it is outnumbered by the invading group.

Chapter III—Individual Behavior

March 5, 1937, Doi Intanon.—While following a group of gibbons for about 40 minutes, I had a good chance to observe types of locomotion. A male of the group was very active. I managed to follow him and get good views of his activity. It seemed that about 90 percent of his locomotion was brachiation, for only occasionally would he run down large main branches of trees. While on slender, terminal limbs, brachiation was the only mode of travel. Once he threw himself outward and downward for 20 feet and, upon touching the next branch, he continued his swinging flight with only the slightest interruption of his forward motion.

March 15, 1937, Doi Intanon.—Schultz finds that a high percentage of the specimens brought into the collecting camp have healed fractures of bones. I believe this to be in large part the result of falls. The speed of the gibbons' travel and their apparent nonchalance in making long jumps would frequently cause them to depend upon the strength of small branches. Since an animal in a brachiating position swings from beneath the support, if a branch breaks, the animal must make its recovery between the broken support and the ground. If there are no lower branches or underbrush to break the fall, the animal must strike the ground with considerable force. The long slender bones of the gibbons probably break more easily than the bones of such types as the macaques.

March 31, 1937, Doi Dao.—When moving rapidly through the forest, gibbons usually brachiate. While the animal is jumping, the arms are held over the head in positions ready for grasping branches. During walking along solid, large base limbs, the arms are generally carried above the shoulder level and extended laterally, where they seem to function as balancing structures. At times, however, when the animal is walking, the arms are used to hold on to collateral limbs as a type of four-point contact during locomotion.

Gibbon locomotion should be visualized as occurring in a network of branches rather than on the ground. There are many variations of patterns from pure brachiation on one extreme to pure upright walking on the other extreme.

May 18, 1937, Doi Dao.—Repeatedly I have seen gibbons climbing up a perpendicular tree trunk using one hand and both feet while they carried food in the other hand.

. . . .

Observations show that gibbons are adept not only at moving over horizontal branches, but also at climbing tree trunks and vines. In climbing trees, even of large diameter, their long arms and hands are well adapted to clasping around the trunk. The deep clefts between great and other toes and between thumb and fingers are of most advantage in such climbing. When climbing, the gibbons' arms are moved up in steps either simultaneously or alternately, while a walking pattern of movement is shown by the feet and legs. The climbing position throws the rump away from the tree trunk and the chest and face close to it.

. . . .

March 31, 1937, Group 3, Doi Dao.—The buff female of Group 3 swung quickly through an open tree and out on a limb. As she was preparing to swing into an adjacent tree, the limb broke, leaving a stub which was about 6 inches long. As the limb broke and fell, the gibbon recovered by turning almost in mid-air and catching the remaining stub of the branch. With extreme rapidity she swung around under and then on top of the limb and then, with only a slight loss of time and momentum, jumped outward and downward 30 feet to an adjacent tree-top.

An important feature of gibbon locomotion is the advantageous use they make of momentum, gravity, and air resistance. Once they have gained an elevation, their locomotion consists of a continuous flow of movement, perfectly coordinated and of a gliding, swinging quality.

April 3, Group 1, Doi Dao.—Several times I have seen the animals of Group 1 making long jumps while the black mother with an infant have gone around to avoid the jump. This would indicate that a large infant is a considerable impediment to the mother, possibly in that it prevents her from assuming advantageous postures and prevents free use of her legs either in taking off or in landing. Then, too, its weight alone would make locomotion more difficult for the mother.

. . . .

The literature describing the locomotion of gibbons in the wild would lead one to assume that they travel exceedingly swiftly through the forest, making it almost impossible to follow and observe them. It is true that, during bursts of speed, gibbons may travel through the trees as if touching branches more for guidance than support, particularly if the general drift of movement is from a high point to a lower one, in which case the animals seem to glide downward at such a rate that it is very difficult to follow them. Nevertheless, these bursts of speed are sporadic and of short duration.

. . . .

Manipulation and Use of Objects.—Gibbons are principally bimanual instead of bipedal in locomotion. Being brachiators, their hands and arms are more highly specialized for support and locomotion than for manipulation. Whereas gibbons excel as brachiators, they are found to be rather poor in fine manipulations as compared with other primates.

The feet of the gibbon are free during brachiation and, when the gibbon swings from a limb by its arms, the feet may be used for manipulation.

.   .   .   .

. . . Objects on flat surfaces present an abnormal situation for the arboreal gibbon; its grasping and manipulatory activities are normally carried out with reference to hanging objects which may be grasped from any angle.

It seems difficult for a gibbon to grasp a number of small objects and hold them—for example, a handful of grapes. The palm of the hand is very narrow as compared with the width of the hand at the base of the fingers. Hence, when a gibbon needs to hold in its hand a number of small objects, its fingers are arranged into a conical-shaped cup. The little finger is held tightly against the palm forming the apex and each succeeding finger is held less tightly, until the second finger forms the edge of an inverted cone which holds the objects.

To supplement the manipulatory capacities of the feet and hands, gibbons use their teeth a great deal for holding objects and for preparation of food. Most fruits which require it are peeled or seeded by the combined activities of feet, a hand, and the teeth.

In the wild, gibbons may be observed using objects to attain certain ends and to produce particular results, and in this they perhaps demonstrate one of the early stages of instrumentation. In crossing a wide space in its path, a gibbon may climb to the very top of a slender tree and sway back and forth until the oscillations sufficiently reduce the space for the animal to jump. Similarly, a gibbon may swing to a vine and cross a space by swinging pendulum fashion from one point to another. During fits of rage, gibbons have been seen repeatedly breaking dead branches and dropping them in the direction of the observer.

Vines with attached food or vines which cling to branches with fruit are pulled in and the food eaten. These examples of the use of objects relate to and suggest box-stacking, the pulling-in technique, and the jumping procedures familiar to laboratory workers. Although the exact capacities of gibbons to use objects as a means to an end remain to be demonstrated by laboratory experiments, I suggest on the basis of field observations that these capacities will be less well developed than those in the cebus or rhesus monkeys. (Recent experiments carried out at Columbia University support this opinion.)

Feeding Activities and Food.—
. . . gibbons like other primates have their own peculiar methods of using their hands, feet and teeth in feeding. . . . While swinging from branches and feeding, the gibbon must use at least one of its arms for support (unless it happens to swing by its feet, an act rarely observed except in play). Being frugiverous and lacking a prehensile tail, the gibbon must travel out to the very ends of fruit-bearing branches and twigs. Being light of weight and having long arms with which to anchor itself, it is possible for the gibbon to swing out to terminal twigs and then, by using its feet, to extend its reach still further for grasping the fruit. Thus brachiation is an adaptation useful in the fruit-eating habits of the gibbon.

.   .   .   .

I have no evidence that gibbons store food. There is little need for this in a habitat similar to that around Doi Dao. Gibbons, however, do frequently gather fruit in their hands or feet and carry it to a place where it may be eaten conveniently. This differs from the feeding habits of howlers, who rarely if ever transport food from the place where it is plucked.

The following field notes describe observations on feeding in gibbons.

March 14, 1937, Doi Intanon.—Almost as soon as I brought a solitary male gibbon into the binocular field, he swung out to the end of a branch and removed a bird's nest from its perch between two twigs. The gibbon then took the nest in his feet and carried it back to a more solid limb, where he again took it into his hands. While he was sitting there, he removed at least two eggs from the nest and ate them. This observation establishes to my satisfaction that gibbons sometimes eat birds' eggs. It is probable that this egg food constitutes an important part of the nutritional needs of this ape. The motor skill shown by this animal in securing and handling the nest should be duly evaluated.

. . . .

April 7, 1937, Doi Dao.—Group 6 was being observed through a natural screen of leafless bamboo clumps. It was moving very near to the ground and there was considerable searching through bamboo husks and bunches of leaves, apparently for insects and larvae.

. . . .

April 16, 1937, Doi Dao.—The buff male of Group 3 showed overt behavior which resembled drinking. He would put his hand against a tree, leave it there for a few seconds, bring it to his mouth, and lick the back of his hand. This behavior continued for about 10 minutes. At first, because of the similarity to drinking behavior, I assumed that he was taking water which was seeping from a hollow in which it had collected. Close inspection of the tree after he left showed that he was apparently collecting ants on the back of his hand and eating them, for there was a large column of ants climbing the tree where he had been feeding.

. . . .

Foods.—In summary, observations and examinations of stomach contents show that gibbons are principally frugiverous but that a considerable amount of leafy mash is also eaten. Perhaps about 80 percent of the food consists of fruits and the rest of a variety of kinds of food. Leaves, buds, and flowers make up most of the remaining 20 percent. Birds' eggs and even young birds are eaten and these, along with various kinds of insects, including ants, must afford proteins necessary to supplement the fruit diet. . . . Honey, of which there is an abundance in the Siamese forests, may be eaten, since captive animals eagerly seek the honeycomb when it is made available to them.

Drinking.—Drinking as a part of feeding activity is highly specialized in the gibbon. Study of several species of arboreal primates shows that they get much of their water by licking dew or rain from leaves and bark or even from their own hair, dampened after a rain. Gibbons also get water in this fashion. However, gibbons have a method of drinking which is typical of them and rarely seen in other primates. Where there is a collection of water, wild gibbons characteristically close their fingers, dip the hand into the water and then suck the moisture from the hairs of the back of the hand and knuckles. Usually the hand is dipped into the water and then brought quickly above the mouth as the head is thrown backward. Thus, the collected drops of water both drip into and are sucked into the mouth. Some gibbons with considerable delicacy dip only the hairs of the back of the hand into the water, while others plunge the entire hand in and collect some water in their poorly formed fist.

. . . .

The sources of water for gibbons are, in the order of their importance:

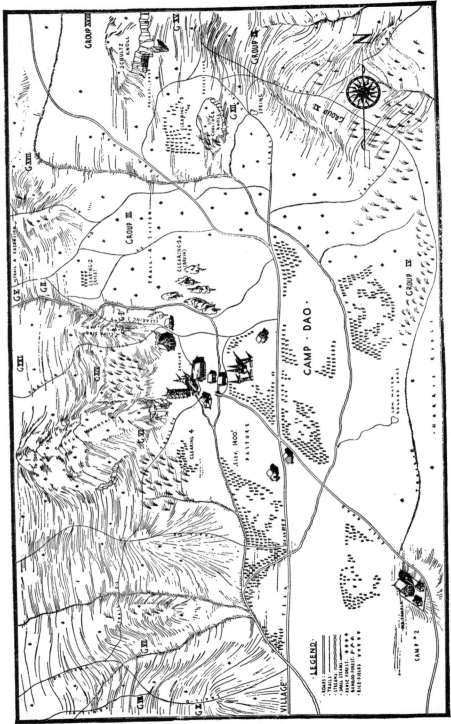

14

1. Water content of fruits and leaves.
2. Surface films of water collected from rains and heavy dews on leaves, bark, and on the animals' own coats.
3. Water collected in the hollows of tree trunks and large limbs. 4. Pools of water, streams, and springs or even water seeping from crevices in rocks. Keen competition among groups occurs around limited sources of water such as seep bogs or springs during long dry seasons.

Chapter IV—Population Studies and Gibbon Families

Censuses of Sample Gibbon Populations.—There are three samplings of gibbon populations on which I wish to report: one on Doi Intanon, one in an isolated forest near the village of Chieng Dao, and one in a section of forest shown on the map, surrounding the Doi Dao Camp.

While working on Doi Intanon, I spent each morning of one week locating, checking, and rechecking the places from which the early and mid-morning calls emanated from groups of gibbons which lived in a valley. These observations were made from several high altitude blinds or platforms built in trees left standing on cut-over mountain tops. These vantage points gave an uninterrupted view of the expanse of densely forested valley below.

The consistency of results in terms of the daily location and relocation of groups by their calls was of interest to me. The resulting scatter diagrammatic map showed that there were apparently about nine locations within earshot of Observation Post No. 3, where groups could be heard each day.

. . . . .

From data gathered at Doi Dao, it was found that the modal group of gibbons contains four animals. By making the rather safe assumption that this mode applied to the groups on Doi Intanon as well, I assume that about 36 gibbons lived in the nine groups in the valley of the Behavior Research Camp on Doi Intanon. The area of this valley is estimated to be four square miles —two miles wide and two miles long. Allowing for probable errors, one can estimate that the number of gibbons in this territory must be somewhere between 35 and 50. Roughly speaking, this means 10 or 12 individuals in two or three groups per square mile.

Lying between the town of Chieng Dao and the village and mountain of Doi Dao, there was a beautiful forest about three quarters of a mile wide and one mile long. The forest was unusually open, relatively free of underbrush and penetrated by a network of trails. In this area, three gibbon groups were located, counted and recounted at least three times until my knowledge of the composition of the groups was almost certain as far as could be determined by gross observations.

The first group in this area, No. 13 . . . had five individuals as follows: (1) An adult black male; (2) An adult black female which carried (3) An infant No. 2,* which was buff colored; (4) A black juvenile No. 2; (5) A black late juvenile No. 3 or young adult.

The second group of this sampling, Group 16, contained four animals: (1) A large black animal judged to be a male; (2) A black female, which carried, (3) A small buff infant No. 1; (4) A black juvenile No. 3.

The third group, Group 19, also contained four animals: (1) An adult buff male; (2) A black juvenile No. 2 or

---

* [These numbers designate the sizes of the young animals.]

No. 3; (3) An adult black female, which carried, (4), A small black infant No. 1.

The compositions of these groups were so different when color and size variations were taken into account that it was possible to identify each group almost as soon as it was entirely seen. It happened, too, that each time the groups were seen, Group 13 was in the western part of the forest, Group 16 was in the middle ranges of the forest, and Group 19 was found in the eastern reaches where this Isolation Forest was separated by a field of low bushes from the forests of the mountain. My observational study of these groups and their accessibility made it possible for me to collect them and learn more accurately the composition of the groups. The three groups were entirely collected.

.   .   .   .

The procedure of first studying and then collecting whole groups of primates instead of shooting individual specimens at random without previous study or plan would seem to be an important advance in collecting techniques, either for taxonomic specimens or for the study of skeletons. Not only does this method have the advantage of enabling one to acquire a system of behavioral data on the animals, but animals collected in this manner yield data on variations or similarities of structures and colors within the family as well as species variations. Structural abnormalities or peculiarities may have a genetic basis which may be inferred and more accurately described if family relationships are known and then noted in the analysis of data.

.   .   .   .

A total of 21 groups . . . studied in the Doi Dao area . . . contained a total of 93 individuals. Excepting solitary animals, which are part of grouping in flux, the groups ranged in size from two to six individuals; the minimum groups consisted of a pair; the largest groups consisted of families with four young. The modal group contained four animals, the adult pair and two young ones. The young ones varied in their stages of development from very early infancy to young adults.

The total population of 93 individuals had approximately 22 adult males and 21 adult females, 11 infants still being carried by their mothers and 39 juveniles, entirely independent of their mothers and ranging in a graded series up to young adults. Considering the different juvenile classifications, it is found that there were 10 of the J1 class, 7 of the J2 class, 6 of the J3 class and 8 of the A (young adult) class. Were the classifications perfectly accurate, and some allowances must be made for errors of estimate, and were the step intervals between classes equal either in terms of the size of the young animals or age, and if the sampling were sufficiently large, the number of individuals in each category should perhaps be equal.

Two satisfactory counts of groups on Doi Intanon, one of which was composed of a pair and another of a pair with two young animals, further supports the above data.

From these data the conclusion can be stated as follows: The mean grouping tendency in gibbons of the species *Hylobates lar* is that of the family: a male and female with their young.

Variations in this grouping pattern are clearly indicated. Two of the groups of the Doi Dao population had no offspring. This type of association indicates to me that the groups are young, i.e., recently formed and that as yet no infant has been born. Reasoning from the same assumption, namely that in fertile pairs the number of young animals in a group indicates within certain limits (perhaps up to six or eight years) the age of the group, then those with three or four immature animals may be considered old groups. In all the groups, the number of infants and juveniles ranged from zero to four.

That there are variations also in the number of adults in the families is indicated by collected groups Nos. 10 and 13. There were three males in Group 10; one was in his prime, another was old if not senile, as indicated by badly worn and broken teeth, and a third was in its very early adulthood. My interpretation of this grouping is that the first male which was in the prime of life was the dominant, supreme male, the old male was probably reproductively ineffectual, and the young male was in a stage just prior to that when he would perhaps separate from his parental group or replace the dominant male.

May 25, 1937, Group 5, Doi Dao.— J3bf and Ab of Group 5 appear to be quite widely separated from the rest of the group for long periods of time. On the basis of group scatter and reasonable inferences from their behavior, it would seem that group cleavage will probably occur between these two animals and the rest of the group.

There is a possibility, however, that the scatter shown by this group is a result of intense play interest as well as perhaps early sexual activity between J3bf and Ab. Almost constant play activity of two animals has the effect of separating them from the rest of the group and of conditioning the animals to each other in a positive and reciprocal manner, preparatory to mating.

April 12, 1937, Group 11, Doi Dao. —An animal which was highly independent was found and distinguished in Group 11. The gibbon is an Ab but its sex could not be learned. It ranges rather widely from the central focus of the group and may at times be seen 150 or 200 yards from Group 11. The relation of this animal to the group scatter suggests that it represents a stage of splitting away from the parent group.

May 13, 1937.—. . . At times the Ab would be separated by more than 150 yards from the others of the group and appeared not to be as responsive to intragroup communicative acts as were the other animals.

An animal commonly associated with Group 11 was also seen at times traveling alone and sometimes making approaches to neighboring groups. A long-time study of this animal and its group relationships convinced me that it represented an animal in the transitional stage of splitting away from its parent group and engaging in general exploratory behavior preparatory to forming the nucleus of a new group with a suitable mate.

I am convinced that the hypothesis which claims that "solitary" individuals are old, ineffective primate males which are driven from their groups is untenable as a complete explanation for extragroup primates. The old, senile, feeble males were tolerated in groups. Some solitary specimens are unquestionably old but others are young and apparently vigorous; hence the social behavior of extragroup animals is not solely a function of factors associated with aging.

The family type of grouping shown to be characteristic of *Hylobates lar* and perhaps other species of gibbons, requires an approximately equal number of males and females to form the families.

CHAPTER V—INTRAGROUP RELATIONSHIPS

An adequate description of groups of primates as wholes depends upon accurate, analytic explanations of the detailed relationships within the groups. Each bisexual, reproducing primate grouping has a given number of qualitatively different relations definable in terms of the kind of individuals involved and their interactive behavior. These constant categories for primate groups are: 1. The relationships among adult males. 2. The relationships among adult females. 3. The relationships of adult males to adult females. 4. The relationships of adult males to young. 5. The relationship of adult females to young. 6. The relationships among young animals of different classes and sex. Thus, there are at least six qualitatively distinct social relations defined in terms of sex and age in the usual primate group. In the forest it was not possible to differentiate sex differences in immature animals, hence further categories in the case of the young are not possible. The six relationships may be abbreviated as follows: 1. male-male, 2. male-female, 3. female-female, 4. male-young, 5. female-young, 6. young-young. Descriptive analyses of these relations help to represent more fully the grouping patterns of gibbon families.

The number of specific intergroup relationships in a particular group is found by applying the simple formula

$$N\frac{(N-1)}{2}$$

[N = number of individuals in the group. Ed.] With the addition of each new individual to a group, the number of specific relations increases by the number already in the group. If there are four animals in a group with six distinct relationships, and a fifth animal is added, then the sum of specific relationships is increased from six to ten. These calculations are based on the assumption that, within the group, each individual has an affective and distinct relationship with every other individual.

. . . .

In the modal family of gibbons with four individuals, there are six distinct relationships and in the maximum group of six there are fifteen such relationships. For purposes of description, however, these relations can be described under the six above listed categories. Each of these will be described separately.

Male-female Relationships.— . . . The association in gibbons is structured around a pair of animals which evidence strong bonds of attachment and form the core of the group. Although it is impossible to observe the establishment of bonds of mating in detail during field observations, nevertheless, by organizing large numbers of observations, the process of mating can be reliably reconstructed.

In the first place, given a parental family with a maturing male, the question arises as to how he obtains a mate. There are several possibilities; either he mates with one of the other siblings in the family, sister or half sister or he mates with a suitable female from another semiclosed group. Also he may mate with his mother, if the dominant male is by some means eliminated from the group. The maturing female has similar possibilities of mating with male siblings or with the father.

An example of mating within the group seemed to have been taking place in Group 1 with the two black young adults. These animals, as far as I could learn, were male and female siblings. . . . It was clearly observable that they were strongly attached to each other and were more closely associated than with others of the group. In fact, during some days for many hours this subgroup of young gibbons would be separated from the rest of the family (male, female, and infant) for many hours and by distances of several hundred yards. Perhaps in this case, a new family was budding off from the parent family in an incest type of mating.

If the young maturing male mates outside of his parent group, he must go through processes of breaking away from the original group, of exploring, and of making contacts with many other groups in his search for a suitable mate. The young adult in Group 11 seemed to exemplify this process. Following this mating comes a process of establishing reciprocal bonds of attachment through what might be broadly viewed as mechanisms of conditioning. The probabilities are that in gibbons the mating bonds are fixed gradually over weeks or even months and that, once established, they are not ended by the completion of any phase of the sexual or reproductive cycle.

It is possible for a young male to find a suitable mate in some group of an adjacent territory during times when the parent groups come near each other. Sometimes neighboring groups actually intermingle for short periods of time. During such periods, a young male may find a suitable female and begin the initial stages of the mating process. Some young males may be completely cut off from the parent group and live temporarily as wanderers who go from group to group, exploring, and eventually finding a mate while living tangentially to other groups. This would account for observed young males which were temporarily separated from groups. Similar contacts to those observed may be repeated many times before a pairing is made since mating depends upon a specific state of maturity and physiological condition.

The foregoing description should not lead to the conclusion that the males are more aggressive in this respect than the females. I have no observations to support this fact. On the contrary, observations in the field and on my captive gibbons tentatively indicate that the males and females are about equally aggressive both in pugnacity and in reproductive behavior. In fact, in two instances of pairings of captive gibbons, females took the initiative. Thus, maturing young female gibbons may go through a parallel process of becoming more explorative with an increased drive for mating, breaking away from the parent group and eventually finding a suitable mate. This would lead to the prediction that in a gibbon population one might expect to find temporary solitary young females as well as young males and there is some data to support this assumption. The breaking away from the parent group by either the maturing male or female is believed to be mainly a result of the heightened sex drive, frustration of this and other drives, and the subsequent exploratory behavior.

The behavior of mated gibbons contrasts sharply with that of males and females in macaque groups or in herds of baboons. In groups of primates which are organized on the mosaic, harem patterns with several males and many females in the large troop, tribe, or clan, there is competition among the males for the females and each male has his particular dominance status. Also, there is competition among the females during estrus for close relations with males and for maintenance of a female hierarchy of dominance. In the gibbon family, the dominance gradient is found between the mated male and female and among the young adults of the family. The activities of the adults may be said to be coaxial, perhaps cooperative, with reference to each other rather than competitive in most social activities.

Sexual Activity.—My observations of copulation and associated behavior in free ranging gibbons were very limited. During hundreds of undisturbed hours of observations on gibbon groups, only two instances of copulation were observed and these indistinctly and incompletely. . . . In all instances observed (including observations on gibbon colonies in Puerto Rico and California) the females were more aggressive than the males. . . .

I have had studies in progress on the estrous cycle of gibbons in Puerto Rico. . . . On the basis of these data it would seem probable that further experimentation will show that gibbons have a period of bleeding which continues for about two days or 48 hours. In one specimen of *Hylobates lar,* the menstrual cycle ranged, during five months, from 21 to 33 days and averaged about 27 days.

. . . .

Two types of evidence show consistently that gibbons do not have a discrete breeding season. First, infants and young animals in all stages of development were to be seen in the gibbon families between the months of February through June 1937. Second, the collected embryos showed considerable range in the stage of their development. . . . It is clear that gibbons give birth to young throughout the year. . . .

A factor worth noting is the percentage of young animals found in gibbon groups. In . . . 21 groups . . . there were 43 individuals classified as adults. These made up 21 pairs, which had 11 infants continuously or usually associated with their mothers, 28 juveniles, and 11 young adults, making a total of 50 young of all classes. . . .

Three characteristics of reproductive behavior in gibbons relate importantly to their grouping patterns and more specifically to the male-female relationship. 1. Apparently there is no definite breeding season; hence copulation may reinforce the male-female bond throughout the year. 2. As compared with macaques or chimpanzees, gibbons seem to have a low degree of sexual drive. 3. Observations on a pair of gibbons in the San Diego Zoological Garden suggest that copulation may take place throughout the menstrual cycle and even during pregnancy, through unquestionably there are marked variations in frequency according to Mrs. Belle Benchley, Executive Secretary of the Garden. These conditions, if experimentally and reliably established, would indicate an equilibrated satisfaction of sexual hunger in a pair of gibbons and reinforcement of the male-female relationships. In gibbons, copulation seems not to be as restricted to an estrous period as has been found with macaques and chimpanzees. This kind of receptivity would seem to compensate for the lack of more than one female for each male and support the family pattern of grouping.

How long does reproduction continue during the life cycle of gibbons? The female, "Pitard," . . . is showing her first menstrual cycle . . . (April 25, 1940). . . . she was known to be approximately seven years of age in June 1937; thus she is menstruating first as she approaches an estimated age of ten years. As yet this is the only meager evidence which I have that suggests that reproduction in gibbons may begin not later than ten years of age in the female and that eight years would be the minimum age for the onset of menstruation.

Some specimens of gibbons have lived in zoological gardens for about thirty-two years (Philadelphia Zoological Garden). A female observed and collected by me carried an infant and this female was described by Schultz as being at the age of advanced senility. This suggests that gibbons continue to have babies rather late in their life cycle.

A rough approximation would seem to be that, given a normal life span of about 30 to 40 years, a gibbon may be effective in reproduction for about 20 years.

The slowness of maturity and growth in infants . . . suggests that not more than one infant is born each two years; hence a single female gibbon probably gives birth to about ten infants during her life. If the interval between the births of young is as much as three years, then a female may only produce six or seven young in her lifetime.

Male - male Relationships.—. . . All facts support the following deductions: 1. When young males have reached maturity, they may become separated from their parental group. Perhaps the negative behavior of the dominant male is an important factor in this separation. 2. Definite proof is lacking to establish the existence in any one group of two vigorous adult males in their prime; thus suggesting that there is strong antagonism between males of the adult age group when the drive for mating is strong. 3. Aging males may be replaced either by maturing intra-group males or by males which break into the group. The aging males may either remain in the group or be separated from it. Whether these separations are temporary or permanent is not known, but it is possible that they might be either, depending on the social behavior of the individual.

. . . . .

. . . the approaches of young adult males to groups and especially to females were strongly repulsed by the group male. The peculiar family social pattern found in gibbons would seem to demand for its maintenance strong antagonism between males (and between females) during the effective stages of their reproductive life. This kind of a relationship is consistent with what is known of the temperament and emotional expressions in gibbons and is consistent with the theories of restricted social relations and aggression.

Male - young Relations. — Very young gibbon infants stimulate the adult males to inspect, manipulate, and groom them. Mild play between a male and an infant, in which the latter is usually the aggressor, may be observed throughout the period of growth.

One of the male's psychosocial functions is that of guarding the infants or juveniles of his family against animals from other groups, against enemies, and against other disturbances such as hunters or observers. A few alarm calls by a young one will bring the male of a family swinging rapidly to its location. Even within the group, the guarding function is shown. During rough play or play fighting, an adult male may interfere while the young ones are struggling.

. . . .

Some time during early adulthood, a change occurs in the relational behavior of a developing young male and the dominant male of the family. Gradually the relationship seems to shift from that of compatibility to antagonistic responses characteristic of gibbons which are strange to each other. The conditioning stimuli which bring this about are little known. Perhaps sexual approaches to the mother are involved and since gibbons are very "jealous," a situation would arise which would induce fighting. This fighting in turn, would weaken the bonds of attachment and establish instead antagonistic relations.

One part of the greeting responses

which occur between gibbons almost invariably involves visual, olfactory, and tactual inspection of the genitalia. When a strange animal is introduced into a group, this inspection is prepotent over every other kind of behavior. Perhaps with the maturation of the young males, rather specific genitalia stimuli become functional in arousing antagonistic responses in the adult males. In this greeting pattern, the approach is exploratory and neutral until the inspection takes place; then the activity takes on a fairly definite quality of friendliness or antagonism. The antagonistic responses are seen clearly in the actions of the adult males when this stage in the greeting pattern is reached.

Female-female Relationships.— The equivalent bisexual dominance which seems to characterize the social behavior of gibbons strongly influences their group organization. The lack of marked behavioral sex differences, except in reproductive activities, make applicable to the female-female relations essentially the same descriptions as have been given for male-male relations. Being equally dominant with the male, the female of a group plays a role very like his in leading, coordinating, and guarding the group. Since the female is specifically attached to a single male within the family group, the situations provocative of competitive activities among females are limited compared with some other primate types. . . . The competition among the females in gibbon groups is limited to the group of maturing daughters, in the main. The young adult female of Group 13, which was almost ready for mating activity (as shown by an examination of her ovaries after she was collected) is an example of the possibility of competition between the group female and the maturing daughter for mating relationship with the group

male. After the female was collected and up until the time that the daughter was shot, she was closely associated with the group male. If this group had been left undisturbed, in all probability the adult female and the maturing daughter would have developed an antagonistic relationship. Also, if the daughter and the male had been left to survive after the adult female was collected, I am convinced that the father and daughter would have mated and formed a new group.

A fact worth special consideration is that in no group other than Group 13, which was collected, was there more than one adult female. There is a possibility that some of the observed young adults, which it was impossible to classify more accurately, were young adult females. However, it would have been expected that in an adequate sampling of gibbon families, some group would have contained two females with babies or dependent young. No such group was found in the 21 groups studied during the four months at Doi Dao nor were two females with young ones observed in any other grouping of gibbons.

.   .   .   .

Female-young Relationships.— No births of gibbons have been observed in the wild.

.   .   .   .

To summarize, almost invariably gibbons carry their infants low down over the pelvis, more or less to one side or the other and sometimes almost over one leg as it is held in a sharply flexed position. Occasionally the infant varies its form of grasping from that of holding around the mother's body and grasping her hair with its hands while holding on to the hair of the groin with its feet, to a position much lower down on the mother's belly where it grasps the legs of the mother from underneath. Not once did I see a young gibbon being carried on its mother's back.

When females carrying young infants stop to rest during the day, the infants usually leave their mothers and engage in various kinds of exploratory activity, such as pulling at leaves and flowers, trying out all kinds of swinging postures and locomotor gaits and generally playing "solitaire." When the infant nurses, the mother is usually seated with her body bent slightly forward. If the infant needs rest or sleep while the mother is quiet, it takes a position somewhere in the flexure of the mother's trunk and is further protected by the mother's long arms and legs. A furry enclosure is thus arranged which may be of considerable importance as a temperature-regulating arrangement for the young infant. In a sense, the mother forms a nest for her young from her own trunk and limbs.

As the infant gibbon matures, changes occur in its activities with reference to its mother. During the first month or six weeks, when it is still very spiderlike, with long, thin, spindly legs and arms and short, downy hair, it rarely if ever leaves its mother; it maintains an almost continuous contact with her. Its first movements away from the mother occur when she is resting and other young animals of the group approach the infant and coax it to play, or at least try to use it as a play object. Beginning by reaching out with its long, thin arms and equally slender legs, it advances to a second stage, involving momentary release of contact with the mother, movement away for short distances, and then hurried returns at the slightest provocation. The focus of behavior for the early infant is its mother; all activities are carried out with continuous reference to her and dependence on her.

The mother in turn usually shows solicitude for the infant. Frequently, before a female starts to travel when her infant is a short distance away from her, she will pull it in and arrange it in a suitable position for carrying before she begins to brachiate.

. . .

Decreasing dependence and increasing independence in the female-infant relationship consists of gradual changes in a number of important behavior patterns. Most important among these are the following: Even the very young infant is almost continuously exploring for foods, reaching, grasping, and carrying objects to its mouth. During the first few weeks of life, the intake of solid foods begins to supplement the mother's milk. Just as the getting of food from the breasts and warmth from her body conditions the infant toward its mother, so the getting of food away from her, accompanied by maturation of motor capacities, stimulates the infant to extend its explorations and become more active. Its need for warmth decreases as it grows a coat of hair. Frequent contacts with other young animals stimulate the infant to play and hence to establish a web of social bonds away from the mother. Increased locomotor capacities make the infant gibbon less dependent on the mother for movement from one place to another. Maturation of communicative behavior, involving movement patterns and sound signals, make less necessary the actual contact control by the mother. These and other factors lead to a gradual weakening of the female-infant bond and finally to actual repulsion by the mother during the weaning period.

. . .

April 10, 1937, Group 1, Doi Dao.— I was watching the black female and black infants 2 of Group 1 when there was a distant shot from a gun. At the time, the infant 2 was swinging and playing about three feet from the mother. When the shot rang out, almost reflexlike, the mother rushed to the infant, pulled it in toward her belly, and it got into position for being carried. In this behavior, care of the young was prepotent over investigatory behavior, fear-flight, or other defense reactions.

.　　.　　.　　.

Young-young Relationships.—As compared with other larger groupings of primates, the number of possibilities of different relations among infant gibbons is quite limited. The gibbon groups observed in this study never contained more than four immature animals (with the possible occasional exception of Groups 7 and 11). This means that there were more frequent and prolonged associations among the several young animals in the group, which probably resulted in the formation of stronger bonds because of their continued reinforcement. . . . in young groups of gibbons, i.e., those not long formed, the firstborn infant would be entirely without a sibling playmate (for example note Group 18) and the number of possible playmates was never observed to include more than three additional siblings. I have reason to believe that once a family is well established with a succession of young ones grading from infancy to early maturity, the grouping pattern and number of animals tend to remain rather constant if births are regular, for as young are born, others reach maturity and become separated from the family.

The number of immature animals in the 21 groups studied at Doi Dao ranged from none to four, the average being about two and a half. Two groups had no young ones, one group had one, eight groups had two, six groups had three, and four groups had four. The modal group therefore contained two young animals.

It is highly probable that the limited number of playmates accessible in gibbon families strongly influences the socialization processes. The infant which develops in the highly organized and exclusive gibbon family unquestionably has fewer opportunities for social relations than the macaque infant, which develops in a group with 15 or 20 young playmates.

The social relations of young gibbons are most often typically and completely expressed in play. From dawn to dusk young gibbons in a family are seldom quiet, except sometimes during the midday rest interval. Even then, although the adults usually remain quiet, the young ones usually play.

.　　.　　.　　.

. . . young gibbons pass through a stage during which they play alone, exploring, trying various forms of movement and postures. They play by themselves, with their hands and feet, and repeat over and over various postures and movements. Play patterns of the social type consist of chasing, catching, wrestling, and biting. Frequently the juveniles chase each other over a circuitous route which has jumps or swings that are repeated many times as the young gibbons engage in a kind of follow-the-leader game.

The amount of play varies in several ways. The diurnal variations include an early morning period of play which takes place before the group begins to move out to feeding places. The next period of most active play behavior occurs as the older animals settle down for the midday interval of rest. There is a third maximum about 4:00 or 5:00 o'clock in the afternoon as the group settles into a proper abode tree for the night. However, at any time when the group is relatively stationary, young animals may be seen playing. When the group is disturbed, and often the playful juveniles are the first to sense a disturbing object, play stops and the young give alarm calls and dash away.

From the point of view of the life cycle, the amount of play increases up to the stage of development classified as juvenile 3 or young adult. With maturation, the amount of play decreases and the decrease seems to be correlated with periods of inactivity in old animals. In addition to other basic physiological factors associated with age and the maturation of sexual behavior, play fighting seems to function to reduce the amount of social play and of general activity. These activities give way to greater differentiation and specialization of behavior and social attachments.

Chapter VI—Territoriality and Intergroup Relationships

Territoriality and Nomadism.— It was found by means of sound localizations that the nine or ten groups of gibbons which lived in the valley near the Behavior Research Camp on Doi Intanon restricted themselves to limited areas and seemingly stayed in them fairly consistently. This was learned through a prolonged daily study from machans (platforms) in trees on the mountain slopes. Records were made on a diagram map of the places where gibbons called. Further suggestions on this subject were obtained from natives who, being familiar with particular sections of forest, would point out that gibbons were regularly to be seen in this or that section or group of trees. When I inquired at native villages as to where gibbons could be found, the reply often was that a group of gibbons lived in a designated valley or tongue of forest. These suggestions, then, pointed to the fact that gibbon groups lived in restricted territorial ranges.

When I moved to camp at Doi Dao, part of the program of observations involved repeated location of a number of groups over a period of months in order to ascertain whether or not groups had definite territories and, if so, what was the extent of their range. During the study, a scatter diagram was kept of locations in which groups were seen. (See the map.) In this way and also by continuously following a group throughout the day and for several consecutive days, the territorial ranges were rather accurately plotted for about 11 groups.

. . . .

The distance covered during a day varied greatly. On some days, Group 1 loitered while feeding within 200 yards of where it had spent the night, and on other days it covered a total of about 1500 yards. Group 3, which had many widely scattered fruit trees within its territory, may have traveled at times as much as 2000 yards during the day.

During April and the first half of May, Group 1 was rarely seen along Trail B on the southeast side of Cliffside Mountain, for at this season the region was parched and dry and the trees leafless. Then Group 1 ranged in the valley close around Clearing 1 and competed with Groups 2 and 3 for access to fig trees which were ripening along the stream. Late in May and during June, Group 1 extended its range to the forest above my camp and to the southeast, where it came into contact with Group 6. The incentive to move in this direction was the ripening of grapes in that region and its lush, springlike vegetation. Thus, the total area in which Group 1 was observed to range was bounded by a line extending 200 yards up Cliffside Mountain (see the map) just southeast of camp, across the depression between Cliffside and Castle Mountain, over the crest of the mountain, over the stream just below Observation Post No. 5 to Clearing 2, and then along a branch of Teak Road to Clearing 3. A line drawn from this point around the clearings and back to the trees above my camp completed the range.

There was an overlapping region between the territories of Group 1 and Group 2. This was a band of forest which extended down from the crest of Cliffside Mountain, included a 100-yard stretch of the cliffside from Observation Post No. 5 west and across the stream bed to Clearing 2. Group 1 was never seen deep within the borders of the range of Group 2. The boundaries between Groups 2 and 5, 1 and 6, 2 and 3 were just as sharply defined.

The amount of territory covered by a group depends on the following factors: 1. Number of animals in the group, 2. Size and kind of forest, 3. Competition from other groups, 4. Availability of all the necessary amounts and kinds of foods, i.e., a variety of fruits and water, 5. Perhaps also disturbance by people or some enemy, 6. Optimum physical conditions, e.g., not too hot and dry but with adequate shade, 7. Previous adaptations.

It may be roughly estimated that Group 1 covered, during the period of the study, between 60 and 75 acres, Group 2 between 30 and 50 acres, and Group 3 between 60 and 100 acres. The territory of arboreal animals should be visualized as being three dimensional, for one important dimension is the height of the forest. In deep, tropical rain forests, the square area covered by a group need not be as great in order for the animals to have the same cubic area as in the low, mixed bamboo and semideciduous forest which predominated near Doi Dao.

Within the heights of the trees which set limits to range, different species of arboreal primates have different altitudinal preferences. Whereas marmosets and capuchin monkeys of Central America, for example, have an altitudinal range which extends from the ground to the topmost branches of trees, gibbons very rarely go either to the very tops of trees or to the ground. The average preference range for gibbons is through the midportions of trees over rather sturdy branches which interlock or are in juxtaposition forming a possible network of trails.

. . . .

When an animal population is organized into groups and herds usually the groupings have definite territorial adaptations; there is established, therefore, an inertia to migration. Particularly is this the case when the groups, families, and herds are mutually antagonistic or competitive. Each group is locked in its own territory by surrounding groups and any migratory movements are blocked according to the strength of the resistance of these boundaries.

. . . .

A group of gibbons in its native habitat is, strictly speaking, not free ranging except within the limits of the territory to which it has become conditioned and which it defends against the encroachment of other groups of gibbons. It would seem that the possession and defense of territory which is found so widely in the vertebrates, including the subhuman and human primates, may be a fundamental biological need. Certain it is that this possession of territory motivates much primate behavior.

Group Interactions.—. . . An individual is strongly enmeshed in its family by positive bonds of conditional responses and yet individuals are separated from groups through the operation of negative or repelling factors. Perhaps it might be well to visualize the factors as being centripetal and centrifugal. The basic question is: How are new groups formed?

Assuming an almost maximum-sized gibbon family consisting of an adult male, adult female, an infant 2, a juvenile 2, and a young adult male, what are the conditions which compel the young adult eventually to leave its parent group? How do the centripetal social bonds or factors become weakened or broken and the centrifugal tendencies strengthened? The changing social status of the individual is a gradual process involving changes in basic motives, particularly those of reproduction, plus the processes of conditioning or learning.

In the first place, with the coming of maturity there is a strengthening of the sex drive with its neural and endocrine correlates. Though the sex drive becomes very strong in the young male in the hypothetical group, there are no possibilities of satiation within the semiclosed family unless copulation could take place with his mother, and this is prevented by the "jealous" guarding behavior of the adult male. Sexual play activities do occur. Increased motivation or drive is followed by or accompanied by an increase in exploratory behavior, i.e., more or less random searching. This increases the centrifugal tendencies, the young male moves farther and farther away from the parent group, and these separations occur with increasing frequency. His excursions bring him into contact with other groups and individuals. When he approaches a group the interactions may range from fighting to affinitive sexual activity.

Secondly, there are forces within the group which tend to drive him away. Adult males are antagonistic to each other except in special relationships. As the young male reaches adulthood, an antagonistic relationship develops with his father, and this must be one of the forces acting to produce centrifugal movements in the young male.

(In macaque groups juvenile males are driven out of heterosexual groups and they live in unisexual groups of young males.)

The process of weaning and the birth of two intermediate young ones may already have weakened the attachment with the mother. Also, whereas formerly there were strong bonds of attachment in play relationships with the other young ones, by this time play fighting has developed and the drive for true play has decreased. Play has come to have painful aspects as the canine teeth have developed and consequently the amount of group-binding play has decreased.

Thus the young male is acted upon by the following kinds of forces which all operate to separate him from his group and to form a new group: 1. Weakening of attachments with the parent group, 2. Increasing motivation which cannot be satisfied within the semiclosed parent group, resulting in consequent frustration, 3. Development of antagonistic relationships with other members of the parent group, especially with the adult male and with the juveniles, 4. Positive incentives which arise from other groups or their individuals. When the forces operating centrifugally are greater than the forces binding the animal to his group, separation occurs. This process of group splitting may be termed apoblastosis, from the Greek meaning unequal division.

Once the young male is separated from his parents and his random exploratory behavior brings him into contact with other groups, a chance relation may be established with a female which is passing through a similar process of splitting away from her parent group or has already become a temporary isolate. Mating of these two individuals may then occur. I have sometimes thought, although I have never been able actually to prove it, that there may be special patterns of vocalizations which bring such animals together.

In some groups where there are two late juveniles or early adults of opposite sex, as is believed to be the case with Group 1, then mating may take place between siblings of the same group. In this instance, apoblastosis involves the separation of two individuals from the parent group, and this probably is a much more gradual process. In this situation, juvenile antagonisms between the young adults shift to sexual attractions. Without sexual frustration, strong positive bonds may be established.

Competition between groups occurs most frequently in border regions of territories. For example, Group 1 met Group 2 in the region between their territories which I have already described, and not anywhere else. Groups 1 and 3 had encounters northeast and east of Clearing 2. I saw Groups 1 and 6 come together only in a narrow strip of territory lying between my camp and the cliff and peak which lay above the temple grounds.

Clear instances of competition for food were observed. Groups 3 and 11 often clashed near the spring on Circle Trail, perhaps in part because each group came there for water, but also because there were several ripening fig trees whose fruit was highly preferred. . . . It may be added that after Group 1 had been driven away, I never again observed it as far advanced toward the territory of Group 6.

The maintenance of a territorial range unquestionably has direct and indirect reference to nutritional needs. If this were solely the incentive for the territorial behavior, the group would follow the shifting food supply, move nomadlike from one place to another and compete with groups which sought

to feed from the same trees. This is not the case. Time and again I have seen Group 1 rush out to meet Group 2 as it approached Clearing 1 and drive it away by persisting calls and the behavior of neither group had direct reference to food trees. When Group 5 moved over a sharp high ridge into a valley, part of which was occupied by Group 21, if one were close enough he could hear the disturbance; whimpering cries of young animals which were antecedent to vigorous calling by adults of the groups. Group 21 would rush out, intercept and divert Group 5, turning it back toward the valley wherein lay its territory.

The processes of conditioning which are operative in establishing a territory have as primary incentives the sources of food and water. Other incentives include arboreal trails which the group has learned, lodge trees in which the group has spent the night, and trees where it has rested and played. The familiar as contrasted with the strange may play a part here. For these spacially localized incentives associated with territorial needs, gibbon groups compete. Just as adult gibbons have a given space surrounding them which is not encroached upon by strangers except in the case of fighting, likewise each group has its involucrum of space from which it drives any encroaching group.

.   .   .   .

Concerted or cooperative action involving more than one group has rarely been observed. When it does occur, it is with reference to some situation or object of disturbance. Once Groups 3, 11, and 12, which were at the time in the same region around the spring on Circle Trail, were greatly disturbed by me and showed a considerable amount of concerted bluffing toward me. Groups 7 and 8 were observed in a like situation. However, in every instance of this kind the groups remained separated and seemed quite as much disturbed by each other as by me. The vocal responses caused by disturbances do act as signals from group to group and hence serve to direct group movements, but apparently among gibbon groups there is a minimum of co-ordinated and cooperative social behavior which cuts across group boundaries, rather the predominating mode of behavior is competitiveness.

In primitive peoples one finds tribal organizations. Situations such as warfare involve the concerted efforts of whole tribes. The origins of such co-operation of groups are difficult to trace in subhuman primates which I have studied. Such cooperation would depend upon more highly developed capacities for language than are to be found in nonhuman primates.

. . . . .

The lack of intergroup coordination would seem to be referable to the primitiveness and simplicity of their symbolic responses. The specificity of individual attachments in the group, which preclude more generalized compatible social relations, may relate to the simplicity of the capacities for symbolic responses (language) and the necessity for direct response (perceptual to stimuli). Expressed differently, it may be said that gibbons have capacities for making complex perceptual social responses and certainly responses to symbolic cues such as gestures or meaningful facial expressions, but they do not have capacities for employing more complex, generalized, "higher level" symbols.

Groups have been described as being semiclosed. Were a group completely closed, it would neither admit an individual into the group nor permit one to leave. The entering or leaving of a group by an individual is dependent upon the equilibrium or disequilibrium

of motivation in the group. In the stable group, for example, there should be approximately balanced male and female sex motivations. The death of a member of a pair would upset the balance. Periods of nonreceptivity of the female would do the same when there is a persisting drive for sexual activity in the male. There are other reciprocal, social drives which must be balanced in the stable group. When the equilibrium is upset, the group may be described as being open in some degree; then either apoblastosis will occur or another animal may join the group.

CHAPTER VII—GROUP COORDINATION, CONTROL, AND INTEGRATION

Group Coordination and Control.—Viewed ontogenetically, the processes of communication between two, or among several individuals in a group begin at birth and involve at first, on the part of the infant, relatively simple reflex responses. The prepotent reflexes found in the newborn primate baby, which have special importance for social conditioning, are well known but may be listed as follows: 1. The reflexes of stance, locomotion, and grasping, 2. The sucking reflexes, 3. The reflexes associated with temperature regulation, 4. Reflexes involving avoidance or negative responses.

The infant's grasping reflexes combined with those of equilibrium and locomotion, in interaction with manipulatory responses of the mother, serve to relate effectively the behavior patterns of the two individuals. The reflex responses of the early infant are random and undirected. It clings to hair, sucks hair, fingers, ear, nipples, or other objects which touch its lips. Shortly after birth it orients itself in space and in reference to its mother's body. It avoids colder regions, objects which are strange, or any objects which startle it. From these reflex responses, which are readily modified or conditioned, evolve responses which are more complex, less random and more differentiated, and more fittingly adapted to the mother's behavior. The mother prevents the infant from clinging to unsuitable parts of her body and forces it to cling in such a way that it will be comfortable for her and will not interfere unduly with her movements. After a short period of training, the infant clings consistently in positions which characterize the carrying of young by gibbon mothers, positions which fittingly relate to the mother's behavior. Random exploratory sucking responses rapidly become specific and then occur directly in relation to the mother's breast and nipples.

Temperature regulation in newborn gibbons has an accessory, social aspect. The infant apparently soon learns to arrange itself at places on the mother's body which are warmer or cooler and, reflexlike, it changes these positions. If the infant is cool, it snuggles close in to the mother's abdominal region. If the mother then responds by folding around it her long arms and flexed legs, the infant is enveloped in a warm, woolly nest more suitable for heat regulation than the nests of most birds.

During the early stage of development in infancy, the reflexlike responses are controlled by the mother's manipulations. This is a stage of social contact control which evolves, through processes of learning or conditioning, to the various levels of gestures and vocal communications. This process is clearly shown by certain gesture responses. For example, during exploratory responses of the very early gibbon infant, it leaves its mother for short distances. If the mother needs to move away while the infant is separated from her, she reaches for the infant, grasps it, and puts it on her belly, and it assumes a position suitable for being carried. Gradually the mother's motor components of these interactive responses with the baby are reduced. Actual grasping and carrying of the infant toward her is replaced by a simpler method. When the mother is ready to move, she merely looks for the infant, assumes a suitable posture for receiving it, and then the infant comes and climbs to its position. Later the stance of the mother, a quick look in the direction of the infant, or a limited movement of the hand is sufficient. In time, the control of the mother may be effected through patterns of sound, signaling the anticipated movement. Thus, actual handling of the infant as a mechanism of social control is replaced through reduction of gross movements, by postural orientation, then by a quick look, and later by postural orientation associated with a sound pattern. This process of cue reduction and fixation is perhaps what Hollingworth has called redintegration. This is one example of how contact control is replaced through learning by more symbolic control.

The gestures described below further illustrate the communication of gibbons through reduced, meaningful patterns.

Affinitive Gestures.—The greeting behavior of gibbons has a large symbolic component. Associated gibbons which are friendly show a striking pattern of greeting, especially after having been separated for a period of time or when two individuals come together for some communal social activity. Characteristically, two such individuals approach each other rather swiftly and then, as they come close together, the tempo of movement slows down. The facial expression involves a muscular pattern which may best be described as being similar to the human smile. The corners of the mouth are drawn back, baring the teeth, and the tongue is often protruded. The quality of every movement is relaxed and gentle. The arms are flexed and held over the head or to the side, if the animals are walking. The legs are drawn up and spread apart if the animals are brachiating. The two approaching animals come into an embrace in which, if the animals are swinging, they clasp one another with one arm and both feet; if they are walking, they use their arms. As they come into the embrace, each gives a little cry which resembles a faint squeal, scarcely audible at a distance of 50 feet, which increases in pitch as the animals reach the climax of the embrace. The embrace lasts for only a few seconds, then the individuals separate. This pattern of greeting symbolizes a disposition to friendly, compatible behavior. So it is that grooming, play, or copulation may follow, while fighting or antagonistic responses are not likely to occur immediately after this greeting embrace.

Grosser motor patterns as well as facial expressions are involved in communicative responses between gibbons. The friendly responses are relaxed and lack the tension observable in antagonistic responses. The tempo of movement is slower and indicates the quality of motives back of the action.

Antagonistic Gestures.—Anyone closely associated with gibbons soon learns the anticipatory expressions and movements which precede and indicate an attitude for attack. The angry or attacking gibbon repeatedly opens and closes its mouth as if smacking its lips and snapping its teeth together. It is tense and restless but there is a slyness in anticipatory movements which one soon learns to interpret. Characteristic rage behavior of shaking supports or stamping up and down repeatedly may

be shown. These movements provoke in associated animals either flight or pugnacious responses; in a sense they are expressive movements symbolizing the animal's motivational state.

Another gesture which is given when a gibbon is annoyed or frustrated occurs as follows: If play becomes too rough or if the animal is frustrated with reference to some incentive, then the gibbon's response consists of throwing back its head, raising its arms to the shoulder level in a flexed position, and shaking back and forth both the head and hands. If this annoyed, frustrated state is sufficiently reinforced, the behavior may change to fighting or attack. The same pattern of behavior may occur when an animal gets wet, is presented with a difficult choice situation, or when it is "bored." Yawning may also be associated with this mood. The sequence of behavior patterns is "understood" by gibbon associates and it exercises a kind of immediate social control.

Vocalizations.—Clearly the only way that an observer has of arriving at the meaning or function of a gesture or pattern of sound produced by an animal is to use the response of associated animals as an indicator. The situation in which the call is given and the response made must also be considered and interpreted. Technically, the problems of studying vocal expressions in primates and their stimulus values may be stated as follows: 1. To describe the stimulus situation in which the vocal pattern occurs, i.e., the specific patterns of stimuli which call forth the vocalization, 2. To describe and measure the sound patterns produced, 3. To describe the responses of associated animals of the same and of other groups including groups of other species. In other words to describe the stimulus value of the produced

TABLE VII

INDICATING NINE TYPES OF GIBBON VOCALIZATIONS AND THEIR PROBABLE FUNCTIONS

Type	Stimulus situation or situations	Subjects	Vocal pattern	Animals responding	Responses	Probable functions
I	a. During travel of group from focus of territory. b. Another nearby group. c. Following Type III calls in alarm situations	Adult males or adult females, more frequently the latter, usually individually	A series of hoots with rising inflection, rising pitch, increasing tempo with climax followed by 2 or 3 notes of lower pitch. Duration 12–22 seconds	Other groups or individuals of same group	Other groups: same vocalizations; at times withdrawal. Same group: Same vocalizations, orientation, rapid swings on high pitched climax	Exploration. Defensive actions. Protection of territory
II	a. Early morning. b. Sometimes while group is moving	Adult males	Single discrete calls, a series but may be repeated over and over. Similar to beginning notes of Type I calls	Animals in neighboring groups	Other groups: similar calls, simultaneously or alternately	Localizes group in its territory. Avoids conflicts
III	When group is surprised by a hunter, observer, or possible enemy	Adult males, adult females, and juveniles, often together	A loud, high-pitched note. A shout. Repeated but not in original series	Mainly in same group but also in nearby groups	Similar calls with avoidance behavior	Alarm, warning defensive
IV	When a member of a group gets lost. Toward the end of a period of alarm calls when group is scattered	Adult males, adult females, juveniles	Single note with rising inflection. Seems questioning at times	Same group	Assembly, searching	Keeps group together and directs attention
V	Not known	Adult males, adult females	High pitched, distinctive. Several seconds duration. Given in series of 3 to 12	Most groups of same region	Similar calls	Not known
VI	When a group is closely pressed by observer or hunter and greatly annoyed	Adult males, adult females	Deep-throated growl	Same group	Aggressive behavior typical of rage response	Defensive
VII	Play situation or when making friendly approach	Young animals	Little chirp or squeal	Play associates. Mother	More play, embracing and greeting behavior	Facilitates play, encourages or stimulates approach
VIII	Disturbed situation, confinement in captivity	Young animals	Fretting cry	All animals present		Begging
IX	During group progression	Adult leading	Chatter or series of clucks	Same group	Following	Means of directing group progression

sound for associated animals, especially for those of the same species, but also, to some extent, for those of different species.

In order to study more completely and objectively the vocalizations of gibbons, recording equipment was used in the Siamese study. A Presto Recorder with play-back attachment, high fidelity recording head, batteries (two 12-volts), transformer, semiportable parabolic reflector, a directional microphone, and 300 feet of cable comprised the essential equipment for making recordings on double-face acetate disks. This equipment was set up in the forest near feeding places, abode trees, and trails where gibbon groups had been observed repeatedly. The reflector and microphones could be shifted about a 300-foot radius from the machine and were placed as near as possible and directed toward the known location of gibbons; it was necessary only to wait until calls began to start making recordings.

.   .   .   .

The frequency with which calls are given throughout the day shows variations in the diurnal cycle and offers a clue to interpreting the function of the various types of calls. Also, the gibbon calls reflect the influence of climate.

.   .   .   .

. . . there are two main periods of calling each day; one during the morning and one during the afternoon. These periods correspond with the times when the animals are on the move; leaving abode trees, searching for food, returning to a place in which to spend the night and so forth. From 11:00 until 2:30 no calls were heard during the fifteen days when ratings were made. However, on April 16th, there was calling at 12:30 and once I heard a series of calls at 7:30 in the evening. The summed ratings for each

day ranged from 5 to 24 points, showing a great variation from day to day. In fact, during some of the windy days in May there was no calling at all.

These ratings were made on the basis of all calls heard by the observer while in forests near camp. On the average, Type I calls could be heard from a distance of about 1000 yards.

Table VII lists nine types of the more prominent and more easily differentiated sound patterns produced by gibbons. In all probability, further study will more clearly define these types, differentiate others, and show sound qualities which are common to some of them. Their functions are extremely difficult to infer and controlled laboratory experiments are urgently needed for further analysis. The fact is clear that these vocalizations as well as other sound patterns not only express excitement in an individual but also they have communicative, signaling value or instrumental value.

.   .   .   .

In gibbons, as well as in howler monkeys, the prominent types of calls by which the two species are best known have been found to function in competitive situations. The barking roars of howlers, like the Type I (see Table VII) series of calls made by gibbons, are produced when two or more groups come together, compete for food or for their established territory. In most situations where rhesus monkeys would fight or make bluffing, driving attacks, howlers, gibbons, and siamangs roar or call back and forth between competing groups. Vocalizations of the kind mentioned are clearly observed to act as buffers to fighting, and actually substitute for fighting as a secondary means of intergroup social control. In addition to the fact that these loud sounds have stimulus values which cause withdrawal, loud sounds may produce startle and avoidance responses. In all probability these particular sounds are sometimes reinforced by actual fighting.

.   .   .   .   .

I have observed a fact which I am not able to interpret to my satisfaction, namely, that when Type I calls are given in a situation involving competition between groups, the sound patterns function as defense or aggressive behavior. When, however, a group is alone and well fed, its members may give Type I calls repeatedly and for long periods among themselves. The latter calling seems to be an expression of excess energy, a type of vocal play (it may correspond to human singing); hence it may be concluded that many of the stereotyped vocalizations of primates are multivalent, i.e., the same sound patterns have several different stimulus values in different situations. Though the sound patterns remain the same, their motivation and biological functions vary, within limits, from one situation to another.

Type I calls are not given by infants. Young gibbons about two years of age first begin to learn to make this series of calls. Considerable improvement in calling may be made for six months or more after the first calls are given. . . .

A marked characteristic of gibbon vocalizations is that calls stimulate similar calls in associated animals. This is true of most types of gibbon calls but it is especially true of Type II. When a group in a particular region has given a series of Type II calls, one nearby group, then another and another, will echo the sound until most of the groups of the region have called. This calling and copying of calling may continue for an hour on some mornings. Likewise, the calls of one individual stimulate another individual to call. It is relatively easy for a person roughly imitating the Type II calls to stimulate calling in captive gibbons. The proc-

ess of stimulus and response resembles that of echolalia, which is sometimes observed in feebleminded persons.

.   .   .   .   .

While collecting specimens for an experimental colony, I have handled at least seven different species of gibbons, including siamangs. I have been impressed with the variations from species to species of the vocalizations. The species differences in calling are marked and these differences persist even when an individual from one species is caged with other species. *Hylobates agalis* has a very different call from *Hylobates lar,* and *Hylobates hoolock* has still a different call. A young specimen of *Hylobates agalis* which was caged with the colony of *Hylobates lar* specimens from October 1938 to July 1939 continued to produce sounds characteristic of her own species. This suggests that vocal patterns are largely structurally ("instinctively") determined and are not easily modified by learning. . . .

. . . 1. Vocalizations coordinate group activity by providing a single kind of dominating stimuli to which all individuals may respond. 2. A vocal pattern may predispose a number of individuals to make common responses to the same or to a variety of stimulus situations. 3. Vocalizations serve to synchronize in time the behavior of the individuals in a group. In addition it seems important to note that vocal responses and reciprocal stimulation may facilitate the overt aggressive behavior of associated animals by enhancing their general excitement. Furthermore, negative withdrawals are produced by some types of sounds and positive, affinitive responses by other types.

In summary, social coordination of behavior first involves actual contact control or manipulation; then through processes of learning similar to that of redintegration, gross expressive movements, i.e., gestures and series of sound patterns, come to have communicative functions. These make up a complex system of signs and signals which coordinate the behavior of individuals.

Even though certain gestures and vocal patterns are just as characteristic of the species *Hylobates lar* as its mode of walking or brachiating and perhaps are similarly determined, nevertheless it is assumed that the efficacy of gestures and vocal patterns depends upon associated effects. In other words, gestures and vocal signals must be instrumented; a warning growl will eventually lose its social function as a warning signal unless reinforced occasionally by a cuff or a bite. The invitational posture almost always observed to precede grooming would not indefinitely stimulate an associated individual to active grooming unless this behavior had its rewarding effect. The chirping cry and invitational behavior to play among young animals would not continue to stimulate playful behavior if the responding animals were always frustrated when reacting to the particular sound stimuli.

. . . . .

Aggressive Behavior.—Though I was much interested in pugnacious activities, while observing gibbons in Siam I did not see an adequate sampling of this kind of behavior. I saw a great deal of general aggressiveness and competitive vocalizations but no actual fights. That these fights do occur is certain, however. Even among the thirty-odd specimens collected at Doi Dao there were found the following: an adult male "slit ¾ inch long in left ear"; an old animal "broken canine tooth"; a young female with an old wound which had become infected and was filled with pus, site over temporal muscle, marked swelling around both eyes; a female with split upper lip; also

an animal with a stiff elbow, a case of "bony ankylosis of humerus and ulna." In addition in captive adult or near adult gibbons where frustrations are greater and the drive for aggression is enhanced, fights regularly occur between some specimens. Adults of the same sex seem to be especially antagonistic. Fights through the wire caging in San Juan result in many finger and hand, toe and foot wounds. In a fight between two adult males, one received a deep arm bite which splintered the left ulna. I am convinced that some of the healed fractures reported by Schultz were produced by the gibbons wounding each other in fights, principally through canine teeth bites, while other fractures have resulted from falls.

The motivation for gibbon fights is characterized by an explosive fit or rage, except in chronically vicious individuals. The attack is swift and telling. The individual attacked is approached, held, and bitten with the keen canine teeth. It is believed that cuts are made by the gibbon embedding the canines, then pulling with the neck muscles like a carnivor. This may open up a clean cut which has the appearance of having been produced by a knife. In adults the attack is usually quickly over, but each may always carry the scars of the battle. When fights did occur in the colony at San Juan, every individual became greatly excited and gave alarm calls and, when possible, other animals would join in either to protect one of the principals or to attack also.

Fighting between young animals usually involves both biting and striking with a clawing movement of the hands. By clawing, even young infants can inflict scratches on human hands. The biting in the young is not serious until the canines are well developed.

Admittedly most of the above description of gibbon fighting is influenced by experience with captive animals. The impression gained from field observations alone, after months of work, is that as the groups are organized there is little intragroup fighting except perhaps during apoblastosis, and that, though they are capable of effective fighting, little intergroup combat occurs, since vocalizations and general behavior in the form of bluffing act as buffers to actual fighting. There is perhaps some relation between the facts that fights rarely occur and that when they do take place they may be very severe.

. . . .

. . . competition among groups of gibbons of the same species is much keener than competition with any other kinds of vertebrates in the region. Gibbon groups are more competitive among themselves than they are with macaque and langur monkeys of the region. I have seen groups of the three kinds feeding seemingly contentedly in the same groups of trees. This would not occur with three gibbon groups of the same species.

A second reason for there being less fighting in naturalistic gibbon groups is that individuals in these groups already have definite statuses and these positions apparently change gradually during maturation and aging. The slow rate of change in gibbon groups gives time for adjustments which do not involve severe stress or frustration. Changes in intergroup relations, i.e., group splitting, formation of new groups, and shifts in territory likewise occur gradually. Hence again in this complex of relations the gradual changes within groups and the absence of frustration permit adjustment without aggressiveness, at least to the degree where fighting occurs.

Dominance.—Young gibbons mainly show their dominance status in play and feeding activities. There is also a positive correlation between dominance and the stage of sexual maturation. (Adult) gibbon males and females are generally equally dominant or aggressive. Likewise, in positive leadership tendencies, they seem quite similar. If there are sex differences in these two respects, field observations did not define them. This lack of behavioral sex differences corresponds to the lack of skeletal sex differences.

The order of progression in wild primate groups gives interesting information about group organization, dominance, and leadership.

May 11, 1937, Group 2, Doi Dao.— Throughout the morning, Ab of Group 2 was leading the group while Jlbf followed closely behind the leader. Mbf and Fbf trailed the two young gibbons at a distance of 30 to 50 yards, these two being rather closely associated.

Repeatedly I have observed Ab in the advance position during group progression. This seems to illustrate a general tendency for late juveniles to anticipate group movements, especially when the group moves over a well-established arboreal pathway to a food tree. It is not true, however, that the group always follows these hyperactive juveniles. Since the infants and juveniles are growing and at the same time are more active than old animals, it seems reasonable to assume that they are more hungry and this may account for their being found often in the forward positions during group progression.

May 18, 1937, Group 5, Doi Dao.— The buff female which carried a black infant 1 led Group 5 throughout the morning until 11:00 o'clock. The female led in any change of direction in the group's movements, with one exception, when the young black adult and the buff juvenile 3 set the pace. The black juvenile 1 and buff juvenile 3 followed the female and infant very closely, while the black male and black young adult were somewhat less closely associated, showing some slight tendency to form a subgrouping. The old male, which I observed for about an hour at very close range, was more independent than the other animals. For long periods of time he followed the group casually and indifferently at a distance of 50 yards.

The group moved slowly from the beautiful spot of deep jungle on Trail A and traveled toward the crest of a sharp ridge to the northwest. Before reaching the crest, Group 5 began calling mildly and inquisitively as if vocally exploring the other side of the crest for cues of other gibbon groups. The immediate response, possibly of Group 17, with voices more intense than those being produced by Group 5, caused the gibbons of Group 5 to change their course, circle sharply, and return to approximately the spot where I had found them earlier in the morning.

. . . the dominance and leadership status of an individual in a group may not depend solely on its aggressiveness but also on such behavior as the degree to which the individual satisfies the sex hunger of the opposite sex, its effectiveness in leading the group to food, its responsiveness in grooming, and especially its effectiveness in defense against strange groups or individuals. Perhaps this aspect of dominance relates closely to what may be defined as a prestige factor.

Grooming.—. . . *March 29, 1937, Group 1, Doi Dao.*—Even though one of the young adults of Group 1 was excited and in the main engaged in exploratory behavior, nevertheless, it groomed itself for a period of about ten minutes. Self- and social grooming need differentiation. although the patterns of prehension are essentially the same. The animal seemed to be mainly occupied in removing reddish soil which covered a large area of its fur. The fur might have been soiled from dirt collected in crevices in the rocks on the hillside.

Just prior to the above observation, this animal, in cooperation with its closest associate in Group 1, had engaged in social grooming. First one animal and then the other would play the active role. The alternation between a dominant and passive role occurred rather regularly.

April 2, 1937, Group 1, Doi Dao.— The two young adults or late juveniles of Group 1 displayed an interesting session of grooming. It began at 11:00 o'clock. As one animal approached the other, it took a relaxed position on its back, to which the first animal responded by beginning and carrying out meticulous and thorough grooming over an area of the chest.

The pattern of grooming involved the use of both hands with which to separate the hair, to hold it in a parted position and remove small particles. These were carried to the mouth.

The two animals alternated regularly; first one and then the other assuming the active role, once each minute to stop-watch time. Having been grooming for about one minute, the active animal would stop, remain quiet or explore for a few seconds, and then assume some relaxed position. In response to this behavior, the animal that had just been groomed would now become active and return the service. The session of grooming lasted ten minutes and during this time there were exactly ten alternations of each animal from the active to the passive role or the reverse.

Areas of the skin groomed were those of the head, especially the ears and neck, the shoulders, down the center of the back, and over the rump. It is interesting to note that precisely these areas are most difficult for an animal to reach during self-grooming. . . . differentiation between self- and social grooming seems important although essentially the same manipulatory patterns are involved. The alternation of grooming and being groomed may relate to an equivalence of dominance in gibbons and to their marked sociability.

The invitational phase of initiating grooming between two animals deserves special attention in connection with communicative interchanges and social coordination. The fact that a gibbon is motivated and receptive for grooming is indicated by the tempo of approach, facial expression, the general body posture, and relaxation in a position suitable for grooming. Almost invariably, when an individual is approached and stimulated by these behavioral qualities, it will respond by active grooming. Its degree of motivation is mainly expressed by the length of time during which grooming continues. If the animal which is approached does not respond adequately, the receptive animal may groom the other animal without invitation and after a short time lie down and relax to be groomed. In gibbons, the exchange of "service" is a marked feature of grooming.

Grooming is important from the viewpoint of group integration; not only does it depend, seemingly, upon a previous state of positive conditioning in the participating animals, but the behavior further enhances and strengthens the social relationship. The reciprocal activity with its common incentives, like copulation, serves to form attachments between animals.

That grooming likewise serves a hygienic function is also true. Healthy specimens have clean fur, clean skin,

and are free from ectoparasites. The coats of fresh-shot specimens are almost without exception clean and free from parasites. When specimens are isolated for shipping, dirty and irritating coat and skin conditions may develop and these conditions may lead to loss of appetite and decline in general physical health.

Group Integration.—The coordination of the behavior of individuals in a group of gibbons depends upon more fundamental processes and conditions of social integration than have been described. Group integration is the product of genetically determined behavior characteristics and learning. The incentives and drives, demands and requirements for adjustments are found in the natural environment of gibbons. The following are some of the drive and incentive relationships which make for learning of social adaptations: The infant's socialization and the mother's attachment to or tolerance for it both grow out of physiological states and involve reciprocal motivational factors. The appearance of the infant after birth coincides with the mother's release from pain and strain. The placenta and birth fluids present an incentive for which the female has an avid hunger. At birth, the infant's grasping reflexes are well developed, and by means of these it makes positive responses to the optimum temperature found near the mother's body. The exploratory responses eventually bring the infant's lips into contact with the mother's breast and nipples and by means of the sucking responses, the infant obtains food. The sucking of the infant also has positive stimulus value for the mother. Through these reciprocal conditioning processes, the infant-mother bond is established. Later, play with other young animals furthers the socializing process.

The total complex of sexual behavior contains many reciprocal drive-incentive relationships which lead to positive conditioning between two or more animals. Through conditioning during primary sexual activity, there may be perseverating effects which maintain the bonds between the animals during periods when no sexual behavior takes place.

Communal association during feeding, play, and rest may likewise serve to reinforce social relations among individuals of a gibbon family. Such behavior as grooming, mutual assistance, cooperative or coordinated guarding and defense may also tend to strengthen group structure.

It is only against a background of previously established drives and conditioning that gestures and vocalizations are effective. It is only against a background of a highly integrated group with means for coordinating all individuals' actions that social control may be exercised.

CARPENTER has also made intensive studies of free-living colonies of howler, spider, and rhesus monkeys, as well as laboratory experiments on these and other primate species. Further quotations from some of his monographs follow.

The Characteristic of Grouping Patterns.—When an adequate sampling of natural groups of any nonhuman primate species is studied, it is found the groups show a central tendency as well as a range of variability. The average group size for howlers is 17.3±6.8. The average group or family of gibbons has four individuals and ranges from two to six. The same group size is characteristic of the siamang. The age of the grouping may relate to its size for, after groups have been long formed and approach the upper limits of size, group splitting or apoblastosis occurs, the parent group is reduced in size, and the nucleus of a new group (or groups) is formed. (The process is very analogous to cell mitosis.)

Studies of grouping patterns show also that usually there are more intragroup males than females. For the howler, this socionomic sex ratio is about 1:3, while for the spider monkeys the ratio is approximately 1:2, and it is estimated that a 1:3 ratio holds approximately for rhesus monkeys. In gibbons which have a characteristic family grouping pattern, the ratio of adult males to females is usually 1:1 although there are a few exceptions.

When the organization of a sample population is studied, including animals which do not, at the time, live in organized heterosexual groups, variations characteristic of species also are found. Howler males live temporarily alone. Excess spider monkey males live in unisexual male groupings, as do the adolescent and nongroup-living adult males of *Macaca mulatta*. It is believed that isolates, both male and female, occur in the gibbon (*H. lar*).

I have found that when male groupings of spider monkeys are collected, young adult, prime, and old ages may be represented in the same group. The adolescent males, perhaps, from about 4 or 5 to 6 or 7 years of age, live in unisexual male groups, while senile individuals may usually live alone or sometimes with one or two very young males. Males in their prime usually but not always live in the organized heterosexual group. Individual males may live in groups, however, and yet not have the chance to reproduce, for, in addition to living in the group, he must have a requisite degree of dominance status or prestige before he can reproduce.

The Characteristic of Dominance.—There is no question but that groups of monkeys and apes are organized around several dominance gradients. By dominance gradient, I mean the order of arrangement of several individuals along a line from low to high dominance. The dominance of one species may vary markedly from that of other species. Furthermore, the dominance status of an individual in a group, as gained by aggression and maintained by aggression, may blend with a prestige factor, i.e., a kind of perseveration of a previous dominance status.

The variability of dominance or aggressiveness from species to species is shown when baboons are compared with howlers, or when langurs are compared with spider monkeys. There would seem to be a genetic basis for this complex kind of behavior which is manifest by the relative degree to which females, food, preferred positions, etc., are exclusively possessed by an individual. In baboon harems a number of females are exclusively possessed by the overlord. Langur males, too, are very autocratic and intolerant of other males. By contrast, howlers tolerate males of the same group.

Rhesus males of the same group show a sharp dominance gradient but they, like howlers, do not possess receptive females exclusively. Rather, in both kinds, a type of rotational mateship occurs during the period of a female's estrus.*

It is the opinion of the present author that Rhesus monkeys living under free range conditions have limited periods of sexual activity within the menstrual cycle. These periods terminate and then re-occur after non-fertile cycles. During the limited estrous period there is a marked frequency of copulation and likewise marked changes in associated behavior traits and social relations. This period corresponds in many respects to "rut," "heat" or estrus in "lower" mammals such as the dog. Nevertheless, there are important differences.

It has become customary to think of estrus as being a physiological state, especially closely connected with the endocrines. It is possible that this concept is too narrow and it would seem more logical to use the term estrus to refer to the total complex of associated changes whch occur near the time of ovulation and lead to possibilities of fertilization. This would include gross anatomical changes, changes in endocrine balances, variations in thresholds of stimulation in the receptors, perhaps also in parts of the nervous system, and subsequent changes in behavior. The latter is a necessary link in the fertilization process. Heape in 1900 defined "oestrus" as the "special period of sexual desire of the female" and again it has been defined as that period when the female actively seeks coitus with a male. Two facts should be noted in this connection: 1. Estrus is a complex of changes

* C. R. Carpenter, "Characteristics of Social Behavior in Non-Human Primates," *Transactions of the New York Academy of Sciences*, Series II, Volume 4, number 8, June, 1942, pp. 251–253

of which behavioral changes are a prominent and essential part, and 2. Estrus is not mere passive receptivity but involves aggressive sexual behavior in the female. The term estrus in this report is used in a broad sense to include anatomical, physiological, and behavioral changes. It is illogical to consider behavioral changes as mere indicators of estrus; behavior traits are essential parts of estrus.*

In almost all natural groupings which have been carefully studied, the male or males play the most prominent role in controlling the group. There is clearly a masculine dominance, with the possible exception of gibbons, in which is found equivalence of sexual dominance.

This does not preclude the fact that, among the females, as among males, there is also a dominance gradient. As compared with that of the males, this female dominance gradient is of a lower slope; i.e., females have less absolute dominance than males and they seem to differ to a smaller degree. Nevertheless, the female gradient overlaps that of the males. This means that some of the most dominant females are more dominant than some of the least dominant males.

When dominance is studied in immature animals it is found that there, too, an unstable gradient exists. Indeed, the status of an individual rhesus monkey begins to be defined during its infancy, after it has begun to engage in social play.

These dominance gradients importantly affect social controls in the groups. The group scatter, or spacing, during feeding, the order of locomotion, and the order of access to estrous females are a few of the behavior modalities in which the order of response is dependent upon dominance and prestige statuses.

That the male dominance gradient is one of the main axes of an organized group, was shown recently by an experimental field study (unpublished). The study demanded continuous observation of Group No. 1 of Santiago Colony for 5 days during each week for a month. Systematic records were kept of all behavior classified as having any degree of aggressiveness. The first week was a control period after which the supremely autocratic male (Diablo) was trapped and held captive. During the third week, No. 174, or male No. 2 in the dominance hierarchy, was trapped and held captive and No. 150 or the No. 3 in dominance order was next trapped. Accumulative systematic records showed changes following each removal.

As soon as the Number 1 dominant male was removed from the group, the territorial range of the group was markedly restricted. The group organization became more fluid and there was an increase in intragroup conflicts and fights. Finally when Nos. 1, 2, and 3 were removed, males Nos. 4 and 5 shifted dominance positions. No. 159, previously dominant over 173, was now superseded by 173.

When the three captive dominant males were released, a dozen females surrounded "Diablo" (No. 1 dominant), while fewer clustered around Nos. 174 and 150. There was marked excitement of a peaceful sort. At one time, six females were photographed grooming Diablo, while three and two respectively groomed 174 and 150. After a marked disruption lasting three weeks, the group was suddenly restructured when the dominant males were released.

* C. R. Carpenter, "Sexual Behavior of Free Ranging Rhesus Monkeys (Macaca Mulatta)," *The Journal of Comparative Psychology*, Vol. 33, no. 1, February 1942, p. 117. Reprinted by permission of the author and the publisher.

The Characteristic of Territorialism.—All types of primates, which have been adequately studied in the field, have been found to show the phenomenon of territorialism. Organized groups have restricted and sometimes quite limited ranges. In some instances these ranges are exclusively possessed by a single group, while at other times and places varying degrees of overlappings are found among neighboring groups. It would seem reasonable to conclude that conditioning and learning importantly determine this territorialism and that these processes relate to the spatial locations of incentives which satisfy basic needs of the individual and the group.

A group of gibbons in its territory is less tolerant (more resistant) of another group of gibbons than it is of a group of langurs or macaques. *H. agalis* and the siamang have been observed to feed peacefully in the same tree. This would not happen without conflict with two groups of the same species. The conclusion may be drawn, therefore, that competition is most keen between organized groups of the same species. And this is so even though the different species have similar food preferences.

The relative dominance of groups and territorial ranges interact. The question has often occurred to me as to why one group, for a while, was more dominant or had right of way over another group and hence had wider freedom of movement. The Santiago studies mentioned above have thrown some light on this question. Group dominance does not relate to the size of the group, for Group 1 was only about one half the size of Group 2 and contained fewer males (7 to 10), but Group 1 always could take precedence over Group 2. The results of field experiments suggest that the determining factor of intergroup dominance is the relative dominance of the autocratic male in one group in relation to the autocratic male of another group. In the experiment, Group 1 lost its freedom of movement and range as soon as "Diablo" was caged.

Characteristics of Interdependence.—Charles Darwin and many natural historians following him have so emphasized "the struggle for existence" and competition that the facts of interdependence in animal societies have not been accurately and fully represented. As a result, the formulated theories and principles of social behavior are faulty, since they are built on inadequate factual bases. An illustration of this is the common expressions which hold that those aspects of human behavior which are untenable, according to a prevailing ethical system, have been derived from an animal level. Extreme egoism, sadism, and masochism are frequently thus designated. By contrast, those activities which are ethically accepted, such as altruism, strong emotional affection, and cooperation, are attributed to man's higher intellectual processes if not to superhuman origins. The naturalistic approach to the study of social behavior leads to the conclusion that anlagen or genetic origins of all kinds of human behavior, competitive and cooperative, egoistic and altruistic, affinitive and antagonistic, have roots in the prehuman levels of the phylogenetic series.

The survival and reproduction of groups of monkeys of a species depend on the social coordination—one may say cooperation—of all the individuals of the group. The survival is quite as dependent upon the epiorganism as on the organism.

Bisexual reproduction requires a degree of coordination of two or more individuals. Particularly on the non-human primate level the young are born without the capacity for independent survival. They are cared for and protected by their mothers in rhesus monkey groups. Otherwise they are killed usually by members of their own parent groups. The play of young monkeys is highly cooperative and it is during that play that many natural reaction tendencies are modified, matured, and established as individual habit systems. Defensive actions may involve the close coordination of all group members in a concerted pattern of attack. In these attacks, individuals are killed, but this is incidental to the fact that the group survives and the species is perpetuated.

The Characteristics of Integration Coordination.—A given number of monkeys and apes does not make or equal what I have been calling a group. Suppose we try this experiment: Raise in isolation animals of the species, but of the right sex and age to compose a group which meets the requirements of the formula for the average group characteristic of a species. These individuals will then be released together. What will happen? Some may so fear others that they flee. Some will be antagonistic and

fight. Others will form into groups and remain together. In general, the synthetic group experiment will not fall together, as had been hoped or predicted, into a single organization. Why? Even though the social drives are operative and social incentives are present, the monkeys have not been conditioned to each other. They have not been socialized—i.e., they have not learned to make fitting responses to each other as complexes of stimuli. What is lacking is what I have called integration.

Social integration is conceived to begin with birth and to involve definable processes of social learning and adjustment. These processes are organic and involve the expressions and satisfactions of physiological drives. From one viewpoint, effective social integration of an individual conditions it in a manner to make it responsive to the communicative acts, motor expressions including gestures, and vocalizations. These communicative acts, involving specific stimuli patterns and fitting responses, constitute the core of group coordination. Let it be remembered that the stimulus aspects of communicative acts cannot be operative except on a background of social integration—i.e., animals which are conditioned to each other.*

Before concluding this chapter, I would like to make several special points about the bearing of the study of lower primate social relations upon anthropology.

1. Human beings have no marked estral cycle. Most lower primates have it. The group marriage of the howler monkey and the harem system of the baboon have apparently arisen in response to this physiological circumstance.

2. The gibbon resembles man in this physiological peculiarity. The gibbon is organized into monogamous* family groups, and there is no reason to believe that human families have ever been formed characteristically in any other way.

* C. R. Carpenter, "Characteristics of Social Behavior in Non-Human Primates," *Transactions of the New York Academy of Sciences,* series II, vol. 4, no. 8, June 1942, pp. 253–257. Reprinted by permission of the author and the publishers.

*Personally I should prefer "monogamous and polygynous" C.S.C.

3. Ground-living primates are in greater danger of attack by enemies of other species than are arboreal primates. That is one reason why baboons live in bands of several adult males with their harems. As Zuckerman has shown, baboons which live in the forest go about in smaller groups than those which inhabit open country. Most human beings who live in open country or park land at a simple level of society are also organized into bands of several families. In most cases, however, sharing food is probably a more important motive than defense.

4. Human beings mature later than any other primates, and hence pass through a longer conditioning and training period, during which they have more to learn.

5. During this learning period, young human beings are taught the proper attitudes of behavior between individuals of different sexes and ages and, when the critical period comes, it is not necessary for the young people to be ejected from the group. Their adjustment is usually further insured by means of puberty ceremonies.

6. The two most vocal primates other than man are the gibbon and the howler monkey. These animals possess resonance chambers in their throats which permit them to make loud calls which can be heard more than a mile away. The mechanical structure of their vocal organs limits them almost entirely to vowels. The resonance chamber of the human vocal apparatus consists of the nasal passages and the various sinuses and air chambers between the palate and the floor of the brain. These chambers permit the formation of consonants and hence a much more varied repertory of semantically meaningful vocal symbols, or in other words, human speech.

7. There is every evidence that the more advanced monkeys and the great apes have a higher capacity for complex behavior patterns and a greater so-called "intelligence" than their life in the wild requires. It is more than likely that man also has kept several jumps ahead of his cultural requirements in the course of human evolution.

Level One

Simple Family Bands

2

read

Gleaners of the Desert: How American Indians Lived in a Submarginal Environment

I N A FEW out-of-the-way places, human beings have survived until recent times, and some may still survive, in a state of social organization no more complicated than those of the subhuman primates. Among such peoples the largest stable or habitual social unit, the only true institution, was the simple biological family with or without a few dependent individuals. Members of a group of this kind would spend most of their time moving about in search of food. Their relations with other family groups would be so infrequent and lacking in regularity that no larger institutional structure would be possible.

All of the peoples so far known who are organized in this way may be divided into two classes, depending on the temperature of the environment in which they live. The first class includes truly primitive people, naked or clothed only in simple robes, using chipped flint cutting tools and fire. They live in deserts, jungles, or chilly coast lands, far from the centers of civilization. They need perform no technical operation which requires elaborate tools, special sources of energy, or the cooperation of many persons. They have been able to remain on a simple level of technology because they can survive nearly naked without freezing.

The second class is composed of peoples living in arctic regions where agriculture is difficult or impossible, where food of any kind is hard to get no matter what techniques are used, and where people have to know how to make good tailored clothing and warm houses to keep alive.

In this section we shall deal with the first category, selecting three examples. The first two are desert peoples. Such groups have been found in the desert west of Alice Springs in Australia, others among the Bushmen of the Kalihari Desert in Africa. The clearest cases, however, come from the drier portions of the Great Basin country of our own nation, in Utah, Nevada, and California, and in adjacent parts of Mexico, particularly Lower California.

Anyone who has driven from the Tioga Pass in the Sierras down to Mono Lake and across southern Nevada to Tonopah will agree that the American desert is not suited to hold many people or to support life on a high level. How human beings managed to live there at all before the days of horses and railroads seems at first glance somewhat of a mystery. The earliest travelers and explorers in this region left certain documents behind, none of which is more graphic or detailed in its account (1846–1878) of aboriginal life than the narrative of the Mormon pioneer, Major Howard Egan.* The following extracts

*Egan, Major Howard R., *Pioneering the West, 1846 to 1878,* William M. Egan, Ed., Salt Lake City, 1917.

illustrate in particular the adaptations of the Indians of the Basin country to their environment—adaptations which are general among peoples living in similar environments at a simple technological level in many parts of the world.

49.—INDIAN CRICKET * DRIVE

I was on a three days' horseback trip in the wilderness, and had for a companion the Indian called "Egan Jack," a trusty, intelligent buck of about thirty years of age. We were on a prospecting or exploring trip to the Northwest of Deep Creek, or Ibapah as the Indians called it. At one place, as we came out of a canyon onto the bench land, we saw quite a number of Indians that were quite busy, some digging trenches and some gathering arms full of the tall wheat grass that grew on the flat in the bottom of the canyon, I asked Jack what they were doing. He said, "Catching crickets for bread." "Well, we will go and see how they do it." We went, and saw that they had dug quite a number of trenches about a foot wide and a foot deep and about thirty or forty feet long, and around like a new moon with the horns uphill.

They had been a number of days at the work, but were now ready for their cricket drive, having five or six of the trenches strung across the bench, the end of each trench joined, or was very close to the end of another. They covered these with a thin layer of stiff wheat grass straw . . . but I thought they were making a mistake, for the crickets could crawl over the ditch on it, but I must wait and see.

As it was getting the hottest time of the day, and therefore the best time for the drive, they were soon ready, . . . Well, there was a few crickets scattered all around, but were more of them above the trenches and near the foothills. . . .

* A local term for grasshoppers.—Ed.

These trenches ran in a north and south direction, the land sloping to the west. The Indians, men, women and children, divided into two parties, one going to the north end and the other to the south end, all carrying a bunch of grass in each hand. They went single file towards the foothills, and making the distance between the parties wider than the length of the trenches. When they had gone what they thought far enough, as judged by the scarcity of grass left by the black insects, the party closed in and, walking back and forth swinging their grass bunches they gradually worked down toward the trenches.

We followed them on horseback and I noticed that there were but very few crickets left behind. As they went down, the line of crickets grew thicker and thicker till the ground ahead of the drivers was as black as coal with the excited, tumbling mass of crickets.

A cricket when disturbed can jump about one foot down hill at a jump and but half that distance up hill, but will never jump up hill if it has any show to avoid it. Well, as we neared the trenches I noticed the Indians were going down slower. Jack said this was to give the crickets time to crawl through the grass into the trenches.

When all had been driven in the Indians set fire to the grass they had in their hands and scattered it along on top of that they had over the trenches, causing a big blaze and smoke, which soon left the crickets powerless to crawl out, if any were left alive when the grass had all burned up, which did not take many minutes. I rode along the line and in some places the trenches were over half full of the dead and legless crickets. I went down below the trenches and I venture to say there were not one out of a thousand crickets that passed those trenches.

They are a scary and excitable, but a clumsy insect, that hardly ever when excited land on their feet, but roll over, then turn their head down hill and jump again. If not molested they seldom ever jump, but travel by crawling. Now the bucks and children had done their part and were sitting around in groups. The squaws were busy gathering up the game.

They had large conical shaped baskets; some of them would hold over two bushels. These the women carry on their backs, held in place by a flat band either over their foreheads or about the shoulders. Now here is what I saw a squaw doing that had a small baby strapped to a board or a willow frame, which she carried on her back with a strap over her forehead:

When at work she would stand or lay the frame and kid where she could see it at any time. She soon had a large basket as full as she could crowd with crickets. Laying it down near the kid, she took a smaller basket and filled it. I should judge she had over four bushels of the catch. But wait, the Indians were leaving for their camp about three or four miles away. This squaw sat down beside the larger basket, put the band over her shoulders, got on her feet with it, then took the strapped kid and placed him on top, face up, picked up the other basket and followed her lord and master, who tramped ahead with nothing to carry except his own lazy carcass. There were bushels of crickets left in the trenches, which I suppose they would gather later in the day.

Having seen enough there we rode on across a narrow valley, and in the foothills came to a large camp of In-dians, the chief of whom I was well acquainted with, and we decided to stay all night with them, . . . We were also getting hungry. We had no provisions of our own, except a couple of rabbits I had killed on the way.

They treated us fine and we had a good time telling and hearing the news. Jack took one of the rabbits and put it to roast on the fire, the other he gave to the chief. When the rabbit was done to his liking, Jack asked the chief if he had any bread; he nodded and called in a low voice the name of his squaw, who came into the tent at once. When told to bring some bread she went out, but returned immediately with a cake of black bread about two inches thick and ten inches in diameter, which she handed to me. I thought it looked too black for pine nut bread, for the latter has a yellow cast and this was decidedly black. Holding the bread in one hand and pointing to it with the other, I asked her if there was pine nuts in it. "Yes," she said unconcernedly. "Is there crickets in it?" "Yes, yes," smilingly. "Sure." Well, I handed the cake to Jack to divide and told the squaw that I would like some pine nuts. She soon brought in some that were all mashed up. These I refused and asked for the "whole" pine nuts. These were soon brought in and I commenced my supper.

The chief noticed that I was slow at shelling the nuts, so he called a young squaw that came in with a basin of water, setting it down near the door, washed her hands in the basin and brought in a flat stone about one foot in diameter and one-half inch thick and another about eight inches long and a couple of inches in diameter. Seating herself between Jack and me, she proceeded to put the mill in motion. She placed a couple of hands full of nuts on the flat stone and taking the other in both hands, gave it a rolling motion over the nuts which cracked the shells so they fell off the kernels, which she rolled off on a piece of sack as clean and plump as I could shell them one at a time. She simply shelled them much faster than both of us could eat them. Well, we had a good supper and breakfast, but Jack ate my share of the bread.

When the crickets are dried the squaws grind them, feathers and all, on the same mill they grind the pine nuts or grass seed, making a fine flour that will keep a long time, if kept dry. Jack says the crickets make the bread good, the same as sugar used by the white woman in her cakes. . . .

[*What the major called "crickets" were grasshoppers. Many peoples in the world collect them and roast them for eating. Not only the Australian aborigines and other food gatherers do this, but also Arabs, who have cultivated grains and domestic animals as their main sources of food. The small hand mill on which the women ground these insects is also the regular equipment of food gatherers as far afield as Australia and Tierra del Fuego. Pine nuts form the staple winter diet of many of the Basin Indians.*]

51.—A Rabbit Drive

One afternoon, while visiting the Indians, I heard them talking of rabbits and, asking them what it was all about, the chief said a rabbit hunt. I said I would like to go along to see how they done it. He seemed pleased at me taking so much interest and said, "Good! Come tomorrow before noon, as we want to start the drive about noon and it is quite a distance to the place. You had better come on horseback."

About the middle of the forenoon next day I was at their camp. Most of the hunters had already started. Going about three or four miles, we came to the place selected for the drive—a piece of sage and rabbit brush land about a mile in diameter. The party I was with stopped, when we saw a fire about a half mile to our right and soon another about the same distance to the left, and then we could see the smoke rising a mile ahead of us. My party soon had their torches at work and the drive was on.

Working all around the circle and towards the center was a continuous ring of fire and smoke, which was gradually closing in and the rabbits were being crowded together thicker and thicker. Each Indian, squaw and papoose had a stick about four feet long, the only weapon they carried. A small boy or girl was just as good as a man, and oh, the fun of it—all laughing and hollering and making as much noise as possible. The rabbits got so dazed by the fire, smoke and tumult that they simply could not run. They would jump a few jumps and sit up trying to see a way out. I saw dozens of them stop within reach of the sticks and many of them were picked up that had not been hit. When a rabbit was seen to pass out of the human ring, someone would follow him in the smoke and put his body in one of the piles of rabbits they had made as they proceeded towards the center, for they could not carry much of the game and do their work at the same time.

When the drive was over the field was a black, fire-swept, but still smoking patch of ground. Talk about rabbits, I am sure there were more caught on that drive than could be packed in a large wagon-bed. It seems that the black-tailed rabbits gather in herds or colonies and these places are noted by the Indians. I learned afterwards that they had intended to attack a smaller colony, but the chief wanted his white friends to see a good, big drive, and he did, and I was well pleased to be present, but thought it was taking too much the advantage of poor Mr. Rabbit, who had no chance to save his life.

The Indians do not like to use fire for a drive, as it takes years for the brush to grow up again. I have seen a drive where no fire was used, but grass nets about two and one-half feet high and two inches or even smaller mesh. A sharp pointed stick a few inches longer than the width of the net was fastened across six or eight feet apart, to act as fence posts, when the sharp end was pressed into the earth. One buck could easily carry a role of one hundred fifty to two hundred yards of the small twisted grass twine nets. Each large family usually have such a role and at times, when living apart from other families, can use them either as traps or to drive; but then, these are only small catches.

The drive I witnessed was when there was six or eight of these nets together. When they had decided just where to run the nets, two of the Indians put the end sticks of their nets together and commenced to unroll their nets, going in opposite directions, sticking each cross stick firmly in the ground as they unrolled, making a rabbit-proof fence. When the first two had placed their nets, two more Indians commenced where they ended and continued the line in the desired direction.

I noticed that when they were through stringing their nets in a kind of semicircle form, there was part of a roll of nets not unrolled at each end. These ends, when they were ready to drive, were strung out, but not in a circle, but flaring straight out from the opening, making a long V-shaped mouth to the field. When the Indians swung across this mouth they began coming in slowly. But every rabbit that was started went into the pen and kept running back and forth to find a place to get through. Vain search, for they were trapped. When the men had reached the opening of the circle the two ends of the net was brought in and strung across the opening, this making a complete enclosure. Then the fun began. All the Indians were inside with sticks, or bows and arrows, picking up the game. Sometimes I could see at one glance five or six rabbits that were entangled in the netting. If the Indians were engaged at one place getting the ones caught, the others were getting into trouble at another place.

It seemed a little strange to me that when a rabbit running along the fence would see a man ahead of him he would turn and run across the circle till he came to the fence, then run along it till he saw someone ahead, then either make a dive at the fence and get tangled, or take another run across lots, but never stopping or trying to hide in the brush in the center, but seemed to know they were trapped.

It took the Indians over a half day to get as many as they wanted. There were many left when they took up the nets and were none the worse off by their little scare.

I have seen the black-tailed rabbits in bands so thick they could not all get in the shade of the sagebrush and I have seen coyotes where there seemed to be dozens and dozens of them in the middle of the day, standing and sitting or laying down, and when approached too close, moving off just fast enough to keep at a safe distance, all of them with full bellies and acted very sleepy. I asked Jack what they were about, he said, "Them coyotes had a rabbit drive last night and now they are resting up and sleeping."

[*Note that in a game drive, or "surround," women and children are not excluded. The more noise the better.*]

52.—MOUNTAIN RAT, FOOD
FOR INDIANS

On one of my days out I came across an old Indian going home with his day's catch of rats. He had a large sheet iron camp kettle nearly filled with them. They had all been caught the night before by dead falls, as we call them, which consists of two sticks about three and a half or four inches long fastened together at their centers by a string that will allow them to spread apart about four or five inches in the shape of the letter "H." One of these, with any convenient flat rock heavy enough to smash and kill a rat, is one dead fall. This Indian had over a hundred of the triggers that he hadn't used, but said he had set the most of them.

His plan was to go up one side of the canyon, setting the traps wherever he saw the sign of rats, and the same down the other side. The next day, taking the same route, gathering the catch and resetting the traps. The rats the Indian had were six to eight inches long, two and a half inches wide and half an inch thick. They were packed as close as he could pack them in the kettle and were quite heavy for the old man to pack to camp, so I carried them for him. At his camp was where I first saw the squaws making rabbit skin robes. This is how it was done:

They had a lot of twine, that had been made of some fiberous bark or grass, and a pile of rabbit skins that had been dried and then rubbed pliable. But it must have been done with care, for a rabbit skin is very tender. These squaws were not making a new robe, but patching up and making an old one larger. The robes are of length to reach from the neck to about the middle of the thighs, say about three or four feet long, and wide enough to reach around the body at the shoulders.

One of the squaws was twisting the strips of skin around a twine that was stretched to two stakes, placed a little past the length of the robe, and as she proceeded the other was following her up and tying that fur rope thus made and laid alongside the previous one close together at about every four inches. They worked back and forth in this fashion till the skins were all used up. There was a strip about two feet wide of new robe attached to the old one. I examined it and found that the tie strings were placed in a straight line across the robe, with the ends of the ties left to attach more robe or to be used to tie the robe together as wanted.

When hung around the neck the person so clothed can stand in a hard rain or snow storm and not one drop of wet will pass through the robe. They are wind and rain proof and almost cold proof. There is no right or wrong side, as both sides are just the same— one solid piece of fur that will stand the wear of years, used as a mattress or bed covering or wind brake. In fact, they never completely wear out.

When the fur at any place gets worn off it is replaced with a few strands of new. This makes an old robe look striped and of different colors. The squaws while at work seemed as happy as a party of white women at a quilting and were talking and laughing just as fast. . . .

[*This technique of making a rabbit-skin robe is a predecessor, in the technical sense, of weaving. By this means a large robe can be made from many small skins. It is also much warmer and stronger than a robe made by sewing the skins together, which would take more work. Major Egan very aptly compares the robe-weaving party to a quilting party. The desire for company rather than the requirements of the work process brings the women together.*]

54.—Pine-nut Harvest

Jack and I were taking a scouting trip high up in the Shell Creek range of mountains, when we came across an Indian who, with his squaw and children, were busily engaged gathering pine-nuts. The man had a long pole with a strong hook fastened to one end. He would reach up in the tree to the pine cones, hook the crook around the branch on which they hung and pull branch and all down, the squaw and children carrying them to a place and piling them up in a heap. When they had collected as many as they wanted that day, the buck had finished his part of the work and could pass the rest of the time sleeping or hunting squirrels just as he pleased.

The squaws and children gathered a little dry brush, which was thrown loosely over the pile of cones and set fire to. The cones are thickly covered all over with pitch, for this reason they make a hot fire, the squaw watching and stirring it up as needed to keep the nuts from burning, as all she wants is to burn the pitch off. When this is done she rakes them back from the fire as a man would do when drawing charcoal.

When the pitch was all burned off the burs, or cones, the squaw spreads a blanket down close to the pile, then taking up one cone at a time, would press them end ways between her hands, which opens the leaves, under which there were two nuts to every leaf. Then shaking the cone over the blanket the nuts would all fall out as clean as you please.

We stayed with them to see the finish, which was not so very long. When the nuts had all been cleaned from the cones they were put in a large basket that would hold over two bushels and was nearly full, the squaw carrying that on her back to a place where they were to be cached and left till wanted. These caches were placed all through the pine-nut grove to save carrying them too far and save time, for the harvest does not last long, for a heavy frost will cause the cones to open and the nuts drop to the ground, where the squirrels and coyotes feast on them.

A pine-nut cone looks like a green pineapple, but some smaller and covered with pitch, that protects them from insects and squirrels. The Indians put them in caches holding about ten bushels or less.

Once on a time when Jack and I were passing along a range where there were a good many pine-nut trees, and as we were getting hungry I asked him if he thought there was any nuts cached there. He said he didn't think they were all cleaned out and would look around. He was not long in locating one, and pushing the large stick of wood aside that was placed on top of the small raise in which the nuts were to be found, he moved off about six inches of dirt and found a tight layer of cedar bark about two inches thick. He dug a hole through this big enough to pass his arm through, which he did, and pulled out a handful of very fine nuts, as fresh as when first put in.

Well, we took about two gallons, covered and left the cache as we found it, minus the few nuts taken.

[Pine nuts formed the principal food of these people. To obtain them required no special or elaborate techniques, no division of labor based on age, sex, or work requirements. The critical factors were finding them, and storing them for the winter.]

55.—Hunting for Water

In traveling through Go-Shute [Gosiute—Ed.] Valley (later called Flower Lake Valley), we were getting very thirsty, having been traveling five or six hours from the last water hole and it being a dry, hot and sultry day I and the horses needed water. The nearest I knew of was about twelve miles distance and that not in the direction of our travel, and our one canteen being empty, I thought we would have to change our course to get water. I asked Jack, "How far to water this way," pointing the way I wanted to go. He said, "I do not know, maybe no water." "Well, are you thirsty?" "Yes." "Well then, think fast and locate water or Indian no better than white man."

We were about the middle of the valley, facing south-easterly, and were among the sand-dunes, which spread a few miles in width and many miles in length through the valley. We had not gone far after this talk when Jack said, "Wait," and pointing to some rat or gopher holes in the side of the sand-dunes, said, "They must have water, I see." Dismounting, he picked a place between the dunes and with his hands scraped off the loose sand to a depth of about six or eight inches to water. He then made the hole nearly a foot deeper and a foot wide, which quickly filled to the water level. Waiting for it to settle, we then tasted it and found it to be a little brackish, but still nice and cool and quite drinkable. Having drank what we wanted, filling the canteen, we let the horses have their turn. They got some, but soon caved the sand in and made the water so riley they would drink no more.

Jack filled the hole up and leveled the sand over it as it was before and said if he did not do it there could not be any more water ever found anywhere near there (Superstition), and I think he actually believed what he said. . . .

[*This method of obtaining water is common to South African Bushmen, Australian aborigines, Sloubbies of Arabia, and other desert peoples in all parts of the world.*]

56.—SQUAWS CATCHING GROUND MOLES

The ground squirrel, or large white bellied mole or gopher, are very numerous in some places on the bench lands along the mountains. One day, while taking a little exercise with Mr. Muncey, the telegraph operator, we rode along the foothills. When we came to the edge of fifteen-mile Creek Hollow and were going down to the creek we came to a ditch about eighteen inches wide and six or seven inches of water running, with a good ripple, to our right, the mountains being to the left. Muncey said, "Who in h--l done this. This water is running up hill." And so it appeared to be. "Well, let us follow it and see where it goes to."

We followed along the ditch until it came out onto the flat, where there was a division, making two streams. A little lower they were again divided. Then we could see about eight or ten squaws very busy, each with a stout stick, digging a trench and leading the water to a gopher hole. The gopher would soon make his appearance in a half-drowned state, get a rap on the head, then put in the sack at the back of the squaw, who would then turn the water into the next nearest hole, with the same result. All of the squaws were hard at work the same way, making a very clean job of it, and very few would be left for a future drowning out. Muncey said he was going to time that young squaw. We saw her divide her part of the water in two streams, thus running it in two holes at the same time. Sometimes she would have three or four streams and then again but one, and according to Muncey's time she had caught between twenty-five and thirty in the half hour.

When we left them some of the squaws had over a half bushel in their sacks and quite a large field to go over yet. It would take a number of days to finish the job.

These rodents are skinned, gutted, then dried the same as beef, only they are dried whole, no bones being removed. Of course, they are also eaten fresh and stewed with Indian potatoes and segos. . . .

[*Note that the women went to the trouble of diverting streams to flood out the rodents. In Owens Valley, California, the Paiutes irrigated wild plants, but had no agriculture.*]

Making Fire with a Stick.—On one of my trips with a comrade we camped for the night just before sundown and soon found out that we had no matches that were dry enough to light a fire with. That did not put us out much and we did not worry a bit, for we could soon make fire with our pistols, but just before we were ready to do it an Indian came up and squat down close to the little pile of wood we had collected.

Then the thought struck me that I would see if an Indian was always prepared to make a fire, so I said to him, "Make a good fire and I will give you something to eat." He jumped up and said, "Give me white fire stick." (Matches.) I told him, "No, they are all wet and no account, and Indian no good either if he could not make fire." He gave a grunt and proceeded to get busy.

He took a stick about eighteen inches long and the thickness of an arrow out of the quiver he carried his arrows in and another flat stick about six inches long, one-half inch thick and three-quarters to one inch wide, there being four or five counter-sunk holes in the flat piece about one-fourth inch deep.

After rubbing some dry cedar bark with his hands till it was very fine, he placed the flat stick on the ground and one end of the long stick which was at one end a little smaller, and putting the largest end in one of the counter-sunk holes, placed his hands together around the top of the stick, which he made to turn around back and forth very fast. As he worked his hands this way, at the same time pressing down all he could, it caused his hands to work down on the stick and he had to place them at the top very often. In about twelve or fifteen minutes he had a few tiny sparks of fire he had made with the sticks, burning the fine ground bark.

After that it was easy, but when the fire was lighted Mr. Indian was in a very sweaty condition. . . . I have seen an Indian make fire by simply rubbing two sticks together. This plan takes longer and harder work. . . .

[*The hand-drill method of fire making described in this passage is the commonest known below the flint-and-steel level. Many people in the world, however, as for example the Andamanese and some of the Australians, are ignorant of fire making and carry embers with them at all times to keep it burning. So great an effort is fire making by the method described above that most people who employ it prefer to keep their fire burning.*]

60.—THE OLD MAN LEFT TO DIE

There is a little spring of very brackish and warm water about a mile north of Fish Spring station and a few rods below the road. Between this spring and the road the Indians had selected as the place to leave a very old man to die. He was totally blind and very poor, hardly any flesh on his bones. He was clad with only a very old and small strip of rabbit skin robe hung about his neck.

The Indians had gathered some sagebrush and made a small semi-circle about two feet high. He was led to the spring and back to the circle and left to die of starvation. Father heard of this from one of the stage drivers and the first time he passed that way was prepared to supply the old man with food and blankets. He told the driver to drive out of the road to the old man's camp.

When they arrived there the old man was down to the spring with his hands down in the water, which was literally alive with fish that were about two inches in length. When he could feel one of them touch the inside of his hands he would grab them and immediately eat them. That was the only way of keeping himself alive.

Father raised him from the spring and tried to make him understand that he would give him something to eat and a blanket to keep him warm. But he soon found that the old man was very deaf and did not seem to understand a word. Father got him back to his camp, gave him enough food to last several days, also a gallon can of water, placed a good new blanket around him and left the old man eating very sparingly of the food, as if to make it last as long as possible.

Father went on his way west, but left word with the stage driver to bring food for him after that every time he passed that way. On his return trip, when he met the driver he asked him about the old man. He said, "He is still alive, but the blanket, water can and grub was gone the first time I passed there. I have left him him food every trip. He seems to be some stronger than when we first saw him."

Father got another blanket, more food and a water can, and when he arrived at that place found the old man sound asleep, curled up about as a dog would for a nap, and getting him awake and placing the bread in one hand and the other on the can of water with the blanket around him left him to himself again.

Father was planning to have the old man moved near the station, where he could be fed at regular times and provided with more shelter and clothing and with means of having a fire when necessary, as the weather was getting quite cold. Too late, for on his next trip out he learned that the old Indian had been taken away and everything that had been given him and even the small semi-circle wind-brake had been burned.

Father's generosity had not been appreciated by the old man's relatives, or the band of Indians that he belonged to, so they made it impossible for him to prolong the life of the old man, who ought to die, and would very soon if let alone.

[*The practice of abandoning the hopelessly ill and aged has been observed in many parts of the world. It is always done by people living in poor environments where it is necessary to move about frequently to obtain food, where food is scarce, and transportation difficult. Such a practice does not imply "cruelty." It is a necessary survival mechanism for the preservation of the able-bodied members of the group and hence of the group as a whole. The student should note, however, that among peoples who are forced to live in this way the oldest generation, the generation of individuals who have passed their physical peak, is reduced in numbers and in influence. There is no body of elders to hand on tradition and control the affairs of younger men and women, and no formal system of age grading. There is no opportunity to hold initiations and puberty schools.*]

61.—How a Young Buck Got His Wife

It was Willow Spring Bill, as he was called, as he had been working here for some time as chore boy. The band of Indians he belonged to lived in the country around Fish Springs. He was very saving of what little money or clothing he got and finally traded for a small bore Kentucky rifle, that had the tube or nipple broken off, therefore useless to the Indian he got it from.

He brought it to me, knowing that I usually had a few extra tubes on hand. He asked me if I would put on one for one antelope skin. (That was the usual price.) "Let me see the skin." "No, I can't get it till you fix my gun so I can shoot antelope." Well, I fixed the gun without taking his note.

About two weeks after I got the skin and traded for a couple more that he had, giving him a few rounds of ammunition, a shirt and a red handkerchief, which he said he wanted to catch a squaw with. He had quit the station. He was now past chore boy. He was a man.

I did not see him again for two or three months, when I chanced to be at Willow Springs. Bill came to the station, a young and good looking squaw at his heels. "Hello, Bill, you catch squaw?" "Yes." "Where you catch him?" "Me catch squaw over to Shell Creek." "When you catch him?" "Two sleeps me catch him. Me go home, Fish Spring."

The young squaw seemed to be very bashful. I asked her if she loved Bill. "Yes," she said, "him very good man, very much like him." And she acted as if she did and I have no doubts she did. But, oh! the difference between white and red people!

I afterwards learned from other Indians just how Bill proceeded to get his wife. She lived in the Shell Creek country with her father, there being no more of the family or relatives left. The father had lost one eye. He was getting old and feeble, so the young girl had a hard time of it gathering enough food for both. There had been many a young buck that wanted her for a wife, but the old man had always driven them off. Well, one day the young Indian Bill made his appearance at the old man's camp and commenced to lay siege to the girl's heart. He made that camp his home and helped out the food supply with game. This went on a month or more. The old man still said no one should take the girl from him. But Bill soon solved the problem. There is no way of finding out just what agreement was made between the boy and girl, but this is what happened:

One afternoon, after coming in from hunting, Bill took his gun all apart and cleaned and oiled it up in fine shape. Then he loaded it ready for work. The girl was busy shelling nuts, the old man sound asleep on the sunny side of the camp, with his face towards Bill, who aimed his gun at the old man's good eye and fired. The ball passed through the eye and the brain, too, killing the old man instantly.

The marriage ceremony was completely over. Bill coolly reloaded his gun, turned to the girl and said, "Come," and the girl picked up her blanket and followed her lord and master and was willing to do so as long as life lasted.

It was two days later that I had seen them at Willow Springs on their wedding tour, apparently as happy as a couple of lovesick millionaires could be and live. All they owned on earth they had on, or carried in their hands. Not much to start married life with, but then they were Indians, whose wants are few.

[The implications of this story are clear. The old man and his daughter lived alone. He needed his daughter to feed him and was not willing to form a third in a family group headed by a younger male. The situation is no more complex than what might be found in a gibbon band described by Carpenter in Chapter 1.]

42.—FATHER'S INDIAN DOCTOR

While Father was out west on the mail line one hot spring-like day before the snow had melted, he had his eyes burned so bad that he was completely blinded and could not stand the least bit of light, and although he kept them bandaged with dead tea leaves, they did not seem to get any better.

After a couple of days of misery, two Indians came to the station where he was. One of them asked one of the men, "Egan sick?" The man said, "Yes, eye sick. No see. Snow no good." "Me see Egan."

The man told Father that there was an Indian there that wanted to see him. "Well, let him come in." He did so. The Buck came up close to Father and said, "Big sick?" Father said, pointing to his eyes. "Eyes big sick; you savey fix them." He had hardly got the words out of his mouth when the Indian jumped and caught Father's head in both hands, and at the same time pushing the bandage out of the way, placed his mouth over one eye and set to sucking with all his strength.

Father said he thought the buck would suck his eye out, if not his brains too. He tried his best to push the Indian off, but he only stayed and sucked the faster. But just before Father had made up his mind to choke him off, the Indian stepped back a little and spit up as much or more than a tablespoonful of blood. After a little rest he said, "Fix more?" Father said, "Fix little, eye big sick." "Alright, little fix." But when he got fastened to the other eye he worked just as hard as before, with the same result, Father trying to push him off, but no go, he was after the blood and he would not let go till he got it.

After about one hour the buck said, "A little more fix eye?" Father said as his eyes felt to be considerable better, he thought he could stand a small dose of the same medicine, and told the fellow, "Fix little bit." Well, he did, but with just about the same force. When he got through he said, "Big Chief see all right two days," which proved true. In two days after the operation Father joined the pack train and went to Salt Lake, his eyes perfectly cured of snow blindness. . . . There was no pain after the dose, but plenty and very severe before.

[The simple but effective treatment which Major Egan received was part of the repertoire of a sucking shaman, a type of medicoreligious practitioner found among primitive peoples the world over. Often the shaman will produce from his mouth some small object, such as a quartz crystal or small pebble, and exhibit it as the cause of the pain, now removed. It is doubtful if the Indian who cured Major Egan of snow blindness was a full-time practitioner, which the landscape in that country could hardly support at a simple food-gathering level of technology.]

A scholarly account of the living habits of the Indians of the Basin region may be found in Professor Julian Steward's well-known monograph, *Basin-Plateau Aboriginal Socio-Political Groups.** A very brief selection from it follows.

ECOLOGICAL DETERMINANTS

The natural environment was a constant. Many important features of the social groups inhabiting it depended upon the manner in which it was exploited by special economic devices and by the subsistence habits entailed. These largely predetermined the population density, imposed limitations upon the size, distribution, and mobility of village groups, and affected the nature of economic cooperation, political controls, and certain property rights. . . . The Shoshonean exploitation of the same environment was so simple that the biological family was, in most respects, necessarily the independent self-supporting unit. Commerce was virtually unknown and specialization was extremely rare. The only true specialist was the shaman, though information showing the extent to which he was relieved of ordinary subsistence activities and supported himself entirely by his practice is not available.

Under native economy Shoshonean units smaller than the family survived only with difficulty. It is probable that individuals were able to support themselves, but were, according to Shoshonean standards, underprivileged. Units larger than the family were transient in most parts of the area.

The individual family was in most respects necessarily the independent economic unit. Subsistence in most of the area was primarily upon plant foods. When gathering these foods, group endeavor might bring the pleasure of companionship, but it did not in-crease the per capita harvest. In fact, because few plants other than the pine nut grew in dense and extensive patches, it usually decreased the harvest. As food shortage was always a real danger it was necessary that families harvest alone or in the company of not more than one or two other families. A woman harvested exclusively for her own family. . . .

It is conceivable that had seed yield been extraordinarily great, specialization in industry might have been possible, so that certain women could have devoted full time to harvesting and traded surpluses for goods made by other women who spent most of their time in manufacturing. This was impossible because the techniques utilized by Shoshoneans for exploiting their limited resources did not permit a woman to gather more plant foods than were absolutely required by her family. Surplus for trade was very unusual. She frequently shared seeds with neighbors and especially with relatives, but was not obligated to do so.

Hunting was the complement to harvesting. Game provided not only essential foods but skins for clothing and materials for certain implements. Most hunting was also on a family basis. Small species, such as rodents and insects, were taken by both men and women. Large game was usually taken by men, while women gathered plant foods. A hunter was obligated, however, to share large game with other members of the village. Thus a family was able to provide most of its wants without assistance. But in time

* Bulletin No. 120, Smithsonian Institution, Bureau of American Ethnology, Washington, 1938.

of dire need other families came to its aid if possible.

But the family was not always the maximum economic unit in hunting. When taking buffalo, antelope, rabbits, deer, mountain sheep, and, under certain conditions, water fowl, fish, and even insects, collective effort increased manyfold what an individual hunter could have procured. The duration of such hunts and the profitable number of participants depended upon special conditions in each case. Among the Western Shoshoni and many of their neighbors game was so scarce that these hunts usually lasted only one to two weeks and never more than six weeks. Participants rarely numbered more than two dozen families. . . .

Several plant and animal species occurred in such great quantities in certain localities during short periods that, even when they were not taken cooperatively, they drew large numbers of families to such localities. Outstanding among such species are pine nuts, which were often a major factor in the location of winter villages, and salmon . . . and grasshoppers, which were sometimes taken cooperatively as well as by single families.

Among Western Shoshoni plant harvesting was the main subsistence activity, game being relatively scarce. For the greater part of the year families necessarily traveled alone or in very small groups and harvested a very large area. They ordinarily ranged 20 miles or more in each direction from the winter village. Their itinerary, though usually the same each year, was not always fixed. Seasonal variation in rainfall and consequently in crop growth frequently required that they alter their routine.

The most permanent association of families was at winter encampments. These were sites where certain families habitually remained during the months when vegetable foods could not be had. Necessary conditions for such sites were accessibility to stored seeds, especially pine nuts, water, sufficient wood for house building and fuel, and absence of extremely low winter temperatures. These conditions were most often fulfilled in the mouths of canyons or within the pine-nut–juniper belt in the mountains, though sometimes broad valleys near fishing streams were chosen. Encampments tended to cluster with respect to mountain masses rather than valleys. But whether they were scattered at intervals of several hundred yards to a mile along streams, were situated at springs on mountain sides, or were clustered in dense colonies depended upon the quantity of foods which could be gathered and stored within convenient distance of each camp. In some places families had to camp alone; elsewhere as many as 15 or 20 could congregate in a true village.

But another factor affecting population distribution was annual variation in seed occurrence. Though a winter encampment was always located near the greatest amount of stored foods, the natural yield was not everywhere and always the same. In some areas, for example, Owens Valley, crops were fairly reliable and villages consequently stable. Elsewhere, especially in the deserts bordering Death Valley, the Great Salt Desert, most of Nevada, and the Snake River, people had to traverse enormous territories, modifying their itinerary considerably from year to year as local rainfall or other factors affected plant growth. The erratic occurrence of the all-important pine-nut crops, for example, required that a family often remain in different localities in successive years. Along and north of the Humboldt River the piñon nut is too scarce to have been an important factor, but other plant species also were unreliable and many had a somewhat similar effect. People consequently were not always able to return to the same winter village.

Western Shoshoni cooperative hunts did not permit permanent associations of families or villages for several reasons. First, these hunts lasted only while the quantity of meat taken was sufficient to feed the assembled crowd—a few weeks. There was rarely a surplus which, being stored for winter, would be a factor in the location of winter villages. Second, alinement of families or villages for hunting was often different for each species. Antelope and rabbits, the most important species in this part of the area, often occurred in different parts of a valley. Moreover, the more important hunts were held only where there was an antelope shaman or rabbit drive director; every valley did not have such men. For communal hunts, therefore, families traveled from their village or from where they happened to be gathering seeds to the most convenient location and often cooperated with very different people in successive hunts. They might join families from across their valley for a rabbit drive, go to a neighboring valley to hunt with its residents in an antelope drive, travel in another direction to a marsh to join a waterfowl drive, and associate with immediate neighbors to hunt deer in their own mountains. If their local pine-nut crop failed the next year they might be thrown into association with still other people for these hunts.

Because the territory exploited by different families was variable as well as overlapping, ownership of food areas would have been impractical. It was absent among Western Shoshoni, excepting possibly the Reese River area.

Among Western Shoshoni and prob-ably Southern Paiute the family was necessarily the economic unit. This family was bilateral rather than patrilineal or matrilineal, first, because an extended family would frequently have been too large to live together; second, because the uncertainties of food and consequently of residence made association with persons other than those of the immediate household uncertain. Under the existing ecology it was physically impossible for groups larger than the village to remain in association during the winter. Though these villages often comprise related families, frequent change of residence prevented this always being so. There was consequently no localized lineage, nor condition for clan development. Social features dependent upon large and prosperous populations were also prevented, e.g., clubs, rank based upon wealth, slavery, and others. Likewise, political organization was minimal. There were no bands.

SOCIAL DETERMINANTS

Festivals were made possible in most of the western area by the temporarily increased food supply produced by rabbit drives, pine-nut trips, antelope hunts, or other communal economic affairs. The essential motivation of festivals, however, was noneconomic. People desired social intercourse with friends and relatives rarely seen during the remainder of the year. They wished to dance and gamble, and, in some localities, to hold religious observances.

The size of groups united by festivals rarely exceeded that produced by communal economic undertakings. In the Western Shoshoni area festivals could be held only at times of communal hunts or when many families were gathering pine nuts or other species at a certain locality. They merely provided an additional motive for assembling together.

. . . warfare was virtually unknown. Shoshoni never fought one another except in family feuds which somewhat disrupted group unity. Upon rare occasions Shoshoni fought their Paiute neighbors, but no organization was entailed.

Shamanistic performances and funerals drew many visitors, but, being informal, were usually attended only by residents of the local village or by people within a convenient distance.

The relationship of kinship to the composition of the sociopolitical group is conspicuously greater among Western Shoshoni than among Northern Shoshoni. Among the former, organization rarely surpassed the bonds of kinship. Relatives sought one another's proximity. Though exigencies of the food quest often forced related families apart, they wintered together if possible. . . .

Stated most briefly, the institutional simplicity of the Western Shoshoni Indians was dependent first on the scarcity of water and hence food in their country, and second and specifically, on the notorious failure of the piñon trees to bear regular annual crops. It is clear from Dr. Steward's discussion that some of these Indians lived on what we have defined as the first level of complexity because they had no institution larger than the family, while others who managed to winter together regularly in the same place developed winter villages with more or less stable leadership.

A third source of material which we shall quote here is Father Jacob Baegert's *Account of the Aboriginal Inhabitants of the Californian Peninsula,** written nearly two hundred years ago. The Indians of whom he wrote are now extinct. Needless to say, he had no training in anthropology. Some of his judgments are subjective, as might be expected. For the most part, however, his account is clear and detailed.

Introduction †

. . . in 1767, by a decree of Charles III, all members of the order of the Jesuits were banished from Spain and the transatlantic provinces subject to that realm. . . . One of the banished Jesuits, a German, who had spent seventeen years in the Californian peninsula, published, after his return to his native country, a book which contains a description of that remote part of the American continent, and gives also quite a detailed account of its aborigi-

* Translated and arranged for the Smithsonian Institution by Charles Rau. Smithsonian Institution, *Annual Report for 1863,* pp. 352–369, Washington, 1864; and *Annual Report for 1864,* pp. 378–399, Washington, 1865.
† By Charles Rau.

nal inhabitants, with whom the author had become thoroughly acquainted during the many years devoted to their conversion to Christianity. . . .

.   .   .   .

Of the peninsula Father Baegert gives a rather woeful account. He describes that region as an arid, mountainous country, covered with rocks and sand, deficient in water, and almost without shade trees, but abounding in thorny plants and shrubs of various kinds. The sterility of the soil is caused by the scantiness of water. "No one," says the author, "need be afraid to drown himself in water; but the danger of dying from thirst is much greater." There falls some rain, accompanied by short thunderstorms, during the months of July, August, September, and October, filling the channels worn in the hard ground. Some of these soon become dry after the showers; others, however, hold water during the whole year, and on these and the stagnant water collected in pools and ponds men and beasts have to rely for drink. Of running waters, deserving the name of brooks, there are but six in the country, and of these six only four reach the sea, while the others lose themselves not very far from their sources among rocks and sand. There is nothing to be seen in Lower California that may be called a wood; only a few straggling oaks, pines, and some other kinds of trees unknown in Europe, are met with, and these are confined to certain localities. Shade and material for the carpenter are, therefore, very scarce. The only tree of any consequence is the so-called mesquite; but besides that it always grows quite isolated, and never in groups, the trunk is very low, and the wood so hard that it almost defies the application of iron tools. The author mentions, further, a kind of low Brazil wood, a tree called paloblanco, the bark

of which serves for tanning; the palohierro or iron-wood, which is still harder than the mesquite; wild fig trees that bear no fruit; wild willows and barren palms, "all of which would be ashamed to appear beside a European oak or nut-tree.". . . But in compensation for the absence of large trees, there is a prodigious abundance of prickly plants, some of a gigantic height, but of little practical use, their soft, spongy stems soon rotting after being cut. Among the indigenous edible productions of the vegetable kingdom are chiefly mentioned the tunas or Indian figs, the aloë, and the pitahayas, of which the latter deserve a special notice as forming an important article of food of the Indians. There are two kinds of this fruit—the sweet and the sour pitahaya. The former is round, as large as a hen's egg, and has a green, thick, prickly shell that covers a red or white flesh, in which the black seeds are scattered like grains of powder. It is described as being sweet, but not of a very agreeable taste without the addition of lemon juice and sugar. There is no scarcity of shrubs bearing this fruit, and from some it can be gathered by hundreds. They become mature in the middle of June, and continue for more than eight weeks. The sour pitahaya, which grows on low, creeping bushes, bristling with long spines, is much larger than the other kind, of excellent taste, but by far less abundant; for, although the shrubs are very plentiful, there is hardly one among a hundred that bears fruit. Of the aloë or mescale, as the Spaniards and Mexicans call it, the fibres are used by the aborigines, in lieu of hemp, for making threads and strings, and its fruit is eaten by them.

. . . In the list of wild quadrupeds are enumerated the deer, hare, rabbit, fox, coyote, wild cat, skunk (Sorillo), leopard, (American panther), onza, (lynx), and wild ram "...[which] cannot be great [in number], for I never saw a living specimen, nor the fur of one in the possession of an Indian; but many skins of leopards and onzas."

．　．　．　．

The feathered tribe does not seem to be very plentiful in California, since, according to Father Baegert, a person may travel one or two days without seeing other birds but occasionally a filthy vulture, raven, or "bat." Among the few which he observed are the red-bird, (cardinal) blue-bird, humming-bird, and an "ash-colored bird with a tail resembling that of a peacock and a beautiful tuft on its head;" also wild ducks and a species of swallow, the latter appearing only now and then in small numbers, and therefore considered as extraneous.

There are some small fish found in the waters of California; but they do not amount to much, and during lent the father obtained his supply from the Pacific, distant 12 leagues from his habitation. . . .

Under the comprehensive, but not very scientific head of "vermin," the author enumerates snakes, scorpions, centipedes, huge spiders, toads, wasps, bats, ants, and grasshoppers. These vermin seem to have been a great annoyance to the good missionary, especially the snakes, of which there are about twenty different kinds in California, the rattlesnake being, of course, the most conspicuous among them. . . . Grasshoppers are represented as a real public calamity. Migrating from the southern part of the peninsula towards the north, they deluge the country, obscuring the sun by their numbers, and causing a noise that resembles a strong wind. Never deviating from their line of march, they will climb houses and churches encountered during their progress, laying waste all fields and gardens over which their pernicious train passes.

Of the climate in California the author speaks well, and considers it as both healthy and agreeable. Being only one degree and a half distant from the Tropic of Cancer, he lived, of course, in a hot region. . . . The greatest heat begins in the month of July and lasts till the middle of October; but there is every day in the year quite a refreshing wind blowing, which begins at noon, if not sooner, and continues till night. The principal winds are north west and south west; the north wind blows only now and then during the winter months, but the east wind hardly ever, the latter circumstance being somewhat surprising to the author, who observed that the clouds are almost invariably moving from the east. He never found the cold severer than during the latter part of September or April on the banks of the Rhine. . . . Fogs in the morning are frequent in California, and occur not only during fall and winter, but also sometimes in the hot season. Dew is said to be not more frequent nor heavier than in middle Europe.

Though the author represents California as a dry, sterile country, where but little rain falls, he admits that in those isolated parts where the proximity of water imparts humidity, the soil exhibits an astonishing fertility. "There," he says, "one may plant what he chooses, and it will thrive; there the earth yields fruit a hundredfold, as in the best countries of Europe. . . . It is only to be regretted that such humid places are of very rare occurrence, and that water for irrigating a certain piece of land sometimes cannot be found within a distance of sixty leagues."

．　．　．

[*This environment seems little better for human occupancy than the desert of which Egan and Steward have written. In place of the piñon nut, the Indians had, as their chief single source of food, the equally unreliable pitahaya cactus,* Lemaireocereus Thurberi *(Engelm.) Britt. et Rose.* Like a number of other desert plants, it fruits only on years when the rainfall lies between a lower and an upper limit. Too much rain will have the same effect as too little. In most of the peninsula, the summer rains are markedly variable. For example, at Mulege on the East Coast, at 27° N. Lat., over a period of six years the mean annual rainfall was 56 mm., with 1 mm. for the driest year and 160 mm. for the wettest. At the southern tip, which is the wettest spot on the peninsula, the figures for a 12-year range were: mean, 142 mm.; driest year, 30 mm.; wettest year, 310 mm.† It has not been possible to determine the exact upper and lower thresholds for fruiting.*

As you will see shortly, these Indians also had no possibility of getting together in large interfamily assemblies with any regularity, until after the arrival of the missionaries. Their institutional complexity therefore remained on the same level as that of the desert Paiutes.]

CHAPTER I—THE STATURE, COMPLEXION, AND NUMBER OF THE CALIFORNIANS; ALSO, WHENCE AND HOW THEY MAY HAVE COME TO CALIFORNIA

In physical appearance the Californians resemble perfectly the Mexicans and other aboriginal inhabitants of America. Their skin is of a dark chestnut or clove color, passing, however, sometimes into different shades, some individuals being of a more swarthy complexion, while others are tan or copper colored. But in new-born children the color is much paler, so that they hardly can be distinguished from white children when presented for baptism; yet it appears soon after birth, and assumes its dark tinge in a short time. The hair is black as pitch and straight, and seldom turns gray, except sometimes in cases of extreme old age. They are all beardless, and their eye-brows are but scantily provided with hair. The heads of children at their birth, instead of being covered with scales, exhibit hair, sometimes half a finger long. The teeth, though never cleaned, are of the whiteness of ivory. The angles of the eyes towards the nose are not pointed, but arched like a bow. They are well-formed and well-proportioned people, very supple, and can lift up from the ground stones, bones, and similar things with the big and second toes. All walk, with a few exceptions, even to the most advanced age, perfectly straight. Their children stand and walk, before they are a year old, briskly on their feet. Some are tall and of a commanding appearance, others small of stature, as elsewhere, but no corpulent individuals are seen among them, which may be accounted for by their manner of living, for, being compelled to run much around, they have no chance of growing stout.

In a country as poor and sterile as California the number of inhabitants cannot be great. . . . A person may travel in different parts four and more days without seeing a single human being, and I do not believe that the number of Californians from the promontory of St. Lucas to the Rio Colorado ever amounted, before the arrival of the Spaniards, to more than forty or fifty

* Diguet, Leon, "Les Cactacees Utiles du Mexique," *Archives d'Histoire Naturelle,* Serie IV, Paris, 1928, p. 170.

† *Köppen-Geiger Handbuch der Klimatologie,* vol. II, section J, p. 54, Berlin, 1936.

thousand souls. It is certain that in 1767, in fifteen, that is, in all the missions, from the 22d to the 31st degree, only twelve thousand have been counted. . . .

However small the number of Californians is, they are, nevertheless, divided into a great many nations, tribes, and tongues. If a mission contains only one thousand souls, it may easily embrace as many little nations among its parishioners as Switzerland counts cantons and allies. My mission consisted of Paurus, Atshemes, Mitshirikutamais, Mitshirikuteurus, Mitshirikutaruanajeres, Teackwas, Teenguabebes, Utshis, Ikas, Anjukwares, Utshipujes; all being different tribes, but hardly amounting in all to five hundred souls.

[*Or an average of forty-five persons per "tribe." This diversity is obviously a function of isolation.*]

. . . all of these petty nations or tribes have their own countries, of which they are as much, and sometimes even more, enamored than other people of theirs, so that they would not consent to be transplanted fifty or more leagues from the place they consider as their home. And, further, the different tribes who live at some distance from each other are always in a mutual state of enmity, which would prevent them from living peaceably together, and offer a serious obstacle to their being enclosed in the same fold. . . . My parish counted far less than a thousand members, yet their encampments were often more than thirty leagues distant from each other. . . .

. . . balsas or little rafts made of reeds . . . are . . . used by my Californians who live near the sea, either for catching fish or turtle, or crossing over to a certain island distant two leagues from the shore.

[*The little balsas were boats made of reeds. The Seri of Tiburon Island still make them. Craft of this kind can be constructed by one man without implements, and hence many of the world's technologically simplest peoples make them, as for example the Tasmanians.*]

. . . no Californian is acquainted with the events that occurred in the country prior to his birth, nor does he even know who his parents were if he should happen to have lost them during his infancy.

. . . the Californians . . . believed . . . that California constituted the whole world, and they themselves its sole inhabitants; for they went to nobody, and nobody came to see them, each little people remaining within the limits of its small district. Some of those under my care believed to be derived from a bird; some traced their origin from a rock that was lying not far from my house; while others ascribed their descent to still different . . . sources.

[*The belief in human descent from natural objects is a very widespread phenomenon. What it is is simply the identification of the people with the landscape on which they live. You will see other examples of this shortly.*]

CHAPTER II—THEIR HABITATIONS, APPAREL, IMPLEMENTS, AND UTENSILS

With the exception of the churches and dwellings of the missionaries, . . . nothing is to be seen in California that bears a resemblance to a city, a village, a human dwelling, a hut, or even a dog-house. The Californians themselves spend their whole life, day and night, in the open air, the sky above them forming their roof, and the hard soil the couch on which they sleep.

During winter, only, when the wind blows sharp, they construct around them, but only opposite the direction of the wind, a half moon of brush-wood, a few spans high, as a protection against the inclemency of the weather. . . . It cannot be otherwise with them; for, if they had houses, they would be compelled to carry their dwellings always with them, like snails or turtles, the necessity of collecting food urging them to wander constantly about. Thus they cannot start every morning from the same place and return thither in the evening, since, notwithstanding the small number of each little people, a small tract of land could not provide them with provisions during a whole year. To-day the water will fail them, to-morrow they have to go to some locality for gathering a certain kind of seed that serves them as food. . . . I am certainly not much mistaken in saying that many of them change their night-quarters more than a hundred times in a year, and hardly sleep three times successively in the same place and the same part of the country. . . . Wherever the night surprises them they will lie down to sleep. . . . They do not live under the shade of trees, as some authors have said, because there are hardly any trees in California that afford shade, nor do they dwell in earth-holes of their own making, as others have said, but, sometimes, and only when it rains, they resort to the clefts and cavities of rocks, if they can find such sheltering places, which do not occur as frequently as their wants require.

Whenever they undertake to construct shelters for protecting their sick from heat or cold, the entrance is usually so low that a person has to creep on hands and feet in order to get in, and the whole structure is of such small dimensions as to render it impossible to stand erect within, or to find room to sit down on the ground for the purpose of confessing or comforting the patient. . . . man and wife hardly can sit or lie down in them. Even the old and infirm are utterly indifferent as to their being under shelter or not, and it happened often that I found old sick persons lying in the open air, for whose accommodation I had caused huts to be built on the preceding day. . . .

As the blue sky forms the only habitation of the Californian Indians, so they wear no other covering than the brown skin with which nature has clothed them. This applies to the male sex in the full sense of the word, and even women have been found in the northern parts of California in a perfect state of nudity, while among most nations the females always covered themselves to a small extent. They did, and still continue to do, as follows: They understand how to prepare from the fibres of the aloë plant a white thread, which serves them for making cords. On these they string hundreds of small sections of water-reed, like beads of a rosary; and a good number of these strings, attached by their ends to a girdle, and placed very close and thick together, form two aprons, one of which hangs down below the abdomen, while the other covers the hind part. These aprons are about a span wide, and of different length. Among some nations they reach down to the knees; among others to the calves, and even to the feet. Both sides of the thighs, as well as the rest of the body, remain perfectly naked. In order to save labor, some women wear, instead of the back-aprons, a piece of untanned deer-skin, or any woollen or linen rag which they can now-a-days obtain. Of the same untanned skin they make, if they can get it, their shoes or sandals, simply flat pieces, which they attach to the feet by coarse strings of the above-mentioned aloë, passing between the big and small toes and around the ankles.

Both sexes, the grown as well as the children, wear the head always uncovered, however inclement the weather may be, even those in a certain mission who understand how to manufacture pretty good hats from palm-leaves, which, on account of their lightness, were frequently worn by the missionaries while on their travels. The men allow the hair to grow down to the shoulders. Women, on the contrary, wear it much shorter. Formerly they pierced the ears of new-born children of the male sex with a pointed stick, and by putting bones and pieces of wood into the aperture they enlarged it to such a degree that, in some grown persons, the flaps hung down nearly to the shoulders. At present, however, they have abandoned this unnatural usage. It has been asserted that they also pierce the nose. I can only say that I saw no one disfigured in that particular manner, but many middle-aged persons with their ears perforated as described above. Under certain circumstances, and on their gala days, they paint different parts of the body with red and yellow color, which they obtain by burning certain minerals.

[*All primitive peoples known use some kind of body paint, usually made of clay and ochre mixed with fat. Lumps of this have been found in caves in association with Neanderthal man, who lived over 50,000 years ago. It was with "lipsticks" of this kind that Cro-Magnon men painted animals on the walls of caves in France and Spain.*]

The baptized Indians . . . observed more decency in regard to dress. The missionaries gave each male individual, once or twice in a year, a piece of blue cloth, six spans long and two spans wide, for covering the lower part of the body, and . . . a short woollen coat. . . . The women and girls were provided with thick white veils, made of wool, that covered the head and the whole body down to the feet. . . . But the women throw aside their veils, and the men their coats, as soon as they leave church, because those coverings make them feel uneasy, especially in summer, and impede the free use of their limbs, which their mode of living constantly requires. . . .

It is not to be expected that a people in as low a state of development as the Californians should make use of many implements and utensils. Their whole furniture, if that expression can be applied at all, consists of a bow and arrows, a flint instead of a knife, a bone or pointed piece of wood for digging roots, a turtle-shell serving as basket and cradle, a large gut or bladder for fetching water and transporting it during their excursions, and a bag made like a fishing net from the fibres of the aloë, or the skin of a wild cat, in which they preserve and carry their provisions, sandals, and perhaps other insignificant things which they may happen to possess.

[*The reason why they had so few possessions is obvious. They were constantly on the move, and could own nothing more than they could carry with them.*]

The bows of the Californians are more than six feet long, slightly curved, and made from the roots of wild willows. They are of the thickness of the five fingers in the middle, round, and become gradually thinner and pointed towards the ends. The bowstrings are made of the intestines of beasts. The shafts of their arrows consist of common reeds, which they straighten by the fire. They are above six spans long, and have, at the lower end, a notch to catch the string, and three or four feathers, about a finger long, not much projecting, and let into slits made for that purpose. At the upper end of the shaft a pointed piece of heavy wood, a span and a half long, is inserted, bearing usually at its extremity a flint of a triangular shape, almost resembling a serpent's tongue, and indented like the edge of a saw. The Californians carry their bows and arrows always with them, and as they commence at an early age to use these weapons many of them become very skilful archers.

In lieu of knives and scissors they use sharp flints for cutting almost everything—cane, wood, aloë, and even their hair—and for disembowelling and skinning animals. With the same flints they bleed or scarify themselves, and make incisions for extracting thorns and splinters which they have accidentally run into their limbs.

The whole art of the men consists in the manufacture of bows and arrows, while the mechanical skill of the females is merely confined to the making of the above-mentioned aprons. Of a division of labor not a trace is to be found among them; even the cooking is done by all without distinction of sex or age, every one providing for himself, and the children commence to practice that necessary art as soon as they are able to stir a fire. The time of these people is chiefly taken up by the search for food and its preparation; and if their physical wants are supplied they abandon themselves entirely to lounging, chattering, and sleep. . . .

[*Note that the term "division of labor" was used 200 years ago.*]

CHAPTER IX—HOW THEY LIVED BEFORE . . . THEIR CONVERSION

I will now proceed to describe in a few words in what manner the unbaptized Californians spent their days.

In the evening, when they had eaten their fill, they either lay down, or sat together and chatted till they were tired of talking, or had communicated to each other all that they knew for the moment. In the morning they slept until hunger forced them to rise. As soon as they awakened, the eating recommenced, if anything remained; and the laughing, talking, and joking were likewise resumed. After this morning-prayer, when the sun was already somewhat high, the men seized their bows and arrows, and the women hitched on their yokes and turtle-shells. Some went to the right, others to the left; here six, there four, eight, or three, and sometimes one alone, the different bands always continuing the laughing and chattering on their way. They looked around to espy a mouse, lizard, snake, or perhaps a hare or deer; or tore up here and there a yuka or other root, or cut off some aloës. A part of the day thus spent, a pause was made. They sat or lay down in the shade, if they happened to find any, without, however, allowing their tongues to come to a stand-still, or they played or wrestled with each other, to find out who was the strongest among them and could throw his adversaries to the ground, in which sport the women likewise participated. Now they either returned to the camping-place of the preceding night, or went a few leagues further, until they came to some spot supplied with water, where they commenced singeing, burning, roasting, and pounding the captures they had made during the day. They ate as long as they had anything before them and as there was room in their stomachs, and after a long, childish or indecent talk, they betook themselves to rest again. In this manner they lived throughout the whole year, and their conversation, if it did not turn on eating, had always some childish trick or knavery for its subject. . . .

. . . they spoke of the course taken by a deer that had escaped them at nightfall with an arrow in his side, and which they intended to pursue the next morning, but they never speculated on the course of the sun and the other heavenly bodies; they talked about their pitahayas, even long before they were ripe, yet it never occurred to them to think of the Creator of the pitahayas and other productions around them.

. . . .

CHAPTER III—OF THEIR FOOD AND THE MANNER OF PREPARING IT

Notwithstanding the barrenness of the country, a Californian hardly ever dies of hunger, except, perhaps, now and then an individual that falls sick in the wilderness and at a great distance from the mission, for those who are in good health trouble themselves very little about such patients, even if these should happen to be their husbands, wives, or other relations; and a little child that has lost its mother or both parents is also occasionally in danger of starving to death, because in some instances no one will take charge of it, the father being sometimes inhuman enough to abandon his offspring to its fate.

The food of the Californians, as will be seen, is certainly of a mean quality, yet it keeps them in a healthy condition, and they become strong and grow old in spite of their poor diet. The only period of the year during which the Californians can satisfy their appetite without restraint is the season of the pitahayas, which ripen in the middle of June and abound for more than eight weeks. The gathering of this fruit may be considered as the harvest of the native inhabitants. They can eat as much of it as they please, and with some this food agrees so well that they become corpulent during that period; and for this reason I was sometimes unable to recognize at first sight individuals, otherwise perfectly familiar to me, who visited me after having fed for three or four weeks on these pitahayas. They do not, however, preserve them, and when the season is over they are put again on short rations. Among the roots eaten by the Californians may be mentioned the yuka, which . . . is not very abundant . . . the Californians . . . roast the yukas in a fire like potatoes. Another root eaten by the natives is that of the aloë plant, of which there are many kinds in this country. Those species of this vegetable, however, which afford nourishment—for not all of them are edible—do not grow as plentifully as the Californians might wish, and very seldom in the neighborhood of water; the preparations, moreover, which are necessary to render this plant eatable, require much time and labor. . . . I saw the natives also frequently eat the roots of the common reed, just as they were taken out of the water. Certain seeds, some of them not larger than those of the mustard, and different sorts in pods that grow on shrubs and little trees, and of which there are, according to Father Piccolo, more than sixteen kinds, are likewise diligently sought; yet they furnish only a small quantity of grain, and all that a person can collect with much toil during a whole year may scarcely amount to twelve bushels.

It can be said that the Californians eat, without exception, all animals they can obtain. Besides the different kinds of larger indigenous quadrupeds and birds already mentioned, they live now-a-days on dogs and cats; horses, asses and mules; . . . on owls, mice and rats; lizards and snakes; bats, grasshoppers and crickets; a kind of green caterpillar without hair, about a finger long, and an abominable white worm of the length and thickness of the thumb, which they find occasionally in old rotten wood, and consider as a particular delicacy.

[*Insect larvae are commonly eaten by all very primitive peoples living in hot or temperate areas. Among the lower primates also they form an important food item. Explorers who have eaten them say that they have an excellent taste and are high in fat content.*]

The chase of game, such as deer and rabbits, furnishes only a small portion of a Californian's provisions. Supposing that for a hundred families three hundred deer are killed in the course of a year, which is a very favorable estimate, they would supply each family only with three meals in three hundred and sixty-five days, and thus relieve but in a very small degree the hunger and the poverty of these people. The hunting for snakes, lizards, mice and field-rats, which they practice with great diligence, is by far more profitable and supplies them with a much greater quantity of articles for consumption. Snakes, especially, are a favorite sort of small game, and thousands of them find annually their way into the stomachs of the Californians.

In catching fish, particularly in the Pacific, which is much richer in that respect than the gulf of California, the natives use neither nets nor hooks, but a kind of lance,—that is, a long, slender, pointed piece of hard wood, which they handle very dexterously in spearing and killing their prey. Sea-turtles are caught in the same manner.

I have now mentioned the different articles forming the ordinary food of the Californians; but, besides these, they reject nothing that their teeth can chew or their stomachs are capable of digesting, however tasteless or unclean and disgusting it may be. Thus they will eat the leaves of the Indian fig-tree, the tender shoots of certain shrubs, tanned or untanned leather; old straps of raw hide with which a fence was tied together for years . . . the bones of poultry, sheep, goats and calves; putrid meat or fish swarming with worms, damaged wheat or Indian corn, and many other things of that sort which may serve to appease the hunger they are almost constantly suffering. . . . For this reason no one took the trouble to clean the wheat or maize, which was cooked for them in a large kettle, of the black worms and little bugs, even if the numbers of these vermin had been equal to that of the grains. By a daily distribution of about 150 bushels of bran, (which they are in the habit of eating without any preparation,) I could have induced all my parishioners to remain permanently in the mission, excepting during the time when the pitahayas are gathered.

I saw one day a blind man, seventy years of age, who was busily engaged in pounding between two stones an old shoe made of raw deer-skin, and whenever he had detached a piece, he transferred it promptly to his mouth and swallowed it; and yet this man had a daughter and grown grand-children. As soon as any of the cattle are killed and the hide is spread out on the ground to dry, half a dozen boys or men will instantly rush upon it and commence to work with knives, flints, and their teeth, tearing and scratching off pieces, which they eat immediately, till the hide is full of holes or scattered in all directions. . . .

[*It is doubtful if the senile blind man was as old as the reverend father believed. Human beings age rapidly under such conditions once they have passed their prime. Under pre-mission conditions it is doubtful that he would have lived as long as he did.*]

I must here ask permission of the kind reader to mention something of an exceedingly disgusting and almost inhuman nature, the like of which probably never has been recorded of any people in the world, but which demonstrates better than anything else the whole extent of the poverty, uncleanness and voracity of these wretched beings. In describing the pitahayas, I have already stated that they contain a great many small seeds resembling grains of powder. . . . these seeds are not consumed in the stomach, but pass off in an undigested state, and in order to save them the natives collect, during the season of the pitahayas, that which is discharged from the human body, separate the seeds from it, and roast, grind and eat them, making merry over their loathsome meals, which the Spaniards therefore call the second harvest of the Californians. . . . I must say in their favor that they have always abstained from human flesh. . . .

They have no other drink but . . . water. . . . When a Californian encounters, during his wanderings, a pond or pool, and feels a desire to quench his thirst, he lies flat on the ground and applies his mouth directly to the water. . . .

. . . They do not cook, boil, or roast like people in civilized countries, because they are neither acquainted with these methods, nor possessed of vessels and utensils to employ for such purposes; and, besides, their patience would be taxed beyond endurance, if they had to wait till a piece of meat is well cooked or thoroughly roasted. Their whole process simply consists in burning, singeing, or roasting in an open fire all such victuals as are not eaten in a raw state. Without any formalities the piece of meat, the fish, bird, snake, field-mouse, bat, or whatever it may be, is thrown into the flames, or on the glowing embers, and left there to smoke and to sweat for about a quarter of an hour; after which the article is withdrawn, in most cases only burned or charred on the outside, but still raw and bloody within. As soon as it has become sufficiently cool, they shake it a little in order to remove the adhering dust or sand, and eat it with great relish. Yet I must add here, that they do not previously take the trouble to skin the mice or disembowel the rats, nor deem it necessary to clean the half-emptied entrails and maws of larger animals, which they have to cut in pieces before they can roast them. Seeds, kernels, grasshoppers, green caterpillars, the white worms already mentioned, and similar things that would be lost, on account of their smallness, in the embers and flames of an open fire, are parched on hot coals, which they constantly throw up and shake in a turtle-shell, or a kind of frying-pan woven out of a certain plant. What they have parched or roasted in this manner is ground to powder between two stones, and eaten in a dry state. Bones are treated in like manner.

They eat everything unsalted, though they might obtain plenty of salt; but since they cannot dine every day on roast meat and constantly change their quarters, they would find it too cumbersome to carry always a supply of salt with them.

The preparation of the aloë, also called *mescale* or *maguey* by the Spaniards, requires more time and labor. The roots, after being properly separated from the plants, are roasted for some hours in a strong fire, and then buried, twelve or twenty together, in the ground, and well covered with hot stones, hot ashes, and earth. In this state they have to remain for twelve or fourteen hours, and when dug out again they are of a fine yellow color, and perfectly tender, making a very palatable dish. . . .

[*The Californians had no vessels and could not boil their food; simple roasting on an open fire is the usual cooking technique employed by hunters and gatherers on this level throughout the world. Note that the Californians knew how to parch insects in a container by tossing them up and down with coals. Also that they ground up the dried remains of food. The only things that kept them from food preservation and storage were the scarcity of food and the necessity of moving about every few days.*]

To light a fire the Californians make no use of steel and flint, but obtain it by the friction of two pieces of wood. One of them is cylindrical, and pointed on one end, which fits into a round cavity in the other, and by turning the cylindrical piece with great rapidity between their hands, like a twirling stick, they succeed in igniting the lower piece, if they continue the process for a sufficient length of time.

The Californians have no fixed time for any sort of business, and eat, consequently, whenever they have anything, or feel inclined to do so, which is nearly always the case. I never asked one of them whether he was hungry, who failed to answer in the affirmative, even if his appearance indicated the contrary. A meal in the middle of the day is the least in use among them, because they all set out early in the morning for their foraging expeditions, and return only in the evening to the place from which they started, if they do not choose some other locality for their night quarters. The day being thus spent in running about and searching for food, they have no time left for preparing a dinner at noon. They start always empty-handed; for, if perchance something remains from their evening repasts, they certainly eat it during the night in waking moments, or on the following morning before leaving. The Californians can endure hunger easier and much longer than other people; whereas they will eat enormously if a chance is given. I often tried to buy a piece of venison from them when the skin had but lately been stripped off the deer, but regularly received the answer that nothing was left; and I knew well enough that the hunter who killed the animal needed no assistance to finish it. Twenty-four pounds of meat in twenty-four hours is not deemed an extraordinary ration for a single person, and to see anything eatable before him is a temptation for a Californian which he cannot resist; and not to make away with it before night would be a victory he is very seldom capable of gaining over himself. . . .

[*The same voracity has been noted for the Bushmen of South Africa. In a land of want and uncertainty, it is a survival mechanism.*]

A priest who had lived more than thirty years in California, and whose veracity was beyond any doubt, assured me repeatedly that he had known a Californian who one day ate seventeen watermelons at one sitting; and another native who, after having received from a soldier six pounds of unclarified sugar as pay for a certain debt, sat down and munched one piece after another till the six pounds had disappeared. He paid, however, dearly for his gluttony, for he died in consequence of it; while the melon-eater was only saved by taking a certain physic which counteracted the bad effects of his greediness. I was called myself one evening in great haste to three or four persons, who pretended to be dying, and wanted to confess. These people belonged to a band of about sixty souls, (women and children included,) to whom I had given, early in the morning, three bullocks in compensation for some labor. When I arrived at the place where they lay encamped, I learned that their malady consisted merely in belly-ache and vomiting; and, recognizing at once the cause of their disorder, I reprimanded them severely for their voracity, and went home again.

CHAPTER IV—OF THEIR MARRIAGES AND THE EDUCATION OF THEIR CHILDREN

As soon as the young Californian finds a partner, the marriage follows immediately afterwards; and the girls go sometimes so far as to demand impetuously a husband from the missionary, even before they are twelve years old, which is their legitimate age for marrying. In all the missions, however, only one excepted, the number of men was considerably greater than that of the females.

Matrimonial engagements are concluded without much forethought or scruple, and little attention is paid to the morals or qualities of the parties. . . . It happens very often that near relations want to join in wedlock. . . .

They do not seem to marry exactly for the same reasons that induce civilized people to enter into that state; they simply want to have a partner, and the husband, besides, a servant whom he can command, although his authority in that respect is rather limited, for the women are somewhat independent, and not much inclined to obey their lords. Although they are now duly married according to the rites of the Catholic church, nothing is done on their part to solemnize the act; none of the parents or other relations and friends are present, and no wedding feast is served up, unless the missionary, instead of receiving his

marriage fees . . . presents them with a piece of meat, or a quantity of Indian corn. . . . As soon as the ceremony is over, the new married couple start off in different directions in search of food, just as if they were not more to each other to-day than they were yesterday; and in the same manner they act in future, providing separately for their support, sometimes without living together for weeks, and without knowing anything of their partner's abiding place.

Before they were baptized each man took as many wives as he liked, and if there were several sisters in a family he married them all together. The son-in-law was not allowed, for some time, to look into the face of his mother-in-law or his wife's next female relations, but had to step aside, or to hide himself, when these women were present. Yet they did not pay much attention to consanguinity, and only a few years since one of them counted his own daughter (as he believed) among the number of his wives. They met without any formalities, and their vocabulary did not even contain the words "to marry," which is expressed at the present day in the Waïcuri language by the paraphrase *tikére undiri* —that is, "to bring the arms or hands together." They had, and still use, a substitute for the word "husband," but the etymological meaning of that expression implies an intercourse with women in general.

They lived, in fact, before the establishment of the missions in their country, in utter licentiousness, and adultery was daily committed by every one without shame and without any fear, the feeling of jealousy being unknown to them. Neighboring tribes visited each other very often only for the purpose of spending some days in open debauchery, and during such times a general prostitution prevailed. . . .

[*We find here a number of customs common throughout the world. Marriage between one man and several sisters is called the sororate. The mother-in-law tabu, by which the son-in-law avoids his wife's mother, is an automatic mechanism to preserve equilibrium, since it avoids sources of potential conflict. The marriage of a man with his own, or even classificatory, daughter, is unusual anywhere. If true it can only reflect the extreme isolation in which these people lived. The "general prostitution" of which Father Baegert speaks is the general sexual license which prevails at ceremonial meetings of simply organized, primitive peoples nearly everywhere. It serves two purposes: to intensify the interaction at meetings, which are very infrequent; to provide the maximum chance for reproduction and hence group survival among people living under the threat of starvation.*]

. . . I have already spoken of the scanty population of this country. It is certain that many of their women are barren, and that a great number of them bear not more than one child. Only a few out of one or two hundred bring forth eight or ten times, and if such is really the case, it happens very seldom that one or two of the children arrive at a mature age. I baptized, in succession, seven children of a young woman, yet I had to bury them all before one of them had reached its third year, and when I was about to leave the country I recommended to the woman to dig a grave for the eighth child, with which she was pregnant at the time. The unmarried people of both sexes and the children generally make a smaller group than the married and widowed.

The Californian women lie in without difficulty, and without needing any assistance. If the child is born at some distance from the mission they carry it thither themselves on the same day, in order to have it baptized, not minding a walk of two or more leagues. Yet, that many infants die among them is not surprising; on the contrary, it would be a wonder if a great number remained alive. For, when the poor child first sees the light of day, there is no other cradle provided for it but the hard soil, or the still harder shell of a turtle, in which the mother places it, without much covering, and drags it about wherever she goes. And in order to be unencumbered, and enabled to use her limbs with greater freedom while running in the fields, she will leave it sometimes in charge of some old woman, and thus deprive the poor creature for ten or more hours of its natural nourishment. As soon as the child is a few months old the mother places it, perfectly naked, astraddle on her shoulders, its legs hanging down on both sides in front, and it has consequently to learn how to ride before it can stand on its feet. In this guise the mother roves about all day, exposing her helpless charge to the hot rays of the sun and the chilly winds that sweep over the inhospitable country. The food of the child, till it cuts its teeth, consists only in the milk of the mother, and if that is wanting or insufficient, there is rarely another woman to be found that would be willing, or, perhaps, in the proper condition, to take pity on the poor starving being. I cannot say that the Californian women are too fond of their children, and some of them may even consider the loss of one as a relief from a burden, especially if they have already some small children. I did not see many Californian mothers who caressed their children much while they lived, or tore their hair when they died, although a kind of dry weeping is not wanting on such occasions. The father is still more insensible, and does not even look at his (or at least his wife's) child as long as it is small and helpless.

Nothing causes the Californians less trouble and care than the education of their children, which is merely confined to a short period, and ceases as soon as the latter are capable of making a living for themselves—that is, to catch mice and to kill snakes. If the young Californians have once acquired sufficient skill and strength to follow these pursuits, it is all the same to them whether they have parents or not. Nothing is done by these in the way of admonition or instruction. . . . The children do what they please, without fearing reprimand or punishment, however disorderly and wicked their conduct may be . . . when their children are now and then slightly chastised for gross misdemeanor by order of the missionary . . . the parents take great offence and become enraged, especially the mothers, who will scream like furies, tear out the hair, beat their naked breasts with a stone, and lacerate their heads with a piece of wood or bone till the blood flows, as I have frequently witnessed on occasions.

The consequence is, that the children follow their own inclinations without any restraint, and imitate all the bad habits and practices of their equals, or still older persons, without the slightest apprehension of being blamed by their fathers and mothers, even if these should happen to detect them in the act of committing the most disgraceful deeds. The young Californians who live in the missions commence roaming about as soon as mass is over, and those that spend their time in the fields go wherever, and with whomsoever, they please, not seeing for many days the faces of their parents, who, in their turn, do not manifest the slightest concern about their children, nor make any inquiries after them. . . .

[Father Baegert was using this exposition of methods of child training among the Indians in order to refute the theories of Jean Jacques Rousseau, much in vogue at the time. Looking at it from a more modern point of view, we see that the child is inhibited as little as possible, and taught only how to survive in a most rigorous environment. Under the circumstances no other teaching could have served him as well. Mass education in the form of puberty ceremonies was probably rarely possible owing to the difficulty of bringing enough persons together for a long enough time.]

CHAPTER VII—THEIR TREATMENT OF THE SICK.—FUNERAL CUSTOMS

With all their poor diet and hardships, the Californians are seldom sick. They are in general strong, hardy, and much healthier than the many thousands who live daily in abundance and on the choicest fare that the skill of Parisian cooks can prepare. It is very probable that most Californians would attain a considerable age, after having safely passed through the dangers of their childhood; but they are immoderate in eating, running, bathing, and other matters, and thus doubtless shorten their existence. Excepting consumption and that disease which was brought from America to Spain and Naples, and from thence spread over various countries, they are but little subject to the disorders common in Europe; podagra, apoplexy, dropsy, cold and petechial fevers being almost unknown among them. There is no word in their language to express sickness in general or any particular disease. "To be sick," they signify by the phrase *atemba-tie,* which means "to lie down on the ground," though all those in good health may be seen in that position the whole day, if they are not searching for food or otherwise engaged. . . .

For the small-pox the Californians are, like other Americans, indebted to Europeans, and this disease assumes a most pestilential character among them. A piece of cloth which a Spaniard, just recovered from the smallpox, had given to a Californian communicated, in the year 1763, the disease to a small mission, and in three months more than a hundred individuals died. . . .

[*This passage dramatically illustrates the fate of many non-European peoples at first contact with European diseases. Probably the most stringent selective factor in human survival is the ability of the organism to resist disease.*]

The patience of the Californians in sickness is really admirable. Hardly a sigh is heaved by those who lie on the bare ground in the most pitiable condition and racked with pain. They look without dread upon their ulcers and wounds, and submit to burning and cutting, or make incisions in their own flesh for extracting thorns and splinters, with as much indifference as though the operation were performed on somebody else. It is, however, an indication of approaching death when they lose their appetite.

Their medical art is very limited, consisting almost exclusively, whatever the character of the disease may be, in the practice of binding, when feasible, a cord or coarse rope tightly around the affected part of the body. Sometimes they make use of a kind of bleeding by cutting with a sharp stone a few small openings in the inflamed part, in order to draw blood and thus relieve the patient. Though every year a number of Californians die by the bite of the rattlesnake, their only

remedy against such accidents consists in tightly binding the injured member a little above the wound towards the heart; but if the part wounded by the reptile is a finger or a hand, they simply cut it off, and I knew several who had performed this cure on themselves or on individuals of their families. Now-a-days they beg in nearly all cases of disease for tallow to rub the affected part, and also for Spanish snuff which they use against headache and sore eyes. Excepting the remedies just mentioned, they have no appliances whatever against ulcers, wounds, or other external injuries, and far less against internal disorders. . . .

They do not, however, content themselves with these natural remedies, but have also recourse to supernatural means, which certainly never brought about a recovery. There are many impostors among them, pretending to possess the power of curing diseases, and the ignorant Indians have so much faith in their art that they send for one or more of these scoundrels whenever they are indisposed. In treating a sick person, these jugglers employ a small tube, which they use for sucking or blowing the patient for a while, making, also, various grimaces and muttering something which they do not understand themselves, until, finally, after much hard breathing and panting, they show the patient a flint, or some other object previously hidden about their persons, pretending to have at last removed the real cause of the disorder. Twelve of these liars received one day, by my orders, the punishment they deserved. . . .

[*Here we see once more the shaman, universal among such peoples. Father Baegert naturally disliked them, for they were his competitors.*]

It is to be feared that some of those who are seized with illness far from the mission, and not carried thither, are buried alive, especially old people, and such as have few relations, for they are in the habit of digging the grave two or three days before the patient breathes his last. It seems tedious to them to spend much time near an old, dying person that was long ago a burden to them and looked upon them with indifference. A person of my acquaintance restored a girl to life that was already bound up in a deer-skin, according to their custom, and ready for burial, by administering to her a good dose of chocolate. She lived many years afterwards. On their way to the mission, some natives broke the neck of a blind, sick, old woman in order to be spared the trouble of carrying her a few miles further. Another patient, being much annoyed by gnats, which no one felt inclined to keep off from him, was covered up in such a manner that he died of suffocation. In transporting a patient from one place to another, they bind him on a rude litter, made of crooked pieces of wood, which would constitute a perfect rack for any but Indian bones, the carriers being in the habit of running with their charge.

. . . the Californians are . . . quiet during their sickness, and die off . . . calmly. . . . As soon as a person has given up the ghost, a terrible howling is raised by the women that are present, and by those to whom the news is communicated, yet no one sheds tears, excepting, perhaps, the nearest relations, and the whole proceeding is a mere ceremony. . . .

[*In fact, a rite of passage, of the simplest possible kind.*]

One of them told me they had formerly broken the spine of the deceased before burying them, and had thrown them into the ditch, rolled up like a ball, believing that they would rise up again if not treated in this manner. I saw them, however, frequently putting shoes on the feet of the dead, which rather seems to indicate that they entertain the idea of a journey after death; but whenever I asked them why they observed this probably very ancient custom, they could not give me any satisfactory answer. In time of mourning, both men and women cut off their hair almost entirely, which formerly was given to their physicians or conjurers, who made them into a kind of mantle or large wig, to be worn on solemn occasions.

When a death has taken place, those who want to show the relations of the deceased their respect for the latter lie in wait for these people, and if they pass they come out from their hiding-place, almost creeping, and intonate a mournful, plaintive, *hu, hu, hu!* wounding their heads with pointed, sharp stones, until the blood flows down to their shoulders. . . .

Chapter VIII—Their Qualifications and Manners

From what I have already said of the Californians, it might be inferred that they are the most unhappy and pitiable of all the children of Adam. Yet such a supposition would be utterly wrong, and I can assure the reader that . . . they live unquestionably much happier than the civilized inhabitants of Europe. . . . Throughout the whole year nothing happens that causes a Californian trouble or vexation, nothing that renders his life cumbersome and death desirable. . . . Envy, jealousy, and slander embitter not his life, and he is not exposed to the fear of losing what he possesses, nor to the care of increasing it. . . . the Californians do not know the meaning of *meum* and *tuum,* those two ideas which, according to St. Gregory, fill the few days of our existence with bitterness and unaccountable evils.

Though the Californians seem to possess nothing, they have, nevertheless, all that they want, for they covet nothing beyond the productions of their poor, ill-favored country, and these are always within their reach. It is no wonder, then, that they always exhibit a joyful temper, and constantly indulge in merriment and laughter, showing thus their contentment, which, after all, is the real source of happiness.

The Californians know very little of arithmetic, some of them being unable to count further than *six,* while others cannot number beyond *three,* insomuch that none of them can say how many fingers he has. They do not possess anything that is worth counting, and hence their indifference. It is all the same to them whether the year has six or twelve months, and the month three or thirty days, for every day is a holiday with them. They care not whether they have one or two or twelve children, or none at all, since twelve cause them no more expense or trouble than one, and the inheritance is not lessened by a plurality of heirs. Any number beyond six they express in their language by *much.* . . .

They do not know what a year is, and, consequently, cannot say when it begins and ends. Instead of saying, therefore, "a year ago," or "during this year," the Californians who speak the Waïcuri language use the expressions, *it is already an ambía past,* or, *during this ambía,* the latter word signifying the pitahaya fruit, of which a description has been given on a previous page. A space of three years, therefore, is expressed by the term "three pitahayas;" yet they seldom make use of such phrases, because they hardly ever speak among themselves of years, but merely say, "long ago,"

or, "not long ago," being utterly indifferent whether two or twenty years have elapsed since the occurrence of a certain event. For the same reason they do not speak of months, and have not even a name for that space of time. A week, however, they call at present *ambúja,* that is, "a house," or "a place where one resides," which name they have now, *per autonomasiam,* bestowed upon the church. They are divided into bands, which alternately spend a week at the mission, where they have to attend church-service, and thus the week has become among them synonymous with the church.

[*Here is an example of culture change at work. In pre-Spanish times the Indians participated in only one repetitive event—the pitahaya harvest. This became their landmark for units of time. With the week-long visits to the church, however, they acquired a new unit. As peoples develop the need for more and more exact timing of events, they invent or take over methods of measuring time to suit their needs.*]

When the Californians visit the missionary for any purpose, they are perfectly silent at first, and when asked the cause of their visit, their first answer is *vâra,* which means "nothing." Having afterwards delivered their speech, they sit down, unasked; in doing which the women stretch out their legs, while the men cross them in the oriental fashion. The same habits they observe also in the church and elsewhere. They salute nobody, such a civility being unknown to them, and they have no word to express greeting. If something is communicated to them which they do not like, they spit out sideways and scratch the ground with their left foot to express their displeasure.

The men carry everything on their heads; the women bear loads on their backs suspended by ropes that pass around their foreheads, and in order to protect the skin from injury, they place between the forehead and the rope a piece of untanned deer-hide, which reaches considerably above the head, and resembles, from afar, a helmet, or the high head-dress worn by ladies at the present time.

The Californians have a great predilection for singing and dancing, which are always performed together; the first is called *ambéra ditì,* the latter *agénari.* Their singing is nothing but an inarticulate, unmeaning whispering, murmuring, or shouting, which every one intonates according to his own inclination, in order to express his joy. Their dances consist in a foolish, irregular gesticulating and jumping, or advancing, retreating, and walking in a circle. Yet, they take such delight in these amusements that they spend whole nights in their performance. . . . These pastimes . . . had to be rigidly interdicted, because the grossest disorders and vices were openly perpetrated by the natives during the performances. . . .

[*Father Baegert viewed the aesthetic activities of the Indians through the lenses of his time and training. It would be interesting to know how a more sympathetic observer would have described them.*]

. . . the natives are exceedingly good runners. I would gladly have yielded up to them my three horses for consumption if I had been as swift-footed as they; for, whenever I travelled, I became sooner tired with riding than they with walking. They will run twenty leagues to-day, and return to-morrow to the place from whence they started without showing much fatigue. . . . I once sent a boy of fourteen years with a letter to the neighboring mission, situated six leagues from my residence. He started at seven o'clock in the morning, and when about a league and a half distant from his place of destination, he met the missionary, to whom the letter was addressed, mounted on a good mule, and on his way to pay me a visit. The boy turned round and accompanied the missionary, with whom he arrived about noon at my mission, having walked within five hours a distance of more than nine leagues.

With boys and girls who have arrived at the age of puberty, with pregnant women, new-born children, and women in child-bed, the Californians observed, and still secretly observe, certain absurd ceremonies of an unbecoming nature, which, for this reason, cannot be described in this book. [. . . *and have thus been lost to science forever.*]

There existed always among the Californians individuals of both sexes who played the part of sorcerers or conjurers, pretending to possess the power of exorcising the devil, whom they never saw; of curing diseases, which they never healed; and of producing pitahayas, though they could only eat them. Sometimes they went into caverns, and, changing their voices, made the people believe that they conversed with some spiritual power. They threatened also with famine and diseases, or promised to drive the small-pox and similar plagues away and to other places. When these braggarts appeared formerly in their gala apparel, they wore long mantles made of human hair, of which the missionaries burned a great number in all newly established missions. The object of the impostors was to obtain their food without the trouble of gathering it in the fields, for the silly people provided them with the best they could find, in order to keep them in good humor and to enjoy their favor. . . .

[*From this we see that the shamans wore special insignia, were given food by their clients, healed by sucking and by casting out evil spirits, controlled the weather (to produce the pitahaya cactus) and performed evil magic (by threatening with famine or disease). They were thus specialists, who performed all of the kinds of ritual needed by their clients individually and as groups.*]

It might be the proper time now to speak of the form of government and the religion of the Californians previous to their conversion to Christianity; but neither the one nor the other existed among them. They were all equals, and every one did as he pleased, without asking his neighbor or caring for his opinion, and thus all vices and misdeeds remained unpunished, excepting such cases in which the offended individual or his relations took the law into their own hands and revenged themselves on the guilty party. The different tribes represented by no means communities of rational beings, who submit to laws and regulations and obey their superiors, but resembled far more herds of wild swine, which run about according to their own liking being together today and scattered tomorrow, till they meet again by accident at some future time . . . .

I made diligent inquiries, among those with whom I lived, to ascertain whether they had any conception of God, a future life, and their own souls, but I never could discover the slightest trace of such a knowledge. . . . I often asked them whether they had never put to themselves the question who might be the creator and preserver of the sun, moon, stars, and other objects of nature, but was always sent home with a *vára,* which means "no" in their language.

[*It is doubtful that Father Baegert had fully explored the ritual beliefs of* these Indians. *The great value of his accounts lies not in this field but in his detailed description of their more overt ways of living.*]

Chapter X—Their Language

The account thus far given of the character and the habits of the Californians will, to a certain extent, enable the reader to form, in advance, an estimate of their language. A people without laws and religion, who think and speak of nothing but their food and other things which they have in common with animals, who carry on no trade, and entertain no friendly intercourse with neighboring tribes, that consist, like themselves, only of a few hundred souls and always remain within their own small district, where nothing is to be seen but thorns, rocks, game, and vermin, such a people, I say, cannot be expected to speak an elegant and rich language. A man of sixty years ran away from my mission with his son, a boy of about six years, and they spent five years alone in the Californian wilderness, when they were found and brought back to the mission. Every one can imagine how and on what subjects these two hermits may have conversed in their daily intercourse. The returned lad, who had then nearly reached his twelfth year, was hardly able to speak three words in succession, and excepting *water, wood, fire, snake, mouse,* and the like, he could name nothing, insomuch that he was called the dull and dumb Pablo, or Paul, by his own countrymen. The story of this boy may almost be applied to the whole people.

Leaving aside a great many dialects and offshoots, six entirely different languages have thus far been discovered in California, namely, the *Laymóna,* about the mission of Loreto; the *Cotshimi,* in the mission of St.

Xavier, and others towards the north; the *Utshiti* and the *Pericúa* in the south; the still unknown language spoken by the nations whom Father *Linck* visited in 1766, during his exploration of the northern part of the peninsula; and, lastly, the *Waïcuri* language, of which I am now about to treat, having learned as much of it as was necessary for conversing with the natives.

The Waïcuri language is exceedingly barbarous and rude but the great deficiency of the language consists in the total absence of a great many words, the want of which would seem to render it almost impossible for reasonable beings to converse with each other and to receive instruction in the Christian religion. For whatever is not substantial, and cannot be seen or touched or otherwise perceived by the senses, has no name in the Waicuri language. There are no nouns whatever for expressing virtues, vices, or the different dispositions of the mind, and there exist only a few adjectives of this class, namely, *merry, sad, lazy,* and *angry,* all of which merely denote such humors as can be perceived in a person's face. All terms relating to rational human and civil life, and a multitude of words for signifying other objects, are entirely wanting.

The word *living* they have neither as a noun nor as a verb, neither in a natural nor a moral sense; but only the adjective *alive. Bad, narrow, short, distant, little,* &c., they cannot express unless by adding the negation *ja* or *ra* to the words *good, wide, long, near,* and *much.* They have particular words for signifying *an old man, an old woman, a young man, a young woman,* and so forth; but the terms *old* or *young* do not exist in their language. The Waïcuri contains only four words for denoting the different colors, insomuch that the natives cannot distinguish in

their speech yellow from red, blue from green, black from brown, white from ash-colored, &c.

They cannot express the degrees of relationship, for instance, *father, mother, son, brother,* nor the parts of the human body, nor many other words, such as *word* or *speech, breath, pain, comrade,* &c., singly and without prefixing the possessive pronouns *my, thy, our,* &c. They say, therefore, *bedáre, edáre, tiáre, kepedáre,* &c., that is, *my, thy, his, our father;* and *bécue, ecue, ticue, kepécue,* that is, *my, thy, his, our mother.* So also *mapà, etapà, tapà,* that is, *my, thy, his forehead. Minamù, einamù tinamù,* that is, *my, thy, his nose; betanía, etanía, tishanía,* my, thy, his word; menembeû, enembeû, tenembeû, my thy, his pain,* &c. But no Californian who speaks the Waïcuri is able to say what the words *are, cue, apà, namù, tanía,* and *nembeû,* express, for *father, forehead, word,* or *pain* are significations which they never thought of using in a general sense, and far less has it ever entered their minds to speak, for instance, of the duties of a father, of a gloomy, a serene, a narrow or large forehead, or to make a long, a flat, or an aquiline nose the subject of their conversation.

They know nothing of metaphors, for which reason the phrase *blessed is the fruit of thy womb* in the "Hail Mary" has simply been replaced by *thy child.* On the other hand they are very ingenious in giving names to objects with which they were before unacquainted, calling, for instance, the door, *mouth;* bread, *the light;* iron, *the heavy;* wine, *bad water;* a gun, *bow;* the functionaries of the mission, *bearers of canes;* the Spanish captain, *wild* or *cruel;* oxen and cows, *deer;* horses and mules *titshénu-tshà,* that is, *child of a wise mother;* and the missionary, in speaking of or to him, *tià-pa-tù,* which means *cne who has his house in the north,* &c.

In order to converse in such a barbarous and poor language, a European has to change, as it were, his whole nature and to become almost a Californian himself. . . .

[*Father Baegert saw clearly the intimate relation between a language and the activities of the people who speak it. A language fits its culture as the skin fits a snake. A language is a mirror image of a culture. You will also notice how many languages there were among so few people—the diversity of languages being a function of isolation, and hence of infrequent interaction between the inhabitants of different segments of the landscape.*

The story of the old man and the boy living together in isolation for five years, between the fifth and eleventh years of the boy's life, is of value to those interested in learning and "socialization." Children normally learn to speak from other children more than from their parents. That is why the children of immigrants, who go to American schools, seldom speak with their parents' foreign accents.]

3

The Canoe Indians of Tierra del Fuego

I N A.D. 1520 Ferdinand Magellan discovered the passage that bears his name, and entered the Pacific Ocean. Having run the gauntlet around the most southerly continental point of land in the world, he found it comparatively easy sailing the rest of the way around the globe. To the south and east of the Straits of Magellan lies one large island, Tierra del Fuego, and a dependent archipelago. The southernmost of the smaller islands bears the name Cape Horn.

In Richard Dana's *Two Years Before the Mast,* you can read about the perils of rounding this landmark. For further details, Charles Darwin's *Voyage of the Beagle* takes you in between the islands and up the length of that cavernous passage, Beagle Channel. In the *Voyage of the Beagle* you can see through Darwin's keen and practiced eyes how the half-naked Canoe Indians of this chilly country looked in 1832, and you can follow the tale of Jemmy Button and Fuegia Basket, the Indians whom Captain Fitzroy had taken to England on an earlier voyage and whom he was now returning.

Charles Darwin spent only a few weeks in Fuegian waters. He did not have a chance to learn the language of the Indians or to study their culture at any length. This task was left to a Scottish missionary, the Reverend Thomas Bridges, who arrived at Ushuaia on Beagle Channel in 1863, and spent the rest of a long and vigorous life caring for the needs of the Indians, as diseases introduced by white men rapidly drove them near extinction. No man ever knew as much about the Indians of the southern Fuegian shores before their decimation as Thomas Bridges, and no man ever will. Dr. Samuel K. Lothrop, who visited Tierra del Fuego and studied the surviving Indians, in 1926, compiled and edited the writings of the Reverend Thomas Bridges which follow, and which are being published here, in their present form, for the first time.

[Preface by Samuel K. Lothrop]

The following account of Tierra del Fuego, by the late Rev. T. Bridges, has been collected from a number of sources; old letters, private or to the South American Missionary magazine, notes for lectures, short articles published at various times, some in English and some in Spanish, and extracts from a diary kept for a number of years, but unfortunately with no great regularity.

It will be understood that in these original fragments there was necessarily a good deal of repetition, so that to publish them entire would have been unsatisfactory. We have therefore tried to arrange them in an order as

83

continuous as possible, whilst keeping, save in a few cases, to the original wording; and inserting fragments, strictly verbatim, from the diary where these seem to have a bearing on the subject. The footnotes have been added where it was thought they might elucidate some point.

. . . .

[The following is Bridges' account.]

Tierra del Fuego, meaning Land of Fire or Fireland, is an extensive archipelago, measuring approximately three hundred and forty miles from Cape Pillar in the West to Cape San Diego in the East, and two hundred and ten miles from Cape Horn in the South to Point Anegada in the North, and consisting of many large islands and an infinite number of small ones.

For the greater part, the country is exceedingly mountainous, and densely covered with forest almost to the limit of perpetual snow. The land rises very abruptly, the valleys between the hills are rather gorges than valleys, being long, narrow and deep. There are numerous deep lakes, but these are generally without fish. The sea, even close to the beach, is also very deep, so that vessels have to anchor closer in shore than is at all comfortable. In parts of the Beagle Channel, not more than two miles across, the water is sixty fathoms.

The South and West, like all mountainous coasts, are much broken up by the sea, very much more so than is shown in the Charts, into numberless peninsulas and islands, presenting an endless diversity of sea surface, in some parts much exposed, in others very sheltered waters surrounded by steep, often precipitous coasts, where the natives (Yahgan and Alaculoof) follow their daily life of fishing and travelling in their canoes.

The surface of the land is as diversified as that of the sea. In one extensive region it forms a continuation of the Southern Patagonian Pampa, in an intermediate region being something between pampa and wooded mountains; in the third forming a continuous chain of bold and closely packed mountains, attaining in the peaks of Sarmiento and Darwin a height of nearly seven thousand feet.[1] In these latter parts the glaciers extend in many places from the upper valleys to the sea, breaking off in huge blocks as they are projected into it by the moving mass behind, and the climate, besides being windy, is very wet.

The name of the archipelago was, I think, derived, not from any volcanic fire but from the many fires seen by its early visitors, and made by the natives. Wherever the two tribes of canoe Indians go, whether into the woods to gather fuel and fungus, or on the water fishing, they almost invariably take fire with them; so that when sailing by night in these waters you see fires on all sides, from the wigwams ashore and the canoes afloat.

Then again the natives were given to setting fire to the camps and woods in Spring and Summer, and in very dry weather extensive areas were burnt, thus tracts of originally forest land are covered with grass. By camp fires the native obtained better growth of berries, as well as clearing the country of thorn bushes. Also it is usual when a person dies to burn his wigwam, setting fire to the grass and bushes of the neighborhood. Thus early visitors may well have called the country Fireland

[1] Or more according to some of the charts, which differ considerably.

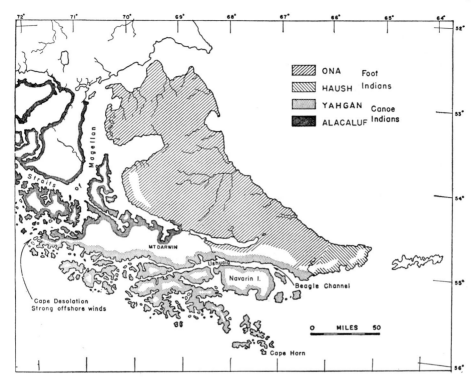

though there is not, and I believe has not been for ages, any volcanic activity.

In Picton Island and the South Coast of Onisin opposite it, much pumice stone is found, which is of great use to the natives for smoothing their arrows.

In some parts iron pyrites is plentiful, and the natives have always been in the habit of using it to obtain fire. They strike two pieces together and receive the sparks either into some dry down of sea birds, or the dry powder of the puff ball. (Extract of diary: Mercury Sound. Feb. 22nd. 1883. Went in quest of the chief source of supply to all Fireland of firestone. We anchored at 1 P.M. in a snug harbour and by our good guide were conducted to the spot. Here we found traces of native labour for centuries past, in large deposits of refuse they had chipped off

at various times. There were great rounded masses of iron pyrites, from which with immense labour they obtain supplies. I am told there is none anywhere else in Alaculoof or Yahgaland. Went up to the head of this water, which is separated from Cockburn Channel by a very narrow isthmus.)

Transparent flints I have nowhere seen, nor any kind of chalk. Blue, Reddish, Yellow and White clays are found abundantly.

[*The use of flint and iron pyrites in making fire alternates with that of the fire stick described earlier. You will note that some of the materials used by the Fuegians came from special places, from which they were distributed throughout the region. The clays of course were used for body painting and decorating ceremonial objects.*]

CLIMATE

In a country so large and of so diversified a surface there are naturally considerable differences of climate, vegetation and animal life. In the excessively humid, cloudy country of Western Fireland frost is almost unknown.[2] The Central and Eastern parts, where the sky is comparatively clear, have four months of sharp frost and in any month one may have frost and snow.[3]

The North and Eastern coasts of Onisin have a windy, sunny climate, with far greater extremes of heat and cold in the Southern and Western parts. The lack of Summer heat is the great fault of the Fuegian climate rather than the winter cold, which I have not known at Ushuaia to be lower than + 12 Fahr. The highest Summer temperature I have observed at Ushuaia has been + 70 Fahr.; the mean Summer temperature for four years has been only 50.50 while the mean winter temperature for the same time was 34.06. The climate is most uncertain, one year differing greatly from another and the daily changes being very great. I speak with certainty on these points, having now had experience of 16 years residence.

(Extract from diary: Ushuaia June 13th. 1884.

In the Southern part of the island wild strawberries of large size and shaped as a raspberry thrive; whilst small black currants, two dwarf arbutus—gush and shanamaim—the sebisa or diddy, two sorts of berberis and in a few parts the Malvina complete the list of edible berries. There is a much larger kind of holly leaved berberis with orange coloured flowers, a very handsome shrub, but its berries, though plentiful, are not good for food.[4]

Among the edible plants used by the natives are celery, two cresses, sea pink and auwunim, a plant with thick, whitish roots, and dandelions. The stems of tussac grass are also used as food in localities where it grows. The seed of one species of grass is also used by the natives as an article of food.

There are also many kinds of tree fungi eaten by the natives; firstly a curiously shaped ahman, yel-lush and koushuf, only found on living or recently dead trees. A variety of ground fungi are also found, but the natives eat none of them. There are a number of other tree fungi, or rather globular parasites, called by the Yahgans amaim.[5] There are ten or more varieties, each produced by one or other of the three kinds of beech tree. These various parasites or fungi ripen at different seasons, according to their kind. They appear to be the fruit of a woody plant which grows round the trunks and branches of trees in large and ever increasing masses. These consist of many plants, having their roots in the substance of the trees. Their surface is very rough and covered with bark, having many eyes or pits, out of which year by year grow the special fruit each kind produces. This woody excrescence does not damage the trees on which it grows; it is very hard and not of a uniform texture when sawn. Some masses of it are found of fully

---

[2] The inhabitants of these parts were accustomed to make, in the centre of their wigwams, a hole from which they would from time to time bail the water with their bark cups, thus keeping the wigwam more or less drained.

[3] On the east coast, near Rio Grande, we have several times between 1908 and 1930 skated in April and once or twice in October.

[4] It is curious that the Yahgans never ate the berry of the edible berberis until they learned from white people to do so, although to the ordinary taste they are more palatable than gush or shanamaim.

[5] The same word they use for berries.

eighty pounds weight, and the whole band is frequently seen covered with these fruits so closely packed as to press each other almost flat. At first they are mere whitish specks but they grow rapidly, some kinds attaining the size of Algerian oranges. With maturity they soften, the skin opens, and they become pitted. These pits of a bright orange colour are full of a gluey juice, in which I believe are found the seeds. The Summer kinds, called by the Yahgans oachij,[6] suchipu and meama, are often dried, smoked and strung for future use.[7] The Autumn and Winter kinds are asuf, c'turn, ushchinij, keem, uiacu and ushuim. All these are identical in composition, though varying in flavour and appearance. They are of an india-rubberish substance which, by reason of its good quality and abundance, may in years to come prove of great commercial value. When boiled for some hours they soften, but refuse to be dissolved, parting with very little of their substance. In this state, eaten with sugar and spice, they are wholesome and enjoyable; the natives always eat them raw. These varieties appear at midsummer, attain their full size by winter, remain frozen as hard as stone on the trees until spring when they ripen and, getting infected with maggots, fall, turn black and decay. The Summer kind called oachij is specially plentiful and literally covers the ground when it falls. With its yellow balls distributed through the branches and twigs of the evergreen beech which alone produces this variety it is a worthy and striking ornament of the Fuegian forest; three months suffice to bring it to perfection. (Extract from S.A.M.S. Mag. 1873

[6] In this writing the *j* in Indian words should be pronounced as in Spanish, or the *ch* in "loch."

[7] These three kinds when ripe have a very sweet juice, quite pleasant to the taste.

page 120: This evening paid George— a Yahgan—a visit. . . . George had been out all day for oachij. He had good success and brought home a large bag full. As usual here he had made a generous distribution among friends and neighbours.

An immense fire was burning, immediately behind which were some twenty lots of stacked oachij, put there to dry and to kill the maggots. This fungus is very generally thus cured and eaten some months after it is out of season. . . . I before leaving proposed prayer, when in came four men. One of these, Tispinges, had this afternoon killed a very large fur seal and supplied his friends and neighbours with a large piece of its flesh. I congratulated him on his success, which was very timely, for lately supplies of food have been scarce. We then praised the Giver of all Good and sang "Son of My Soul.")

In Fireland the forests, which extend for many long miles in unbroken length and depth, contain only five sorts of trees, viz. the evergreen beech (nothofagus-betuloides), the deciduous beech (nothofagus pamilio), and the stronger scented deciduous beech (nothofagus antarctica), the winter's bark (or drimys), and the cypress or yew.

Besides these there are tree-like bushes of mugoo (or embrothrium) whose lovely scarlet flowers appear twice a year, the leush or leña dura, valuable as food for cattle during winter, when it flowers, seeds, and is in full leaf; the holly leaved berberis before mentioned and various others.

The yew is found only in the Western Andean district where also one sees thickets of fuchsia almost impenetrable and of considerable height, which flower profusely. In these parts also grows the phelesia, a beautiful flowering shrub. These are not found in the dryer and Eastern districts. The wild currant grows everywhere and reaches a good height.

(Extract from diary: Sept. 27th. 1885. Friday night we spent at Fortescue Bay. Here landed in various places, and went into Port Gallant. Came across a native encampment on Wigwam Island, literally embowered in giant fuchsia and currant bushes, winter's bark and leña dura. It is a beautiful position and wonderfully sheltered.

The natives always select prominent places to dwell in, whence they can at once pop out into the open waters.

Wednesday Sept. 30th. The veronica grows on New and Lennox Islands as woods, and as massive bushes on other ocean girt islands; for it prospers best where it can receive the spray of the sea waves. . . . its wood is useless save as fuel. The drimys or ushcuta flowers in January and February, and is at this season singularly beautiful. It produces in great abundance its fruit or seeds, very piquant and pleasant smelling. Its soft white bark is, like the whole tree, very peppery; and this tree is singularly free from false growths and the attacks of insects, to all of which the beeches are very liable. Its wood is very sappy and heavy, but dries light and brittle; it is of little value as wood, but its saplings when split serve the Yahgans for lining their canoes, and its aromatic wood for fuel. Neither it nor the evergreen beech grow on the Northern side of Onisin.

From the yew the natives make excellent lances, but with an immense amount of labour. It tapers rapidly and is hard and very knotty, but tough and durable and of straight growth, it is also very heavy. The natives prefer the wood of the shushchi or evergreen beech for lances, as it is heavy and easily worked. Also the bark of the same is exclusively used for canoes and water buckets. They prefer the wood

of the c'turn for bows, chelia, or holly leafed berberis for arrows, and the leña dura for clubs; it is very heavy and takes a high polish like ivory. The bark of this tree they used in preference for water cups.

ZOOLOGY

The animal life of the country comprises: the guanaco, found only in Onisin and Navarin Islands, the ctenomys, or coruro, found only in the North and East, eaten by the Ona; foxes of large size.[8] Dogs are never eaten, nor are their skins used; to eat a dog would be almost as bad as cannibalism, a custom which does not exist among the Indians of Tierra del Fuego. There is also a small bat, loathed by the natives on account of its compound nature.[9]

The land nutria is found in Western Tierra del Fuego and besides this there are two kinds of water otter and four of seals, four classes of porpoises and whales of several kinds, all much valued as food by the natives. Seals and otters supply them with good furs, and oil which they eat with berries, fungus, and salad; from whales and porpoises they procure oil and sinew, as well as meat. The sinew they convert into bowstrings, fishlines, cord for all purposes and nets (these made with the same knot used in Europe). The skins of the hair seal the Ona use for making quivers, the Yahgans and Alaculoof as hut coverings, mats to sleep on and thong for all uses. When the Yahgans will cut up a hide into thong they first deprive it of its hair. This they do in the following manner; they spread it on the floor of the wigwam hair side up, then cover it with grass and broken moss and thoroughly wet it with urine. They then sit and sit on it to cause

[8] The Ona sometimes eat these, the Yahgans only when much pressed by hunger.

[9] And feared also by the Ona as a bringer of bad luck.

fermentation, after which they can easily wipe and scrape off the hair.[10] Formerly their only cutting instruments were shells and stones and it must have been a lengthy task to flay and cut up an animal, and convert its hide into thongs. The shell of the mussel (mytel chilensis) makes a very good knife and chisel, making and keeping a very keen edge; with it they used to crop their hair in mourning, an unpleasant operation.

The birds number at least 90 varieties, among which are four kinds of geese, five of duck, five of widgeon and teal, two swans, three snipe, a woodpecker, a woodcock, a partridge, the banduria or ibis, a lovely kingfisher, the humming bird, and a number of others. The condor is sometimes seen, and there are two large hawks or rather eagles, seven other hawks, four owls, and four vultures.

The sea and beach birds are chiefly the following: mollymauks, albatross, eight kinds of gull, four of grebe, four of penguins, a large sea vulture, the sea hawk or Cape hen, various petrels, two black fishing gulls, four kinds of shag, oyster-peckers, curlews, etc.

Insect life is very scarce, comprising two dragon flies, three butterflies, six or seven moths, a wasp, seven flies, a mosquito, beetles among which is the beautiful Lady cow and a peculiar tree beetle, a small snail, a slug, and not a few others. The beaches swarm with insect life, and there are many specimens of the vegetating animal forms, including coral, sponge, and sea anemones red, white, and green. The principal fishes are: mullet of large size, the hapaim, yapacama, hama, lasahrr, ushcupatabailapaiaca, which are all choice and large fish.

(Extract from diary: Ushuaia July

[10] The Ona do not practice this form of tanning.

17th. 1877. The weather very cold. This morning the thermometer stood at +14 Fahr. and all day it has not risen higher than +19 in the shade. Today most of the men who left for Yahga in nine canoes returned with a large quantity of the excellent mackerel like fish called ushcupatabailapaiaca—the rough tailed fish. They are found in dense shoals and stabbed with spears.)

The hapaim and the lasahrr are particularly rich; the former is marked and shaped like a mackerel, attaining a length of over three feet and often weighing more than twenty pounds. Besides the above are the luj or black cod, the pejerrey or smelt, umushapum, or spine fish, the yamala yahgu, the hasyuna and the ilaimush, all fish of good size and quality. Among the smaller fish are the valuable syuna, the gaiyis, the tulluj and the onoali also much valued for food. The following should also be mentioned; sprats of two kinds, at times very plentiful, shrimps and the uca, a kind of sucker fish much prized by the natives for its gristle-like flesh and rice-like eggs.

(Extract from S.A.M.S. Mag. 1877 page 109: From letter dated Ushuaia Feb. 6th. 1877. There has been a remarkable supply of ia-ca-si, a native term including the class of fish represented by sprats and mackerel, inclusive of such birds, and even seals, as prey upon them. Sprats were so plentiful as to be left repeatedly in dense masses on the shores around us, and for some days the air was scarcely fit to breathe through the stench of millions of sprats which literally covered the shores of the inlet. Four kinds, or rather five, of fish are found in company with the sprats, which are decidedly larger than those found around the coasts of England. These five kinds of larger fish are excellent in flavour and richness, and their livers supply the natives with abundance of oil during the season. The excitement among the natives when the shoals approached the shore was intense. This was always by night, and the shores were closely watched. The noise made by the approaching myriads of fish was like that of quickly rippling water, we could even hear it though some four hundred yards off. The natives, provided with dips for sprats and spears for the larger fish, obtained large quantities and lived meanwhile on fish only.

Another cause for thankfulness is an extraordinary supply of the chief winter fungus, called usuf, but now in its immature state maceenik. This is a great standby for at least five months and much appreciated by the natives.)

The onoali mentioned above is a scaleless fish, marked like a serpent, with a round, long, tapering body. Its flesh is peculiarly white, firm and good. I should have mentioned two classes of conger eel-like fish, which live in pairs in cavernous pools. The natives seek them at low water, wading among the rocks in quest of their retreats, which are betrayed by the refuse of their food found in front of them. The natives thrust in their spears in quest of these fish, which seek to avoid the spears, keeping head on to their enemies. The natives, sure of their presence, repeat the thrusts until they strike them in the head and thus draw them out on the spears. Where they find one they are sure of finding its companion. The fish resort to these abodes early in the spring, apparently to rear their young.

Their flesh is very white and good but apt to be infested with flesh worms. Several sorts of fish, especially the luj, are very liable to the attacks of a parasitic animal, which doubtless kills large numbers of them.

(Extract from diary: Ushuaia Sept. 3rd. 1882. The natives are wretchedly provided with canoes and thus they find it much more difficult to obtain necessary food. This scarcity of canoes is very deplorable, and criminal on their part, as when they might make them they will not. The whale meat the natives brought from the East gives them a most detestable smell, so that to be much with them is very disagreeable; but under the present circumstances blubber is a great stand-by and highly valued by them. We have not had a fish brought for sale for some four months and do not expect any for two months more. These people are as a rule six months with and six months almost without fish. The mussel is decidedly the staff of life and sometimes almost the sole food of the people through the Winter. It is very pleasant to hear the cheerful notes of the chumuj (i.e. zonotrichia canicapilla) which have just now returned. Their coming has always been hailed by the natives, who fondly interpret the varied notes of this bird as full of different meanings.)

Two edible crabs are found, of which the kind called akeeya is a fine Crustacean. The hermit crab is also found, making its abode in the shells of paush and other volutes. There are seven sorts of edible mussels, of which four are very fine; of limpets five sorts are eaten, three of which are of large size. Of whelklike shellfish there are five varieties used by the natives, two of which attain so large a size that one will suffice for a meal. One species of these has a part which must be abstracted before it is eaten, as it is highly poisonous; this species the Yahgans call danawa. There are also two kinds of shellfish allied to the cockle which live in the kelp beds, nipping between their shells the leaves of this plant. They can change their abode at pleasure, darting about with a jerky, wavy motion by alternately thrusting out and closing their shells; these are very choice eating. I must not forget the sea urchin called, on account of its innumerable spines, uppush, the name of the troublesome burrs which are the seeds of the plant known as Austral Rose. These sea urchins are very plentiful in Western Fireland, where they form the most important article of native food. There are a great many small shell fish, some of which are prized by the natives for the making of necklaces and pendants.

I do not pretend in any of the above lists of animal or vegetable life to be complete, as I am sure there are other forms not a few of which more extensive research will bring to light.

In Fireland there are no pumas, serpents or other noxious animals or reptiles. The fox is the only beast of prey, and the minute lizard of Onaland the only reptile found. There are no deer or hares.

[*The environment depicted by Bridges and Lothrop is chilly and wet, but not too cold for human habitation, provided that the people have some means of keeping warm and dry, indoors and out, after exposure. The abundant vegetation and the marine fauna provide enough food and materials to sustain life on a simple technological level.*]

Indians

The natives of Tierra del Fuego are of three tribes, Yahgan, Ona and Alaculoof, whose languages point to a perfectly separate origin for each of the three; Yahgan is decidedly the most euphonious.

Being better acquainted with the Yahgan tribe than with any of the others it has come to pass that Yahgan terms predominate in this paper. Thus the Yahgan name for their Northern neighbours is Ona, and by this term that interesting tribe of Tehuelche descent is now known to the world, as also their country by its Yahgan name

Onisin (land of the Ona) and the Channel South of it, Beagle Channel, Onashaga (or Ona Channel).

But whilst the Yahgans had a name for the main island, they had no one name for Hoste Island, and whilst they have names for every locality, every creek or tiny island, which sufficiently serve their purpose, they often have no name for the larger divisions of land and water. Thus this port of Harberton has no native name, though its ten localities have their distinctive names, besides those of the headlands. The sixteen mile coast of the Bay of Ushuaia has no less than fifty-six names.

The Yahgans occupy both shores of the Beagle Channel from Cape Good Success in the East to Desolation Bay in the West and all the islands to the South as far as Cape Horn (Ushtanush) and sometimes have travelled as far as Ildefonso, which they call Yecapasiyoosha (they call Staten Island Chuanisin). They are preeminently a fish-eating people, and their wigwams are generally within a few yards of high water mark.

It grieves me sorely to say that the Yahgan tribe, which thirty-six years ago certainly numbered at least three thousand persons, as lists of names and families I have made fully prove, now counts no more than four hundred.

(Extract from S.A.M.S. Mag. 1884 page 223: From letter dated June 2nd. 1884. I have lately taken an almost perfect census of the Yahgan tribe, which numbers two hundred and seventy-three men, all of whose names I have registered under their several clan names. Their wives and other adult females number three hundred and fourteen; at least sixty of these are widows and unmarried, and the actual number of children enumerated is three hundred and fifty eight, making a total of nine hundred and forty five. Of orphan and young children I feel there are not a few oversights, say fifty five, which would bring up the Yahgan tribe to one thousand. The number of adults includes the youths of over seventeen years. The number of boys among the children as greatly exceeds the girls as the women do the men, making the sexes equal. This shows that the females reach maturity considerably earlier than the men, and this is certainly the case. Youths of nineteen or twenty you would frequently mistake for fourteen or fifteen. For instance, I am now sending Tymuran to Keppel Island; I had thought him to be thirteen or fourteen but on looking into my registration of births I find he will be twenty years old in August.)

The fearful mortality commenced in 1860, the year following the massacre of the "Allen Gardiner's" crew. Between that year and 1863 there was a great mortality in all parts, owing to a number of diseases, when the population was reduced by nearly one half. At this time in many cases the slightest wound mortified and death resulted. Many fell dead suddenly, others died after short illnesses. The natives wandered about in fear of their lives; but when in 1863 I first visited Tierra del Fuego the natives were still numerous and a few days sufficed to bring together three or four hundred persons, attracted by the news of the vessel's arrival. Other and similar diseases followed, among them a sort of small-pox, and the loss still continued, not only in parts touched by the Mission but all through the Channel.

Finally there has been a fearful increase of pulmonary complaints and an epidemic of measles, which in one year reduced the tribe from over eight hundred to four hundred. From these data it appears that these people at no distant day will cease to exist, unless a great change should take place among them. The mortality is decidedly greater among men than women and there is no doubt that immorality is one of the chief causes of this great decay of a hardy and muscular race. Yet these natives have usually been described as a great deal worse than they were. I well know they were bad enough, as all ignorant lawless people must be, but they were falsely reported to be cannibals, and the sketches of them have been rather caricatures than likenesses. They did neither eat flesh nor fish in a raw state, they never married any blood relation, however distant; to do so was utterly abominable to them. On the other hand they were very immoral and low in their conversation and conduct, and their many offenses against the dearest rights of their friends and neighbours kept the community in a chronic state of unrest and fighting. Few were without scars, and many deaths occurred through personal violence.

[*The white man's diseases here as elsewhere had their dread effect. The "immorality" of which Mr. Bridges spoke was the general promiscuity at infrequent meetings, also noted by Father Baegert in Lower California, and serving the same purposes in both places.*]

(Extract from diary: Ushuaia, March 24th, 1872. Hatushwaianges very ill from the effect of injuries received from Couilij who was jealous of him. March 28th. This morning at about 2:30 Hatushwaianges died. During his illness he has been most kindly cared for by Pinooinges and his wife. He has been in a very dull state for some days past and complained of pain, principally in the neck and chest. I fear that the violence of Couilij has caused his death. March 31st. There have been some few demonstrations of anger by one and another for the death of Hatushwaianges, and Couilij has had to give away his blubber [13] and other things, and in other ways to suffer.

[*The stranding of a whale was to the Yahgans a windfall comparable to the ripening of the pitahaya in Lower California. It brought people together. When they came together, they made merry and held ceremonies, both at once.*]

April 8th. Today a party of sixteen canoes arrived with intent to avenge the death of Hatushwaianges, Couilij made his escape and walked round the shore Eastward. The other natives asked me to help them and to speak to the avengers, I asked them all to be as passive as possible and told them I would be with them and do what I could.

The occupants of the sixteen canoes, having landed, lost no time in meeting the people here. All on both sides, men and women, were armed with sticks, spears or paddles and all who were connected with Hatushwaianges or Couilij indicated the same by the paint on their faces.[14] Before the two parties met I intercepted the avengers and asked them to be reasonable and just and not ignorantly to hurt innocent people. They would not, however, be detained but hastened on and Meacol presented himself as the chief object of their revenge, being the nephew on his mother's side of the manslayer. He was quite alone and the three principal avengers in turn threw large stones at him, but purposely avoided hitting him, as was very evident. There was much shouting and rushing about, great noise and confusion, much threatening and fierceness of manner but very few blows. Meacol, after the affair was over, was obliged to lay down the principal of his possessions to further appease the angry feelings of the dead boy's relatives.

[*Here as so often elsewhere, there is a fine line between ritual and actual combat. Both serve to restore equilibrium.*]

There was much talking throughout the rest of the day. Four of the canoes left this afternoon. The rest were made welcome to the various wigwams here. We are very thankful to our merciful God Who did not suffer this affair to be a very serious one.[15]

The last mention of the above affair is under date July 11th. 1872. (Went to see Couilij who has been hurt by a cousin of the boy Hatushwaianges of whose death he was the cause. His head is much hurt and he received several blows about the body but he is not dangerously injured.)

(Extract from S.A.M.S. Mag. 1875 page 13: From letter dated Ushuaia May 2nd. 1874. Today seventeen canoes arrived, with people from many places. There was a little commotion made by the newcomers on landing, which was feared by some would prove serious. I must describe it. Last night, unknown to any of the people

[13] A large supply of this commodity had just been brought from an immense whale stranded near Pacawaia, some twenty miles to the Eastward.

[14] Hatushwaianges' relations having their faces covered with white spots on a black ground, Couilij's with white bands on a red ground.

[15] It probably would have been more serious had the writer of the above not been present. Though he always went unarmed among the natives, the influence of a perfectly fearless man, bent on keeping the peace as much as possible, certainly had a good effect. Even when warned that a very bad tempered Yahgan was waiting for an opportunity to brain him with a hatchet he only, when the man came to the gate as though to speak to him, scolded him for his foolishness and pulling aside his skin mantle took the hatchet from him.

here, the above arrived and put up at Hamacuhr. Some of the people here heard the voices of many at Hamacuhr Shadatoo, i.e., make a loud tremendous shouting, as is the manner of those who have blood to avenge. Not knowing what might have occurred elsewhere, and who might unhappily find themselves deeply concerned, many were anxious, and two men came to me to ask for hoes wherewith to defend themselves; I refused them kindly and besought them to be slow to anger and fight and only to take slender rods. However before the people landed we learned from a fishing canoe which came in before them that there was nothing serious to fear. The canoes kept together, and the men landed at Entrance Point, and were all disguised with paint and charcoal, so that I could not readily recognize many whom we knew well. The women and children remained in the canoes, put out a little from the shore, and moved very slowly forward. The men came along, many armed with clubs. One man, Lasapowloom, a vigorous, active young fellow, acted the champion and challenger, and stood prominently forward to meet the foremost and most excited of the opposite party. Like the man who confronted him, he had a broad band of white from his chin downward, and his head was bound with the skin of a kelp gander with the white down on it; his hair was also whitened. He had a white stone in either hand. His antagonist, who came leaping along making much noise, was armed with a club. He kept on demanding what iacasi (a term for seals, penguins, mollimauks and other sea birds, and deep water fish) would let him kill someone, as though he thirsted for blood.

[I presume that the man had reference to the spirit-owners of these creatures, rather than to the birds, animals,

etc. themselves.]

He held his club ready to use it, and they both spoke excitedly and loudly to each other. Presently Lasapa threw one of his stones a full yard behind his opponent's heels, and ran after his stone to pick it up. Presently, looking where I heard much noise, I saw two other highly painted fellows engaged in loud vociferation and earnest gestures, each with an arm round the other's neck, and bobbing their heads each to the other. The rest stood quietly looking on, and presently the people dispersed to the various quarters they had meanwhile been invited to. I was highly amused to learn that Lasapa acting the part he did was according to custom, called Tsworoo or the storm of wind; the man who met him was called Tumootsworoo or the one who invites the storm to rage against him. Now we learn that there has been an accident, but the parties interested have been and still are a little suspicious of foul play. A month or more ago we had news of a canoe upsetting and all being lost. Then we heard a rumour of one of the men in the canoe, with the connivance of his sister, the ill-treated wife of his companion in the canoe, killing him and then sinking him and the canoe in deep water. We now hear that the skeleton of the woman has been found, and nothing yet discovered either of the canoe or the men.)

[This is a highly informative passage. There has been trouble. People have been drowned in a canoe during a storm. Their relatives, highly disturbed, relieve their feelings to some extent by accusing others of foul play, probably by influencing the spirit who controls the storms. The opposing parties stage a ceremony, a rite of intensification, which serves to restore balance in the relations of all concerned. Note the elaborate face and body painting, and the representation *of forces of nature by actors, who stage a mock combat. One of them calls upon the spirits which govern the animals, birds, and fish which furnish the Yahgans their food. Unwittingly Bridges has told us much about the ritual beliefs and practices of the Yahgans in this brief narrative.*]

The Yahgans were very quarrelsome and touchy and the weaker were very careful not to offend the stronger and to be courteous in their manners and language, often dissembling with smiles and words of peace their hatred and disapproval.

Having no fixed principles they were utterly unreliable, being solely guided by what was expedient or gratified their passions. Many considerations kept them from coming to blows more often; each person represented all his kindred, and by his misdeeds exposed them to the consequences and himself to their displeasure.

Cannibalism was an utter impossibility from the very nature of native society, in which human life is a very sacred thing, and for this reason—all the relations of the murdered person were in honour bound to avenge his death. I have heard of periods of sharp hunger, when continued bad weather prevented their obtaining supplies either from the woods, the sea or the shore. At such times they have eaten their hide shoes and thongs but never has anyone proposed to eat a human being.[16]

The lives of the old women who have been reported as the usual victims of cannibalism were as sacred as those of any other persons, because they had sons and daughters, nephews and nieces, younger brothers and sisters, who felt as such towards them, and

none dared to suggest their deaths.

The Yahgans occasionally hastened the end of their relatives by strangulation. This was kindly meant and there were good reasons for it. It was only resorted to in cases of long continued unconsciousness and utter weakness, preceding death, when the dying person neither ate nor drank, spoke nor moved. The act was done openly and with the consent of all except that of the victim, who was too inanimate to do anything. This act was called tabacana and it was done to any class of person in the above hopeless condition, either man or woman.

[*This is a clear exposition of the practice of destroying the aged and hopelessly ill, found among all peoples living simply in difficult environments. It eliminates the generation of elders in the society, with effects which we can understand more easily when we come to a society in which the elders can be preserved.*]

The Yahgans had great faith in dreams and were consequently often troubled with anticipation of death without reason. They feared death because of the suffering and misery attending it and because it was the end of life. Great consideration was shown to the sick, they were well tended and as far as possible their wishes were fulfilled. The nursing chiefly fell to the lot of the women. At the last closing scene all friends and relations were expected to be present and to make the occasion important by their united lamentations. It was a great gratification to the sick to have their friends around them and so much honour shown them.

Immediately after death the body was enwrapped in skins and branches of trees, and either burned in the shell

---

[16] In bad weather the tides in the Beagle Channel ebb very little; owing to the effect of the South and South West winds the falling tide, which runs out in great part through the Murray Narrows, is driven in before the shell fish on the beaches are uncovered.

heaps around the wigwam or publicly burned and the embers scattered about; or it was taken to some almost inaccessible shelf of rock, and there deposited. The wigwam in which the death occurred was burned and the family left the place, not returning for some months. For mourning they cropped their hair close round the crown of the head and painted their faces black with charcoal and oil. Friends painted theirs red, with mixture of black according to the degree of relationship. Also there were regular systems of painting by which the nature of the death of the departed was indicated. Thus for death by drowning the pattern was black bands with white edges, if by violence it was black or red with white spots, if natural a plain black. For marriages and births also special paintings were used. Mourning for the dead was kept up a long time and no one dared mention the dead by name. If anyone did so it gave great offence and begat a disturbance often ending in fatal frays.

[*The mourning practices of the Yahgans may be taken as typical of people living at a simple technological and institutional level. Leaving the place of death and forbidding the mention of the name of the deceased are standard practices serving to intensify the separation of the individuals concerned from the deceased. The standard rationalization is fear of the ghost, a ritual symbol of the relations between the living and the dead. As soon as the disturbance caused by the death has been allayed, belief in that particular ghost peters out.*]

The Yahgans formerly had the vaguest and most ridiculous notions of the rest of the world. They looked upon ships as moving countries or compound animals rather than the work of men's hands. Their knowledge did not extend beyond the limits of their trav-

els, and they in their ignorance considered themselves stronger, wiser and more cunning than their foreign visitors, and I think they were, in the sense of wrestlers, not wrong in the first instance, i.e. in their own way of wrestling, which was a fair trial of personal strength. Capt. Fitzroy discouraged wrestling between the sailors and the natives because the latter proved the stronger.

The Yahgans believed in ghosts and in a number of supernatural beings and in wild men of the woods. The ghosts were supposed to live in lonely caves in the forest and were much feared. Persons from time to time believed they had seen these spirits and gave accounts of the apparition. The Hanush, beings shaped as men, lived, alone or in groups, in the woods but with no women or children; they were constantly watching to surprise and kill any man, woman or child possible.

The Cushpij were spirits which at night could make themselves visible but not tangible. They were malign, and the Yahgans associated them with sickness and death; to call a person Cushpij was a great insult.

[*To identify shooting stars with dead shamans simply emphasized the importance of these ritual experts. It may be noted also that the different kinds of supernatural beings and evil spirits symbolize the different kinds of danger to which people are subjected—getting lost in the woods (the Yahgan were sea people), being killed by occasional Ona raiders, stumbling about and falling in the night, taking sick, etc. There was also some confusion between evil spirits and strangers*].

The Asasyu or Apunanusiaula, people of the West, were much feared.

They were believed to be assassins of wonderful power and wickedness, travelling all night in their large wooden canoes and hiding so well by day that they could never be seen, but stories were told of one and another who had seen them by night yet managed to escape. [*These wooden boat people were Alakalufs*].

From another Ms.: The natives travelled long distances in their canoes and were venturesome in trusting themselves with comparative strangers. Thus I know several natives of Cuchawulaf who come to Ushuaia in the East and in the opposite direction as far as Port Gallant and Mercury Sound; this distance is considerably over two hundred miles.

GAMES

The Yahgans were very fond of wrestling, of which they had several kinds. Out of their wrestling matches many quarrels arose. The manner of wrestling was this: a wrapt up otter skin served as the gauntlet, which the challenger would place at the feet of him he sought as an antagonist from the circle of players and witnesses. Never more than one pair wrestled at a time. They were encouraged by their highly excited witnesses and partisans. The object of the wrestlers was to floor one another. They fairly grasped each other under the arms and never used the legs to wrest the opponent's feet from the ground. They lifted and then would toss aside and bring the opponent down with all possible weight on one leg and thus try to force him down. They never tried more than twice when those matched proved equal.

Another game was with a ball made of the large webbed foot of the Mollimauk, stuffed with down. The players formed in a ring and tossed the ball from one to another, keeping it thus flying about as long as possible. Another game was the following: the players squatted on the ground on their feet, holding each other under the arms

and between the knees, thus forming a compact row. They would then sing or chant and would begin rolling simultaneously from right to left, to the measure of the time. Sooner or later the row of rolling and slowly advancing players would upset, when there would be much laughter.

They had other diversions which were of a semi-religious, dramatic nature.

[*So casual did the rituals of the Yahgan seem to Bridges that he dealt with them in the same context as games.*]

To carry on these they constructed elongated log wigwams with openings at either end. The dwelling wigwams were always round, whether made of logs or branches. Women and children were denied entrance to these special huts. In them the lads were disciplined and initiated into their status as men. These wigwams were called keena; boys uninitiated were called tamum, those in the course of initiation Ushwoala. The initiation of the boys and girls took place when they were between fourteen and sixteen years old. The lads were taken in hand by their uncles and elder brothers or other male relatives, the lasses by their aunts or elder sisters. The lads were initiated and trained in the keena, the lasses in the common dwellings but always in the absence of any men and boys. Abstinence from food was exacted from both; and the fasting of the lads was often severe, resulting in many instances in leanness and debility. Also for several years the youths were expected to abstain from the use of certain kinds of fish and shell fish and of certain parts of whales, etc. Both sexes received, after a longer or shorter season of abstinence, good moral precepts with reasons for observing them, whereby their friends honestly thought to fit them for their future life. For example, stealing and lying were forbidden because they brought suffering and trouble; diligence, generosity, and faithfulness in marriage were enjoined because they ensured peace and happiness. Adultery was condemned as a crime, an adulterous person was likened to a rotten tree, which has only to be touched to fall. But, as elsewhere all the world over, though their precepts were right their lives were wrong and in consequence the precepts had little or no effect. Vice was forbidden because it was hurtful, righteousness enjoined because it was beneficial; the lads were enjoined to be faithful to their clannish duties of vengeance, and fortitude was strongly required. No boy could marry until he had undergone this discipline. Neither sex received any cruel treatment while it was in progress, though the fasting of the lads was sometimes over severe.

One piece of worldly advice given to the younger men was to take as a first wife an old woman, because such would give them little trouble and much help. This was often followed, though never, I am sure, from inclination, but only from necessity, because marriageable girls were scarce and always bespoken by men already married. Widows did not long continue so, in fact a single adult man or woman was a rarity. All the rites connected with the keena were reserved for times when considerable numbers were gathered together to observe them, and give due eclat to the various performances. The Ushwoala or lads under training, besides gathering wood for the keena fires, where it was wastefully used, were obliged to make many fires on the eminences around and when abroad were accompanied by a guard to see that they did not break the rules as regards fasting, and visit the dwelling

wigwams to get a meal. The lads behaved very meekly and did not gaze about them but kept their eyes steadily downwards.

The men meanwhile would be occupied in the keena, painting and variously disguising themselves with bark hats and smearing themselves with blood, procured by pricking the inside of their noses, to represent various characters. Some would appear as an evil being called Chinugoo, others as another evil spirit known as Tanoowa, others again represented Ushoomeena and others Laiacakeepa, a female demon. When all was ready, the women and children being seated outside their wigwams, these variously disguised men, unrecognisable even to their nearest relatives, would rush forth with club, spear or bow in hand; dancing and leaping about frantically, threatening the women with their weapons and often speaking most offensively but in no case harming anybody. They would then, having thoroughly wearied themselves with their wild antics, rush back to the keena in the same manner as they had rushed out of it, chanting vociferously. In the keena they would rest and, amidst roars of laughter, discuss the merits of the different actors. Secrecy was strictly enjoined upon the newly initiated ones, at the peril of their lives, on the secrets and cheatery they had been made privy to. The natives had not the least idea of propitiating by their performances any being whatsoever. These rites sometimes occupied many days, and they were times of great disorder and license.

All dances and amusements were accompanied with singing or chanting, for the varieties of which they had special names, derived from birds and plants. None of their chantings had any meaning though the words were diversified. The tunes were very monotonous, yet when men, women and children united they sounded well enough. The natives keep in time together: the men without exception have tenor voices of very good compass.

All the singing of the Yahgans whether jovial, religious, vengeful or for mourning is accompanied with swayings of the body. The Doctors when seeking inspiration sang, or rather chanted, mourners made loud and long continued lamentations, chiefly left to the women; persons seeking revenge for murder of relatives loudly chanted, with violent motions of the body, thus seeking to excite themselves to violence and all when gathered round the wigwam fire were glad to amuse themselves by singing divers chants and relating and hearing traditions of the past.

Under the name "keena", which simply means "hut" of "wigwam" Bridges was apparently describing the *shiehaus* or Yaghan puberty ceremony, which faded out or went underground about 1870. It was revived in 1922 in order to initiate Father Martin Gusinde, S.J. whose work was not published (in German) until 1937, after Lothrop wrote. Lothrop who knew about Gusinde's findings, has this to say about the *shiehaus*.*

For the *shieháus* ceremony a large domed hut, elliptical in outline, was erected near the encampment. The framework was of split saplings an inch or two in diameter, bent and set up to form archlike ribs, and secured in place by a few horizontal beams. These timbers were held together by lashings of gut. At either end of the hut were doors, one large to admit spectators, one small for the use of the candidates. On the roof they piled branches of the evergreen antarctic beech to afford shelter to those within, but the sides were left open to the weather. Rows of logs staked in place on the floor divided it into a central gangway flanked by benches, built up by branches covered with skins. In the middle of the gangway burned a fire.

The house we have described was the type used by the central and western Yahgan. The eastern Yahgan, I was informed, did not use a domed hut for this rite, but a pointed conical wigwam like that seen among the Ona.

To beautify the initiation lodge, the flat inner surface of the split saplings constituting the framework was painted with red, white, and black paint. Broad boards, inserted at regular intervals in the frame, received similar decoration. When a ceremony was in progress the hut was further adorned with small painted tablets hung from the roof, while an additional touch of color came from painted wands which often were wedged in the frame of the house when not in use.

Two hundred feet or so from the initiation lodge a second and smaller hut was erected to serve as a cookhouse where meals for the candidates and officials were prepared.

The paraphernalia used during the ceremony consists of heron-plume headbands worn by the officials, kelp-goose down headbands worn by the others present, a narrow hide headband painted white worn by the initiate during part of the ceremony, a small stick also painted white used for

* Samuel K. Lothrop, "Indians of Tierra del Fuego," *Contributions,* Vol. X, Museum of the American Indian, Heye Foundation, New York, 1928. With permission of author and museum.

scratching, and various painted wands. The scratching stick is assigned to all the Yahgan by Koppers (1925), but I was told that it was used only by the easterners. The wands were held in the hand during the singing and dancing, and were swung in time to the music. When not in use they were thrust upright in the ground or stuck in the frame of the lodge. If one fell on the ground it was considered an evil omen. I was told that these wands were not in use among the easterners. The men in charge of the ceremony kept at hand a seal-hide thong adorned with closely spaced red dots; it was used to tie up any candidate who became unruly.

The oldest and most experienced of the men present assembled before the ceremony and agreed on the time and manner in which it was to be conducted. From their number they chose one who was both respected and well liked to be the master of ceremonies. Another they selected as the official instructor of the candidates, while others they designated "policemen." Their duties were to assemble the candidates in the lodge—by force if necessary— to see that they were submissive at all times, to sit on the roof during the ceremony and ward off any threat from without, and to communicate with the cookhouse when necessary. Finally each candidate had three godparents, two of his own and one of the opposite sex. Their part was to see that the candidates fulfilled all the ritual properly and to help them as much as possible, for it was to the credit of the godparents if their adopted children did well. In addition to the candidates and the officials, most of the grown people came to celebrate the ceremony. Places were taken in family groups, while the initiates sat with their godparents. All sat with their legs crossed under them and with

arms akimbo, thereby taking up as little room as possible so that a large number might receive the warmth of the central fire.

For the first three days of the initiation, candidates maintained a strict fast, for their allowance of food was only from three to five mussels a day. Their water supply was also limited and had to be consumed through a hollow bird bone. At night they were forced to maintain their cross-legged position, with the exception of four to six hours when they were allowed to sleep. If they relaxed at any other time they were pushed back into position by the older people and perhaps beaten for their lapse.

During the day the initiates received instruction in the art of making a living. The men instructed the boys in the methods of hunting, how to make tools and weapons, how to build canoes and houses, etc. Similarly the women taught the girls how to gather mussels and fungi, how to make baskets, buckets, and necklaces, how to rear children, etc.

At nightfall all the candidates were taken to the beach and forced to bathe in the icy water of the ocean. After the first bath the boys received a sort of tattooing on their chests, consisting of three lines of scratches into which they rubbed red paint. This was not real tattooing, because the cuts were not deep enough to retain the color permanently.

The greater part of the *shieháus* ceremony was filled with singing and dancing. By means of song they sought both to communicate with and to keep at a distance the *Yetaite,* a great evil spirit, who, the candidates were told, might seriously injure the occupants of the initiation lodge. Dancing served to neutralize the evil of his presence. To frighten him, the walls of the hut were beaten with sticks. Candidates were told to follow directions exactly or the *Yetaite* would seize them. Sometimes the *Yetaite* actually appeared—a man fantastically painted. Finally the candidates were told who it was and were warned that the real *Yetaite* was much worse than what they had seen.

The master of ceremonies usually was the leader in the singing, though sometimes this duty was assigned to another old man. The dances, which usually came late at night, were named for certain animals. Both the melody and the movements suggested characteristic peculiarities of this animal.

The moral instruction of the candidates they divided between the godparents and the official teacher, at whose feet the initiates had to sit from time to time. They were taught to be altruistic in thought and conduct, and to exhibit the virtues of hospitality and generosity. Respect for the aged was inculcated, for all must grow old in time. The boys they taught to be peaceful and not to make enemies, to treat women with respect, to help the young and the blind. The girls they told to rise early in the morning to get their water and wood, to care faithfully for their husbands and children, not to fuss about trifles, nor to repeat gossip. Behind these instructions stood

a certain amount of religious sanction, for the evil *Yetaite* threatened them, while the supreme *Watauinewa* observed their every action. This moral code set a standard for the tribe to which in practice they did not adhere too rigidly.

After some days of instruction the ceremony came to a close. At a given hour the candidates assembled behind a curtain at one end of the hut. One by one they were called forth with the master of ceremonies dancing beside them and were ceremonially surrendered to their godparents and therewith accepted as members of the tribe. The godfather gave his child three gifts: a finely woven *gaiïchim* basket adorned with feathers, a bird bone like the one used to drink with, and a scratching stick.

In the final hours of the last evening the women took charge under the leadership of an old woman. She and the older women sang, seated in the central part of the lodge. Finally a mock battle between the sexes was staged.

Such then was the *shiehàus* ceremony. On it the Yahgan believed their well-being depended, and without it no one could have any standing in the community. In fact each individual repeated the performance two or more times, but received preferential treatment after the first course.

These are first-rate eyewitness accounts of an initiation ceremony. In it the Yahgans sought to instruct their young people in the essentials of good behavior and to prepare them for adult life. The course could last only as long as the food supply held out, and very often it was possible to hold such a meeting only at the time of a special windfall, such as the stranding of a whale. To make up for the brevity of the instruction, the intensity and emotional content were high. The restrictions on eating, sleeping, and sitting in comfortable positions, and the presence of masked performers did much to impress the young people and make them remember what they learned at such a time.

For those that sought to become shamans, the Yaghans held a graduate school called the *kina* (not Bridges's "keena"). Gusinde graduated from this one too.

The Yaghans' shamans' school*

There are several ways in which a putative shaman may acquire his guardian helper. A man walking in a forest alone may be approached by one of the numerous spirits that live in old tree-trunks, and the latter offers to be the man's guardian. Or he may encounter the spirit of a sea animal on the shore. Or in a dream he may see a giant whale. This is the most powerful spirit that a shaman could have as his familiar. A man who dreams of the giant whale has received an imperative call that he cannot resist.

A man with a strong call, from a whale or whatever, may be in a state of semitrance for a few days, fasting and avoiding his fellows. Other people notice his condition and talk about it, and an established shaman may invite him to join himself and others in a session of a shamans' school. When they get enough candidates they will assemble in a secluded place where there is likely to be enough food to feed several families for some time. There they build a conical log house like that of the Men's House ceremony, and the session may last several months. During this time the candidates and their teachers sleep and eat in the house, and must remain chaste for the duration of the course, even if a few frightened women should be admitted as semicandidates who may never expect to become first-class shamans.

The leader is the most prominent among the shamans on the staff, and a few middle-aged men who are not shamans serve as helpers, to provide food and firewood and to prevent disturbance. In the evenings male visitors may be allowed in to observe quietly the candidates' progress.

Everyone in the house is completely naked, and every shaman and male candidate paints himself all over with pieces of lime or dried white clay, shredded off with his teeth and mixed with saliva. When this coat has dried they scratch lines through the paint on each other's bodies. Female candidates, helpers, and visitors paint the upper parts of their bodies white, with red lines running from the corners of their mouths to their ear lobes. This is, apparently, a second-class uniform.

Everyone has his own, assigned seat. The candidates sit with their legs out straight. Each candidate keeps his head from touching the wall behind him with a pad of soft, spongy, rotten wood taken from one of the trees in which guardian spirits live, and if he lays his head on the ground this spiritual insulator must serve as a pillow.

At about four in the afternoon the routine starts with singing, and this keeps up until about two or three in the morning when Sirius and Procyon, the stars into which the Yoaloch brothers were transformed, reach their highest point in the sky. At dawn the candidates awake and are fed, all of the food, such as it is, being cooked in the house. A candidate starts with three mussels a day, plus a mussel-shell of water drunk through a bone tube. Later his ration is cut to two mussels, and finally to one. If mussels are in short supply a fish tail may be substituted for each bivalve. After this meager breakfast, his only meal, each candidate remains silent until noon. On some days they are then sent out after firewood, or, under the supervision of women, to collect mussels, which they cannot then eat.

Like many other hunting peoples, the

---

*C.S. Coon, *The Hunting Peoples.* Boston: Atlantic-Little Beens, 1972, pp. 396-9; after Martin Gusinde, *The Yamana,* New Haven: HRAF, 1961, Vol. 5, pp. 1320-1339.

© by author, permission granted by author and publisher.

Yaghans believe that a shaman's body is differently constituted from those of other persons, and that the transformation begins here at this school. Each novice takes a ball of fine shavings scraped from wild barberry wood, mixes it with dry white paint, and rubs it on his cheeks, a half hour or so at a time, at frequent intervals throughout the day. This rubbing is supposed to remove his cheek skin and to grow three new layers which are progressively more sensitive, until the last layer of ultra-sensitive skin spreads over his whole body, growing invisibly larger, so that he can feel things about him that his visible body cannot touch, some as much as one hundred yards away. The shamans attentively watch this progress, which they apparently can see. The novice that gets a whole new skin first is considered their most promising candidate.

While these skins are growing and expanding, the shamans frequently hold their cupped hands over the fire and pour its warmth over a novice's head, and they also put warmth into the latter's mouth with one hand. These two movements are said to remove a wall of fog from in front of the novice's eyes so that he can see his guardian spirits and sing to them. The songs they sing are those taught them by their guardian spirits at the time they first appeared to them. Every once in a while one of the shamans puts himself into a trance by singing softly and swaying. Then he falls over, and the novices imitate this performance. Or he may begin suddenly to sing louder, which means that the spirit has entered him and is doing the singing, and gradually this animated singing peters out and dies down as the spirit leaves him. In the evening, the shamans may tell each other about the visits they received from their guardian spirits that day.

Sometimes the spirit-visits become contagious. During the singing one shaman may cry out: "My spirit is coming quite close!" He stands up, bending over; he touches each of the other men and asks: "Who are you?" and receives an evasive answer: "Oh, I am just a native of this part of the country." Others leap up and announce the arrival of their spirits, until the house is full of them, and excitement rises. During the session attended by Gusinde a female candidate named Emilia, whose first husband was a great shaman, pushed a spirit into the fire, whereupon the spirit shot a magical disease object with his sling, but Emilia caught it in one hand and rubbed it invisibly into the hand of Santiago, a male candidate, saying: "I now give it to you!" Then Emilia caught another spirit from the ice on Cape Horn and rubbed it into Gusinde's body.

After such a session the spirits leave one by one, until only one person continues singing, and in a weak voice; but someone may start another round, and so on again until it is time to go to sleep.

In this school candidates are taught to communicate with spirits in dreams during trances, but they also learn more active tricks, such as sleight of hand and swallowing and vomiting up disease objects. This latter type of instruction is probably given privately because it is too secret to be revealed to the mixed audience at the sessions described.

Returning to Mr. Bridges' narrative, we find a vivid account of the practices of Yahgan shamans.

The men when they passed thirty or forty years of age sought for excitement and importance by entering the ranks of the Doctors or yecamush. They were prepared by fasting and much incantation to some indefinable but apparently evil spirit called yapachal, to act as medicine men and exorcists. They were favoured with dreams, had power to procure good weather and drive away bad. They prescribed cures of this or that bark and also were credited with powers to exorcise the cause of sickness, or by witchcraft to cause sickness and death. When under the influence of the yapachal they pretended to be insensible to outward things, the burning of the fire and the presence of their friends. They at such times acted as though really possessed. I have seen one yecamush rush up on the fire, scatter the burning embers among the assembled people and dance on the hot ashes; one must suppose he burned even his tough skin considerably.

They oftentimes handled the sick very roughly, when in this wrought up state, excited through much chanting and violent contortions, they exorcised the pain and its cause from the body of the sufferer, pretending to do this by the hands and suction and to swallow the malady and its cause, which was supposed to be an arrow or spear pointed flint called yecush, of which the doctors always professed to have a supply in their stomachs. The cause of sickness they could present at their pleasure and could pass it off again in an invisible form into the air and thence again receive it in visible form and swallow it.

The natives, strange as it may seem, had great faith in these doctors' alleged powers and entertained some fear of them; but this state of things has long since passed away. There are no more doctors, the keena drama is no longer performed and mourning for the dead is more reasonable.

(Extract from Diary: July 27th, 1872. On Tuesday afternoon we had a most interesting session. During the morning the sewing party [1] had much conversation concerning the power of

[1] Men who were learning to make clothes for themselves.

Yecamush in regard to yecush, etc., and a clear trial was proposed to decide the important question. At two P.M. a large party assembled in the chapel which was warmed and comfortable. Two oldish men and renowned doctors performed, Meecungaez and Usiahgulum. The former first performed, being placed on a table at the end of the room. He would make us believe, if he could, that we saw the yecush in his hand, asserting it was there; but we asserted the contrary and after many vain attempts and acknowledgments of want of power he gave up, vanquished.

Usiahgulum, after being searched, was then seated on the table with a like result. These two men acknowledged that in our presence they could not perform and that the power to do such things was leaving them. . . . I think almost all were glad to see for themselves the exposure of imposture. The two actors were not angered at all and the whole thing went off very happily. When it was over we spent the rest of the afternoon playing games in the field, which were very much enjoyed.)

To lessen pain in the limbs or body bleeding was often resorted to by means of light but numerous cuttings near the affected part. Headache was relieved by making the nose to bleed by cutting it within the nostrils, as also by clipping the hair. The men often practice abstinence from food from early morning until night, thinking it manly so to do and tending to good health and efficiency in hunting. To delay, when out hunting, to gather berries or other food, or to take with them food from wigwam to eat by the way would be looked upon with disfavor as unworthy of a man and as tending to laziness and inefficiency.

The Yahgans differ much among themselves in features, stature and mode of life. In the Western parts, owing to the broken nature of the ground, the rank growth of vegetation in the preeminently wet climate, the abundance of thorny shrubs and the absence of open spaces and beaches, walking is very little practised and the canoe is not only a conveyance but to a very large extent the home of the native, where not a few births occur and many a night is spent. In consequence the natives' limbs are distorted, their legs crooked and ill developed and their stature small. But in parts further East where the land is more open and there are guanaco to hunt and distant lakes to visit for catching birds and gathering eggs, the natives are taller and better grown than the others by virtue of their different modes of life. We have had many proofs through the space of twenty-five years experience that you have only to alter the manner of life of a people to completely change their physical development and that in one generation. But apart from the Mission influences, amongst the natives of Tierra del Fuego, even among the Yahgan tribe, the variations are immense. Some have lank hair while others have theirs crisp and curly, some have flattened noses with the bridge very much depressed, some are remarkably stout, others are of very fair stature and bulk; the shortest among the women measured four feet six inches and the tallest among the men five feet nine inches.

(Extract from diary: Ushuaia, March 6th, 1871. This morning I measured some fifteen of the men here. The tallest was Pinoinges five feet five inches, the shortest four feet seven and seven eighths inches. The average height is five feet two and one half inches. I afterwards measured eight, whose several heights when put with the others make the average height to be five feet two and three-quarters

inches. The individuals were from parts widely scattered and of the canoe Indians I think this is a very fair average.

Ibid. March 27th, 1871. Some of the old trousers given me for the natives are much too large for them in every way. The sight of such gigantic garments created much merriment among the natives; they greatly wondered there could be men sufficiently large to fill them.)

Manners and customs also vary considerably. In some parts one wife was the rule, in other parts many had two wives, some three and a few as many as four. Girls were given in marriage from fourteen years onward. Not infrequently before they became settled in life they had had many husbands, for the marriage relationship was not secure unless children were born to unite the parents in a common care for them. In no case has a woman been known to have more than one husband at a time, but successively some have had ten or even more.

Whilst children belonged to the clan of their father yet their mother's relations were equally dear to them as their father's and were equally bound to befriend and defend them and to avenge their wrongs.

Ucuhr, wigwam or house, is also the term for relatives of kindred, answering exactly to our word house or household. Marriage with very distant clans was infrequent from the natural unwillingness of women to separate themselves so entirely from their own people. When a man married more wives than one they were generally sisters, which fact tended greatly to strengthen the family party. A wife was by no means wholly in her husband's power and she had quite as much liberty as was good for her; not a few men are domineered over by their wives. But on the whole the family life was happy and correct; what the wife caught or obtained was her own, the husband only used of it what his wife gave him, and she did not ask his permission when she would make presents to her friends.

Children were generally born in the open air, and this of necessity and from proper feeling, the wigwams occupied jointly by several families, offered no privacy. The expectant mother with her nearest female friends withdrew. Shortly after the birth the party returned, a friend carrying the young child. Within a few days after birth the child was dipped in the sea, with the idea of strengthening it.

Unnatural births were always destroyed and wisely so. For unimportant defects, or such as proved themselves later as for instance deafness, no one was destroyed but only for enormities. Though deaf or dumb men never married, unless it were an old woman, a deaf woman would be a wife and have children; the men remained single because usually no woman would marry such.

The children are decidedly small at birth and to this fact may be chiefly attributed the mother's immunity from danger.

More pleasure was expressed at the birth of a son than of a daughter and mothers were always proud to tell how many children they had. Infanticide was rare and when it occurred was generally the mother's act, on account of being deserted by her husband or annoyance at the complaints of her neighbours over the child's crying. Generally the children were tenderly cared for by their parents and friends and encomiums of every kind were expressed in order to please the parents as also to express the honest affection of loving friends. In the absence of the mother any other woman would feed the child rather than let it suffer.

Mothers of young children tend them most carefully and give themselves up to their maternal duties much more entirely than is the case with most civilized people, scarcely ever putting them out of their arms, and nourishing them amply to a very late age.

Children did much as they pleased, like everybody else; there were no schools to attend, no lessons to learn. They early, for pastime, prepared themselves for their future life; spending their time, if boys, in practising throwing or slinging stones, spearing or shooting arrows at a mark, or in attempting to make the various articles of native property; the girls in threading berries as necklaces, paddling in the canoes, making reed baskets, or in attempts at painting faces, etc. The children's help was required in all the duties of native life.

Girls and boys were, by their proud parents, often laden with a profusion of native necklaces of bone or shells and their faces painted as attractively as possible.

The division of labour was, I consider, very fair, the women were not imposed upon. The men gathered the fuel and the fungus, the women cooked, fetched water, paddled the canoe and fished. In journeys the men paddled as well as the women. The men tended the fires, made and mended the canoes and prepared material for them. The men hunted otters, seals, guanacos, foxes, birds and fish of every description. The women had charge of the canoes and could invariably swim well but it was a very rare thing for a man to be able to swim. The reason was that it was absolutely necessary for the women to swim but not at all so for the men. The Yahgans, like the Alaculoof, often live in districts where there are no beaches for many miles on which it is possible to haul up their canoes. They must therefore anchor them off the steep shore. In such cases on coming to shore the husband and family land. The husband goes up into the forest to collect fuel for the wigwam and starts the fire. The others bring up the supply from the canoe. The mother, meanwhile, paddles the canoe a few fathoms off into the kelp and taking some of its long branches secures them to a paddle, which she passes under the thwarts. Having done this she steps overboard and swims ashore. In the wigwam she finds a good fire, whereby she warms and dries herself. When the canoe is to be used she swims off to it, gets in and brings it ashore. She goes then to the wigwam fire. The husband or elder children make a fire in the canoe.[2] They also take down the things that will be wanted and when all is ready the party embark with their dogs and all their worldly possessions.

Native property consists of the canoe and its furniture of paddles, spears, bark or wooden buckets, bailers, slings, fishlines of plaited whale sinew, clubs, bows and arrows, drinking bones, shells or bark cups (the wing bone of an albatross is much used for drinking from the deep, narrow buckets), reed ropes, two kinds of baskets and a sort of hand net also of reeds, round wooden boxes fitted with covers, bags of divers kinds of skin and gullets for oil, paints, tinder and firestone, spear and arrow heads, thongs for various purposes, bone awls, chisels, smoothing and sharpening stones, wedges of bone for splitting bones on wood, wood shavings scraped by shells in the making of spear shafts, etc., and used as towels and pocket handkerchiefs and other odds and ends.

[2] On a turf put upside down and usually with some shingle or sand on top; the canoes always leaked more or less so the fire did no harm.

Necklaces made of different kinds of small shells, also of shag's bones (the smaller bones of the wings only are used) cut into small pieces about one eighth of an inch in length are threaded on a strong string of plaited whale sinew. Fine plaited cords of whale sinew are also worn coiled round the neck. Wreaths neatly made from the fine feathers of handsome birds are used as head bands; they also used the skin of the kelp gander, the down of which is of a snowy white, as a sort of cap.

The canoes are made of the bark of the evergreen beech, they are formed of five or more pieces; the bottom piece which is very thick, the tumagaia which are joined to the end of the bottom piece, and rise to a point at either end of the canoe and the unchapai, or two side pieces shaped like a bow, each made of one or more pieces of bark. The seams are sewn with whale bone or if that can not be had with wood fibre and wadded with the stringy seed stems of the wild celery. They are then wadded with grass, moss and mud and lined closely with split stems of sapling Winter's Bark. They are kept in shape and are strengthened by shafts of wood sewn down firmly on the inner rim of the canoe, meeting and crossing at the point of the tumugaia. Cross pieces or thwarts of leña dura are notched and sewn firmly down to the rim at proper distances, dividing the canoe into compartments called Apun, the fireplace, Keepacuchin, the women's seat, Muaskemana, the bow and Ushtaca, the stern. Outside of the bark forms the outside of the canoe; as it is very rough it is necessary to chip off to a smooth surface all the rough parts which would impede the canoe. The canoes vary very much in size, some can carry three quarters of a ton, others scarcely half a ton. They are old and worn out after six months service and are made twice a year, in Spring and Autumn. The former are called Hacua, the latter Een-anan, i.e., Winter canoe. The natives are specially careful to make the latter well. (Ushuaia, January 29th, 1874. Today Wanigulashan and his son, with their wives and daughters, left in order to make a canoe before the bark becomes fast to the trees, which it does towards the end of February and loosens in October, leaving five months for canoe making.)

The Yahgans' chief weapons are their spears of three kinds, slings (these with no hole in seat, they are very dexterously used, the stone is invariably sent forth in the second twirl round the head), and clubs. These weapons are also and chiefly used in getting their food. The spear heads are usually of bone; of whale, seal, guanaco or man, but never of their friends, and are of all lengths from 9 inches to 3 feet, the shafts from 5 to 20 or more feet. The large single or double notched spear is called Oain and is used in fighting and in killing large game as guanacos, seals, porpoises and whales. The shaft is called Kushooma, and varies in length from 16 to 20 or more feet. A thong is attached to the shaft some five or more feet from the butt and the other end is secured to the bone head; the head is then hitched into a groove and is kept there by the tightness of the fit and the aid of the thong, which is on stretch, when the animal is struck the head is soon disengaged from the shaft, which now impedes the animal's escape.

The many notched spear is called Shooshoaia, from Shoosha, a penguin and ooia, a spear, it is used in spearing birds and fish; its shaft is known as Shooshoaishuia and is securely bound to the head. The smallest spear, Eenij, is also used for fish and birds, its slender shaft is Ahgamoosh and it is simply a small Kushooma.

A three pronged spear called Seeta is also used for catching crabs and another called Umba of three or more prongs for fish.

They used three kinds of clubs, the largest of which, called Yoj, is pointed at one end. The second is called Wosin and the third Kueea; this is the smallest and is also used as a missile.

The Yahgan devices for obtaining food were many and ingenious, I can but mention a few; they varied greatly according to the nature of the locality. Wild geese were caught in considerable numbers by the following simple device: across narrow valleys leading to lakes frequented by birds little sticks were thrust in long rows into the ground, with openings here and there. In these openings were secured whalebone nooses. The geese on landing from the lake would walk along this fence seeking openings to pass through; they did not think of flying over. On finding openings they attempted to pass and were caught securely by the neck. They catch steamer ducks thus: at the edge of the woods, on the shore a man builds a little bower or simply secretes himself in the bushes there. A captive bird is in his possession. This, hearing its fellows without, calls to them or if the man has no captive he cleverly imitates the call of the drake when he sees any of these birds near. Hearing it the other birds draw nearer and nearer; the man holds a long slender rod with a fine noose attached to it; this he uses discreetly. Before very long one or other of the ducks puts its big foot in the noose, is tripped and disappears into the bower. The others, not seeing any enemy, are very excited but do not go away, still hearing the decoy bird within and the noosed rod is carefully thrust out again to catch another bird. In open situations nooses of fine whalebone secured to a small stick are placed on points frequented by birds, which are thus caught.

Among other ways the following is practised for catching cormorants: a strip of wood is formed into a hoop; to this are attached short lines with bait on their ends; inserted and securely bound at their lower end in the bait are two or three finely pointed bits of hard wood, of about 1½ inches length, the upper ends slightly opening outwards. These points draw inward on being swallowed with the bait, and present no difficulty; but the shag, finding the bait attached to something, tries to disgorge it; this is, however, impossible as now the upper points open and stick into the gullet of the bird.

Another way of catching these birds is to approach the cliffs on which they roost in the darkness of night. The natives cover over the fire in the canoes and have prepared flambeaux of bark beforehand. Suddenly these are ignited and the cover of the fire thrown off when the astonished birds, startled out of sound sleep, drop down in a semi-conscious state into the sea, where the occupants of the canoes kill all they can.

A third and very successful way of catching these birds is this: before they return to some islet where they are accustomed to spend the night in large numbers two or more native men secrete themselves there under the stones and seaweed so that the birds cannot see them. In due time the canoe leaves, the men not forgetting to keep some fresh water for their use in case bad weather prevents the return of the canoe on the morrow. Evening draws on and with it the birds assemble. When it is quite dark the hidden men creep forth to do their work. Their art is to seize the birds singly over their wings, so as to prevent a flutter or cry. They kill each bird by biting its head, and hold it firmly until it is quite dead; they then deposit it on the stones and treat another and another in the same way, until by some mishap the alarm is given and the startled birds make off into the sea. These birds sleep soundly with their heads under their wings.

(Extract from S.A.M.S. Magazine 1875, page 9: Ushuaia, April 10th, 1874. Now is the penguin and loggerhead duck season. The latter are now in the height of moulting and many are chased and taken. It is wonderful that any should be still in these waters. Hunters of elephants, lions and tigers in the tropics would not be more alive to the excitement of these hunts and the recital and hearing accounts of such than these natives are in speaking of the capture of these birds in their canoes. April 11th. A cloudy, dull day and very calm. Some natives went out to spear penguins and loggerhead ducks. *Ibid.* page 12, April 25th. A very fine day. Almost every man and woman in the place is away after a whale, which they have been attempting to kill yesterday and today. They are a long way Eastward and are still out on the water.

April 26th. This evening some ten or more canoes came, each having a share of the poor whale, which literally was killed by inches, having received into its body about a hundred spears and from first to last was being followed and wounded from Friday 4 P.M. to last evening at 10 P.M. The meat looks very good and has not the least smell. It was a young female about 18 feet long. This is the first instance since we have been here (about four years) of the natives killing a whale when free in its own element. They, the natives, were thoroughly fagged out. *Ibid.,* page 13,

April 20th. The natives have suffered much temporary pain from eating the whale and I hear that this is usual at first, but passes off with the continual use of whale meat.)

(Extract from S.A.M.S. Magazine 1878, page 79: Ushuaia, November 17th, 1877. We have lately heard of a sad canoe accident. Three or more canoes were out by night in Ponsonby Sound spearing sea gulls by torch light, when a heavy Southwest gale sprang up and six persons were lost; all were nearly so but the others were resuscitated by the kind offices of other natives. The persons lost were Amiananges, his two wives and three children. We well remember the particular night this sad accident happened; it blew fearfully, was excessively dark and there was a strange luminosity over the sea which looked like silver.

(From S.A.M.S. Magazine 1881, page 251: Several accidents have happened to canoes, one of which was broken by an infuriated wounded sea elephant and the five persons it held were drowned.)

The natives catch fish without hooks. They bait their lines with the tail of a small fish. Some luckless fish swallows the bait and is then quickly, yet without any jerk, drawn near to the surface. Unaware of danger and reluctant to lose its food, it retains it. No sooner is it within a few inches of the surface than the skilled hand of the fisher grasps it and it is deposited in the basket with its fellows, the bait is drawn out of its mouth and the line thrown over to catch another.[3]

Of course there were times, regulated rather by the weather than anything else, of plenty and of want; but the natives had no idea of a feast as such, or of commemorating any

event or day by feasting or mourning.

Having no numbers beyond three and no terms for definite divisions of time, as e.g., weeks, months, years, they could not distinguish one time from another. Again, they had no idea of the length of a month as measured by the moon for the same reason. Yet they used the terms for different states of the moon to indicate the time when they had done or intended to do this or that. Again, they had a variety of terms for different seasons of the year but none of these of definite length. They were loosely used as suitable for the time of year. In this loose manner Arina, Keesi, Hanislush, Eena, meant Spring, Summer, Autumn, Winter. Hanislush means red leaves, referring to the prevailing tints of the woods in Autumn. Besides the above they have terms such as the following: the season for canoe making, the egg season, the hatching time, etc. No one knew how old he was, and the knowledge of none extended backwards more than three or four generations. They universally used their fingers for counting, which for them served very well.

Each grown person had his or her place in the wigwam and the several wives of a man had each her appointed place as respected the seat of her husband, from which she derived her title. Thus the first or rather principal wife, for sometimes the first in respect of time became second or third in respect of rank, was spoken of as Wahyusin, i.e., the one on the door side, because her place was invariably on that side of her husband. The second was called Ushushpai because she sat next her husband on the inner side, and the third Cuchiellahco, i.e., next beyond on the inner side of. Thus each knew her place when they went into any fresh dwelling, but usually a man had not more than one or two wives at a time.

[3] This sort of fishing was always done in the kelp where the woman's brown hand, lying among the leaves, was not easily seen.

(Extract from S.A.M.S. Magazine 1875, page 218: The natives are always buying and selling, exchanging canoes and everything and their manner of doing so is very unsatisfactory. Here is a sample that occurred a few days ago. Palahlaian, a man about thirty-eight, has three wives, three little children and a good canoe. Another man, a visitor here, not living with Palahlaian, intends to give his canoe to Palahlaian. Palahlaian does not wish it, and hears of it indirectly and is troubled what to give in return. He told me all about it. Palahlaian at length is told that such and such a canoe is his, not, however, by the giver. Palahlaian then seeks him and gives him a large axe, well handled. Thus there is no mutual agreement previously made, and most of their transactions are performed in this loose manner. Marriages are brought about in much the same way . . . there are no arrangements, no agreements between the various parties. This horrible looseness prevails through everything. [*The habit of continually exchanging objects, although it may not always make sense to the orderly mind of an European, fulfills an important purpose —to keep relations between individuals at a high enough level of frequency so that in time of need channels for more useful exchange will already be open. We will see more elaborate developments of this same principle shortly.*] The begging and stealing propensities of the natives discourage laying up stores of fuel or food and engender slyness. When they sell skins or other things to us they aim to do so unknown to their fellows, in order to keep what they receive for themselves.)

It seems to be the rule among ignorant races to have no special name for themselves, though they invariably have for the tribes around them; in default of such names they are content to use for their own tribe terms meaning man, person, people. Thus a Yahgan, wanting to know whether one of his tribe was aboard would ask "Undagaratayamana?" i.e., "Is there a man or a person on board?" He did not consider the English or others persons in the same sense as he did his own people.

This word, yamana, applied specially to mankind, is highly significant. It plainly points to the idea of man being the highest form of life. The word means living, alive; as a substantive it means life; as a verb it means to live, recover life or health. Wiamanana means to give life to, restore to health, to heal.

I gave these natives the name Yahgan because it was convenient. The Murray Narrows, near which our Mission was established, called by the natives Yahga, may be considered the centre of their land and the language as spoken there was that I learned and its purest form, being the mean between its varieties spoken Southward, Eastward and Westward. For these reasons Yahgan seemed a suitable name and is now known everywhere.

Three classes of names were current among the Yahgans. First, those derived from the place of birth, as Sechunges, Usiehguloom, Washanges (men) and Tuspilikeepa, Ashailikeepa, Calagatamuatamolikeepa (women). By these people were generally called, oftentimes they had no other name. But if you asked a person his name and he happened to have only that of the place of his birth, he would tell you that he had no name, because to the native mind the family name was preeminently the name of the individual. These family names, to a great extent, have in process of time lost their meaning, being largely of very remote origin.

Children seldom received their parents' name, but usually those of their uncles and aunts and of grandparents. Of these family names the following are samples: Lasapa, AiamInaez, Palahlaian, Meacol, Cushchin, Chingalaian, Pataez, Lacoazkeepa, Aiawahr, Hanyuitan. (Extract from "Voice of Pity," vol. 13, page 176: The natives have an idea that naming children early stops their growth and since children so often die in early infancy and it is considered evil to name the dead, if the child had no name the parents are not vexed by hearing it.)

The third class of names were epithets descriptive of some peculiarity of manner, feature or accident. These latter were often handed down as family names, when of course they became no longer suitable. Of this class I will only give translations; Long, Red or Pointed Nose; Flat, Broad or High Forehead; Long, Short or Bow Legs; Hairy Face; Broken Hand or Foot; and a great variety of others, many of which were highly objectionable but which through constant repetition the natives used almost unconsciously of their meaning. (Extract from diary: January 25th, 1872. Ootatoosh very much desired to drop the name of Ootatoosh, which means narrow or small neck, and to be called, as is the custom, by the name of his father's father, Meacol, to which, of course, we have assented.)

But names of any class were to a large extent tabooed when the bearer was present, or in the presence of his relatives after his death. In place of naming persons present they were indicated by the positions they occupied in the canoe, the wigwam or the field with respect to the person speaking or spoken to, or in some other covert manner. Thus instead of saying "Aiaminaez gave me this," they would rather say, "He in the bow or stern," or "He on this side or that side of the wigwam gave me this." Such phrases are very difficult to us because we have no concise terms for them but such terms the Yahgans have in abundance, the following will serve as samples: Inga, Ura, Usha, Ila, Hoamatu, Sicu, and many others. All these, in the absence of suitable terms, we should translate, he, she, or they, but to the Yahgans they all have further reference to place and direction, with respect to the person speaking, spoken to or spoken of.

The natives gave very sensible names to the different parts of the country, observing much method in this matter. Thus Navarine Island they called Wulla; Wullaia or the bay of Wulla is so called because it is the largest bay in the Island and Button Island, situated in this bay is called Wullayeshca, namely the Island of Wulla; Gable Island is called Wulla Lanuj, i.e., the end of Wulla.

The language is very rich in number of words and its structure is regular and ample. It consists of 45 sounds, of which 16 are vowels. The natives had not the least idea of writing and knew nothing of words as such. They could well use their language but they could not give one a sentence word by word. Their language had to be learned by inference rather than direct information.

(Extract from S.A.M.S. Magazine, page 128: It is utterly impossible at first to get hold correctly of the pronunciation of a new language from the lips of a savage. He cannot, before he is taught, pronounce words of his own tongue slowly and distinctly. Often have I, until I was ashamed, made the Indians pronounce words so repeatedly that they have called me deaf, being unable to satisfy my mind as to whether I had it correctly, and after all being compelled to write it down when dissatisfied with my pronunciation and consequently with my spelling of the word.

Ibid., 1878, page 11: The cause of the difficulty these natives find in speaking, reading and writing English is the middle sound they give in their own language to C and G, P and F, D and T, Ch and J, S and Sh; U, A, and E, which sound in their language so nearly approximate as to render it difficult to determine which is which. They cannot with certainty tell the difference between Et and At, red and rat.)

At length, however, it was acquired and accurately written with a phonetic alphabet. This goes on the system of a letter for every distinct sound and each sound to have its especial letter. Thus the task of reading and writing it is rendered most easy and the pronunciation is definitely fixed. But though rich in sounds and numbers of words and, like their appliances of life, eminently adapted to the use of the natives in their former state it proves a very poor means of educating them for a higher life, as it is sadly wanting in definite terms, for ideas which the natives had never entertained.

For example they have no terms for authority and no laws, even parental rule was very weak. The only term usable for obey is Urumana, which means rather to assent, agree, yield, than to obey. For our ideas of duty, as expressed in the words ought, should, owe, the Yahgans have no adequate terms, even as they had no proper conception of them. The only word by which one can express owe is ushari, to promise, because what one owes one in a sense promises to give. They have no word for to pay, it can only be rendered by the word tago, to give. For equal they have no equivalent nor have they any name whatever for any fraction; thus it is impossible to say in Yahgan "two and a half," "one and a quarter," etc.

Let us turn for the moment to Lothrop's account:

According to Mr. Fred Lawrence, of Remolino, generally regarded as the best living authority on the Yahgan language, in the old days there were five distinct dialects, distributed as follows:

1. Central dialect, including Ushuaia and Murray narrows. This is the speech recorded in the Bridges dictionaries.

2. Eastern dialect, spoken from Harberton eastward and on Lennox Island, New Island, etc.

3. Western dialect, found from Cape Divide westward.

4. Wollaston Islands dialect.

5. New Year's Sound dialect, spoken to the south and west of False Cape Horn and on the southern part of Hoste island.

These dialects are said to have differed from one another as much as Scotch from Cockney; that is to say, they are mutually intelligible but there was wide variation in accent and the choice of words. The fact that considerable divergence once existed within such a small geographical limit indicates that but little movement of the tribe as a whole had taken place for centuries, at least.

And then back to Bridges:

Yahgan has fully thirty thousand words, is beautifully constructed and susceptible of endless composition. Its nouns, pronouns and verbs have three numbers, viz., singular, dual and plural, each complete in its various changes for case, tense, interrogative, positive and negative forms. It is particularly rich in pronouns and verbs, and, owing to the eminently social life of the people who spend so large a part of their lives in talking and, both men and women, in giving lengthy harangues, called by them Teehamuna, they perfectly keep up the knowledge of their language and early learn to speak it well. Children were not confined to the society of their parents and a few busy servants but intimately mixed with the whole community. Everyone knew everyone and each item of news was well discussed. The wigwam life of ease and sociality is eminently favourable to talk. I expect the gypsies, for this reason, are a very forward people with their tongues. The natives among themselves gathered round the wigwam fire, their wants generously supplied (for as a rule they had abundance of food), were very animated and spent a large part of their time in lively conversation and exuberant merriment, laughing as much to please others as to express their own pleasure. Their laughter was very natural and hearty and it was excessive in degree. I feel safe in saying that in actual work the natives did not spend more than one-twelfth of their time, whereas we spend fully five-twelfths of ours in occupations forbidding much conversation.

(Extract from Diary, June 13th, 1877: This afternoon visited two wigwams; the first was so crowded with natives and crabs and so dense was the smoke, that I could not stay three minutes. In the other I spent some time and right welcome to the inmates was my visit. There were three men, five women and seven children in this wigwam and three fires lit in different parts.)

APPENDIX*

One custom the Yahgans had in old times and of which, oddly enough, we have found no mention among those of our father's papers in our possession; was to tie something tightly around the neck to induce partial strangulation; they said that in this half stupefied state they saw beautiful colours. Our father was once called to the aid of a young woman who had lost consciousness through binding her neck too tightly and whom the other Indians thought to be dead or dying; she however recovered.

Another thing of which we can find no mention is that the Yahgans formerly, both men and women, sometimes suffered, or pretended to suffer, from a sort of madness which took the form of running frantically without, apparently, any fixed idea. All the bystanders would give chase, and when at last caught the person would be thrown or dragged into the water, which appears always to have had a calming effect.

We used to think this simply hysteria or sham to arouse a little excitement and probably often was so, but we have since known of two similar cases which certainly seemed genuine. One, a small boy of mixed Ona and Yahgan blood, we were told would sometimes at night, when sitting with his friends, suddenly rush away without any reason and greatly to the inconvenience of the said friends who felt obliged to follow and catch him—a difficult task as on these occasions he ran very fast. The other was an Ona man named Coiyoat, not at all an excitable character, who on one occasion climbed, in this condition, a steep cliff. He was not especially active—rather the opposite—but only one, a very agile man, could follow him. The others made a detour and

* By Miss Alice Bridges

captured the runner after a long chase. This same man once when camping out alone with one of our brothers asked him, it being a fine night and full moon, to tie him up for the night, saying that he feared to run away and perhaps injure himself. He said that on one occasion, also at full moon, he had come to his senses in a thick wood a long way from his encampment and had walked some distance before recognising where he was. Of course this might have been a case of sleepwalking, but on the other occasion the noise made by the pursuing band of Indians would put this out of the question.

The fact which impressed the early voyagers most about the Yahgans was their ability to keep alive with so little clothing in a raw, chilly climate. Although there were few days in the year that would be considered comfortable out-of-doors for an ordinary American youth, there were also few in which one ran the risk of freezing. Winter temperatures were not nearly as cold as in the Middle West, or even in New England. If an American youth went about in this climate clad only in a sealskin tied over his back, he would probably catch cold in a few hours, and might even die of pneumonia.

The Yahgans must have developed an immunity to pulmonary diseases over generations of selection, but to other epidemic ailments they were peculiarly susceptible. Between the visit of the *Beagle* and the establishment of the mission of Ushuaia, the population was reduced by nine tenths. This is a dramatic instance of selection on the basis of inherited immunity to diseases, probably the most drastic kind of selection to which human beings are exposed. Death from measles, smallpox, and other white-man's diseases mowed the aboriginal peoples of the world down ahead of him, in Fuegia as in many other places.

You will observe that Bridges spoke about clans, and gave some details about the obligations of clan members to avenge each other, and about their face-painting insignia. Among people like the Yahgans a clan is simply a number of persons who consider themselves related by bilateral descent. It is not an exclusive body. Its members do not necessarily live together or work together. A given individual may consider himself related to two other persons who do not deem themselves related. You yourself probably have cousins, and they in turn have cousins who are no kin of yours. With a system like that of the Yahgans, and our own, it is impossible to draw a circle around a list of names and say, "These people are one kin, and belong to no other." The crowd of men who joined together on a raid to avenge a murdered relative may have had a temporary leader, but it is doubtful if precisely the same group ever reassembled. In the same way the people who conducted initiation ceremonies were together because food was plentiful at that place at that moment. A whale had stranded, or some other windfall had occurred. Being together, they took the opportunity to enjoy each others' company, to instruct the young, and to train shamans. While these were the Yaghans' only well-organized activities that their circumstances allowed them to develop, they fell short of the institutional level through changes in personnel and irregularity of meetings.

4

The Seal Eskimos: Simplicity Through Poverty

IN THE examples which we have so far presented, we have been dealing with peoples who were noted for a simple technology. The environments in which they lived, though rigorous, permitted them to survive without elaborate means of keeping cool or warm, of utilizing natural resources, or of performing skilled actions. Whatever their origins and histories, they were truly primitive peoples.

There are other parts of the world in which no one can survive unless he is extremely skilled. The inhabitants of these regions must have developed elaborate means of dealing with the rigors of the environment before they can have reached their present homes. Men who go on a polar expedition lead simple lives while they are in the Arctic. Mountain climbers who are scaling Mount Everest have no elaborate system of relations while they are aloft. And the people who make their homes in cold places and far northern climes live simply all of the time, because they are always there. The environment will not permit a complex set of human relations. The paths by which far northern peoples have arrived at their present level of institutional complexity may be divergent, and again far different from those taken by the peoples in Chapter 2, but the environmentally fostered results are at least superficially the same. We shall now deal with the second kind of institutionally very simple people.

All along the arctic coasts of North America from the Aleutians to Labrador, and on the Siberian side of the Behring Straits, on the arctic islands of Canada, and on Greenland, live the well-known Eskimos. These people endure a much more rigorous climate than that of the Yahgans; if they did not have adequate clothing they would die.

All Eskimos do not have equal advantages. Those inhabiting the shores of Alaska and Greenland are able to hunt walrus and whales, which provide them with great quantities of animal fats needed for fuel in their lamps, to heat their houses, and to cook their food. Those who live along the shallow seaways around the Boothia peninsula, just west of Hudson Bay, have to make out with a few seals, for the larger sea mammals have too deep a draft for these waters and stay away. Although the Alaskan and Greenland Eskimos who have more food to eat and more fuel to burn can live in villages of some size and permanence, their poor relations in between are unable to form larger or stabler social units than those of the Yahgan.

As an example of these most hard pressed of Arctic peoples, I offer the following vivid, personal, and exciting passages from Knud Rasmussen's report * of his expedition to this region between 1921 and 1924.

* "The Netsilik Eskimos," *Report of the Fifth Thule Expedition*, 1921–1924, Vol. VIII, No. 1–2. Copenhagen, 1931.

Cut off from the surrounding world by ice-filled seas and enormous trackless wastes, a little handful of people calling themselves Netsilingmiut (the Seal Eskimos) have been suffered to live their own life, entirely untrammeled by outside influence, right up to the present time.

According to the census I made of them, there were around Pelly Bay 32 males and 22 females, on Boothia Isthmus 39 males and 27 females, at Murchison River 22 males and 15 females, at Bellot Strait 10 males and 8 females, and finally at Adelaide Peninsula 47 males and 37 females. In other words, this gives in all 259, namely 150 males and 109 females. The marked excess of males over females was not due to any greater mortality among the females, but to infanticide. . . .

. . . .

The Netsilingmiut have not received their group name: "the people who live where there are seals" because seals were particularly abundant in their territory; this is by no means the case, unfortunately. They have more probably received it because, after a life in the interior, they have for some reason or other separated from the Caribou Eskimos and moved down to the coast. The inland dwellers, with whom they still maintained intercourse via Back River, have then given them a group name that was characteristic of their country and their new mode of living.

. . . .

It is astonishing how much the Netsilingmiut know about the land they live in, be it natural conditions and fauna or its early history. Though they had no previous knowledge of paper and pencil, they were remarkably quick in outlining the shape of their great country, and, having done so, could put in all the details with remarkable certainty. Obviously the distances in these hand drawings cannot always be correct; but all islands, peninsulas, bays, and lakes are reproduced so accurately that finding one's way from place to place is an easy matter even to an utter stranger to the country. This geographical knowledge is of course accompanied by a most intimate acquaintance with the animals and their habits—a knowledge on which their whole existence depends.

. . . .

The traditions of the Netsilik have it that they are a people that have come into the country from elsewhere and have taken it from the original inhabitants. Where they came from is a question that is rather vague to them. They know merely that when their forefathers came to their present hunting grounds the lands were already populated with Tunrit. . . .

They say that in the earliest times it was the Tunrit that made the country "inhabitable," which means that they did all the work that made it possible to hunt the caribou and catch the salmon with the gear they had invented themselves and the hunting methods that were used. It was the Tunrit that found the places where the caribou crossed the waters, and they built cairns in various parts of the country and thus compelled the animals to follow certain paths so that while on land they could be hunted with the bow and arrow from . . . [blinds] or pursued in kayaks at . . . crossing places either over lakes or wide rivers. They it was, too, that found the fishes in the rivers and set up . . . dams and fish weirs built of stones at the places where the salmon run, so that those that were shut in could be speared with the leister.

. . . .

. . . They spoke the same language as the Netsilingmiut, though there was a dialect difference that is still remembered in some traditions.

.   .   .   .

The Tunrit are described as big, strong people who were so good natured as to be almost timid and therefore easily took flight. As a rule their inland life in summer and autumn coincided with that of the Netsilingmiut as far as hunting and fishing were concerned; but, in contrast to the present population, they loved the sea when it was not covered with ice and preferred to choose settlements where there were plenty of whales, walruses, and seals, and these they hunted in their kayaks. They were skilled at musk-ox hunting, too, and bold bear hunters.

It is so long since the Tunrit hunted marine animals in the land of the Netsilik that now everything is changed. At that time great marine monsters such as whales, white whales, and narwhales traveled along by the coast. Nowadays they are only to be found up at Bellot Strait. But the memory of their once having frequented the waters round King William's Land is preserved not only in the whalebone houses there and the many implements of whalebone to be found everywhere in the old ruins, but also in the whale . . . skeleton buried in soil and sand about 14 kilometers from the mouth of Pfeffer River, presumably about 25–30 meters above sea level. And what is more, old men say that there is another big whale skeleton far inshore at Saitoq, east of Shepherd Bay, and in the same bay near Lake Qorngoq many skeletons of white whales have been discovered; and further inland still, close to Lake Qissulik, there is a quantity of driftwood that is now so old and rotten, worn by wind and weather, that it crumbles at a touch. Now the fairways are said to be so shallow that not even the bearded seal

from Queen Maud's Sea runs in through Simpson Strait, and nowadays the sole quest of the seal hunters is the little fjord seal. . . .

[*This is graphic evidence of the fact that the land has risen, forbidding access to large sea mammals, and impoverishing the environment. The Netsilingmiut are Caribou Eskimo who moved northward from the interior; the Tunrit were their whale-hunting predecessors. Both are Eskimo.*]

It was not always an easy matter to obtain people's true meaning as to how they appraised the white man. . . . Often one had the feeling that they regarded him in quite the same manner as many white men look upon the Eskimo—as being inferior to themselves, as a sort of powerful barbarian to whom particular deference was due, because he was bigger and stronger than themselves and had an outfit and instruments of power far in excess of their own. . . . A further fact that increased their respect was that they always believed the white man's resources were inexhaustible. . . . But above all was their invention of the firearms, which made them both terrible enemies and impossible to compete with in the struggle for food. On the other hand, the Eskimos were always their superiors in their ability to live in their cold land, in building snow huts, in driving dogs and in paddling a kayak. In these very elementary accomplishments the white men were always inferior, and in many ways quite dependent upon the Eskimos themselves while in their country. . . . All these points of view were explained to me one day by old Kuvdluitsoq, and in conclusion he as it were summarized his views and his appraisal in the following sentence:

". . . It is generally believed that white men have quite the same minds as small children. Therefore one should always give way to them. They are easily angered, and when they cannot get their will they are moody and, like children, have the strangest ideas and fancies."

. . . .

There is scarcely any country on earth that presents conditions more severe and inclement for man than the most easterly parts of the Northwest Passage, for it lies waste and bare of all that is otherwise considered necessary to life; and yet there the Netsilingmiut for generations have known how to wage the struggle for existence, in such a manner that strangers coming among them will involuntarily receive the impression that it is a people who desire no better hunting grounds than these, the very ones where their ancestors developed that special culture which they have faithfully handed down from father to son.

Winter takes up most of their lives, a hard, stormy winter, already beginning in September and lasting right into spring—the middle of June. In the winter months proper they have to contend with the severe cold, which constantly fluctuates between −30° and −50° C, and in spring, when warmer weather really should set in, it is often so raw and stormy that it is a matter of great difficulty to obtain food. In May, June, July, and August they are livened up on exceptional occasions—that are remembered—by a few warm days when nature awakes and everything seems to be growing. Then one is sensible of such mildness around that all adversity is forgotten and it feels wonderful to be alive. But such periods are brief, a few days at the outside, and one is again left at the mercy of a climate in which warm clothing and a healthy, hardened constitution are necessary for survival.

Snow begins to fall in September, sometimes even toward the end of August, and it lies until June. As early as September the fjords are iced over, and in October the sea ice lays a covering that does not disappear until sometime between July and August the next year.

. . . .

Qaqortingneq said to me: "You have seen us happy this summer; we have been happy, not only because we have enjoyed living together with entirely new people in our village, who came to us from far away and yet could speak our tongue. You also came to us with ammunition for our guns and with iron for our ice-hunting harpoons. . . . In times like these we often feel we have so much food that we will not be able to eat it all. But whoever does that forgets the many, many days in winter when we can find no food at all; he forgets that the caribou go away from our country and that even the seals may disappear or snowstorms prevent us from finding their breathing holes. And so the man that is wise never lolls about idle when the weather is good; he can never know what bad days may eat up his meat caches and drive him and his family into starvation.

. . . .

"Three winters before your coming (1919) seven people starved to death up there close to Kingaq (Cape Britannia); they had spent the summer in King William's Land as we had, but their hunting had not been good; there were not caribou enough and scarcely any trout. As soon as the ice would bear they tried sealing, but that failed because the ice was all cut up by the currents owing to the mild weather, and they could catch no cod either.

". . . in the dark time, when the sea ice was cut by currents, they starved to death. [*He names the seven persons*] . . .

"The year after there were still more

who died of hunger . . . [*He names eighteen persons*]. They had spent the summer at Naujatoq on Adelaide Peninsula and perished in the easterly part of Simpson Strait. Constant snowstorms was the cause, and it seems that the men have been ill, too, possibly some sickness contracted through eating year-old, putrid stores."

. . . .

In the following I will in Samik's own words give some accounts of famine. He himself was a good hunter and a respected shaman.

. . . .

"You know Tuneq, the brother of Itqilik; you have met him and his present wife; you have lived with them and seen that he is a happy man, a man who likes to laugh and a man who is always good to his wife.

"One winter, many years ago, hunting was a failure. Day after day went by and nobody had anything to eat. People died of hunger or froze to death, and the quick lived on the dead. Then Tuneq suddenly became disturbed in his head. He began to consult the spirits, and it was not long before he began to do so through his own wife. He used her as a medium. . . . He did it in this way: he tied a line to one of her legs and made her lie on the platform; then he tugged at her leg and let the spirits answer through her leg. He did this often, and it was not long before he said he had received the answer that he was to save his own life by eating his wife. At first he only cut small pieces from her clothing and ate them, drinking water with it to help him to swallow it. People who saw him say that he behaved like a man possessed of a wild and evil spirit. Bigger and bigger were the pieces he cut from her clothing; at last her body was quite exposed in many places. The wife knew that the spirits had said her husband should eat her, but she was so

exhausted that it made no impression on her. She did not care. It was only when he began to feel her, when it occurred to him to stick his fingers in her side to feel if there was flesh on her, that she suddenly felt a terrible fear; so she, who had never been afraid of dying, now tried to escape. With her feeble strength she ran for her life, and then it was as if Tuneq saw her only as a quarry that was about to escape him; he ran after her and stabbed her to death.

"After that he lived on her, and he collected her bones in a heap over by the side platform for the purpose of fulfilling the taboo rule required of all who die. He was going to hold death-taboo over her for five days. But people say that the ghost of his wife often walked through her own bones, Tuneq waking up at night as the bones he himself had gnawed began to rattle. Sometimes they moved up and down, and it happened that the man sitting up on the platform would be hauled off during the night by some invisible power. And when he then suddenly awoke there was no one in the snow hut, only the bones lying over by the side platform, rattling.

"This was shortly before Amundsen came to our land [1903]; Tuneq had not yet taken another wife at the time he became Amundsen's adoptive son, and was to have gone with him on the ship to the white man's land.

"In the same famine, Tuneq's brother Itqilik ate his younger brother. . . .

". . . his younger brother was frostbitten in both feet so that he was unable to walk. Gangrene set in, and as his feet were quite numb, Itqilik cut them off his living brother and ate them. Later they agreed that Itqilik might just as well try to save his life by eating the whole of his brother, who was doomed anyhow. Then Itqilik killed him with his knife and lived on his body till he reached a place where men lived. . . ."

.   .   .   .

The most glaring consequence of the struggle for existence is manifested in the way in which they try to breed the greatest possible number of boys and the fewest possible girls. For it is solely economy that lies behind the custom that girls are killed at birth, if they have not already been promised to a family where there is a son who some day is to have a wife. These murders of newborn girls are not at all committed as the outcome of crudeness of mind nor because they underrate the importance of the female to the community; they are quite well aware that she is indispensable. When it happens, it is only because the struggle for existence is so hard, because the experience of generations is that the individual provider is unable to feed more than the most necessary members of the family. . . .

.   .   .   .

They hold the view that if a woman is to suckle a girl child it will be two or three years before she may expect her next confinement. But if she has not to suckle, she may expect another child comparatively soon after; so they encourage the number of births—when it is a girl that is born—either by killing it or giving it away immediately after birth, and then hope that the next one will be a boy.

A hunter must take into consideration that he can only subject himself and his constitution for comparatively few years to all the strain that hunting demands. Competition is keen, and if he has no very special natural gifts and enjoys no unusually good health, he need not be very old before he can no longer hold his own with the young. Now if he has sons, they will as a rule be able to step in and help just when his own physique is beginning to fail.

Thus it is life's own inexorability that has taught them the necessity of having as many sons as possible. Only by that means may they be certain that they will not need to put the rope around their own neck too early; for it is the common custom that old people, who can no longer keep themselves, prefer to put an end to their life by hanging rather than drag themselves through life in poverty and helpless old age.

.   .   .   .

On King William's Land I asked all the women at Malerualik how many children they had borne and how many girls they had put out of the way. I went into every single tent and spoke with every one of them. The result was the following . . . list, showing 96 births for 18 marriages and 38 girls killed . . . of the 259 souls in the Netsilik tribe only 109 are females, whereas 150 are males. Despite the high birth rate the tribe is moving towards extinction if girl children are to be consistently suppressed.

As an example of fertility I was informed that a certain Imingasruk, about sixty years old, whom I met in Committee Bay, had had twenty children; of these ten little girls had been killed, four died of disease, one son had been lost in a kayak, and there were alive four sons and one daughter; I met them, all splendid constitutions, handsome and powerful Eskimos. When I enquired whether they did not regret the killing of so many girls they answered: "No, for without killing she would not have had so many children, and if she had had to suckle all the girls, who were born before the boys, she would have had no sons now." Now she loved her boys, who gave her and her husband an old age free of care, but had no sentiment about those that had been killed, whom she had scarcely ever seen.

.   .   .   .

[*Rasmussen's account of the rigorous environment in which these Eskimos live, and their means of keeping alive in extremity, needs no elaboration. It is clear that among these people, as among those studied in the last chapter, there is little chance for an elder generation to develop, or for large or stable institutions to be formed. One can easily imagine that during the long periods of the last glacial advance, many small groups in Europe and Asia must have been just as hard pressed for survival as these Eskimos.*]

We will now make a closer examination of what life is like in the different seasons, and, as our starting point, take the early winter, when all the new clothing with which they have to withstand the cold is ready. This skin clothing has been made under both taboo and festivity; for from the day that the last caribou left the country all hunting is temporarily suspended while industrious seamstresses in new, warm snow huts are occupied from morn till eve. Evenings and nights are passed in song feasts after joyous banqueting on caribou meat and frozen salmon.

[*In order to survive the Eskimo must perform each of their special tasks in its proper season. This seasonal division of labor is enforced by stringent tabus, under the sanction of a belief in the disaster which will follow a breach of custom.*]

When at last everything is finished— for not another stitch may be put in when out on the ice the sun is again high in the heavens the following spring —they remove the camp from land and start out on their way to where the seals congregate. This breaking up from . . . "the place where the clothes are made," or "the sewing place," takes place at varying times all according to whether there is meat enough and they can afford to take a holiday close to the winter caches. In some years they have to go out to the breathing holes at the end of November, whilst there are years when they may wait until January or February.

Once out on the ice, this represents the commencement of a life of constant moves and journeys; they remove to a new hunting area as soon as there are no more seals at the camp that was first chosen. These journeys to new grounds may be long or short, all depending upon whether the hunting is good or bad. As a rule the distance is six to ten miles. The appearance of the seal is closely bound up with the manner in which the ice happens to lie. If the winter ice comes over a fjord suddenly and at the same time lies far out to sea, it often happens that only a few seals get into the usual hunting places. But if the ice forms so that the inner part of the fjord is first covered, while there is open water for some time outside, the animals have more time to come into the open sea, and then hunting is profitable.

In seasons when hunting is bad they have to move incessantly from place to place, and the winter becomes a hard one, not only for the hunters themselves but especially for the old people. The treatment of the aged, of course, varies with the individual. Here, as everywhere, there are helpful and sympathetic, or hard-hearted sons and sons-in-law, and the fate of the old people lies in their hands. . . .

I made exhaustive enquiries as to the treatment of the aged, and the only case of heartlessness that I came across was that of an old woman by name Kigtaq. She was the mother of a woman named Terigssaq, who was married to Arfeq. When they moved from camp to camp she was often left out on the ice in mid-winter, clad only in a thin inner jacket and no thick, warm outer coat. Even in bad weather she often had to sleep out on the ice as she had not caught up with the others. . . .

I took up this case of Kigtaq and asked whether it was not thought wicked that more care was not taken of an old woman. To this Samik answered: "No one here among us wishes harm to old people. We ourselves might be old some day. Perhaps there are those among us who think Arfeq might take better care of his mother-in-law, particularly by giving her better clothes. But others excuse Arfeq, in that he has been so unlucky in his hunting that he has barely been able to procure furs for his wife and his children, and people think he must first and foremost attend to them; for not only are they more closely related to him, but they have their lives before them and they must live long, whereas there is no future for an old worn-out woman. Then again there are others who think that Arfeq should allow his mother-in-law to ride on his sledge, or at any rate go back for her when he has built his snow hut, while others say that he only has two dogs and with his wife has to help to drag his sledge from place to place. And if he has to be at the breathing holes next morning at the proper time to secure food, he cannot travel backwards and forwards between the old and the new camp to salvage an old woman. He has the choice between helping one who is at death's door anyhow, and allowing his wife and children to starve. This is how it is, and we see no wickedness in it. Perhaps it is more remarkable that old Kigtaq, now that she is no longer able to fend for herself, still hangs on as a burden to her children and grandchildren. For our custom up here is that all old people who can do no more, and whom death will not take, help death to take them. And they do this not merely to be rid of a life that is no longer a pleasure, but also to relieve their nearest relations of the trouble they give them."

.   .   .   .

If they only had decent sledges and sufficient dogs, their winter life would be a much easier one . . . various primitive types of sledges of skin they use, and one can only admire the ingenuity with which they help themselves when no wood is to be had. For it was a long way to where there was wood. And in addition, a journey for the purpose of getting driftwood has as a rule to be paid for by bad summer hunting; for they would have to go right down to Queen Maud's Sea, to the north coast of King William's Land, or the region about Matty Island, and even then there was no saying that they would get anything out of their journey in these regions where wood is almost nonexistent.

.   .   .   .

So rare was driftwood that the Netsilingmiut believed it only grew on the bottom of the open sea. . . .

.   .   .   .

In a snow hut it is always the woman who begins the day. She gets up first in the morning and tends the lamp, which as a rule is all but extinguished in the evening before going to sleep. This is done not only because they do not mind sleeping in a cold room, but because they have to economize with the oil. For the blubber supplies they can put aside for the winter are astonishingly small, even in the spring months when most seals are caught. It is kept in a seal skin that has been removed whole, cuts being made only at the head and hind flippers. A blubber bag of this kind is reckoned to hold the blubber of five medium sized seals. . . . On the ice round about King William's Land there are only very few families that had more than three or four . . . for the winter. These families were in fact looked upon as being very well-to-do. . . .

But to return to the early rising woman. As soon as she has got her big blubber lamp burning at full blaze she removes the block of snow that closes the entrance passage . . . and this means that the house is open to any one who cares to make a morning call. . . .

The woman's next task is to put food over the lamp for her husband, usually consisting of a strong blood soup with blubber or boiled seal meat in it. This first meal is eaten by him naked, just as he is after his night's rest, and lying on the platform. While breakfast is being prepared the footwear and what else may have been hung over the drying rack to dry is attended to. This rack is always in the form of a half circle. . . . The lamp itself is . . . set on three upright sticks . . . so that its heat will not melt the snow, or on two pieces of wood laid longitudinally under the lamp. . . . The Greenland drip-basin for the oil that always oozes out of the lamp . . . is here substituted by a piece of sewn seal skin that is called . . . "the kneeling place"; . . . The lamp, and everything belonging to it, is not only the woman's property but as a rule has been hewn out of soapstone by her.

People living together in a hunting camp feel closely attached to one another in many ways. They mostly have a strong feeling that they cannot manage singly but need one another's help in the daily hunting. Therefore the men call their hunting companions . . . "those with whom I live on the firm ice," an expression that has come to mean: "the one with whom I have sought refuge." The thought is always this: "If I do not catch anything, I will surely get food for myself and my family from the others in the camp."

The moral is of course: "I expect you to do for me what I do for you." These are all views that naturally grow in places where it is difficult to obtain food. Caches that have been kept from the summer hunting are therefore always considered to be common supplies in a camp on the sea ice; it is expected that the owners will share them when they bring them in, so that all will have a part. If caribou meat or frozen trout is brought home, it would cause a most painful stir if all were not gathered to a festive meal—by invitation, of course. The man who brings a cache in . . . fulfills his obligations by adding a song feast to the meal, and this sets the donor in still higher relief. Song feasts are always a sign that there is meat and good days at a camp and hunters who can afford to feed others. Consequently the guests manifest their pleasure at the host's being able to "afford to sing" by eating without stint before the singing begins.

.   .   .   .

The difficulty of procuring dog feed necessitates the keeping of very few dogs. Many have only one, some two to four, and only very few of the most skilled hunters can permit themselves the luxury of what may be called a real team of seven to eight dogs. The result is that they are not used for traction in the same sense as in other regions, where walrus hunting gives a surplus of meat of quite different dimensions. Among the Netsilingmiut there is never anything to spare, and therefore they have to draw the sledges themselves and be content with a couple of dogs to assist. . . .

As a draught animal it might well be dispensed with. But a breathing-hole hunter without a dog might just as well stay at home and suck his thumb. If he has a dog, a hungry one for preference, it will lead him over the ice with distended nostrils in order to get the scent of something eatable, and it is from wonderfully long distances that it will suddenly prick its ears, lift its tail, and rush away, not stopping until with unfailing certainty and without wavering a moment it has taken its master to a breathing hole.

. . . .

The seal is only caught from the ice. Open-water hunting is not known. . . .

. . . .

Breathing-hole hunting is a wonderful method and can be developed into a great art through years of practice and experience. Training begins early, at the age of twelve or fourteen, and . . . the Netsilingmiut are considered to be experts by all other tribes. . . .

. . . .

All the men of the settlement go out together, each with his dog. As soon as a breathing hole has been found they all throw their harpoons at it, trying to hit it. The lucky thrower gets the hole, even if it may have been another who first discovered it.

. . . .

. . . quite early in the morning, while it is still half dark outside, Inŭtuk and I are awakened by a pail of boiling seal blood being put before us. Drowsily we slobber up the hot liquid with its plentiful admixture of train oil, for we know from experience that it is the only meal we may expect to have for the next ten or twelve hours. Then we quickly get into our clothes and tumble out of the snow hut. As usual there is a fresh breeze blowing and it is bitingly cold. Our fellow hunters are there already and, fifteen men strong, we race over the ice. Finding a breathing hole without the aid of a dog is a matter of pure chance; not only is it difficult to discover, but there are not many of them. But sometimes the foxes form a guide, for they often place their excrement on the ice dome. Today, however, we all

have a dog on a leash, and its fine nose is working incessantly up into the wind, sniffing and smelling from the moment we left the camp. We are three hours wandering about before the first hole is found, and we immediately flock round it in order to hit the small opening in the snow with our harpoons; Inŭtuk is the lucky one, and I remain with him while our comrades go on over the ice; gradually we see that they take up a position at other holes, some of them so far away that we can just discern them as small dots out on the white snow.

With the certainty of great experience Inŭtuk now makes his arrangements for the hunt. First he cuts away the whole of the uppermost layer of snow, exposing the little dome down on the firm ice. With his tuk he opens the frozen ice at the place where the seal usually breathes and then scoops out the small lumps of ice that fill up the opening with his ilaut of musk-ox horn. He "feels" his way under the ice until he knows whether the little opening through which the seal is to be harpooned is in the middle or to one side of the dome itself. He knows that this investigation is of vital importance to the direction in which the harpoon has to be thrust. The seal always comes up with its back to the ice and, if the ice is thick, the breathing hole from the surface of the ice down to the water forms a large funnel-shaped basin which the body of the seal by no means fills, so that one might very easily thrust the harpoon past it, even if the upper opening of the hole is hit truly. That is why it is so important and necessary to work out beforehand the position the seal will occupy in the ice funnel. These investigations completed, a small snow dome is again built up over the hole, just as it was before the snow was shoveled away. With the harpoon a hole is then made through the snow so that this and the opening in the ice are in line, thus ensuring that at the critical moment the harpoon meets with no resistance.

Now Inũtuk takes out his fine, ingeniously thought-out down indicator, [*a simple but ingenious device made of a piece of swan skin and a caribou sinew. This gives him warning of the approach of a seal*] places a single piece of swansdown between the "straddle legs" of the caribou sinew, and puts it down through the hole so that it hangs in the upper rim of the hole with the "arms" up, while the "legs" with the swansdown go down into the opening, but no further than that they can easily be seen from above.

Now all preparations have been made, and Inũtuk spreads his tutEriAq [fur box] out before the breathing hole and stands on it. Having done so, he stands as motionless as a statue, harpoon in hand and eyes fixed intently on the swansdown, which is just visible through the opening in the snow. Hour after hour goes by, and I realize what a fund of patience and hardiness is required when this hunting has to be pursued in a storm and in a temperature of about −50° C.

Four hours seems to me an eternity, and yet it is nothing; it sometimes happens that a man will stand twelve hours at a stretch when it is necessary to get food for those who are starving up in the icy snow hut; indeed when times are bad, when a quick catch means life or death, particularly to the hunter himself, exposed as he is all the time to wind and weather, it may happen that a man will stand almost without a break day after day at a breathing hole, taking only the shortest possible rests at home in the snow hut. I have heard of a man who spent two and a half days at a breathing hole, sometimes standing, sometimes sitting, but awake all the time.

Inũtuk and I had just about decided to abandon the hunt at this hole and to try to find another one, when we caught sight of a man who had got his harpoon firmly into a seal. As soon as the happy hunter had got his catch hauled up on to the ice we ran over to him for the purpose of partaking of the feast, which always assumes the character of a ceremony on account of the gravity with which it is eaten. All knelt down, the man who had made the catch on the right side, the others on the left side of the seal. The hunter cut a tiny hole in the belly, through which he took the liver and a piece of blubber. This done, the hole was closed up again with wound pins so that no blood would run out and go to waste. The liver and blubber were cut up into small squares and eaten in the same kneeling position. Whenever I took part in one of these meals I felt something fine and affecting in the manner in which they knelt to "the daily meat."

.   .   .   .

Toward the end of May the dome over the breathing hole melts and the opening is fully exposed in the ice. They are no longer difficult to find then, and, if there is a sufficient number of people in the camp, men, women and half-grown children scatter over the ice, as far as possible all provided with a harpoon and line, and every one takes up a position by a breathing hole. . . . The whole stretch of ice is taken into possession over as great an area as can be manned, and then the seals are gradually compelled to come up to a hole even if there is someone there, for the many fruitless attempts they have made to come up and get air make them bewildered and half mad; their dizziness overcomes their fear and they fall an easy prey. If . . . there are numbers of seals, and there are people enough, a big kill can be obtained.

. . . o't'uq is the term for a seal that lies up on the ice to sleep. . . .

It is surprising how few o't'uq there are in the Netsilingmiut hunting areas, presumably because the weather is always windy and snowy. Not until well into May and in the beginning of June do they become numerous, but by that time the ice is so watery that it is almost impossible to crawl up to the seals without making a noise . . . the hunter crawls over the ice, but stops every time the seal he is stalking wakens and looks at him. As long as his prey is observing him he has to roll about in the snow exactly like another wet seal that has just come up out of the water. The o't'uq, which is very suspicious at first, at last believes it is another seal that like itself has come up to bask in the sun, and by and by takes no more notice of the hunter, who at last gets so near that he can jump up and harpoon it. . . .

. . . . .

itErtulErinEq is particularly associated with a locality that is called Tuat. . . .

The hunter builds a snow hut over one of the small open cracks that are formed here at Tuat on account of certain particularities of the current. As soon as these cracks form, the seals naturally abandon their breathing holes and then move along by the cracks, where they can rise at any time and get their breath. The hut must be so built that the interior is as dark as possible. This is easy enough if only the blocks for building the house are cut thick enough. The doorway is . . . covered over with several layers of skin hung one over the other so that no light may penetrate . . . it is necessary to get the seal out of the house very quickly.

That part of the crack in the ice that runs through the house is now entirely covered over with a piece of ice which has been worked so that in the middle there is a hole of just the same shape as a breathing hole. This piece of ice must be so thick that the artificial breathing hole may have a relatively wide opening underneath, whereas at the top it ends in the usual little "blow hole." The migrating seals now move along by the crack as is their wont, rising and diving while seeking their food. For some reason or other the small man-made breathing hole seems to have a special fascination for them, and in going up into it to breathe they are harpooned in just the same way as out on the ice in winter. . . .

. . . . .

There are naturally very definite rules as to the manner in which the booty is shared among the hunters who have been out together. The rules apply especially to breathing-hole hunting, however, as this is pursued at a season when every bite of food procured is of importance. In spring, when everybody has food enough, it is no uncommon occurrence that a man retains the whole of the seal himself. . . .

Apart from the skin, the man that catches a seal only keeps the entrails, head, blood, the fat of the back and head, and the hind flippers and tail bone—in other words not a single piece of real meat. So little is his share if there are many men out together and all have to have a part. Thus if there are only two men in a hunting camp, the seal is divided across the middle. A man may have the right to a share even if he has not been out with the party, whether his absence may have been due to sickness or to work that could not be put off; he receives as his rightful share the same piece as he would give of his own kill to the other man.

. . . . .

In the ordinary breathing-hole hunting the shares play such an important role that at many villages there are most complicated rules for dividing a seal. They have in fact special amulets for luck with hunting shares; and sometimes it happens that, while their boys are still quite small, parents decide which parts of a seal their sons undertake to give each other for the rest of their lives while they live at the same village. . . .

[*The division of meat is always attended by strict rules among hunting peoples, and these rules are always so constituted that the group has the maximum chance of survival. The people who share meat together form the largest natural group among the Eskimo.*]

As soon as it is brought into the house the seal must be dealt with exactly in accordance with ancient observance. It must never be laid on the dirty and trampled snow floor. Before being taken in, snow is carried in and trodden out over the floor so that the seal will lie on fresh clean snow. It offends the soul if its body is allowed to lie on a place where a woman has walked. . . .

The careful hunter will always dip a piece of snow into the water-pail and let the water drip down into the seal's mouth. It is said that seals are always thirsty, and that they often let themselves be killed just to get a drink of water. For the thrust of the harpoon that kills it does not hurt and simply feels like a slight smarting. It is the belief that all seals know where killed animals are usually treated well, and therefore they always make their way to such people. . . .

[*Seal hunting provides these Eskimo with most of their food during the winter. It is a tricky business requiring skill and endurance, and governed to a certain extent by chance. No wonder the treatment of the seal is surrounded by ritual.*]

About the beginning of June, after the last seal hunts and the wet removals on melting ice, they [the hunters] lie up on land and dry their clothing; their worn and blubber-smeared garments are seen to and on the whole everything is made ready for the great season, summer and autumn, that is to be spent in fishing for trout and hunting caribou.

The caribou have already begun to make their appearance in April, singly or in small flocks. . . . And afterwards they come into the country steadily and regularly. They are shy, and in the old days were almost impossible to get with bow and arrow; but now, when guns are used, matters are different and, on trips into the interior, individual animals are brought down as early as in the latter part of April. For the sun is high up and it is not so serious a matter to blend the hunting of caribou and seal as in the cold and dark months.

As soon as the snow has melted away they move into the summer districts and settle down for the next four months. This is the time of the tent camps round lakes and rivers, the happiest season of the year, when the summer sports are entered into with zest and nobody ever neglects an opportunity to excel at hunting and fishing. In this period all the old and infirm become rejuvenated and gather strength to bravely withstand the rigors of the darkness and the frost of winter.

.   .   .   .

At the first part of the season trout are the principal form of food, but there was some sporadic caribou hunting with bow and arrow; the hunters concealed themselves behind talut, which were built right up to the paths usually followed by the game, and there they could lie for days and wait. . . . it has been practically impossible to hunt caribou that remained in the country during the winter when it was cold. The creaking snow made it quite impossible to get within suitable range, and the cold interfered in another manner too, even if the hunter had special fingered mittens designed for handling the bow and arrow, it was very slow sport in cold weather. The fingers became numb, not to speak of the fact that no hunter could hold out having to lie motionless hour after hour in windy weather on the cold snow. It was reckoned to be quite an achievement, a song was composed about it, if caribou were shot out of season before the great herds gathered. On the mainland this was not until the end of June, when mighty herds slowly made their way northwards—cows with their tiny calves, heifers, and young oxen. But even though hunting them gave a rich yield in numbers of animals killed, their meat did not go far because they were so lean, while their skins were useless for clothing. The great harvest of meat was always reaped in autumn. . . .

. . . . .

In those days it was a great and constant problem to get skins enough for the winter. For outer and inner coat four skins each were required, two each for inner and outer trousers, and one for footwear. This made seven skins for a grown man, six for a woman, and three or four per child, so that taking a small family of husband, wife, and three half-grown children, twenty-five skins had to be procured from caribou killed in the season when the fur was serviceable, i.e., in August–September, and this without counting an extra suit for the husband, who, always out in every sort of weather, could certainly do with it.

But this was not all. There had to be platform skins too, and with rugs at least six skins, and sleeping skins at least three, the total at a modest estimate was twenty-nine to thirty skins

without counting those for the tent sheet, eight to sixteen according to size. Before firearms were introduced it had certainly been difficult for most Eskimos to get so many, and in most cases they managed by the help they received from those who were well supplied. . . .

Of the scores of the best hunters I may mention: Eqaluk, 80 caribou; Qaqortingneq 76; Niúnauq 70; Tarrajuk 61; Inútuk 55; Alorneq 53; Itqilik 29; a score of twenty to thirty in the actual season, i.e. in the period when the skin was serviceable for garments, was the most common and, as anyone will understand, this cannot be said to be any overwhelming total. As a consequence they had to resort to a great extent to bear skin. . . .

[*The variation in number of animals killed by the different hunters is great. Also the number killed is important. The Eskimos know how to count; they need to know. In upper palaeolithic sites in Europe, tally sticks give the scores of animals killed by earlier hunters, and engravings on the bones and antlers depict the animal killed—the reindeer, cousin of the caribou.*]

When hunting with the kayak at the crossing places, the usual method was for the kayaks to lie concealed on the opposite side of the water to that from which the caribou were driven out, although when required by the terrain they might sometimes be on the same side. There was always a race. Two brothers have become famous for their quickness and their arrogance. Of them Qaqortingneq tells:

"Aklaussaq was down at a crossing place and was hunting caribou together with Kuvkilik's two sons, and used to paddle out with them in his kayak when the caribou swam across. But as he never could keep up with them and was always left behind, he finally got into the habit of shouting:

"'Kuvkilik, dear little Kuvkilik, I can't keep up with your two sons in my kayak. So give me a little meat for my wife to put into our empty pot.'

"But Kuvkilik used to answer exultantly: 'You are right! Nobody can paddle as fast as my sons.'

"Once, however, when autumn was approaching, Aklaussaq's wife said to him one day:

"'How is it that you never catch a caribou?'

"'I'm only waiting for them to be nicer and more meaty,' he answered.

"One day he took his paddle down, an old-fashioned kayak paddle . . . it is made with hollows for the hands at the place where one holds the paddle.

"He hid himself at the crossing place, and barely had he got down to his kayak when two bulls sprang out into the water; those who were waiting to pursue them only held back until the caribou had got so far out that, from where they lay hidden, they could see water between the swimming caribou and the land. As soon as they had got so far out that the men from their hiding places could see them swimming out in the lake, Aklaussaq pushed off. Then one of Kuvkilik's sons said mockingly:

"'Go on, paddle after them as fast as you can; for you are only waiting for them to be so nice and meaty that you can be bothered to kill them!'

"The two brothers laughed at him, for they were sure that he would not catch up with the animals and that they would overtake him and kill them. But Aklaussaq got there first and pierced them with his spear.

"From that day Aklaussaq was always the fastest kayak in the Netsilik tribe, and the two brothers were always left far behind; but their old father Kuvkilik shed many a tear over it."

．　　．　　．　　．

During the whole of the period when caribou were hunted their skins had only to be dried, and had not to be cured or sewn. There was a very strict taboo against making clothes before the great caribou hunt on the migrating animals had been brought to an end and people had moved into ice houses or snow houses. But if there were a case of urgency and a pressing necessity that a man should have a new garment before the sewing season, snow had to be collected from different drifts until they had sufficient for a house just large enough to accommodate the seamstress. The skins out of which she had to make the clothing had not to be prepared in the usual way, and in particular had not to be softened with the bone scraper which broke down the tissue, nor with the very sharp sAko't, which scraped off all the small shreds of flesh and completed the curing and softening of the skin. All that could be done was to moisten the skin on the fleshy side with water, roll it up, stamp it together and lash it with seal thong. Then it was left until the moisture had made its way through, after which the preparation was completed by softening it with the feet. . . .

．　　．　　．　　．

The Netsilingmiut imagine the "Land of the Blessed" as a place where joy never dies and where every day it must manifest itself in play. It would seem that this ideal existence had already been realized in life at the fishing place, where every single day they played and carelessly noised and laughed for at least five or six hours—people of all ages and of both sexes. Their day formed itself almost as follows: First the labor of procuring the daily food. This was restricted to ten minutes twice, sometimes three times, a day; but even these ten minutes' work was to them a sport, with contests and larks to the accompaniment of cries and deafening laughter.

The fishes were caught down in the little stream that joined the two lakes together. A stone dam had been built in it, blocking it completely. Out in the middle was the [gashge], a round weir of stones forming a separate enclosure, ten meters long, parallel with the flow of the river, four meters wide measured at right angles from the course of the river. This [gashge] had an uk'uAq: a gateway in the end facing the lake from which the river flowed. The trout that followed the stream and tried to get from the upper lake to the lower one had necessarily to pass through the uk'uAq into the [gashge], for both to the right and to the left of the uk'uAq ran a stone wall about ten meters long right into the banks of the river. These were called san'Erutit (those that run across the course of the river). The [gashge] was furnished with a number of traps built of stones and roofed with large flat stones; they tapered off inwards and had a length of two meters with an opening of barely half a meter wide. These traps, which were built close together outside the stone setting of the [gashge], were called [situsharfet] (those to glide down into); into each trap there was of course an opening from the [gashge] itself.

The fish usually approached at midnight or early in the morning before sunrise, and sometimes in the afternoon when the sun was low. Only at these times did the Eskimos catch them and during the rest of the day fishing was strictly forbidden, for then the fish were to be left in peace. Everybody fished at the same time. No one had to approach the [gashge] till the local "superintendent of fisheries" had shouted the signal over the whole settlement: ". . . Now we'll all go down!"

This cry was always greeted with joyous howls from all the tents, but nobody ever walked down to the river; it was always a wild race of men, women and children, from the most decrepit, hobbling and stumbling old veterans to the youngest fleet runners, some fully dressed, others half naked, most of them bare legged, despite the fact that the water was icy cold and the air more than chilly. They seemed to be oblivious to cold. They stopped a short distance from the river, where the leisters with their long shafts were deposited, and then four or five men stole forward, leister in hand, towards the lake whence the fish usually came. Cautiously they crept up to just outside the brink, careful lest their shadows should fall on the water. Twenty or thirty meters from the [gashge] and the san'Erutit they suddenly rushed out into the river and then walked downstream, waving arms and leisters, wading towards the opening of the [gashge] inside the stone walls of the san'Erutit . . . then one could see how the many fish that had accumulated shoaled hurriedly towards the [gashge]; only here and there did one leap over the stone dam and continue on toward the other lake. Most of them ran between the open uk'uAq into the [gashge]. When there were no more fish in the river a man sprang to the uk'uAq and closed it with a large flat stone, and then all the trout were shut up in the weir.

The closing of the uk'uAq was the sign that the fishing could begin and, careless of the cold water or their clothes, which became saturated, the whole impatient flock of people tumbled into the river and into the [gashge], where they began to spear the fish that had collected in it. The fish dashed wildly about, in between the legs of the Eskimos, who stabbed away with their leisters with no pretense at any system, the sole object being to be the one to catch the most fish, and it was always a riddle to me that in this scuffle, with the leisters incessantly darting in and out of the water, apparently at random, the people preserved their toes unscathed; there was never anyone that got so much as a scratch on leg or foot. Each fisher carried in his hand a qorqaut: a long bone needle on a thong, with a toggle of wood at the other end. When a fish is caught the needle is stuck through it, preferably so as to break the backbone, then he goes on again, often trailing five or six fish behind him at the end of the thong.

It is not all the fish that are taken with the leister, for many of them slip into the traps and hide there; the salmon has the well-known peculiarity that it never turns in a trap and tries to get out the way it came in; on the contrary, they press forward in the narrow part of the trap in order to get out in the direction they were proceeding. Thus the fish that have got into the traps are doomed and are regarded as the private property of those who built the trap. There man and wife usually fish in company, one holding the leister at the entrance to the trap for safety's sake, while the other removes a stone at the inner end, whence the scared fish allows itself to be taken without resistance.

Later on in the summer season, or the beginning of autumn, there is often such a wealth of fish at Amitsoq that, in the course of fourteen days, every family can catch so much that they are able to make three or four caches of good, fat trout for the winter. Each cache represents between two and three hundred kilograms. . . .

[A leister is a spear with several curved and notched points at the end, looking something like a hatrack. It is more efficient for catching closely swimming fish than a single-pointed spear. You will observe that in fish-ing, which is a group operation, a special person gives the signal to begin. This is true of group activities in other societies, for example acorn picking in California, olive picking in Morocco, and buffalo shooting among the Plains Indians. It preserves order and ensures a greater efficiency in collection and distribution than random individual efforts.]

Some variation in the day's events was caused by many small, affecting customs. For instance it is a very important event, and one to be celebrated, when a small boy catches his first fish. Thus I one day happened to see Pugutaq (the wooden tray) catch his first fish. The boy was no more than six years old, so that it was his mother that had to do most of the catching. He was too small to wade out in the river, so she had to carry him out to the [gashge]. There he had to hold the leister himself, but had to be assisted in spearing the fish, and afterwards in pushing the qorqaut through it. But as soon as this was done she broke out into loud joyous cries and announced to the settlement that her son had made his first catch. Later on the day was celebrated with a great feast, consisting of all the trout possessed by the family. It was arranged in the usual manner, the women eating by themselves and the men likewise; they never eat together, as the men are afraid of bad hunting if they eat in company with unclean women, which might scare the animals away. . . .

[This is an example of a conflict between symbolic configurations as discussed in the Appendix (Sec. 7). The men do the hunting. Their hunting activities interfere with their relations with their women, and vice versa. Thus the whole realm of hunting and that of the relations between sexes are virtually antagonistic. This conflict is extended to the symbolic level. The *meat eaten symbolizes the relations between men (the interaction component) which are part of the hunting activity. Menstruation and pregnancy, which are critical and noticeable attributes of women, symbolize the relations of men with women. The two sets of symbols must be kept apart to reinforce the separation of the men from the women while the former are hunting.]*

All work has a natural distribution, roughly characterized by the fact that it is the man who procures food while the woman does all the housework. Her contribution to the upkeep of the home is set at a high value, and a clever seamstress enjoys genuine esteem. The woman has not only her special duties but also her rights; in her marriage she has her own property, her particular possessions being recognized as the lamps, pots . . . , ulo, sewing needles, meat trays of wood . . . , water containers . . . and the large horn ladles for boiled meat and soup, almost always of musk-ox horn. She brings all these things into the marriage as her trousseau and retains them in the event of a separation. . . . Itqilik's wife Unalerssuaq, who had no soapstone cooking pot in her marriage outfit, bought one and paid for it—of course with her husband's approval—with a newly born child. Naturally a soapstone pot is not so high priced if the family is in the vicinity of one of the places where soapstone is to be had, so that this particular bargain may be explained by the fact that the Itqilik family was right up at Arvetoq (Bellot Strait), and there it was impossible to get any of this material.

. . . .

Divorce is common as long as there are no children, and there are women who go through seven or eight trial marriages before they finally settle down.

Their pleasure in their offspring is great, and children always unite parents closely. If they cannot beget children a little adoptive child usually has the same effect and influence. Adoptive children are always bought, and the price paid for them varies greatly, although it is always high. Eqatlijoq, for instance, had bought her adoptive son for a soapstone cooking pot and a kayak, both very precious objects. They are usually bought when newly born, the reason being, of course, that a mother who does not intend to rear her child does not want the trouble of nursing it, especially as this also would mean that her next child would be so much the later in coming. In winter these little adoptive babies are brought up on seal soup, or on caribou soup in the caribou season; the foster mother first takes the soup into her mouth and keeps it until it has come to a suitable temperature, and only then does she gulp it into the infant's mouth. It needs no saying that this feeding gives most children violent diarrhoea, of which many of them die. This happens especially when the foster mother in her eagerness to make the soup more nourishing puts blubber or caribou fat in it. But if the foster child survives the first difficult period it thrives well and begins to eat meat even at the age of twelve months, although the foster mother chews it first and then passes it into its mouth.

. . . .

Most young men and women are "engaged" before they are born, which means that the parents agree that their children are to have each other. If the parents of an engaged couple live so far apart that they rarely or never see each other, the natural thing is that when they grow up they enter into a temporary marriage with another. As far as the woman is concerned this happens at a very tender age, thirteen to fifteen. One young man, Angutisugssuk, who lived in King William's Land, called a man right up at Repulse Bay his father-in-law. Angutisugssuk was then twenty years old and unmarried, because his mother-in-law had not yet given birth to his "intended." And so for the time being he was "second husband" in the house of Tarajorqaoq.

.   .   .   .

Polygamy is known, but of course it cannot be general owing to the great inferiority of women as to number. If a man has more than one wife it is consequently always a sign of good standing and especial skill as a hunter. Though jealousy is no unknown feeling, concubines usually get on well together. Polyandry is also practised, it being no rare occurrence for a woman to have two husbands. A grown man is a helpless being if he has no woman to make his clothes, and so it will happen that a husband will call a good comrade who is alone to share his wife with him. It is seldom, however, that these marriages run smoothly, especially if the men are young, for it very often ends in one of them being killed. Naturally, a wife can never ask a good friend to come in as a partner in her marriage; this is a right that exclusively belongs to the husband.

Wife exchanging for short periods often takes place, especially between men who are usually song-fellows at festivals. . . . Husbands have almost always a certain man to whom they hand the drum when they have sung their song. This man, who has to sing a song in reply, is called his iglua: his song-comrade or song-fellow. . . . Two such men who usually follow one another at a song festival are considered to be so closely associated that not only after the ceremony but at all times when they feel inclined, they can exchange wives. Some religious appraisement undoubtedly lies behind this fellowship. It involves both advantages and obligations; for instance, if a man is about to set out on a long journey—perhaps to trade—and his wife is with child, sick or in some other manner unfit to go with him, he can borrow the wife of his iglua to accompany him, giving his own in exchange. This form of wife-exchange is necessary in a community living the nomad life of Eskimos.

Husbands have a very free hand in their married life and it is considered to be quite in order for them to have intercourse with any woman whenever there is an opportunity. . . .

. . . a woman who has given herself to another man usually gets a thrashing from her husband, even if she herself was not the inciting party. Cases do occur, however, where it is the gallant lover that is called to account, and the difference is then settled by a bout of fisticuffs. All men are clever and trained boxers. A fight of this description is usually fought without spectators. The contestants strip to the waist, face each other and then pound away at shoulders, arms and head until one of them retires and declares himself beaten. After an encounter of this kind the two are good friends again.

.   .   .   .

I said that men fight among themselves for a wife, for a simple consequence of the shortage of women is that young strong men must take women by force if their parents have not been so prudent as to betroth them to an infant girl. The little settlement up at Bellot Strait was established by men who found their surroundings too hot for them because they had stolen their wives and incidentally, in the heat of strife, had sent the husbands into the great silence. Abduction need not always end in bloodshed, however. Just before I arrived at King William's Land a young man, Inorajuk, had lost his wife under circumstances which he himself described as follows:

"Last winter I visited a snow-hut camp with people from Victoria Land just at the time when the warmth of the sun begins to return and the seals have young. I went there to trade, and my sledge party consisted of Seqineq and his wife, my wife and my little daughter. My trading was soon completed, but I was compelled to stay the day over on account of snowstorm. On that day my wife was invited to a house to eat boiled seal meat; but scarcely had she gone inside when my comrade Seqineq came running up to me and told me that the people at the settlement intended to steal my wife.

"There were fourteen men and their wives in the camp. I hurried to the house where my wife was being kept shut in, and by using my fists I succeeded in getting her out into the open. But then all the men and their wives came out after me with the exception of Seqineq, who was kept shut in because he would help me. After a long fight I had to give in at last, because my opponents had pulled all my clothing off and it was impossible for me to fight out in the snowstorm, which numbed all my muscles. Then I had to leave the camp alone with my little daughter, and since then it has been impossible for me to get my wife back."

.   .   .   .

In the old days a tribe was really at war with all others outside of its own hunting grounds, and many are the tales that have been handed down of strife, murder, in fact massacre. After the entry of the white man into the Hudson Bay district, perfect peace was established between the tribes in the east, but they were still at loggerheads with all tribes to the west, especially the people from Victoria Land.

One would think that in these waste and desolate regions they would feel pleasure when they came across people who could be company for them; far from it. To this day it is customary, when a sledge party approaches a settlement, that it does not drive right up to the door. An informal arrival like that might give rise to fright and misunderstanding, which would quickly lead to hostilities. And the fact must never be lost sight of that human life was never at any time taken too seriously.

It is astonishing how suspicious they were in former times, but an instinct of insecurity like this can only have arisen because experience showed that there was reason for it. As evidence of this an old man told me the following:

When they broke camp in his grandfather's day and moved from one hunting place to another, they drove sledge behind sledge, many in company, in a long line, the first breaking the trail. As there were only few dogs, men and women had to pull too. During such a removal the snow knife was never released from the hand and as a rule a man also had his sealing harpoon with him. A man in the procession could not stop to make water without great risk, for the one who walked in front might easily get the idea that the man for some reason or other would strike him down from behind, and this suspicion alone might be a sufficient cause of bloodshed. They did not trust each other; even if they apparently were the best of friends they could never be sure that the one had not evil intentions. So it is no wonder that they were doubly cautious when meeting strangers.

When the sledges had been stopped at a distance of about a mile from the settlement a woman was sent up to tell who they were and that no hostile feelings were entertained. Only when the truce bearer had been well received could the rest drive up without hesitation. . . .

[*Interpersonal relations are seen to rest on the simplest and most direct basis possible among these Eskimo. They are limited by the shortage of food and of other necessary materials. Soapstone, needed for lamps and pots, comes from a distance, and a lamp is as valuable as a child. Marriage provides the maximum service of the opposite sex for each person. Like everyone else the Eskimo are human, and their affairs are regulated for the greatest convenience of the largest number; everything that they do seems designed for survival. The vagueness of rules and regulations in interpersonal relations reflects the catch-as-catch-can nature of their adjustment to their environment.*]

Angatkut, or shamans, are people possessed of special gifts that can bring them in communication with the spirits of the earth, the air and the sea. By means of these preternatural beings they can see "the things that to others are hidden," and they can help their fellow men who have got into danger, either on account of sickness or on account of continuous misfortune on their hunts, or if, attacked by an enemy, they have become possessed of an evil spirit.

Angatkut can get into communication with the supernatural in two ways, either by holding a seance or through qilanEq. These methods of calling up spirits correspond in every way to those that are customary among the Iglulingmiut, and, as among the latter, a special spirit or shaman language is employed.

An ordinary seance is held in a snow hut or a tent, preferably in a subdued light; it is said that the spirits do not care to appear in full daylight. When a shaman is going to summon his helping spirits for some purpose or other the whole village is invited to attend the ceremony. He conjures them by singing special spirit songs; among the Netsilingmiut these spirit songs were not necessarily about anything particular nor set to any special melody. It is simply said that there is a certain song which, when sung, has the effect that the spirits like to come. Every angatkut has his own particular song, and it puts him into a trance. It is then believed that the spirit summoned takes up its abode in his body and simply speaks through his mouth. And so, as soon as he has fallen into a trance, he always speaks in a voice that is not his own, often a deep, resonant bass, at other times in a shrill falsetto, and, if some animal is his helping spirit and it now dwells in him, he imitates the voice of that animal.

A helping spirit is called an apershaq: one that exists to be questioned, and there may be a great difference in these apershät. For instance, a certain Unaraluk, a man who was one of the less prominent angatkut, had such eminent helping spirits as the sun and the souls of his deceased father and mother. Another shaman, Iksivalitaq, had the moon spirit, a sea scorpion and one of his father's dogs—remarkably enough a dog that was alive, a young animal still in use.

An angatkut does not choose his own apershaq. They come to him of their own volition, and then he must not be afraid of them. If he is, he will never secure them as helping spirits. Tiagssaq, the wife of Samik, was a shaman in her younger days but abandoned the cult when she began to have children. Her expressed reason was that she could not sleep at night for fear of her helping spirits.

There is no particular place in hut or tent for an angatkut when summoning his helping spirits. Either he walks about the floor singing, or he sits on the platform uttering the various sounds that are characteristic of the spirit that has possessed him.

The other method of getting into touch with one's apershaq is the so-called qilanEq, which means that "something happens by means of tying something fast." It is just the same as the Iglulingmiut method. The shaman ties a line to one of his own legs or the head or leg of another; then he jerks the line to the continuous accompaniment of a monotonous repetition of: ". . . where are those (spirits) I must bind fast to me?" After having been called for some time a spirit takes up its abode in the body that has been tied to the line, and one communicates with it by continually jerking the line. When the part of the body to which it is tied becomes so heavy that one cannot lift it, the spirit is there and ready to answer the questions put to it. Usually the shaman has some idea of the breach of taboo that may have been the cause of the misfortune or sickness that is now to be averted or cured. He addresses a number of questions to the spirits, pulling at the line all the time. When the line cannot raise qilaq (that to which it is tied), i.e. either his own leg or another's head or leg, it means that he has named one of the causes of the sickness or bad hunting. That is how the spirits answer.

The Netsilingmiut themselves are very emphatic in pointing out that they no longer have great shamans among them. The whole art rests upon traditions from olden times, and the respect for shamanizing is really only created by what people know from the old tales a shaman *should* be able to perform, if only he is sufficiently well up in his art. . . .

. . . . .

All that I was unable to get anything like exact information about was the special training of shamans, so I must presume that preparation is of a rather casual character. Disciples are led out into the bosom of nature by an experienced shaman who is willing to help them, and there in solitude they receive visions, a simple result of the fact that they are firmly convinced that they are there to witness something supernatural. Hallucinations in this nervous state are very common, and the teachers themselves do all they can to surround the disciple with a mysteriousness that increases his agitation.

. . . . .

Once during a visit I had an opportunity of seeing Ugtugpagluk shamanizing. While I was in her tent she suddenly had a violent attack of hysterics, apparently for no reason whatever; she spoke wildly, screamed, sang, and shouted aloud, tumbling to and fro on her platform, until finally she went into a trance. In that state she put some fur from a hare's foot into her mouth and spit it straight out again, and then it had become caribou fat. Just before the seance we had eaten a very fat caribou tongue, and she had apparently kept some of this in her mouth and later on, by chewing it together with the white hare fur, made it look like a piece of tallow. As soon as the hare fur had been transformed into tallow she came to herself again, resumed her natural voice and explained that it had been a helping spirit that had possessed her and compelled her to make tallow of the hare fur. Her husband and all the audience were very much impressed by this trick.

. . . . .

These events took place in the month of October, just when the first long and dark evenings had commenced; the darkness had undoubtedly affected their minds. They said then that evil spirits were prevalent in our village and, although we had no fewer than five shamans at the place, they were fully occupied every evening with their invocations. They were two men and three women. Every evening they rushed out into the darkness to fight against the spirits, and they always returned with torn clothing. Sometimes they were also bloody on arms and hands. No one imagined the possibility that they may have torn their garments themselves or taken blood with them and smeared themselves with it. No one ventured out after nightfall at that time. . . .

[*The Eskimo make most ingenious houses. They heat them, and cook their food, with soapstone lamps, using the blubber of sea mammals as fuel. They cut and sew the world's best arctic clothing. As hunters they are superb. But they are forced to live in small, impermanent, and widely separated groups. In their rigorous environment, with many chances for illness, accident, and death, disturbances are common, and these disturbances need spiritual attention. The Eskimo shaman, who concerns himself with the restoration of equilibrium (see Appendix, Sec. 16) to individuals and the small groups which exist, operates on the same level of sophistication, and employs the same kind of symbols, as the shamans of the Indians of Lower California and the Yahgans. It is therefore evident (and this can be tested with other Arctic peoples) that the ritual development of a people is a function of their social complexity rather than of their technological skill.*]

One very rarely sees men or women at their work without their humming a song. They have all their songs, both men and women. And sometimes it happens that children, half in play, half in earnest, make up songs and deliver them among playmates when playing song-festivals in a little snow hut that they have built themselves. Great

pains are taken to put the words together nicely and skilfully so that there is melody in them, while at the same time they are pertinent in expression. A man who wants to compose a song may long walk to and fro in some solitary place, arranging his words while humming a melody which he also has to make up himself.

With Orpingalik, who of all Netsilingmiut was the most poetically gifted man, I often discussed the significance of song, not merely as a herald of festivity in the qagsge but also as a valve for their sorrows and cares. [*To him his songs are*] not only . . . just as necessary . . . as his breath, but they are his comrades in loneliness.

In the following I have attempted to reproduce Orpingalik's views on how a song is born in the human mind. His poetic narrative of course was not the product of a single question, but the result of a most intimate conversation which I have recorded summarily, but retaining his own expressions and illustrations.

. . . . .

. . . "Songs are thoughts, sung out with the breath when people are moved by great forces and ordinary speech no longer suffices.

"Man is moved just like the ice floe sailing here and there out in the current. His thoughts are driven by a flowing force when he feels joy, when he feels fear, when he feels sorrow. Thoughts can wash over him like a flood, making his breath come in gasps and his heart throb. Something, like an abatement in the weather, will keep him thawed up. And then it will happen that we, who always think we are small, will feel still smaller. And we will fear to use words. But it will happen that the words we need will come of themselves. When the words we want to use shoot up of themselves —we get a new song."

I have previously compared life at a fishing place with that in "the Land of the Blessed." Everybody does just what he pleases and almost invariably that which amuses him or her at the moment. Onerous duties are for the long cold winter. "In summer people must flourish in exactly the same manner as the soil they live on," explained Samik one day. The form of pastime that is most in vogue is games, and . . . it is impossible to obtain any really vivid impression of life in summer if some of the favorite variations are not mentioned here. . . .

Naturally enough, the people usually chose the games that provided both warmth and exercise, and hour after hour they would devote themselves to these simple and naïve pleasures, oblivious to everything else.

A particular favorite was a cross between hide and catch. All the players stand in a circle, close together, with heads bent, while one conceals himself; when he is found he is pursued, and the first to touch his bare body must then hide, and the game begins all over again. Or they sit down in a long row while one walks along and kicks all the foot-soles of those seated; then he walks over their toes, next over their shins, and every time he has completed the round he butts them in the stomach. Finally he goes around behind them, tickles each one on the body with his foot and runs away, when all the others jump up and pursue him; when he is caught he must tear a tuft of hair from his coat and give it to the one who is now to take his place. Or they play "keeping silent," with firmly closed mouth. The one who laughs first is given a comical name which he must answer to for the rest of the day. Or they play bears and try to attack all the others who jump about, the one who is "on" having to crawl on all fours. There was also a ball game, in which as many as

possible had to take part. They split up into twos and these partners try to throw the ball to each other. Every kind of trick is allowed; they fight with their opponents, trip them up, and push from behind, with shrieks of laughter all the time, and once this game is properly started, old and young participating, it might well last the whole day and never seem to weary. Next day they would start again. Man and wife were oftenest partners, and I was forced to admire their pretty treatment of each other. I have rarely been among people where the men praised their women so much, while the women never tired of lauding the splendid qualities of their husbands.

A curious game, a particular favorite among the children, was . . . [the spirit game], in which they imitated and parodied shaman seances and the general fear of evil spirits with a capital sense of humor. They held complete and true shaman seances, fought with imaginary enemies just as the grown-ups do; in fact they even used the same formulas that they had heard their parents utter when really in fear and danger. Although this game was absolute blasphemy the grown-up audience writhed with laughter, just as if they took a certain satisfaction in seeing the evil and inexorable gravity of life made the subject of farcical burlesque. Some hours later it might happen that an attack of illness, or perhaps a bad dream, would rally the grown ups to a seance during which they desperately sought to defend themselves against hidden enemies, with exactly the same means as the children had mocked in play. When I mentioned this remarkable circumstance to my friend Kuvdluitssoq, and enquired of him whether it was really prudent to mock the spirits, he answered with the greatest astonishment pictured in his face that the spirits really understood a joke.

This last point made by Rasmussen is a very important one. People like the Yahgans, Eskimos, and others whom we shall study later on do not separate their activities into mutually exclusive and conflicting categories, as we do. They offer up a prayer, or small sacrifice, as an essential part of a work activity. They combine humor with ritual, ceremony with trade, and sex with both ritual and trade. The difference is that they belong to but one group, or institution, apiece; it is the same people who are concerned in each activity. We have separate economic, political, and religious institutions, carrying on their activities independently. An individual who trades with one group of persons worships with another, and is politically identified with still others. That is why we have conflicts where the Eskimos do not.

5

The Story of the Reindeer Lapps

JUST to show that a simple institutional life and perhaps an equally simple out-look on the great unknown is not the property of any one race or collection of races, we can examine the culture of a group of white people who have been living under extreme environmental conditions in the far north of Europe for centuries. These are the Lapps, the hardy reindeer herders whose domain covers parts of four nations, Norway, Sweden, Finland, and the Soviet Union.*

Over thirty years ago a middle-aged Lapp who had lived a hard, full life in the open air, and who was famous throughout Lapland for his skill at hunting wolves, learned to read and write. He, Johan Turi, sat down in a log cabin and wrote out the story of his people in his own language. A friend translated it into Danish, and it was published in Copenhagen. Later it has appeared in a number of languages. The following selections are from the English edition.† Cutting this material was almost as painful as amputating a finger.

Telling about the Lapps, where they first lived, what were their circumstances, what they lived on, and from whence they come.—No one has ever heard that the Lapps came to this land from any other place. From the very earliest times they have been up here in Lappland; and when, in the beginning, the Lapps lived by the seacoast, there wasn't a single other person living here, and that was a good time for the Lapps. In olden times the Lapps lived all over the Swedish side too, then there weren't any settlers in the land, and the Lapps never knew that there were any other folk in the whole world.

I think that at first they lived by catching fish, wild birds, and reindeer, and trapping bears and all kinds of wild beasts. I think this because you find Lapp names in the fishing places on lakes where the present-day Lapps don't fish any more. And a still greater proof that the Lapps had lived for long, long ages in the same place is the pits to be found in the earth everywhere where the Lapps have been. These pits were their homes, they dug pits like wild beasts.

*Although this material on the life of the Reindeer Lapps is ample in many respects, it does not include enough precise data on relations between groups of Lapps, and those between Lapps and outsiders, to permit an accurate allocation of these people to any specific level of complexity. Probably this varies between Lapp groups and has also changed during the last century as Scandinavians, Finns, and Russians have moved northward. I place the Lapps here for convenience in teaching.

† Translated (Danish) by Emilie Demant Hatt; translated (English) by E. Gee Nash. Jonathan Cape, London; Harper & Bros., New York, 1931. By permission of the publishers.

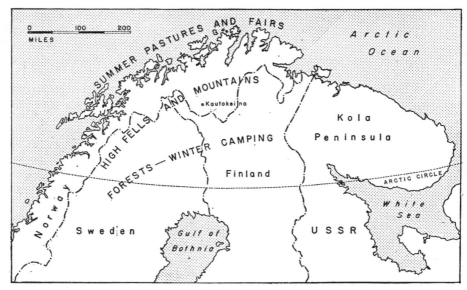

The country of the Lapps

And the greatest number of these pits are to be found on the sea coast, and on the banks of lakes and rivers, and in those places where the animal roads pass, such as points where the great clefts in the fell sides meet, and on tracks between lakes.

Now such was the Lapp nature that they began to long for the wild reindeer. They saw a lot of wild reindeer, and they began to catch them and watch over them. In the winter, when the snow was thick in the forest, they began to follow them on their skis, till the wild reindeer tired, and then they took the most tractable of them, but it was probably hard to keep them together. And when they had got a few tame ones it was easy, with their help, to catch more. In the hot months, when the reindeer run in flocks, they like to go in among the high crags, and then the Lapps followed them and shut them up till they were hungry, and had got used to the sight and smell of human beings.

At that time the Lapps first began to make sacrifices to *seites* [1] in order to get more reindeer, or so that the herds should increase. In olden days the Lapps used to worship idols so that the herds should be large, and their herds grew big from next to nothing, and they were the most beautiful reindeer; but these *seite* herds only last during the owner's lifetime, their children are always poor. And the Lapps usually fear that their children will be poor if they have *seite* herds, and even I who write this have heard it said that such and such a Lapp owned a *seite* herd, and that the herd would be only fleeting. Now the folk had not so much time for catching fish, for they all turned to catching reindeer, and they caught so many that they began to live in *sidas*.[2] They found out where it was best to take the herd at different

[1] Idols of wood or stone to which sacrifices are offered. The name *seite* is also given to the place of sacrifice.

[2] The name given to a collection of Lapp tents, together with their herds. This name is also given to a single tent with its herd, or herds.

times of the year, and they discovered that it was best to migrate just as the Lapps do to this day. In those days it was easy to live, for there were no settlers . . . neither Norwegian nor Swedish.

Then they used to spend the winter far south, until the settlers came and frightened them until they gave up going so far south. In the summer they went to Norway, and stopped by the seacoast, and kept their herds in the forests, and up on the fells, just wherever they pleased.

At that time the Lapps didn't know that there were any other folk in the world and the Lapps who lived in the south began to move toward the high fells in the north, and those who lived by the seacoast moved up to the high fells too, and they met, and they were so terrified of one another that they ran away and hid, for each thought the others were Stallos and Uldas.[3]

And at that time the Lapps didn't know that there was a God, but they believed in worshipping something, for when they sacrificed it helped them and so they made offerings to *seites*.

.   .   .   .

About the late summer, and the Lapp migrations southward from Norway, when, according to their nature, the reindeer begin to long for the south.[4]—When the grass begins to wither then the reindeer begin to long for reindeer-moss and in Havland (Norway) there is very little moss, it is almost all grassland. Then, in those districts where it is not possible for several families to travel together—in those places where there are five or eight thousand reindeer—the Lapps begin to separate the herds.

In olden times Lapps did not use reindeer stockades,[5] but separated the herds on some level table land. If there is a narrow cape projecting out into a lake in the neighborhood, this is a specially good place. The separating is done like this:—The Lapps begin to frighten one part of the herd, they poke the reindeers' behinds with sticks, and they go away, and the rest of the animals they leave in peace. This part of the herd that is left when the others have driven away their animals is unmixed, and they drive it away so far that it can't be seen, so that it shan't mingle with the other part. The other part is still a mixed herd, and they let it rest there, and then they begin separating this in the same manner . . . by poking them behind. Some animals run off at once to the other edge of the herd, but others are so bold that they go back again, and won't let themselves be driven away, not even if you beat them, and then you must run after them till you get them away, and that makes a lot of trouble, for the reindeer that have been left get frightened, and if it's an impatient man who is running after them, then he frightens them all the more. In this separating of the different herds it's no good being strong, or quick at running, but you must be clever at separating, and this cleverness consists of being quiet, and trying not to move quickly. Those who get angry, and begin to spring about after the reindeer, and set the dogs on them, they make the reindeer run and mix together, and so the work is all to do again. And that often causes anger, where there are impatient folk it is difficult to separate the herd, and it makes a lot more work; but when folk are clever at separating

---

[3] Lapp trolls.
[4] When Turi uses the word south he means the Swedish side of the ridge of high fells that forms the boundary between Norway and Sweden.

[5] Enclosures into which the Lapps drive the reindeer when they are to be milked or separated.

it goes twice as quickly, and twice as easily too. And so, when there is a little flock (separated) they drive it away to where the first flock has been put. And so day ends, and the owners gather together to consult as to where it is best to take each little herd; and when they come to a decision as to where they will put them the watchers go out to each flock. There are now three flocks (two separated flocks and one mixed flock) and when the weather is good the watchers can easily hold the herds together, and in the morning the watchers come back with the herds, and so they start separating again. And as the mixed herd is now smaller they start separating from both sides, and the mixed herd is left in the middle, and that is the worst time. Then, if the men are quiet and clever everything goes fast and well; but if they are impatient and clumsy, and if some begin to run about, then the others have to run about too, and then they run into one another, or the reindeer mix together, and then they start to set the dogs on them, and then the reindeer run together worse than ever. And if there are any unmarked animals or animals that have been marked in the summer with other men's marks, and the men recognize their reindeer, then there is a great outcry, and they rush about, and spoil the whole separating. If they come to blows it is even worse, and the herds mix together till it is all to do over again the next day . . . and some men get so angry that they begin to kill other men's reindeer.

When they have finished separating the herds, then they set out on the way southward; and if it is fine weather then it is a pleasant wandering southward over the high fells, but when it is a bad year there is bad weather early in the late summer in Havland, and when they are ready to move they can't

get the herds together, and when they get the herds together there is already rain and snow and everything is wet. And when it is cold the tent cloth stiffens so that you can't fold it, and you have to dry it on the poles, and make a great fire to dry it with, and dry, too, all the clothes the folk have on, for those who have been out have their clothing wet through to their skin and they are so frozen that their legs swell and will hardly bend, and if they are out and can't get a fire they freeze to death.

.   .   .   .

When they set off all their belongings are loaded on pack reindeer, the children too, big and little. And then the strings [6] set off, and the herd isn't far away. And when they are late in starting it gets dark before they reach their camping place, and that is very dangerous. Then the pack reindeer grow so frightened that they begin to spring about, and their packs fall off, and the reins break, and the reindeer run off into the wilderness, and in the dark you can't see where they go, and so you have to let those reindeer run. And the children fall off the reindeer, and the reindeer run over them and trample on them, sometimes until they are almost killed. But you must go on with the reindeer that you still have hold of, and it is hard to find the way. When you reach the place where you have decided to camp for the night you untie the reindeer, and they are tired out and the day is already gone. Now you must make haste to put up the tents before the dark comes, for the nights are already beginning to get dark. And so the tents are put up as fast as can be. Some put up the tents, and others cut

[6] A "string" is a line of reindeer, either carrying packs or drawing sledges. They are linked together by leather thongs. Each string is led by a Lapp.

wood . . . there is still birch wood [7] and when the fires are lighted they begin to eat, reindeer milk and cheese . . . and the folk have bread too in these days but they had not in olden times. And water is put on to boil and they put *juobmo* [8] milk into the water and then they drink it. The women hasten to unpack the children and tend them, and the older children are warmed, for it is even worse for them than for the tiny children in the cradles, for they have no such shelter as the cradles give. And when those who have been with the strings have eaten and drunk, those who have been driving the herd come up to the tents with it, and others go off to watch it all night. And when it is dark and rainy you can't see in front of your feet and you knock against stones or walk into bogs or lakes, or against trees; and you can't see the reindeer either, only hear them. And the reindeer watcher must walk round and round the animals, and keep this up all night and not let the dogs chase the reindeer, for the dogs split the herd up into flocks and they begin to run when the dogs chase them. And when it is morning he drives the herd back to the tent, but at this time of the year the nights are not yet long. And in the morning the first work is to go out and find the pack reindeer that broke away with their burdens, and when there isn't any snow, it's not so easy to track them, and when you get to the place where they broke away you go in the direction in which they went, and on your way you may find one pack but the others are still missing. And when you've looked for them one day then you can't stop to look another day. So there are two pack reindeer and their burdens missing, and those you must leave behind. And it is night again, and the reindeer watchers go out again to the herd, and this night's work is like the last. And when they come back again with the herd in the morning the folk start off again and they go up to the high fells where there are no more birches and now they must camp where there is no wood.

The Lapps have a superstition . . . how it goes with the first day's traveling so it will be with the whole journey; if they meet with any misfortune on the first day then there will be nothing but misfortunes all the time. And if that *sida* has bad luck on the first day then they believe that misfortune will follow them on the whole journey. But what is to happen will happen! Once, it was on a very bad journey, when the strongest folk must lead the strings, there was a pregnant woman along, and she dared not be with the strings, so she went instead and drove the herd [9] and the child was born on the journey and there was nothing for that woman to do but to tuck it into the front of her tunic and go on driving the herd till she reached the place where the tents were to be put up. And when she reached the tents, then for the first time she could get into a bed . . . such as the Lapps have now, and there was a scarcity of wood in that place, and they looked after her according to Lapp custom. But the whole *sida* couldn't stop there, and so they went on and they left be-

[7] They have not yet got above the tree belt.
[8] Milk prepared with sorrel. First you gather the plant whose name is *juobmo* (sorrel) and cook it, and mix it with the milk and then hang it up in a reindeer's stomach to dry.

[9] It can be extremely exhausting work to lead a string, as they often meet with misfortunes that call for both strength and quickness, in addition to which the strings travel without rest until they reach their camping place, while the herd stops here and there to eat and rest, therefore it is less exhausting to go with the herd.

hind one tent and two people and they tied up their pack reindeer.[10]

· · · ·

About the care of children.— When the child has been successfully born it is wrapped in a reindeer-calf skin, till water is warmed to wash it in. Then it is wrapped in linen and in a reindeer-skin and laid in the cradle, and there it lies both night and day when the Lapps are journeying, or when they are stopping still, both summer and winter. The cradle is made of hollowed out wood and the hollow is just the size of the child, and the head end is made higher with a hood of bent wood which holds up the cradle-covering so that the child is not suffocated.

For the benefit of students interested in physical anthropology, I may add that the Lapp cradle without question flattens the child's skull and produces a protuberant forehead. The traditional brachycephalic head form of the Lapps is artificial.

The life of the nomadic Lapps has changed considerably during the last hundred years, owing to the increasing settlement of the far north by Norwegians, Swedes, and Kvaens (Finns). In the old days the Lapps used to pasture their reindeer during the summer on the grass along the shores near the North Cape. Here the various herds would get mixed up and would need to be separated before the fall migration over the high fells to the forests of Sweden, where they wintered. During the summer, fairs were held along the coast, at which the Lapps traded reindeer meat and skins for metal and other manufactured goods.

Here I tell something of the condition of the children on migration. —When the children are little and light, then it is easy to sling them in their cradles on one side of a pack reindeer, just as the Lapps always carry their burdens . . . that is twenty kilos on each side of a reindeer; but if the child cries a lot, then it is difficult for the mother to give it the breast when it is on the reindeer, but she has to do it and she manages somehow.

About bigger children. When the children are bigger and heavier so that a reindeer cannot carry them slung on one side like a burden . . . when they are about four years old . . . then they must already ride on the animal's back, whether it is good weather or rain or snow, and then they freeze, and grow so tired, till in the end they can't stop on the reindeer any longer. It's so cold on a reindeer's back because the wind blows from beneath, and from every direction. The children who can be carried as packs slung on to the reindeer can be much better sheltered and those children keep very warm in the cradles. And when a child has grown so big that a reindeer cannot carry it, it must run along as best it can, though it is very hard for it, especially in bad weather, when there is rain and sleet; and it gets so tired that at last it can't move another step and then someone has to carry it, when it is a migration of twelve miles or more.

And it is just as difficult for the weak, old folk, they get exhausted on the long journeys and then they have to spend the night out in the wilds, and

[10] If, in a case like this, you do not tie up the pack reindeer, they go off with the free herd, and the folk are left without any means of traveling.

then they freeze terribly and some have died on migrations, and there hasn't been time to look for them, and many years afterwards folk have seen their bones, but no one has bothered about them any more than if they were reindeer bones.

. . . .

[*Once a Lapp has passed his physical prime, he ages rapidly, and grows very thin. Although I have no absolute statistics to prove this, I am confident from other evidence that few Lapps live to a great old age. There is no class of wise old men among them, any more than among the Eskimos or Yahgans. The exigencies of the environment make this impossible among a people with even the high technical skill of the Lapps.*]

About milking.—Sometimes it was the custom to smear the udders of reindeer cows with reindeer dung so that the calf would not suck; another way was to tie wool round the tops of the teats, but then if a cow got lost, her teats fell off. This was done so that the calf could not suck, because if it sucks, it sucks all the time, and then there is no milk left to be milked.

That was in the time before the Lapps came from the east and taught the others how to tend reindeer . . . as soon as they had learnt this, then the herds began to increase. Jukkasjärvi Lapps had never been able to tend the herds properly, and so they had not increased till the land was full of reindeer, as it is at this time.

About reindeer sicknesses.—In the disease we call *slubbo* there come swellings between the two halves of the cleft hoof and they begin to matter. In *njunevikke,* the muzzle becomes scurfy, and it spreads to the tongue and the mouth and goes down the throat and so into the lungs and kills the reindeer. In *gaerdne* the reindeer's cow's udder becomes scurfy and swells

up, and it begins to matter so that the whole udder falls off, and the reindeer cow licks it and then it attacks the mouth and goes down into the lungs and kills it. In *tjakkaravikke* the bull's genital organs swell up till they are very big. In *ruodno* they walk with drooping hind quarters as if they were about to make water, but nothing comes; and this disease begins in the urine opening, and goes up into the bladder, and then matter spreads to all the entrails and the animal dies. In *livcavikke* the reindeer sometimes looks quite well but it gets thin, and sometimes the hind quarters will not stop upright but are dragged along, and this disease happens in the winter too, but the other diseases cease in the winter, except *slubbo,* which sometimes goes on through the winter, but is never so severe as it is in the summer, because in the winter time only an occasional reindeer has it.

. . . . .

Here I will tell about the enemies of the reindeer. Something that has never been written before. —The bears are bad; if a bear finds a herd of reindeer cows he kills many calves when he finds that he can get them; but he can't get many big reindeer, and if he gets one he eats it all up, but if you come upon him while he's eating then he is angry and springs up and tears folk to pieces. And if you follow him in the spring, then he is angry and goes to one side of the trail, and hides; and when you come along he attacks you and smashes your head. Many a time bears have killed Lapps.

The wolf is the reindeer's worst enemy, it kills reindeer all the year round, and at every season. One kind of wolf is such a robber, that if he comes to a herd that has been collected, he will kill as many as he can overcome, sometimes ten or twenty in a night. And in the winter when the snow is deep he kills forty and even seventy in a night.

About the Wolverine.—The wolverine too is bad during the winter. When the snow is deep he can get at the reindeer, and he too can kill ten in a night. And in the spring, on the snow crust, he kills reindeer and many calves; and if it is a hard spring and the reindeer are starved and weak then the wolverines kill many reindeer. And the arctic fox, and the ordinary fox, kill too; in the spring they kill many calves before they have their growth. And the eagle too kills reindeer calves, it is even worse than the arctic fox; the eagle kills one-year-old calves too.

The settlers' and the Norwegians' dogs bite the calves, and the Lapps' own dogs occasionally bite the calves. And the flies are in some sort the enemies of the reindeer. When it gets warm so many insects wake to life, and they follow the reindeer, and when they settle upon them they hang fast in a second. There is one sort that goes up the nostrils and lays its eggs up there, and they hatch out into grubs which kill the reindeer in the spring when they are weakened. And there is another insect that fastens itself to the reindeer's back, and it brings forth maggots, and in the spring these kill many weakened reindeer, by burrowing into their backs. And the reindeer are so frightened of these insects that they run here and there, and rush up on to the highest mountains and crags where it is colder and where there is a lot of snow, and glaciers.

Reindeer's eating and resting times.—Reindeer rest when the dawn begins to break, and that is called the dawn rest. And then they feed till mid-day, and then they rest the mid-day rest; and then they feed until evening, and then they rest the twilight rest; and then they eat until mid-night, and then they rest the midnight rest. It is only where there is good pasture that reindeer have these fixed resting times, when they rest all at once; because, in hungry years, the reindeer do not all find food at the same time. When there are two watchers, as there generally are, and when they have found the herd, then each goes to his own side, and they circle the herd outside the outermost animals. But if they are clever watchers they hold the herd together and drive it to the tents for the dawn rest, but then they must begin to drive it whilst it is still dark, so that they reach the tents when it is just beginning to get light, for that is their resting time.

And as soon as it begins to be a little light they begin to milk the reindeer cows, and when the milking is done then other watchers take the herd out for the day, and in the evening they bring it back to the tents and then they milk again. And the other watchers have slept during the day, and now they go out with the herd. And when they do that they call it a half-watch.

When the Lapps have reached the south side of the high fells, then they begin to stop a little longer in those places where there is pasture for the reindeer, even if the wood supply is bad. But they do not stop in the same places each year. And when they come to those places where they generally stop in the spring and where they have left their winter clothes and their winter utensils, food and sledges, they stop in the neighborhood to change into their winter clothes and leave their summer clothes. And they stop in that neighborhood during the reindeer's rutting season.

The rutting season begins at Mikkelsdags-tid (September 29th) and the real rutting time only lasts for two weeks. And at that time the Lapps castrate the young bulls before the pairing has begun. They castrate them in this way. . . . You castrate the bulls that you do not want to get thin while they are mating. First you catch the animal with a lasso and force it down to the ground but at that season they are so strong and so savage that it is very dangerous, you must be quick and strong-handed. When you have got the bull down, one holds down its head while the other goes behind it and puts his head down between its back legs, holding its hind quarter with his hands, and then with his teeth he bites through the skin below the testicles; but he must take care that he does not stretch the sinew. And when it is bitten through, then you must squeeze with your fingers until it is as smooth as gruel. And then you cut a mark in the hide to show that it has been castrated.

. . . . .

Now it begins to be time to leave the rutting camps.—Now the rutting is finished, and the reindeer cows cease to allow the calves to suck, and now it is the best milking time, when the reindeer cows have a lot of milk, and if you do not milk every day the cows dry up, and the milk is finished with for that year. And at that time the Lapps have a lot of work as they have to move their camps and milk and watch their reindeer. And at that time the reindeer are very uneasy, when the bulls have tired of holding the herd together.

And when you have got back to the *sida* everyone makes haste to change their summer clothes and put on their winter ones. And the summer articles are left hanging up in a birch tree, or else you make a very high *suonjer*,[11] and they hang there through the winter

until you come there again in the spring. And when they have all changed their clothes and got everything in order, then it is time to migrate. As yet there is little snow, every stone and tuft is bare, but move you must because the pasture for the reindeer is finished.

Now we travel with strings of sledges.[12]—Each sledge has its own particular purpose; the first is the driving sledge; the second is the children and puppy sledge; the third sledge carries the household utensils; the fourth carries the bedclothes, and the fifth is the tent sledge. The housewife leads this string, and it is called the tent-string. And in the second string there is fish and meal, and the fine church clothes and the better food stuffs . . . coffee, butter and dried meat . . . and in that string there are covered sledges carrying chests with lids; and if the spring food is being carried there is another string, and it is a heavy one.[13]

[11] A framework of three birch trees resting against one another, in the branchy tops of which things are hung up; it is mostly used for hanging freshly slaughtered meat.

[12] A Lapp sledge (*gieres*) is built like a little boat with a pointed prow. Behind, it is cut off square. Underneath, it is furnished with a flat keel about one and a quarter inches deep and about six inches broad. The length of the sledge is about five feet and the breadth about eighteen inches, and the depth is about nine inches. The shape and decoration vary according to the different uses to which the sledges are put. Baggage sledges are generally open at the back. Covered sledges, in which the finer foodstuffs are carried . . . meat, frozen milk, butter, etc., are divided into two compartments and secured under lock and key. The Lapps' personal driving sledges are extremely elegant in shape and are decorated with cut-out ornamentation on the stern, and the backboards, which often have beautiful iron mountings, go so high up that they form a little back rest.

[13] At the beginning of winter the Lapps slaughter those reindeer that they intend to use for spring and summer food. The meat is laid in sledges, and a well-off Lapp will often have several sledges full of frozen meat which he carries with him till he comes

Now, when they start off, the ground is so covered with tussocks that the sledges are thrown from tussock to tussock, and from stone to stone, and the wildest reindeer spring to one side, and go behind trees, so that the sledges get stuck behind stones and tussocks; and the children cry when the sledges bump so hard that their heads can't put up with it . . . but they have to put up with it. Yet sometimes you have to set the children upon the reindeer, or carry them as if it were summer; but it is not so bad when there comes more snow, then the children are better off in the sledges. The tussocks and the stones are not so bare, but the birches and firs are rather bad even when the snow is deep. It is the very worst traveling when you first take to the sledges, but the children keep warmer when you travel with sledges, but for all that the sound of children crying and dogs barking can be heard from far away.

Now the *sida* has reached a camping place and they begin to set up the tents, some set up the tents and others cut wood; the housewife and the girls cut branches (for the floor covering of the tent). But if a woman has a little baby and it cries a great deal, then she has no time to do any work, but she must feed the baby and rock it. And if the child falls asleep or stops its crying, then she too goes and cuts branches. And when the tent is ready, first you lay branches on the sleeping places and then bring in the bed clothes and then the cooking utensils are put in the *boaššo*.[14] And then you make a fire

and it is cheerful when there is a fire in the tent. And if there is no water in that place, then you have to melt snow, and then you begin to get the food out of the food bags and begin to eat, and then it is pleasant. The present-day Lapps have coffee, and coffee cooking is the first thing they do as soon as the water is warm, or the snow melted. Where the pasture is good you don't need to watch the reindeer, not if there are no wolves in the neighborhood. And the Lapps think that it is pleasant when the pasture is good and they have moved to a fresh place.

The place where they have stopped is on the south side of the high fells in the birch forests that are above the fir belt. And they stop there until the snow gets a little deeper. There is moss everywhere in the fir forests, and where there are thick fir forests and many low fir-covered mountains there is always food, even in a bad year; and when there are many hills and valleys, then there is good food too in a bad winter. And in the birch forests there is plenty of moss but in the birch forests there is no food in the winter, when the snow begins to be deep, if the land is flat and it is a long way from a river. It is as if rivers ate snow, the snow is always thinner near a river than it is upon the ridges. And if there are a great many birches then there is no reindeer moss, unless there are willows in between, and in some places there is moss and no reindeer moss . . . except here and there a little bit. About spruce lands. In the spruce forests there is a lot of moss and very little reindeer moss, and in the spruce forests the snow is much thicker and harder. It is as if the spruce and the birch attract the snow; but there is a power in the air which acts upon the snow.

And when it is time to go from this place it is already Yule and it is dark

---

to his storehouse, or to the place where he is going to salt and dry the meat when it thaws in the spring. But if he has time, and opportunity, he can bring it to the storehouse straight away, so that he does not need to carry it with him on migration.

[14] The part of the tent opposite to, and farthest from, the door, where the Lapps keep household utensils and food.

and cold, and then it is really terrible to travel when the day is already ended before you are ready to move from the camping place and so you have to travel in the dark. The draft reindeer are afraid and spring to one side, and entangle the sledges behind trees and then it's a job to get them loose again. And then sometimes the reindeer strangle to death when a sledge is entangled behind a tree and the rest of the string in front are pulling on the neck thong, and you don't manage to get there in time and cut it, you must do that if you want to keep life in the reindeer. And at that time there is slush on the lakes and rivers and then the strings are very apt to stick. When it is cold the sledges stick fast in the slush as it freezes and then the reindeer can't move them. And when the whole string has stuck fast, then you are helpless, and you must wade in the slush up to your knees, even if it is thirty or forty degrees of cold. And many a one has been very ill when his feet were frozen. And I who write this have worked at all the things I describe above, those things that the present-day Lapps work at.

The Lapps' biggest festival is Yule.—The Lapps have many customs on *ruottabaeivve* (Yule eve) they make everything ready that they will need to use during the holy days. They slaughter reindeer and sew everything they will need during the holy days, and they cut a great quantity of wood. And when they've got enough to last over the holy days they take all the brushwood away and stack the wood evenly, very evenly, no piece of wood must stick out in case Stallo's string of sledges should catch in it, and behind the wood pile they set up a branch so that Stallo can tie his string there while he goes into the tent to drink water. If he cannot find any water he sucks the brains out of one or another, and

so the Lapps take care to see that there is water and that the kettle is quite full so that Stallo shall not have the power to do anything (evil). And when the holy day has come, then they do not do any other work than watch the reindeer and keep fires in the tents and eat and drink what they need and look after the children so that they don't make a noise. And during Yuletide they live the most beautiful life, and don't do any work unless something happens that they have to work. If wolves come and kill the reindeer they have to go and flay them, and for such work you don't see evil spirits because it is necessary to do it; and for everything that it is necessary to do you are not guilty, because you have to do it even if you do not want to. Sometimes the Lapps must even travel during the holy days with the whole *sida,* when there is such bad pasture for the reindeer that there is nothing to do but go to another place. Neither is that their fault because the move is a necessity. And there is a law about even these things, that no one shall be punished unless he is guilty.

Now they begin to travel again and to move to the spots where they will stop during the winter, some near at hand, and some farther away. For those who travel far south it is difficult; and if they go on to the settlers' ground they have to pay much money, and if they do not pay as the "masters say" then it goes ill with the Lapps. But the settlers are permitted to have hay standing out in the open the whole of the winter every year, and if the reindeer eat it, then the Lapps must pay, and if they don't pay the whole sum then the settlers come to the tents in flocks and beat on the tents, and beat the reindeer and the menfolk are frightened and go off into the wilds, because the settlers threaten them and strike them and do all manner of things. And so it is best to pay what they ask, because when you pay it is convenient, as the reindeer have very good pasture where there is plenty of reindeer moss, and then you don't need to run much on skis, and the herds get fat. And when it is time to travel again it is good traveling for those *sidas* who have been on the settlers' taxed lands where there is reindeer moss.

Really the Lapps have almost the same nature as reindeer, both of them migrate north and south, in the way they are used to migrating, and both of them are a little shy, and because of this shyness they have been driven away from everywhere, and so the Lapps must now stop where there are no other folk than Lapps, that is on the naked high fells; and they would stay there always, if only they could keep themselves warm and feed their reindeer herds. And the Lapps are weather-wise and they have learnt something of weather wisdom from the reindeer; and the Lapps easily keep themselves warm and easily find their way; they can find their way in the dark too, and in the fog, and in blizzards . . . , at least a lot of the Lapps can. And all that concerns skiing and running comes natural to them.

In olden times the Lapps spent the winter in the fir forests, and lived in peace, each on his own mountain.

And when the pasture came to an end because the snow everywhere was scraped up, then they went on to another mountain or to another spot which had not been grazed over . . . where reindeer have been feeding the scraped-up snow gets so hard that the reindeer cannot get through (to the mosses underneath). And where there is good pasture, then it is pleasant, and there is not too much work to do skiing after the reindeer, unless there are wolves about.

In bad years the reindeer run down

the fell slopes and the Lapps follow them till they reach the coast, and some of them used to stop there too, until the settlers came and frightened them up the fells again and hunted the Lapps farther and farther up the fells, until the high fells stopped and the Lapps went over the fells, and farther still.

And even other folk began to work with reindeer, but they would not follow the reindeer from place to place because they did not want to travel like the reindeer travel, and so they began to live in one place, and built themselves houses, and caught wild reindeer and fish.

About work in the tents.—When the Lapps have reached their winter camping places they each begin to work at their own tasks. The men look after the reindeer and everything that concerns the herds, and if they have time they mend the sledges which have been broken during the migration . . . that is if they know how to do it, but if they do not know how to do it, then they have to pay some poor Lapp who has no work, nor food, and so there are two to help one another. And if those men who are clever with their hands have time, and are diligent, then they make new sledges, and skis, and everything that Lapps need. Driving-sledges, covered sledges, and chests with lids are very dear . . . ah, those who have the time and can make these things! . . . All the Lapps' summer and winter articles cost a lot of money. Some men know how to make everything, but others don't know the least thing about handicraft work, and it is a great pity when it is a man who knows nothing about handicrafts. And it is even worse when a housewife is not clever. She who must sew all the clothes, and do everything that is a Lapp woman's work. And cooking too is a Lapp woman's work.

When you have reached winter quarters you do have a little time as you are stopping longer in one place. And so the women busy themselves with their work, now that they have time to unpack the sledges, and take out the things. During migration you can't take the things out; on a journey it is too big a work to pack up more things than just food and clothes. And so they begin to look to the clothes that have got wet on their travels and that have rotted and torn; and when they have finished with them, they begin to sew new clothes, and shoes, and everything that is made of reindeer skin, while it is mild weather; because you can't do handiwork when it is so cold that the tent cloth gets frosty on the inside, in spite of the fire burning so high that it flames through the smoke hole. Then it is a big work to get wood to keep the fire in and look after the children so that they are not frozen or frostbitten. And when it is such a severe cold that it is forty degrees of frost, there is such a frost-fog inside the tent that you can't see anything on the other side of the fire.

And when you bake in such cold weather the dough freezes between each cake that you make and bake, and so you are obliged to let the dough lie quite close to the fire. The cakes are baked in a frying pan made of iron and some are baked on the embers until they are stiff and then they set up against a piece of wood to cook in front of the fire and those cook very well and quickly, as many as you like. And another method is to put the raw cakes on a flat stone and turn them till they are cooked. In the olden days the cakes were baked on twigs under the fire, when the wood was bad and there was haste to cross the fells.

Coffee is roasted in a frying pan, and the ways of grinding it are many; you can grind it with a round stone upon a flat stone, and another way is to make a hole in a log of wood, and then take another piece of wood and pound the coffee till it is broken up; and another way is to put the coffee in a leather bag, and then beat it with a piece of wood against a slab of wood until the coffee is finely broken up. (Now, the Lapps use a little round coffee-mill of brass which anybody can buy in Skibotten, where they are made exclusively for the Lapps.) Old-time Lapps used *duovlle,* and corn, and birch sap instead of coffee. *Duovlle* is is a fungoid growth found on birches. It is gathered in the summer, dried in the smoke of the tent, and ground like coffee. It has a sweet taste, like birch sap. It is also used for tanning the tent cloths and gives them a reddish color.

And they made bread of tree moss (the long sort that grows on pine and fir trees) and of reindeer moss, and of *guolmas* (the soft part of pine and fir bark), mixed with a little meal . . . at that time there was very little meal up here in Nordland. The bark bread was made in this way. The outer bark was taken off the fir, and then you flayed off the inner bark, and then it was dried very dry, and then it was ground until it was meal. You made a hole in a piece of birch, and then you made a sharp-edged tool out of birch wood, and then you scraped the bark until it was as fine as meal. And they helped out the food supply with plants. They cooked *fadno* (one year old angelica) in water, and then they put it in a reindeer's stomach, and mixed it with milk, and then they put it in blood gruel, and it was very good in the winter. And they collected a lot of *boska* (two year old angelica), and salted it and ate it. And sorrel is much in use even to this day.

About reindeer slaughtering.— Reindeer slaughtering is the concern of the men folk. When a Lapp has taken a reindeer out of the herd, he leads it to the *boaššo*-side of the tent to sharpen the knife so that it is really sharp and clean, and will kill the reindeer quickly. If the knife is not really clean it will not kill the animal quickly and it will suffer a long time before it dies. Some knives are bad for killing, if they are of hard steel then they are good for killing with, but soft steel is very bad. And when the Lapp has got everything ready he comes out, and he takes a comrade with him if there are any folk about. And then they throw the reindeer and stick the knife into its chest and then they loose it from the rein; and if it is a good knife then it cannot get up even once, but if the knife is middling good then it gets up and falls down again at once, and if the knife is bad then it lives for a long time and if it gets loose then it can go for a long way before it falls dead.

When the reindeer is flayed, you catch the blood in the reindeer's own stomach . . . the stomach is washed clean with water or with *sænjas* (granulated snow) and you take a little of the blood in a special vessel and with it you make blood sausages, if the reindeer is so fat that there is enough fat for them. And the women wash the intestines in the tent. The first meal is the back, the liver and blood sausages, and if it is a big household then they need more, but if it is a little household then they don't need so much. When a reindeer has been slaughtered and the pot is cooking, the first thing to do is to put the brains in to cook, and when they have cooked a little you take them out and mix them with *guolmas*-meal (bark meal) and the fat from the top of the pot, and then you eat it and it is wonderfully good, and it is a medicine for folk's stomachs. And I who write this have often eaten it.

The second meal of reindeer is the legs, marrow bones and head, and after that the rest of the meat is cooked just as you like. And it is Lapp custom that one night there shall be gruel and the next night meat. And meat is only cooked in the evening, and during the day the Lapps eat fish and bread, and if they have it, butter . . . but it is only an occasional Lapp who has butter . . . and with their food they drink coffee.

The thighs and the tongue of the reindeer killed in late winter are sold, but the reindeer that are slaughtered first for spring and summer food they are called "spring meat and sledge meat" [15] and of that, not the least little bit is sold. They are slaughtered first in the winter, and the meat is packed in sledges, and only in the spring, at the calving places, do the Lapps begin to eat that, and to dry it. And for that meat they choose the fattest reindeer, because in the spring all the reindeer are thin in those tracts where there is bad reindeer moss, and their hides are riddled with maggot holes, and so the Lapps slaughter in the winter all that they need for the spring.

The Lapps generally slaughter their reindeer near the tents, and carry any meat they are going to cook into the tent in the skin; that's what folk do who slaughter their own reindeer.

· · · ·

And now the time draws near for the Lapps to migrate north from their winter camping places.—The Lapps are not in a hurry to move earlier than the week before Valborgsdag (Walpurgis day, May 1st), unless it thaws earlier and then freezes again and makes a hard crust. But the first cows begin to calve about Valborgsdag, and you must be in the calving places when the cows begin to calve, so that you must move in a hurry to be in the calving places by Valborgsdag. And

[15] See footnote 13

when there is a hard snow crust, then there is no pasture for the reindeer in the fir forests, and then you must travel night and day until you reach the high fells. On the high fells there is pasture or at least snow-free ground. That is a hard time for the Lapps when sometimes they have to watch for three twenty-four hours on end, and sometimes in hard springs they have to watch for a week. And it often happens, when they reach the high fells, that they have to watch the reindeer on account of the wolves.

Here I tell about the war against wolves.—It is very hard for the Lapps when there are wolves about, then you must watch, be it never such bad weather and never so cold. The watching goes like this: in the day the herd is gathered together into a flock, and when it begins to get dusk, the night watchers go out, and they watch till midnight; and then other watchers come up and the first ones can go home, but it is hard to find the way in the dark and worse if there is fog or bad weather. But some folk find their way whatever the weather is like, but all are not equally clever at finding their way, some get lost and have to spend the night in the wilds. And that watching is very hard work if you are to hold the wolves at bay; you must run on your skis without ceasing and you must shout as loud as you can, if you stop shouting then the wolves come in a second. And if a wolf comes and follows the reindeer, in the neighborhood of the watcher, so that he sees it, and is near to it, then he must take care not to shout with his mouth turned towards the wolf, but he must turn it in the other direction when he shouts, if he doesn't do this the wolf will take away his voice and he will lose it. And when the wolf comes he is such a *noaide* [16] animal that he makes folk

[16] *Noaide*: cunning in magic. [Translator's note.]

sleep, and when you are asleep, then he can frighten the herd and separate a little flock, and when he has got that little flock separated then he drives it away and kills as many as he can catch. The most I have heard of is seventy killed in a night, but from a watched herd he cannot generally get so many, especially if it is good weather; but when a wolf comes to an unwatched herd, then he will kill a whole flock in a night. . . .

About wolf hunting on skis.—When you are on skis, you kill a wolf like this. You ski after it when the snow is deep and will bear skis, if you are an active and clever Lapp. And when you have caught him up, you hit him with the ski-staff on the head, or on the neck under the ear, or over the root of the tail, or on the nose, just on the black nose-tip, which is very tender; in other places he won't feel anything, however hard you hit. But the man must be quick, one who does not loose his staff or his skis, a wolf is very quick at snapping at the staff with his mouth, and he snaps at the skis too, and shakes them till the man falls off them, and when the man falls out of his skis, then the wolf leaps upon him, and bites him, wherever he can get at him; but the Lapp has his knife to defend himself with, he grips the knife and strikes like lightning, but the wolf sometimes bites him somewhere, sometimes badly and sometimes not so badly. There is a special art . . . when the wolf seizes hold of a man's arm, the man must thrust his hand into the wolf's jaws, right down his throat, and then squeeze the lowest part of his gullet, and then the wolf cannot bite, and with the other hand, the man must strike with his knife, and then there is no danger. But if the wolf manages to get a grip with his teeth on a foot, or in the middle of the arm . . . it is dangerous if he gets a grip on the elbow joint . . .

then he bites, and his teeth go right through the arm; and if he gets a hold of a leg, that too is very dangerous when he bites there, because the wolf has such long teeth that they go through the leg, and then the leg stiffens so that it cannot be bent.

It has often happened that wolf hunters have been so badly bitten that they nearly died, and in any case they were very ill for a long time, sometimes a month, and sometimes the whole winter, and the scars of a wolf bite last as long as a man lives. They use their spears too, but yet the wolves manage to bite them, although it is a great help when you have a spear.

To chase a wolf on skis is the very worst thing there is for ruining folks' health. Then you must ski till the blood comes into your mouth, and you get so hot that you must uncover the whole of your chest. And when you have been skiing for the whole of a long day, then you sweat so that all your clothes nearest the skin are wet, and you are so tired that you can hardly manage to get back. But if you manage to get down into the forest, and there is deep snow and plenty of it, not too hard and not too soft, and the tracks do not lead up towards the high fells,[17] then it is sometimes easy to catch him; if only you are not bitten, you will catch him. . . .

About bear hunting.—A method of hunting bears is to have a spear, and you must stab like this, the spear must lie hidden under your arm with the spear shaft far behind your back, and when the bear rushes on you, then you must cast yourself quickly backwards and then the bear is stuck on the spear. And then you must turn round and

drive the spear deeper into the bear and force him down to the ground.

Sometimes you find a bear when it has gone to sleep in its den. You find it like this. In the autumn, during the first snows, you find a bear's tracks, and you follow them until he begins to make curved tracks, and then you go round them. And when you have been all round them, then you let be for that day, and the next day you go out and go round them again. When you have gone right round an animal that you are going to hunt, then the animal is much braver or bolder and it is much easier to shoot it.[18]

And if the bear has not gone his way, then he has gone to sleep there, and then you must go round again, each time in smaller circles, till you see where the hole is that he has gone in by. And then you must let him be for that time, and after a week go and look again, and then you must set a mark before the opening, so that you can see if he is still there when you come to shoot him later on. And when the snow is thick, then you go to kill him. Then there must be three men, two hold crossed sticks across the door opening and the third must be ready to hit the bear on the head when he comes out to see what it is when they shout to him. And when he sticks his head out he looks to see how many there are, and if you don't manage to hit him, then, when he comes out for the second time, he is like a raging fire, and you can't hit him; but when he comes out for the first time, it is easy to hit him if you are not too afraid. And the men must be there with the sticks so that they can hold him back, so that he does not come out

[17] On the high fells the thin snow does not hold the tracks, and they are easily lost; added to which it is harder for the ski runner to overtake the wolf than it is farther down in the forests, where the snow is deep and soft and hinders the wolf's progress.

[18] About this encircling Turi wrote in another place—you encircle every beast that you wish to catch. If you go round it, then the animal can't get out, if it isn't frightened; you will almost always catch the animal that you encircle.

too quickly, before he is hit on the head; afterwards they let him out, and just as he gets out he dies. . . .

Bears can be caught in snares also, and will be hanged in them when it is a man who knows how to set snares. The snare must be six inches up from the earth, then he will hang fast in it. And the bear has teeth, but he will not bite the rope but cast his urine on it, and then try to bite it off in that place where the urine has burnt the rope. And it will not be long before it gets so weak that it breaks. And the man who has a snare must look at it often. And in this way many bears have been killed. And the rope must be tanned with bark so that the bear cannot smell it. You must make a fence right across the place where the bear generally comes, and an opening in the fence, and put the snare in the opening. . . .

More about bears.—The bear is a wonderful animal, who lives all through the winter without eating. And he is not angry with a person who comes up to him and does not do anything to him. He has promised that he will not do any harm to one who comes to him in his den. . . .

The bear has the sense of one man and the strength of nine men, and that is why he is not afraid of many people, but he is afraid of two brothers, because a brother does not love his own life better than his brother's life.

About wolves.—The song of the wolf begins like this: *"Over nine dales he springs in a twilight, voia voia, nana nana—Over nine dales he springs in a twilight, voia voia, nana nana—"*

Baergalak (the Devil) made the wolf . . . Ibmel (God) breathed life into him through his nostrils. And therefore the wolf will only do evil like Baergalak. The old Devil had no power to make anything, but he had power to spoil things that were already made. But he was an angel, God's best angel,

and God was angry when he began to do much that did not become him, and that time he made the wolf. And that is why those learned in *noaide* arts have the power to turn human beings into wolves even to this day. In the olden times magic-cunning men knew many arts; against the wolf they used this method . . . when you come upon a fresh wolf track you take your knife and cut out a square piece from the bottom of the slot and then you turn it round three times in the direction in which the wolf has gone and say: "Jesus Christ bless *juoksat*,[19] forward, forward, over water and land, forward, forward." But you must not cross the track before you have said this. And you must say it as many times as there are wolves.

And the wolf can magic a bullet, so that it will not reach its mark; or so that the gun misses fire; but there is a remedy against this, you must first sight with the butt and then with the muzzle and then you will hit.

And the wolf is such that he brings sleep over those who are watching for him, when he is at his lair, or by his prey. And when you are watching a reindeer herd, because of wolves, then too the wolf can bring sleep upon you. And the wolf has one man's strength and nine men's cunning. And he who will hunt the wolves skilfully, he must know all the wolf's names in the Lapp dialect of that tract where the wolves are, and he must think of nine ways of trapping him, when he goes to hunt him, and he must keep till the last the one he intends to use.

In olden times the *noaide* folk changed thieves into wolves; and they could magic folk who could not say

[19] This word is an old troll word which means "forward," but which cannot be directly translated. Turi says:—"Such troll words are always different from ordinary words." You must not cross the track because that prevents the spell from working.

"Our Father" or the Lord's Prayer in three tongues,[20] and those who willfully killed folk, or innocent people, the *noaides* could turn into wolves. And when they had got them ready, then they ordered: "Now rush on a reindeer, take fresh meat!" And then they rushed on a reindeer, and when they tasted blood from the reindeer, then they turned into wolves. And they turned many folk into wolves, and many proofs of this have been found. Such proofs as finding under certain wolves' hides (while flaying them) things belonging to the people they used to be . . . flint and steel and tinder, and sulphur cups too. . . .

[*Like many other peoples, the Lapps consider wolves and bears to be supernatural, or at least to partake of human intelligence. The* noaide *folk mentioned are shamans. The student will observe the convenient blending of Christianity with old pagan belief to serve the ritual needs of the Lapp way of living.*]

About fishing.—Lapps who migrate to Norway in the summer have no time to fish, except in the spring when the lakes are first open, and then they fish with a hook that they themselves have made of tin. And on it they put as bait a little bit of red or yellow stuff, until they catch a fish, and then they put on a little piece of the fish's belly skin, and that is much better.

In the autumn they fish with snares in the small brooks; in the autumn there are a great number of small fish in the little brooks. And sometimes, but not often, they fish with nets and sweep nets. And they also shoot pike in the spring, in among the sedges in the swamps. The pike spawn in the spring, and the grayling and the perch,

[20] In northern Norway and Sweden, in addition to their own tongue the Lapps speak Finnish; presumably the third tongue is Swedish or Norwegian.

and the char and the white-fish and the gray salmon spawn in the autumn. If it thunders in the spring, before the ice on the lakes has melted, it will be a fishless summer, at least in some of the lakes; for the fish are frightened and go deep down for the whole of the summer, the summer after thunder has rolled over the ice covered lakes.

But it needs not only cleverness in fishing, you must be lucky too. And the old folk made many sacrifices for luck in fishing. They sacrifice to the *seites* mostly for the sake of trapping-luck, but also for reindeer luck. And for good health they made offerings, and to this day some folk make offerings to the churches for the sake of human beings. For trapping luck you must make an offering to some poor person, or to some one who is not too heathen, or an evildoer. And you make offerings also to folk who have some malformation . . . or are very lame, so that they have hard work to provide for themselves, or to some very old poor folk who have difficulty in supporting themselves . . . the folk who give to them have luck. And some lay preachers have luck, too, but you must prove who has luck, and some people have really good luck.

Here is a little explanation about these offerings.—You promise something to the church if everything goes as you want it to. And it is the same when you promise something to a human being; but that which you have promised, you must give. And in the olden days it was in this way that folks sacrificed to the *seites,* when they went off hunting they made a promise to them; some *seites* were content if they got the horns, but others wanted a whole leg, and it was understood that not the least little bit of meat must be missing. A fish *seite* would not want more than half the fat, and then the fish were driven into the net, as many as the man could handle. And some *seites* would have a whole living reindeer and it must be decked out with all kinds of finery, with cloth and woolen yarn, and silver and gold. And some people sacrificed children too. And it is not so long ago since the last sacrificing *noaide*-man was alive. The last was Kumen and his wife, and his father Dobar, who sacrificed a ten-year-old boy, together with a reindeer. . . .

[*The* seites *are the spirit-owners of the different kinds of birds, animals, and fish used for food. We have seen exactly the same concept among the Yahgans. The Lapps sacrificed to them to insure success in critical ventures. Giving offerings to poor people in order to improve one's luck is a ritual mechanism fostering the survival of the Lapp community. The Lapp shaman was an all-purpose practitioner, healing and casting spells and influencing the weather.*]

Another tale about the frog.—Once there was a woman who was going over a bog and she saw a stone in the bog, and she stepped upon it. But it was no stone, it was the frog's mother, who was as big as a man's head. And so the frog hooked fast to her foot, so that she could not get loose in any other way but by beating her off with her ski stick. And then the foot began to hurt where the frog had hung on to it. And she too was taken to the Lulea doctor, but she too died. And as a child she had mocked at frogs, and they first injured her, when she happened to step on the mother of the race. And that happened to Lunte Andaras' wife at Vuoskojaure.

. . . .

And in this book there is all about Lapp doctoring; but not about *noaide* arts. And when those who know all about everything that is described in this book . . . and there are not many who know these arts . . . do not recognize folks' sicknesses, then they are apt to think that it is a fatal sickness, or that specters or ghosts have been set upon the sick person, and that it is the work of *noaide* folk.

About ghost roamings.—When the dead travel, they fly in the air like birds, sometimes higher, sometimes lower. And when they are out wandering, then there is a roaring louder than the wildest storms, and a still greater roaring is made by the specters. And when they wander, they do not move high up, but where they go forward the trees are bent to the earth, and some trees are broken. And when you hear that, it is the specters. But they are not seen by all, only by some folk, and innocent beasts see and hear them plainly enough, even when they do not make such a noise that folk hear them. And a ghost is headless, and, when they travel, they fly the one above the other, and most of them have bodies only up to their shoulders, and some of them bodies only to their middles.

And specters are those souls that are half sinful and half Christian. They do not get to Hell or to Heaven. And they can only exist in the air. And they want to find work and it is in them that the *noaide* folk find their best helpers, when they begin to work magic.

And the sign that a specter is about a human being is that that human being begins to see and hear much that others do not see. And he speaks of the matter, how there are specters about him, and what they will do, and of who it is that has set them upon him, and he talks a little about other folks' affairs too. And what such folk say is for the most part true. And he who is about to exorcise a specter from some person, he talks a strange tongue, and then he reads to the sick person some words in a strange tongue (and the sick person must repeat the words). And when the person talks the strange tongue when he is exorcising a specter or a devil, it is so wonderful that it is impossible to describe it. He gets in a state of frenzy [21] when he sees specters or devils upon folk, and he sees all such things and he is able to drive them out. And such folk can do harm as well, if they want to, but such folk will never do harm unless wicked people begin to press them too hard, but if they are in dire need, then they too have permission to show their strength.

The last great Lapp *noaide* was Dopar, who also made sacrifices to *seites* . . . sometimes reindeer, and once, when he could not prevail against another *noaide*, he sacrificed a ten-year-old child, one that could already ride upon a reindeer. One time he was trying his strength with another *noaide* and he could not prevail except by sacrificing a reindeer and a child. And he chose out the most beautiful white-flecked pack reindeer and put decorations upon it, all kinds of finery, silver and cloth, and woolen yarn, red and yellow, and all kinds that he knew of, and that the Lapps use for decorations. And he bound these decorations in all the places wherever he could. And he put blankets on the reindeer and he set the child upon it and pointed with his finger in the direction in which the reindeer was to go. And the reindeer set off at once on its way and neither of

[21] Turi likens this state to that called *liikutuksia* (literally "movement"), the state into which the Lapps are thrown by the revivals held by Laestadian preachers. They proclaim their sins aloud and, with sobs and shrieks and cries and the most extraordinary noises, they beg God for forgiveness. Each one has his own "melody," and the whole mingles into a dreadful choir, which is nerve-racking to a sober listener. The whole congregation embrace one another in an unbroken rocking movement. This state of ecstasy can last for several hours, and is followed by great fatigue, but the latter quickly disappears in the eating and coffee-drinking that generally follows.

them was ever seen again. And so he prevailed over the other *noaide* until the latter had to make peace. And it ended by those two *noaides* never more trying their strength against one another. And Dopar was such a *noaide* that he could see whatever he wished in a cup of *brännvin*. And he saw when his host [22] in Norway died . . . and he too was a great *noaide,* and Dopar was his reindeer watcher. And Dopar too used the magic drum, and he used a wooden vessel also. And his son, Kumet, used a magic drum of birch wood . . . it must be made of those growths that come in the top of birch trees, and which the Lapps call *biega vissir*.[23] And he who found such a thing had found a very great thing, according to their ideas.

[*Turi refers here to contests between shamans. These are also characteristic of the Eskimos in Alaska and Greenland, the Chukchi of Siberia, and many other peoples. The Maidu of California, as we shall see presently, hold similar contests. They serve as a prime means of entertainment during dull moments when there is little work to be done.*]

About the magic drum.—The magic drum was a *noaide* instrument, and it was made in the following way. In it you put rings, and nine twigs from *Accis-oedne's* reindeer reins. And they struck it with a hammer of copper or horn, and they whistled, and sometimes they ground their teeth. And then they were ready to work magic. When *noaides* are working magic they heat the pot chain till it is quite red.

[22] When the Lapps, on a "church visit," or some similar journey, reach inhabited parts, they each have their special host among the settlers; the latter takes them in and is, in a manner of speaking, their friend. Generally it is the settler whose reindeer the Lapp is minding.

[23] A pathological excrescence on the birch trees.

and then they strike about with it as much as they can, and grind their teeth as much as they can. And they turn their fur coat and their hood back to front. But these *noaides* did not swear nor did they steal.

And such a *noaide* who is fully qualified and still has his teeth, he is in full power.

And old-time *noaides* were such that some of them have flown, and some of them have driven to church behind wolves, and when they reached it, they unharnessed the wolf, and it disappeared. And when they were ready to drive back again, the wolf appeared again, and then the *noaides* drove past all the other drivers.

And some *noaides* were such that when they were working magic, they left their bodies as if dead, and the life went off to work with *Birrus* (the Devil's angel) to do evil to some person or other. And if anyone touched his body, it (the soul) went its way, and those two, the soul and the body, never came together again. And such *noaides* were called "wood-rotting" *noaides* . . . the most powerful *noaides,* who could rot a tree by merely looking at it.

. . . .

There was a *noaide* whom even I (J. Turi) have seen and whose name is Johan Goven. And he lived in Kistrand, Porsanger, in Norway, and he was a really strong *noaide*. He traveled widely round the seacoasts of Norway, and he was in Ivgo (Skibotten) for all the markets. And he was such a one that he could cure sick folk. And at market times a great many folk came together. And it is plain that where there are many folk together, and many sorts of folk, then there are also the sorts of folk who steal each other's possessions. And then folk discovered that J. Goven was such a one that he could make thieves bring back the stolen goods; and so, when

thieves had been stealing, then folk went straight to Goven and told him what had been stolen. And so he made the thief come back with the stolen goods; however far he had got he had to come back, whether he was a Lapp or a Norwegian. And in the end the thieves grew afraid and dared not steal any more when they knew Goven was there. And sick folk gathered together at the markets so that they could see Goven, and so that he might possibly heal them. And he cured many sick folk without any medicine. And he used a little medicine too, but he cured most of them without medicine. And he freed folk from the spirits of the dead. Neither have I ever heard that he did harm to anybody, or sent ghosts to anyone, although he could have done it if he had wanted to.

. . . .

One *noaide* method is to take the froth from a dead man's mouth, and put it in a bottle. And then they give it to a person and that person dies. And the person who has begun to use this method, must give it to another person before two years have passed. If, before two years have passed, he has not given it to somebody, then it begins to injure him and in the end it kills him. And therefore, in order to save his own life, he is obliged to give it to some chance person, and he may give it to some quite innocent person.

And *noaides* make use of dead folks' teeth, and churchyard mold or sand, and these are used in exactly the same way. And these arts are wicked and dangerous, because the one who uses them may happen to kill someone whom he doesn't want to, and so it is a dangerous art. But they are still used here among the Lapps because they are easy, and no one can escape them, not even a *noaide* himself. But if you can manage to throw it up at once, then you can live . . . a person who has drunk the things described above.

. . . .

About Stallos.—Stallos are those folk who are half human and half troll or devil. They were strong, and cunning in magic, and the giants were very nearly the same kind of folk, but the giants did not hate mankind as the Stallos did. Stallos killed folk and ate them up. The giants were strong, and they were big too, and learned in *noaide* arts. These two (Stallo and the Giant) often fought, but they often went about together also.

One time they went off to a gold tree, to pick the gold leaves; and they only had one eye between them, and that one eye belonged to the giant (that Stallo never had any eyes since the day his servant burnt them out, Stallo's servant burnt out his eyes, he poured boiling lead into them while he was in his service, and ever since that time Stallo has been blind). So now he couldn't see anything, but as the giant had an eye they got along all right. And a little fellow followed them to see where the gold tree grew. So Stallo climbed up into the tree and began to pick the gold leaves, but as he hadn't any eyes, he couldn't see anything, and so he asked the giant to lend him his eye, so that he could see to pick the leaves. So the giant handed up the eye, but the little fellow snatched it, and the giant thought that Stallo had taken it. And so Stallo asked again: "Give me the eye, quick!" and the giant said: "I've given you the eye!" And so they quarreled, and grew very angry, and fought until they tore each other to pieces. And the man took the gold leaves, as many as he could carry, but that man could never find the place again. The Stallos and the giants hid it.

When dead Stallos were carried to their own houses, they came to life again. Their life was in a little house, and in the house there was a cask, and in the cask there was a sheep, and in the sheep there was a hen, and in the hen there was an egg, and in the egg there was life!

The Stallos made a contract between themselves that none of them should go into the others' territory, and that they should not even visit one another. When they made this law they were by Stallojaure.[24] And each one of them kept this law.

. . . .

The story of what happened to the Stallo who lived by Stallojaure. —Once when a Christian Lapp was on a journey, he came to this Stallo's tent. And the Lapp had a pretty daughter and a son. And the Lapp was tired, and he was hungry too; and Stallo gave him food to eat. And he ate it, for all he couldn't fancy it, because Stallo had cooked lots of folk in that same pot; but he was obliged to eat. And when he had eaten, Stallo said: "Will you give your daughter to my son?" and the man dared not refuse, so he promised him his daughter, and they made arrangements where they would hold the wedding. At that time there were no banns to bother about, they did nothing more than come together and take one another's hands, then it was all in order. Now that Lapp knew where the Uldas lived, and he was friends with them, so he went off to the Uldas and asked their advice, because he didn't want to give his daughter to Stallo's son. When he came to the Uldas' house, the Ulda grandmother said at once: "*Voi, voi,* to think that you have promised your daughter to be Stallo's daughter-in-law!" Then the

24 On the map Talojarvi. This mountain and the other places named here are to be found east of Torneträsk. Turi's placing of these and other place names are for the most part incorrect and merely folk-etymological.

Lapp said: "Do you know any way out?" The Ulda answered: "I don't know for certain, but if you will come here on your way to Stallo's tent, I shall have some advice for you." So the Lapp went home. And he told his folk what had happened. Then they set off to hold the wedding. And on their way, they came to the Uldas' house, and the Uldas advised them: "You must go by the 'night-side' (the north) of Kuortovare, for Stallo has dreamt that if you come from the 'night-side' of the mountain it will be dangerous, and he will ask you at once, which side of the mountain you come from . . . the 'night-side' or the 'day-side' (the south)." (So when Stallo asked them) they answered: "We came by the 'day-side.'" And so he was not afraid. And they began to hold the wedding. And they hung two big pots over the fire. And when the meat was cooked, the Lapp's son rose to his knees and lifted off one pot, and Stallo said to his son: "Now you get to your knees and lift off the pot like that other boy did." And when he began to lift off the pot his bride said: "Shall I help you?" Then Stallo said: "He's strong enough, he can lift it down alone!" But when he was about to lift it, the bride seized hold of the handle, as if she would help him, but she lifted it so high that the boiling fat poured down inside the bridegroom's furs, and his stomach and testicles were burnt, but he told nobody that he was burnt so badly. And so they began to eat, and a great many Lapps had come to the wedding, and they ate and drank; but the bridegroom, who was dying, he did not eat, he went outside and lay down, and his bride sat by his side, she saw well enough that he could not live. And so they went down to the lake to play, as was the custom among the Lapps in the old times, when they had eaten a wedding feast. And the Lapps had cut many holes in the ice and covered them with snow, and laid big logs of wood by the side of them. And the women were very busy cooking drinks till the men came back. And the Lapp women knew well enough what trickeries were toward.

And they knew that Stallo's wife had an iron pipe that was dangerous, if she sucked through it then there was danger about. So they stole her iron pipe and put the mouthpiece in among the glowing embers, then they started going over each other's heads for lice. And the menfolk were playing out on the lake. Stallo had a cloth over his eyes, and the others sprang round him pulling at his furs, and Stallo snatched at them. And when he caught one of them he said: "Njauka, Njauka. Now I shall have some fresh meat. This one shall be my evening meal!" And he bit their clothes so deeply that there came meat between his teeth, and after that they sprang quicker than ever. And when he caught another one he said: "Njam, Njam! That's good, now I've got some meat for tomorrow." And he bit so deeply that the pain was terrible, and he grew angry too. So they sprang about till at last they got Stallo to fall into one of the holes in the ice, and then they started to beat him on the head with the logs of wood, till Stallo began to shout to his old woman: "Now suck with your iron pipe!" And when she heard her man's voice, she began to look about for her iron pipe, but she couldn't find it, and she could hear from his voice that Stallo was in dire distress; then the Lapp woman who was searching her head said: "What's that burning in the fire?" When she caught sight of the pipe she snatched it up, and started sucking the red-hot end, and her throat was filled with burning embers, and she burnt her throat and her stomach and she died on the spot. And the

Lapp and his comrades beat Stallo until he died. And the son died at the same time as his mother. But Stallo lived a little longer. And when Stallo was dead they fetched stones, and tied them round his neck, and sank him in a hole in the ice. And that's why Stallojaure is a lake very poor in fish. And Stallo's old woman and his son are buried on the east shore of the lake. And the burial place is there to this day. And ever since then, that ground has been accursed, so that all the folk there are tainted, and they are so quarrelsome that they are worse than any other folk in the neighborhood. . . .

[*The tube which Stallo's wife used was a sucking tube, part of the standard equipment of shamans all over the Arctic region, and particularly in North America. Pairs of sucking tubes have been found in New England Indians' graves. They are of course made of stone or bone, not of iron. To the Lapps, iron was a magical substance. Like many other simply organized peoples the Lapps have many myths to explain the configuration of the landscape. We shall see presently that the Australian aborigines employ similar narratives as an essential part of their ritual beliefs and practices.*

Who were the Stallos? It seems unlikely that they were wholly the product of the Lapps' imaginations. Scandinavian archaeologists have found remains of a stone-age culture in northern Norway, which may easily have continued until the time of Christ, the date at which the first arrival of persons identifiable as Lapps in that region has been set. The Stallos may thus have been isolated survivors of a people of paleolithic-mesolithic tradition. This conclusion, however, is wholly conjectural.

The Uldas, about whom Turi next speaks, need no historical counterpart. They are ground spirits, or fairies, the personification of the disturbances which occur when people perform antisocial acts—that is, break the rules, making life harder for others. They can be compared directly to the "good People" in Ireland.]

About the Uldas.—The Uldas are the folk who live underground, and in the rocks. And they are descended from the race that our first forefathers bound under the earth. Uldas are strange folk of whom it is not good to know what they are, nor from whence they came in the beginning, or if they are human beings or not, but they too are Adam's children. And they have reindeer, and their reindeer are much handsomer than the Lapps' reindeer. The Uldas' reindeer are white, or white-patched, or light-gray and white-patched, and they have white muzzles, or are speckled with white in all manner of ways. Sometimes they show them to the Lapps, such Lapps as they take a fancy to, and they give them away too, if a man does what he should do. If you see the Uldas' herd, you must not lose sight of it for a moment until you can cast steel over it . . . a knife, or even only a sewing needle, and if you manage to cast steel over it you get all the animals you've thrown over. And reindeer a man gets from the Uldas are always white-patched. When a man has such a herd with many white or white-patched animals, the Lapps call it an "Ulda herd." The Uldas do not care for all kinds of folk, they care for those who have black hair and are honest and can talk well, so that it pleases them. Some Uldas are very clever at *joiking*, the Lapps often hear them, and they first learnt *joiking* from the Uldas. And the Uldas are dressed like the Lapps, and they watch their reindeer and shout, and their dogs bark and bells clang, but you don't see anything. And if one says to another: "Listen, do you hear that?" Then you don't hear anything any more. Sometimes the Lapps hear crying, and then it's just the same, if one says to another that he hears something, then it stops. But it means that those who hear it will weep. When the Lapps are traveling in the wilds, and it is rainy weather, they seek shelter under a stone, or in a crack in the rocks, and sometimes they come upon a beautiful house, and there is a lot of gold and silver there and food too. And the folk (the Uldas) quickly invite them to eat, and if you eat you can never get out again, but if you don't eat, the Uldas can't keep you there, and so they drive those folk out. And dogs see the Uldas too, and some folk never see or hear anything at all . . . not the least thing . . . but the dogs see them, and bark, but not so furiously as they bark at ghosts or churchyard specters.

Telling how the Uldas change children with the Lapps.—The Uldas are dangerous too, they like to take pretty, black-haired children in exchange for their old parents, whom they do not care to provide for, and Uldas' old folk live a long time and grow very old. And this happens when the Lapps leave a child alone in a tent, or hanging in its cradle from the branch of a tree,[25] or by the side of a stone. And the worst is to leave a child alone if it has no marked silver about it. And so the Lapps put silver and other such things in the child's cradle. In a boy child's cradle they generally put a knife, and in the girl child's they put a sewing needle (one of the triangular ones that they use to sew leather with) and a fire steel (flint and steel) and a ring for hanging sewing things on. But if there are none of these things, and the child is lying alone, then it is easily exchanged. And when the child

[25] A Lapp woman often hangs the cradle containing her child on the branch of a tree when she is outside and has some work to do.

is exchanged it still looks the same, but it does not grow or talk as a child ought to, and it does not walk, and it has not the same nature as an ordinary child; and it is much uglier too, and its eyes are uglier. And such folk as I have described are certainly nothing but those that the Uldas have exchanged for their old parents; but those who were exchanged children, they grow well enough, and talk like other folk, but they are always a little different in looks and nature. And the Uldas never exchange their prettiest children, but they always take the prettiest children.

Now I will tell how the Uldas live in all kinds of earth, and if folk happen to set up their tent over their dwelling place, they are disturbed, because they sleep in the day and wake up in the night, and so they are bad-tempered, but not towards all, and they tell them to go away. And if you obey they don't do anything, but if you don't obey, they won't give you any peace to sleep in, they rumster about in the night till you don't know what is happening, but you won't get any peace to sleep in, and sleep won't come although you don't see anything. And they come in dreams and talk. Some folk they ask quite politely to go away from that place that is on the top of their dwelling place, and when you go away it is always quite quiet. But the Uldas are not so good towards all folk, they don't tell them that they want them to go away, but they only plague them, and kill their creatures and at last they begin to kill the human beings too, if you don't know enough to go away. And if you swear badly.

And to this day the Uldas exist like other folk. And the Lapps see them often and hear them constantly. And the Uldas are very handsome, those that folk have seen. Now and again a boy has seen an Ulda girl, and she was so beautiful that he wanted to get nearer to her, and when he got nearer he thought, "If only she were mine!" Then the girl disappeared, and the young man stood alone, and was very unhappy. And the next day he went back to the same place, and then he heard an Ulda girl *joiking* and it seemed to him it was the same girl; and for a long time he listened to the beautiful *joiking,* such beautiful *joiking* as he had never heard before, and the boy learnt *joiking* from that Ulda girl, and he taught other Lapps to *joik.* And some Lapps have learnt many *noaide* arts from the Uldas, and Uldas are so good to some folk that they tell them all that is happening. And if they know of something evil that is going to happen, they tell about it; and they help and give advice as to what shall be done. Such folk get on wonderfully well, and it is those folk whom the Uldas help who are the most skilled in *noaide* arts. And the Uldas take care of the reindeer herds too, so that they don't die; but you must pay toll to the Uldas. This toll paying must be done like this: in some special place you put money or something, copper or brass or silver, and you must throw it into a big moraine, or in the water where nobody can ever find it. And you must say to the Uldas, "This I give to you." And to this day the Lapps often give things to the Uldas, sometimes they pour some coffee out on to the ground, or sometimes *brännvin,* and say: "Drink you too of my coffee, and help me."

[*The Uldas thus serve not only to prevent people from performing deeds which will disturb others, but they furnish a convenient explanation for unusual qualities in people.*

Turi next writes about Lapp esthetics. Moving about as they do, and living in small groups, they have little chance for elaborate musical instruments or stage properties, and it is only natural that their chief artistic medium is poetry through song.]

    •   •   •

About Lapp song.—The Lapp song is *joiking.* This is a way of recalling other folk; some are remembered with hate, some with love, and some with sorrow. And often these songs concern certain places, or animals . . . the wolf, and the reindeer, and the wild reindeer. And this form of song is as I describe it below.

Now the one girl says to the other girl, "*Joik* about your beloved Nilas." Nilas was handsome in the opinion of all the girls, and all the girls wanted to have him for a husband, and so they *joiked* about him a lot. And the name of this (kind of) song is *loutte.* And so she begins to sing Nilas' song:

Voia voia, nana nana, very clever, very lovely, very gentle.

Voia voia, nana nana, when he runs, he moves like a bird, voia voia, nana nana.

And then the other girl begs: "Now sing your beloved's *joik.*" And the first girl says: "I have no lover." The other says: "O! That you have." The first says: "Well, who is it that you think is my lover?" "I mean Matte." The first says: "Matte doesn't bother about me, he has those who are better than me." She's a waggish girl, she doesn't tell the other that she has a lover, because her lover is Nilas.

And so she wants to hear if the stupid one thinks that she will get Nilas. But Nilas has never thought of taking her, Nilas likes the waggish girl. He often sang that girl's *joik* like this:

Voia voia, nana nana, very gentle, very loving, very clever,

voia voia, nana nana, big and lovely, best girl in the country, voia voia, nana nana.

But when Nilas saw the waggish girl coming, he didn't *joik* any more. And the waggish girl *joiked* to Nilas that his dearest was Ani . . . that was the stupid girl's name. And the waggish girl's name was Elle. And so she *joiked* to Nilas:

The best boy in the district, deceiving Ani, voia voia, nana nana,
The best boy in the country, voia voia, nana nana,
Who took another boy's beloved, voia voia, nana nana,
And left Matte weeping.

And Nilas feared that he would not get the waggish girl. Matte too loved Elle, and Elle had promised to take Matte, and Matte believed that she was in earnest, and he too *joiked* often to Elle:

Voia voia, nana nana, best beloved,
Very clever, very lovely, voia voia, nana nana,
This is the best girl on this high fell, voia voia, nana nana.

But when Matte heard that Nilas had given Elle betrothal gifts, then he wept and *joiked*:

Voia voia, nana nana, sad deceiver.

And he wept and sorrowed, until he nearly lost his reason, and he grew bitter against Nilas, and killed his reindeer, and when he had drunk himself full, then he *joiked* and swore like this:

Voia voia, nana nana, Birru Baergalak, Now I'll kill all Nilas' reindeer.
Satan's false Elle's rotten trousers; still are many, many like her, voia voia, nana nana.

And so he wept a little more, and *joiked*. And Matte thought to himself: "I'm silly to be angry at Nilas and Elle; I shall find as good a girl, an even better girl." His sister Ingir said to Matte: "The boys don't look at Andaras's Marja, but she's a fine girl, and she will be rich." Ingir was a young girl, and a sensible girl. And Matte said to Ingir: "Do you think that Marja will take me?" Ingir answered: "I don't know, but I will ask Andaras's Marja if she will take you." And then Matte liked his sister, when she would help him to get a wife.

And so one Sunday, Ingir went to the *sida* where Marja was. And so she met Marja and asked her: "Will you promise to take my brother, Matte?" Marja answered: "Matte does not care for anybody but Lodne's Elle." Ingir said: "It's not quite like that; you must believe me when I say that it is so. You two are made for one another." Marja said: "How do you know that we two are made to be happy in marriage?" Ingir answered: "I have dreamt it, and what I dream is always right."

Marja answered: "If things are like that, then I will promise that you can come here after another week, when I have thought about it; will that do?" And so they separated. And Ingir went home. And then she went to her brother and told him what she had heard. And when they told their mother and father, they liked it very much. And after a week had passed, then they went again to Marja. And in the old days it was customary, when a young man came courting, for a girl to go to meet him and unharness his reindeer, and that was a sign that she would take him. And if the girl did not come and unharness his reindeer, then the young man drove round the tent, and between the tent and the woodpile. And if the girl did not come and unharness his reindeer even then, the man knew that the girl would not have him. And some men never even stepped into the tent, they drove straight back. And Marja knew all this, how everything should be done, and when she saw Matte coming, she went toward him and unharnessed his reindeer, and so Matte went into the tent and made his greetings, according to Lapp custom. Among the Lapps it is customary to take a person round the neck and press nose to nose. And Matte did this, and he kissed her for such a long time that it seemed as if he would never be done. And not till then did they begin to talk and drink a little *brännvin* . . . at that time there was no coffee. And so they got married the same day, and Matte went home. And then Marja's father, Andaras, ordered her to fetch her church reindeer and give it to Matte. And when Marja had fetched the reindeer, then Matte drove home and Marja sat in the sledge. And when they took leave of one another, they took each other round the neck and kissed. And those two thought that nothing else was necessary. But then father-in-law Andaras said: "You two will have to make yet another journey before you are finished. You must go to the church father, and get permission." And then Matte said: "Has Marja another father, or has Marja another husband, or what is it?" Matte did not know that one needed permission from the church fathers, or as it is now called, marriage.

When Matte set off for the second time (to Marja) he was still afraid that the church father would snatch his wife from him. He'd got a little bit funny in the head. And in courting times the mind is often a little wild, especially in those who have that sort of blood. The explanation of why some folk have such weak blood that it is rather easy to upset them is that some people are of such an amorous nature that at that time they can think of nothing else. And that is why it is as if they lose their wits. And some folk are still in love afterwards, but it is not everyone who is in love afterwards. And when all the marriage affairs have been put in order, then they generally get as clear in their heads as they were before.

And when Matte drove to Marja for the second time, he took his ex-change reindeer to Marja's *sida*. (The bride and the bridegroom always exchange reindeer as a sign of their acceptance of one another.) And so they greeted one another as before. And they began to drink *brännvin* again and to talk of the young pair, what they should do. And how, in the morning, they would drive to the church father. But Matte was afraid that he would lose his Marja to the church father. He had no wish to go there, but when Marja's father said it was necessary to do it, then they set off. They took with them three reserve reindeer, and sledges, in which there was meat and reindeer milk. And when they began to drive, father-in-law Andaras took the reserve reindeer, and Marja and Matte each drove a reindeer, and they drove their exchange reindeer. And those reindeer were snow-white, and there was a lot of finery on the harness, cloth of all kinds. On the reindeer's girth and on the halter. The girth goes round the middle of the reindeer, and the halter is on the head . . . the band with which you steer the reindeer, like the bridle on a horse. And so they drove off, and the reindeer sprang until the snow smoked, so that they could not keep their eyes open, nor could they even breathe. And then it is dangerous if the sledge swings behind a tree or behind a stone, then you are easily killed. And when the reindeer had run for a short stretch, then they were a little tired, and then they began to go more quietly, and then it is pleasant to drive, and then they began to *joik* like this:

Voia voia voia voia, nana nana nana
  nana
splendid   reindeer,   springing,
  springing,
voia, voia voia, nana nana nana,
  reindeer springing like the wind-
  storm,

voia voia voia, nana nana nana,
  reindeer springing like a gunshot,
voia voia voia, nana nana nana
  finest horns among all reindeer,
voia voia voia, nana nana nana.

And now the reindeer began to be hot and thirsty, and so they kept snapping at the snow, to cool their heat and slake their thirst. And so Matte drew in his reindeer, and all the reindeer stopped to breathe.

There are certain places where you let the reindeer eat snow, and make water; it is dangerous if you drive too far at a stretch. If the reindeer do not make water, then they get bladder stoppage, and then they can't make water. And when Ingir saw that all the reindeer had made water, then she began to *joik.*

To the young pair we wish good luck, voia voia, nana nana,
  the young pair shall be rich, voia voia, nana nana,
They shall have lovely children, voia voia, nana nana,
  lovely little Marja, shining like a light, voia voia, nana nana,
Now we drive on again, voia, voia, voia, voia, nana, nana, nana, nana,
  the great reindeer springing on again, voia voia, nana nana.

Level Two

The Band Contains
Several Families

6

The Andaman Islanders

IN THE selections which you have read so far, you have learned how whole cultures work, in five different parts of the world. In each you have read how peoples of different races have managed to live at different levels of technical competence in different environments. One thing in particular they all seem to hold, or have held, in common, for various reasons—a social structure of rock-bottom simplicity. As far as I can tell from the information at hand, the largest institution to which any of them belong was the family, and the individuals belonged to only one institution of any kind, and for a good reason: scarcity of food.

In the long selection that follows—Radcliffe Brown's study of the culture of the Andamanese Negritos* and one of the great classics of ethnography,—for the first time in his book you will be reading about a people who live in an environment where desert suns do not blister, nor cold winds off the poles freeze, and where food is abundant all the year, and their social structure is thereby a little more complicated.

The Andaman Islands are part of a chain of islands stretching from Cape Negrais in Burma to Achin Head in Sumatra. This line of islands forms a single geographical system, as it were a submarine range of mountains, the highest points rising here and there above the surface of the ocean. . . . The Andaman Group itself consists of the Great and Little Andaman with their outlying islets, and occupies a distance approximately north and south of about 210 miles. . . .

The Great Andaman may be regarded as one island, although it is divided by narrow sea water creeks into four areas, often spoken of as separate islands and called North Andaman, Middle Andaman, Baratang, and South Andaman. It is a long narrow stretch of land with a much indented coast, surrounded by many smaller islands. . . . The length of the Great Andaman with Rutland Island is nearly 160 miles, while the breadth from sea to sea is nowhere more than 20 miles. The Little Andaman lies to the south of the Great Andaman, about 30 miles distant from Rutland Island, from which it is sep-

* A. R. Brown, *The Andaman Islanders.* The University Press, Cambridge, 1922. Reprinted by permission of the author.

arated by a shallow strait with a maximum depth of only 21 fathoms. The island is about 26 miles long from north to south and about 16 miles wide.

Viewed from the sea the islands appear as a series of hills, nowhere of any great height, covered from sky line to high-water mark with dense and lofty forest. The hill ranges run approximately north and south, in the same direction as the islands themselves, and attain a greater elevation on the east than on the west. The highest point of the North Andaman is Saddle Peak (2402 feet), that of Middle Andaman is Mt. Diavolo (1678 feet), while the South Andaman has the Mt. Harriett Range (1505 feet), and in Rutland Island there is Mt. Foord (1422 feet). There are no streams of any size. The water drains from the hills into tidal creeks running through mangrove swamps, often many miles in length. The coast is broken by a number of magnificent harbours. The shores are fringed with extensive coral reefs, and on these and in the creeks there is abundance of fish and molluscs.

The islands, save for the clearings of the Penal Settlement, are covered with dense tropical forest. There are few mammals, the only two of any size being a species of pig (*Sus andamanensis,* Blyth) and a civet cat (*Paradoxurus tytlerii,* Tytler). The other mammals are a few species of rats, a tree shrew and some species of bats.* Of birds there are many different species, some of them peculiar to the islands. The reptiles include a considerable number of species of snakes, and a few species of lizards, or which the most noteworthy is the large Monitor lizard (*Varanus salvator*).

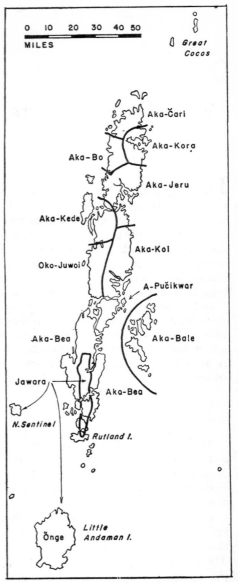

Andamanese tribes (*after A. R. Brown*).

---

*The pigs were domestic swine introduced about A.D. 1585, along with pottery making, probably by Indonesians, rather than Muslim Malays, who ate no pork. The pigs then went feral and the pottery degenerated (Lidio Cipriani, *The Andaman Islanders,* London and New York, 1966. The Carbon-14 date was A.D. 1582 ± 80 years, R-86). The civet-cats, tree shrews, and rats, all parasites, probably came as stowaways on Malay ships.

The climate is warm and moist, and fairly uniform throughout the year. The mean temperature for the year at Port Blair is about 86° F. (80° F. on the wet-bulb thermometer). The lowest temperatures are recorded in January and February, and the highest in March, April, or May. The average lowest temperature in the South Andaman over a period of seven years is 66.7° F., the minimum during that period being 63° F. The average highest temperature in the shade for the same period was 96° F., the maximum being 97°. The average diurnal variation is 10°.

The average rainfall of seven stations in the Penal Settlement of Port Blair, for a period of seven years, was 138 inches per annum, the average of the different stations varying from 104 to 172 inches. For the same period the average number of rainy days in the year was 177, the minimum being 160 and the maximum 196.

The islands are sufficiently far from the Equator to have a single well-defined rainy season. The greater part of the rain falls during the southwest monsoon, which lasts from the middle of May to the middle of November. The northeast monsoon extends over the other six months of the year, which include the dry and hot seasons. . . . Many of the violent cyclonic storms that sweep across the Sea of Bengal seem to form themselves a little to the south of the Andamans. Cyclones of exceptional violence struck Port Cornwallis in 1844 and Port Blair in 1864 and 1891. . . .

There are numerous references to the Andamans in the seventeenth and eighteenth century, and all of them show that the islands were feared and avoided. During these and the previous centuries wrecks must have occurred in considerable numbers, and it is probable, from what is now known of the

natives, that the mariners would be immediately slain. . . .

There is one way in which the life of the Andamanese was affected by the vessels that visited or were wrecked upon their shores, since it was by this means that they learnt the use of iron. It is impossible now to determine the date at which they became acquainted with the metal. The earliest reference to the subject is in an account of a visit to the Andamans in 1771, where it is shown that the natives were at that time aware of the value of iron.[1] Until the middle of the nineteenth century the only supply of the metal was from wrecks, of which there have always been a fair number. . . .

Although of one race throughout, the Andaman Islanders are divided into several groups, with differences of language and culture. There are two main divisions, which will be spoken of as the Great Andaman Group and the Little Andaman Group respectively. The Great Andaman Group includes all the natives of the Great Andaman with the exception of those of the interior of the South Andaman who are known as *Jarawa*. The Little Andaman Group includes all the inhabitants of the Little Andaman, those of the North Sentinel Island and the *Jarawa* of the South Andaman. . . .

The natives of the Great Andaman Group are divided into tribes, of which

[1] The account is that of a visit to the Andamans in 1771 by John Ritchie, published in the *Indian Antiquary,* Vol. XXX, 1901, pp. 232 *seq.* Two natives came off to the ship in a canoe, and Ritchie writes: "I gave them some nails and bits of old iron which pleased them much; and about three in the afternoon, they went into the canoe, and tried hard to pull the chain plates from the vessel's side. They went astern when this would not do, and dragged strongly and long at the rudder chains; but these were too well fixed; and at last, they went towards the shore at an easy rate, looking at their nails, and singing all the way."

there are ten, each with its own distinctive language or dialect, and with a name. The following is a list of these tribes, passing from north to south :—
Aka-Cari, Aka-Kora, Aka-Bo, Aka-Jeru, Aka-Kede, Aka-Kol, Oko-Juwoi, A-Pucikwar, Akar-Bale, and *Aka-Bea.* In each case the name is given in the form in which it is used by the tribe itself. . . .

The natives of the Little Andaman refer to themselves as *Onge* (men). It is probable that the so-called *Jarawa* of the South Andaman have the same word. . . .

Judging from what it is possible to learn about the habits of the natives, and the food supply available, I should estimate that the former population of the islands (in 1858) was about 5500. An estimate for the proportion of the different groups is as follows :—

line is of more importance to the Andamanese than the actual area of their country. The natives of the Little Andaman are not able to harpoon turtle and large fish, which constitute an important element of the food supply of the tribes of the Great Andaman.

. . . When the islands were first occupied by the British, before depopulation had affected their institutions, the natives of the Great Andaman were to be found living in small communities scattered over the islands, mostly on the coast, but some of them in the forest of the interior of the island. Each such community, which will be spoken of as a "local group," was independent and autonomous, leading its own life and regulating its own affairs. Each group had occasional relations with other neighbouring groups ; visitors might pass from one to another ; or

Area	Estimated former population	Density per square mile
North Andaman (four tribes)	1500	2.75
Middle Andaman with Baratang and Ritchie's Archipelago	2250	2.5
South Andaman (Aka-Bea and Jarawa)	1200	2.0
Little Andaman and North Sentinel	700	1.75
Total	5650	2.25

With regard to the comparative density per square mile of the different groups it may be pointed out that the reason for the smaller density of the South Andaman is the fact that the *Aka-Bea* and *Jarawa* were living there at war with one another, and the territory was therefore probably not so fully occupied as in other parts of the islands where boundaries between neighbouring tribes were well defined. The food supply of the Little Andaman does not seem to be so abundant as that of the Great Andaman in proportion to its area. It must be remembered that length of coast

the two groups might meet together for a few days and join in feasting and dancing. On the other hand there were often quarrels between neighbouring groups, which might result in a state of feud between them for many months. Between communities separated from one another by a distance of only 50 miles or even less there were no direct relations whatever. The members of one community kept to their own part of the country, only leaving it to visit their friends within a narrow radius.

These local groups were united into what are here called tribes. A tribe consisted of a number of local groups all speaking what the natives themselves regard as one language, each tribe having its own language and its name. The tribe was of very little importance in regulating the social life, and was merely a loose aggregate of independent local groups.

The local groups are further distinguished by the natives themselves as being of two kinds according as they lived on the coast or inland. This division was independent of that into tribes. Some tribes consisted of coast dwellers only, while others included both coast dwellers and forest dwellers.

Within the local group the only division was that into families. A family consists of a man and his wife and their unmarried children own or adopted.

These are the only social divisions existing among the Andamanese, who were without any of those divisions known as "clans" which are characteristic of many primitive societies.

The natives of the Great Andaman (leaving aside the *Jarawa,* who by language and culture belong to the Little Andaman division of the race) are divided into ten tribes, each occupying a certain area of country. Each tribe consists of a number of persons who speak what is regarded by the natives themselves as one language. That the tribe is fundamentally a linguistic group is shown by the tribal names. These are all formed from a stem with the prefix *aka-,* which prefix is used in the languages of the Great Andaman to convey a reference to the mouth, and thereby to the function of speech. . . .

Although the natives themselves thus recognize and give names to ten distinct languages, all of them are closely related. There is, on the whole, not a great deal of difference between two neighbouring languages. A man of the *Aka-Jeru* tribe could understand without any great difficulty a man speaking *Aka-Bo.* On the other hand many of the languages included two or even more distinct dialects. . . .

Leaving aside the *Aka-Bea,* the average extent of territory occupied by a tribe was about 165 square miles. Of the nine tribes the largest, as regards area, was the *Aka-Kede,* with over 300 square miles, while the smallest was probably the *Aka-Cari,* with less than 100 square miles. Save in the case of the *Akar-Bale* tribe, which occupied the islands of Ritchie's Archipelago, it is difficult to find any marked geographical features that might be supposed to have determined the extent and the boundaries of the different tribes.

The *Aka-Bea* tribe was in an abnormal position as there was no recognized boundary between them and the *Jarawa.* Together, these two divisions of the Andamanese occupied an area of about 600 square miles. The *Aka-Bea* seem to have kept more to the coast while the *Jarawa* occupied the interior of the South Andaman and Rutland Island.

If the estimate previously given of the former population of the islands be correct, the nine tribes (leaving aside the *Aka-Bea*) would have formerly contained about 3750 persons of all ages. . . .

Besides the division into tribes, and independent of it, the Andamanese recognize another division into coast dwellers and forest dwellers. In the *Aka-Bea* language the coast dwellers are called *Ar-yoto,* while the forest-dwellers are called *Erem-taga.* The difference between them is due solely to the difference in their food supply. The *Ar-yoto* obtain much of their food from the sea. They are expert in fishing and turtle hunting. They make canoes and use them not only for hunting but also for travelling from one camp to another. Some portion of their food they also obtain from the forest, edible roots and fruits and the flesh of the wild pig being the chief. On the other hand, the *Erem-taga* rely solely on the forest and the inland creeks for their food supply. Their only use for canoes is in the creeks. They are entirely ignorant of such matters as turtle or dugong hunting, but they are more at home than the coast dwellers in the forest, and are generally more skilful at pig hunting. The advantage certainly rests with the coast dwellers, for they have both the sea and the forest to draw upon for their sustenance. . . .

Each tribe formerly consisted of a number of independent local groups. The local group, and not the tribe, was the land-owning group, each one owning or exercising hunting rights over a certain recognized area. At the present time, owing to the breakdown of the local organisation, through the settlement of the islands, and the resulting decrease of population, it is difficult to ascertain what area of country was occupied by each of these local groups. In many cases it would seem that the boundaries between two neighbouring groups are not very clearly defined, there being portions of forest over which the members of both hunted when the groups were at peace. There is no doubt that in the more favourable localities, particularly on the coast, the country occupied by a single group was smaller than in places of less abundant food supply. It is probable that the forest dwelling local groups occupied considerably larger areas in each case than the coast groups. Some of the coast dwelling groups seem to have occupied areas of less than ten square miles. . . .

From the information that I was able to obtain from the natives them-selves, I came to the conclusion that an average local group consisted of from 40 to 50 persons of all ages, the average number of local groups to a tribe being about 10. This would give the average extent of country occupied by each local group as about 16 square miles, but some groups certainly had a larger territory than this and some had smaller. . . .

A man or woman is generally regarded as belonging to the local group in the country of which he or she was born. There is nothing, however, to prevent a person from taking up his residence with any other local group if he so wishes, and if the members of that group are willing to welcome him. It would seem that there were a fair number of such cases in which a man or a woman left his or her own local group to join another. In particular, when two young people belonging to different groups got married they might fix their residence either with his or with her parents.

The local group, as stated above, was characterised as the land-owning group. A man might hunt over the country of his own group at all times, but he might not hunt over the country of another group without the permission of the members of that group. . . .

Within the territory of each local group there are a number of recognized camping places. During the greater part of every year the members of the local group would be found living together at one or other of these. Some of these camping grounds have been in use for many centuries, as is shown by the heaps of refuse many feet deep, chiefly consisting of the shells of molluscs and the bones of animals. Such kitchen middens, as they have been called, are to be found in numbers all around the coast of the islands.

In the case of the coast-dwelling communities the camping sites are always close to the seashore or to a creek, so that they can be reached by canoe. In the case of those dwelling inland this is of course not so. In any case one of the chief factors determining the choice of the site is the existence of a supply of fresh water. This is of extreme importance in the case of a site to be occupied during the dry season when fresh water becomes scarce.

Within their own territory the local group is what we may speak of as semi-nomadic. The coast dwellers rarely reside continuously at the same spot for more than a few months, but shift from one camp to another, moved by different causes. If a death occurs the camp is deserted for several months, and a new one is occupied. A change of camp often takes place at a change of season, some spots presenting particular advantages, such as shelter from the prevailing wind, or better hunting or fishing, at certain times of the year. Another cause of the abandonment of a camp by the coast dwellers is that all refuse is thrown away close to the camp, and after a few months the decaying vegetable matter thus accumulated renders the spot uninhabitable. The natives seem to find it easier to move their camp than to clear away their refuse. The truth is, perhaps, that they are so accustomed to change their camp from one spot to another, in order to make the best use of the natural resources available, that there is no necessity for them to take those sanitary measures that would be essential if they wished to remain for many months continuously at the same place.

The forest dwellers are less nomadic in their habits than the coast dwellers. One of the reasons for this is that as they cannot convey their belongings from one place to another by canoe, but must carry them overland, the moving of a camp is a more tiresome business with them than it is with the coast dwellers. During a great part of the year the forest dwellers were accustomed to remain at one camp, which was thus the chief camp of the group. In particular they would spend there the whole of the rainy season. During the cool and hot seasons they would leave the chief camp for a few months, leading during that time a more nomadic life, living in temporary hunting camps and paying visits to their friends in other groups. At the opening of the rainy season they would return once more to the main camp.

The camps of the natives of the Great Andaman may be distinguished as being of three kinds. Of the first kind are what may be spoken of as permanent encampments. Certainly every group of the forest dwellers, and probably every group of the coast dwellers, had its permanent encampment, which was, so to speak, the headquarters of the group. At this spot there would be erected either a communal hut, or a carefully built village. . . .

A large communal hut took some little time to erect. The posts had to be cut and erected, this being the work of the men, and the palm leaves had to be collected and then made into mats by the women. Once the hut was built it would last for several years, and if it were in fairly constant use, particularly if it were not abandoned in the rains, it might be used, with a little occasional patching, for ten years or even more.

Among the coast dwellers it was more usual to erect at the headquarters a semi-permanent village. . . .

The village occupied a small clearing in the forest close to the seashore at a place called *Moi-lepto* in the country of the *Akar-Bale* tribe. A spring or soak close to the village provided the fresh water. The site is a favourite one as it is well sheltered, and is within convenient distance of good fishing and turtle hunting grounds. It was formerly one of the chief camping places of the local group known as the *Boroin wa* (Hill people).

The village was composed of eight huts, ranged round a central open space, and all of them facing inwards towards the centre. This open space is kept clear and clean for dancing, and is simply the village dancing ground. Each of the single huts was occupied by a family group, consisting of a man and his wife with their children and dependents. One hut was occupied by an old widower and a bachelor. . . .

In the simplest form the hut consists of a sloping roof made of palm leaves, erected on four posts, two taller ones at the front and two short ones at the back. . . . If more shelter is required a second roof is added in such a way that the top of one overhangs the top of the other. In some cases a third roof may be added on one side. . . .

A second kind of camp was made when the natives did not intend to stay more than two or three months. Such camps were erected by the forest folk during the dry season, or at any time when they were compelled to leave their chief camp through the death there of one of their number. Such a temporary camp is always put up in the form of a village, and never as a communal hut. The huts are similar to those already described, but are made more carelessly. The thatching leaves, instead of being made into mats, are simply tied in bundles on to the rafters. A hut of this kind will last quite well for three months or so and it can be built very rapidly at any place where there is a sufficient supply of thatching leaves. . . .

A third kind of camp remains to be briefly mentioned, which we may call the hunting camp. A hunting party (which may include women as well as men) spending a few days away from one of the main camps will erect for themselves a few huts or shelters consisting of nothing more than a simple lean-to of leaves.

Caves or rock shelters suitable for human occupation are almost unknown in the Andamans. . . . I was told by the natives that on one of the islands off the west coast of the North Andaman there is a rock shelter of a fair size that was formerly used as one of their chief camps.

The following figure will give an idea of the Andamanese village and its arrangement. In hunting camps which are intended only to be occupied for a few days or a few weeks, this arrangement is not observed, but the huts or shelters are placed so as to give shelter from the prevailing wind with no particular regard to the respective position of the different units.

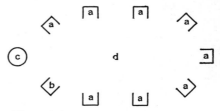

Plan of Andamanese Village
a. Huts of married people.
b. Bachelors' hut.
c. Public cooking place.
d. Dancing ground.

The constitution of the local group is illustrated by the arrangement of the village. The whole village consists of a number of separate huts, each hut occupied by a family. A family consists of a man and his wife and such of their children own or adopted as are not of an age to be independent. Besides the families each group necessarily contains a small number of unmarried men and widowers and some unmarried girls and widows. The unmarried men and widowers without children occupy a separate hut (or huts) which we may speak of as the bachelors' hut. Mr. Man states that the spinsters (i.e., the unmarried women who are of marriageable age) and widows occupy a hut of their own similarly to the bachelors.[1] In the camps that I visited I did not find any such spinsters' hut; the girls and widows were living in the huts of some married relative, generally the parent or foster parent. [*This was due either to a regional difference or to depopulation C.S.C.*].

All the huts face inwards towards an open space which is the dancing ground of the village, and, except in exposed situations, are generally open in front. At some convenient spot on one side of the dancing ground is to be found the communal cooking place of the village. This is generally close to the bachelors' hut, as it is the bachelors who attend to such cooking as is carried on there. Besides the public cooking place each family has its own fireplace in its own hut, on which a fire is kept continually alight. In the village two or more families may build their huts adjoining one another in such a way that they become for all practical purposes one hut, of which each family retains its own special portion. Two brothers will thus often make a sort of common household.

The communal hut, in the way in which it is arranged, and even in the way in which it is built, is really a village with all the huts drawn together so that each one is joined to the one next to it and the roofs meet in the middle. In the centre of the hut there is an open space corresponding to the dancing ground of the village. It is even used as a dancing ground, though for this purpose it is somewhat small. It is the public part of the hut. Around this are arranged the different families, each occupying its own special portion of the hut, which is marked off by means of short lengths of wood laid on the floor. The public cooking place is sometimes inside the hut, and there is the space marked off for the unmarried men. The advantage of the communal hut is that it affords a better protection from the weather; its disadvantage is that it leaves almost no room for dancing.

Thus it may be seen that the arrangement of the camp shows very plainly the constitution of a local group, consisting as it does of a few families. Each group seems to have contained, on the average, about ten families, with a few unmarried males and females.

The Andaman Islanders depend for their subsistence entirely on the natural products of the sea and forest. From the sea they obtain dugong, turtle (both green and hawksbill), an enormous variety of different sorts of fish, crustaceans (crabs, crayfish and prawns) and molluscs. Fish and crabs are also to be found in the salt-water creeks which in many places penetrate inland for some miles. From the forest they obtain the flesh of the wild pig, wild honey, and a large number of vegetable foods—roots, fruits, and seeds.

The life of the forest folk is more simple and uniform than that of the coast people and we may therefore consider it first. During the rainy season, which lasts from the middle of May to the end of September, the local group lives at its headquarters camp, which, as we have seen, formerly often took the form of a communal hut. During this season animal food is

[1] Man, E. H., "The Andaman Islands," *Journal of the Anthropological Institute,* vol. VII, Aug. 1877, p. 108.

plentiful, as the jungle animals are in good condition; on the other hand there is not much vegetable food to be obtained. The following brief account will give an idea of how the day is spent in such a camp at that time of year. Some time after sunrise the camp begins to be astir. The various members of the community make a meal of any food that may have been saved from the day before. The men start off for the day's hunting. At the present time dogs are used for pig hunting. These dogs were obtained in the first instance from the Settlement of Port Blair, and their use in pig hunting was learnt from the Burmese convicts. Nowadays every married man has at least one dog. Before the dogs were obtained, hunting was a pursuit requiring a great deal more skill than it does at present. A hunting party consists of from two to five men. Each man carries his bow and two or three pig arrows, and one of the party carries a smouldering firebrand. They make their way through the jungle until they find the fresh tracks of a pig, or follow up some of the usual pig runs until they come upon the animal feeding. In former days much skill was required to creep noiselessly through the jungle until they were sufficiently near either to discharge an arrow, or, if the jungle were more open, to rush in upon the animal shouting and shoot it before it could escape. At the present day it is the dogs that scent out the pig and bring it to bay, when the natives shoot it with their arrows.

When a pig has been killed it may be tied up, and carried to the camp on the shoulders of one of the hunters, or a fire may be lighted then and there and the pig eviscerated and roasted. A cut is made in the abdomen and the viscera removed. The cavity is filled with leaves, the joints of the legs are half severed and the carcase is placed on the fire and turned over and shifted until every part is evenly roasted. It is then removed from the fire, the burnt skin is scraped clean, and the meat is cut up. Meanwhile the intestines or some of the internal organs are cooked and eaten by the hunters. The meat is tied up in leaves and is carried to the camp. If the pig be carried home whole the process of roasting it and cutting it up is performed in exactly the same way at the public cooking place of the camp, the meat being distributed only after it has been thus partially cooked.

If the hunting party should come across a civet cat (*Paradoxurus*) or a monitor lizard they would endeavour to kill it, but the main object of every hunting party is to obtain pork. Snakes and even rats are killed and eaten. Birds, though plentiful in the islands, are not often obtained, for the density of the jungle and the height of the trees in which the birds conceal themselves, make it very difficult for the natives to shoot them with their bows and arrows. A man does not care to risk the loss of his arrow in a chance shot at a bird. The Andamanese do not trap either birds or animals, though some of the birds, particularly the rail, might be very easily caught in traps.

As the hunting party traverses the forest they may come across roots or fruits or seeds, or wild honey, and these are collected and carried home. In the rainy season only small combs of black honey are to be found, and these are generally consumed by the hunters on the spot.

The provision of the vegetable food of the community is the work of the women, who must also supply the camp with firewood and water. While the men are away hunting the women, attended by the children, cut and carry the firewood, and either remain in the camp making baskets or nets or other objects, or else go into the forest to look for fruits and seeds. Thus by midday the camp may be quite deserted, save perhaps for one or two old men and women, and a few of the children.

In the afternoon the women return with what food they have obtained and then the men come in with their provision. The camp, unless the hunters have been unsuccessful, is then busy with the preparation of the evening meal, which is the chief meal of the day. If a pig has been brought home whole it is cooked at the public cooking place and is then cut up. The meat is distributed amongst the members of the community and the woman of each family then proceeds to cook the family meal. The pork, after it has been roasted and cut up, is further cooked by being boiled. The family meal is prepared at the fire that each family has in its hut. The meal is a family one, partaken by a man and his wife and children. The bachelors cook and eat their own meal, and the unmarried women also eat by themselves.

After the meal is over, darkness having by this time fallen, the men may spend an hour or two in dancing to the accompaniment of a song sung by one of them with the help of a chorus of women. In that case they would probably eat another meal after the dance was over. Another favourite amusement for the evening is what may be called "yarning." A man sits down with a few listeners and tells them, with few words, and with many dramatic gestures, how he killed a pig. The same man may go on with tale after tale, till, by the time he finishes he has killed twenty or thirty pigs. Finally the whole camp retires to rest and nothing is to be seen but the dim light of the little fires burning in each hut or in each of the family quarters.

On a day when there is plenty of food left from the day before, or on a day of stormy weather even when food is not too plentiful, the men may remain in camp instead of going hunting. They busy themselves with making weapons and implements, such as bows, arrows, adzes, etc.

On occasions when game is not very plentiful a party of hunters may stay away from the camp for a few days, not returning till they have been successful in obtaining a fair supply of food. The women and children and old men, with perhaps a few of the able bodied men also, remain at home, and provide for themselves as well as they can, the women devoting their time to collecting what vegetable foods are in season.

At the end of the rainy season there comes a brief period of unsettled weather, called by the natives of the North Andaman *Kimil,* and by those of the South, *Gumul.* During this season some of the vegetable foods begin to be available, though not in any quantities. At this time of the year, the natives are able to obtain and feast upon what they regard as great delicacies, the larvae of the cicada and of the great capricornis beetle. The cool season, when fruits and roots are plentiful, begins at the end of November. The forest dwellers leave their main encampment during this season. Some of them go off to pay visits to their friends of other local groups. Such visits may last two or three months. Those who remain occupy temporary camps in convenient places. The men join the women in looking for roots and fruits, and do not spend so much of their time in hunting. Some of the men visit the main camp at intervals of a few days to see that it is all right. As the cool season gives way to the hot season (March to May) honey begins to be plentiful. At that time hunting for pig is almost abandoned. The pigs are in poor condition, and even when one is killed it is often left in the jungle by the natives as not being good enough to eat. On the other hand everyone is busy collecting honey. This is work in which both men and women join, though it is the men who climb up the trees and cut down the honeycomb. The natives have no means of keeping the honey for more than a very short time, as it rapidly ferments. While it is plentiful they almost live on it, supplementing it with roots and fruits and with fish, if they are near a creek. Towards the end of the hot season, the fruit of the *Artocarpus chaplasha*, which is a favourite food of the natives, becomes ripe. The men and women, at this time, spend much of their time collecting the fruit. When it is collected the fruit is broken open and each of the seeds is sucked to obtain the juicy pulp or aril with which it is surrounded, and which has a very pleasant taste. The seeds are then partly boiled and are buried in the ground to remain there for a few weeks, when they will be dug up again and cooked and eaten. Any natives who may have been away from home on a visit return before *Artocarpus* comes into fruit in order to take their share in collecting it and providing a supply of the seeds for consumption in the rainy season. The natives then return to the headquarters camp and make any necessary repairs to the hut in preparation for the rainy season, which begins about the middle of May.

The coast dwellers are not quite so much influenced by the seasons as the forest dwellers. They can fish and collect molluscs all the year round. In the rainy season they divide their time between hunting pig in the forest, and fishing or turtle hunting. They do not need, however, to remain at the same camp during the whole of the rainy season, but after a month or two at one place can move to what they hope to find better hunting grounds. During the cool and hot seasons they pay visits to one another. In the fine weather the men often go off on turtle-hunting expeditions for several days, leaving the women and children and older men in the village, where they provide for themselves with vegetable food and with fish and molluscs from the reefs.

It is during the fine weather that there take place the meetings of two or more local groups that are an important feature of the social life of the Andaman Islanders. . . .

Besides their food, which they must find from day to day, the natives have need of nothing save their weapons and implements. Of these each person makes his own, each man making his own bow, arrows, adze, etc., while the wife makes her baskets, nets and so on.

The economic life of the local group, though in effect it approaches a sort of communism, is yet based on the notion of private property. Land is the only thing that is owned in common. The hunting grounds of a local group belong to the whole group, and all the members have an equal right to hunt over any part of it. There exists, however, a certain private ownership of trees. A man of one of the local groups of the coast may notice in the jungle a tree suitable for a canoe. He will tell the others that he has noticed such a tree, describing it and its whereabouts. Thenceforward that tree is regarded as his property, and even if some years should elapse, and he has made no use of it, yet another man would not cut it down without first asking the owner to give him the tree. In a similar way certain men claim to possess certain *Artocarpus* trees, though how the ownership in these cases had arisen I was unable to determine. No one would pick the fruit off such a tree without the permission of the owner, and having received permission and gathered the fruit, he would give some part of it to the owner of the tree.

A pig belongs to the man whose arrow first strikes it, though if the arrow merely glanced off and did not remain in the wound it would not give any claim to ownership. A turtle or a dugong or big fish belongs to the man who throws the harpoon with which it is taken. A honeycomb belongs to the man who climbs the tree and cuts it down. The fish that a man shoots belong to him, and to a woman belong the roots she digs up, the seeds that she collects, the fish or prawns that she takes in her net, or the molluscs that she brings from the reefs. Any weapon that a man makes belongs to him alone to do what he pleases with, and anything that a woman makes is her own property. A man is not free to dispose of the personal property of his wife without her permission.

In the village each family erects and keeps in repair its own hut, and the wife provides the hut with the firewood and water needed. In the case of a communal hut it would seem that this is really an example of a possession common to the whole group. This is so, however, only in appearance. The hut is built by all the different families, but each family is regarded as owning a certain portion of the hut when it is finished, and it is the family that keeps this part of the hut in repair.

A canoe is cut by a number of men together. From the outset, however, it is the property of one man, who selects the tree and superintends the operation of cutting it into shape. He is always one of the older men, and he enlists the services of the younger

men to help him. When finished, the canoe is his if he wishes, and he can do what he pleases, giving it away, if he wishes, and no one has any share of ownership in a canoe on the ground that he helped to make it.

While all portable property is thus owned by individuals, the Andamanese have customs which result in an approach to communism. One of these is the custom of constantly exchanging presents with one another. When two friends meet who have not seen each other for some time, one of the first things they do is to exchange presents with one another. Even in the ordinary everyday life of the village there is a constant giving and receiving of presents. A younger man or woman may give some article to an older one without expecting or receiving any return, but between equals a person who gives a present always expects that he will receive something of equal value in exchange. At the meetings that take place between neighbouring local groups the exchange of presents is of great importance. Each of the visitors brings with him a number of articles that he distributes amongst the members of the group that he visits. When the visitors depart they are loaded with presents received from their hosts. It requires a good deal of tact on the part of everyone concerned to avoid the unpleasantness that may arise if a man thinks that he has not received things as valuable as he has given, or if he fancies that he has not received quite the same amount of attention as has been accorded to others.

It is considered a breach of good manners ever to refuse the request of another. Thus if a man be asked by another to give him anything that he may possess, he will immediately do so. If the two men are equals a return of about the same value will have to be made. As between an older married man and a bachelor or a young married man, however, the younger would not make any request of such a nature, and if the older man asked the younger for anything the latter would give it without always expecting a return.

Almost every object that the Andamanese possess is thus constantly changing hands. Even canoes may be given away, but it is more usual for these to be lent by the owner to his friends.

[*People are giving each other things, more than is really necessary. Does not this build up a habit of exchange, which would have a survival value in time of need?*]

It has been stated above that all food is private property and belongs to the man or woman who has obtained it. Every one who has food is expected, however, to give to those who have none. An older married man will reserve for himself sufficient for his family, and then will give the rest to his friends. A younger man is expected to give away the best of what he gets to the older men. This is particularly the case with the bachelors. Should a young unmarried man kill a pig, he must be content to see it distributed by one of the older men, all the best parts going to the seniors, while he and his companions must be satisfied with the inferior parts. The result of these customs is that practically all the food obtained is evenly distributed through the whole camp, the only inequality being that the younger men do not fare so well as their elders. Generosity is esteemed by the Andaman Islanders one of the highest of virtues and is unremittingly practised by the majority of them.

Within the local group there is no such things as a division of labour save as between the two sexes. In the coastal groups every man is expected to be able to hunt pig, to harpoon turtle and to catch fish, and also to cut a canoe, to make bows and arrows and all the other objects that are made by men. It happens that some men are more skilful in certain pursuits than in others. A skilful turtle hunter, for example, may be an indifferent pig hunter, and such a man will naturally prefer to devote himself to the pursuit in which he appears to most advantage.

The division of labour between the sexes is fairly clearly marked. A man hunts and fishes, using the bow and arrow and the harpoon; he makes his own bows and arrows, his adze and knife, cuts canoes and makes rope for harpoon lines. A woman collects fruits and digs up roots with her digging stick; she catches prawns and crabs and small fish with her small fishing net; she provides the firewood and the water of the family and does the cooking (i.e., the family cooking, but not the common cooking, which is done entirely by the men); she makes all such objects as baskets, nets of thread, and personal ornaments either for herself or her husband.

There is no organized government in an Andamanese village. The affairs of the community are regulated entirely by the older men and women. The younger members of the community are brought up to pay respect to their elders and to submit to them in many ways. It has already been shown how, in the question of food, the elders get the best share. When it is a question of shifting camp to some better hunting ground the opinion of the older men would weigh against that of the younger if they disagreed. It must not be thought, however, that the older men are tyrannical or selfish. I only once heard a young man complain of the older men getting so much the best of everything. The respect for seniority is kept alive partly by tradition and partly by the fact that the older men have had a greater experience than the younger. It could probably not be maintained if it regularly gave rise to any tyrannical treatment of the younger by the elder.

The respect for seniors is shown in the existence of special terms of address which men and women use when speaking to their elders. In the languages of the North Andaman there are two such terms, *Mai* or *Maia,* applied to men, with a meaning equivalent to "Sir," and *Mimi,* applied to women. These words may be used either alone or prefixed to the personal name of the person addressed. A younger man speaking to an older one whose name was Bora would address him either as *Mai* (Sir), or as *Maia Bora* (Sir Bora). . . . .

In the legends of the Andamanese these titles are nearly always prefixed to the names of the legendary ancestors. . . .

Besides the respect for seniority there is another important factor in the regulation of the social life, namely the respect for certain personal qualities. These qualities are skill in hunting and in warfare, generosity and kindness, and freedom from bad temper. A man possessing them inevitably acquires a position of influence in the community. His opinion on any subject carries more weight than that of another even older man. The younger men attach themselves to him, are anxious to please him by giving him any presents that they can, or by helping him in such work as cutting a canoe, and to join him in hunting parties or turtle expeditions. In each local group there was usually to be found one man who thus by his influence could control and direct others. Amongst the chief men of several friendly local groups it would generally happen that one of them, by reason of his personal qualities, would attain to a position of higher rank than the others. Younger men would be desirous of joining the local group to which he belonged. He would find himself popular and respected at the annual meetings of the different groups, and his influence would thus spread beyond the narrow limits of his own small community.

There was no special word to denote such men and distinguish them from others. In the languages of the North Andaman they were spoken of as *er-kuro,* "big."

Such men might perhaps be spoken of as "chiefs," but the term is somewhat misleading, as it makes us think of the organised chieftainship of other savage races. . . .

Of authority the leading men have little or none, but of influence they have a good deal. Should any one venture to oppose a popular chief he would find the majority of the natives, including many of his friends, siding against him. . . .

Women may occupy a position of influence similar to that of the men. The wife of a leading man generally exercises the same sort of influence over the women as her husband does over the men. A woman, however, would not exercise any influence over the men in matters connected with hunting. They do have a good deal of influence in connection with quarrels either of individuals or of local groups.

There are certain men, and possibly sometimes women, who have an influence over their fellows owing to their being credited with the possession of supernatural powers. . . . It sometimes happens that a chief (the leading man of a local group) is at the same time a medicine man, but the two positions are entirely distinct and separate, and a man may be a medicine man who possesses none of the qualities that are necessary for a head man.

There does not appear to have been in the Andamans any such thing as the punishment of crime. We may distinguish two kinds of anti-social actions which are regarded by the natives as being wrong. The first kind are those actions which injure in some way a private individual. The second are those, which, while they do not injure any particular person, are yet regarded with disapproval by the society in general.

Amongst the anti-social actions of the first kind are murder, or wounding, theft and adultery, and wilful damage of the property of another. . . .

Quarrels sometimes occur between two men of the same camp. A good deal of hard swearing goes on, and sometimes one of the men will work himself up to a high pitch of anger, in which he may seize his bow and discharge an arrow near to the one who has offended him, or may vent his ill-temper by destroying any property that he can lay hands on, including not only that of his enemy but also that of other persons and even his own. At such a display of anger the women and children flee into the jungle in terror, and if the angry man be at all a formidable person the men occasionally do the same. It apparently requires more courage than the natives usually possess to endeavour to allay such a storm of anger. Yet I found that the slightest show of authority would immediately bring such a scene to an end. A man of influence in his village was probably generally equal to the task of keeping order and preventing any serious damage from taking place. It was probably rare for a man so far to give way to his anger as to kill his opponent.

Such murders did, however, occasionally take place. The murderer would, as a rule, leave the camp and hide himself in the jungle, where he might be joined by such of his friends as were ready to take his part. It was left to the relatives and friends of the dead man to exact vengeance if they wished and if they could. If the murderer was a man who was much feared it is probable that he would escape. In any case the anger of the Andamanese is short-lived, and if for a few months he could keep out of the way of those who might seek revenge, it is probable that at the end of that time he would find their anger cooled.

[*Notice how casual and rudimentary their system of laws seems to be. When so few persons are involved, individual adjustments may be made.*]

A man who is liable to outbursts of violent anger is feared by his fellows, and unless he has other counterbalancing qualities, he is never likely to become popular. He is treated with outward respect, for every one is afraid of offending him, but he never acquires the esteem of others. . . .

Quarrels were more likely to occur at the meetings of different local groups that took place in the fine weather, and such quarrels might occasionally end in the murder of some one. In such a case the quarrel would be taken up by the group of the murdered man, and a feud would be set up between them and the local group to which the murderer belonged. Such was one of the common causes of origin of the petty warfare that formerly existed in the Andamans. . . .

The frequent occurrence of serious quarrels is prevented both by the influence of the older men and by the fear that everyone has of the possible vengeance of others should he in any way offend them.

There are a number of actions which, while they do not offend any particular person, are regarded as being antisocial. One of these is laziness. Every man is expected to take his proper share in providing both himself and others with food. Should a man shirk this obligation, nothing would be said to him, unless he were a young unmarried man, and he would still be given food by others, but he would find himself occupying a position of inferiority in the camp, and would entirely lose the esteem of his fellows. Other qualities or actions that result in a similar loss of esteem are marital unfaithfulness, lack of respect to others and particularly to elders, meanness or niggardliness, and bad temper. One man was mentioned to me as being a bad man because he refused to take a wife after he had reached the age when it is considered proper for a man to marry. In recent times at least one man has refused to undergo the privations connected with the initiation ceremonies. This was of course a case of gross rebellion against the customs of the tribe, but there was no way of punishing him or of compelling him to conform, save by showing him that he was an object of contempt and ridicule to others. Probably such a refusal to conform to tribal customs would not have taken place before the British occupation of the islands.

Another class of wrong actions consists in the breaking of ritual prohibitions. There are, for example . . . a number of actions which it is believed may cause bad weather, such as burning beeswax or killing a cicada. There is, however, no punishment that can be meted out to any one who does any of these things. The punishment, if we may call it so, is a purely supernatural one, and it strikes not only the offender but everyone else as well. In the legends of the Andamanese there are one or two stories related of how one of the ancestors, being angry, deliberately performed one of the forbidden actions and thus brought a storm that destroyed many human beings.

There are other ritual prohibitions the nonobservance of which is supposed to bring its own punishment on the offender, who, it is believed, will be ill.

The medicine men . . . are credited with the power to work evil magic, and by its means to make other people ill, and even to kill them. A man suspected of evil magic might be liable to the vengeance of those who thought that they had been injured by him, but though the practice was regarded as reprehensible it does not seem that the society ever acted as a whole to punish a man suspected of it.

Children are reproved for improper behaviour, but they are never punished. During their years of infancy they are much spoilt, not only by their parents but by every one. During the period of adolescence every boy and girl has to undergo a somewhat severe discipline. . . . This probation, if it may be so called, is enforced by a unanimous public opinion. The discipline lasts until the man or woman is married and a parent, or if childless as so many now are, until he or she has settled down to a position of responsibility. . . .

As, in the languages of the Andamans, there are few words serving to denote relationship, and on the contrary a developed system of terms denoting social status, so in the social organisation of the Andamans there are very few special duties between relatives, and the conduct of persons to one another is chiefly determined by their respective social positions. This will become evident as we proceed, and it will thus be shown that there is a close connection between the way the natives denote relationships and the way in which their social life is affected by questions of relationship.

We have already seen that in the Andamanese social organisation the family is of great importance. A family is constituted by a permanent union between one man and one woman. In one of its aspects this union is a sexual one. By marriage a man acquires the sole right to sexual congress with the woman who becomes his wife. At the same time it is the duty of a married man to avoid sexual relations with other women whether married or unmarried. Promiscuous intercourse between the sexes is the rule before marriage, and no harm is thought of it. The love affairs of the boys and girls are carried on in secret, but the older members of the camp are generally fully aware of all that goes on. What generally happens is that after a time a youth forms an attachment with some girl and a marriage between them results from their love affair. . . .

Beyond the prohibition of the marriage of near kin, I could not find any restriction on marriage. A man may marry a woman from his own local group or from another, from his own or from another tribe. . . . It is probable that the majority of marriages, or at any rate a large proportion, were between persons belonging to different local groups.

Marriages are arranged by the older men and women. Children are sometimes betrothed by their parents while they are still infants. . . .

When the parents of a youth who is of suitable age to be married perceive that he has formed an attachment with a girl, they take it upon them to arrange a marriage. The matter is first of all talked over between the young man and his parents. The man's parents do not themselves speak to the girl's parents of the matter, but request some one or more of their friends to do so. From the moment that the possibility of a marriage exists the man's parents avoid speaking to the girl's parents. Any communication between them is carried on through a third person. They send presents to each other, of food and other objects. The recipient of such a present hastens to make a return of equal value. If the marriage is arranged the parents on each side become related to one another by the relationship denoted in *Akar-Bale* by the word *aka-yat.* . . .

When a marriage has finally been arranged an evening is appointed for the ceremony. In the North Andaman this is as follows. The bride is seated on a mat at one end of the dancing ground, her relatives and friends sitting near her. Torches or heaps of resin are lighted near by, so that the ceremony may be seen by the on-lookers. The bridegroom is seated with his friends at the other end of the dancing ground. One of the older and more respected men addresses the bride, telling her that she must make a good wife, must provide for her husband such things as it is the duty of a wife to obtain or make, must see that he does not run after other women, and must herself remain faithful to him. He then addresses the bridegroom to the same effect, and taking him by the hand or arm, leads him to where the bride is seated and makes him sit down beside her. The relatives and friends weep loudly, and the young couple look very self-conscious and uncomfortable. The shyness of the young man is such that he often attempts to run away, but he is caught by his friends, who are prepared for such an attempt. After some minutes the officiating elder takes the arms of the bride and bridegroom and places them around each other's necks. After a further interval he again approaches and makes the bridegroom sit on the bride's lap. They sit so for some minutes and the ceremony is over. The other members of the community generally have a dance on such an occasion, but in this the newly wedded pair do not join. A hut has already been prepared for them, and all their friends make them presents of useful objects with which to start housekeeping. They retire shyly to their new hut, while their friends continue dancing. The day after the ceremony the bride and bridegroom are decorated by their friends with white clay. For a few days the newly married couple are very shy of each other, hardly venturing to speak to or look at one another: but they soon settle down to their new position in the life of the community. During the early days of their marriage they are abundantly supplied with food by their friends. They are not addressed or spoken of by name, but if their names be A and B, the husband is called "the husband of B" while the wife is called "the wife of A". . . .

During their infancy the children are in the care of the mother. Children are, however, such favourites with the Andamanese that a child is played with and petted and nursed not only by his own father and mother but by everyone in the village. A woman with an unweaned child will often give suck to the children of other women. Babies are not weaned till they are three or four years old.

Before the children can walk, they are carried about by the mother, and sometimes by the father or other persons, in a bark sling. . . . After they can walk the children generally accompany their mothers in their expeditions near the camp for firewood or vegetables. When they are not with their mothers, they amuse themselves with games in the village or on the beach. All the children of the coast villages learn to swim when they are very young, in fact almost as soon as they learn to walk, and many of their games are conducted in the water.

When a boy reaches the age of five or six his father makes him a toy bow and arrows, and sometimes a toy canoe. From this time the boy begins to learn the occupations of men and begins to pick up knowledge about the animals and trees and fishes of his country. The girl, accompanying her mother on her expeditions to gather roots and seeds, or to catch fish or pick up molluscs on the reefs, learns what it is necessary for women to know.

Until the age of about eight to ten a child lives with his parents, having a place in the family hut, and a share of the family meal. The children are treated with extreme kindness, and are never punished, and hardly ever scolded. Should the parents die the children are adopted by friends or relatives, and such adopted children are treated by the foster parents in exactly the same way as their own children.

At the age of ten, or a little before, a change is often brought about in the life of a child, owing to the custom of adoption. . . . A man and his wife . . . adopt children belonging in a local group other than their own. The adopted child lives with his or her foster parents, having a place in their hut and a share of their meals. From about the age of ten children of both sexes begin to be of service to their parents or foster parents in many ways. The foster parents treat their adopted children in exactly the same way that they would treat their own children, and the children, on the other hand show the same regard and affection to their foster parents that they do to their own parents, and assist them in every way that they can. Their own parents come to visit them at regular intervals.

The period of childhood is brought to an end at about the age of puberty by certain ceremonies. . . . After the beginning of these ceremonies a boy ceases to live in the hut of his parents or his foster parents, and must live with the young unmarried men and widowers in what has been called the bachelors' hut. From this time until he marries, his services are constantly required by his parents or by his foster parents, and he is expected to obey them and help them in any way he can. It is only after his marriage that he becomes relatively independent and free to please himself in his own actions, and even then he is required to provide his parents or his foster parents with food and to serve them in any way they may need.

A girl, during the period between the beginning of the initiation ceremonies and her marriage, continues, at any rate, in some cases, and in these days, to live with her parents or with foster parents. Mr. Man states that the unmarried women and girls occupy a spinsters' hut similar to the bachelors' hut. It is possible that this was the former custom. I found instances of an unmarried girl occupying a place in the hut of a married couple who made use of her services and controlled her conduct, regarding her in the light of a foster daughter. On one occasion I found two unmarried girls occupying a separate hut adjoining that of a married couple, who looked after the girls who occupied it.

The position of an unmarried girl is very similar to that of an unmarried youth. She is required to help her elders, in particular either her parents or her foster parents, i.e., the married couple under whose care she is for the time being.

After marriage a son continues to help his parents, providing them with food and seeing that they are comfortable. If either a man or a woman lives in a local group other than that of his or her parents, he or she pays frequent visits to them.

From the time that a youth or girl ceases to belong to the family household, his or her duties to the parents are really only the same in kind as the duties that every young man and woman owes to all the older men and women. Though there is no difference in kind, yet a man or woman is expected to show more affection and respect for his or her own parents than to other persons of the same social standing.

The only other relationship, besides that of husband and wife and that of parents and children, which exists inside the family is that between children of the same parents. The conduct of brothers to one another depends on their respective ages. The younger is expected to give way to the elder, while the latter protects and looks after the former. The relation of sisters to one another is similar.

The duties of a man and woman to his or her relatives, other than those to parents, brothers and sisters, and even to some extent the duties to these near relatives, are not distinguishable in kind from the duties he or she owes to other persons who are not relatives. Thus a young married man owes certain duties to all the older married men of about the age of his father. These duties are the same in kind as those towards his own father and his foster father, the only difference being that he must defer more to his own father than to other men, and must be more constant in his attentions to him. I could not discover any way in which a man distinguished, in his dealings with them, his father's brother from his mother's brother. They are both of them older men whom he must respect and to whom he must make presents of food. Similarly a father's sister is not distinguished, so far as I could discover, from a mother's sister. A man treats both of them in much the same way that he treats his own mother, or any other woman of the same age.

There is only a slight difference in connection with parents-in-law. A man would not be so familiar with his parents-in-law as he would with his parents or their brothers or sisters, and treats them with more deference and respect. This is borne out by the *Akar-Bale* custom of applying to a father-in-law or mother-in-law the same term of address (*Mama*) that is used in speaking to grandparents and others to whom it is required to show particular deference.

In the same way there is very little difference between the way a man conducts himself towards his elder brother and his conduct towards any other man of the same age. Brothers are often close comrades, putting their huts next to one another in the same village, joining together whenever possible in hunting or fishing expeditions, and so on; but a man may have a comrade who is not his brother, whom he will treat in exactly the same way.

The general attitude of a married man to other married men somewhat younger than himself is very much that towards a younger brother. As between men and women one special duty appears in this connection. A married man may not and will not have any close dealings with the wife of a man younger than himself. It is not considered fitting that he should speak to her. If he wished to have any communication with her, he would do so through some third person. It would be regarded as a wrong thing to do if he were ever to touch her. The only explanation that the natives give of this custom is by saying that a man feels "shy" or "ashamed" towards his younger brother's or friend's wife. The custom is exactly the same with respect to the wife of any younger man, whether a brother, a cousin, or a stranger.

This custom depends on the distinction between older and younger. A man may be on terms of familiarity with the wife of a man older than himself, whom he would treat much as he would an elder sister.

There is one special relationship which has peculiar duties attaching to it, and this is the relationship between the father and mother of a man on the one hand and the father and mother of the man's wife on the other. In the *Akar-Bale* language such persons are said to be *aka-yat* to one another. A man or a woman will not have any immediate dealings with a person who is his *aka-yat*. He will not speak to him, and if they should meet or be sitting near to one another they would avoid looking at each other. On the other hand a man is constantly sending presents to his *aka-yat*. The natives say that two persons in this relation feel "shy" or "ashamed." (There is only one word in Andamanese for these two English words, *ot-jete* in *Aka-Jeru*.) The shyness begins at the moment when a marriage between their respective children is first discussed as a possibility, and lasts apparently till death. . . .

The main features of the relationship system of the Andaman Islanders may be briefly summed up. The duties that one person owes to another are determined much less by their relation to one another by consanguinity and marriage than by their respective ages and social status. Even within the family, which nevertheless is of importance, the duty of a child to a parent is very little different from his duty to any other person of the same age. There is very little of any special customs relating to conduct towards different kinds of relatives. Corresponding to this we find very few terms to denote relationships and a considerable development of the terms which denote age and social status.

Thus a man's duties to his elder brother are much the same as those towards the other men of the same age, and we find that there is no word for "elder brother" but only a term by which a man distinguishes all the men of his own generation older than himself from those who are younger. Similarly there are no duties that a man owes to his father's brother or to his mother's brother which he does not also owe, in perhaps a less degree, to other men of the same age, and there is no term by which he can distinguish his father's brother from those others. . . .

Two neighbouring groups, whether of the same tribe or of different tribes, might be either friendly towards one another or unfriendly. Friendly relations were kept alive by several of the customs of the Andamanese, by the intermarriage of members of different groups, by the adoption of children from one group to another, and by the fact that a man of one group might take up his residence more or less permanently with another (particularly when he married a woman of that group, or was adopted when a boy by one of the men belonging to it). All these customs served to bind some persons in the one group to persons in the other, and thus prevent the two groups from becoming entirely unfriendly to one another.

When two neighbouring local groups were friendly to one another communication between them was kept up by visitors from one group to another, and by occasional meetings of the whole of the two groups.

Either a single person or a family might at any time pay a visit to another camp, staying a few days or weeks or even longer. A man would, however, only go visiting when he was sure of a welcome. Such visits were most frequent in the fine months of the year (December to May). As a

husband and wife in many instances belonged to different local groups they would, if living with the man's parents, pay a visit every year to the parents or other relatives of the wife. The parents of a child that had been adopted by a member of another local group would make a point of visiting the child when they could. Visitors to a camp would always take with them presents to be given to their hosts. A visitor was hospitably entertained, being given the best of the food, and joined his hosts in their hunting and fishing expeditions. The duty of hospitality is one upon which the Andamanese lay stress.

The meetings of two or more local groups were organised from time to time by the more prominent men. The time and place of the meeting would be fixed and invitations sent out to the neighbours. The visitors, men, women, and children, would arrive at the appointed time, and would be accommodated as well as possible by the hosts. During the first few hours, as the natives themselves told me, everyone would feel a little shy and perhaps frightened, and it would take some time for the feeling to wear off. The visitors would bring with them various objects, such as bows, arrows, adzes, baskets, nets, red paint, white clay, and so on. These were given by the visitors to their hosts, and other presents were received in return. Although the natives themselves regarded the objects thus given as being presents, yet when a man gave a present to another he expected that he would receive something of equal value in return, and would be very angry if the return present did not come up to his expectations. A man would sometimes mention, when giving his present, that he would like some particular object in exchange, but this was the exception and not the rule, and the process cannot be spoken of as barter. In certain cases it undoubtedly served a useful economic purpose. Thus if a local group had no red ochre or white clay in their own country they could obtain these commodities by exchange with others who had. In the case of a meeting between forest and coast dwellers, the former could obtain such things as shells, red paint made with turtle fat, and other objects with which they could not provide themselves in any other way. It was in this way also that the iron obtained from a wreck on one part of the coast would be spread over a large area. For the most part, however, as each local group, and indeed each family, was able to provide itself with everything that it needed in the way of weapons and utensils, the exchange of presents did not serve the same purpose as trade and barter in more developed communities.

The purpose that it did serve was a moral one. The object of the exchange was to produce a friendly feeling between the two persons concerned, and unless it did this it failed of its purpose. It gave great scope for the exercise of tact and courtesy. No one was free to refuse a present that was offered to him. Each man and woman tried to out-do the others in generosity. There was a sort of amiable rivalry as to who could give away the greatest number of valuable presents.

[*Trading here is masked by ritual. Through their ceremonial actions the two parties pave the way for economic exchange. You will see much more of this before we are through.*]

The visitors remained with their hosts for a few days. The time was spent in hunting, feasting and dancing, and in the exchange of presents above described. The hosts made every effort to provide the camp with plenty of good things. The guests took their share in the hunting and fishing expeditions. Every evening was spent in singing and dancing. Some of the men were sure to have composed new songs for such an occasion.

Such meetings as these were sometimes the means of bringing to an end past quarrels between the local groups, but occasionally they were the cause of new quarrels. The hosts, or some of them, might think that they had been shabbily treated in the matter of presents, or the guests might complain that they were not well enough entertained. It often needed a man of strong influence to maintain harmony in the camp. Angry words might lead to the rapid breaking up of a meeting, and even result in a feud between the two groups.

Quarrels between individuals, as we have seen, were often taken up by friends on each side. This was particularly the case when the two opponents belonged to different local groups. Before the days of the settlement of the islands there often arose in this way petty quarrels between neighbouring local groups. In some instances there appear to have been feuds of long standing; in others there was a quarrel, a fight or two, and the enemies made peace with one another, until a fresh cause of disagreement should arise.

It does not seem that there was ever such a thing as a stand-up fight between two parties. The whole art of fighting was to come upon your enemies by surprise, kill one or two of them and then retreat. A local group that had some grievance against another would decide to make an attack. They might seek and obtain the aid of friends from other local groups. The men who were to take part in the expedition would paint themselves and put on various ornaments and join in a dance. They would then set out, either by land or by sea, in the direction of the encampment they meant to attack. Their weapons consisted of bows and arrows, and they carried no shields or other defensive weapons. They would not venture to attack the enemy's camp unless they were certain of taking it by surprise. For this reason such attacks were generally made either in the evening when the camp would be busy with the preparation of the evening meal, or at early dawn, when every one would be asleep. The attacking party would rush the camp and shoot as many men as they could. If they met with any serious resistance or lost one of their own number they would immediately retire. Those attacked, if they were really taken by surprise, were generally compelled to save themselves by flight. Though the aim of the attacking party was to kill the men, it often happened that women or children were killed. The whole fight would last only a few minutes, ending either with the retirement of the attackers before resistance, or the flight of those attacked into the jungle. A wounded enemy would be killed if found.

Such attacks and counterattacks might be continued for some years, thus establishing a feud between two neighbouring local groups. More usually, however, after one or two such fights peace would be made. In the tribes of the North Andaman there was a special peace-making ceremony. . . . All peace negotiations were conducted through the women. One or two of the women of the one group would be sent to interview the women of the other group to see if they were willing to forget the past and make friends. It seems that it was largely the rancour of the women over their slain relatives that kept the feud alive, the men of the two parties being willing to make friends much more readily than the women.

.   .   .   .

During the latter part of the period of pregnancy, and for about a month after the birth of the child, the mother and father must observe certain restrictions. In particular there are certain foods that they may not eat. The statements of different informants on this matter did not quite agree with each other, and it seems that there were slightly different rules in different tribes. According to an *Akar-Bale* informant the man and woman may not eat dugong, honey and yams; they may eat the flesh of small but not of full-grown pigs and turtle. An informant of one of the Northern tribes said that the woman may not eat full-grown pig, *Paradoxorus,* turtle, dugong, the fish *komar,* monitor lizard, honey and yams; her husband may eat these things but must carefully avoid eating certain fishes.

The natives give two different reasons for these rules. One is that if these foods be eaten by the parents the child will be ill. The other is that the parents themselves will be ill. The latter is the explanation most commonly offered.

The baby is named some time before it is born, and from that time the parents are not addressed or spoken of by name. For example, if the name chosen be *Rea,* the father will be spoken of as *Rea akamai* (Rea's father) instead of by his own name. The mother may be referred to as *Rea it-pet,* from the word *it-pet* meaning "belly." This practice is continued till some weeks after the birth, when the use of the names of the parents is once more resumed.

In childbirth the woman is assisted by the matrons of the camp. She is seated in her hut in the village on fresh leaves, and a piece of wood is placed at her back for her to lean against. Her legs are flexed so that her knees may be clasped by her arms. The only manipulation is pressure exerted on the upper part of the abdomen by one of the attendant women. The umbilical cord is severed with a knife, formerly of cane or bamboo, but in these days of iron. The afterbirth is buried in the jungle. The infant is washed and then scraped with a *Cyrena* shell. After a few days he (or she) is given a coating of clay (*odu*).

If a baby dies and within a year or two the mother again becomes pregnant, it is said that it is the same baby born again, and the name of the deceased child is given to it. Thus one woman had three children of the same name, the first two having died soon after birth. According to the native ideas this was really the same child born three times. It is only those who die in infancy that are thus reincarnated.

In the Northern tribes it is believed that a woman can tell the sex of her unborn child. If she feels it on the left side it is a male, because the men hold the bow (the typical masculine implement) in the left hand. If she feels it on the right side it is a female, because it is in her right hand that a woman holds her fishing net.

A married man who is childless and desires a child will wear a *ciba* (sling of bark used for carrying children) round his shoulders when he is sitting in camp. . . . If a childless woman wishes to have a child she may catch, cook and eat a certain species of small frog.

At a place called *Tonmuket* in the North Andaman there is a spot to which it is said that women may resort if they wish to become pregnant. On the reef at this spot there are a large number of stones which, according to the legend, were once little children. The woman who desires a child walks out on to the reef when the tide is low and stands upon these stones. It is believed that one of the baby souls will enter her body and become incarnate.

[*The women believe that the stones represent babies, which can enter their bodies and make them pregnant—a naive rationalization of a type common to . all peoples lacking in biological knowledge. This reaches into the peasant population of Europe—a preliterate concept.*]

In the North Andaman there is some sort of association between the unborn souls of babies, the green pigeon and the *Ficus laccifera* tree. The same name, *Reŋko,* is used to denote both the green pigeon and also the *Ficus laccifera,* of the fruit of which the pigeon is very fond. The belief of the natives is sometimes stated by saying that the souls of unborn children live in the *Ficus* trees, and that if a baby dies before it has been weaned its soul goes back to the tree. Another statement of the natives is that it is when the green pigeon is calling that the soul of a baby goes into its mother. The *Ficus* is to a certain extent tabu. I was told that the tree must not be cut or damaged. Nevertheless the natives do cut the tree in order to obtain the bark of the aerial roots from which they prepare a fibre that they use for making personal ornaments. There is no tabu in connection with the green pigeon, which may be killed and eaten. . . .

The life of an Andaman Islander is divided into three well-marked periods, corresponding roughly with the physiological periods of childhood, adolescence, and maturity. The first period lasts from birth till about the advent of puberty; the second lasts from puberty till after marriage; the third extends from marriage to death.

During the period of childhood the boy or girl lives with his or her parents, or, in the later years of the period, with adopted parents, having a place in the family hut and a share in the family meal. A girl continues to live with her parents or with her adopted parents until she marries. When boys have finished growing, and have reached the condition of young men, they cease to live with their parents or adopted parents and, until they are married, they occupy a bachelors' hut of their own, and have their own meal.

Every boy and girl has to undergo the operation of scarification. This is begun when the child is quite young, and a small portion of the body is operated on. The operation is repeated at intervals during childhood, until the whole body has been scarified. A small flake of quartz or glass is used, and a series of fine incisions made in the skin. The usual method is to cover a small portion of the skin with a number of parallel rows of short cuts. The choice of the design (if it can be called such) rests entirely with the person who performs the operation, who is in all cases a woman. The incisions leave scars that can usually only be seen when close to the person. . . .

The only reason that the natives give for this custom is either that it improves the personal appearance, or else that it helps to make the child grow strong.

In the case of a girl the period of childhood is brought to a close by a ceremony that takes place on the occasion of her first menstrual discharge. The ceremony I describe is that in use in the Northern tribes, but I believe that the ceremony of the Southern tribes is very similar. On the occurrence of the first menstrual discharge the girl tells her parents, who weep over her. She must then go and bathe in the sea for an hour or two by herself. After that she goes back to her parents' hut or to a special shelter that is put up for the occasion. She is not

required to go away from the camp. All ornaments are removed from her, only a single belt of *Pandanus* leaf being left, with an apron of *cainyo* leaves. Strips of *Pandanus* leaf are attached round her arms near the shoulders and round her wrists, and others are placed as bands crossing her chest from the shoulder to the waist on the opposite side, and crossing her abdomen from the iliac crest on the one side to the trochanter of the other. These are so attached that the long loose ends hang down at the girl's side. Bunches of leaves, either *celmo* (*Tetranthera lancoefolia*) or, if these be not obtainable, *poramo* (*Myristica longifolia*) are fastened beneath her belt before and behind. Other leaves of the same kind are placed for her to sit upon. . . .

Thus covered with leaves the girl must sit in the hut allotted to her, with her legs doubled up beneath her and her arms folded. A piece of wood or bamboo is placed at her back for her to lean against, as she may not lie down. If she is cramped she may stretch one of her legs or one of her arms, but not both arms or both legs at the same time. To feed herself she may release one of her hands, but she must not take up the food with her fingers; a skewer of *cainyo* wood is given her with which to feed herself. She may not speak nor sleep for 24 hours. Her wants are attended to by her parents and their friends, who sit near her to keep her from falling asleep.

The girl sits thus for three days. Early every morning she leaves the hut to bathe for an hour in the sea. At the end of the three days she resumes her life in the village. For a month following she must bathe in the sea every morning at dawn.

During the ceremony and for a short time afterwards the girl is not addressed or spoken of by name, but is referred to as *Alebe* or *Toto*. The meaning of the first word is not known. *Toto* is the name of the species of *Pandanus* from which women's belts are made and the leaves of which are used in the ceremony. On the occasion of this ceremony the girl is given a new name, her "flower-name," and from this time till after the birth of her first child she is never addressed or spoken of by the name which she had as a child, but only by the name given to her at this ceremony. The name given is that of a plant or tree which is in flower at the time. If the ceremony takes place when the *jili* is in flower she is called *Jili;* if when the *jeru* is in flower, she is named *Jeru,* and so on. These names will be mentioned again later in the present chapter.

After this ceremony the girl is said to be *aka-ndu-kolot.* For some time afterwards she must not have her head shaved, and she must not use red paint or white clay.

I was not able to learn much about the native ideas in connection with the menstrual function. According to the account given me by one informant I gathered that the girl's first menstrual discharge is supposed to be due to sexual intercourse. The man's breath goes into her nose and this produces the discharge. It is believed that if a man were to touch a girl during this period, either during the ceremony or for some time after it, his arm would swell up.

At every recurrence of the menstrual period a woman is required to abstain from eating certain foods. According to an *Akar-Bale* informant these are, in that tribe, pork, turtle, *Paradoxurus,* honey and yams. An *Aka-Cari* informant added to the above list dugong, monitor lizard, and the fish *komar.* If she ate any of these things at such a time she would be ill. This continues throughout her life till the climacteric. A menstruating woman is not required

to leave the camp, as she is in many savage communities.

From the moment of the ceremony just described the girl enters a new condition which is denoted in the *Aka-Jeru* language by the word *aka-op* (*aka-yaba* in *Aka-Bea*). This word means that the person to whom it is applied is under certain ritual restrictions, chiefly concerned with foods that may not be eaten.

In the case of a boy there is no physiological event so clearly marked as there is in that of a girl. It rests with the relatives and friends to decide when the boy is to become *aka-op.* It would seem that in the Southern tribes there is no ceremony on this occasion. Among the Northern tribes the boy is made *aka-op* by means of a ceremony that consists of making the scars on his back that are customary in these tribes.

When the friends and relatives of a boy decide that he is old enough to have the incisions made in his back a dance is held in the evening, and the boy is required to dance through the whole night till he is tired. As soon as morning breaks he is made to bathe in the sea for two hours or so. He is then seated in some convenient place, not in a hut. The boy kneels down and bends forward till his elbows rest on the ground in front. One of the older men takes a pig-arrow and with the sharpened blade makes a series of cuts on the boy's back. Each cut is horizontal, and they are arranged in three vertical rows, each row consisting of from 20 to 30 cuts. When the cutting is finished the boy sits up, with a fire at his back, until the bleeding stops. During the operation and for a few hours following it the boy must remain silent. There is no treatment of the wounds to produce raised scars. The scars are much more noticeable on some men than on others.

The boy does not receive a new name on this occasion, but for a few weeks his own name is dropped and he is addressed and spoken of as *Ejido*. From this time the boy is described as being *oko-taliŋ-kolot,* this being the masculine term corresponding to *aka-ndu-kolot* for girls. From the time the cuts are made on his back the boy becomes *aka-op* and is under certain restrictions as to what foods he may eat.

When the wounds on his back are thoroughly healed similar cuts are made on his chest. . . .

During the period that a boy or girl is *aka-op* he or she is required by the customs of the tribe to abstain from eating certain foods. The exact rules in this matter differ from tribe to tribe. More particularly there are important differences between the coast-dwellers on the one hand and the jungle-dwellers on the other. The general principle, however, is in all cases the same. The boy (or girl) must abstain from all the chief foods of the people, and since he could not abstain from them all at one time without starving, he takes them in turn. It is in the order in which the different foods are forbidden that the chief differences occur.

In the *Aka-Cari* tribe of the North Andaman, where all are coast dwellers, the boy or girl during the first part of the *aka-op* period must not eat turtle, dugong, porpoise, *komar* (a fish), hawksbill turtle, the two kinds of edible grubs . . . the monitor lizard, the flying fox . . . certain birds (perhaps all birds), certain shellfish, the four varieties of mangrove seed . . . three edible roots . . . and a large number of other vegetable foods. . . . A certain number of fishes must be added to this list. This period is brought to an end by the turtle-eating ceremony which will be presently described. After this ceremony, turtle, which is one of the

chief foods of the *Aka-Cari,* may be eaten, although certain parts of the turtle (such as the intestinal fat) are still forbidden, and the youth is also allowed to eat many of the other foods previously forbidden. On the other hand he is now required not to eat pork and a number of other foods both animal and vegetable. During this second period certain minor ceremonies take place, as for instance on the first occasion on which turtle's eggs are eaten. This period is brought to an end by the pig-eating ceremony. After that the youth is again free to eat pork. As turtle and pork are the two most important foods the ceremonies and observances in connection with these occupy a position of greater importance. After the pig-eating ceremony the youth is made free of one food after another, until some time after he is married he becomes free to partake of any of the foods available. In the case of some of the more important foods, such as honey, dugong, porpoise, the fish *komar,* etc., there is a sort of minor ceremony. The only ceremonies of any importance in this tribe are the turtle-eating and the pig-eating ceremonies.

In the forest-dwelling communities of the North Andaman things are necessarily different. These people only eat such foods as turtle, dugong, etc., when they are visiting their friends on the coast. The three most important ceremonies amongst these people are the *nyuri*-eating, the pig-eating and the honey-eating ceremonies. (The *nyuri* is a fish that is found in the creeks.) According to my informants of the *Aka-Bo* tribe the foods that must be avoided during the first part of the abstention period are all species of fish found in inland creeks . . . the monitor lizard, sucking pig, two species of snake . . . a number of vegetable foods and also honey. After the *nyuri-*

eating ceremony the different kinds of fish mentioned may be eaten, but the youth or girl must then abstain from pork. . . .

When the older men decide that it is time for a boy who has been abstaining from turtle to be released from the restriction, a turtle-hunting expedition is arranged, and this is continued until a fair number of good turtle are captured. The best of these is selected, killed, and cooked. The youth is seated in a hut, either that of his parents, or one placed at his disposal by a friend or one specially built. All his ornaments are removed. (In the case of a girl one belt of *Pandanus* leaf is retained.) He is seated on leaves of the *Hibiscus tiliaceus,* or if these be not obtainable, on those of the *Myristica longifolia,* and a bundle of the same leaves is placed under his folded arms so as to cover his belly, while another bundle is placed at his back where there is some sort of rest provided for him to lean against. He must sit still with folded arms and with legs stretched out in front, the two big toes clasping each other. He sits facing towards the open sea, and a fire is placed near him, generally just beyond his feet.

Some man is chosen to take charge of the ceremony. This may be one of the older men of the community to which the youth belongs or a distinguished visitor, if there be any such present in the camp at the time. This man selects some of the meat and fat of the cooked turtle, placing them in a wooden dish. He comes to where the youth is seated, while the friends and relatives gather round. Taking some of the fat he rubs it first over the lips and then over the whole body of the youth, while the female relatives of the latter sit near and weep loudly. When the youth's body is thoroughly covered with fat the man who is performing the ceremony takes some burnt

oxide of iron, such as is used for making red paint, and rubs it over the youth's whole body, except the hair of his head. He then takes a piece of turtle fat and places it in the youth's mouth, feeding him thus with a few mouthfuls which the youth eats in silence. At this point the weeping of the relatives is taken up again with renewed vigour and then gradually comes to an end. Having fed the youth the man then proceeds to massage him. He first stands behind him and placing his hands on his shoulders presses down on them with all his weight. Then he seizes a roll of flesh on each side of the youth's belly and shakes it up and down as though to shake down what has been eaten. The arms are next massaged and the wrists and knuckles are forcibly flexed so as to make the joints "crack." The legs are similarly massaged, either with the hands or with the feet, the performer (in the latter case) standing on the outstretched legs of the youth and rolling the muscles beneath his feet. The joints of the toes are forcibly bent with the hand to make them "crack" if possible. A mixture of clay (*odu*) and water has been prepared in a wooden dish. The performer dips his hands into this and spatters it over the youth's body from head to foot, either by holding his hands near the youth and clapping them together, or by jerking the clay off his fingers with a flicking motion. During the whole of these proceedings the youth sits passive and silent.

The first part of the ceremony is now over. The food tray containing turtle meat and fat, cut into small pieces, is placed beside the youth and he is provided with a skewer of the wood of the *Hibiscus tiliaceus,* as he may not touch the meat with his fingers. He must sit in the same position with legs outstretched and arms folded and surrounded with *Hibiscus* leaves. To feed himself he may unloose one arm, and when his legs are cramped he may double them up beneath him. He may not lie down nor speak nor sleep for 48 hours. During this period he may eat nothing but turtle and drink nothing but water. The man in charge of the ceremony sits behind him and gives him instructions as to what foods he may and what he may not eat after the ceremony. Some of the men and women take it in turn to sit beside the youth, attending to his wants and talking or singing to keep him awake.

On the morning of the third day a belt and necklace are made of pieces of the creeper called *terkobito-balo,* i.e., "centipede creeper" (*Pothos scandens*), and these are placed round the youth's waist and neck. On this day he is permitted to sleep. Either on the same day, or early the next morning, he has a bath in the sea, to remove some of the red paint and clay, and he is then decorated with red paint made of red ochre and turtle fat, and with white clay (*tol-odu*). The red paint is put on in stripes over his body, and his ears are daubed with it. The white clay is put on in a zigzag pattern to be described later, the lines of white clay alternating with those of red paint. This decoration is done by female relatives.

Early on the morning of the fourth day, soon after daybreak, the whole village is astir. One of the older men takes his stand by the sounding board used for marking time at dances, and the women sit down near him. The youth comes out from his hut and stands in the middle of the dancing ground, and five or six men stand round him in a circle, each of them facing towards the youth. Each of the men, including the youth, holds in each hand a bundle of twigs of the *Hibiscus tiliaceus* or, if such be not obtainable, of the *Myristica longifolia*. The man

at the sounding board sings a song, beating time with his foot, in the usual way, on the sounding board, and at the chorus the women join in and mark the time by clapping their hands on their thighs. The song may be on any subject and is selected by the singer from his own repertory. A song referring to turtle hunting is preferred. During the first song the dancers stand at their positions on the dancing ground, lifting up their leaf bundles at short intervals and bringing them down against their knees. The singer then commences a new song or repeats the former one, and when the song comes to an end the youth and those with him begin their dance. Each dancer flexes his hips so that his back is nearly horizontal. He raises his hands to the back of his neck, so that the two bundles of leaves in his hands rest on his back. With knees flexed he leaps from the ground with both feet, keeping time to the beating of the sounding board, which is about 144 beats to the minute. At the end of every eight jumps or so, the dancer brings his hands forwards, downwards, and backwards, giving a vigourous sweep with the bundles of leaves, which scrape the ground at each side of his feet, and then brings back the bundles to their former position. They dance thus for 15 or 30 seconds and then pause to rest. The dance is repeated several times, until the youth is tired out. As the dance is extremely fatiguing, this does not take long.[2]

The youth then returns to his hut and resumes his former position. He may now, if he wishes, talk to his friends and he may sleep. He must retain the bundles of *Hibiscus* leaves and the necklace and belt of *Pothos* leaves. The dance is sometimes re-

[2] I believe the dance is intended to imitate the movement of a turtle as it swims through the water.

peated in the afternoon. It is in any case repeated on each of the two days following, and after that the youth resumes his ordinary life. For a week or two he may not touch a bow and arrow. The *Pothos* leaves are worn till they are faded and are then discarded. The paint on the body wears off and is not renewed, but his ears are kept painted with red paint. For some weeks the youth is supposed to be in an abnormal condition and is carefully watched by his friends. . . .

[*No clearer description of puberty ceremonies has ever been written. You will observe that in this, as in other truly primitive cultures, the majority of rituals are Rites of Passage. (See Appendix, sec. 16.) An emphasis on Rites of Intensification comes at a later stage of complexity, as among the Aztecs and Romans.*]

. . . In the Great Andaman three different substances are used for painting the body. These are (1) a common clay of which different specimens are grey, yellow or pink, called *odu* in *Aka-Jeru* and *og* in *Aka-Bea;* (2) a fine white pipe clay which is rarer than the common clay and is more highly prized, called *tol* or *tol-odu* in *Aka-Jeru* and *tala-og* in *Aka-Bea;* (3) a red pigment made by mixing burnt oxide of iron with animal or vegetable fat or oil, called *keyip* in *Aka-Jeru* and *koiob* in *Aka-Bea.*

The common clay (*odu*) is used in three different ways. After the death of a relative a man or woman smears himself all over with this clay and plasters it on his head. From this custom a person who is mourning for a dead relative is called *aka-odu* in *Aka-Jeru* or *aka-og* in *Aka-Bea.* The same clay is used at a certain stage of the initiation ceremonies, as described above, being spattered over the initiate in the turtle-eating and pig-eating ceremonies. The third and most common use of this clay is to decorate the bodies of men and women with patterns called (in *Aka-Jeru*) *era-puli.* These patterns are always made by the women, who decorate each other and their male relatives. The clay is mixed with water in a wooden dish or a shell and the mixture is applied to the body with the fingers. There is an almost infinite variety in the patterns employed, although there are a certain number of what may be called usual designs. Each woman vies with others in her endeavours to produce some novelty of detail in her designs, and a successful innovation is immediately copied by others. I was able to watch the rise and development and ultimate disappearance of "fashions" in this connection in one of the camps of the North Andaman. . . .

[*Changes in fashions have no reference whatever to change in complexity of societies. This is of universal application.*]

These patterns are made in the afternoon after the men return from their day's hunting, and always either just before or just after a meal.

If a man be asked what pattern he is painted with, he replies by mentioning the food that he has just eaten. A man who has been eating turtle will say that the painting on his body is *cokbi-t'era-puli,* turtle pattern, while if he has been eating pork he will call it *ra-t'era-puli,* pig pattern. . . .

Of special patterns I was only able to discover two. One of these is called *kimil-t'era-puli* and is used only to paint a person who is *aka-kimil,* i.e., who has just been through one of the initiation ceremonies. Another special pattern is called *tot-t'era-puli (Pandanus* pattern), and is used, I believe, to decorate a girl after the ceremony of her first menstruation.

The fine white clay called *tol-odu* in *Aka-Jeru* is used in a different way and on different occasions. When it is used to ornament a body, it is always applied in one customary pattern. The name of this pattern in *Aka-Jeru* is *or-cubi-t'era-bat,* from the name of a species of snake, *or-cubi.* . . . The pattern is built up of zigzag lines. . . . The face also is decorated. These patterns are made by the women. It is one of the duties of a wife to decorate her husband in this fashion when occasion requires.

The only reason that the natives give for ornamenting themselves in this way is that it makes them "look well." On the occasion of a big dance many of the performers are thus ornamented. This is always so at the dances held when two or more local groups meet together. There are certain special occasions, already mentioned in this chapter, when the use of the "snake pattern" is required by custom. One of these is the dance at the end of mourning. During the period of mourning the mourners are forbidden to make use of this form of decoration. The same pattern is used to decorate a bride and bridegroom after their marriage. In the initiation ceremonies the youth or girl is decorated in this way before the dances at the turtle-eating and pig-eating ceremonies. The same pattern is also made on a corpse before burial.

In all these cases the whole body is decorated. On less ceremonial occasions, such as an ordinary dance when there are no visitors of importance in the camp, a man frequently has his face alone decorated with white clay. . . .

The third kind of material used for painting the body is red paint. This is applied in two different ways. When a man or woman is ill he or she is generally to be seen with some part of his body smeared with red paint. For colds and coughs the chest and neck are painted. In fevers red paint is smeared on the upper lip. Besides the medical use of red paint, if we may call it so, there is a ceremonial use, the pigment being used in combination with white clay, lines of red paint being applied to the body between the lines of clay of the snake pattern. It is used in this way to decorate the body of a dead person for burial, and on ceremonial occasions such as the dance at the end of mourning and the dances in connection with the initiation ceremonies. . . .

In the North Andaman, and possibly in the South also, there was a ceremony by which two hostile local groups made peace with one another. When the two groups have agreed to make friends and bring their quarrel to an end, arrangements are made for this ceremony. The arrangements are made through the women of the two parties. A day is fixed for the ceremony, which takes place in the country of the group that made the last attack. In the village of this group the dancing ground is prepared, and across it is erected what is called a *koro-cop.* Posts are put up in a line, to the tops of these is attached a length of strong cane, and from the cane are suspended bundles of shredded palm leaf (*koro*). . . . The women of the camp keep a lookout for the approach of visitors. When they are known to be near the camp, the women sit down on one side of the dancing ground, and the men take up positions in front of the decorated cane. Each man stands with his back against the *koro-cop,* with his arms stretched out sideways along the top of it. None of them has any weapons.

The visitors, who are, if we may so put it, the forgiving party, while the home party are those who have committed the last act of hostility, advance into the camp dancing, the step being that of the ordinary dance. The women of the home party mark the time of the dance by clapping their hands on their thighs. I was told that the visitors carry their weapons with them, but when the dance was performed at my request the dancers were without weapons. The visitors dance forward in front of the men standing at the *koro-cop,* and then, still dancing all the time, pass backwards and forwards between the standing men, bending their heads as they pass beneath the suspended cane. The dancers make threatening gestures at the men standing at the *koro-cop,* and every now and then break into a shrill shout. The men at the *koro* stand silent and motionless, and are expected to show no sign of fear.

After they have been dancing thus for a little time, the leader of the dancers approaches the man at one end of the *koro* and, taking him by the shoulders from the front, leaps vigorously up and down to the time of the dance, thus giving the man he holds a good shaking. The leader then passes on to the next man in the row while another of the dancers goes through the same performance with the first man. This is continued until each of the dancers has "shaken" each of the standing men. The dancers then pass under the *koro* and shake their enemies in the same manner from the back. After a little more dancing the dancers retire, and the women of the visiting group come forward and dance in much the same way that the men have done, each woman giving each of the men of the other group a good shaking.

When the women have been through their dance the two parties of men and women sit down and weep together.

The two groups remain camped together for a few days, spending the time in hunting and dancing together. Presents are exchanged, as at the ordinary meetings of different groups. The men of the two groups exchange bows with one another. . . .

The Andaman Islanders believe in the existence of a class of supernatural beings which I propose to denote by the term "spirits." The native name for his spirits is *lau, lao,* or *yau* in the languages of the North and Middle Andaman, and *cauga* in the South Andaman. While all spirits are denoted together by the term *lau* or *cauga,* there are certain special classes of spirits. There are, for instance, spirits that haunt the jungles of the islands. . . .

There are other spirits that live in the sea. Although these may be included under the term *Lau* or *Cauga,* when it is used in a general sense, yet there is a special name for the sea spirits, *Jurua* in the North Andaman, and *Juruwin* in *Aka-Bea.* The *Jurua* are beings of the same nature as the *Ti-miku Lau,* with the difference that they live in the sea, while the latter live in the forest.

In the South Andaman the natives also speak of another class of spirits who live in the sky and are called *Morua* or *Morowin.* . . .

The Andamanese relate legends . . . which concern doings of mythical ancestors. As all Andamanese, when they die, become *Lau,* these ancestors are of course included under that term. They are often distinguished from the spirits of persons recently dead by being denoted as *Lau t'er-kuro,* from the word *er-kuro* meaning "Big," and applied to human beings to denote importance of social position. Just as a man who occupies a prominent position in his tribe is called a "big" man (*er-kuro*), so the ancestors of the Andamanese legends are called "big" spirits. . . .

The name *Lau* or *Cauga* is also applied by the Andamanese to the natives of India and Burma whom they see in the Penal Settlement of Port Blair. . . . Natives of the North Andaman told me that in former times (before 1875) they applied the term *Lau* to Europeans also, not distinguishing them from other light-skinned aliens. . . .

The spirits of the forest and the sea are believed to be generally invisible, but there are tales of men and women who have seen them, and their personal appearance is sometimes described. The descriptions vary considerably from one informant to another. One of the commonest statements is that they are light or white skinned. (The Andamanese vocabulary does not allow of any distinction between white and a light grey or a light shade of colour.) One man, however, said that the forest spirits were black (or dark) while the sea spirits are white (or light). I was told several times that the spirits have long hair and beards (the Andamanese having, as a rule, no beard, and their hair, being frizzy, never growing to any length). Their arms and legs are said to be abnormally long, while they have only small bodies. Though there is no uniformity in the way in which the natives describe the spirits of the jungle and the sea, there is a notable tendency to associate them with the grotesque, the ugly, and the fearful. There is a common belief that the spirits, both of the jungle and of the sea, carry about with them lights, which several men and women claim to have seen.

In reply to the question as to how the spirits of the forest and the sea originated, the natives all agree in saying that they are the spirits of dead men and women.

The jungle spirits live in a village (or villages) in the forest. There is a belief that mortals wandering by themselves in the jungle have been captured by the spirits. Should the captive show any fear, my informants said, the spirits would kill him, but if he were brave they would take him to their village, detaining him for a time, and then releasing him to return to his friends. A man to whom such an adventure has happened will be endowed for the rest of his life with power to perform magic. He will pay occasional visits to his friends the spirits. The natives told me of one such man who died not many years ago. At irregular intervals he used to wander off into the jungle by himself and remain absent for a few hours, sometimes for a day or two. He returned to the village after such an absence looking strange and wearing ornaments of shredded palm leaf (*koro*) which he claimed had been placed upon him by the spirits.

Save for persons who have made friends with them, and have thereby become endowed with magical powers, all contact with the spirits of the jungle and the sea, or with the spirit of a dead man, is dangerous. The spirits are believed to be the cause of all sickness and of all deaths resulting from sickness. As a man wanders in the jungle or by the sea, the spirits come invisibly and strike him, whereupon he falls ill, and may die. A man or woman is more likely to be attacked by the spirits if he or she is alone, and it is therefore always better to be in company when away from the village. The spirits rarely venture into the village itself, though they may prowl round it, particularly at night. They are more dangerous at night than during the day.

There are many objects that are believed to have the power of keeping spirits at a distance, and thus of preserving human beings from the danger of sickness. Amongst the most important of these are fire, arrows, human bones, bees'-wax, and red paint.

A man or woman leaving a hut to go only a few yards at night will always carry a firebrand as a protection against spirits that may be prowling in the neighbourhood. If the night be dark a torch is carried in addition to the firestick.

The Andamanese never whistle at night, as they believe that the noise of whistling would attract spirits. On the other hand they believe that singing will keep the spirits away.

The spirits that haunt the woods and waters of a man's own home are regarded as being less dangerous to him than those of a country in which he is a stranger. A man of the *Aka-Cari* tribe who was with me in Rutland Island had a cold on his chest. He asked me for permission to return to his own country, explaining that the spirits of Rutland Island were, so to speak, at enmity with him, and that if he stayed longer he would be seriously ill, and perhaps die, while on the other hand, the spirits of his own country were friendly towards him, and once he was amongst them he would quickly recover. . . .

The Andaman Islanders personify the phenomena of nature with which they are acquainted, such as the sun and the moon. . . . Different statements, not only of different informants, but even of the same informant, are often quite contradictory. For example, it is sometimes said that lightning is a person, and at other times it is said that lightning is a firebrand thrown across the sky by a mythical being named *Biliku*. These two statements, which to all logical thinking are incompatible, are both given, and apparently both equally believed, by the same person. Many examples of such contradictions will be found in what follows, and it is important to point out their existence beforehand.

About the sun and moon, the most usual statement in all the tribes is that the sun is the wife of the moon and the stars are their children. In the North Andaman the moon is *Maia Dula* (*Aka-Cari*) or *Maia Cirikli* (*Aka-Jeru*), the sun is *Mimi Diu* and their children the stars are *Catlo,* the larger ones, and *Katan* the smaller. *Catlo* is the name of a species of finely marked beetle, and *katan* is the name of the common firefly. Individual stars or constellations are not recognized.

Another version from the same tribes is that the moon (*Dula*) is female, and has a husband named *Maia Tok,* while the sun (*Diu* or *Torodiu*) is male.

In the *Aka-Jeru* tribe there is a belief that the moon (*Maia Cirikli*) can, when he wishes, turn himself into a pig, and come down to earth and feed on the things that the pigs eat. There is a legend that on one occasion the moon thus turned himself into a pig and came down to earth to eat the *cuei* fruit. A man named *Maia Coinyop* met the moon (in the form of a pig) in the forest, and shot him with an arrow. *Cirikli* (the moon) took out his knife and killed the unfortunate *Coinyop,* cutting off his head, which he left behind, and taking the body up to the sky where he ate it.

In the *A-Pucikwar* tribe the most common statement is that the moon (*Puki*) is male and that the sun (*Puto*) is his wife. A different statement from the same tribe is that the moon is female and is the wife of a being named *Tomo.* *Tomo* seems to be to some extent identified with the sun. Thus one informant said that it is *Tomo* who sends the fine weather, and that it is he who sends the daylight every day. Where *Tomo* lives, in the sky, it is always day and is always fine. When the natives die their spirits go up to the sky and live with *Tomo.* . . . according to some of the legends, *Tomo* is the first ancestor of the Andamanese. . . .

A belief about the moon which is found in all the tribes, both of the North and the South, is that he will be very angry if there is any fire, or any bright light, visible when he rises in the evening shortly after sundown. At such times the natives are careful to cover up their fires so that they only smoulder without flame. . . .

In all parts of the islands the rainbow is believed to have some connection with the spirits of the jungle or of the sea. One very common statement is that it is a bridge of cane that stretches between this world and the world of departed spirits. It is along the rainbow that the spirits travel when they visit the earth. . . .

Among the most important of the Andamanese beliefs are those relating to the weather and the seasons. These are under the control of two beings named *Biliku, Bilik* or *Pulaga,* and *Tarai, Teriya,* or *Daria.* There are a certain number of points in which the statements of one informant may differ from those of another in connection with these two mythical beings, but there are also a certain number of points on which there is absolute unanimity in all the tribes of the Great Andaman.

[*Like other very primitive peoples, the Andamanese have no codified system of rationalizations. Many field men would have been content to take down one version only. You will notice that the phenomena about which contradictory statements are made are the ones which create the least disturbance; those about which all agree are the critical ones.*]

The first belief in which there is entire unanimity is that of the connection of *Biliku* and *Tarai* with the two chief winds that are known in the Andamans. *Biliku* lives in the northeast

and is connected with the northeast monsoon. *Tarai* lives in the southwest and is connected with the southwest monsoon. . . .

It comes about, in this way, that the year is divided into two portions, one of which is specially connected with *Biliku* (*Puluga*), while the other is specially connected with *Tarai* (*Deria*). These two seasons are not quite of equal length. The *Tarai* season lasts only while the southwest monsoon is blowing, which, in an average year, is between four and five months. The other seven months are connected with *Biliku* and are divided into three portions, (1) the stormy season of October and November, (2) the cold season of December to February, and (3) the hot season of March and April.

There are many points relating to *Biliku* and *Tarai* about which there is no general agreement amongst the tribes, or, in some cases, even within the same tribe. In the North Andaman *Biliku* is regarded as female, and is called *Mimi Biliku*. This is so in all the four tribes, *Aka-Cari, Aka-Bo, Aka-Kora,* and *Aka-Jeru*. A statement that is frequently made by the natives of these tribes is that *Tarai* and *Biliku* are husband and wife. While this is the most common statement, there are, however, other versions of the matter. . . .

[*The general confusion as to whether these deities are male or female shows that it makes little difference. Men and women in Andamanese society play about equally important roles, and either can become a shaman. In societies where the tasks and positions of authority of men and women are sharply differentiated, no such confusion will occur.*]

. . . One *Aka-Kede* man, from the southern part of the tribe, said that *Biliku* was male. . . .

Rain and thunder and lightning that come with the southwest wind are believed to be due to *Tarai*. Storms that come during the season connected with *Biliku* are made by *Biliku* and are due to her anger. When a big storm comes the natives say, *"Biliku* is angry." Lightning is explained as being a firebrand thrown by *Biliku* across the sky when she is angry, and thunder is said to be her voice growling. Another explanation of lightning is that it is a pearl shell, called *be* in the North Andaman, thrown by *Biliku,* the bright flash of the mother-of-pearl being seen as it crosses the sky. Still another statement from the North Andaman is that *Biliku* makes the lightning by striking a pearl shell (*be*) against a stone.

Although *Biliku* is generally mentioned when a native is asked about lightning, yet *Tarai* also wields the lightning and the thunder. On one occasion when I was talking to a native I referred to the thunder and lightning that were at the moment coming up from the southwest, making a remark to the effect that *Biliku* was getting angry about something, and was corrected by him with "No, that is *Tarai."*

There are a certain number of actions that are believed by the natives to arouse the anger of *Biliku* (*Puluga*), and thereby cause storms. There are three of these that are of importance.

1. Burning or melting bees'-wax.
2. Killing a cicada, or making a noise, particularly a noise of cutting or banging wood, during the time that the cicada is "singing" in the morning and evening.
3. The use of certain articles of food, of which the chief are the seeds of the *Entada scandens,* the pith of the *Caryota sobolifera,* two species of *Dioscorea* (yam), and certain edible roots, of which may be mentioned those called in *Aka-Jeru labo, mikuli, ji,* and *loito.*

In this matter there is an entire unanimity of belief in all the tribes of the Great Andaman. All the natives agree in saying that any of these three actions causes the anger of *Biliku* or *Puluga* and so brings bad weather.

The natives do, as a matter of fact, melt all the bees'-wax they obtain, in order to purify it, and render it suitable for use in the various ways in which they employ it. Also they do make use of all the plants mentioned under (3) whenever they are in season. They give various explanations of this variance between their precepts and their actions. Some of my informants said that though these actions may bring rain and storms, yet they would rather submit to bad weather than go without some of their most prized vegetable foods. Others again say that there is always a chance that *Biliku* may not notice that the plants have been disturbed, particularly if no fragments are left lying about the camp, and if, when taking the roots, the creepers are not disturbed. Another statement is that it is really only during the season of storms, called the *Kimil* season in *Aka-Jeru,* that it is dangerous to eat these foods, that is, during the months of October and November. After this season has passed there is no longer any danger of violent storms and the foods in question may be freely eaten. Nevertheless the natives do eat these foods in the months of October and November. . . .

In all the tribes of the Great Andaman I found a belief that *Biliku* or *Puluga* will be angry if anybody makes a noise, particularly a noise of chopping, breaking, or banging wood, during the time a cicada is singing. The cicada "sings," as the natives call it, during the short interval between dawn and sunrise, and during that between sunset and darkness. It is at these times that no noise may be made. The

Andamanese do observe this custom, and refrain from making any noise at such times. For instance, if a man were singing, he would cease until the cicada were silent again. In all the tribes I found that this prohibition was connected in the minds of the natives with *Puluga,* the reason of the custom being always explained to me by saying that any breach of it would infallibly bring bad weather. In the North Andaman the cicada (*mite*) is commonly spoken of as the "child" of *Biliku.* . . .

As regards the prohibition against killing the cicada, this seems to refer only to the imago. So far as I was able to observe, the natives do carefully avoid killing the cicada in its fullgrown form. On the other hand the grub of the cicada is regularly killed and eaten, being regarded as a delicacy. It is only eaten during the months of October and November.

In connection with the cicada, and with the weather, there is a rite which was described to me, but which I did not see performed. According to the account given of this rite, which is called "killing the cicada," its purpose is to produce fine weather. It takes place in December, at the end of the season during which they eat the grub. When the time agreed upon for the performance of the ceremony arrives, all the members of the community are careful to be in the camp before sunset. As soon as the sun sets and the cicadae begin their shrill cry, all the men, women and children present begin to make as much noise as they possibly can, by banging on the sounding board, striking the ground with bamboos, beating pieces of wood together, or hammering on the sides of canoes, while at the same time shouting. They continue the noise, which entirely drowns that of the cicada, until after darkness has fallen. The rite may be

performed, I believe, two or more times, on successive evenings. My informant explained the rite by saying that the natives have been eating the cicada, and the rite is intended to "kill" those that are left. After the rite the cicada disappears and is not seen or heard for some weeks, and there follow four months of fine weather with little rain. . . .

[*"Killing" the cicada, which means really helping it out by making noise, for the cicada is noisy at this time, is a ritual means of assisting nature. Since the song of the cicada is a "sign" linked to the end of the rainy season, making more noise insures the arrival of good weather. This is magical rationalization. More fundamentally, the change of seasons is a cause of disturbance, and the ritual of noisemaking serves to pull the camp together—an increase of interaction always found in a Rite of Intensification. You will see more of this before you have finished the book.*]

The only punishment that *Biliku* ever inflicts on human beings when she is angry with them for any reason is to send violent storms. The way to stop a storm seems to be to frighten *Biliku.* One means of doing this is to throw the leaves of the *Mimusops littoralis* in the fire. These leaves explode with the heating of the juices and make a crackling or popping noise, which it is said that *Biliku* dislikes. I believe, however, that if any one were thus to burn *Mimusops* leaves during fine weather, it would be regarded as most likely to cause a storm. The most efficacious means of stopping a storm is to do some of the things that *Biliku* most dislikes. To burn bees'-wax, or to go into the jungle and damage or destroy the creepers that belong to her, these are the heroic remedies against *Biliku's* anger. . . .

There are, amongst the Andamanese

certain individuals who are distinguished from their fellows by the supposed possession of supernatural powers. These specially favoured persons correspond, to some degree, with the medicine men, magicians or shamans of other primitive societies. . . .

. . . it is more usual for men to become famous in this way than women. There is no very clear dividing line between those who are *oko-jumu* or *oko-paiad* and those who are not; one person may possess the powers in only a slight degree, so as scarcely to differentiate him from others, while another may be much more highly gifted. . . .

The powers of a dreamer, supernatural as they are, can only be acquired by supernatural means, through contact in one way or another with the spirits (i.e., the *Lau* or *Cauga*). One way of coming into contact with the spirits is by death. If a man should, as the natives put it, die and then come back to life again, he is, by that adventure, endowed with the power that makes a medicine man. One man of the *Aka-Kora* tribe was pointed out to me as having obtained his powers in this way. It would seem that during a serious illness he was unconscious for some twelve hours or so, and his friends thought that he was dead. A medicine-man whom I met with in the *A-Pucikwar* tribe was said to have died and come to life again three times. Another man, whom I did not meet, was described to me as a great *oko-jumu,* and from the description given it seemed to me that he was subject to epileptic fits. . . .

Another way in which a man can acquire magical powers is by direct communication with the spirits. A man who died a few years ago was believed by the natives to have once met with some spirits in the jungle, and to have acquired in this way the powers of an *oko-jumu*. He used to go off into the jungle by himself at intervals and hold communication with the spirits with whom he had made friends. From such a visit he had returned with his head decorated with shredded palm-leaf fibre (*koro*) which had, so he said, been placed on him by the spirits. This man had a reputation as a powerful *oko-jumu*.

In a less degree the powers of an *oko-jumu* may be obtained through dreams. It is believed that certain men have the power of communicating with the spirits in dreams, and such men are *oko-jumu*. If a man or boy experiences dreams that are in any way extraordinary, particularly if in his dreams he sees spirits, either the spirits of dead persons known to him when alive or spirits of the forest or the sea, he may acquire in time the reputation of a medicine man.

A man may claim some degree of magical power, and yet his claims may not be recognized by others. Each *oko-jumu* has to make his own reputation, and to sustain it when made. This he can only do by demonstrating his powers to others. Once this reputation is his, he not only receives the respect of others, but also makes a considerable personal profit. Every one is anxious to be on good terms with one who is believed to have extraordinary powers. Hence a man who is an acknowledged *oko-jumu* is sure to receive a good share of the game caught by others, and presents of all kinds from those who seek his good will.

As the name implies, and in whatever way his power may have been obtained, an *oko-jumu* is privileged to dream in a way that less favoured persons do not. In his dreams he can communicate with the spirits of the dead. In dreams, also, so the natives say, he is able to cause the illness of an enemy or to cure that of a friend.

[*Here we see shamanism—religious activity—at its simplest level. The idea that death and rebirth are involved in the acquisition of spiritual power simply means that the prospective shaman goes through a Rite of Passage. This is almost universal. So is the belief in the importance of dreams. Primitive man cannot explain dreams—nor can we entirely—and tends to take them literally. The shaman can both cure and injure. He is a physician, spiritual guide, and weather priest all in one.]*

. . . . When a person is ill the *oko-jumu* is often consulted as to the best means of treating the patient. His treatment is often limited to the recommendation, or the application, of some one or other of the recognized remedies. He may undertake to dispel the spirits that are supposed to be the cause of the disease, which he does by addressing them and conjuring them to go away, or by the use of one or other of the substances and objects that are believed to have the power of keeping spirits at a distance. . . . It is believed that in his dreams he can communicate with the spirits and can persuade them to help him to cure the sick person.

Besides their power of causing or curing sickness, the *oko-jumu* are credited with being able to control the weather. As has been shown, the Andamanese believe that the weather is under the control of two beings named *Biluku* and *Tarai*. There is, however, an alternative and contradictory belief, which is also held, that the weather is controlled by the spirits, and particularly by those of the sea. The means taken by magicians or others to prevent bad weather can be divided into two kinds according as they are directed against *Biluku* or *Tarai,* or against the spirits of the sea. As an example of the very simple rites which are performed for this purpose, two cases may be quoted. One of the *oko-jumu* of the Northern tribes, now dead, once stopped a very violent storm by crushing between two stones a piece of *Anadendron paniculatum* and diving with it into the sea where he placed it under a rock on a reef. A more recent example is very similar. A man still living, named *Jire Pilecar*, who was, in a way, the successor of the man formerly mentioned, is said to have stopped a violent storm by using the leaves and bark of the *Ficus laccifera* in the same way, that is by crushing them and placing them under a rock in the sea. In both these cases it would seem that the rite was directed not against *Biliku* and *Tarai,* but against the *Jurua.*

Apart from his power to communicate directly with the spirits, the *oko-jumu* owes his position to a superior knowledge of the magical properties of common substances and objects. This knowledge he is supposed to obtain from the spirits. However, a lesser degree of knowledge on such matters is possessed by everybody. Thus in the treatment of sickness there are a number of magical remedies of which anyone can make use without consulting an *oko-jumu*.

A complete enumeration of all the things that are believed to possess magical properties is, of course, not possible, but the following notes refer to all the most important.

We may consider first of all the magical properties of mineral substances. One of the most important of these is red ochre. Yellow ochre, which is found in pockets in many parts of the islands, is collected and burnt, when it turns red, and the powder so obtained is either used by itself or is made into a paint with pig or turtle fat. The powder is mixed with water and taken internally. Red paint is applied to the throat and chest for coughs and colds and sore throats, and round the ear for earache. When a man feels unwell he often smears red paint on his upper lip just below his nostrils.

In this way, the natives say, the "smell" of the paint cures his sickness. The paint is sometimes used as a dressing for wounds or centipede bites. . . .

White clay (*tol-odu* in *Aka-Jeru*) is sometimes used medicinally, both externally and internally. The commoner clay (*odu* in *Aka-Jeru*) is plastered on sores, and has the effect of keeping off flies, if it does nothing else.

An olive-coloured earth (called *culŋa* in *Aka-Bea*), found in certain springs, is prized as a remedy. It is mixed with water and taken internally as a general remedy for all sorts of complaints. . . .

The *Anadendron paniculatum* is a plant from which the Andamanese obtain a valuable fibre, which they use for their bow strings, and for thread with which to make their arrows and harpoons. A number of magical properties are attributed to this plant. Rheumatism is supposed to be due to the "smell" of the plant getting into the system when the fibre is being prepared. The "smell" of the green plant, or of the fibre until it has been thoroughly dried for some days, is believed to frighten away turtle. A man who had been preparing the fibre would not dream of joining a turtle-hunting expedition, for his presence in the canoe would be sufficient to drive away all the turtle. A turtle-hunting expedition would be a failure if a piece of the green creeper were in the canoe. A man who has been handling the plant may not cook turtle, for the meat would be "bad," i.e., uneatable. The same thing would happen if turtle meat accidentally came in contact with a piece of the plant. All this applies only to the green creeper, and not to the fibre after it has been properly prepared and dried. The fibre itself is used for binding the heads of turtle harpoons, so it is evidently regarded as harmless.

If a piece of the *Anadendron* creeper were burnt in the fire the natives believe that it would drive all the turtle away from the neighborhood, or, according to another statement, that there would be a great storm.

So far we have considered the properties of the plant only in so far as they make it dangerous to handle. It has other and beneficial properties. It is said that a man swimming in waters infested with sharks would be safe from them if he had a piece of the *Anadendron* creeper with him, in his belt or necklace. The creeper is also supposed to preserve anyone who carries it from the attacks of the sea spirits (*Jurua*). . . .

The *Tetranthera lancoefolia* is a small tree from which the natives obtain the wood for the shafts of their pig arrows. The leaves of this tree are believed to have the power to keep away the spirits of the forest. They are used in the pig-eating ceremony described in the last chapter. The wood is shredded and made into plumes, and these plumes are believed to have magical properties. They are worn by a man who has killed another, and are believed to protect him from the vengeance of the spirit of the dead man. . . .

[*You will observe that the substances considered magical are those most commonly used. They represent the greatest amount of interaction in which the Andamanese participate. Thus they symbolize that which is critical in their relations to the environment and to each other.*]

We may now turn to animals and animal substances. Magical properties are attributed to beeswax, particularly to black bees'-wax. In a case of pleurisy black bees'-wax was heated until it was soft, and then smeared over the man's chest. Bees'-wax is believed to keep away the spirits of the forest. . . .

Mention has already been made of the magical value attributed to human bones. They are esteemed as a means of driving away spirits, and therefore of curing or preventing sickness. A human jawbone was hanging in my hut in such a position that it could swing in the wind. The natives attributed to this the illness from which I and several of them were suffering at the time, and asked me to put the bone away in a basket, where it could not move.

Bones of animals are made into ornaments in the same way as human bones, and magical properties of a similar kind seem to be attributed to them.

Of other objects possessing magical properties the most important is fire. Fire is believed to have the power of keeping away spirits of the sea and of the forest. A fire is always kept alight beside a sick man or woman. For dysentery stones are heated in a fire and the patient is required to defecate on to these.

In conclusion, mention must be made of one favourite remedy of the Andamanese, namely scarification. The part of the body that is the seat of pain is scarified, as the forehead for headaches, the cheek for toothache. A number of very small incisions are made in the skin close together, with a sharp flake of quartz or glass. The incisions are just deep enough to cut through the skin and cause a little blood to ooze out, but not so deep as to produce a flow of blood. The operation is the work of women. It is probably more frequently used than any other remedy except red paint and human bones.

If you have read this last selection carefully, you cannot fail to have a picture of a whole culture on the level of simple bands composed of several families. Perhaps you noticed something new, something that we have not encountered before. That is the development of age grading among the Andamanese. All the other people we have known have lived in such rugged environments that life becomes immensely difficult once a person has passed his physical prime. The premium is on strength and the ability to bring in food. Power is to the strong. The Andamanese, however, can stay in one place for weeks, even months at a time. There is enough food for everyone. Old people can live on, and their judgment, based on decades of experience, is appreciated. Strong and strict rules of behavior between young, prime adult, and old, make a comfortable life possible past the age of maximum physical efficiency. If you can afford to feed older people they will form a top level in the social structure, which will in turn give it stability.

If you are interested in the way the treatment of children from birth onward influences their "socialization," or adjustment to life in the community, you will find no better evidence than this. You probably noted how the child is trained to interact with the members of the group as a whole rather than with his own family alone. Crawling around from hut to hut to suckle from various women in turn, and the custom of fosterage, make the child a citizen more than a son.

Aside from these theoretical considerations, the study of the Andaman Islanders has a historical and geographical value. These people are Negritos, like the Congo Pygmies, the Negritos of the Philippines, and a number of other groups between Central Africa and New Guinea. They form a link in an ancient chain of forest people, and more than that, they are the only Negritos known who live by themselves and have even a language of their own. We will have more to say about the Negrito problem in Chapter 11.

7

The Ancestors Walk: The Arunta of Central

Australia

IN THE Andamanese we saw for the first time what happens when older people are preserved and are able to take the lead in the events of a community. Another example is that of the Arunta (modern ethnographers spell it Aranda), one of the many tribes of hunters who occupy the great central and northern grasslands and desert-border regions of Australia. Australia is the home of early types of plants (the eucalyptus family) and of mammals (monotremes and marsupials). Geographically it is the most isolated large land area in the world not covered during parts of the Pleistocene by glacial ice. Human beings at some past time or times ferried themselves across the then narrower waters separating the continent from New Guinea and Indonesia, and brought into Australia an archiac way of life, which their descendants preserved until about a century ago in some parts of the continent. In a few of the most barren areas some aborigines still lead a tribal life.

Of the many books written about Australian tribes, none has attained the fame of Spencer and Gillen's *The Arunta,* a two-volume classic from which the following selection is taken.* The reader must remember that the Australian aborigines are true survivors of Pleistocene man; they are physically archaic, they chip their flints in recognizable forms which archaeologists can identify, and if anywhere in the world we can say that fossil men still live on, it is here. The Arunta live near Alice Springs, in the Macdonnell Ranges, in the middle of Australia.

The Arunta is, or rather was, one of the largest tribes in Central Australia, and still occupies a tract of country extending from the Macumba River on the south to seventy miles north of the Macdonnell Ranges, a total distance of about 400 miles. Thirty years ago, when first we studied it, its members must have numbered at least 2000, now they cannot be more than 300 or 400. . . .

The Arunta tribe is divided into a large number of small local groups, each of which occupies, and is supposed to possess, a given area of country, the boundaries of which are well known to the natives. In speaking of themselves, the natives will refer to these local groups by the name of the locality which each of them inhabits. . . . Often also a number of separate groups occupying a larger district will be spo-

* From Baldwin Spencer and F. J. Gillen, *The Arunta. A Study of a Stone Age People.* London, 2 volumes, 1927. By permission of The Macmillan Company, publishers.

213

ken of collectively by one name, as, for example, the groups living along the Finke River are often spoken of as Larapinta men, from the native name of the river. In addition to this, the natives speak of different divisions of the tribes according to the direction of the country which they occupy. Thus the east side is called *Iknura,* the west side *Aldorla,* the southwest *Antikera,* the north side *Yirira,* the southeast side *Urlewa. Atua iknura mbainda* is applied to men living on the east, and so on.

Still further examination of each local group reveals the fact that it is composed largely, but not entirely, of individuals who describe themselves by the name of some one animal or plant. Thus there will be one area which belongs to a group of men who call themselves kangaroo men, another belonging to emu men, another to Hakea flower men, and so on, almost every animal and plant which is found in the country having its representative amongst the human inhabitants. The area of country which is occupied by each of these, which will be spoken of as local totemic groups, varies to a considerable extent, but is never very large, the most extensive one with which we are acquainted being that of the witchetty grub people of the Alice Springs district. This group, at the time when we first knew it in 1896, was represented by exactly forty individuals (men, women and children), and the area of which they were recognized as the proprietors extended over about 100 square miles. In contrast to this, one particular group of "plum tree" people was only represented by one solitary individual, and he was the proprietor of only a few square miles.

[*Totem. I will come to this a little later.*]

With these local groups we shall subsequently deal in detail; all that

need be added here in regard to them is that groups of the same designation are found in many parts of the district occupied by the tribe.

Within the narrow limits of his own group the local head man or Inkata takes the lead; outside of his group no head man has of necessity any special power. If he has any generally recognized authority, as some of them undoubtedly have, this is due to the fact that he is either the head of a numerically important group, or is himself famous for his skill in hunting or fighting or for his knowledge of the ancient traditions and customs of the tribe. Old age does not by itself confer distinction, but only when combined with special ability. There is no such thing as a chief of the tribe, nor indeed is there any individual to whom the term chief can be applied.

[*Inkata. The local unit is the largest one that has a chief and a definite form of government. Meetings of larger units are international conferences.*]

The authority which is wielded by an Inkata is of a somewhat vague nature. He has no definite power over the persons of the individuals who are members of his group. He it is who calls together the elder men, who always consult concerning any important business, such as the holding of sacred ceremonies or the punishment of individuals who have broken tribal custom, and his opinion carries an amount of weight which depends upon his reputation. He is not of necessity recognised as the most important member of the council whose judgment must be followed, though, if he be old and distinguished, then he will have great influence. Perhaps the best way of expressing the matter is to say that the Inkata has, *ex officio,* a position which, if he be a man of personal ability, but only in that case, enables him to wield considerable power not only over the members of his own group, but also over those of neighbouring groups whose head men are inferior in personal ability to himself.

[*The Inkata calls a council of elders. This is a very common form of local government; in fact, the commonest in the world. It depends, of course, on the preservation of men past their physical (but not their mental) prime.*]

The Inkata is not chosen for the position because of his ability; the post is one which, within certain limits, is hereditary, passing from father to son, always provided that the man is of the proper designation—that is, for example, in a kangaroo group the Inkata must of necessity be a kangaroo man. To take the Alice Springs group as an example, the holder of the office must be a witchetty grub man, and he must also be old enough to be considered capable of taking the lead in certain ceremonies, and must of necessity be a fully initiated man. The present Inkata inherited the post from his father, who had previously inherited it from his father. The present holder has no son who is yet old enough to be an Inkata, so that if he were to die within the course of the next two or three years, his brother would hold the position, which would, however, on the death of this brother, revert to the present holder's son. Of course it occasionally happens that the Inkata has no son to succeed him, in which case he will, before dying, nominate the individual whom he desires to succeed him, who will always be either a brother or a brother's son. The Inkataship always descends in the male line, and we are not aware of anything which can be regarded as the precise equivalent of this position in other Australian tribes, a fact which is to be associated with the strong development of the local totemic groups in this part of the continent.

The most important function of the Inkata is to take charge of what we may call the sacred storehouse, which has usually the form of a cleft in some rocky range, or a special hole in the ground, in which, concealed from view, are kept the sacred objects of the group. Near to this storehouse, which is called *Pertalchera*, no woman, child or uninitiated man dare venture on pain of death.

[*The sacred storehouse. These people cannot carry many objects with them. Their holiest objects, the sacred churingas (bull-roarers),* must be kept in a safe place, free from the prying eyes of women and children. A sacred storehouse is a cleft in the rocks, or a pile of stones, which the uniniated avoid. The whole area immediately surrounding it is holy. From the sacred storehouse has arisen historically, in some regions, the temple.*]

At intervals of time, and when determined upon by the Inkata, the members of the group perform a special ceremony, known under different names, such as *Intichiuma* and *Mbanbiuma,* in various local groups, which will be described later on in detail, the object of which is to increase the supply of the animal or plant bearing the name of the particular group which performs the ceremony. Each group has such a ceremony of its own, which can only be taken part in by initiated men bearing the group name. In the performance of this ceremony the Inkata takes the leading part; he it is who decides when it is to be performed, and during the celebration the proceedings are carried out under his direction, though he has, while conducting them, to follow out strictly the customs of his ancestors.

[*Increase ceremony. An example is given at the end of this chapter.*]

* A slat of wood tied to the end of a thong, so called because whirling the slat causes an intermittent roaring.

As amongst all savage tribes, the Australian native is bound hand and foot by custom. [*Old men everywhere are conservative. They see to it that things are done exactly the same way, generation after generation. This has a survival value among stone-age Australians but it would produce chaos in a rapidly changing civilization such as ours.*] What his fathers did before him that he must do. If during the performance of a ceremony his ancestors painted a white line across the forehead, that line he must paint. Any infringement of custom, within certain limitations, is visited with sure and often severe punishment. At the same time, rigidly conservative as the native is, it is yet possible for changes to be introduced. We have already pointed out that there are certain men who are especially respected for their ability, and, after watching large numbers of the tribe when they were assembled together for months to perform certain of their most sacred ceremonies, we have come to the conclusion that at a time such as this, when the older and more powerful men from various groups meet together, and when, day by day, and night by night, around their camp fires they discuss matters of tribal interests, it is quite possible for changes of custom to be introduced. At the present moment, for example, an important change in tribal organisation is gradually spreading through the tribe from north to south. Every now and then a man arises of superior ability to his fellows. When large numbers of the tribe are gathered together—at least it was so on the special occasion to which we allude—one or two of the older men are at once seen to wield a special influence over the others. Everything, as we have before said, does not depend upon age. At this gathering, for example, some of the oldest men were of little account; but, on the other hand, others not so old as they were, but more learned in ancient lore or more skilled in matters of magic, were looked up to by the others, and they settled everything. It must, however, be understood that we have no definite proof to bring forward of the actual introduction by this means of any fundamental change of custom. The only thing that we can say is that, after carefully watching the natives during the performance of their ceremonies and endeavouring as best we could to enter into their feelings, to think as they did, and to become for the time being one of themselves, we came to the conclusion that if one or two of the most powerful men decided upon the advisability of introducing some change, even an important one, it would be quite possible for this to be agreed upon and carried out. That changes have been introduced—in fact, are still being introduced—is a matter of certainty; the difficulty to be explained is how, in face of the rigid conservatism of the native, which may be said to be one of his leading features, such changes can possibly even be mooted. The only possible chance is by means of the old men, and, in the case of the Arunta people, amongst whom the local feeling is very strong, they have opportunities of a special nature. Without belonging to the same group, men who inhabit localities close to one another are more closely associated than men living at a distance from one another, and, as a matter of fact, this local bond is strongly marked—indeed. so marked was it during the performance of their sacred ceremonies, that we constantly found it necessary to use the term "local relationship." Groups which are contiguous locally are constantly meeting to perform ceremonies; [*Meetings between adjacent local groups are frequent enough to build up stable relations. These are needed*

for trade and for help in lean years.]
and among the Inkatas who thus come
together and direct proceedings there
is perfectly sure, every now and again,
to be one who stands pre-eminent by
reason of superior ability, and to him,
especially on an occasion such as this,
great respect is always paid. It would
be by no means impossible for him to
propose to the other older men the introduction of a change, which, after
discussing it, the Inkatas of the local
groups gathered together might come
to the conclusion was a good one, and,
if they did so, then it would be adopted
in that district. After a time a still
larger meeting of the tribe, with head
men from a still wider area—a meeting
such as the Engwura, which is described in the following pages—might
be held. [*Meetings of whole "tribes,"
that is of clusters of local groups speaking the same language in most cases,
carry this principle still further.*] At
this the change locally introduced
would, without fail, be discussed. The
man who first started it would certainly have the support of his local
friends, provided they had in the first
instance agreed upon the advisability
of its introduction, and not only this,
but the chances are that he would have
the support of the head men of other
local groups of the same designation
as his own. Everything would, in fact,
depend upon the status of the original
proposer of the change; but, granted
the existence of a man with sufficient
ability to think out the details of any
change, then, owing partly to the strong
development of the local feeling, and
partly to the feeling of kinship between
groups of the same designation, wherever their local habitation may be, it
seems quite possible that the markedly
conservative tendency of the natives in
regard to customs handed down to
them from their ancestors may every
now and then be overcome, and some

change, even a radical one, be introduced. The traditions of the tribe indicate, it may be noticed, their recognition of the fact that customs have varied from time to time. They have, for
example, traditions dealing with supposed ancestors, some of whom introduced, and others of whom changed,
the method of initiation. Tradition also indicates ancestors belonging to particular local groups who changed an
older into the present marriage system,
and these traditions all deal with special
powerful individuals by whom the
changes were introduced.

In addition to the Inkata, there are
two other classes of men who are regarded as of especial importance; these
are the so-called "medicine men," and,
in the second place, the men who are
supposed to have a special power of
communicating with the *Iruntarinia* or
spirits associated with the tribe. Needless to say, there are grades of skill
recognised amongst the members of
these two classes, in much the same way
as we recognise differences of ability
amongst members of the medical profession. [Men of these three special
types] . . . have a definite standing
and are regarded as, in certain ways,
superior to the other men of the tribe.
. . . while every group has its Inkata,
there is no necessity for each to have
either a medicine or an *Iruntarinia*
man, and . . . in regard to the position of the two latter there is no such
thing as hereditary succession.

[*Note that two kinds of shamans
have branched off through specialization—the healer and the diviner. In the
societies discussed so far, the shaman
has been an all-purpose practitioner.*]

In their ordinary condition the natives are almost completely naked,
which is all the more strange, as kangaroo and wallaby are not by any means
scarce, and one would think that their
fur would be of no little use and com-

fort in the winter time, when, under the perfectly clear sky, which often remains cloudless for weeks together, the radiation is so great that at nighttime the temperature falls several degrees below freezing point. The idea of making any kind of clothing as a protection against cold does not appear to have entered the native mind.

[*The Arunta have no clothing. They can own only what they are able to carry, and clothing is less necessary than weapons and implements.*]

The aboriginal is a pure nomad, living entirely on vegetable food and animals that he finds in the bush. Nothing comes amiss: acacia seed, lily roots and stems, yams, honey of the wild bee and honey ant, grubs, kangaroos, emus, snakes, rats, frogs—in fact everything edible is eaten, even some things, such as certain flies and pounded anthill clay, that we should scarcely call by this name. He stores nothing, except for a few days, in preparation for a ceremony, and has no idea of agriculture or domestication, partly perhaps because the animals around him, such as kangaroos, are not adapted to act as beasts of burden or givers of milk, but still more because he believes that, by means of magic, which plays a large part in his life, he can increase their numbers when he wishes to do so. When food is abundant he eats to repletion, when it is scarce he tightens his waistband and starves philosophically.

Under ordinary conditions the members of each local group are constantly to be met with wandering in small parties consisting of one or two families, often, for example, two or more brothers with their wives and children, over the land which they own, camping at favourite spots where the presence of water holes, with their accompaniment of vegetable and animal food, enables them to supply their wants.

Each family, consisting of a man and one or more wives and children, accompanied always by dogs, occupies a *mia-mia,* which is merely a lean-to of shrubs so placed as to shield the occupants from the prevailing wind, which, if it be during the winter months, is sure to be from the southeast. In front of this, or inside if the weather be cold, will be a small fire of twigs, for the black fellow never makes a large fire, as the white man does. In this respect he certainly regards the latter as a strange being, who makes a big fire and then finds it so hot that he cannot go anywhere near to it. This forms the family hearth where the cooking is done, and around which they sit and talk. In addition, on cold nights there will be a small fire between each two persons, with a supply of small wood handy to replenish it if anyone wakes.

[*Furthermore, they keep warm by an ingenious arrangement of fires, reducing the need of clothing still further.*]

Early in the morning, if it be summer, and not until the sun be well up if it be winter, the occupants of the camp are astir. Time is no object to them, and, if there be no lack of food, the men and women all lounge about while the children laugh and play. If food be required, then the women will go out, accompanied by the children, and armed with digging sticks and *pitchis,* [*A pitchi is a troughlike wooden bowl, carried by the woman. She uses it to dig with, and as a container*] and the day will be spent out in the bush in search of small burrowing animals such as lizards and small marsupials. [*The women and children go out on their daily rounds after "slow game," as elsewhere.*] The men will perhaps set off armed with spears, spear throwers, boomerangs and shields in search of larger game, such as emus and kangaroos. The latter are secured by stalking, when the native gradually approaches his prey with perfectly noiseless footsteps. Keeping a sharp watch on the animal, he remains absolutely still, if it should turn its head, until once more it resumes its feeding. Gradually, availing himself of the shelter of any bush or large tussock of grass, he approaches near enough to throw his spear. The end is fixed into the point of the spear thrower, and, aided by the leverage thus gained, he throws it forward with all his strength. Different men vary much in their skill in spear throwing, but it takes an exceptionally good man to kill or disable at more than twenty yards. Sometimes two or three men will hunt in company, and then, while one remains in ambush, the others combine to drive the animals as close as possible to him. Euros (a form of kangaroo) are more easily caught than kangaroos, owing to the fact that they inhabit hilly and scrub country, across which they make "pads," by the side of which men will lie in ambush while parties of women go out and drive the animals towards them. On the ranges the rock wallabies have definite runs, and close by one of these a native will sit patiently, waiting hour by hour until some unfortunate beast comes by.

[*Australians kill animals with spears, thrown by hand or with the spear thrower. Bows were unknown to the natives of that continent.*]

In some parts the leaves of the pituri plant (*Duboisia Hopwoodi,* the native name for which is *unkulpa*), are used to stupefy the emu. The plan adopted is to make a decoction in some small water hole at which the animal is accustomed to drink. There, hidden by some bush, the native lies quietly in wait. After drinking the water the bird becomes stupefied, and easily falls a prey to the black fellow's spear. Some-

times a bush shelter is made, so as to look as natural as possible, close by a water hole and, from behind this, animals are speared as they come down to drink. It must be remembered that during the long dry seasons of Central Australia water holes are few and far between, so that in this way the native is aided in his work of killing animals. In some parts advantage is taken of the inquisitive nature of the emu. A native will carry something which resembles the long neck and small head of the bird and will gradually approach his prey, stopping every now and then, and moving about in the aimless way of the bird itself. The emu, anxious to know what the thing really is, will often wait and watch it until the native has the chance of throwing his spear at close quarters. Sometimes a deep pit will be dug in a part which is known to be a feeding ground of the bird. In the bottom of this a short, sharply pointed spear will be fixed upright, and then, on the top, bushes will be spread and earth scattered upon them. The inquisitive bird comes up to investigate the matter, and sooner or later ventures on the bushes, and, falling through, is transfixed by the spear. Smaller birds, such as the rock pigeons, which assemble in flocks at any water hole, are caught by throwing the boomerang amongst them, and larger birds, such as the eagle hawk, the down of which is much valued for decorating the body during the performance of sacred ceremonies, are procured by the same weapon.

It may be said that, with certain restrictions, which apply partly to groups of individuals and partly to individuals at certain times of their lives, everything which is edible, animal and plant alike, is used for food. So far as cooking is concerned, the method is primitive. Many of the vegetables, such as the Irriakura (the bulb of *Cyperus rotundus*), may be eaten raw, or they may be roasted in hot ashes. Very often large quantities of the pods of an acacia will be gathered and laid on the hot ashes, some of which are heaped up over them, and then the natives simply sit round and "shell" and eat the seeds as if they were peas—in fact, they taste rather like raw green peas. Perhaps the most standard vegetable diet of the natives in this part of the Centre is what is called by the natives in the north of the Arunta, Ingwitchi-ka, and by white men usually Munyeru. This is the seed of a species of Claytonia. The women gather large quantities and winnow the little black seeds by pouring them from one *pitchi* into another so that the wind may carry off the loose husks, or else, taking some up in their hands, they blow the husks away. When freed from the latter, they are placed on one of the usual grinding stones and then ground down with a smaller stone held in the hand. Water is poured on every now and then, and the black, muddy-looking mixture tumbles over the side into a receptacle, and is then ready for eating either raw or after baking in the ashes. Munyeru seems to take the place amongst these tribes of the Nardoo (the spore cases of *Marsilea quadrifolia*), which is a staple article of food in the Barcoo district and other parts of the interior of Australia.

[*Collecting, winnowing, and grinding seed—this technological sequence goes back to the simplest ways of living. Yet from this humble beginning probably developed agriculture.*]

The native has no pottery; he carries water in a wooden trough or *pitchi,* and sometimes, especially amongst the more northern tribes, his bags, made of grass, rushes or split cane, are so closely woven as to be able to hold honey, but he has nothing in which water or food can be heated.

In the case of animals, the larger ones are usually cooked in more or less shallow pits in the ground. An opossum is first of all disembowelled, the wool is then plucked off with the fingers and the body placed on the hot ashes. A rock wallaby is treated in much the same way, except that the hair is first singed off in the fire and then the skin is scraped with a piece of flint. The ashes are heaped up over the body, which, when partly cooked, is taken out and an incision made in each groin; the holes fill and refill with fluid, which is greatly appreciated and drunk at once. The animal is then divided up, the flint at the end of the spear thrower being used for this purpose. When cooking an Echidna the intestines are first removed. Then a small hole is dug, the bottom is sprinkled with water, and the animal placed in it. The back is covered with a layer of moist earth or sand, which is removed after about a quarter of an hour, and hot ashes substituted, which are removed after a few minutes. The skin with the quills is next cut off with a flint, and the body is then placed amongst hot ashes till cooked.

When a euro or kangaroo is killed, the first thing that is always done is to dislocate the hind legs so as to make the animal what is called *atnuta* or limp. A small hole is cut with a flint in one side of the abdomen, and after the intestines have been pulled out, it is closed up with a wooden skewer. The intestines are usually cooked by rolling them about in hot sand and ashes, any fat which may be present being carefully removed, as it is esteemed a great delicacy. One of the first things to be done is to extract the tendons from the hind limbs. To do this the skin is cut through close to the foot with the sharp bit of flint which is attached to the end of the spear thrower. A hitch is next taken round the tendon with a stick, and then, with one foot against the animal's rump, the man pulls until the upper end gives way. Then the loose end is held in the teeth, and, when tightly stretched, the lower end is cut through with the flint and the tendon thus extracted is twisted up and put for safe keeping beneath the waist girdle, or in the hair of the head just behind the ear. These tendons are of great service to the natives in various ways, such as for attaching the barbed points on to the ends of the spears, or for splicing spears or mending broken spear throwers. Meanwhile a shallow pit, perhaps one or two feet deep, has been dug with sticks, and in this a large fire is made. When this burns up, the body is usually held in the flames to singe off the fur, after which it is scraped with a flint. Sometimes this part of the performance is omitted. The hind legs are cut off at the middle joint and the tail is either divided in the middle or cut off close to the stump. When the fire has burnt down, the animal is laid in the pit on its back with its legs protruding through the hot ashes, which are heaped up over it. After about an hour it is supposed to be cooked, and is taken off, laid on green boughs so as to prevent it from coming in contact with the earth, and then cut up, the hind legs being usually removed first. In some parts where the fur is not singed off, the first thing that is done after removing the body from the fire is to take off the burnt skin. The carver assists himself, during the process of cutting the body up into joints, to such dainty morsels as the heart and kidneys, while any juice which accumulates in the internal cavities of the body is greedily drunk.

When cooking an emu the first thing that is done is to pluck it roughly; an incision is then made in the side, the intestines are withdrawn, and the inside is stuffed with feathers, the cut being closed by means of a wooden skewer. A pit is dug sufficiently large to hold the body and a fire lighted in it, over which the body is held and singed so as to get rid of the remaining feathers. The legs are cut off at the knee joint, and the head is brought round under one leg, to which it is fastened with a wooden skewer. The ashes are now removed from the pit, and a layer of feathers is put in; on these the bird is placed, resting on its side; another layer of feathers is placed over the bird, and then the hot ashes are strewn over. When it is supposed to be cooked enough, it is taken out, laid on its breast, and an incision is made running round both sides, so as to separate the back part from the under portion of the body. It is then turned on to its back, the legs are taken off and the meat is cut up.

The leaves and small twigs of the pituri plant (*Duboisia Hopwoodi*), called by the natives *Unkulpa* or *Ungulpa,* are used as a narcotic. They are dried, broken up, packed tightly into woven string bags, each holding two or three pounds weight, and then traded over long distances. Though the plant grows on the sand-hill country around Lake Amadeus and Ayer's Rock, the greater part of that used by the Arunta and neighboring tribes, such as the Dieri and Urabunna, appears to come from the northwest, in the interior of Queensland, distant at least 200 miles. It is made up into small "plugs," which are passed from mouth to mouth and chewed. When not in use, they are carried behind the ear or, sometimes, in a hole bored through the nasal septum. . . .

[In making the plugs,] the leaves are dried in the sun; then twigs of a species of cassia bush are burnt to ashes and the latter pounded up with the Duboisia, mixed with a little water and made into a plug, the chewing of which has a soothing effect.

[*Note that pituri, a narcotic, is one of the most widely traded objects. In this it is comparable to tobacco, opium, and alcoholic drinks in other cultures.*]

It is curious that, though the true tobacco plant, *Nicotianum suaveolens,* grows plentifully in parts of the Arunta country, the natives have not discovered its narcotic properties.

The tracking powers of the native are well known, but it is difficult to realise the skill which they display unless one has seen them at work. Not only does the native know the track of every beast and bird, but after examining any burrow he will at once, from the direction in which the last track runs, or even after smelling the earth at the burrow entrance, tell you whether the animal is at home or not. From earliest childhood boys and girls alike are trained to take note of every track made by every living thing. With the women especially it is a frequent amusement to imitate on the sandy ground the tracks of various animals, which they make with wonderful accuracy with their hands. Not only do they know the varied tracks of the latter, but they will distinguish those of particular men and women. In this respect the men vary greatly, a fact which is well known to, and appreciated by, those in charge of the native police in various parts of the interior of the continent. Whilst they can all follow tracks which would be indistinguishable to the average white man, there is a great difference in their ability to do so when they become obscure. The difference is so marked that while an ordinary good tracker will have difficulty in following them while he is on foot, and so can see them close . . . a really good one will unerringly follow them up on horse- or camel-back. Not only this, but, strange as it may sound

to the average white man whose meals are not dependent upon his ability to track an animal to its burrow or hiding place, the native will recognise the footprint of every individual of his acquaintance.

Whilst in matters such as tracking, which are concerned with their everyday life, and upon efficiency in which they actually depend for their livelihood, the natives show conspicuous ability, there are other directions in which they are as conspicuously deficient. This is perhaps shown most clearly in the matter of counting. At Alice Springs they occasionally count, sometimes using their fingers in doing so, up to five, but frequently anything beyond four is indicated by the word *oknirra,* meaning much or great. . . . Time is counted by "sleeps" or "moons," or phases of the moon, for which they have definite terms; longer periods they reckon by means of seasons. They have further definite words expressing particular times, such as morning before sunrise (*ingwuntagwunta*), evening (*ingwūrila*), yesterday (*tmirka*), day before yesterday (*tmirkairpĭna*), tomorrow (*ingwunta*), day after tomorrow (*ingwuntairpĭna*), in some days (*ingwuntalkura*), in a short time (*ingwuntanma*), in a long time (*ingwunta arbarmaninja*).

[*This is counting or time reckoning on a simple level, to suit the cultural needs of the Arunta.*]

The vocabulary is rich in terms denoting everything in their environment. Every animal and plant has its own name, each species, except the very small and insignificant ones, being recognised. Every feature in the landscape has its special name. . . .

In many respects their memory is phenomenal. Their mental powers are simply developed along the lines which are of service to them in their daily life.

However, to return to the native camp once more. (There are two distinct kinds of camps, the more or less temporary one made out in the bush, and the main central camp, of each local group, called *Tmara mbainda,* which is permanently located at one special spot and has a very definite organisation, so far as the sections of the tribe to which the various members belong are concerned.) If we examine their weapons and implements of various kinds—that is, those usually carried about—they will be found to be comparatively few in number and simple. A woman has always a *pitchi*—that is, a wooden trough varying in length from one to three feet, which has been hollowed out of the soft wood of the bean tree (*Erythrina vespertilio*), or it may be out of hard wood such as mulga or eucalypt. In this she carries food material, either balancing it on her head or holding it slung on to one hip by means of a strand of human hair or ordinary fur string across one shoulder. Not infrequently a small baby will be carried about in a *pitchi*. The only other implement possessed by a woman is what is popularly called a "yam stick," which is simply a digging stick or, to speak more correctly, a pick. The commonest form consists merely of a straight staff of wood with one or both ends bluntly pointed, and of such a size that it can easily be carried in the hand and used for digging in the ground. When at work, a woman will hold the pick in the right hand close to the lower end, and, alternately digging this into the ground with one hand, while with the other she scoops out the loosened earth, will dig down with surprising speed. In parts of the scrub, where the honey ants live, that form a very favourite food of the natives, acre after acre of hard sandy soil is seen to have been dug out, simply by the picks of the women in search

of the insect, until the place has the appearance of a deserted mining field where diggers have for long been at work "prospecting." Very often a small *pitchi* will be used as a shovel or scoop, to clear the earth out with, when it gets too deep to be thrown up merely with the hand, as the woman goes on digging deeper and deeper until at last she may reach a depth of some six feet or even more. Of course the children go out with the women, and from the moment that they can toddle about they begin to imitate the actions of their mother. In the scrub a woman will be digging up lizards or honey ants, while, close by, her small child will be at work, with its diminutive pick, taking its first lessons in what, if it be a girl, will be the main employment of her life.

So far as clothing is concerned, a woman is not much encumbered in her work. She usually wears around her neck one or more rings, each of which is commonly formed of a central strand of fur string, round which other strands are tightly wound till the whole has a diameter varying from a quarter to half an inch. The two ends of the central strand are left projecting so that they can be tied behind the neck, and the ring thus made is thickly coated with grease and red ochre. A similar kind of ring is often worn on the head, and, amongst the younger women especially, instead of, or perhaps in addition to, the hair neck ring, there may be worn a long string of the bright red beads of the bean tree. Each bead is bored through with a fire stick, and the pretty necklet thus made hangs round the neck in several coils, or may pass from each shoulder under the opposite armpit.

North of the Macdonnell Ranges the women wear small aprons formed of strands of fur string suspended from a waist string, and on the forehead they often wear an ornament composed of a small lump of porcupine-grass resin, into which are fixed either a few kangaroo incisor teeth or else a number of small bright red seeds. A short strand of string is fixed into the resin, and by means of this the ornament is tied to the hair, so that it just overhangs the forehead.

The men's weapons consist of stone knives, axes, shield, spears, boomerangs and spear thrower, all of which are constantly carried about when on the march. The shields, though they vary in size, are of similar design over practically the whole Central area. They are uniformly made of the light wood of the bean tree, so that their actual manufacture is limited to the more northern parts, where this tree grows. The Warramunga men are especially noted for their shields, which are traded far and wide over the Centre. Every Arunta man has at least one of them. Each has a distinctly convex outer and a concave inner surface, in the middle of which a space is hollowed out, leaving a bar running across in the direction of the length, which can be grasped by the hand.

In the Ilpirra, Arunta and Luritcha tribes the ordinary spear is about ten feet, or somewhat less, in length; the body is made of Tecoma wood and the tip of a piece of mulga, which is spliced on to the body and the splicing bound round with tendon. Close to the sharp point a small curved barb is attached by tendon, though in many this barb is wanting. A rarer form of spear is made out of heavier wood, such as the desert oak (*Casuarina Descaineana*), and this is fashioned out of one piece and has no barb.

The spear thrower is perhaps the most useful single thing which the native has. It is in the form of a hollowed-out piece of mulga from two feet to two feet six inches in length, with one end tapering gradually to a narrow handle, and the other, more suddenly, to a blunt point, to which is attached, by means of tendon, a short, sharp bit of hard wood which fits into a hole in the end of a spear. At the handle end is a lump of resin, into which is usually fixed a piece of sharp-edged flint or quartzite, which forms the most important cutting weapon of the native.

[*It may interest potential archaeologists to learn that flint blades can be hafted in resin or gum without any special shaping of the butt.*]

The boomerangs are not like the well-known ones that are met with in certain other parts and made so that when thrown they return to the sender. The Central Australian native does not appear to have hit upon this contrivance; or, at least, if he ever possessed any such, the art of making them is now completely lost; his boomerang has a widely open curve, and the flat blade lies wholly in one plane.

In addition to these weapons, a man will probably carry about with him a small wallet which is made simply of part of the skin of some animal, or perhaps of short strips of bark tied round with fur string. In this wallet he will carry a tuft or two of feathers for decoration, a spare bit or two of quartzite, a piece of red ochre, a kind of knout which has the form of a skein of string, and is supposed, by men and women alike, to be of especial use and efficacy in chastising women, and possibly he will have some charmed object, such as a piece of hair cut from a dead man's head and carefully ensheathed in hair or fur string. If the man be old it is not at all unlikely that he will have with him, hidden away from sight of the women, a sacred stick or bull-roarer, or even a sacred stone.

[*In some tribes they carry bull-roarers tied up in their long hair.*]

In the south of the Arunta tribe, the women weave bags out of string made of fur or vegetable fibre, in which they carry food, etc., but these are not found in the northern parts.

One of the most striking and characteristic features of the Central Australian implements and weapons is the coating of red ochre with which the native covers everything except his spear and spear thrower.

As regards clothing and ornaments, the man is little better off than the woman. His most constant article is a waist belt made of human hair—usually provided by his mother-in-law. On his forehead, stretched across from ear to ear, is a *chilara* or broad band made of parallel strands of fur string, and around his neck he will have one or more rings similar to those worn by the women. His hair will be well greased and red-ochred, and, in the Luritcha and southern Arunta, may be surmounted by a pad of emu feathers, worn in much the same way as a chignon, and tied on to the hair with fur string. If he be at all vain, he will have a long nose-bone ornament, with a rat tail or perhaps a bunch of cocka-too feathers at one end, his *chilara* will be covered with white pipe clay on which a design will be drawn in red ochre, and into either side of his chignon will be fastened a tuft of white or brightly-coloured feathers. His only other article of clothing, if such it can be called, is the small pubic tassel which, especially if it be covered with white pipe clay, serves rather as an ornament to attract the eye than as a covering.

[*You will note that the Arunta, like most outdoor peoples who form the subject matter of anthropology, use red ochre as body paint. It is hard to say how much this serves them as a protection and lubricant, in addition to its symbolic value.*]

Such are the ordinary personal belongings of the natives which they carry about with them on their wanderings.

When many natives are camped together for some time it can easily be seen that the camp is divided into two halves, each separated from the other by some such natural feature as a small creek, or very often, if the camping place be close to a hill, the one half will erect its *mia-mias* on the rising, and the other on the low ground. Every individual belongs to one or other of the four sections called Panunga, Bultara, Purula and Kumara, and in camp it will be found that the first two are always separated from the last two. (In the northern part of the tribe each of these four divisions is further divided into two subsections.) This is most clearly marked in the case of the main permanent camp of each local group.

During the daytime the women are sure to be out in search of food, while the men either go in pursuit of larger game, or else, if lazy and food be abundant, they will simply sleep all day, or perhaps employ their time in making or trimming up their weapons. When conditions are favourable everyone is cheerful and light-hearted, though every now and then a quarrel will arise, followed perhaps by a fight, which is usually accompanied by much noise and little bloodshed. On such occasions, if it be the women who are concerned, fighting clubs will be freely used and blows given and taken which would soon render an ordinary white woman *hors de combat,* but which have comparatively little effect upon the black women; the men usually look on with apparent complete indifference, but may sometimes interfere and stop the fight. If, however, two men are fighting, the mother and sisters of each will cluster round him, shouting at the top of their voices and dancing about with a peculiar and ludicrous high knee action, as they attempt to shelter him from the blows of his adversary's boomerang or fighting-club, with the result that they frequently receive upon their bodies the blows meant for the man whom they are attempting to shield.

[*Dr. Norman Tindale, of the Adelaide Museum, once told me that in the band he lived with for several months fights were commonest in the early morning before sunrise, when the people were cold and irritable.*]

As a general rule the natives are kindly disposed to one another—that is, of course, within the limits of their own tribe; and, where two tribes come into contact with one another on the borderland of their respective territories, there the same amicable feelings ar maintained between the members of the two. There is no such thing as one tribe being in a constant state of enmity with another so far as these Central tribes are concerned. Now and again, of course, fights do occur between the members of different local groups who may or may not belong to the same or to different tribes.

We have already spoken of the local groups as being composed mainly of individuals each of whom bears the name of some animal or plant; that is, each such group consists, to a large extent, but by no means exclusively, of men and women of, what is commonly spoken of as, a particular totem. . . . in these tribes, there is no such thing as the members of one totem being bound together in such a way that they must combine to fight on behalf of a member of the totem to which they belong. If, for example, a large number of natives are gathered together and a fight occurs, then at once the Panunga and Bultara men on the

one hand, and the Purula and Kumara on the other hand, make common cause. It is only, indeed, during the performance of certain ceremonies that the existence of a mutual relationship, consequent upon the possession of a common totemic name, stands out at all prominently. In fact, it is perfectly easy to spend a considerable time amongst the Arunta tribe without even being aware that each individual has a totemic name, whilst, on the other hand, the fact that every individual belongs to one or other of the sections, Panunga, Purula, etc., is soon apparent. This is associated with the fact that in these tribes, unlike what obtains in so many of the tribes whose organisation has hitherto been described, the totem has nothing whatever to do with regulating marriage, nor, again, does the child of necessity belong either to its mother's or to its father's totem.

[*Totems in this sense are objects which serve as symbols of the relations between the members of the group so designated. If you belong to an athletic club called "The Bears," you may wear a representation of a bear sewn on your sweater. If beyond this you and your fellow members swear that you will not kill or eat bears, since they are your brothers, and you make up some story about how the founder of your club was once helped or saved by a bear, and if after much repetition this story comes to be believed, then the bear is your club's totem.*

In Spencer and Gillen's account, it is not athletic clubs that have totems, but marriage classes. Supposing that everyone you knew was divided into four groups, the bears, wolves, eagles, and crows. The bears had to marry eagle women, wolves had to marry crow women, and so on. If you were a bear, your wife would have to be chosen from the eagles. How do you know which of the four you belong to?

You inherit your group membership from your mother. If you are a male bear, your son will be an eagle. The bears do not all get together at any special time for any particular purpose, any more than do all the people in your city who are named Johnson. A marriage class is not a natural group, or institution.]

In many works on anthropology it is not unusual to see a particular custom which is practised in one or more tribes quoted in general terms as the custom of "the Australian native." It is, however, essential to bear in mind that, whilst undoubtedly there is a certain amount in common as regards social organisation and customs amongst the Australian tribes, yet, on the other hand, there is great diversity. Some tribes, for example, count descent in the maternal line, others count it in the paternal line. In some tribes totems govern marriage, in others they have nothing to do with the question. In some tribes a tooth is knocked out at the initiation rite, in others the knocking out of the tooth may be practised, but it is not part of the initiation rite, and in others, again, the custom is not practised at all. In some tribes the initiation rite consists in circumcision and perhaps other forms of mutilation as well; in others this practice is quite unknown. . . .

[Tooth knocking, as practiced among the Arunta, is common to many primitive hunters and was practiced by early peoples in North Africa and Europe. We know this from their skulls.]

We may, in general terms, describe the Arunta native as being somewhat under the average height of an Englishman. His skin is of a dark chocolate colour, his nose is distinctly platyrhinic with the root deep set, his hair is abundant and wavy, and his beard, whiskers and moustache are well developed and usually frizzled and jet black. His supraorbital ridges are well developed, and above them the forehead slopes back with the hair removed so as artificially to increase its size. His body is well formed and very lithe, and he carries himself gracefully and remarkably erect with his head thrown well back.

Naturally, in the case of the women, everything depends upon their age; the younger ones—that is, those between fourteen and perhaps twenty—have decidedly well-formed figures, and, from their habit of carrying on the head *pitchis* containing food and water, they carry themselves often with remarkable grace. As is usual, however, in the case of savage tribes the drudgery of food collecting and childbearing tells upon them at an early age, and between twenty and twenty-five they begin to lose their graceful carriage; the face wrinkles, the breasts hang pendulous, and, as a general rule, the whole body begins to shrivel up, until, at about the age of thirty, all traces of an earlier well-formed figure and graceful carriage are lost, and the woman develops into what can only be called an old and wrinkled hag. . . .

A very striking feature of both men and women are the body scars in the form of great ridges of keloid tissue.

Every individual has a certain number of them raised on his body and arms, but very rarely on the back. They are made by cutting the skin with a piece of flint, or, at the present day, glass is used when obtainable, and into the wound thus made ashes are rubbed or the down of the eaglehawk, the idea being, so they say, to promote healing, and not, though the treatment probably has this effect, to aid in the raising of a scar. In some cases they may stretch right across the chest or abdomen. As a general rule the scars are both more numerous and longer on the men than on the women, but no definite distinction can be drawn in this respect. . . .

There is, apart from ornament, no special meaning, so far as their form or arrangement is concerned, to be attached at the present day to those cicatrices, nor could we discover anything in their customs and traditions leading to the belief that they had ever had any deeper meaning. (Certain of them, both on men and women, are made at special times in connection with initiatory and mourning ceremonies.) Vague statements have been made with regard to marks such as these, to the effect that they indicate, in some way, the particular division of the tribe to which each individual belongs. . . . [However,] so far as the Arunta and other Central tribes are concerned, they have no significance at the present day as indicative of either tribe, class, section or totemic group.

In addition to these, every man will be marked, usually on the left shoulder, but sometimes on the right as well, with irregular scars which may form prominent cicatrices, and are the result of self-inflicted wounds made on the occasion of the mourning ceremonies which are attendant upon the death of individuals who stand in certain definite relationships to him, such, for example, as his *Irundera* or father-in-law, actual or tribal. Not infrequently the men's thighs will be marked with scars indicative of wounds inflicted with a stone knife during a fight.

Just like the men, the women on the death of certain relatives cut themselves, and these cuts often leave scars behind. Sometimes writers have described these scars and regarded them as evidence of the cruel treatment of the women by the men, whereas, as a matter of fact, by far the greater number of them, which are often a prominent feature on a woman's body, are the indications of self-inflicted wounds, and of them she is proud, as they are the visible evidence of the fact that she has properly mourned for her dead. . . .

In some cases both men and women knock out one of the upper incisor teeth, but this is purely a matter of individual choice, and has nothing to do with initiation. It is most frequently done amongst the northeastern Arunta in what is known as the Quatcha or water country.

As a general rule, both men and women are well nourished, but naturally this depends to a large extent on the nature of the season. When travelling and hungry the plan is adopted of tightening the waist belt; indeed, this is worn so tight that it causes the production of a loose flap of skin, which is often a prominent feature on the abdomens of the older men. . . .

In regard to their character, it is, of course, impossible to judge them from a white man's standard. In the matter of morality their code differs radically from ours, but it cannot be denied that their conduct is governed by it, and that any known breaches are dealt with both surely and severely. In very many cases there takes place what the white man, not seeing beneath the surface, not unnaturally describes as secret murder, but, in reality, revolting though such slaughter may be to our minds at the present day, it is simply exactly on a par with the treatment accorded to witches not so very long ago in European countries. Every case of such secret murder, when one or more men stealthily stalk their prey with the object of killing him, is in reality the exacting of a life for a life, the accused person being indicated by the so-called medicine man as one who has brought about the death of another man by magic, and whose life must therefore be forfeited.[1] It need hardly be pointed out what a potent element this custom has been in keeping down the numbers of the tribe. No such thing as natural death is realised by the native: a man who dies has of necessity been killed by some other man, or perhaps even by a woman, and sooner or later that man or woman will be attacked. In the normal condition of the tribe every death meant the killing of at least one other individual. . . .

[*The discovery and identification of the criminal is the work of the second kind of medicine man or shaman—the diviner. He is a specialist whom we have not previously encountered.*]

With regard to their treatment of one another, it may be said that this is marked on the whole by considerable kindness—that is, of course, in the case of members of friendly groups, with every now and then the perpetration of acts of cruelty. The women are certainly not treated usually with anything which could be called excessive harshness. They have, as amongst other savage tribes, to do a considerable part, but by no means all, of the work of the camp, but, after all, in a good season this does not amount to very much, and in a bad season men and women suffer alike, and of what food there is they get their share. If, however, rightly or wrongly, a man thinks his wife guilty of a breach of the laws which govern marital relations, then undoubtedly the treatment of the woman is marked by brutal and often revolting severity. To their children they are, we may say uniformly, with very rare exceptions, kind and

considerate, carrying them, the men as well as the women taking part in this, when they get tired on the march, and always seeing that they get a good share of any food. Here again it must be remembered that the native is liable to fits of sudden passion, and in one of these, hardly knowing what he does, he may treat a child with great severity. There is no such thing as doing away with aged or infirm people; on the contrary, such are treated with especial kindness, receiving a share of the food which they are unable to procure for themselves.

Infanticide is undoubtedly practised, but, except on rare occasions, the child is killed immediately on birth, and then only when the mother is, or thinks she is, unable to rear it, owing to there being a young child whom she is still feeding, and with them suckling is continued for it may be several years. They believe that the spirit part of the child goes back at once to the particular spot from whence it came, and can be born again at some subsequent time even of the same woman. Twins, which are of extremely rare occurrence, are usually killed immediately as something which is unnatural; but there is no ill-treatment of the mother, who is not thought any the less of. We cannot find out what, exactly, lies at the root of this dislike of twins in the case of the Arunta and other tribes. Possibly it is to be explained on the simple ground that the parent feels a not altogether unrighteous anger that two spirit individuals should think of entering the body of the woman at one and the same time, when they know well that the mother could not possibly rear them both, added to which the advent of twins is a very infrequent event, and the native always has a dread of anything which appears strange and out of the common. In connection with this it may be noted

---

[1] At the final mourning ceremonies of an old man held recently, when the men were leaving the grave one of the older ones jumped on to it and shouted out, "We have not found the Kurdaitcha who killed you yet, but we will find him and kill him."

that on the very rare occasions on which the child is born at a very premature stage as the result of an accident, nothing will persuade them that it is an undeveloped human being; they are perfectly convinced that it is the young of some other animal, such as a kangaroo, which has by mistake got inside the woman.

[*The Arunta keep their old people alive by giving them special food and care. They can afford to. Distances are not as great here as in Lower California, and cold presents no problem. If the population is to be kept down, it is by infanticide.*]

On rare occasions, children of a few years of age are killed, the object of this being to feed a weakly but elder child, who is supposed thereby to gain the strength of the killed one.

When times are favourable the black fellow is as light-hearted as possible. . . .

There is, however, in these, as in other savage tribes, an undercurrent of anxious feeling which, though it may be stilled and, indeed, forgotten for a time, is yet always present. In his natural state the native is often thinking that some enemy is attempting to harm him by means of evil magic, and, on the other hand, he never knows when a medicine man in some distant group may not point him out as guilty of killing some one else by magic. It is, however, easy to lay too much stress upon this, for here again we have to put ourselves into the mental attitude of the savage, and must not imagine simply what would be our own feelings under such circumstances. It is not right, by any means, to say that the Australian native lives in constant dread of the evil magic of an enemy. The feeling is always, as it were, lying dormant and ready to be called up at once by any strange or suspicious sound if he be alone, especially at nighttime, in the bush; but, on the other hand, just like a child, he can with ease forget anything unpleasant and enter perfectly into the enjoyment of the present moment. Granted always that his food supply is abundant, it may be said that the life of the Arunta native is, for the most part, a pleasant one. . . .

The preceding selection was from Spencer and Gillen's introduction. In order to give the student some idea of the details of a ceremony, I append their famous account of the Witchetty Grub ritual.

Intichiuma (Mbanbiuma) of the Udnirringita or Witchetty Grub Totem.—When the ceremony is to be performed by the Choritja group at Alice Springs the men assemble in the main camp, and then those who are about to take part in the proceedings leave the camp quietly, slinking away to a meeting place not far off, the women and men who do not belong to the totem not being supposed to know that they are gone.[1] A few, perhaps two or three, of the older men of the totem stay in camp, and next morning they ask the men who do not belong to the totem to return early from their hunting. Every man leaves his weapons behind, because he must go quite unarmed and without any decoration of any kind; even the hair girdle, the

[1] This account refers to the ceremony as we saw it enacted in 1896. The name of the ceremony in the Choritja group is Intichiuma, and as this is the most elaborate of these ceremonies known and was the first to be described, the local name is retained. It is the exact equivalent of *Mbanbiuma* in other groups.

one constant article of clothing worn by men, must be left in camp. They all walk in single file except the Alatunja,[2] who sometimes takes the lead and at others walks by the side of the column to see that the line is kept. On no account must any of the men, except the very old ones, eat any kind of food until the whole ceremony is over; anything which may be caught in the way of game has to be handed over to the old men. The procession usually starts late in the afternoon, so that it is dusk by the time that a special camping ground near to the Emily Gap is reached, and here they lie down for the night.

At daylight the party begins to pluck twigs from the gum trees at the mouth of the Gap, and every man carries one in each hand except the Alatunja, who carries nothing save a small *pitchi* or wooden trough,[3] which represents the *Meimba* in which the Inkata carried his store of *Kuruna* and Churinga in the Alchera. Walking again in single file, they follow—led by the Alatunja —the path traversed by the celebrated Intwailiuka, the great leader of the witchetty grubs in the Alchera, until they come to what is called the *Ilthura oknirra,* which is placed high up on the western wall of the Gap. In this, which is a shallow cave, a large block of quartzite lies, and around it are some small rounded stones. The large mass represents the *Maegwa*—that is, the adult animal. The Alatunja begins to sing and taps the stone with his *Meimba,* while all the other men tap

[2] In the Choritja group, which was a very large and important one amongst the Northern Arunta, the head man was called *Alatunja.* This is the equivalent of the terms *Inkata* and *Chantchwa* used in other parts.

[3] This is not especially made for the purpose, but is an ordinary small *pitchi*, such as the women use for scooping the earth out of burrows, and is always provided by a daughter of the Alatunja.

it with their twigs, chanting songs as they do so, the burden of which is an invitation to the animal to lay eggs. When this has gone on for a short time they tap the smaller stones, which are *Churinga unchima*—that is, they represent the eggs of the *Maegwa.* The Alatunja then takes up one of the smaller stones and strikes each man in the stomach with it, saying, *Unta murna oknirra ulquinna* (You have eaten much food). When this has been done the stone is dropped and the Alatunja strikes the stomach of each man with his forehead, an operation which is called *atnitta ulpailima.* Leaving the *Ilthura,* the men descend from the range to the bed of the creek in the Gap, and stop under the rock called *Alknalinta*—that is, the decorated eyes—where, in the Alchera, Intwailiuka used to cook, pulverise and eat the grub.

[*"Alchera." According to the Arunta their ancestors performed marvelous deeds in olden times. But their concept of time is different from ours; the Alchera not only preceded the present era, but also coexists with it; it is still going on.*]

The Alatunja strikes the rock with his *Meimba,* and each man does the same with his twigs, while the older men again chant invitations to the animal to come from all directions and lay eggs. At the base of the rock, buried deeply in the sand, there is supposed to be a very large *Maegwa* stone.

[*In this ritual they act out the whole cycle of the life of a grub. They are assisting nature, participating in its actions. To say that they are trying to increase the food supply is too simple a rationalization. Some of the increase ceremonies which have been observed since Spencer and Gillen's day have nothing to do with food. What they are actually doing, although they themselves may not know it, is to reenforce*] *their own relationships with each other by the symbolic mechanism of repeating the acts of the Alchera heroes, with whom they all feel identified.*]

Certain drawings . . . on the rock face on the western side of the Gap represent the *Churinga ilpintira* and *Ilkinia* of the Udnirringita *Knanja,* and were originally placed there by Numbakulla when he wandered over the country "making" it and settling upon *Knanja* places. Others represent feet, shoulders and bodies of Alchera ancestors. One design in particular . . . indicates the position of the camp where the Alchera women painted themselves and then, as is suggested by the great slanting line, peered upwards, watching the Inkata Intwailiuka performing *Intichiuma,* because, in the Alchera, women were allowed to see and even perform sacred ceremonies.

It was at this spot that Intwailiuka used to stand while he threw up the face of the rock numbers of *Churinga unchima,* which rolled down again to his feet; accordingly the Alatunja does the same with some of the Churinga which have been brought from the storehouse close by. While he is doing this the other members of the party run up and down the face of the rocky ledge, singing all the time. The stones roll down into the bed of the creek and are carefully gathered together and replaced in the store.

The men now fall once more into single file and march in silence to the nearest *Ilthura,* which is about a mile and a half away from the Gap in the direction of Alice Springs. The Alatunja goes into the hole, which is four or five feet deep, and scoops out with his *Meimba* any dirt which may have accumulated in it, singing as he does so a low monotonous chant about the *Uchaqua.* Soon he lays bare two stones which have been carefully covered up in the base of the hole. The larger one is called *Churinga uchaqua,* and represents the chrysalis stage from which the adult animal emerges; the smaller is one of the *Churinga unchima* or eggs. When they are exposed to view, songs referring to the *Uchaqua* are sung, and the stones are solemnly handled and cleaned with the palm of the hand. One by one the men now go into the *Ilthura,* and the Alatunja, lifting up the *Churinga uchaqua,* strikes the stomach of each man with it, saying again, "You have eaten much food." Finally, dropping the stone, he butts (this is the only word expressive of the action) at each man in the abdomen with his forehead. He also rubs their stomachs with the *Churinga unchima.* . . .

There are altogether some ten of these *Ilthura,* in each one of which is a *Churinga uchaqua,* and each *Ilthura* is visited in turn by the party and the same ceremony is repeated.

When the round of the *Ilthura* has been made and the same ceremony enacted at each one, then a start is made for the home camp. When within a mile or so of the latter they stop and decorate themselves with material which has been purposely brought to the spot. Hair string is tied round their heads, and *Chilara* or forehead bands are put on, beneath which twigs of the *Udnirringa* [4] bush are fixed so that they hang downwards. Nose bones are thrust through the nasal septum, and rat tails and topknots of cockatoo feathers are worn in the hair. The Alatunja is but little decorated; he has only the *Chilara* across his forehead, and the *Lalkira* or nose bone. Under his arm he carries the *Meimba,* and in his hand a twig of the *Udnirringa* bush. While the men walk along

[4] The totemic animal takes its name from this shrub, on which the grub feeds. It is a species of Eremophila.

they keep their twigs in constant motion, much as if they were brushing off flies. The totem *Ilkinia* or sacred design is painted on the body of each man with red ochre and pipe clay, and the latter is also used to paint the face, except for the median line of red. When the decorations are complete a start is again made, all walking in single file, the Alatunja at the head with his *Meimba* under his arm. Every now and then they stop, and the old Alatunja, placing his hand above his eyes, as if to shade the latter, strikes an attitude as he peers away into the distance. He is supposed to be looking out for the women who were left in camp. . . . The old man, who had been left in charge at the camp during the absence of the party, is also on the lookout for the return of the latter. While the men have been away he has built, away from the main camp, a long, narrow wurley, which is called *Umbana,* and is intended to represent the chrysalis case from which the *Maegwa* or fully developed insect emerges. Near to this spot all those who have not been taking part in the ceremony assemble, standing behind the *Umbana.* Those men who belong to the other moiety of the tribe—that is, to the Purula and the Kumara—are about forty or fifty yards away, sitting down in perfect silence; and the same distance further back the Panunga and Bultara women are standing, with the Purula and Kumara women sitting down amongst them. The first-named women are painted with the totem Ilkinia of red and white lines; the second are painted with lines of white faintly tinged with red. When the old man at length sees the party approaching he steps out and sings:

"*Ilkna pung kwai, Yaalan ni nai, Yu mulk la, Naan tai yaa lai.*"

The Alatunja, as the party comes slowly along, stops every now and then to peer at the women. Finally all reach the *Umbana* and enter it. When all are inside they begin to sing of the animal in its various stages, and of the *Alknalinta* stone and the great *Maegwa* at its base. As soon as the performers enter the wurley, the Purula and Kumara men and women lie face downwards, and in this position they must remain until they receive permission to arise. They are not allowed to stir under any pretext whatever. The singing continues for some time; then the Alatunja, in a squatting position, shuffles out of the *Umbana,* gliding slowly along over the space in front, which has been cleared for a distance of some yards. He is followed by all the men, who sing of the emerging of the *Maegwa* from its case, the *Umbana.* Slowly they shuffle out and back again until all are once more in the wurley, when the singing ceases and food and water are brought to them by the old man who had remained in camp and built the *Umbana.* This, it must be remembered, is the first food or drink which they have partaken of since they originally left the camp, as, except in the case of the very old men, it is imperative that the ceremony be carried out without any eating or drinking on the part of the participants. When it is dusk they leave the wurley, and go round to the side away from that on which the Purula and Kumara men are lying, so that, to a certain extent, they are hidden from their view. A large fire is lighted, and round this they sit, singing of the witchetty grub. This is kept up till some little time before daybreak, and during all that time the women of the right moiety must stand peering about into the darkness to see if the women of the other moiety, over whom they are supposed to keep watch, continue to lie down. They also peer about, watching the *Intichiuma* party just as the women did in the Alchera.

Suddenly the singing ceases, and the fire is quickly put out by the Alatunja. This is the signal for the release of the Purula and Kumara men and women, who jump to their feet, and these men and all the women at once run away to the main camp. The *Intichiuma* party remains at the wurley until daylight, when the men go near to the *Ungunja*,[5] make a fire and strip themselves of all their ornaments, throwing away their *Udnirringa* twigs. When all the *Uliara, Imitnya, Lalkira* and cockatoo feathers are removed, the Alatunja says, "Our *Intichiuma* is finished, the *Mulyanuka* must have these things or else our *Intichiuma* would not be successful, and some harm would come to us." They all say, "Yes, yes, certainly"; and the Alatunja calls to the *Mulyanuka* (*i.e.* men of the Purula-Kumara moiety), who are at the *Ungunja*—that is, the men's camp—to come up, and the things are divided amongst them, after which the old man, who before brought them food, goes to the various camps and collects a considerable quantity of vegetable food which is given to him by the women. This is brought back and cooked and eaten by the fire, where they still remain. During the afternoon the old man again visits the camp, and brings

back with him some red ochre and the fur string which belongs to the various members of the party, and, just before sundown, the old men rub red ochre over their bodies and over those of the younger men, thus obliterating the *Ilkinia* and the painting on the face. The men then put on their arm strings, etc., and return to their respective camps, and with this the main part of the ceremony is brought to a close. When all is over, the *Meimba* or *pitchi* of the Alatunja is held in great regard, and the Panunga and Bultara women enjoy the privilege, each in turn, of carrying it about.

The Udnirringita includes what may be called three subtotems associated with three allied species of grubs called Unjailga, Yippija and Alkneja. The Udnirringita Alatunja is the head of the group, Yippija and Alkneja having no separate Alatunjas or *Intichiuma* ceremonies; they are, as it were, included in the main one. The Udnirringita Alatunja, at times, requests the Unjailga head man to perform the ceremony, the decorations and details of which are the same as if it were performed by the former himself. After the ceremony, in each case, all four kinds of grubs are supposed to increase.

It is clear from Spencer and Gillen's account that the Arunta have worked out a very stable way of living which gives them the maximum chance of survival on their landscape. Their "goodness of fit" to the earth, with its plants, its animals, its supplies of flint for knives and of ochre for ceremonies, is as perfect as anything in nature. We must remember that time spent in ceremonial is not time wasted, for it is the mechanism by which people maintain their relationships with one another which in turn makes it possible for them to live off the land in the most efficient manner possible.

One thing that Spencer and Gillen did not stress, for they probably did not at that time have the information, was the variability of the annual rainfall. In Australia it is not simply the amount of rain that falls each year that makes the

[5] The *Ungunja* is a special part of the main camp where the men assemble, and near to which no woman may go. In the same way the women have their special part, called *Lukwurra*, near to which no man may go.

difference between much food and little, dense and sparse populations. In some places, as around Port Darwin, much rain falls, but it falls all at once, floods the land, and flows and evaporates away. So the seasonal variation is a second factor. A third is the variation between wet and dry years. In a country where this kind of variability is great, a number of bands may feed well off a piece of landscape for two or three years, and the next year not a drop will fall. The roots will wither, and the kangaroos hop away. This is the time when people need kin in distant places, places where there has been rain, and that is why it is so important to have regular interband meetings and extensions of kinship by means of marriage classes. Your reception will be much more cordial if you seek refuge among kin and among persons with whom you have been initiated, than if you throw yourself on strangers.

Another equally important reason for interband relations is trade—pituri, ochre, spear shafts, soft wood for shields, and flints are carried hundreds of miles in Australia, since each has its special region of abundance. In order to let these articles pass, peace must be maintained.

In these intercamp meetings, we come to the threshold of institutions larger than the simple band, but that threshold is not crossed. The Inkatas at the meetings maintain their sovereign rights, as did Roosevelt, Churchill, and Stalin at their historic meetings. The people go home, once the ceremonies are over, like Yale students from a visit to Cambridge after the annual football game. International good will has been built up, but union is not now.

Level Three

The Rise of Specialists and Multiple Institutions

8

The Kurnai of Gippsland: Food Gathering in a Rich Environment

IF YOU will look at a modern population-density map of Australia, you will find that the white people are now concentrated along the eastern seaboard and the southeastern shores. They live where there is the most rainfall, where its seasonal distribution is most equable, and where approximately the same amount falls each year. In aboriginal times also this area was most densely populated. The best country, from the food-gathering point of view, was the coastal region from Melbourne to Brisbane. Varying from fifty to a hundred miles in width, it is separated by the highlands and steppes to the north and west by a mountain chain called the Great Dividing Range.

This coastal region is part plain and part hills; part forest and part parkland. The most favored section of it all is Gippsland, to the east of Melbourne and west of Cape Howe, at the very southeastern corner of Australia. This country held the densest native population in Australia, except for the region on the banks of the Murray River, near its mouth.

The chief reason for this density, which probably reaches one person per square mile, was the abundance of water in a temperate, equable climate. Thirty to forty inches of rain fall every year in Gippsland. It rains every month of the year, and the annual variation (variation between years) is small. Up in the mountains in back of the coastal region as much as sixty inches fall in some places, much of it in the form of snow. This water runs off through Gippsland, following the courses of many streams and forming a succession of ponds and marshes. Down near the sea the coast is lined with long white sandy beaches and a whole succession of salt lagoons formed by waves breaking over the sandbars at high tide.

Inland, toward the mountains, the trees are high and thick-boled, and animal life scarce; here there is little food. But nearer the coast the trees are smaller, and the strong winds off the ocean blow many of them down. Patches of grass are common, and there is more feed for animals. Vegetable foods are abundant—including lily bulbs in the fresh-water streams and swamps; ferns, the tender shoots of which can be eaten raw; several kinds of berries; and grass seeds. Any native looking for grubs can find a fallen tree without much search, and by simply lifting off the bark will find dozens of slow-crawling pupae, white and fat, in the rotten wood. Bees, wasps, and ants are numerous, and much wild honey may be had for the climbing. Edible snakes and various kinds of lizards, frogs, and terrapins are easily caught. No one need go hungry in such a country.

In the salt lagoons as in the open sea, oysters, crayfish, squid, and fish abound, including red snappers and several kinds of game fish. Black swans, which may

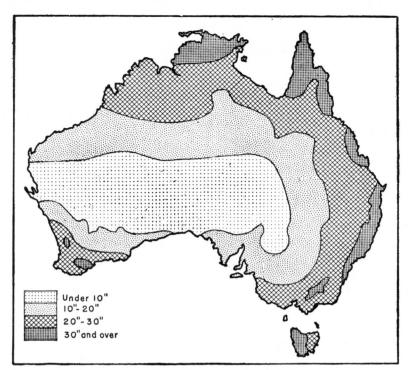

Australia. Mean annual rainfall.

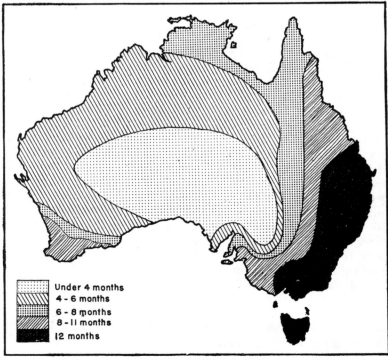

Australia. Number of months with 1 inch or more rainfall per year.

238

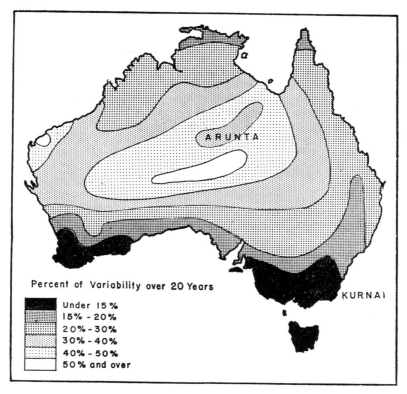

Australia.   Rainfall reliability.

still be seen in flocks of several hundreds, make these inland waters their home. Pelicans too are permanent residents, while tens of thousand of migratory ducks, flying all the way from Siberia, end their annual trip at Gippsland. All of these birds lay eggs, and these eggs form an important part of the aboriginal menu. To it may be added the usual, and some unusual, Australian mammals—kangaroos, wallabies, opossums, and koalas (Australian teddy bears)—as well as the famous duckbilled platypus.

The rainfall is as great in Gippsland as in Eastern Massachusetts or on the coast of Georgia; the annual temperature range so slight that barefooted savages, if they keep out of the mountains in the wintertime, can go hunting all the year round; and food is equally abundant at different seasons. That is why single "tribes," the largest local political unit, which averaged as many as three thousand persons each, could live in territories as small as 25 by 35 miles. Since the variation in food supply from season to season was so little, these people were able to maintain permanent villages, and a hunter seldom needed to sleep away from home for more than a few nights at a time.

With permanent villages, in which old people and children could live the year round, it was possible to accumulate material possessions. Important among these were warm opossum-skin robes, softened by slitting the skin in various patterns with a flint knife and sewing them together. Grass seeds and lily bulbs would keep for some time, as would swans' eggs. There was no need to eat all of one's food on the day that it was gathered.

With permanent villages, it was worth while to take some care in house building, and these people made houses of fallen logs, easily stripped bark, and earth. Such a house would hold an entire family.

It will be better to let someone else tell this story, someone who was there and saw it. That man was A. W. Howitt, whose book, *The Native Tribes of Southeast Australia,** is just as great a document as that of Spencer and Gillen for the desert-dwelling Arunta.

. . . . It is in the coastal districts that one finds the most favourable conditions for the native tribes, though at the head of the Great Australian Bight the desert extends nearly to the sea, for the Nullarbor Plains are waterless, and beyond them the desert [extends] to where Sturt Creek ends in the northern parts of West Australia. Yet the Yerkla-mining people who live there are better off than those who inhabit the desert, having not only the land, but also the sea, from which to procure food. The advantages of the coast lands increase on coming eastwards; and from the Gulf of St. Vincent the country afforded ample food supplies, from the lakes at the Murray mouth and the country bordering on them and the sea. Still more favourable conditions existed in Victoria, and especially in Gippsland, where again extensive lakes and adjacent country afforded an unfailing supply of fish and game. The tribes of the New South Wales coast enjoyed similar advantages, the principal difference being that the climate becomes warmer on proceeding northwards, and the food supplies more varied in character, until on the Queensland coast the tropical influence is met with. For instance, where the scope of my work ends, the blacks hunt the tree kangaroo, and ponds and lagoons furnish edible plants in abundance. The high mountains of the Dividing Range, which commences in

Central Victoria, and its accompanying tablelands, extend northwards the whole length of the coast. In many parts they isolated the tribes of the coast from those inland, though there were tracks here and there by which friendly meetings or hostile raids took place between some of the tribes. The character of the coastal country itself also frequently isolated the tribes to some extent from their immediate neighbours. . . .

I use the word "tribe" as meaning a number of people who occupy a definite tract of country, who recognise a common relationship and have a common speech, or dialects of the same. The tribes-people recognise some common bond which distinguishes them from other tribes, usually a tribal name, which may be their word for "man," that is, an aboriginal of Australia. . . .

In all the native tribes of Australia there are geographical divisions of the community determined by locality, and also divisions of the tribe on which the marriage regulations are based. The former are distinguished by certain local names, while the latter are denoted by class names, or totems, and more frequently by both class names and totems. . . .

An entire community, tribe, nation, or whatever it may be termed, is divided socially into two exogamous intermarrying moieties, which for shortness may be designated A and B. In

* London, 1904. Reprinted by permission of The Macmillan Company, publishers.

some parts of Australia these two principal moieties or classes have become divided, each into two sub-classes. In Central and Northern Australia, there has been a further division of the sub-classes, resulting in eight sub-classes, and the same process has taken place in Northern Queensland. . . .

As I have said, the tribe is also divided into a number of lesser groups, say X, Y, Z, etc. (I take these for the sake of convenience, but there may be many more) ; these divisions of the tribe are local, and therefore differ essentially from the classes or totems, which are groups of the social organisation. In order to prevent confusion between the lesser division of each of these different organisations of the tribe, the term "clan" is used for the subdivision of a tribe which has descent in the male line, and "horde" for that in which there is female descent. The clan and the horde are each therefore a geographical division of a tribe. . . .

In order to make clear the definition of the terms I use, the following is given:

1. Nation is used to signify a group of tribes.

2. Tribe is used in the sense [just] given.

3. Horde, the primary geographical division of a tribe having female descent, for instance, the Ngadi-ngani below.

4. Clan, the primary geographical division of a tribe with descent in the male line, for instance, the Krauatungalung.

The alliance of the tribes forming the nation comes into view on the occasion of one of the great ceremonies being held; all the tribes which form the nation may attend the ceremonies and take part in them, a bond which holds the hordes or clans of a tribe together. . . .

The Bunurong tribe, whose eastern bounds were at Anderson's Inlet, were there met by the Kurnai, also a coast tribe, which occupied almost the whole of what is now Gippsland. This great area, 200 miles in length by about 70 in width, lies between the seacoast and the Dividing Range. It was divided into five portions, each of which was inhabited by a clan of the Kurnai. These five clans spoke three dialects, more or less unintelligible to each other. The dialects spoken were Nulit by the Brayakaulung, the Brataualung, and the Tatungalung, the Muk-thang or "excellent" speech by the Brabralung, and Thangquai or "broad" speech by the Krauatungalung.

The clans were divided into lesser groups, each of which had a special name, derived in some cases from their principal locality, while in other cases it was the local group which gave the name to the locality. For instance, a large section of the Brataua clan lived on the upper waters of the Avon River, and were called Kutbuntaura or fire carriers. This name was also that of their country, with the suffix *wurk,* meaning "land" or "country."

Such large sections were again divided and subdivided, each subdivision having its own tract of hunting and food ground, until the unit was a small group of kindred, frequently an old man, his sons, married or unmarried, with their respective wives and children. Such an instance was that of the *Bunjil-baul,* or men of the island, who lived on Raymond Island in Lake King, and who not only claimed that island, but also all the swans' eggs laid upon it, as their own exclusive property. Although it was separated from the mainland, which was the country of the Brabralung, by merely a narrow channel, and from that of the Tatungalung by several miles of lake, the *Bunjil-baul* claimed to be "partly Tatungalung, and partly Brabralung, but mostly Tatungalung."

Each male received the name of *Bunjil-baul* at his initiation. The oldest male of the family had authority over the others, but they were all collectively *Bunjil-baul*.

Any stranger who took swans' eggs on this island without the permission of one of the *Bunjil-baul* had to fight them, but there was no prohibition against friendly tribesmen who might visit the island taking any other kind of food or game.

Taking such a family as the tribal unit of the Kurnai, it was the aggregation of such families which formed what may be called a division, inhabiting a larger area, and the aggregate of the divisions formed the clan. . . .

The Narrinyeri tribe was divided into eighteen local clans, each inhabiting a different tract of country. That is to say, in each of fourteen there was one totem only; in three there were three each, and in one there were two. . . .

The Kurnai is a tribe without class divisions. . . . the local organisation . . . controls marriage in so far that it can only properly take place between members of certain reciprocal localities. . . .

At the time when Gippsland was settled after 1842 the oldest man in the Kutwut division of the Brataua clan, who lived on the Albert River, said that the fathers of his people came from the west, from a country where there were a great number of blacks. A Wurunjerri legend relates that long ago Loän, who may be described, in the words of Mr. Andrew Lang, as a "non-natural man," wandered from the Yarra River, following the migration of the swans, first to the inlets of Western Port Bay and then to Corner Inlet, between Wilson's Promontory and the mainland where he took up his abode. This is far within the country of the Kurnai, whose legends also speak of him living there with his wife Loäntuka, as the guardian of the Brataua clan.

To judge from the similarities of language, from tradition, and from common customs, the Kurnai may be considered an offshoot of the Kulin, and to have probably carried with them the Kulin class system. If the Kurnai use of the name Bunjil points to the former name of a class, then the reverence which they show to Ngarugal, the crow, may also indicate the second class name. The crow is said to be the friend of the Kurnai. It was wrong to kill a crow, and doing so, they thought, would bring on stormy weather. Tankowillin, a man whom I have mentioned elsewhere, said when I spoke to him about this belief, "I know that I would not kill and eat crow, but I have often eaten his children without his doing me any harm." Crows have a habit of following people in the bush, flying from tree to tree, and peering down at the person followed while doing so; the Kurnai say that a crow understands their language, and answers their questions by its caw, which is their affirmative *ngaa*.

Each Kurnai received the name of some marsupial, bird, reptile, or fish, from his father, when he was about ten years old, or at initiation. A man would say, pointing to the creature in question, "That is your *thundung;* do not hurt it." In two cases I know of, he said, "It will be yours when I am dead." The term *thundung* means "elder brother," and, while the individual was the protector of his *thundung,* it also protected its "younger brother," the man, by warning him in dreams of approaching danger, or, by coming towards him in its bodily shape, it assisted him, as in the case of the man Binjil-bataluk mentioned elsewhere, or was appealed to by song charms to relieve sickness.

The *thundung* of the Kurnai known to me are as follows:

Narut	wombat
Jirha	kangaroo
Barlajan	platypus
Gliun	water-hen
Blit-buring	a small bird
Gwanamurrung	eagle hawk
Thurung	tiger snake
Bibing	sea salmon
Burra	small conger eel
Noy yang	large conger eel

The *thundung* are clearly the equivalents of the totems of other tribes, and form a vestigiary survival of a class system. . . .

. . . the Kurnai have . . . totems, that is, certain marsupials, and birds, fish, and reptiles, which are the *thundung* (elder brothers) of men, and *bauung* (elder sisters) of women. Under the influence of male descent these names are restricted to certain localities, and not scattered throughout the tribal country. As I have indicated in the chapter on marriage, a man brings his wife to his own locality; she does not transmit her *bauung* name to her children, but he transmits his. The names are therefore perpetuated from generation to generation in the same locality, and in this manner have become localised. In the sense, however, that they are common to the members of certain families in the same tract of country, they are still group totems.

Usually the *bramung* or younger brother of one of these totems will not injure or kill his *thundung,* nor willingly see another person do so, but there are exceptions to this; for instance, men of the conger-eel totem at the Snowy River eat it; and I have known a man of the kangaroo totem eat that animal. . . .

There are two birds which the Kurnai reverence: the emu-wren and the superb warbler, which are the sex totems, and no man would think under any circumstances of injuring his "elder brother," *Yiirung,* or any woman her "elder sister," *Djiitgun.* Thus, as to these sex totems, the usual totemic taboo exists. The totem is the protector of the individual, and the individual protects his totem. . . .

The Kurnai had no class divisions. And although there are survivals of totems in this tribe, they do not affect marriage. Under the influence of paternal descent these animal names are segregated into localities somewhat in the manner that the class names of the Wurunjerri and Bunurong tribes were.

This is easily seen when one considers that a man brought his wife into his own district, excepting in the occasionally occurring cases among the Kurnai where a man joined the clan of his wife and lived in her district.

But in taking her to his own district she did not transmit her name to her children, but he did, and as this would be done generation after generation under paternal descent, the *thundung* names (totems) became fixed in definite localities.

As, moreover, a man could not marry a woman belonging to his own district, he necessarily married some woman whose *thundung* name differed from his, thus still following unconsciously the exogamous rule.

There was no betrothal in this tribe, nor was there an exchange of sisters by those men who married, except in such rare cases as to prove the rule. Therefore there was no social organisation in this tribe in the sense in which I use the term. . . .

Marriage was forbidden in the division, but not always in the clan or tribe. . . . It was also a general rule that those living on the course of the same river were considered to be too nearly related to each other to marry. . . . The rule was that the divisions mutually obtained wives from each other, where the right of intermarriage existed. Yet to this general rule I have found an exception. Gliunkong, the survivor of the Bunjil-baul, who lived on Baul, now called Raymond Island, in Lake King, Gippsland, said to me that they did not travel far from the lakes for wives, but that men from distant places had to come to Baul for theirs. . . .

The Kurnai man, with the rare exceptions mentioned, could acquire a wife in one way only, namely, by running off with her secretly, and with her own consent. Marriage, therefore, was by elopement, and this was brought about in different ways. A young man who was so fortunate as to have an unmarried sister, and who also had a friend similarly provided, might arrange with him that they should take each other's sisters, these being of course consenting parties, for under the peculiar conditions of this tribe the choice of a husband rested altogether with the woman. Or a man might send a message to a girl he fancied, or a girl might even send a message to a young man, such as, "Will you find me some food?"

A young man who had been initiated at the *Jeraeil,* and had served a certain probation, was qualified thereby to take a wife. He would go on a visit to his relatives in that locality from which his mother had come, or to one of the other localities with which his own had marriage relations; and seeing some girl that he fancied, and the feeling being reciprocated, the two would elope. Of the numerous ways in which marriage by elopement was brought about, there are two which are worthy of special notice. If it happened that there were marriageable girls, but that the marriageable young men did not take

the initiative, the women set it going by killing a *Yiirung* (emu-wren), that is, one of the "men's brothers," and casually letting the men see it. Then the men became very angry because one of their brothers had been killed. The young men who might be suitors got sticks, the girls took their digging sticks, and a fight commenced between them, at which many blows were struck, heads were broken, and blood flowed. Even the married men and women joined in the fight. The following day the young men killed a *Djiitgun* (superb warbler), that is, a "woman's sister," and in consequence caused another fight, perhaps worse than the former. After a time, the wounds and bruises having healed, one of the eligible young men and one of the girls meeting, and being inclined towards each other, he looking at her would say, *"Djiitgun?"* to which, if she responded to the understood meaning of the term so used, she would reply *"Yiirung; what does the Yiirung eat?"* He in reply says, "He eats so and so," mentioning kangaroo, opossum, or some other game. This constitutes an offer and its acceptance, and the couple then on a favourable occasion elope.

The second instance to be given is that of the *Bunjil-yenjin,* a medicine man, whose specialty was the arrangement of marriages by elopement spells. *Bunjil* is a praenomen applied to men who have some special qualification. . . . It was the business of the *Bunjil-yenjin* to aid the elopement of young couples. For instance, when a young man wanted a wife, and had fixed his mind on some girl, whom he could not obtain from her parents, he must either go without her, persuade her to run off with him, or call in the aid of the *Bunjil-yenjin.* In the latter case his services were retained by presents of weapons, skin rugs, or other articles. The *Bunjil-yenjin* then lay down on the ground in or near the encampment; next to him was the young man, and beyond him his comrades. The *Bunjil-yenjin* then sang his song, and the others all joined in with him.

The following is one of these songs, of which there were very many used on such occasions, and it is said to have been a very powerful one. One of my Kurnai informants, whose wife was one of the girls that eloped at the *Jeraeil* above mentioned, said in speaking of it, "That *Yenjin* made the women run in all directions, when they heard it."

Bara-burni	*Wangur*
Roll up the twine,	Jaw,[1]
molla	*tallo-burni*
down there	little twine
tallo	*karagan*
little	sweetheart
ngella-galli	*kernanga*
I go first	the hollow (to)
gola	*yinna.*
before	you.

. . . this performance—ceremony, it might even be called—was well known to all the camp, for there was no concealment, and even if done at a little distance, there was always some female friend to carry the news to the girl, and say, "There is so and so singing a *Yenjin* about you."

When the *Bunjil-yenjin* thought his magic was strong enough, he ceased his song. In one case, when one of my informants was present, Bunjil-gworan was the *Bunjil-yenjin,* and the girl's parents covered themselves as if asleep.

Before the youth could avail himself of the spell, something more had to be done, and probably in the above-mentioned case it preceded the covering up of the parents. Another medicine man had to use his art to send them to sleep. At the time of the *Jeraeil* which I men-

tioned a few pages back, this man was the renowned Bunjil-daua-ngun mentioned later on, and his proceeding was as follows. Being paid by the youth with weapons, opossum rugs, and other things, he stuck his magical spear thrower into the ground, slanting towards the camp of the parents, and with such an inclination that after a time it fell down. By its side he placed his *Bulk,* and at a little distance his *Yertung,*[2] and beside it his *Gumbart* (nose peg). He then sang his song, and when the spear thrower fell down the charm was completed, and the parents were believed to be in a magical sleep. Tulaba, before mentioned, was the youth in this case, and might now run off with his sweetheart, but only after a formality which shows that the final choice rested with her. Stealing round to the back of her parents' camp, in which she was sitting, he touched her with a long stick, and she being ready to run off, pulled the end as a signal. He then left, and the girl, having her bag (*Batung*) packed up, in fact, having her trousseau ready, flitted after him.

In the case which I am now describing, the proceedings were not yet over. After a time the old people, according to my informant, Mr. Lucas, woke up, and finding their daughter gone, the old man summoned those of his kindred who were at the camp, to assist him in singing a song which should make the young man's legs become so weary that he would not be able to effect his escape. Finally, he took his spear thrower, and, holding it loosely in his hand, made blows with it towards different points of the horizon. When it made a sound like a crack, it indicated the direction in which the runaways had gone.

On the occasion of the elopement, the

---

[1] Wangur was the name of the girl to whom this *yenjin* was addressed.

[2] A small bone instrument used for extracting splinters from the hands or feet.

man gave notice to his *Brogan,* that is, those who were initiated at the same *Jeraeil* as himself. They met him, and the girl at some appointed place, and had the right of access to her. This right, having been exercised, is at an end. No sexual licence occurred in this tribe beyond this; except when the *Aurora Australis* was seen, when they thought it to be *Mungan's* fire, which might burn them up. The old men then told them to exchange wives for the day, and the *Bret* (the dried hand of one of their dead kinsfolk) was swung backwards and forwards with cries of "Send it away."

While there were medicine men who assisted those who wished to elope, there were other medicine men who aided the pursuing kindred to discover them. Such a one was Bunjil-bataluk, whose familiar was a tame lace lizard, which is said to have gone in front of him to show where the pursued couple were. If such a couple could escape, and remain away for a long time, their offence against the tribal customs might be overlooked, especially if a child had been born to them while away. But if caught, the girl was severely punished. The women, including her female kin-

dred, beat her with their digging sticks, her father or brother might spear her through one or both feet, to prevent her running away again, or she might be cut down the back by a blow from a *Tundiwung,* or be even killed. Her husband would be attacked by the men, and even by the women, other than his own kindred, the men with their weapons, and the women with their digging sticks, sharpened at the point, to stab him in the stomach if possible. His friends would try to prevent the others from attacking him, and usually a severe fight was the result. He might even have to save himself by flight. Yet after all this the two would go away again on the first opportunity. Finally the affair blew over and they settled down among the married people, who indeed had themselves gone through the same experience. . . .

There can be no doubt that the old people of the Kurnai winked at this practice of marriage by elopement. In by far the greater number of cases they themselves had obtained a wife or husband in this manner, and yet when their daughter married in the same way they were furious at it, and punished her with severity. . . .

One offense that no one winked at, apparently, was the violation of the rule that a man's first wife should be older than his second, third, and so on. Age superiority would give her the prestige needed in dealing with her husband's other consorts. This is graphically illustrated by a case history from the account of the Reverend George Taplin, one of the first missionaries in southern Australia.*

. . . One of the worst battles we had lasted at intervals for six days. It arose out of a quarrel between a husband and wife. Solomon Baalpulare had a young wife, Tungkungutte. After she had lived with him some years he brought an older woman home to

his wurley as a second wife. Now, a wife amongst the heathen Aborigines has no objection to her husband taking another spouse, provided she is younger than herself; but this woman was Tungkungutte's senior, and consequently mistress of the camp. Solo-

* Taplin, George. "The Narrinyeri," in *The Native Tribes of South Australia.* Edited by J. D. Woods, Adelaide, 1879.

mon refused to listen to his first wife's remonstrances, so she fled to her tribe at Lake Albert. Solomon gathered his tribe and came to Point Macleay and met the other tribe. He demanded his wife; her friends refused to let her return to him. Then they fought, and he nearly killed his wife's brother; indeed, he ultimately died of the wound which he received. But it was all of no use—he could not get his wife back. They fought day after day, until I was sick of the hoarse shouts and yells. At the conclusion Solomon offended some of the second and intruding wife's friends, and so they turned to and gave him a thrashing. This finished the affair. Very few were killed in these combats, but many received dangerous and disabling wounds. . . .

When someone commits a breach of custom, then we see how strong are the forces which act to restore equilibrium within a group. It is an incident like this that serves the anthropologist in place of experimentation. In this case one wonders if the breach were not due to an outside force—the presence of the missionary. Perhaps Solomon thought that with the missionary at hand he could get away with it.

Returning to Howitt:

Among the Kulin there was a Headman in each local group, and some one of them was recognised as being the head of all. Some were great fighting men, others were orators, and one who lived at the time when Melbourne was established, was a renowned maker of songs and was considered to be the greatest of all.

If a Headman had a son who was respected by the tribes-people he also would become a Ngurungaeta in time. But if he were, from the native point of view, a bad man, or if people did not like him, they would get some one else, and most likely a relative of some former Headman, such as his brother or brother's son.

A Headman could order the young men of the camp to do things for him and they would obey him. He might, as I have heard it put, say to the young men, "Now all of you go out, and get plenty of 'possums and give them to the old people, not raw but cooked." Similarly the wife of the Ngurungaeta could order the young women about.

Each Headman had another man "standing beside him," as they say, to whom he "gave his words." This means that there was a second man of somewhat less authority, who was his comrade, or rather "henchman," who accompanied him when he went anywhere, who was his mouthpiece and delivered his orders to those whom they concerned. When the Headman went out to hunt with his henchman, or perhaps with two of them, if he killed game, say a wallaby, he would give it to one to carry; if he killed another, the other man would carry it, and it was only when he obtained a heavy load that he carried anything himself. . . .

The Wurunjerri tribe of the Woëworung-speaking people gives a good example of the manner in which the lesser divisions (clans) were arranged, and of the relation to them of the Ngurungaeta. In order to make clearer what I shall have to say about the Headman, it will be necessary to say that when Melbourne was established, the tribe was divided into three parts. One, called Kurnaje-berring was subdivided into those who, under their Headman Bebejern, occupied the country from the Darebin Creek to the sources of the Plenty River, and those who, under their Headman Billi-billeri, lived on the east side of the Saltwater River, up to Mt. Macedon. The second division lived about the Yarra Flats, under their Headman Jakki-Jakki, and occupied also the country on the northern slopes of the Dandenong Mountains. The third division was the "real Wurunjerri," who dwelt on the western side of the Saltwater River, and as far as Mt. Macedon, under their Headman Bungerim.

Immediately adjoining the Wurunjerri country, on the west side, was that of the Kurnung-willam who were also Woëworung, and whose Headman was called Ningu-labul, but was named by the white men "Captain Turnbull." He was a great maker of songs, which, as Berak said, "made people glad when they heard them," but when he sang one of them to me, it had the contrary effect, for it made him shed tears. Ningu-labul came of a family of gifted singers, for his father and grandfather had been renowned song makers, and this, as well as his own poetical power, was the cause of his great authority as a Ngurungaeta, not only in his own tribe, but also in those adjoining. The case of this man shows how headmanship was hereditary in a family, whose members were gifted beyond their fellows. . . .

Most of the Headmen were related to each other by marriage, and thus in a family such as that of Ningu-labúl, where there was a tendency for authority to become hereditary, there was the germ of a practice which, under favourable circumstances, might have established a privileged family, such as some of my correspondents have spoken of.

In tracing out these connections between the several Headmen, it became clear to me that they exercised much influence in making the Ngurungaetas. Thus it was Ningu-labul, whose influence made Bebejern and Billi-billeri Headmen. The former and other old men made Bungerim a Ngurungaeta.

The right to hunt and to procure food in any particular tract of country belonged to the group of people born there, and could not be infringed by others without permission. But there were places which such a group of people claimed for some special reason, and in which the whole tribe had an interest. Such a place was the "stone quarry" at Mt. William near Lancefield, from which the material for making tomahawks was procured. The family proprietorship in this quarry had wide ramifications, including more than Wurunjerri people. On the one side it included the husband of Billi-billeri's sister, one of the Headmen of the Kurnung-willam, who lived at Bacchus Marsh, and who was named Nurrum-nurrum-biin, that is, "moss growing on decayed wood." On another side it included Ningu-labul, and in another direction Bebejern, the son of an heiress in quarry rights, from whom an interest came to Berak through his father Bebejern. But it was Billi-billeri, the head of the family whose country included the quarry, who lived on it, and took care of it for the whole of the Wurunjerri community. When he went away, his place was taken by the son of his sister, the wife of Nurrum-nurrum-biin, who came on such occasions to take charge, when it may be assumed, like Billi-billeri, he occupied himself in splitting stone to supply demands. The enormous amount of broken stone lying about on this mountain shows that generations of the predecessors of Billi-billeri must have laboured at this work.

When neighbouring tribes wished for some stone they sent a messenger to Billi-billeri saying that they would send goods in exchange for it, for instance, such as skin rugs. When people arrived after such a message they encamped close to the quarry, and on one occasion Berak heard Billi-billeri say to them, "I am glad to see you and will give you what you want, and satisfy you, but you must behave quietly and not hurt me or each other."

If, however, people came and took stone without leave, it caused trouble, and perhaps a fight between Billi-billeri's people and them. Sometimes men came by stealth and stole stone. I have heard Berak speak of such a case, and the manner in which it was met is described further on. . . .

A side light is thrown on the position and powers of these Headmen by a passage in Knopwood's account of Colonel Collins' attempt to form a settlement in Port Phillip Bay in the year 1803. A party who were surveying "at the northwest point of the bay" were met by a number of natives, who, on a shot being fired over their heads, "ran away a small distance, but soon approached again with the king, who wore a very elegant turban crown and was always carried upon the shoulders of the men. Whenever he desired them to halt, or to approach, they did it immediately." The fact that he was carried by his men may, however, mean no more than that he was from some cause unable to walk. . . .

In the Yuin tribe there was a Headman in each of the local divisions. He was called *Gommera,* and, to be fitted for the office, must be a medicine man, be aged, able to speak several languages (dialects), be skilful as a fighting man, and be, above all, able to perform those feats of magic which the *Gommeras* exhibit at the initiation ceremonies. . . .

The power of these men is riveted on the younger men by the impressive instructions which are given at the initiation ceremonies, as to the implicit obedience to be given to their orders, and also by the apparently supernatural powers which they exhibit thereat. But the *Gommeras* also admonish their people directly, as when one of them stands up by his camp fire and tells those present about the old laws which they must obey. . . .

When any of them went into the town, they were immediately pointed out by their companions, or those natives who resided in it, in a whisper, and with an eagerness of manner which, while it commanded the attention of those to whom it was directed, impressed them likewise with an idea that they were looking at persons remarkable for some superior quality even among the savages of New South Wales. . . .

In the Kurnai tribe, age was held in reverence, and a man's authority increased with years. If he, even without being aged, had naturally intelligence, cunning and courage, beyond his fellows, he might become a man of note, weighty in council, and a leader in war; but such a case was exceptional, and, as a rule, authority and age went together. The authority of age also attached to certain women who had gained the confidence of their tribespeople. Such women were consulted by the men, and had great weight and authority in the tribe. I knew two of them who, being aged, represented the condition of the Kurnai before Gippsland was settled. Together with the old men, they were the depositaries of the tribal legends and customs, and they kept alive the stringent marriage rules to which I have referred elsewhere, thus influencing public opinion very strongly. Possibly the reason for this may have been in part that in this tribe the women take part in the initiation ceremonies up to a certain point.

When Gippsland was settled in 1842, there were two principal Headmen who were recognised as their *Gweraeil-kurnai,* or Great Men. One lived in the northern and the other in the southern part of the district. These men were the recognised leaders. One was a great fighting man; the other less so, but he was also a great medicine man. There were also Gweraeil-kurnai in the local divisions, and it is significant that some of these men gave their names to the divisions, of which they were respectively the Headmen. . . .

At the Jeraeil ceremonies he [Bunbra] was the leader, and it was mainly his voice that decided questions which arose and were discussed at meetings of the initiated men. When during the ceremonies two of the novices were brought before the old men charged with having broken some of the ceremonial rules, it was Bunbra who spoke last, and his directions as to them were followed.

In one of the intervals of the ceremonies at the Jeraeil, when I was sitting with some of the old men; they spoke of the old times, and what was very unusual, of the old men who were now dead, and of their great actions. I could understand then how they came to be the Gweraeil-kurnai of the tribe. One of these they mentioned was a man of the Brataualung clan, who in a fight with one of the other clans, ran ahead of his men and broke the legs of some of the enemy with his hands, leaving them to be killed by his followers. So also another man of the Brayaka, who lived near where Rosedale now is, used in wet winters, when the ground was very soft with rains, to run down the old men kangaroos, and thus catch them with his hands, and kill them. Another old hero was Bruthen-munji, whom I have mentioned before. It

was said that he ran down one of the Brajerak, at a place now known as Blackfellow's Gully, near Buchan, and held him till his brother, another fighting man of renown, came up and killed him with his club. . . .

In the old times the Headmen, and other prominent men of the Kurnai tribe, took an active part in dealing with breaches of tribal customs or native morality. It was by the Gweraeil-kurnai and the other old men that important matters were decided, such as the *Jeraeil* ceremonies, the arrangement of the *Nungi-nungit,* and raids on other clans, or neighbouring tribes. But in all cases these men were in touch with the men somewhat younger than themselves, and had probably discussed with them the matters which the elders dealt with. . . .

Among the Kurnai, when a man had been called upon to appear and submit to an ordeal by weapons, for some death which he had been supposed to have caused by magic . . . he was attended by his kindred and by that branch of the tribe to which he belonged. He was called *Wait-jurk,*[1] and the aggrieved person, that is, one of the near kindred, was called *Nungi-nungit,* which also applied to all his kindred who took part in the ordeal. They also were respectively supported by their section of the tribe.

In the proceedings, the aggrieved party and the accused were each at the ordeal accompanied by the *Gweraeil-kurnai* of their section of the tribe. The proceedings were conducted by the old men according to the ancient traditions, that is, as they would put it, "as their fathers did." . . .

A good instance of the *Nungi-nungit* was one in which the man Bunbra, otherwise, *Jetbolan,* was the defendant, and which occurred about the year 1850.

[1] "Murderer."

A brother of the Tulaba before mentioned awoke in the night and saw Bunbra standing over him, who said he had come for some fire. The next day the man fell sick, and told his friends that Bunbra had "caught him," that is, that he had placed some magical spell on him. By and by he died, and his male kindred sent a message to Bunbra desiring him to come to a *Nungi-nungit*. At the time and place appointed he duly appeared, accompanied by many of his clan, the Tatungalung, and also of the Krauatungalung, who were their friends.

The meeting was held on the Tambo River between Swan Reach and Lake King. The two parties faced each other at a little distance, in the manner described, and Bunbra had two shields for his defence, one for use and the other in reserve. The other side were armed with *Kunnin* for throwing, and boomerangs. It may be mentioned that the latter used in these ordeals are not those which return to the thrower, but the fighting boomerang which does not return. The proceedings commenced by Bunbra saying, "I want to tell you that I did not hurt that poor fellow." The reply was, "You must fight." Boomerangs were then thrown, as my informant said, "like a flight of parrots." Bunbra dodged or successfully warded them off. At last a *Kunnin* was thrown, which passed through his thigh, but which he drew out, and threw back at his assailants. The women then rushed in between the two parties and stopped the fight, and the feud was at an end. . . .

In all the tribes I refer to there is a belief that the medicine men can project substances in an invisible manner into their victims. One of the principal projectives is said to be quartz, especially in the crystallised form. Such quartz crystals are always, in many parts of Australia, carried as part of the stock-in-trade of the medicine man, and are usually carefully concealed from sight, especially of women, but are exhibited freely to the novices at the initiation ceremonies. . . .

The Kurnai fastened some personal object belonging to the intended victim to a spear thrower, together with some eagle hawk's feathers and some kangaroo or human fat. The spear thrower was then stuck slanting in the ground before a fire, and over it the medicine man sang his charm. This was generally called "singing the man's name" until the stick fell, when the magic was considered to be complete. Those who used this form of evil magic were called *Bunjil-murriwun*, the latter word being the name of the spear thrower. It was, as the Kurnai say, made strong, that is, magically powerful, by being rubbed with kangaroo fat. . . .

An instance of the manner in which the spear thrower is used, or rather in which Tankowillin wished to use it, came under my notice in the year 1888. He came to me and asked for the loan of a spear thrower which I had and which he thought to be of special magical power, because it had been used at the *Jeraeil* ceremonies. He informed me that he wanted it to catch one of the tribe who had married a relation of his, a widow, without the consent of her kindred, and also far too soon after the death of her husband, indeed so soon that "it had made all the poor fellow's friends sad, thinking of him." When I refused him the use of the *Murriwun*, he said it did not matter, for he and his friends had made a very strong stick to point at him with, singing his name over it, and spitting strong poison over it. . . .

The practice of using human fat as a powerful magical ingredient is widely spread over Australia, and consequently the belief is universal that the medicine men have the power of abstracting it magically from individuals, or also of actually taking it by violence accompanied by magic. This is usually spoken of by the whites as taking "the kidney fat," but it appears to be the caul fat from the omentum. . . .

A very intelligent Jupagalk man gave me the following account of what he saw, as a boy of about ten years of age, of the fat-taking practice by the medicine men of his tribe. He spoke as follows:

"When I was a boy, I went out one day with some of the men to hunt. We were all walking in a line, when one of them hit the man in front of him on the back of the neck and knocked him down. Two or three of the men held me tight so that I could not run away, for I was very frightened. Then the man cut open the one he had knocked down, by a little hole in his side below his ribs, and took out his fat. After that he bit the two edges of the cut together, and sang to make them join, but he could not succeed. He then said he could not do this because some one had already taken this man's fat before, as he could see the marks on the liver, and that whenever a man had been opened and closed up, no one could do it again. As they could not wake the man up, they buried him. They smoked the fat over a fire and took it away wrapped up tightly in a cloth. They wanted it to carry with them to make them lucky in hunting."

The Kurnai called this practice *Bretbung,* or "with the hand." The men who practised it were called *Burraburrak,* or "flying," and also *Bret-bung mungar worugi,* or "with the hand from a long distance." They were believed to throw their victims into a magic trance by pointing at him with the *Yertung,* which is a bone instrument, made of the fibula of a kangaroo, corresponding to the *Yulo* of the natives of northwestern Victoria. In the Kurnai tribe men have died believing themselves to have been deprived of their fat, although there were no signs of violence on their bodies. At the same time there is no doubt that the taking of fat was actually practised. An informant on whom I can rely tells me that when a boy, not long after Gippsland was settled, he saw an old man roasting fat which they had taken from a blackfellow, whom they had knocked down with a club. This they ate, and told the boy that they would now have the strength of the other man. The alleged victim of this action did not die, but was killed some time after by his own people for some tribal misdemeanour.

The effect of dreams in which the sleeper believed that he had fallen into the hands of such a medicine man may be seen from a remark made by my Wurunjerri informant, that "Sometimes men only know about having their fat taken by remembering something of it as in a dream." . . .

The following account of the practice of a celebrated *Bangal* of the Jupagalk tribe was given to me by one of the men who were present, and I record it as nearly as possible in his own words. "A blackfellow was very ill, and at dusk the *Bangal* came to see him. At dark he went off for a time. By and by we saw a light afar off, and as it seemed to be above the treetops to the eastward, it looked at first like a star. Then it went round to the west, and kept coming nearer and nearer. At last we saw the *Bangal* walking along the ground carrying a piece of burning rag in his hand. His legs were covered with something like feathers, which could be seen by the firelight, and the people said that they were *Bangal's* feathers. He sat down by the poor fellow, saying that he had been over to the Avoca River, where he found a man who had the rag tied on a yam stick roasting it before a fire. He then rubbed the place where the man was sick, and sucked out some pieces of stone and glass. The man then soon got better." . . .

A peculiar feature in the Kurnai magic is that the functions of the *Birraark* are separated from those of the medicine man (*Mulla-mullung*). The former combined the functions of the seer, the spirit medium, and the bard, for he foretold future events, he brought the ghosts to the camp of his people at night, and he composed the songs and dances which enlivened their social meetings. He was a harmless being, who devoted himself to performances which very strikingly resembled those of the civilised "mediums." A man was supposed to become a *Birraark* by being initiated by *Mrarts* or ghosts, when they met him hunting in the bush; but, that they might have power over him, he must at the time be wearing a *Gumbart,* that is, one of those bone pegs which the Australian aborigine wears thrust through the septum of his nose. By this they held him and conveyed him through the clouds. Some say that he was conveyed hanging to a *Marrangrang,* which was described as being either like a rope or else something on which the *Birraark* can sit. But whatever it was like, the *Mrarts* went first and the *Birraark* last. It is said that, when they reached the sky, the leading *Mrart* gave a signal, and some one inside opened a hole and looked out. This, it is said, was a *Gweraeil-mrart,* in fact a Headman of ghostland, as a Kurnai man remarked to me when speaking of this matter, "like a *Gweraeil-kurnai."* As the *Birraark* climbs through the hole last, the *Mrarts* put a rug over his head, all but a place through which he can see the people there, the women beating their rugs, and the men danc-

ing. Looking on, he learns new songs and dances (*Gunyeru*), which he afterwards teaches to the Kurnai. But he must not on any account laugh. One *Birraark* was away from his camp for a time, and on returning he told his people that when aloft with the *Mrarts* he could not help laughing, because two *Mrarts* caught hold of him by the sides and tickled him. As a penalty they kept him with them for some time, after which his tribes-people called him [by a special name].

A *Birraark* might not eat any part of a kangaroo that had blood on it, nor carry home a kangaroo that he had killed. Others did this for him, and gave him some part of it free from blood. Nor might he kill any man. If he did any of these things, the *Mrarts* would never again take him up aloft.

Having been thus introduced to the land of ghosts, he could return there at will, calling on the *Mrarts* to carry him on the *Marrangrang,* or as I have heard it said, to take him along the *Wau-unga-nurt,* the path or track to the sky, along which the *Yambo* (spirit) travels after death.

One of the best remembered of the *Birraarks* was a man of the Brabralung clan named Mundauin. It is related of him that he became a *Birraark* by dreaming three times that he was a kangaroo, and as such participating in a kangaroo *Gunyeru,* or dancing cor- robboree. He said that after dreaming of the kangaroos, he began to hear the *Mrarts* drumming and singing up aloft, and that finally one night they came and carried him away. A man who was in the camp on the occasion of one of his manifestations said as follows:

"In the night his wife shouted out, 'He is gone up.' Then we heard him whistling up in the air, first on one side of us and then on the other, and afterwards sounds of people jumping down on the ground. After a time all was quiet. In the morning we found him lying on the ground, near the camp where the *Mrarts* had left him. There was a big log lying across his back, and when we woke him and took the log off, he began to sing about the *Mrarts,* and all he had seen up there." . . .

Rain makers and weather changers are important persons in most parts of Australia, but especially in those parts of the continent which are subject to frequently recurring periods of drought. . . .

Among the Kurnai there were rain makers, and also those who caused rain and storms to cease. The former were to be found in each clan, and the methods use for producing rain by the *Bunjil-willung,* or rain men, were to fill the mouth with water and then squirt it in the direction appropriate to the particular clan, and each one sang his especial rain song.[2] The Brayaka squirted water, and sang, towards southwest (*Krauun*); the Brayaka and Tatungalung did this in the same direction; the Brabralung and the Krauatungalung squirted water towards the direction of the southeast, the east winds (*Belling*) being from their rainy quarter. From these several directions the rain came in Gippsland; and when, for instance, a southwesterly rain came to the Brabralung they said that it was the Brayaka who sent it, and so on with the others. These rain makers could also bring thunder, and it was said of them, as of the other medicine men, that they obtained their songs in dreams. I have before spoken of one of the Brayaka Headmen who was credited with the power of calling up the furious west

[2] *Willung* is rain. The Kurnai say that the frogs when croaking in chorus in the swamps are "singing for rain," and that the big sonorous bull-frogs are the *Bunjil-willung.*

winds, whence he derived his name of *Bunjil-kraura.* His song by which he stopped the gales which prevented his tribes-people from climbing the tall trees in the western forest, ran thus—

"*Kutbuna-wang Kraura,*"

from *Kutbun* to bear or carry, *Wang* a bond, or something tied, and *Kraura,* the west wind. I did not hear the song by which he caused the western gales to arise, but I have no doubt that it was of the same character. When these gales came, he was propitiated by presents to send them away. . . .

The belief of the Kurnai is that the *Mulla-mullung* obtains his power in dreams. The ancestral ghosts either visited the sleeper, and communicated to him harmful or protective chants and knowledge, or they completed his education elsewhere. . . .

Tankli, the son of Bataluk the Lace-Lizard, gave me an account of how he became a *Mulla-mullung,* which is as follows:

"When I was a big boy about getting whiskers I was at Alberton camped with my people. Bunjil-gworan was there and other old men. I had some dreams about my father, and I dreamed three times about the same thing. The first and the second time, he came with his brother and a lot of other old men, and dressed me up with lyre-bird's feathers round my head. The second time they were all rubbed over with *Naial* (red ochre), and had *Bridda-briddas* [3] on. The third time they tied a cord made of whale's sinews round my neck and waist, and swung me by it and carried me through the air over the sea at Corner Inlet, and set me down at *Yiruk.* It was at the front of a big rock like the front of a house. I noticed that there was something like an opening in the rock. My father tied

[3] A *Bridda-bridda* is a kind of kilt which the men wore in front and behind hanging from the cord which was wound round the waist as a belt.

something over my eyes and led me inside. I knew this because I heard the rocks make a sound as of knocking behind me. Then he uncovered my eyes, and I found that I was in a place as bright as day, and all the old men were round about. My father showed me a lot of shining bright things, like glass, on the walls, and told me to take some. I took one and held it tight in my hand. When we went out again my father taught me how to make things go into my legs, and how I could pull them out again. He also taught me how to throw them at people. After that, he and the other old men carried me back to the camp, and put me on the top of a big tree. He said, 'Shout out loud and tell them that you are come back.' I did this, and I heard the people in the camp waking up, and the women beginning to beat their rugs for me to come down, because now I was a *Mulla-mullung*. Then I woke up and found that I was lying along the limb of a tree. The old men came out with fire sticks, and when they reached the tree, I was down, and standing by it with the thing my father had given me in my hand. It was like glass, and we call it *Kiin*. I told the old men all about it, and they said that I was a doctor. From that time I could pull things out of people, and I could throw the *Kiin* like light in the evening at people, saying to it *Blappan* (go!). I have caught several in that way. After some years I took to drinking, and then I lost my *Kiin* and all my power, and have never been able to do anything since. I used to keep it in a bag made of the skin of a ring-tail opossum, in a hole of a tree. One night I dreamed that I was sleeping in the camp, and my wife threw some *Kruk* [4] at me, and after that my *Kiin* went out of my bag, I do not know where. I have slept under the tree where I left it, thinking that my power might come back, but I have never found the *Kiin,* and I never dream any more about it.". . .

According to Taplin, the native belief in the powers of the shamans was not always hard to shake.

. . . There used to be a class of doctors amongst the natives called kuldukke men. They were great impostors; their impositions and lying became notorious around the lakes. Their method of procedure was by dancing, whistling, incantations, and squeezing the diseased part. They used by sleight-of-hand to produce extraordinary substances from those parts which were afflicted. I knew a white man who for a joke submitted himself to the kuldukkes, in order to cure an attack of rheumatism in the shoulder. The doctors muttered charms, and whistled, and blew, and danced, and at last produced a small piece of the leg of an old chair, which had been kicking about in the back yard for weeks before, and solemnly declared that they had extracted it from the diseased shoulder. These kuldukkes soon ceased to exert influence amongst the natives, and their practice has died out. One circumstance which contributed to this result was the following :—There was an intelligent native at Goolwa, named Solomon. He used to be regularly employed by settlers in that neighbourhood. One day Solomon went to work after breakfast, leaving instructions with his wife to make a couple of dampers for their dinner. This was

[4] *Kruk* is menstrual blood.

soon accomplished, and two dampers and a small cake awaited the return of their owner to his midday meal. Just then a lot of kuldukke men passed the hut, and looked in rather inquisitively. Presently they told Solomon's wife, who was known to be a superstitious body, that they could see a spirit, the dreadful Melapi, coming across the ocean, and that he would be certain to hurt her husband unless he were driven away. This they offered to do by their enchantments if she would give them one of those dampers. The poor foolish woman believed their story, and one of the dampers was soon devoured. The kuldukkes then began dancing, whistling, pointing spears, and muttering charms in a very energetic manner. In a quarter of an hour they came and said that their strength was insufficient, and that they must have another damper. With a sigh the wife handed over a second fee. They then danced about still more vigorously, and made demonstrations which might fairly be supposed sufficient to frighten a demon; and then they came and told the woman that the mighty deed was done, her husband was safe, the evil spirit had departed; and then they rapidly followed his example. Just then Solomon appeared in sight, ready for dinner. Extremely long was the face which he pulled when he heard the story, and found there was only a very small cake remaining for his meal. With a deeply injured expression, he said to his wife, "What for, you big one stupid, let em kuldukke men cheat you? Him no look out Melapi, him only look out my dinner." . . .

Back again to Howitt.

The makers of Australian songs, or of the combined songs and dances, are the poets, or bards, of the tribe, and are held in great esteem. Their names are known in the neighbouring tribes, and their songs are carried from tribe to tribe, until the very meaning of the words is lost, as well as the original source of the song. It is hard to say how far and how long such a song may travel in the course of time over the Australian continent. . . .

In the tribes with which I have acquaintance, I find it to be a common belief that the songs, using that word in its widest meaning, as including all kinds of aboriginal poetry, are obtained by the bards from the spirits of the deceased, usually of their kindred, during sleep in dreams. Thus, as I have before said, the *Birraark* professed to receive his poetic inspirations from the *Mrarts,* as well as the accompanying dances, which he was supposed to have seen first in ghostland. . . .

I have mentioned songs which are accompanied by rhythmical gestures or by pantomime, which greatly adds to the effect. A favourite one which I have seen describes the hunting of an opossum, and its extraction from a hollow log by the hunter, who is the principal singer, and his assistants. Every action of finding the animal— the ineffectual attempt to poke it out of its retreat, the smoking it out with fire, and the killing of it by the hunters as it runs out—is rendered, not only by the words of the song, but also by the concerted actions and movements of the performers in their pantomimic dancing.

A very favourite song of this description has travelled in late years from the Murring to the Kurnai. It was composed by Mragula, who, it may be mentioned, was a song maker in his tribe, the Wolgal, describing his attempt to cross the Snowy River in a leaky canoe during flood. The pantomimic action which accompanies this song is much fuller than the words, and is a graphic picture of the pushing off in the canoe, the paddling into the stream, the gaining of the leak, and after an ineffectual attempt to bail the water out by hand, a hurried return to shore. Then the hole being carefully stopped with adhesive mud, the performers again put off and paddle across. The words are in the Wolgal language, and therefore quite unintelligible to the Kurnai. . . .

Among the Kurnai, when a man died, his relatives rolled him up in a 'possum rug and enclosed it in a sheet of bark, cording it tightly. A hut was built over it, and in this the mourning relatives collected. The corpse was placed in the centre, and as many of the relatives as could find room lay with their heads on it. There they lay lamenting their loss, saying, for instance, "Why did you leave us?" Now and then their grief would be intensified by some one, for instance, the wife, uttering an ear-piercing wail *"Penning-i-torn"* (my spouse is dead), or a mother would say *"Lit-i-torn"* (my child is dead). All the others would then join in with the proper term of relationship, and they would cut and gash themselves with sharp stones and tomahawks until their heads and bodies streamed with blood. The bitter wailing and weeping continued all night, only the more distant relations rousing themselves to eat until the following day. After this had continued for several days the mourners unloosed the body to look at it, and thus renewed their grief. If by this time the hair had become loose, it was plucked off the whole body, and preserved by the father, mother, or sis-

ters in small bags made of opossum skin. Then the body was once more rolled up, and was not again uncovered till it had so far decomposed that the survivors could anoint themselves with oil which had exuded from it. The Kurnai say that this was to make them remember the dead person. Sometimes they opened the body and removed the intestines to make it dry more rapidly. The body in its bark cerements was carried with the family in its wanderings, and was the special charge of the wife, or of some other near relative. Finally, the body having, perhaps after several years, become merely a bag of bones, was buried or put into a hollow tree. Sometimes the father or mother carried the lower jaw as a memento.

The most remarkable custom connected with the dead was that of the *"Bret"* or hand. Sometimes the Kurnai cut off one hand of the corpse, or both hands, soon after death, which they wrapped in grass and dried. A string of twisted opossum fur was attached to it, so that it could be hung round the neck and worn in contact with the bare skin under the left arm. It was carried by the parent, child, brother, or sister. The belief of the Kurnai was that at the approach of an enemy the hand would push or pinch the wearer. Such a signal being experienced, the hand would be taken from the neck and suspended in front of the face, the string being held between the finger and thumb. The person would then say, "Which way are they coming?" If the hand remained at rest, the question would be again put, but now facing another way, and so on. The response being that the hand vibrated in some direction, and it was thence that the danger was coming. My informants have told me that the swinging of the *Bret* was sometimes so violent that the string broke.

In one case which I heard of, the *Bret* did not respond to its wearer, who said to it, *"Munju! Munju! Wunman? Munju! tunamun nganju, brappanu mabanju,"* that is, "There! There! Where? There! Speak me to (or) throw dingo-to." That is, he would throw it to the wild dogs. . . .

For many years I had known a medicine man of the Wolgal tribe, the before-mentioned Yibai-malian, and through him became acquainted with one of the principal *Gommeras* of the Yuin. On several occasions I had spoken with Yibai about the initiations, and to his surprise he found that I knew much about them; and I also produced to him several of the bull-roarers from different parts of Australia. Thus at last he came to look on me as one of the initiated, and in consequence spoke to me unreservedly on the otherwise forbidden subjects. I then arranged with him that one of the most influential of the Yuin *Gommeras,* who lived at Twofold Bay, should come up to Manero with some of his men and meet me on the occasion of my next visit to that part of New South Wales. At this meeting, amongst other things, we discussed the advisability of holding a *Kuringal,* and it was at last decided that one should be held. I was greatly struck by the manner in which the old man received a bull-roarer which I had made for the occasion, it being the facsimile of those with which I had played as a boy. I drew it from a small bag and secretly presented it to him, saying: "This I used when I was a lad, and you know that these *mudthi* were first made by that great one (pointing upwards), and that he ordered your fathers to hold the *Kuringal,* and to make your boys into men." He and Yibai, who was standing by him, each placed his hand over his mouth, and looked at the bull-roarer for some moments. Then the Yuin *Gommera* Brupin said: "Yes, that is it," and he called the three men whom he had brought with him, and holding the bull-roarer before him said: "This is a *mudthi* which he (pointing to me) has brought from a long way off. It is the same as that which we know of, and which was given to our fathers by that great *Biamban* you know about." The men looked at it with every appearance of awe, but said nothing, and then returned to their fire.

When we parted it was understood that I should send up my messenger to Brupin, who would consult with the other *Gommeras,* and I shortly after sent a man of the Krauatun Kurnai as my messenger to the Yuin to ask them to call together a *Kuringal,* and to let me know when they were ready, and I would go up to help them. . . .

He carried from me the bull-roarer which I had shown to Yibai-malian and Brupin, and delivered it with my message to the latter at Bega. In going to and from that place he journeyed on foot a distance of about four hundred miles over some of the most mountainous country in Southeast Australia. He made the journey a second time before the arrangements were completed, and he brought back a message to me that Brupin would send his messenger carrying my *mudthi* to the principal *Gommera* of the Kurial, who lived at the Shoalhaven River, asking him to bring his people to a meeting on the east side of the Bega River, not far from the coast.

Word was sent to me when the Murring were assembling. Being, so to say, in the position of a *Gommera* of the Kurnai, I was told that I was to bring a contingent of my men to the meeting; and I accordingly arranged with my messenger that he was to take certain of the Kurnai, starting from the Snowy River mouth, and meet me on the upper waters of the Delegate River. . . .

The ceremonial meeting having been called, that part of the community which took the initiative prepares the ground, and gets everything ready for the arrival of the various contingents; some spot being selected where a good supply of food is obtainable. . . .

. . . the proceedings commence about the time when the contingents are expected to arrive.

Assuming that the Bunan was to be attended by the clans from Moruya, Bega, and Twofold Bay, that is, by both the Kurial and Guyangal, and that the meeting was to be near Bega, the following would be the procedure as the contingents arrived.

The people from Braidwood, Ulladulla, and Shoalhaven would accompany those from Moruya. With them, people from Broulee would occasionally come. Next would arrive those from Queanbeyan, then the Grungatta from beyond Shoalhaven, with whom there might be even some from Jervis Bay; and all these people are true Kurial.

The Wollongong people did not attend this ceremony, because they go to one farther up the coast. The people from Twofold Bay would arrive about the same time, and bring with them some of the Bemeringal from the country along the coast range, being some of those living to the east of the Ngarigo.

The limits within which people would come may be roughly stated as Jimberoo, Kangaroo Valley, Nowra; but at this latter place were Bemeringal, that is, those who lived upon the high tableland, who went to the ceremonies at Goulburn. Nor did the Bemeringal come to these ceremonies from as great a distance as the country of the Ngarigo. . . .

The Yuin ceremonies of initiation were attended by people from a district included by Shoalhaven River, Braidwood, the southern part of Manero, and Twofold Bay. At the termination of these ceremonies, when the novices had gone away into the bush for their time of probation, and when the people were about to separate, there was held a kind of market, at which those articles which they had brought with them for exchange were bartered. It was held at some clear place near the camp, and a man would say, "I have brought such and such things," and some other man would bargain for them. A complete set of articles is one *Ngulia* or belt of opossum-fur string, four *Burrain* or men's kilts, one *Gumbrum* or bone nose peg, and a complete set of corrobboree ornaments. It was the rule that a complete set went together. Weapons might be given in exchange, and a complete set of these is "two hands," that is ten, fighting boomerangs (*Warangun*), being the straight-going one; the same number of grass-tree spears (*Gumma*); one of each kind of shield, namely the *Bemata,* used for stopping spears, and the *Millidu,* used for club fighting; one club (*Gujerung* or *Bundi*), and one spear thrower (*Meara*).

The women also engaged in this trade, exchanging opossum rugs, baskets, bags, digging sticks (*Tuali*), etc.

Not only were these things bartered, but presents made to friends and to the Headmen by the other men. The women also gave things to the wives of the Headmen. A Headman who was held in great esteem might have as many things given to him as he could well carry away.

Not only were articles which the people made themselves bartered, but also things which had some special value, and had perhaps been brought from some distant place. Such an instance I heard of at one of these meetings many years ago. An ancient shield had been brought originally from the upper waters of the Murrumbidgee River, and was greatly valued because, as my informant said, it had "won many fights." Yet it was exchanged, and carried away on its farther travels.

There is a natural tendency for certain occupations to become hereditary. The office of medicine man, for instance, and that of song maker have been already mentioned, as well as that of Headman, as being in some cases hereditary. One instance remains, which is, so far, the only one which has come to my knowledge. In the Herbert River tribes the various trades, if one may use that term, are hereditary, so that there are hereditary tree climbers, canoe, shield, spear, and boomerang makers, fishermen, rainmakers or medicine men, hunters, messengers or heralds. Among the women are yam hunters, hut makers, basket makers, etc. The tribal rain maker is also an hereditary shield maker. . . .

As we read Howitt's account, several matters which we have not met before in this book appear.

1. The people are organized into permanent villages, with chiefs, and these chiefs meet with each other regularly. A number of compound political institutions had either arisen or were on the point of arising at the time when the English came.

2. The chiefs, called Gommeras, were political specialists, with "henchmen" to act as their deputies and carry their burdens, in one case to carry the chief himself. These chiefs inherited their positions in some cases, but in any case had to be men renowned for some special skill, at fighting, composing or singing songs, and at magic. The families of these chiefs intermarried, and a supervisory class or caste had appeared in at least a rudimentary form (p. 249).

3. The totemical marriage classes of the desert country were not needed here. Instead we have a system of marriage dependent on local exogamy without totemic designation (p. 244). However, the entire Kurnai nation had its totem, the crow (p. 243) ; the individual had his own totem, serving as familiar spirit in the case of shamans ; and the two sexes had their own totems (p. 244). Thus nation, individual, and sex were symbolically designated.

4. Marriage by exchange (p. 245) is one of the world's commonest systems. The story (p. 245) of how the women start action in making the men notice them by killing the male totem shows the utility of sex totemism. It also illustrates the close physiological relationship between fighting and mating.

5. There is much individual specialization in work techniques, although none of them appear very complicated. These specializations seem to have been inherited. However, there is no indication that specialists married daughters of their own fellow craftsmen, and hence no evidence of a caste system. No organization of craftsmen into guilds is seen. In the Kurnai we seem to have been on the threshold of a more complicated social structure than is usual among food-gathering peoples.

6. Trade was considerable. Billi-billeri's ax-blank quarry (p. 249) is a classic example of a concentrated source of special materials. Opossum-skin robes seem to have been the chief currency received in return for ax blanks. Blankets, robes,

and sheets of cloth are standard media of exchange in many countries. They come in handy units, and are easily standardized. During the initiation ceremonies, to which people came from distant regions, the participants opened a market and carried on a brisk trade (p. 259). As in so many other places throughout history, ceremony served as a cover for trade.

7. Shamans are no longer all-purpose healers and magicians, but are now divided according to three specialties, healing, divining, and rain making. The healers use quartz crystals, as do many of the American Indian shamans. The rain makers squirt water out of their mouths in mimetic magic, as do Southwestern Indians. The magical fear of menstrual blood is a commonplace. Here it is considered hostile not so much to hunting, which is not very critical, but to the power of the shaman, which is. Shamans make ritual use of human kidney fat, symbolizing the man himself and his life energy (p. 253). They perform remarkable surgical operations while their victims are unconscious. Some of these may be imaginary, the rational *post rei facto* explanation for aches and pains, but others were probably real. See Lloyd Warner's *A Black Civilization* * for a full account, with several case histories.

8. Here as elsewhere the death of a man in his prime creates much disturbance (p. 258) and to restore equilibrium the magicians must find a scapegoat. Hence the rationalization that the man died from evil magic, or one of these mysterious surgical operations, and hence the search for the evildoer, and his punishment. This is a very common procedure in Negro Africa and elsewhere. Among the ancient Scythians the king's death was attributed to someone having sworn "by the king's hearth" and having then broken his oath.

9. We are told that a bard sang a song in an unintelligible language, with gestures, and that the audience understood. What they understood was the "gestures." The Australians had a sign language as perfectly suited to their needs as that of the Plains Indians.

* New York: Harper & Brothers, 1937.

9

The Northern Maidu: Acorns and Winter Dances
in the Sacramento Valley

THE Kurnai were able to keep on living in their bounteous environment until the middle of the nineteenth century. One factor and one alone kept peoples with more efficient technical methods and more complicated systems of organization from taking their land away from them before that time. That factor was isolation. Isolation, however, cannot be measured in terms of space alone. Peoples living a few hundred miles apart may be effectively isolated by details of the environment.

For example, the Indians of the Southwestern United States grew maize (Indian corn). They still do. Maize requires summer rains for maturation. In the Southwest, impressive thunderheads form, usually in July, and when the clouds burst the maize receives the needed water. Across the desert in California, the landscape may appear much the same, but the rains fall in the winter, and the summer is a time of drought. California enjoys what geographers call a Mediterranean climate. This sequence of winter rain and summer drought is ideal for small grains, such as wheat and barley. These cereals developed in a similar climate in the Old World, which is useless for maize without elaborate irrigation. Many anthropologists believe that this is the principal reason why the Indians of California never became farmers.

Even without farming, they were able to obtain abundant supplies of food from the landscape—at least those living in the richest parts of the state had this good fortune. Among other peoples so fortunately situated were the Maidu, one of the principal "tribes" of the Sacramento Valley and adjacent sierras. Their country reached from the eastern bank of the Sacramento River to the arid lands over the mountains, and from the site of the modern city of Sacramento to Lassen Peak, Eagle Lake, and Honey Lake. Their territory covered an area 135 miles long and 70 miles wide, about 9000 square miles in all, including the main valley land, foothills, and small mountain valleys. The Maidu probably numbered about 9000 before they succumbed to the inevitable white man's diseases. Between 1820 and 1840 most of them died, leaving the land conveniently empty for the gold seekers. Kroeber estimates a population density of 3 per square mile in the valley proper, with less than 1 in the hills and high valleys. He also lists some 99 Maidu villages, of which he can locate 72 on the map. The average population of a village was 90 persons. Each village had an average area of 94 square miles, an area 9 by 10 miles. In the valley the villages would take up less room than in the uplands.

In the valley each village usually consisted of a number of hamlets, or groups of two to six houses, one of which was a "sweat house," about which more later. One village, at what is now Quincy, California, had 6 hamlets with 22 houses and 4 sweat houses; another, at Taylorsville, had 3 hamlets with 22 houses and 3 sweat houses. In each village one of the sweat houses was larger than the others and served as dance house for the entire village population. The number of persons in each of these villages probably averaged around 150. The average Maidu rarely traveled more than two villages away from home in his lifetime. There was no element in their emotional needs or in their technological adjustment to their environment that made wide travel necessary, and more distant people were usually hostile.*

Let us now continue by reading from the monograph of the earliest student who concerned himself with these people, my own teacher and predecessor, Roland B. Dixon.†

The methods of manufacture of knives and of spear and arrow points do not differ from those usually employed by Indians in other portions of the continent. The materials used were various: a rather hard black basalt being used in many cases for knives and spearheads; while obsidian, obtained largely in trade, was used for arrow points, and in some cases also for knives. Flint and jasper were also used. Near Oroville was one of the best known spots for getting flint, from a cave on or near Table Mountain. The opening to the cave was very small, but, once in, the size was such that a man could stand upright. A person going to get flint must crawl in, and then throw ahead of him beads or dried meat as offerings to the spirits for the flint he was about to take. A person was allowed to take only so much flint as he could break off at a single blow. The flint obtained, the person had to crawl out backwards. If the regulations were not complied

with, the person would have bad luck; the flint would not chip well, or would fail to kill. . . .

In the manufacture of acorn flour, they were accustomed to use either the smooth, flat surface of some large bowlder or ledge, or else a flat slab or block of stone of irregular shape sunk into the floor of their houses. On this flat surface the pulverization of the acorns took place. In the course of time, from the constant pounding, a hole or cavity would be worn in the surface of the stone. In all cases noted, these cavities were distinctly funnel-shaped, coming to a rather sharp point at the bottom. . . .

The pestles used for pounding the acorn meal are of different sizes, but are substantially of the same type. Generally cylindrical, with a circular or oval cross section, they vary from fifteen to thirty-five centimetres in length, with a diameter ranging from six to almost ten centimetres. . . .

Metates and mullers were in use

* Most of the above is abstracted from Kroeber, A. L., *Cultural and Natural Areas of Native North America,* Berkeley, 1939; Kroeber, A. L., *Handbook of the Indians of California,* Bulletin 78, Bureau of American Ethnology, Washington, 1925; also consulted were Gifford, E. W., *Clans and Moieties in Southern California,* University of California Publications in Ameican Archaeology and Ethnology, no. 2, pp. 115–219, 1918; and Loeb, E. M., *The Eastern Kuksu Cult,* Univ. of Calif. Pubs. in Amer. Arch. and Ethn., vol. 33, no. 2, pp. 139–232, 1933.

† "The Northern Maidu," *Bulletin American Museum of Natural History,* Vol. XVII, 1905. Reprinted by permission.

chiefly for grinding the grass seeds and other seeds, of which a considerable variety were used for food. The metate is merely a slab of coarse-grained stone, set at a low angle; the muller being a smaller piece of the same stone, convenient to grasp in the hand.

Stone [smoking] pipes . . . would seem to have been at all times objects of value, and to have been, on the whole, somewhat scarce, a wooden pipe being far more common. All pipes were of the tubular form. . . . The pipes were drilled by means of a piece of deer antler, which was pounded with another stone, till, after a long time, the cavity was made. Sometimes sand was added, which accelerated the work. . . .

Shamans wore pendant from the neck obsidian knives, which were regarded as of great value and mysterious power. . . .

With the exception of their excellent bows and arrows and their very crude dugout canoes, the Maidu made little, if any, use of wood for implements. Small trees were felled by the laborious process of hacking with sharp flints held in the hand, or roughly hafted. . . . Once felled, the trunk was commonly burned in two where desired. Large trees they did not attempt to cut down, but utilized such as were blown down by the wind or burned down in forest fires. . . .

Shell was used only for ornament and for currency. The white, disk-shaped beads common to all this coast region were largely used by the Maidu. They were obtained apparently from the Wintun, who, in their turn, probably obtained them from the Pomo and Yuki along the coast. From the statements made by the Indians, it would appear that the beads were obtained either in the finished or partly finished state. In the latter case, they were already drilled and strung on cords, but

were not yet rounded and smoothed. This finishing was accomplished in the usual manner, by rolling the string of imperfect disks between two stones, thus grinding them to perfect circles. Abalone was used largely for ear ornaments and for necklaces. The shell was used in irregular or rectangular pieces, and was hung pendant from cords, either by itself, or in connection with the ordinary white disk beads. It was obtained, like the latter, from the Wintun. Dentalium was also known and highly prized. It was used, however, but little, because of its rarity. . . .

Among the Northwestern section, the method and plan of [house] construction were as follows: A suitable site being selected, where the soil was soft and no large rocks were to be encountered, an excavation was made to a depth of not over one metre, and over a circular area from six to twelve metres in diameter. The ground was loosened by the aid of digging sticks, and then gathered into baskets, in which it was carried off and dumped, to be used later in making the earth covering. Spring was the season usually selected for building a house, as at that time the earth was soft, whereas later in the summer the ground becomes hard and baked. The excavation having been completed, the posts which support the roof beams were next procured. These posts, when possible, were of oak, and were cut, brought to the site, and set up with much ceremony. . . . In all cases, there were . . . two main posts—one standing behind, and the other in front of, the fireplace. . . . On either side of these two posts, and halfway between them and the walls, was generally a row of shorter posts, four in number, thus making ten in all. The two main posts were from three to six metres in height, whereas the shorter posts were from two to three metres. . . . The sides of the excavation were left vertical, and lined or walled with logs, either whole or split, set on end, or with large slabs of bark, forming thus a solid wooden wall around the interior of the house. From the edge of the excavation, then, the long beams to support the roof were leaned toward the centre, resting on the posts already set, and tied to them securely with grapevines or osiers. In some cases rude sockets seem to have been made for the beams to rest in; in other cases a crotch post was used. On these beams as a basis, cross poles were laid; and on these, again, large pieces of bark, branches, leaves, and pine needles; and lastly, a heavy covering of earth, generally from twenty to fifty centimetres thick. In the centre of the roof, at the top, an opening was left for a smoke hole. This was covered, when necessary, by a skin, a basket, or a slab of bark. Directly in line with the two main posts, a doorway was made, less than a metre wide and from one metre to a metre and a half high; and a passage was built out about two metres in length, slanting up from the floor of the house to the level of the ground outside. . . .

In the construction of these earth lodges, several families generally took part; and these occupied the house when finished. In the case of the large dance houses, the whole village seems to have joined to a greater or less extent; and, since they all helped, all had a right to the use of the house. . . .

The earth-covered lodge seems to have been the traditional and the most common type of dwelling among the Maidu. The earlier explorers in Maidu territory describe this form almost exclusively; and from the myths, and the statements of the people themselves, we may believe that all save the poorest originally lived in these well-built structures. The large houses accommodated several families, each of which had its recognized portion of the interior. It seems that the chief or head man of the village occupied the largest and the best house; and that this was sometimes, but not always, also the dance or sweat house of the village. In large villages there was almost always a special structure, larger than the dwelling houses, for this purpose. . . .

The size of villages seems, as would be expected, to have varied much. In some, there were as many as twenty or more earth-covered lodges. In other cases, a village, or, rather, settlement, would consist of but a single lodge. . . .

The collection and preparation of acorns for food were among the most important industries of the Maidu, in common with most of the Central Californian tribes. At the time in the autumn when the acorns are ripe, everyone is busy. The men and larger boys climb the trees, and, by the aid of long poles, beat the branches, knocking off the acorns. The women and smaller children gather these in burden baskets, and carry them to the village, storing them in granaries or in the large storage baskets in the houses.

The first step in the preparation of the gathered nuts is to remove the shell and dry the meat. This, as well as all other labor in connection with the preparation of the acorn, is done by women only. The acorns are usually cracked by means of two stones, the acorn being placed point down on one, and the butt-end being struck several sharp blows with the other. The acorn is thus cracked in halves, and the shell is then separated from each half by the aid of the teeth. The split meats are then spread in the sun, where they rapidly become dry.

The preparation of acorn meal from the dried nuts is carried on with or without a mortar or milling basket. Perhaps most commonly this mortar basket is dispensed with. Selecting a flat rock or bowlder, or using a flat stone sunk in the floor of the house, the woman sits cross-legged, or with legs extended, on the ground, and, in the absence of a mortar basket, spreads out a couple of quarts of dried acorns in a circle. Holding the pestle in the one hand, she strikes regularly in the centre of this circle, and with the other hand constantly gathers, and sweeps back under the descending pestle, the acorns that scatter with each blow. The pestle is changed from one hand to the other now and then, thus insuring an even pounding of the acorns, and resting the hands and arms. When a considerable quantity of acorns has thus been reduced to meal, the finer flour must be separated from the coarser particles. In this process, several handfuls of the meal are placed on one of the flat winnowing baskets or trays, and are tossed and caught several times. . . .

The flour must next be sweetened by removing the bitter element present. For this purpose a spot is selected where the soil is sandy and soft. Here a circular depression is scraped out to a depth of five or seven centimetres, and the earth heaped up in a little wall round about the excavation. The diameter of these bowl-like hollows may vary from one third of a metre to a metre. The acorn flour, being first damp-ened, is carefully plastered over the whole interior of the hollow, the layer of dampened meal being about five centimetres thick. Over this layer of meal a few small cedar sprigs or boughs are laid, so that in pouring on the water the meal shall not be disturbed. Warm water, heated in baskets by hot stones, is now poured gently on the cedar boughs, and allowed to trickle through until the hollow is filled to the brim.

Slowly the water soaks through the layer of meal, and is absorbed by the sandy soil. As soon as the first water has soaked away, a second lot is poured in, this time somewhat hotter; and so on, until finally water at boiling point is used. From time to time the wom-an tastes the flour, until she finds that every trace of the bitter principle has been dissolved out. The sweetening process is then completed, and the flour is ready for its final cooking. . . .

[*We must not forget that in the Mediterranean countries of Europe and North Africa, acorns are still eaten as emergency food in times of famine. The oak was sacred to the ancient Greeks, as to the Maidu. Archaeolo-gists will recognize in the stone- and shell-working techniques of the Maidu a parallel to the late Mesolithic and Early Neolithic in the Old World.*]

Grasshoppers and locusts were eaten eagerly when they were to be had. . . . Angleworms were much relished. They were collected in considerable quantities by planting a pole in the ground in a favorable spot, and then working this pole round and round, running around it at the same time, and stamping hard upon the ground. The worms quickly came to the sur-face, and, when gathered, were gen-erally cooked into a thick soup.

Eels were speared, split, and dried. In preparing them for food, they were usually cut into small pieces, and stewed. Salmon were split, and dried by hanging them over a pole. When thoroughly dry, the fish was usually pounded up till it was reduced to a coarse flour, and kept in baskets. It was eaten dry, as a rule.

Deer and other meat was cut into strips and dried. Usually this was done in the sun; but occasionally a fire was lighted under the drying meat to hasten the process, and to smoke the product slightly.

Salt was used sparingly, but was highly prized. It seems to have been obtained largely from local salt deposits and springs, but considerable is declared to have been brought from deposits of some size near the Marysville Buttes. . . .

That portion of the Maidu living in the mountains depended much more on game than did the lowland people, and they were much more skilful hunters . . . .

[*The mountain Maidu, obtaining a surplus of game, traded dried venison and deerskins to the people of the valley.*]

Except on their hunting trips, the Maidu seem not to have been travellers. They rarely went far from home, even on hunts. It seems that twenty miles was an unusual distance to go, and few went to greater distances from their homes. This restriction of travel was in part due to the rugged nature of the ground, and in part to the hostility of the different villages toward each other. Villages were at times abandoned, it seems; but the move was but a few miles at most, and after several years the original site was often reoccupied. The inhabitants of any one village thus knew only a small section of country, and all lying beyond was *terra incognita*.

In the mountains there was, to be sure, the annual change from the settled winter life in the earth lodges and permanent homes along the streams, to the wandering summer life on the ridges in temporary shelters; but the area traversed in the wandering was very restricted, and each village, or group of villages, guarded very jealously the territory it considered its own.

. . . The Northeastern Maidu traded with the Achoma'wi Indians, getting chiefly beads, and giving in exchange bows and deer hides. With the Piutes and Washos there seems to have been little trade or intercourse. With the Northwestern Maidu, those in the higher Sierra traded for beads, pine nuts, salt, and salmon, giving in exchange arrows, bows, deer hides, and several sorts of food. In exchange the beads were counted, not measured by strings. For each ten beads a stick was laid down as a counter. Tobacco grew plentifully in the region about Honey Lake, and was traded from there quite extensively. The Northwestern Maidu traded chiefly with the Wintun, and the principal article secured was beads. For currency, the circular, disk-shaped shell beads were the standard. As just stated, they were counted, and not measured in strings, but seem always to have been kept in strings. Woodpecker scalps appear not to have been used as an exchange medium here, as they were so largely on the Klamath River.

. . . The principal weapons in use among the Maidu were the bow and the spear. The bows made in the mountain sections, where yew could be be obtained, were regarded as superior to others, and were quite an article of trade. . . . The back of the bow was covered with a layer of sinew, generally the back sinew of the deer. . . . Each strip or shred of the sinew, as it was put on, was dipped in glue prepared from scraped and boiled salmon skins. The layer being thus built up of the required thickness, the bow was placed in the sun and carefully dried, great pains being taken that in the drying the sinew layer did not crack. As soon as a crack appeared, it was at once smoothed over, and the sinew pressed together again. When the sinew layer was wholly dry, the bow had to be painted. To this end the paint (most commonly a greenish mineral pigment obtained in trade from the extreme northern boundary of the State, or just across it in Oregon) was mixed with salmon glue, and applied with the end of a feather. As a rule, the bow was wound with a narrow strip of fur or buckskin at the grip. . . .

The spears in use were rather heavy, with a shaft two metres or more in length, and were exclusively for thrusting. The shaft was usually wrapped with sinew for four or five centimetres, about thirty centimetres back of the point. The latter was commonly of obsidian, from ten to fifteen centimetres in length, and was securely tied with sinew in a groove in the end of the shaft, and still further secured by pitch. . . .

For defence, the Maidu has two sorts of armor,—the elk hide, and the stick or slat armor. The former was but slightly used, and was merely a stiff, heavy piece of skin covering the body from the shoulders to the knees, suspended from the shoulders by cords. The stick armor was much more in use, and more serviceable. . . .

The warfare of the Maidu was merely raiding and ambushing. Owing to the lack of any feeling of tribal unity, there was little in the way of combined attack on an enemy on any considerable scale. Several villages, indeed, would at times band together against a common enemy, but apparently these unions were not lasting or of any great size. Warning of attacks was commonly given by means of signal smokes and fires; and attacks were usually made at dawn, or just before. In fighting, great reliance was placed on dodging. The fighters stood with their sides toward the enemy, so as to present a small mark, and kept in constant movement from side to side, dancing about and capering, so that it might be difficult for their opponent to hit them. Prisoners, if men, were usually killed. Women were carried off by their captors, but very often managed to escape

after a short time. Many stories of such escapes are told. Slaves were not taken or used. As a rule, the slain were scalped, and, it is asserted, a scalp dance was held on the return of the party, the scalps being suspended from a pole, while all the visitors and their wives danced about. . . .

Besides the intervillage enmities, the Maidu had many outsiders to contend against. The Northeastern Maidu were particularly embroiled with the Washo, the Achoma'wi, and the Yana (Kombo). The valley people seem to have had the Yana on the north, and at times the Wintun, as their chief enemies. . . .

[Football] . . . seems to have been much more common in the mountains than in the Sacramento Valley, and was played exclusively by men. Two poles were set up about seven metres apart, and four or six players ranged in line with each pole, the players standing from thirty to fifty metres apart, and forming parallel lines. The two end men farthest from their respective goals each had a buckskin ball stuffed with deerhair, and varying from fifteen to twenty centimetres in diameter. At a given signal each kicked his ball toward his goal, and ran after it. The second man in the line then kicked it on farther to the third, who in his turn kicked it to the fourth; and thus it was passed from one to another, that side being the winner whose ball was first to reach the goal. The game was the occasion of great excitement, villages playing against each other usually; and it was a great favorite when any considerable gathering of Indians took place. . . .

The women had a game somewhat similar to the men's football, played however, with different implements. It was played usually by six players, though at times an unlimited number took part. The players had a stick about one hundred and twenty-five centimetres long, with which they tossed either a buckskin rope, plaited of several strands, and usually about thirty centimetres in length; or a couple of sticks, fifteen centimetres long and five in diameter, tied to the ends of a buckskin cord about ten centimetres in length; or a rope or bundle of frayed cottonwood bark. Two goal posts were set up, as in the men's football game, and the game was played in the same manner, the rope or sticks being tossed from one player to another by means of the poles. . . . In the Sacramento Valley the game was played with two acorns tied together by a string, and was played only once a year, at the time of the annual burning. The men's football was also, in this region, played only at this same time, and both seem to have had somewhat more of a ceremonial character than elsewhere. . . .

The favourite game, however, of the Maidu, was, and still is, the so-called "grass game," played for a stake, and, like all gambling games, played with great earnestness, and often for days at a time without stop. . . .

The implements used in the game are two sticks or "bones" about six centimetres in length, and from one to two centimetres in thickness. . . . One of these . . . is plain: the other . . . either has a thong or cord tied about the centre, or is scratched deeply in a ring, and this filled with pitch or charcoal. . . . In addition to these bones, there are used counting sticks known as de'mi. These are nowadays merely splinters of wood, roughly of the same size and length. . . . The chief variations in the game are in the number of these counting sticks which are used. . . .

In playing the game, two players play on a side; and, as the game is usually played in the dance house, two sit at the right, and two at the left, of the door, with the fire between them. Before each pair of players is a pile of dried grass, in which the "bones" are wrapped in playing the game. The stake played for may be anything. It may be given by one of the players, it may be contributed to by all the players, or it may be the result of contribution by the players and the spectators together. In the last case, any outsider or spectator who puts anything into the stake is entitled to the same proportion of the winnings, if his side wins; he having to bet, at the time he contributes, which side he thinks will win. All being in readiness, and the de'mi being equally divided between the two sides, the game commences. Each of the two players on one side has a pair of "bones." Taking one in each hand, each of the two players begins to sing his gambling song or songs, waving his hands about, changing the bones rapidly from hand to hand, now high in the air, now low down near the ground, now behind his back. He seizes a mass of the dried grass, and, wrapping each bone in a handful of grass, continues to shift and change the bones, singing the while, and swaying his body back and forth and from side to side in time with the rhythm of the song. Both men sing the same song, although sometimes they sing different words. Meanwhile the two players on the other side watch the whole performance with intense earnestness. At last, after perhaps four or five minutes of this preparation, the two players who have been shifting the bones stop, and, holding their hands tightly clinched, and usually pressed tight against the breast, they continue to sing their songs in a somewhat suppressed tone, and sway gently in time as before. Suddenly one of the players on the opposite side claps his hands once, twice, or three times, and shouts, thus designating the hands in which he thinks the marked or unmarked bones are, darting or throwing out his hand or hands violently at the same moment. As each of the two players holding the bones has one of both kinds, it follows that these four bones may be in any one of four possible arrangements. A, sitting on B's right, may have the marked bone in his right hand, while B holds his in the left, the two bones being thus far apart,—on the outside, as it were, of the pair of players; or A may have his marked bone in the left, while B has it in his right, thus bringing the bones together in the middle; or A may have his marked bone in the left, while B has it in his left also; or each may have the marked bone in his right hand. For each one of these four possible arrangements there are special phrases or cries, and often each arrangement has a dozen or more such. . . .

In general, although there are two players on the guessing side, only one does the guessing. As long as he is successful, the other keeps still; but, should the guesser prove unlucky, he ceases, and the other partner tries his luck. The guess having been made, the two players holding the bones open their hands, and show which hands the bones are actually in. If those guessing guess wrongly, they throw over two de'mi. If, however, they guess correctly, both pairs of bones are tossed across the fire to them, and they, in their turn, become the ones who hold the bones, while those who have just held the bones become the guessers. Should the opponents guess correctly the location of one blank bone only, then a single pair of bones is tossed across, and the side which has just "rolled" or held the bones does so again; this time, however, the single remaining pair of bones being used by one of the players only. If the opponents again guess correctly, this remaining pair of bones is tossed across, and the opponents become the "rollers." If they fail, they have to return the first set, and begin all over again. . . .

[There are several ways of playing this game, depending on the number of counters used and the system of counting. Each side keeps its original counters separate from its winnings, and does not begin paying off with the winnings until the original counters are all gone.]

In any case, the game is played until one side or the other gets all the counters. . . .

In the foothill region the grass game was often played as follows. A party of men from one village would go to another village to gamble. They would sit down outside the dance house on arriving, and make sixteen new de'mi. These being finished, they make up a stake, each member of the party contributing something. One of their number is then deputed to take this into the dance house. The residents then have to add to this stake an equal amount. The chief of the village then calls in the visitors, who come in, and seat themselves on the side of the house nearest to their own village. The new de'mi are then divided, and the game begun. None may eat anything till one game has been won. . . .

In the regular grass game the players are always in great earnest. The players who "roll" or shift the bones get into a dripping perspiration from the violence of their movements and the energy they put into their singing. The opponents stare with wide-open eyes, and watch every flutter of an eyelid, in their endeavor to determine in which hand the bone is held. Their faces work, they become much excited, and are absorbed, to the exclusion of all else, in the game. Village plays against village, or parties within the village contend against each other; and at times the games continue for twenty-four or even thirty-six hours without a stop, the long game in particular well deserving its name. Into the myths the game enters constantly; and we find great players mentioned—those who had passages through their arms and body, so that they could transfer the bones back and forth unknown to the opponents, and thus, by cheating, win all. The myths all speak of the custom of rival chiefs playing for each other's people, the winner carrying the loser and all his people away as slaves, or killing them. We also find rivals playing for each other's eyes and hearts. . . .

Each village—or, in the case of small villages close together, each little group of villages—had a head man or chief. The position was in no case hereditary among the Northern Maidu, but seems to have been so among the more southern villages. The chief was chosen largely through the aid of the shaman, who was supposed to reveal to the old men the choice of the spirits. [*By shaman Dixon here means the yukbe, a dreaming shaman, the head of the village hierarchy. He must not be confused with the more numerous sucking or healing shamans.*] Generally, some person of mature years was selected; and wealth, ability, and generosity were strong arguments in favor of a given man's choice. Once chosen, he held his place only so long as he gave satisfaction. Should his conduct be displeasing to the people, he could be deposed, and a new chief put in his place. This was also brought about through the exertions of the shaman, who was supposed to declare the spirits' will in the matter. The functions of the chief seem to have been largely advisory, although a man of strong character and ability generally had what practically amounted to mandatory powers. There seems to have been, as a rule, a rather indeterminate council, composed of the older members of the Secret Society, and with these men the chief was supposed to consult. Apparently the chief often led the people

of the village in war . . . although a special war leader was often selected instead, who was noted for his bravery. Among the Northern Maidu, the chief seems not to have fared much better than the other members of the community. He had to hunt and fish as well as the others; and while he received his share of all meat and fish distributed, yet there seems to have been no larger portion given to him, as a rule, than to others. The Southern Maidu, however, particularly along their line of contact with the Moquelumnan people to the south, gave the chief a more important position in this matter. He had his choice of all meat killed, and sometimes there were young men who gave the chief the whole product of their chase at times. In this there was an approximation to the custom among the Moquelumnan people, where the chief was supplied regularly with food by the village. The chief usually occupied the largest house; and where there was no separate structure for use as a dance house, the chief's large house was often used for the purpose. In any case, he was regarded as having special rights in the dance house; and at his death it was not infrequently torn down or burned. . . .

The area owned by each community was very definite, and its exact limits were known and marked. Practically the same system seems to have been in force throughout the region occupied by the Northern Maidu. There are definite traditions of meetings held by several different communities to agree upon and mark out these boundaries, and at these meetings marks were adopted to designate the territory owned by each community. In the case of the communities occupying the western part of Butte County among the Northwestern Maidu, there were, according to information obtained by

Mr. Spencer, four of these communities or "tribes" which thus entered into an agreement. The Bald Rock people adopted as their mark a crescent with upturned horns; the Bidwell Bar people selected a Latin cross; the people about Oroville took three vertical parallel lines; and the villages near Mooretown and Swede's Flat had a combination of the last two designs. The whole area occupied by this group of four "tribes" was divided by boundary lines, each section forming a rude square, the corners being marked by the designs of the abutting tribes. The method of marking was to peck or scratch the design into a large bowlder or outcrop of rock. The lines connecting these corners were carefully determined, and, although apparently not marked, their position was known and remembered with exactness. Each tribe or group of communities kept its boundary lines constantly patrolled by men, who were to see that no poaching took place, and that the rights of each tribe were respected. These men were, it is said, selected by the chief every week, and two or more deputed to guard each side of the area. The men were chosen for their bravery and steadiness, those who had quick tempers, or had shown lack of judgment, not being thought fit. The men were marked while on duty by a single tail feather of the magpie, worn upright in the hair. The guards met and exchanged accounts once or twice a day. They were armed with bow and arrow, but only used them as a last resort. Game shot or wounded by a person within his own tribe's territory might be followed by the hunter, if it crossed the line into a neighboring tribe's land, only for a certain distance. If he could dispatch the animal within this limit, he was free to take it away with him. Should he fail, or follow it beyond this distance, the guardians

along the boundary were supposed to take the meat away. Any person belonging to the tribe into whose land the stranger had thus come could kill such wounded game, and carry it off. The underbrush was commonly burned out every year by each tribe in its own territory, to make hunting more easy. In time of war, these boundaries are said to have been guarded still more carefully; so that, if the attacking party were not driven off, at least an alarm could be given. . . .

The regulations in regard to different crimes were few and simple. Theft and murder, if commited on another tribe, were right, and involved no blame. Theft among one's own tribe was generally punished by reprisal if possible, the aggrieved taking something of about equal value.[1] Murder of a tribesman, or indeed of any person, involved usually blood revenge. In the Sacramento Valley region the murderer is killed, if possible, by some of the members of the murdered man's family. If it be impossible to reach him, then any member of his village will be killed instead. If the family of the murdered man are willing, the revenge may be compounded for by a payment of beads, etc. In case the affair lies between two villages, then a party from each side dresses as if for war; and they then meet, and sit down to a conference, at which the amount to be paid is discussed and settled. In the foothills the same general customs were in force. There was a distinct effort, in attempting to revenge a murder, to kill the offender in exactly the same way as he had killed the victim in the first place. If he had used a bow and arrow, the avenger would also; if he had used a stone or club, so would the avenger. . . .

. . . Gatherings of a social as dis-

[1] Theft, if unpaid for, gave the right to the aggrieved to kill the thief.

tinguished from a ceremonial nature were common. One village, or a man in that village, would invite other villages to a feast, or, as it is generally called, a "soup dinner." When it had been decided to hold such a festival, the shaman, as a rule, was requested to prepare "strings." These were cords on which a number of knots were tied, the number corresponding to the number of days between the time of sending out these "strings" and the date of the festival. As many strings were prepared as there were families that were to be invited; and when all were ready, they were sent out by messengers, who distributed them to the different families asked. Each day the head of the family untied a knot, or cut it off; and thus all knew when the time had come, and all arrived together. Such notices were usually sent out one or two weeks in advance. At these festivals the chief amusements were gambling, and games of various sorts; and abundant supplies of acorn soup and mush were provided. This was supplemented by other kinds of food; and after a couple of days of feasting and merrymaking, the guests went home. The season most favored for such gatherings seems to have been the summer months; for in winter the food supply was less abundant, and indulgence in any games except the gambling-games was impossible. . . .

Puberty ceremonials are held only for girls among the Maidu, although in one sense the initiation ceremonies of the Secret Society may be considered as puberty ceremonies for the boys. Inasmuch as, however, these initiations may occur at any age up to middle life, it seems they should not be regarded as puberty ceremonies proper. . . .

[*They are actually rites of passage for consecutive age grades, as in Australia and elsewhere, and only loosely associated with puberty.*]

[In the Sacramento Valley region] at the time of a girl's attaining puberty, she notifies her mother of the fact, and the latter at once communicates the news to all the relatives and friends. That evening all these friends and relatives, men and women, assemble at the girl's house. The fire is covered with ashes, and all present gather in a ring about the fireplace, sitting on the ground. Each person holds two stones, which they beat together in time to the songs sung. The girl herself sits alone, and some distance apart from the others, in the northwest corner of the house, covered over completely with mats and skins. No man or boy may come near her. The whole gathering now begins to sing, beginning always with the "grasshopper song." Other songs follow this, in which the different roots, seeds, and food products gathered by women are mentioned. A mistake made by any singer causes him or her to be sent out of the house at once. These songs are kept up throughout the night; and then at dawn all go out, and, standing on the top of the house, sing the final song, "Elaki ya'-mandi lai'dam yowowau'no" ("Manzanita hill-on the dawn"; i.e., the dawn begins to show on the manzanita hill). This song finished, all return to the house, and are given a feast by the girl's parents. The same proceedings are carried out on the next night again; and so on for perhaps a week. The ceremony is known as do'ngkato or yo'-pokato. The girl is known throughout the ceremony as do'mi. Except during the singing at night, she has to remain in a small separate hut called the do'mim uyi.

She may eat no meat or fish for five days. She may not feed herself, but has to have her mother, or other older woman, feed her. She has a basket, plate, and cup for her own use. She must use a scratching stick for scratching her head. At the end of five days she takes a warm bath in the do'mim uyi, and, while still having to remain in the hut, and use the scratching stick, she may now feed herself. After five days more she goes to the river and bathes, after which her parents give a big feast. At this feast any person may ask the parents for anything that pleases the guest's fancy, and the parents are obliged to give it. This even goes so far as having to give a daughter in marriage if she is asked for. At the feast the girl in whose honor it is given dresses in her best, and much effort is expended in display at this time. At each subsequent menstrual period the woman has to seclude herself for three or four days in the do'mim uyi, and must abstain from fish and meat, must not touch or come near a man or boy, and may not handle any food except that which she herself is to eat. . . .

[*Among the Northeastern Maidu, people assemble from villages all around, and for several nights, after the dancing, there is a general indulgence in sexual license.*]

. . . In the Sacramento Valley section, when a man wanted to marry, he sent a friend with a gift of beads to the family of the girl. The present would be given to the father of the girl, who would keep it if he and his wife and the other relatives considered the gift large enough, and the match a desirable one. . . . The consent of the girl was always necessary, and was obtained usually by the suitor before sending the gift to her parents. If accepted, the man usually went to live with the girl's family, if they were members of his own village. If his wife was of another village, however, she invariably came to live with him. For a period of some months, at least, the husband hunted and fished for the family of his wife. Often, if she were from another village, the pair would make a long visit with her family about six months after the marriage.

There seems to have been no very general rule as to whether the man should choose his wife within or without the village. On the whole, there would appear to have been a slightly greater practice of local exogamy. Many men were monogamous; but those who could afford it generally had two or more wives, although the chief was the only one, usually, who had as many as four. If a man had more than one wife, there seems to have been no noticeable difference in rank between them, all having equal rights. Should a wife prove unfaithful, her father was obliged to take her back again, and repay the husband the purchase-money or gift made at the time of marriage. The levirate, while not compulsory, was usually complied with. The ordinary customs in regard to the mother-in-law were in force, mother-in-law and son-in-law not looking at or speaking to each other. The woman always covered her head when she met her daughter's husband. . . .

. . . There is some difference in the customs relating to death and burial in different portions of the Maidu area. In the Sacramento Valley region the usual custom appears to have been burial, and not cremation. The body of the deceased was dressed in the best the family could afford, and decorated with strings of beads, and with feather ornaments of various sorts. It was placed on a bear skin, and, the knees being bent closely, so that the body was in a squatting position, it was then wrapped and roped up by some of the older men into a ball. Sometimes several skins were used, but, as a rule, one was all that could be afforded, The grave was dug generally close to the village, as, were it at a distance, enemies might dig up the body for the beads. The grave was usually from about a metre to a metre and a half in depth, and over it a mound of earth was heaped. Some food was placed in the grave with the body, as well as bow and arrows, pipe, etc. The body being buried, all went back to the house, and wailed for some time; and, although the wailing began at once after death, it was now continued with redoubled energy. . . . In mourning, the widow cut her hair short, and covered her head, face, neck, and breast with a mixture of pine pitch and charcoal obtained from charring the wild nutmeg or pepper nut. This pitch she was obliged to wear until it came off, generally many months. Often there was a longer period set, as a year or more, and it was then renewed. The widow must remain in the house continually during the daytime, and was allowed to come out only for a short time after dark. This she must continue until the time of the "burning." There are said to have been no food restrictions. A man in mourning had to cut his hair short, and also wore the pitch. He must not gamble or dance till the "burning" was over. During the period while the widow remained in the house, she was constantly occupied in making baskets and other things which were to be burned for the deceased at the next "burning" that was held. Generally all relatives aided her in this. . . .

. . . By far the most important of the ceremonials and customs in connection with death and burial among the Maidu, and one of the most important of all their ceremonials, was the annual so-called "burning," or "o'-stu." . . .

As a rule, a burning ground, once chosen, is used for many generations. Sometimes a burning ground is abandoned for lack of people, the village or villages to whom it belongs having largely died out. As a rule, however, the ground is kept up even when the number of survivors of a village is very small. A man always desired to be buried in the same place as his ancestors. Several villages generally have a burning ground in common. Should a man move away from home, he would, when he died, be buried in the burning ground of his native village. . . .

Every burning ground is ruled by one or more members (generally shamans) of the tribe or village in whose territory it is situated. . . . the relatives may not take part in the burning until they have received a membership string or necklace for the ground in which the body was placed. After the body is buried, therefore, the mourners got to those who are in charge of the ground in question, and apply for such a string, so that they may take part in the next burning which is to be held. The owners or overseers of the burning ground then give the applicant a string, for which payment had to be made in beads, furs, food, or other things. The so-called "strings" are necklaces of beads and cord, the number of beads and their arrangement varying with every burning ground, so that from the string one can tell at once to what ground the person wearing it belongs. The arrangements of beads on the cord are varied thus:

o—o—oo—o—o—oo—o—o
oo—o—oo—o—oo—o—oo
ooo—o—ooo—o—ooo—o—ooo, etc.

Having received such a string, the recipient is entitled to burn (or "cry") for a period of five years. At the end of this time, if no other member of the family has died, the person may burn the string, or tell the one from whom it was received that he wishes it to be burned. When this occurs, he receives from the original giver the equivalent of the price paid for it. The strings are worn, while they are in the hands of the mourner, constantly as a necklace. Should other members of the family die before the five years are up, the string may be kept till five years from the date of the most recent death. . . . strings may be issued by the individual mourners, to any persons whom they wish to invite to come to the burning which they expect to hold for their dead. The recipient must give in return a few baskets or something of that sort, and is entitled to attend all burnings by the issuer, until the latter redeems the string. This is done, as above described, by paying back to the person property equivalent in value to that which he originally gave for it. The string, thus redeemed, is then burned. The whole affair of redemption and burning of the string takes place at one of the regular burnings. In some cases, if the person issuing the strings is wealthy, he or she may give property to the recipient when issuing the string, in which case the recipient must pay this back, when the string is called for to be redeemed. The time of the burning is set by the votes of all who have strings for that particular ground. If a person has many relatives to burn for, the other members will not hasten the matter, but let the person have plenty of time to get things ready. The burning comes, however, as a rule, in the latter part of September, or early October, although it may be put off until somewhat later. Every family may hold one of these strings, but no more. They must be kept with great care, never given away or traded, and never sold.

The date being finally set by the members, as above stated, in consultation with the shaman, knotted strings are distributed to all who are to be present; and in the usual manner, by untying or cutting off one knot every day, they all arrive together. The village in whose territory the affair is to occur has to supply the guests with food. Each member of the local group gives as much toward this general store as he can. All such food is then collected in baskets in a great pile. The whole number of guests having arrived, the shaman calls for the food to be brought, and then divides it among the people as he sees fit. Usually, it is divided with regard to the size of the families, a family of six getting twice as much as one of three. In distributing the food, the chief or shaman calls the name of the oldest male member of that family, who then comes forward, and receives the share for the whole family, which he then divides among them. Any person who comes late, after the food has been distributed, must be looked out for by those who have already received food.

The whole party being assembled, the ceremony begins the evening before the actual burning. This preliminary ceremony is participated in only by the chief mourners. There is little regular order in the affair. About sunset they gather at the burning ground and wail and mourn at the graves, crying thus for several hours. Often the graves are covered by the mourners with a thin layer of flour, and then of earth. Members begin and stop when they please, and drop away one by one, going back to the camp to sleep. The purpose of this prelimiary cry is to give notice to the dead that the burning is to take place.

The following morning and early afternoon are spent in repairing the brush fences about the burning ground, and in gathering the poles to be used for the suspension of gifts. These brush fences or enclosures . . . are usually from twenty to thirty metres in diameter, or less, and are made by piling up brush of any kind about a low, roughly circular earthen embankment about twenty centimetres high. The brush is leaned against poles running between crotched posts, and forms a fence from one to two metres in height. In this fence there are generally two openings left—one at the eastern and one at the western side, the latter generally the wider. Sometimes but one such opening is made, and then invariably on the western side. In the centre a huge pile of wood is placed for the fire, which is lighted when the ceremony itself begins. . . .

The fences having been repaired, and plenty of wood gathered for the fire, all eat their dinner, the local residents partaking of their own supplies of food, the visitors depending on what had been given them, as already described. Each family eats by itself; and, although it may eat with others, it is not customary.

The meal over, the preparation of the poles is begun. Each mourner may have as many poles as he or she wishes and can fill; and each person will be given space according to the amount of property on the poles he has. Some have large quantities to burn, some but little, but the amount of goods does not increase the respect felt for the person. All the property to be burned by each mourner is brought to the burning ground the day before, but no display is made of it till the evening of the burning itself. If the night is bright, one is supposed to wait until dusk before beginning to prepare the poles and display the property. There is, however, complete individual freedom, and any person may begin to prepare his poles earlier if he desires. Each article which is to be burned in honor and for the use of the dead is, if possible, tied to a pole. Shirts have sticks placed in the arms to hold these out. The shirt is then hung to the pole by a string from the collar. The first shirt is tied at the top of the pole, and others successively below it till the pole is filled to within about one metre of the ground. In a similar manner other articles of clothing for men or women —skins, beads, necklaces, etc.—are tied to other poles. It is customary to have a separate pole for each sort of thing to be burned, all the shirts being on one pole or on several poles, all dresses on others, and so forth. People help each other in the preparation of their poles.

The poles are usually from five to eight metres long, and are either stripped of bark or not, as the person prefers. When these poles are all ready, each family carries its poles, with their loads of goods, to the centre of the burning ground, and digs a hole about fifty centimetres deep for each group of from five to ten poles to stand in. The poles are then placed in the hole, and earth firmly stamped down about them. The groups of poles are arranged roughly in rows, on the north and south sides of the fire. In 1904 one pole to which baskets were attached was not set in the ground, but thrust into the brush fence, so that the pole leaned inward at an angle of about 45°. The baskets on this pole were not used in the ceremony. The poles being thus set, the heavier articles, and such as could not well be attached to the poles, are piled on the ground at the foot. This would include such things as large baskets, flour, acorns, dried meat, fish, etc. . . . This all accomplished, each family gathers about its poles, and sits by them till all have finished. The large fire in the centre has not yet been lighted, but many small fires are lighted outside the enclosure for cooking purposes and for light. There is usually one such fire for each family.

After some time, one of the members of the local tribe, holding a member's string for this burning ground, comes forward and lights the fire. The task is usually given to some old man. So soon as the fire is lighted, any member may, if he chooses, sell or exchange any articles he has brought for the burning; and there is often considerable bargaining among the people for a time. If no trading takes place, or, if trading occurs, when it is over, the chief or shaman makes the opening address. Of this the following, delivered in 1900, may serve as an example:

"Don't fail to hear me! Don't fail to hear me! Light up the fire, it is not long till daylight. Our people are all ready. We have assembled here to mourn and cry again. We want no trouble. We are here to cry, and not for trouble. Do not drink whiskey. Hear me, all you boys! Do not drink any whiskey and get drunk. Come, here, every one, and from every place, and help us cry! If you assist us, we, in our turn, will assist you. I, as your chief, will lead you in all things. Come, one and all! While we are here, if any one has a member string, and he has finished with it, I am ready to receive it. If no one has one to give up, we will begin."

As soon as this address has been made, the speaker begins crying, and this is the signal for the others to begin also. The chief or shaman, having begun the crying, throws on the fire a few pine nuts, acorns, pieces of dried meat or fish. In no case, however, is anything yet taken from any of the poles, or the piles at their bases. All present now join in the wailing. From time to time individuals throw bits of food and small offerings taken from the piles on the ground into the fire, and in this manner the night passes till nearly dawn. The mourners stand back to the fire; and after gently swinging the article to be burned to and fro before the body, it is then swung over the fire and dropped in, the right hand being at the same time thrown up above the head, or simply to the head. In wailing, some moan or wail in a low tone, others scream loudly, and all use different expressions and exclamations, which are addressed to the dead. Some of these are the following: "Pity my poor boy!" "Where are you, my darling girl?" "Why, oh why, did you die, my boy?" "Oh, my husband!" "Come back, my poor sister!" "Brother, brother, brother, no more!" "My child, my child!" "Father, father, father, pity me!" At early dawn the stripping of the pole begins. Any person may start when he wishes, without waiting for the others. The poles are lifted from the holes, and the articles removed, either by the person who is giving them or by any friend who is willing to assist. As the objects are removed, they are thrown into the fire, singly or in armfuls. This is done always by the person who is giving the things. At this stage in the ceremony generally, the member and invitation strings are redeemed. Baskets and other property for this purpose are brought and placed on the poles, just as other property is. New strings are also given out at this time. As soon as any one thus begins to take down the poles, it serves as a signal for all to begin, and a general stripping of poles at once takes place. It is at this time that the ceremony reaches its climax of excitement and importance. The older men and women sway their bodies from side to side, and sing and wail, and there is intense excitement among all. The fire is often nearly smothered by the great amount of things thrown into it; and, under these circumstances, a halt must be called till the fire can burn up again. While the things from the poles are being put on the fire, and to a less extent during the earlier wailing, the mourners pat their heads rapidly with their hands, and blow forcibly every now and then, expelling the air from the lungs violently, as if to blow away unseen things. As the dawn approaches, and the last of the goods are being thrown into the fire, the wailing and moaning increase, if possible, in intensity, and the older women try to throw themselves into the fire, having to be restrained by the men. Old men are wiping away the tears that stream down their faces, and many are prostrated by the fatigue and excitement. As soon as all the poles are stripped, the remaining articles piled at the bases of the poles are thrown on; and this continues till all has been destroyed.

After a short interval, during which the assembly secures a little rest, the chief or shaman makes his closing address: "Don't fail to hear me! Our burning is ended. I command you all to go to the dance house. We are all tired. At the dance house we have food for all. There we will eat, for it is not well to go home hungry. You may gamble there. The fire is burning in the dance house, and the house awaits your coming. Gamble and make merry, but let us have no trouble or disturbance. Let us go! I will lead the way." This speech over, the assembly adjourns to the dance house, and there, after a little food and sleep on the part of the men (the women being usually scattered about in the various other houses), there is for a day or more a constant succession of games, gambling, and feasts. Then one by one the visitors start for home, and the village returns to its former quiet life.

At the burning held at Mooretown in 1900 there were about a hundred and fifty poles filled with objects, so the amount of property sacrificed was not small. There were dresses, shirts, baskets, two poles of earrings, one of knitted caps, three bear hides, one coyote hide, one pole of raccoon skins, and one of chinchilla-cat skins, etc. There were about three hundred pounds of flour, birch-seed flour, pine nuts, dried eels, dried fish, etc. There

were also a number of hats for boys, men, and women. The approximate value of the goods burned was about two hundred dollars; the value in baskets destroyed was about equal; and in skins the money value was about thirty-five dollars. Thus nearly five hundred dollars' worth of property was burned at this single burning. In this same year there were burnings held at four or five other places in Maidu territory; and while the amount of property consumed was probably considerably smaller in all cases, yet the aggregate must have been over a thousand dollars.

. . . After sacrificing thus for three or four years, it seems to be felt that enough has been done; and, as a rule, the family does not continue to offer property for a relative at the burnings for more than four or five years. Occasionally, however, some will continue the offerings for a long period; and one case was noted of a woman who had burned for ten or twelve years for her husband, and she had declared that it was her intention to continue to "burn" every year until she should die. . . .

The ceremonial of the burning in the region of the Sacramento Valley was, so far as known, substantially the same as above described from the foothill area. The ceremony has at present, however, gone almost completely out of use. . . .

In the Sacramento Valley region, when a person dies, the soul or ghost stays in or near the body for three or four days. Then it starts off, and travels everywhere that the man or woman has ever been in life, tracing step by step his or her journeyings throughout their whole extent, and in particular visiting every spot on which the person had spat. Besides thus traversing once more the scenes of the earthly life, the ghost is apparently supposed also to act over again every deed performed in the flesh. This done (and it would seem that it is accomplished with miraculous rapidity), the ghost sets out toward the Marysville Buttes, a group of volcanic peaks in the centre of the great expanse of the Sacramento Valley opposite Marysville; and here, entering a mysterious cave which is often spoken of in the myths, finds a supply of spirit food, of which it partakes, and then passes up into the Hi'piningkodo ("the above-land"), to the Yo'ngkodo ("the flower land"), to the Ku'kinimkodo ("the spirit land"), whence it never returns. The ghosts seen by people, by shamans, and, it would seem, perhaps also those who are supposed to be present at the burnings, are the ghosts of persons who have not yet finished the pilgrimage described as preceding their departure. . . .

[Accounts of the creation of the world vary. In one] . . . the world was formed from a robin's nest found by the Creator floating on the primeval sea. After the world was made, the germs of the present Indian people were prepared by him also; and after ineffectual attempts to overcome the maliciousness of Coyote, the Creator departed from this world, travelling towards the east, into which he disappeared. Various relics of his presence in the world are pointed out, among them the stone canoe in which he and all the other people took refuge, when, in his third and final unsuccessful attempt to destroy Coyote, he caused a great flood to cover all the world. This canoe is still to be seen, it is said, on the summit of Keddie Peak, just north of Indian Valley. The sites of his and Coyote's dance houses may be seen as huge circular depressions at Durham, and the scenes of many of his adventures are accurately known and pointed out. . . .

The Maidu believe that the whole country occupied by them is thronged with mysterious powers or spirits known as ku'kini. These spirits are particularly associated with prominent rocky peaks, crags, or cliffs, with rapids or waterfalls, and with lonely mountain lakes. There are spirits under the earth who are very powerful; there are also many in the sky. These beings are regarded as residing at definite spots, to which in particular the shamans go to gain power. Every shaman must have one or more of these as his guardian spirit or spirits, and they aid him in all that he does. He also, of course, may have the different animal spirits. Those of the rocks and little lakes are, however, very powerful. At times the shaman calls them to the dance house; and they are supposed to enter by the smoke hole, and hang head downward therefrom. They are in appearance like people, but always have the tongue lolling; and, as they hang head downward, the tongue reaches to the ground.

. . . To stop storms, feathers or wild-pepper wood are burned, or the leaves of various sorts of oaks.—To cause rain or storms, recourse is had to smoking ceremonially, and praying for rain by the shaman.—Rain is also sure to result from the telling of stories about the water snake, or from chasing frogs. —If one tells stories in the daytime, many believe the narrator will become crooked.—The spots in the moon are thought to be a frog. Others recognize in them the face of the Creator.— If the moon, in its first quarter, stands with the points of the crescent upwards, it denotes a good season for fruit, good weather, freedom from sickness; should it stand with points directed horizontally, it denotes a poor season, bad weather, and sickness.

. . . The shaman was, and still is, perhaps the most important individual among the Maidu. In the absence of any definite system of government, the word of the shaman has great weight: as a class they are regarded with much awe, and as a rule are obeyed much more than the chief. As the beliefs and customs in connection with the shaman vary considerably, they may best be considered geographically.

In the Sacramento Valley region it is not necessary for a man's ancestors to have been shamans in order for him to become one. Sometimes, while out hunting, he may see something in the woods that makes him fall down unconscious. The being or animal, whichever it is, then talks to him while he is this trance, and tells him what he is to do. When the man recovers, he spits blood and a whitish secretion of some sort, and then feels perfectly well again. He goes home, but tells no one of his experience, and goes without meat for some days. He never tells any one what he saw till he grows to be an old man. After this first meeting, the same animal or being constantly appears to the man, and gives him advice and help. In other cases a man dives for a fish or for shellfish, but fails to come up. He is thought to have seen something mysterious under the water, and is hunted for, and pulled out. If he revives, he is sure to become a shaman. Soon after the experience he falls sick, and has to be sung over by other shamans. He lies on the north side of the fire, feet toward the blaze. One shaman sits by his side all the time, while others sit about, singing. This is continued all night; and then at dawn two of the men lift the patient, and hold him in their arms, while all present dance. All this time blood is running at intervals from the patient's mouth. There seems to be in this region considerable instruction of the young shamans by the older ones. The older shamans are supposed to have

something about as long and large as a finger, sharp at each end. This they are supposed to insert in the candidate's nose. If he can get it out without help, he will be a shaman; if he has to have assistance, he is a failure. A shaman can by means of these si'la, as they are called, tell whether a man is a real shaman or not. He simply throws it at him: if it makes him bleed, the man is an impostor.

In doctoring a patient, the shaman has always to fast for a time. He wears a netted cap and a raven feather stuck into it. The pain or disease is sucked out, and is shown to the patient and friends. It is usually a small object with feathers on it. As soon as this object (the o'meya) is extracted, it is at once buried. Should the first shaman be unsuccessful, a second is called. Immediately on getting the o'meya out of the body of the patient, the shaman falls to the ground insensible. He revives after a while, and spits the o'meya out. Should a shaman fail to cure a patient, he gets no pay, but is not killed as a penalty, as was the case in the region to the north. If a man frequently has bad dreams, he is taken to the dance house, and the chief has to dance and sing over him. He uses, in this dance, a long-handled cocoon rattle, called so'loya. The patient lies on the ground, head away from the fire and toward the east. All the important men and shamans come in; and the chief, in dancing, stands by the main post in the dance house. When all is over, he washes the man's face, and pours water over his head. Then the man must go and swim and bathe, as also must the chief. Then both may eat meat again, from which they are debarred while the ceremony is going on. For such a ceremony a very large price is asked.

To kill an enemy, a shaman must be highly paid. To accomplish the result, the shaman merely goes to the enemy, and allows his own shadow to fall on the man. Then he goes to the river and bathes, and prays to his spirit guardians, saying, "I want so and so to die"; or the shaman may, as if in fun, merely touch or poke the victim with an elder stick, which is hollow, and contains some sort of "medicine." This method causes death very quickly. Formerly there was a special rattlesnake shaman in every village, who sucked the poison out, and cured people. These rattlesnake shamans had special ceremonies of their own. . . .

[Among the Northeastern Maidu,] some shamans are particularly successful in curing certain diseases. Some are able to cure the bites of bears, others those of snakes, etc. This specialization, and particularly the close connection of dreaming of the bear with curing bear bites, etc., does not seem so much developed here as just to the north, among the Achoma'wi. . . .

There are apparently at least two sorts of shamans—one the shaman proper (or yo'mi), whose main duties are the cure and causing of disease; and the other the "dreamers" (or ne'-tdim mai'du), whose abilities are largely those of being able to communicate with the spirits, and with ghosts of the dead. A man may be a "dreamer" and not a shaman, but nearly all shamans are also "dreamers." [*Since Dixon's time the meaning of the word shaman has been greatly extended. In its present sense, all these men were shamans.*] These "dreamers" hold meetings during the winter months, usually every few weeks. The meetings are held in the dance house, and the affair is always preceded by a feast or "soup." Strings are sent out as for a burning or other ceremonial, and the knots cut off or untied daily, till the date set has arrived. Guests are expected to arrive at the place where the affair is to be held a day or so before the ceremony proper. The day and night before the ceremony are given up to games, gambling, and trading. At dusk on the day set, men, women, and children all gather in the dance house; and then, after an hour or two of chatting and quiet, the shaman declares himself ready. The smoke hole is then partly covered, the fire completely banked with ashes, and the interior of the dance house made perfectly dark. No one is allowed to smoke, to speak, or to leave the house. The ceremony is described as follows: Taking his position at the main post of the dance house (the one back of the fire), the shaman begins to sing, shaking his cocoon rattle and beating with it on the post. The lips are given a peculiar quivering motion, making the voice tremble and quaver. After some time spent thus, the spirits are supposed to arrive, and answer the questions the shaman puts to them. The tone of his voice changes, and in an assumed tone he answers his own questions, the answers being supposed to come from the spirits present. Besides the shaman, there is always present at these affairs a pehei'pe or "clown." He apes the shaman in everything, repeats after him everything he says, and in every way tries to make the spectators laugh. . . . At these meetings the ghosts of the dead are often present, and convey their desires to their relatives. They and other spirits give directions as to when feasts are to be held, hunts made, or raids on neighboring villages undertaken. In no case do they attempt to foretell the future. . . .

Among the shamans of this section there was formerly, it seems, an annual dance, at which each shaman endeavored to overcome the others by means of his "poison" or charms. The dance was held in the dance house, and shamans from all about were invited to attend. Women shamans were present as well as men. During the ceremony every shaman tried to overcome the rest; and, although there were spectators present, they were not in danger, as the charms were directed only against the shamans. Each dancer had his or her peculiar dance and motions. Before the beginning of the dance, all fasted for a day or more. The shamans being assembled, the head shaman of the village where the dance was held announced the beginning of the ceremony. Certain rules had to be followed. No person who was not present at the beginning of the dance was allowed to enter it at a later period. No arms, knives, arrow points, sharp bones, sticks, or mysterious packages were allowed to be brought in, and none could be used as ornaments. Any person touching another was debarred from the remainder of the dance, and any one who should draw any blood from another was killed. The dancers were allowed to wear any sort of feather ornaments they chose. The rules being stated, and all being ready, the shamans from each village gathered together in little groups by themselves. A fire was lighted with the fire drill, and fed with dry manzanita wood, which had been carefully inspected by all the shamans to see that no poisonous roots had been mixed with it. The pehei'pe was the leader, and danced naked. No songs were sung, nor was there any beating of time with drum or sticks. Shamans held cocoon rattles, but that was all in the way of musical instruments that was allowed. In dancing, the body was swayed from side to side, and the hands held against the breast, and then thrown forcibly out and away from the body, palms out, as if warding off evil influences. The throwing out of the hands was used also to throw "poison" at the other dancers, an object also accomplished by

breathing strongly and forcibly. As the dance continued after an hour or two one shaman after another dropped out of the circle. Some were taken with violent pains in the stomach; others in the back, breast, head, or limbs. Some bled from the nose. Those who first recovered from their attacks, supposed to be the effect of the charms and "poison" sent out by the other shamans, attended to those who succumbed later, sucking out the "poison" or pain that had been thrown at them. Thus the dance continued till only one man was left, and he was declared the chief shaman of all. . . .

When the dancing came to an end, all having succumbed but one, all the participants went to a spring near by, and washed themselves carefully. All then returned to the dance house, and, seated in a circle, smoked the stone pipe and prayed, thus removing all traces of the charms and "poisons" which had been used in the dance. That no evil influence might survive, one shaman was deputed to remove such lingering traces as might be left on the body of the clown. This was done by blowing smoke over his body, as he sat near the centre of the house; and the action was accompanied by exhortations to the "poison" to go away, and leave all free from ill effects. . . . At the conclusion of the purification of the pehei'pe, a feast or "soup" was given, and all gambled, and many games were played. This ended the whole ceremony. . . .

[The most elaborate and spectacular ceremonies of the Maidu were those which formed the dramatic cycle of the winter season. These required an institutional framework of some complexity, including a leader (the head shaman), a head instructor (the chief), special prompters, dance-step teachers, and a clown. The actors performed before an audience composed largely of women and children.]

Certain general features characteristic of the dances may advantageously be considered before taking up in detail the description of the dances themselves. As a whole, there seem to be two different types—those dances in which no animal representations occur, and those in which these representations are an integral part of the ceremony. Where animals are represented, particularly in the region of the Northwestern Maidu, the dancers wear either the skin of the animal in whole or in part (as in the Bear, Deer, and Coyote dances), or ornaments which in some way symbolize the animal or bird in question. In none are any masks worn. In these dances, the personators of the animals endeavor to imitate the actions of the animal, and to utter its characteristic cries. The purpose of these animal dances (confined very largely to the Sacramento Valley area) is said to be varied. Some—like the Deer, Duck, and Turtle dances—have for their purpose the increase of the animals in question, that food may be plenty, and seem to have as an important feature a prayer or address in which the animal is besought to multiply and increase. Other dances, such as the Bear dance, are to soothe and pacify the animal, and render it less likely to attack hunters. Other dances still, like the Coyote dance, seem to refer to the Coyote myths at times, and the part the Coyote played in the creation and during the time of the "first people." One of the dances of the Sacramento Valley people, although not an animal dance, seems to have for its purpose the one which was referred to in the first class of animal dances; namely, the increase of the food supply of the people, acorns here being desired instead of game. We may, I think, reasonably regard the striking of the main post, therefore, by the dancers in the a′ki dance, as symbolical of the striking of the branches of the oaks in the autumn in the process of gathering acorns.

An interesting feature of both types of dances in the Sacramento Valley region is that of the bringing of a bundle of sticks by one of the participants in the dance, which bundle is presented to the chief or head man, as far as there is any. There are as many sticks in the bundle as there are men in the village; and each of these men subsequently has to make a payment to the chief of a few small skins or some beads. At least in the area occupied by the Northwestern Maidu, the dances seem to be under the direction of a leader or master of ceremonies, who himself takes part at times. The same person seems to fill the place every year, but this is not certain. Another person of importance is the clown. He is both clown and speaker for the chief or leader, mimicking the words and actions of the dancers, and, when the leader or chief wishes to speak, serving as his spokesman. As a clown he is constantly performing knavish tricks, and attempting to induce the spectators to laugh. He has his regular position in the dance house, at the foot of the front post; whereas the leader stands just back of the main post, near the drum and the men who are beating it. In the creation myth we find the clown mentioned with the Turtle as occupant of the canoe into which the Creator descended, and as playing a minor part in the events of creation.

In all the dances, and among all sections of the Maidu, great importance is attached to the main post of the dance house. As stated in speaking of the shaman ceremonies, the guardian spirits, when they appear, always sit on the top of this post, or cling to it, and the semi-sacredness which the post has may in part come from this fact. The post before the door is important, but not nearly so much so as the main post. In the dances, at least, of the Northwestern Maidu, the dancers as a rule, when not circling the fire, are formed into two lines—one on the north and one on the south side of the fire—on the left and right hand sides respectively of the door. When this is not the case, the dance is first held on the one side, and then repeated on the other side, of the fire. The rattles used in the dances in this same area, and in general throughout the whole Maidu territory, are always the split-rattle or clapper variety. They are carried by the dancers, and struck on the palm of the hand.

Throughout the whole series of dances, particularly among the Sacramento Valley people, four is very clearly the sacred number, and most individual features of the dances are repeated four times. The ceremonial circuit is also plainly sinistral or contraclockwise. The introduction of comic interludes (apart from the antics of the clown) is a feature of considerable interest among the Northwestern Maidu, and, from rather uncertain hints, may once have been much more common than the descriptions given me declare. . . .

In the Sacramento Valley region occupied by the Maidu, there seems to have been a regular dance season, beginning some time in October, and continuing through the winter until April or May. The season began and ended with a dance known as the he'si; and between these came two or three other great dances at stated periods, and a host of lesser dances, each of which might, it seems, be danced more than once, if desired, in the course of the season. The greater dances, however, were held but once a season.

The he'si was in some ways the most important of all the dances. . . . In it, as in the other greater dances, there seems to be a distinct attempt to represent various spirits and mythological beings. The dance is held in October or early November, the exact date being set by the chief and the leader of the Secret Society. Only men are allowed to be present in the dance house, although women and children sit outside on the roofs of the houses, and watch what they can. The men of the village being assembled in the dance house, in the early morning the ceremony begins by the approach of the ma'ki and his attendant yo'hyoh. The ma'ki wears the long feather cloak, which is itself called ma'ki. . . . Besides the cloak, he wears stuck in his hair, or rather in the feather bunch which covers and conceals his head, two sticks, to the end of each of which a single eagle feather is tied firmly. These two sticks are stuck in, one on each side of the head, pointing backward, and resembling, as described by my informant, the horns of a goat. He is followed by a yo'hyoh, who wears similar (?) feather sticks in his hair, is painted black, and, except for a skirt of shredded tule about his waist, is naked. A feather collar of some sort is worn around the neck. Both ma'ki and yo'hyoh have dressed at some hidden place, and come slowly to the door of the dance house just at dawn. They enter, and the ma'ki addresses the men assembled. He has brought with him a bundle of small sticks, one for each man present; and these sticks he gives to the chief. He then removes his feather cloak (it is uncertain whether publicly or behind a mat hung up at the back of the dance house), and each man present gives to him beads, feathers, or other property, according to his ability. This is all immediately handed over by the ma'ki to the chief, and it becomes his property. The yo'hyoh then goes out, but returns to the dance house about the middle of the morning, and dances. He carried a split-stick rattle in each hand. He is accompanied by another being, called ma'si. This person wears a feather band about his forehead, feather plume-sticks in his hair, and a black feather bunch at the back of his head. In his right hand he carries an arrow, and in the left a bow. He wears a breech-cloth only. The yo'-hyoh and ma'si dance side by side on the left side of the fire. They dance here twice; i.e., dance and rest, then dance again. This over, they pass around back of the fire, and dance similarly twice on the right or south side. In the afternoon, about two o'clock, a new sort of dancer appears, known as si'li. These si'ling ku'kini are six or eight in number, and wear feather bands on the forehead, feather plume sticks in the hair, and have a long fringe of women's hair tied about the forehead under the feather band, this hair fringe hanging down over the face, and concealing it wholly. They also wear a net (with feathers attached?) over the shoulders, head, and body, extending to the ground, and belted at the waist with a feather belt. In their left hands they carry bows; and in the right, spears. Their bodies are painted black all over. One after another they file into the dance house, and dance in line around the fire, contraclockwise. The leaders of the ceremonies put angelica root (ta'su) into the fire at this time. After the root has been put in the fire, the si'li cease their circling, and dance slowly on the same spot for some time. After this has gone on a while, they stop, put away their feather ornaments, bows, etc.; and all present sweat, dancing around the fire the while. They dance thus for a time, then rest, then dance again, and again rest, till they have danced four times, when all suddenly rush out of the house and plunge into

the river. The following day the yo'-hyoh comes in the morning again, accompanied, as before, by the ma'si. This time, however, there seem to be two yo'hyoh. One stops outside, and the other comes into the dance house. The si'li come again, as before, and dance, and then come the yo'mpui. Of these there are a dozen or more, each dressed and decorated a little differently from his fellows. All, however, are painted red all over, some having white streaks or spots also. They wear the feather band, and also apparently skirts of shredded tule. They come out one at a time, and dance similarly to the si'li. No angelica root is, however, put in the fire. When their dance is finished, every one, as before, sweats, and jumps into the river. While all the people have thus gone to the river, the ma'ki and yo'hyoh come out of the dance house, and pass in procession around it four times contraclockwise. This is for the purpose of preparing the dance house for its occupancy during the winter, and to make it "good." This over, they go to a secret spot, remove their costumes, and go back to get them at night, when they will not be seen. . . .

The Deer dance (su'mingkasi) is held, it would seem, generally about March, and is one of the most important of this class of dances. It begins at night, when, all women being out of the dance house, the fire is covered; and two men, without decoration or ornaments, go around and around the fire in the darkness, while the others present say, "Hoi, hoi!" After thus going around for some time, the spectators say, "Ts, ts, ts!" The two men then stop. After a while they again go around, and again stop; and this is done four times. Next morning very early these same two men go off to the woods; and one dresses in a feather cape, wearing on his head a deer's head with the antlers on. In each hand he carried a stick, painted black and white to represent the forelegs of the deer, and held thus, the man leaning on them as on two canes. The second man is merely the helper, and aids the deer man to dress. They come to the dance house, and, as usual, bring the bundle of sticks, and the usual payment takes place. Then the dance proper begins. Two men wear a headdress known as bo'topi, consisting of two long sticks, perhaps seventy-five or a hundred centimetres long, projecting forward. A very long feather band is worn, and also a feather crown (?), or perhaps only buzzard-feather sticks. Two other men wear the immense dö headdress, with its thirty or forty radiating twigs, in this case the twigs being feathered with chicken-hawk feathers. They also have feathers of the tail of the magpie stuck in their hair, and a band of badger skin about the forehead. The two men wearing the bo'topi come out from the dressingroom first, and, following the leader, first go toward the fire, then turn sharply to the left, make a complete turn, and then, going in front of the drum, pass around the fire contraclockwise back to the point where the sharp turn was made. The first of the two men stops here; the second goes on, and takes a position on the north side of the drum, symmetrical with that of the first man on the south side. The two men wearing the dö now come out, and, omitting the first turn and circle, pass around the fire as did the others, one stopping on the south and the others on the north side of the drum. Other men then follow, wearing the dö headdress, but with white goose feathers instead of those of the chicken hawk. These take their position behind the pair of men on either side of the drum, and then follow them, as they dance slowly for-

ward to the door and back. The next night the young men go out to the woods and paint their bodies black and white in spots, like fawns. The two men who wore the bo'topi paint themselves in stripes of black and white, as do also the two men wearing the dö. The two bo'topi enter first, followed by the dö; and, last of all, the crowd of young men painted to represent fawns. These latter form a line, half on the north side, half on the south side, of the house. The two bo'topi and two dö then dance back and forth east and west, between the two lines. They dance four times, and then stop. Apparently six or eight men then appear, wearing feather capes and deer heads. They dance in a squatting position, keeping the back to the fire, and going around contraclockwise. After four circuits, they stop, and turn their faces to the fire. They then go back to the drum, and lie on the ground; while the leader (ma'si), holding tule bunches in his hands, sings. They then get up and dance again, and again stop and lie down, repeating the whole four times. Then everyone cries; and the shaman, taking his cocoon rattle, sits by the foot of the main post and prays. The prayers are apparently that the deer may be numerous, and that people may get many.

. . . The Maidu of the Sacramento Valley had a definite dance or ceremonial season, lasting from some time in October till the following April or May. During this period there were a large number of different dances and ceremonials celebrated, of which some at least were to be held but once a year, and seem to have come at stated times. The other dances could, it appears, be held more than once in a season, but were not always so held. In the he'si, the dance which opens and closes the dance season, and in many other dances, mythical or supernatural beings seem to be represented, of which the most important are the ma'ki, the yo'hyoh, and the si'lin ku'kini. The ma'ki is a being sometimes seen in the forest by hunters, who at once fall into a deep sleep, in which they dream. No ill effects are said to follow the encounter. The yo'hyoh are also seen occasionally; but to see them is far more dangerous, for a person almost always dies shortly afterwards. What the nature of the si'lin ku'kini is, is not clear. The ma'ki is apparently always impersonated by the same person at the dances. He has a helper, who assists him in dressing. This helper always succeeds the ma'ki when the latter dies. At the death of a person who has impersonated the ma'ki, the helper for the first time puts on the costume of the ma'ki, and follows the body to the grave. When the grave is dug, the new ma'ki gets into the grave with the body of the former impersonator, and, while the members of the Secret Society form a circle about the grave to conceal the proceedings from the uninitiated, the feather costume of the deceased is placed upright on a pole in the grave, the new ma'ki secretly joining the ring of members of the society. When the grave is filled in, it appears to the other spectators as if the ma'ki had been buried with the dead. The new ma'ki then proceeds at once to make a new costume for himself. None of these beings have been mentioned in any myths that have thus far been secured. The yo'hyoh are sometimes spoken of as "ghosts," but satisfactory information as to the nature of these three classes of beings has not yet been obtained. The beings are regarded as actually present at the dances, and all details as to the costume and ornaments are kept strictly secret from all but members of the Secret Society. . . .

The clown, who plays so important a part in most of the ceremonies of both the foothill and Sacramento Valley people, is a personage of much interest. He always wears a necklace of "crooked acorns,". . . and is much respected by all persons. He seems always to be eating; and at the beginning of a dance, when he is called for, he generally appears munching a huge piece of acorn bread. Very strong arguments are generally necessary on the part of the shaman to induce the clown to stop eating, and take his proper part in the ceremony. The following is given as a typical dialogue between the shaman and the clown.

SHAMAN. Where have you been, Clown?

CLOWN. I have been lying down. I am ill, and have pains in my stomach. I found some medicine that never fails, if there be only enough of it (here he takes a bite of the bread, and sits down by the fire).

SHAMAN. Why don't you put away that bread, and wait till the dance is over before eating?

CLOWN. Then I can't get any.

SHAMAN. Who is going to steal your bread?

CLOWN. I don't know. Perhaps you might.

SHAMAN. Where did you get your bread?

CLOWN. I brought it with me. Didn't you see me coming in with a big loaf?

SHAMAN. I saw you come in with nothing but your cane.

CLOWN. No, no! I had the bread under my arm. On the other hand, I would not lie about a loaf of bread.

SHAMAN. Put away that bread, and go out on top of the dance house. I am going to talk to our people, and you must help me.

CLOWN. No, it is dark, and I am afraid.

SHAMAN. What are you afraid of? Are you a woman?

CLOWN. Yes, I am a woman. Would you like to marry me?

SHAMAN. Stop your joking and go out at once. I will take care of your bread until you have finished. (Here the clown breaks off a piece of the bread, and, putting it under his arm, gives the rest to the shaman. He then goes out and gets up on the roof of the house.) Are you there, Clown?

CLOWN. Yes, I am here. Don't eat my bread! Oh! the ants up here are eating me up.

(The shaman here begins his speech to the people.)

SHAMAN. Don't fail to hear me! Don't fail to hear me! We are going to have a dance in which both women and men must take part.

CLOWN. Don't fail to hear *me!* Don't fail to hear *me!* You are going to have a dance in which you all must take part.

SHAMAN. We come here not for trouble.

CLOWN. I come here not for trouble.

SHAMAN. But we came here to dance and feast.

CLOWN. But you came to dance. I came to eat and gamble.

SHAMAN. Bring on the soup.

CLOWN. Bring on the soup! Bring on the bread! Bring on the fish! Bring on the meat! Ha, ha, ha! Don't fail to hear *me!* Don't fail to hear *me!*

SHAMAN. Bring on some wood! How can we gamble without wood?

CLOWN. Bring on wood, all of you! How can I gamble or keep warm?

SHAMAN. Bring on the soup! Bring on the bread! Bring on the fish! Bring on the meat! We are all hungry.

CLOWN. Haa-a-a-a-a! I am going down! (Here the clown comes down from the roof, and re-enters the dance house. As he enters, he speaks again.) Bring on the soup! Bring on the bread! Bring on the fish! Don't fail to hear me! Haa-a-a-a-a! Come on, come on! Fill up my old woman's burden basket! Haa-a-a-a-a!

The clown then goes to the base of the main post, where his pipe is always placed. This pipe has a peculiar form, and is larger than other people's. He fills it, if possible, from the shaman's supply of tobacco, and then smokes, puffing out as much smoke as possible. Between the puffs he calls out, "I like acorn bread! I like deer meat! I like fish! I like soup! Be good to me, be good to my old woman!"

Here men enter, bringing the food. At once the clown jumps up, puts away his pipe, and shouts, "Haa-a-a-a-a!" He then goes from one basket to another, tasting of each, and endeavors to steal for himself the one that tastes best. He is, however, detected by the shaman, and forced to put the basket back. The shaman reprimands him sharply for his actions, but the clown pays little attention, and continues doing all sorts of knavish tricks. When the dance begins, the clown starts off with great vim; but as soon as the shaman turns his back, the clown's efforts become less vigorous, he dances half-heartedly or on one foot, and often produces a piece of acorn bread from under his arm, and eats that. As soon, however, as the shaman's attention turns toward him, he at once begins to dance frantically again. . . .

Among the Sacramento Valley and foothill members of the Maidu in the northern portion of their area, there was a society, or series of societies, membership in which was obtained only by a regular initiation, and the position and power of which were considerable. . . .

[*What Dixon called the Secret Society was simply the entire group of adult males, with a few exceptions to be explained shortly. These males passed through two stages of initiation, during which they were first novices, or Yo'mbussi, and later Ye'poni, or full initiates. In the sense that the term "Secret Society" implies an association, it is misleading in this context.*]
. . . . Its leaders were the leaders, in reality, of the tribe or community, and to a very large extent, if not wholly, regulated the dance organization. Boys were initiated into the society generally at about the age of twelve or fourteen, although in some cases a man was twenty or over before he was selected for a member by the older men. The time chosen for the initiation was during some one of the more important dances. The old men, members of the order, having decided which boys or young men were to be initiated, went at night to their houses and dragged them out without a word of explanation. They were carried to the dance house; and the chief and the leader of the society . . . took each neophyte in turn, and, each holding him by an arm and a leg, walked slowly around the dance house, swinging the boy gently from side to side . . . and singing. . . . The door of the house was fastened, so that the candidates might not escape. Each candidate was carried thus once around the house, and then placed on the floor, to the north of the drum. When all had thus been treated, the older members of the society danced. If the initiation took place at the time the he'si was being held, the clown talked, turning to the south first . . . to the east . . . to the north . . . and to the west . . . [addressing each]. As he spoke thus to each point of the compass, the boys were sent out of the house, under guard each time, and shouted toward that point to which the clown had just spoken. [Then] . . . the boys re-entered the house, and the doors were again fastened. For some time the boys had to remain in the house, refraining from all flesh foods, and subject to various regulations not specified. At the close of this period of seclusion, during which the older men had been instructing the boys in the myths and traditions of the people, the he'si dance was held, and the new members were taught the various dances.

Dixon had the disadvantage of working with a remnant population, but, since he did his field work over seventy years ago, it was a much livelier remnant than it was when described by others later. The burnings were still going on, although the dances had apparently been largely abandoned. One thing that Dixon apparently missed, and Loeb discovered, was that the feather making lay in the hands of a class of specialists. These were men called *suku,* who were responsible for the highest artistic achievements of these people. The *suku* were transvestites; they wore women's clothing, did not marry, and were not initiated with the other men. It is hard to say to what extent they practiced homosexuality, if at all.

From Dixon's account we see people living a settled life, spending the whole slack winter season in carrying on a round of ceremonies which could only serve to keep people occupied, to re-enforce lines of authority, and to build up relationships between neighboring villages. The internal lines of authority were needed to control the annual round of salmon fishing, acorn gathering, etc.; inter-village relations were needed to keep the channels of trade open. Since all the obsidian came from the north, all the shell beads from the coast, all the yew for bows from one place, all the green paint to rub on them from another, and since different kinds of pine nuts passed between different environmental subareas, it is clear that the village was far from self-sufficient. What is more important is that there were no technological tasks that required much interaction, and none that used any force greater than that of two or three individuals' muscles.

The most characteristic aspect of Maidu culture was their response to the alternation of the seasons. Nearly all the food was obtained during the summer. Games were very important to serve as routines of interpersonal and intervillage interaction during the slack times in warm weather; dances—which could be aptly described as dramatic performances—during the rainy and chilly season. These dramas, indeed, provided the framework for the Maidu's most complex institution. Ritual and ceremony, furthermore, required more specialization and the manufacture of finer products than work routines. Although there were but two main classes of shamans, "seers" and healers, the latter were again specialized according to the kind of disease.

Each Maidu male might belong to a number of natural groups—his village, a special dance company, a burning group, a company of shamans, etc. What we have here is a number of overlapping institutions with a certain amount of specialization and a considerable regional interdependence in trade.

10

Traders of the Trobriands

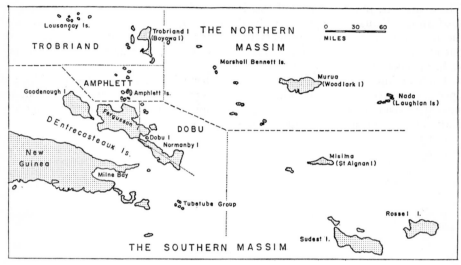

The Massim District, including the Trobriand Islands (*after Malinowski*).

So FAR we have been dealing entirely with nonagricultural peoples. Except for the Lapps, all were food-gatherers as well. The student must not gather the idea that there is an inevitable progression in institutional complexity from flint knappers to ax polishers to metal users, or from hunters to farmers to manufacturers. Historically these are the sequences that seem to have occurred, but when we study contemporary peoples many other factors, particularly differences of environment and time, throw this pat progression off the rails. We can find some farmers on level two, others on our own level; some food gatherers who use rifles and burn kerosene lamps. We can find whole civilizations in which gifted sculptors built high white temples of limestone, without benefit of metal tools. This does not mean that there is no order in the world, only that we must study all the angles, instead of one or two.

The peoples of the Pacific, the Melanesians, Polynesians, and Micronesians, were all farmers, and all used polished stone or polished shell cutting tools. They varied in institutional complexity with the sizes of their islands, with their distance from the shore, with their distance from other islands, and for other reasons. Many excellent monographs on these people have been written, but none that can

292

surpass the exciting story of the Trobriand people of Melanesia,* written by the late Bronislaw Malinowski, one of our truly great social scientists.

The coastal populations of the South Sea Islands, with very few exceptions, are, or were before their extinction, expert navigators and traders. Several of them had evolved excellent types of large seagoing canoes, and used to embark in them on distant trade expeditions or raids of war and conquest. The Papuo-Melanesians, who inhabit the coast and the outlying islands of New Guinea, are no exception to this rule. In general they are daring sailors, industrious manufacturers, and keen traders. The manufacturing centres of important articles, such as pottery, stone implements, canoes, fine baskets, valued ornaments, are localised in several places, according to the skill of the inhabitants, their inherited tribal tradition, and special facilities offered by the district; thence they are traded over wide areas, sometimes travelling more than hundreds of miles.

Definite forms of exchange along definite trade routes are to be found established between the various tribes. . . .

There exists . . . a very extensive and highly complex trading system, embracing with its ramifications, not only the islands near the East End, but also the Louisiades, Woodlark Island, the Trobriand Archipelago, and the d'Entrecasteaux group; it penetrates into the mainland of New Guinea, and exerts an indirect influence over several outlying districts, such as Rossel Island, and some parts of the Northern and Southern coast of New Guinea. This trading system, the Kula . . . is an economic phenomenon of considerable theoretical importance. It looms paramount in the tribal life of those

natives who live within its circuit, and its importance is fully realised by the tribesmen themselves, whose ideas, ambitions, desires and vanities are very much bound up with the Kula. . . .

Leaving the bronzed rocks and the dark jungle of the Amphletts . . . we sail North into an entirely different world of flat coral islands; into an ethnographic district, which stands out by ever so many peculiar manners and customs from the rest of Papuo-Melanesia. . . .

We now enter an opaque, greenish sea, whose monotony is broken only by a few sandbanks, some bare and awash, others with a few pandanus trees squatting on their air roots, high in the sand. To these banks, the Amphlett natives come and there they spend weeks on end, fishing for turtle and dugong. Here is also laid the scene of several of the mythical incidents of primitive Kula. Further ahead, through the misty spray, the line of horizon thickens here and there, as if faint pencil marks had been drawn upon it. These become more substantial, one of them lengthens and broadens, the others spring into the distinct shapes of small islands, and we find ourselves in the big Lagoon of the Trobriands, with Boyowa, the largest island, on our right, and with many others, inhabited and uninhabited, to the North and Northwest.

As we sail in the Lagoon, following the intricate passages between the shallows, and as we approach the main island, the thick, tangled matting of the low jungle breaks here and there over a beach, and we can see into a palm grove, like an interior, supported by pillars. This indicates the site of a

*Argonauts of the Western Pacific, George Routledge and Sons, Ltd., London, 1922. Reprinted by permission of the publishers.

village. We step ashore on to the sea front, as a rule covered with mud and refuse, with canoes drawn up high and dry, and passing through the grove, we enter the village itself. . . .

Soon we are seated on one of the platforms built in front of a yam house, shaded by its overhanging roof. The round, grey logs, worn smooth by contact with naked feet and bodies; the trodden ground of the village street; the brown skins of the natives, who immediately surround the visitor in large groups—all these form a colour scheme of bronze and grey, unforgettable to anyone, who, like myself, has lived among these people. . . .

The great variety in their physical appearance is what strikes one first in Boyowa. There are men and women of tall stature, fine bearing, and delicate features, well formed nose and chin, and an open, intelligent expression. . . . And besides these, there are others with prognathic, negroid faces, broad, thick-lipped mouths, narrow foreheads, and a coarse expression. . . . The better featured have also a markedly lighter skin. Even their hair differs, varying from quite straight locks to the frizzly mop of the typical Melanesian. They wear the same classes of ornaments as the other Massim, consisting mainly of fibre armlets and belts, earrings of turtle shell and spondylus discs, and they are very fond of using, for personal decoration, flowers and aromatic herbs. In manner they are much freer, more familiar and confident, than any of the natives we have so far met. As soon as an interesting stranger arrives, half the village assembles around him, talking loudly and making remarks about him, frequently uncomplimentary, and altogether assuming a tone of jocular familiarity.

One of the main sociological features at once strikes an observant new-comer—the existence of rank and social differentiation. Some of the natives—very frequently those of the finer looking type—are treated with most marked deference by others, and in return, these chiefs and persons of rank behave in quite a different way towards the strangers. In fact, they show excellent manners in the full meaning of this word.

When a chief is present, no commoner dares to remain in a physically higher position; he has to bend his body or squat. Similarly, when the chief sits down, no one would dare to stand. The institution of definite chieftainship, to which are shown such extreme marks of deference, with a sort of rudimentary court ceremonial, with insignia of rank and authority, is so entirely foreign to the whole spirit of Melanesian tribal life, that at first it transports the ethnographer into a different world. . . .

Another sociological feature which forcibly obtrudes itself on the visitor's notice is the social position of the women. Their behaviour, after the cool aloofness of the Dobuan women, and the very uninviting treatment which strangers receive from those of the Amphletts, comes almost as a shock in its friendly familiarity. Naturally, here also, the manners of women of rank are quite different from those of low class commoners. But, on the whole, high and low alike, though by no means reserved, have a genial, pleasant approach, and many of them are very fine-looking. . . . Their dress is also different from any so far observed. All the Melanesian women in New Guinea wear a petticoat made of fibre. Among the Southern Massim, this fibre skirt is long, reaching to the knees or below, whereas in the Trobriands it is much shorter and fuller, consisting of several layers standing out round the body like a ruff. . . .

The highly ornamental effect of that dress is enhanced by the elaborate decorations made in three colours on the several layers forming the top skirt. On the whole, it is very becoming to fine young women, and gives to small slender girls a graceful elfish appearance.

Chastity is an unknown virtue among these natives. At an incredibly early age they become initiated into sexual life, and many of the innocent looking plays of childhood are not as innocuous as they appear. As they grow up, they live in promiscuous free-love, which gradually develops into more permanent attachments, one of which ends in marriage. But before this is reached, unmarried girls are openly supposed to be quite free to do what they like, and there are even ceremonial arrangements by which the girls of a village repair, in a body to another place; there they publicly range themselves for inspection, and each is chosen by a local boy, with whom she spends a night. . . . Again, when a visiting party arrives from another district, food is brought to them by the unmarried girls, who are also expected to satisfy their sexual wants. At the big mortuary vigils round the corpse of a newly deceased person, people from neighbouring villages come in large bodies to take part in the wailing and singing. The girls of the visiting party are expected by usage to comfort the boys of the bereaved village, in a manner which gives much anguish to their official lovers. There is another remarkable form of ceremonial licence, in which indeed women are openly the initiators. During the gardening season, at the time of weeding, the women do communal work, and any strange man who ventures to pass through the district runs a considerable risk, for the women will run after him, seize him, tear off his pubic leaf, and ill-treat him orgiastically in the most ignominious manner. Side by side with these ceremonial forms of licence, there go, in the normal course of events, constant private intrigues, more intense during the festive seasons, becoming less prominent as garden work, trading expeditions, or harvesting take up the energies and attention of the tribe.

Marriage is associated with hardly any public or private rite or ceremony. The woman simply joins her husband in his house, and later on, there is a series of exchanges of gifts, which in no way can be interpreted as purchase money for the wife. As a matter of fact, the most important feature of the Trobriand marriage is the fact that the wife's family have to contribute, and that in a very substantial manner, to the economics of her household, and also they have to perform all sorts of services for the husband. In her married life, the woman is supposed to remain faithful to her husband, but this rule is neither very strictly kept or enforced. In all other ways, she retains a great measure of independence, and her husband has to treat her well and with consideration. If he does not, the woman simply leaves him and returns to her own family, and as the husband is as a rule economically the loser by her action, he has to exert himself to get her back—which he does by means of presents and persuasions. If she chooses, she can leave him for good, and she can always find someone else to marry.

In tribal life, the position of women is also very high. They do not as a rule join the councils of men, but in many matters they have their own way, and control several aspects of tribal life. Thus, some of the garden work is their business; and this is considered a privilege as well as a duty. They also look after certain stages in the big, ceremonial divisions of food, associated with the very complete and elaborate mortuary ritual of the Boyowans. . . . Certain forms of magic—that performed over a first-born baby, beauty magic made at tribal ceremonies, some classes of sorcery—are also the monopoly of women. Women of rank share the privileges incidental to it, and men of low caste will bend before them and observe all the necessary formalities and taboos due to a chief. A woman of chief's rank, married to commoner, retains her status, even with regard to her husband, and has to be treated accordingly.

The Trobrianders are matrilineal, that is, in tracing descent and settling inheritance, they follow the maternal line. A child belongs to the clan and village community of its mother, and wealth, as well as social position, are inherited, not from father to son, but from maternal uncle to nephew. This rule admits of certain important and interesting exceptions, which we shall come across in the course of this study.

Returning to our imaginary first visit ashore, the next interesting thing to do, after we have sufficiently taken in the appearance and manners of the natives, is to walk round the village. In doing this, again we would come across much which, to a trained eye, would reveal at once deeper sociological facts. In the Trobriands, however, it would be better to make our first observations in one of the large, inland villages, situated on even, flat ground with plenty of space, so that it has been possible to build it in the typical pattern. In the coastal villages, placed on marshy ground and coral outcrop, the irregularity of the soil and cramped space have obliterated the design, and they present quite a chaotic appearance. The big villages of the central districts, on the other hand, are built one and all with an almost geometrical regularity.

In the middle, a big circular space is surrounded by a ring of yam houses. These latter are built on piles, and present a fine, decorative front, with walls of big, round logs, laid crosswise on one another, so as to leave wide interstices through which the stored yams can be seen. . . . Some of the storehouses strike us at once as being better built, larger, and higher than the rest, and these have also big, ornamented boards, running around the gable and across it. These are the yam houses of the chief or of persons of rank. Each yam house also has, as a rule, a small platform in front of it, on which groups of men will sit and chat in the evening, and where visitors can rest.

Concentrically with the circular row of yam houses, there runs a ring of dwelling huts, and thus a street going all round the village is formed between the two rows. . . . The dwellings are lower than the yam houses, and instead of being on piles, are built directly on the ground. The interior is dark, and very stuffy, and the only opening into it is through the door, and that is usually closed. Each hut is occupied by one family . . . that is, husband, wife and small children, while adolescent and grown-up boys and girls live in separate small bachelors' houses, harbouring some two to six inmates. Chiefs and people of rank have their special, personal houses, besides those of their wives. The chief's house often stands in the central ring of the storehouses facing the main place.

The broad inspection of the village would therefore reveal to us the rôle of decoration as insignia of rank, the existence of bachelors' and spinsters' houses, the great importance attached to the yam harvest—all these small symptoms which, followed up, would lead us deep into the problems of native sociology. Moreover, such an inspection would have led us to inquire as to the part played by the different divisions of the village in tribal life. We should then learn that the *baku,* the central circular space, is the scene of public ceremonies and festivities, such as dancing . . . division of food, tribal feasts, mortuary vigils, in short, of all doings that represent the village as a whole. In the circular street between the stores and living houses, everyday life goes on, that is, the preparation of food, the eating of meals, and the usual exchange of gossip and ordinary social amenities. The interior of the houses is used only at night, or on wet days, and is more a sleeping than a living room. The backs of the houses and the contiguous groves are the scene of the children's play and the women's occupations. Farther away, remote parts of the grove are reserved for sanitary purposes, each sex having its own retreat.

The *baku* (central place) is the most picturesque part, and there the somewhat monotonous colour scheme of the brown and grey is broken by the overhanging foliage of the grove, seen above the neat fronts and gaudy ornamentation of the yam houses and by the decorations worn by the crowd when a dance or ceremony is taking place. . . . Dancing is done only at one time in the year, in connection with the harvest festivities, called *milamala,* at which season also the spirits of the dear return from Tuma, the nether world, to the villages from which they hail. Sometimes the dancing season lasts only for a few weeks or even days, sometimes it is extended into a special dancing period called *usigola.* During such a time of festivities, the inhabitants of a village will dance day after day, for a month or longer, the period being inaugurated by a feast, punctuated by several more, and ending in a big culminating performance. At

this many villages assist as spectators, and distributions of food take place. During an *usigola,* dancing is done in full dress, that is, with facial painting, floral decorations, valuable ornaments, and a headdress of white cockatoo feathers. . . . A performance consists always of a dance executed in a ring to the accompaniment of singing and drum beating, both of which are done by a group of people standing in the middle. Some dances are done with the carved dancing shield.

Sociologically, the village is an important unit in the Trobriands. Even the mightiest chief in the Trobriands wields his authority primarily over his own village and only secondarily over the district. The village community exploit jointly their garden lands, perform ceremonies, wage warfare, undertake trading expeditions, and sail in the same canoe or fleet of canoes as one group.

After the first inspection of the village, we would be naturally interested to know more of the surrounding country, and would take a walk through the bush. Here, however, if we hoped for a picturesque and varied landscape, we should receive a great disappointment. The extensive, flat island consists only of one fertile plain, with a low coral ridge running along portions of the coast. It is almost entirely under intermittent cultivation, and the bush, regularly cleared away every few years, has no time to grow high. A low, dense jungle grows in a matted tangle, and practically wherever we move on the island we walk along between two green walls, presenting no variety, allowing of no broader view. The monotony is broken only by an occasional clump of old trees left standing—usually a tabooed place—or by one of the numerous villages which we meet with every mile or two in this densely populated country. The main element, both of picturesqueness and ethnographic interest, is afforded by the native gardens. Each year about one quarter or one fifth of the total area is under actual cultivation as gardens, and these are well tended, and present a pleasant change from the monotony of the scrub. In its early stages, the garden site is simply a bare, cleared space, allowing of a wider outlook upon the distant coral ridge in the East, and upon the tall groves, scattered over the horizon, which indicate villages or tabooed tree clumps. Later on, when the yam vines, taro, and sugar cane begin to grow and bud, the bare brown soil is covered with the fresh green of the tender plants. After some more time still, tall, stout poles are planted over each yam plant; the vine climbs round them, grows into a full, shady garland of foliage, and the whole makes the impression of a large, exuberant hop yard.

Half of the natives' working life is spent in the garden, and around it centres perhaps more than half of his interests and ambitions. And here we must pause and make an attempt to understand his attitude in this matter, as it is typical of the way in which he goes about all his work. If we remain under the delusion that the native is a happy-go-lucky, lazy child of nature, who shuns as far as possible all labour and effort, waiting till the ripe fruits, so bountifully supplied by generous tropical Nature, fall into his mouth, we shall not be able to understand in the least his aims and motives in carrying out the Kula or any other enterprise. On the contrary, the truth is that the native can and, under circumstances, does work hard, and work systematically, with endurance and purpose, nor does he wait till he is pressed to work by his immediate needs.

In gardening, for instance, the natives produce much more than they actually require, and in any average year they harvest perhaps twice as much as they can eat. Nowadays, this surplus is exported by Europeans to feed plantation hands in other parts of New Guinea; in olden days it was simply allowed to rot. Again, they produce this surplus in a manner which entails much more work than is strictly necessary for obtaining the crops. Much time and labour is given up to aesthetic purposes, to making the gardens tidy, clean, cleared of all debris; to building fine, solid fences, to providing specially strong and big yam poles. All these things are to some extent required for the growth of the plant; but there can be no doubt that the natives push their conscientiousness far beyond the limit of the purely necessary. The non-utilitarian element in their garden work is still more clearly perceptible in the various tasks which they carry out entirely for the sake of ornamentation, in connection with magical ceremonies, and in obedience to tribal usage. Thus, after the ground has been scrupulously cleared and is ready for planting, the natives divide each garden plot into small squares, each a few yards in length and width, and this is done only in obedience to usage, in order to make the gardens look neat. No self-respecting man would dream of omitting to do this. Again, in especially well trimmed gardens, long horizontal poles are tied to the yam supports in order to embellish them. Another, and perhaps the most interesting example of non-utilitarian work is afforded by the big, prismatic erections called *kamkokola,* which serve ornamental and magical purposes, but have nothing to do with the growth of plants. . . .

Among the forces and beliefs which bear upon and regulate garden work, perhaps magic is the most important. It is a department of its own, and the garden magician, next to the chief and the sorcerer, is the most important personage of the village. The position is hereditary, and, in each village, a special system of magic is handed on in the female line from one generation to another. I have called it a *system,* because the magician has to perform a series of rites and spells over the garden, which run parallel with the labour, and which, in fact, initiate each stage of the work and each new development of the plant life. Even before any gardening is begun at all, the magician has to consecrate the site with a big ceremonial performance in which all the men of the village take part. This ceremony officially opens the season's gardening, and only after it is performed do the villagers begin to cut the scrub on their plots. Then, in a series of rites, the magician inaugurates successively all the various stages which follow one another—the burning of the scrub, the clearing, the planting, the weeding and the harvesting. Also, in another series of rites and spells, he magically assists the plant in sprouting, in budding, in bursting into leaf, in climbing, in forming the rich garlands of foliage, and in producing the edible tubers.

The garden magician, according to native ideas, thus controls both the work of man and the forces of Nature. He also acts directly as supervisor of gardening, sees to it that people do not skimp their work, or lag behind with it. Thus magic is a systematising, regulating, and controlling influence in garden work. The magician, in carrying out the rites, sets the pace, compels people to apply themselves to certain tasks, and to accomplish them properly and in time. Incidentally, magic also imposes on the tribe a good deal of extra work, of apparently unnecessary, hampering taboos and regulations. In the long run, however, there is no doubt that by its influence in ordering, systematising and regulating work, magic is economically invaluable for the natives.

. . . The primitive Trobriander . . . works prompted by motives of a highly complex, social and traditional nature, and towards aims which are certainly not directed towards the satisfaction of present wants, or to the direct achievement of utilitarian purposes. Thus, in the first place, as we have seen, work is not carried out on the principle of the least effort. On the contrary, much time and energy is spent on wholly unnecessary effort, that is, from a utilitarian point of view. Again, work and effort, instead of being merely a means to an end, are, in a way an end in themselves. A good garden worker in the Trobriands derives a direct prestige from the amount of labour he can do, and the size of the garden he can till. The title *tokwaybagula,* which means "good" or "efficient gardener," is bestowed with discrimination, and borne with pride. Several of my friends, renowned as *tokwaybagula,* would boast to me how long they worked, how much ground they tilled, and would compare their efforts with those of less efficient men. When the labour, some of which is done communally, is being actually carried out, a good deal of competition goes on. Men vie with one another in their speed, in their thoroughness, and in the weights they can lift, when bringing big poles to the garden, or in carrying away the harvested yams.

The most important point about this is, however, that all, or almost all the fruits of his work, and certainly any surplus which he can achieve by extra effort, goes not to the man himself, but to his relatives-in-law. . . . about three quarters of a man's crops go partly as tribute to the chief, partly as his due to his sister's (or mother's) husband and family.

But although he thus derives practically no personal benefit in the utilitarian sense from his harvest, the gardener receives much praise and renown from its size and quality, and that in a direct and circumstantial manner. For all the crops, after being harvested, are displayed for some time afterwards in the gardens, piled up in neat, conical heaps under small shelters made of yam vine. Each man's harvest is thus exhibited for criticism in his own plot, and parties of natives walk about from garden to garden, admiring, comparing and praising the best results. The importance of the food display can be gauged by the fact that, in olden days, when the chief's power was much more considerable than now, it was dangerous for a man who was not either of high rank himself, or working for such a one, to show crops which might compare too favourably with those of the chief.

In years when the harvest promises to be plentiful, the chief will proclaim a *kayasa* harvest, that is to say, ceremonial, competitive display of food, and then the straining for good results and the interest taken in them are still higher. We shall meet later on with ceremonial enterprises of the *kayasa* type, and find that they play a considerable part in the Kula. . . . The Trobriander works in a roundabout way, to a large extent for the sake of the work itself, and puts a great deal of aesthetic polish on the arrangement and general appearance of his garden. He is not guided primarily by the desire to satisfy his wants, but by a very complex set of traditional forces, duties and obligations, beliefs in magic, social ambitions and vanities. He wants, if he is a *man,* to achieve social distinction as a *good gardener* and a good worker in general. . . .

In every community in the Trobriands, there is one man who wields the greatest authority, though often this does not amount to very much. He is, in many cases, nothing more than the *primus inter pares* in a group of village elders, who deliberate on all important matters together, and arrive at a decision by common consent. It must not be forgotten that there is hardly ever much room for doubt or deliberation, as natives communally, as well as individually, never act except on traditional and conventional lines. This village headman is, as a rule, therefore, not much more than a master of tribal ceremonies, and the main speaker within and without the tribe, whenever one is needed.

But the position of headman becomes much more than this, when he is a person of high rank, which is by no means always the case. In the Trobriands there exist four totemic clans, and each of these is divided into a number of smaller sub-clans,—which could also be called families or castes, for the members of each claim common descent from one ancestress, and each of them holds a certain, specified rank. These sub-clans have also a local character, because the original ancestress emerged from a hole in the ground, as a rule somewhere in the neighbourhood of their village community. There is not one sub-clan in the Trobriands whose members cannot indicate its original locality, where their group, in the form of the ancestress, first saw the light of the sun. Coral outcrops, water holes, small caves or grottoes, are generally pointed out as the original "holes" or "houses," as they are called. Often such a hole is surrounded by one of the tabooed clumps of trees alluded to before. Many of them are situated in the groves surrounding a village, and a few near the sea shore. Not one is on the cultivable land.

The highest sub-clan is that of the Tabalu, belonging to the Malasi totem clan. To this sub-clan belongs the main chief of Kiriwina, To'uluwa, who resides in the village of Omarakana. . . . He is in the first place the headman of his own village, and in contrast to the headmen of low rank, he has quite a considerable amount of power. His high rank inspires everyone about him, with the greatest and most genuine respect and awe, and the remnants of his power are still surprisingly large, even now, when white authorities, very foolishly and with fatal results, do their utmost to undermine his prestige and influence.

Not only does the chief—by which I shall designate a headman of rank—possess a high degree of authority within his own village, but his sphere of influence extends far beyond it. A number of villages are tributary to him, and in several respects subject to his authority. In case of war, they are his allies, and have to foregather in his village. When he needs men to perform some task, he can send to his subject villages, and they will supply him with workers. In all big festivities the villages of his district will join, and the chief will act as master of ceremonies. Nevertheless, for all these services rendered to him he has to pay. He even has to pay for any tributes received, out of his stores of wealth. Wealth, in the Trobriands, is the outward sign and the substance of power, and the means also of exercising it. But how does he acquire his wealth? And here we come to the main duty of the vassal villages to the chief. From each subject village, he takes a wife, whose family, according to the Trobriand law, has to supply him with large amounts of crops. This wife is always the sister or some relation of the headman of the subject village, and thus practically the whole community has to work for him. In olden days, the chief of Omarakana had up to as many as forty consorts,

and received perhaps as much as thirty to fifty percent of all the garden produce of Kiriwina. Even now, when his wives number only sixteen, he has enormous storehouses, and they are full to the roof with yams every harvest time.

With this supply, he is able to pay for the many services he requires, to furnish with food the participants in big feasts, in tribal gatherings or distant expeditions. Part of the food he uses to acquire objects of native wealth, or to pay for the making of them. In brief, through his privilege of practising polygamy, the chief is kept supplied with an abundance of wealth in food stuffs and in valuables, which he uses to maintain his high position; to organise tribal festivities and enterprises, and to pay, according to custom, for the many personal services to which he is entitled.

One point in connection with the chief's authority deserves special mention. Power implies not only the possibility of rewarding, but also the means of punishing. This in the Trobriands is as a rule done indirectly, by means of sorcery. The chief has the best sorcerers of the district always at his beck and call. Of course he also has to reward them when they do him a service. If anyone offends him, or trespasses upon his authority, the chief summons the sorcerer, and orders that the culprit shall die by black magic. And here the chief is powerfully helped in achieving his end by the fact that he can do this openly, so that everybody, and the victim himself, knows that a sorcerer is after him. As the natives are very deeply and genuinely afraid of sorcery, the feeling of being hunted, of imagining themselves doomed, is in itself enough to doom them in reality. Only in extreme cases, does a chief inflict direct punishment on a culprit. He has one or two hereditary henchmen, whose duty it is to kill the man who has so deeply offended him, that actual death is the only sufficient punishment. As a matter of fact, very few cases of this are on record, and it is now, of course, entirely in abeyance.

Thus the chief's position can be grasped only through the realisation of the high importance of wealth, of the necessity of paying for everything, even for services which are due to him, and which could not be withheld. Again, this wealth comes to the chief from his relations-in-law, and it is through his right to practise polygamy that he actually achieves his position, and exercises his power.

Side by side with this rather complex mechanism of authority, the prestige of rank, the direct recognition of his personal superiority, give the chief an immense power, even outside his district. Except for the few of his own rank, no native in the Trobriands will remain erect when the great chief of Omarakana approaches, even in these days of tribal disintegration. Wherever he goes, he is considered as the most important person, is seated on a high platform, and treated with consideration. Of course the fact that he is accorded marks of great deference, and approached in the manner as if he were a supreme despot, does not mean that perfect good fellowship and sociability do not reign in his personal relations with his companions and vassals. There is no difference in interests or outlook between him and his subjects. They sit together and chat, they exchange village gossip, the only difference being that the chief is always on his guard, and much more reticent and diplomatic than the others, though he is no less interested. The chief, unless he is too old, joins in dances and even in games, and indeed he takes precedence as a matter of course.

In trying to realise the social condi-tions among the Trobrianders and their neighbours, it must not be forgotten that their social organisation is in certain respects complex and ill-defined. Beside very definite laws which are strictly obeyed, there exist a number of quaint usages, of vague graduations in rules, of others where the exceptions are so many, that they rather obliterate the rule than confirm it. The narrow social outlook of the native who does not see beyond his own district, the prevalence of singularities and exceptional cases is one of the leading characteristics of native sociology. . . .

The most important chief is, as said, the one who resides in Omarakana and rules Kiriwina, agriculturally the richest and most important district. His family, or sub-clan, the Tabalu, are acknowledged to have by far the highest rank in all the Archipelago. Their fame is spread over the whole Kula district; the entire province of Kiriwina derives prestige from its chief, and its inhabitants also keep all his personal taboos, which is a duty but also a distinction. Next to the high chief, there resides in a village some two miles distant, a personage who, though in several respects his vassal, is also his main foe and rival, the headman of Kabwaku, and ruler of the province of Tilataula. The present holder of this title is an old rogue named Moliasi. From time to time, in the old days, war used to break out between the two provinces, each of which could muster some twelve villages for the fight. These wars were never very bloody and of long duration, and they were in many ways fought in a competitive, sporting manner, since unlike the Dobuans and Southern Massim, there were neither head-hunting nor cannibalistic practices among the Boyowans. Nevertheless, defeat was a serious matter. It meant a temporary destruction of the loser's villages, and exile for a year or two. After that, a ceremony of reconciliation took place, and friend and foe would help to re-build the villages. The ruler of Tila-taula has an intermediate rank, and outside his district he does not enjoy much prestige; but within it, he has a considerable amount of power, and a good deal of wealth, in the shape of stored food and ceremonial articles. All the villages under his rule, have, of course, their own independent head-men, who, being of low rank, have only a small degree of local authority.

In the West of the big, Northern half of Boyowa (that is of the main island of the Trobriand Group) are again two districts, in past times often at war with one another. One of them, Kuboma, subject to the chief of Gumil-ababa, of high rank, though inferior to the chief of Kiriwina, consists of some ten inland villages, and is very im-portant as a centre of industry. Among these villages are included those of Yalaka, Buduwaylaka, Kudukwaykela, where the quicklime is prepared for betel chewing, and also the lime pots made. The highly artistic designs, burnt in on the lime pots, are the speciality of these villagers, but un-fortunately the industry is fast decay-ing. The inhabitants of Luya are re-nowned for their basket work, of which the finest specimens are their produc-tion. But the most remarkable of all is the village of Bwoytalu, whose in-habitants are at the same time the most despised pariahs, the most dreaded sor-cerers, and the most skilful and in-dustrious craftsmen in the island. They belong to several sub-clans, all originat-ing in the neighbourhood of the village, near which also, according to tradition, the original sorcerer came out of the soil in the form of a crab. They eat the flesh of bush pigs, and they catch and eat the stingaree, both objects of

strict taboos and of genuine loathing to the other inhabitants of Northern Boyowa. For this reason they are de-spised and regarded as unclean by the others. In olden days they would have to crouch lower and more abjectly than anyone else. No man or woman would mate with anyone from Bwoytalu, whether in marriage or in an intrigue. Yet in wood carving, and especially in the working out of the wonderful, round dishes, in the manufacture of plaited fibre work, and in the produc-tion of combs, they are far more skil-ful than anyone else, and acknowledged to be such; they are the wholesale man-ufacturers of these objects for export, and they can produce work not to be rivalled by any other village.

[*Skilled artisans are social outcasts in many cultures. This goes with a local or ethnic division of labor and trade, in areas without strong central governments, as we shall see later.*]

The five villages lying on the west-ern coast of the northern half, on the shores of the Lagoon, form the district of Kulumata. They are all fishing vil-lages, but differ in their methods, and each has its own fishing grounds and its own methods of exploiting them. The district is much less homogeneous than any of those before mentioned. It possesses no paramount chief, and even in war the villages used not to fight on the same side. . . .

In the southern part of Boyowa, there is first the province of Luba, oc-cupying the waist of the island, the part where it narrows down to a long isthmus. This part is ruled by a chief of high rank, who resides in Olivilevi. He belongs to the same family as the chief of Omarakana, and this southern dominion is the result of a younger line's having branched off some three generations ago. This happened after an unsuccessful war, when the whole tribe of Kiriwina fled south to Luba, and lived there for two years in a temporary village. The main body returned afterwards, but a number remained behind with the chief's brother, and thus the village of Olivilevi was founded. Wawela, which was formerly a very big village, now consists of hardly more than twenty huts. The only one on the Eastern shore which lies right on the sea, it is very picturesquely situated, overlooking a wide bay with a clean beach. It is of importance as the traditional centre of astronomical knowledge. From here, for generation after generation up to the present day, the calendar of the natives has been regulated. This means that some of the most important dates are fixed, especially that of the great annual festival, the *Milamala,* always held at full moon. Again, Wawela is one of the villages where the second form of sorcery, that of the flying witches, has its main Trobriand home. In fact, according to native belief, this form of sorcery had its seat only in the Southern half, and is unknown to the women in the North, though the Southern witches extend their field of operation all over Boyowa. Wawela, which lies facing the East, and which is always in close touch with the villages of Kitava and the rest of the Marshall Bennetts, shares with these islands the reputation of harbouring many women who can fly, kill by magic, who also feed on corpses, and are especially dangerous to seamen in peril.

Further down to the South, on the Western shore of the Lagoon, we come to the big settlement of Sinaketa, consisting of some six villages lying within a few hundred yards from one another, but each having its own headman and a certain amount of local characteristics. These villages form, however, one community for purposes of war and of the Kula. Some of the local headmen of Sinaketa claim the highest rank, some are commoners; but on the whole, both the principle of rank and the power of the chief break down more and more as we move South. Beyond Sinaketa, we meet a few more villages, who practice a local Kula. . . . The Southern part of the island is sometimes called Kaybwagina, but it does not constitute a definite political unit, like the Northern districts.

Finally, south of the main island, divided from it by a narrow channel, lies the half-moon-shaped island of Vakuta, to which belong four small villages and one big one. Within recent times, perhaps four to six generations ago, there came down and settled in this last mentioned one a branch of the real Tabalu, the chiefly family of highest rank. But their powers here never assumed the proportions even of the small chiefs of Sinaketa. In Vakuta, the typical Papuo-Melanesian system of government by tribal elders—with one more prominent than the others, but not permanent—is in full vigour.

The two big settlements of Sinaketa and Vakuta play a great part in the Kula, and they also are the only two communities in the whole Trobriands where the red shell discs are made. This industry, as we shall see, is closely associated with the Kula. Politically, Sinaketa and Vakuta are rivals, and in olden days were periodically at war with one another.

Another district which forms a definite political and cultural unit is the large island of Kayleula, in the West. The inhabitants are fishermen, canoe builders, and traders, and undertake big expeditions to the western d'Entrecasteaux islands, trading for betel nut, sago, pottery and turtle shell in exchange for their own industrial produce.

. . . All departments of tribal life, religion, magic, economics are interwoven, but the *social organisation* of the tribes lies at the foundation of everything else. Thus it is essential to bear in mind that the Trobriands form one cultural unit, speaking the same language, having the same institutions, obeying the same laws and regulations, swayed by the same beliefs and conventions. The districts just enumerated, into which the Trobriands are subdivided, are distinct politically and not culturally; that is, each of them comprises the same kind of natives, only obeying or at least acknowledging their own chief, having their own interests and pursuits, and in case of war each fighting their own fight.

Again, within each district, the several village communities have each a great deal of independence. A village community is represented by a headman, its members make their gardens in one block and under the guidance of their own garden magician; they carry on their own feasts and ceremonial arrangements, mourn their dead in common, and perform, in remembrance of their departed ones, an endless series of food distributions. In all big affairs, whether of the district or of the tribe, members of a village community keep together, and act in one group.

Right across the political and local divisions cut the totemic clans, each having a series of linked totems, with a bird as principal one. The members of these four clans are scattered over the whole tribe of Boyowa, and in each village community, members of all four are to be found, and even in every house, there are at least two classes represented, since a husband must be of a different clan from his wife and children. There is a certain amount of solidarity within the clan, based on the very vague feeling of communal affinity to the totem birds and animals, but much more on the many social duties, such as the performance of cer-

tain ceremonies, especially the mortuary ones, which band the members of a clan together. But real solidarity obtains only between members of a sub-clan. A sub-clan is a local division of a clan, whose members claim common ancestry, and hence real identity of bodily substance, and also are attached to the locality where their ancestors emerged. It is to these sub-clans that the idea of a definite rank attaches. One of the totemic clans, the Malasi, includes the most aristocratic sub-clan, the Tabalu, as well as the lowest one, the local division of the Malasi in Bwoytalu. A chief of the Tabalu feels very insulted if it is ever hinted that he is akin to one of the stingaree eaters of the unclean villages, although they are Malasi like himself. The principle of rank attached to totemic divisions is to be met only in Trobriand sociology; it is entirely foreign to all the other Papuo-Melanesian tribes.

As regards kinship, the main thing to be remembered is that the natives are matrilineal, and that the succession of rank, membership in all the social groups, and the inheritance of possessions descend in the maternal line. The mother's brother is considered the real guardian of the boy, and there is a series of mutual duties and obligations, which establish a very close and important relation between the two. The real kinship, the real identity of substance is considered to exist only between a man and his mother's relations. In the first rank of these, his brothers and sisters are specially near to him. For his sister or sisters he has to work as soon as they are grown up and married. But, in spite of that, a most rigorous taboo exists between them, beginning quite early in life. No man would joke and talk freely in the presence of his sister, or even look at her. The slightest allusion to the sexual affairs, whether illicit or matrimonial, of a brother or sister in the presence of the other, is the deadliest insult and mortification. When a man approaches a group of people where his sister is talking, either she withdraws or he turns away.

The father's relation to his children is remarkable. Physiological fatherhood is unknown, and no tie of kinship or relationship is supposed to exist between father and child, except that between a mother's husband and the wife's child. Nevertheless, the father is by far the nearest and most affectionate friend of his children. In every so many cases, I could observe that when a child, a young boy or girl, was in trouble or sick; when there was a question of some one exposing himself to difficulties or danger for the child's sake, it was always the father who worried, who would undergo all the hardships needed, and never the maternal uncle. This state of things is quite clearly recognised, and explicitly put into words by the natives. In matters of inheritance and handing over of possessions, a man always shows the tendency to do as much for his children as he is able, considering his obligations to his sister's family.

It is difficult, in one phrase or two, to epitomise the distinction between the two relations, that between a boy and his maternal uncle, and that between a son and a father. The best way to put it shortly might be by saying that the maternal uncle's position of close relation is regarded as right by law and usage, whereas the father's interest and affection for his children are due to sentiment, and to the intimate personal relations existing between them. He has watched the children grow up, he has assisted the mother in many of the small and tender cares given to an infant, he has carried the child about, and given it such education as it gets from watching the elder ones

at work, and gradually joining in. In matters of inheritance, the father gives the children all that he can, and gives it freely and with pleasure; the maternal uncle gives under the compulsion of custom what he cannot withhold and keep for his own children.

A few more words must be said about some of the magico-religious ideas of the Trobrianders. The main thing that struck me in connection with their belief in the spirits of the dead, was that they are almost completely devoid of any fear of ghosts, of any of these uncanny feelings with which we face the idea of a possible return of the dead. All the fears and dreads of the natives are reserved for black magic, flying witches, malevolent disease-bringing beings, but above all for sorcerers and witches. The spirits migrate immediately after death to the island of Tuma, lying in the Northwest of Boyowa, and there they exist for another span of time, underground, say some, on the surface of the earth, though invisible, say others. They return to visit their own villages once a year, and take part in the big annual feast, *milamala,* where they receive offerings. Sometimes, at this season, they show themselves to the living, who are, however, not alarmed by it, and in general the spirits do not influence human beings very much, for better or worse. In a number of magical formulae, there is an invocation of ancestral spirits, and they receive offerings in several rites. But there is nothing of the mutual interaction, of the intimate collaboration between man and spirit which are the essence of religious cult.

On the other hand, magic, the attempt of man to govern the forces of nature directly, by means of a special lore, is all-pervading, and all-important in the Trobriands. Sorcery and garden magic have already been mentioned.

Here it must suffice to add, that everything that vitally affects the native is accompanied by magic. All economic activities have their magic; love, welfare of babies, talents and crafts, beauty and agility—all can be fostered or frustrated by magic. In dealing with the Kula—a pursuit of immense importance to the natives, and playing on almost all their social passions and ambitions—we shall meet with another system of magic, and we shall have then to go more into detail about the subject in general.

Disease, health, or death are also the result of magic or countermagic. The Trobrianders have a very complex and very definite set of theoretical views on these matters. Good health is primarily of course the natural, normal state. Minor ills may be contracted by exposure, overeating, overstrain, bad food, or other ordinary causes. Such ailments never last, and have never any really bad effects, nor are they of immediate danger. But, if a man sickens for any length of time, and his strength seems to be really sapped, then the evil forces are at work. By far the most prevalent form of black magic is that of the *bwaga'u,* that is the black sorcerer, of whom there are a number in each village. Usually even in each village there are one or two men more or less dreaded as *bwaga'u.* To be one does not require any special initiation except the knowledge of the spells. To learn these—that is, to learn them in such a manner as to become an acknowledged *bwaga'u*—can only be done by means of high payment, or in exceptional circumstances. Thus, a father will often "give" his sorcery to his son, always, moreover, without payment; or a commoner will teach it to a man of rank, or a man to his sister's son. In these two latter cases a very high payment would have to be given. It is important as a characteristic of

the kinship conditions of this people, that a man receives sorcery gratis from his father, who according to the traditional kinship systems is no blood-relation, whereas he has to pay for it to his maternal uncle, whose natural heir he is.

When a man has acquired the black art, he applies it to a first victim, and this has always to be some one of his own family. It is a firm and definite belief among all the natives that if a man's sorcery is to be any good, it must first be practised on his mother or sister, or any of his maternal kindred. Such a matricidal act makes him a genuine *bwaga'u.* His art then can be practised on others, and becomes an established source of income.

The beliefs about sorcery are complex; they differ according as to whether taken from a real sorcerer, or from an outsider; and there are also evidently strata of belief, due perhaps to local variation, perhaps to superimposed versions. Here a short summary must suffice.

When a sorcerer wants to attack someone, the first step is to cast a light spell over his habitual haunts, a spell which will affect him with a slight illness and compel him to keep to his bed in his house, where he will try to cure himself by lying over a small fire and warming his body. His first ailment, called *kaynagola,* comprises pains in the body, such as (speaking from our point of view) would be brought by rheumatism, general cold, influenza, or any incipient disease. When the victim is in bed, with a fire burning under him, and also, as a rule, one in the middle of the hut, the *bwaga'u* stealthily approaches the house. He is accompanied by a few night birds, owls and nightjars, which keep guard over him, and he is surrounded by a halo of legendary terrors which make all natives shiver at the idea of meeting a sorcerer on such a nocturnal visit. He then tries to insert through the thatch wall a bunch of herbs impregnated with some deadly charm and tied to a long stick, and these he attempts to thrust into the fire over which the sick man is lying. If he succeeds, the fumes of the burnt leaves will be inhaled by the victim, whose name has been uttered in the charm, and he will be seized by one or other of the deadly diseases of which the natives have a long list, with a definite symptomatology, as well as a magical etiology. Thus the preliminary sorcery was necessary, in order to keep the victim to his house, in which spot only can the mortal magic be performed.

Of course, the sick man is on the defensive as well. First of all, his friends and relatives—this is one of the main duties of the wife's brothers—will keep a close watch over him, sitting with spears round the hut, and at all approaches to it. Often have I come across such vigils, when walking late at night through some village. Then, the services of some rival *bwaga'u* are invoked (for the art of killing and curing is always in the same hand), and he utters counterspells, so that at times the efforts of the first sorcerer, even should he succeed in burning the herbs according to the dreaded *toginivayu* rite, are fruitless.

Should this be so, he resorts to the final and most fatal rite, that of the pointing bone. Uttering powerful spells, the *bwaga'u* and one or two accomplices, boil some coconut oil in a small pot, far away in a dense patch of jungle. Leaves of herbs are soaked in the oil, and then wrapped round a sharp stingaree spine, or some similar pointed object, and the final incantation, most deadly of all, is chanted over it. The the *bwaga'u* steals towards the village, catches sight of his victim, and hiding himself behind a shrub or house,

points the magical dagger at him. In fact, he violently and viciously turns it round in the air, as if to stab the victim, and to twist and wrench the point in the wound. This, if carried out properly, and not counteracted by a still more powerful magician, will never fail to kill a man.

I have here summarised the bare outlines of the successive application of black magic as it is believed by sorcerer and outsider alike to be done, and to act in producing disease and death. There can be no doubt that the acts of sorcery are really carried out by those who believe themselves to possess the black powers. It is equally certain that the nervous strain of knowing one's life to be threatened by a *bwaga'u* is very great, and probably it is much worse when a man knows that behind the sorcerer stands the might of the chief, and this apprehension certainly contributes powerfully towards the success of black magic. On the other hand, a chief, if attacked, would have a good guard to protect him, and the most powerful wizards to back him up, and also the authority to deal directly with anyone suspected of plotting against him. Thus sorcery, which is one of the means of carrying on the established order, is in its turn strengthened by it.

If we remember that, as in all belief in the miraculous and supernatural, so also here, there is the loophole of counterforces, and of the sorcery being incorrectly or inefficiently applied, spoilt by broken taboos, mispronounced spells, or what not; again, that suggestion strongly influences the victim, and undermines his natural resistance; further that all disease is invariably traced back to some sorcerer or other, who, whether it is true or not, often frankly admits his responsibility in order to enhance his reputation, there is then no difficulty in understanding why the belief in black magic flourishes, why no empirical evidence can ever dispel it, and why the sorcerer no less than the victim, has confidence in his own powers. At least, the difficulty is the same as in explaining many contemporary examples of results achieved by miracles and faith healing, such as Christian Science or Lourdes, or in any cure by prayers and devotion.

Although by far the most important of them all, the *bwaga'u* is only one among the beings who can cause disease and death. The often-mentioned flying witches, who come always from the Southern half of the island, or from the East, from the islands of Kitava, Iwa, Gava, or Murua, are even more deadly. All very rapid and violent diseases, more especially such as show no direct, perceptible symptoms, are attributed to the *mulukwausi,* as they are called. Invisible, they fly through the air, and perch on trees, housetops, and other high places. From there, they pounce upon a man or woman and remove and hide "the inside," that is, the lungs, heart and guts, or the brains and tongue. Such a victim will die within a day or two, unless another witch, called for the purpose and well paid, goes in search and restores the missing "inside." Of course, sometimes it is too late to do it, as the meal has been eaten in the meantime! Then the victim must die.

Another powerful agency of death consists of the *tauva'u,* nonhuman though anthropomorphic beings, who cause all epidemic disease. When, at the end of the rainy season the new and unripe yams have come in, and dysentery rages, decimating the villages; or, when in hot and damp years an infectious disease passes over the district, taking heavy toll, this means that the *tauva'u* have come from the South, and that, invisible, they march through the villages, rattling their lime gourds, and

with their sword clubs or sticks hitting their victims, who immediately sicken and die. The *tauva'u* can, at will, assume the shape of man or reptile. He appears then as a snake, or crab, or lizard, and you recognise him at once, for he will not run away from you, and he has as a rule a patch of some gaudy colour on his skin. It would be a fatal thing to kill such a reptile. On the contrary, it has to be taken up cautiously and treated as a chief; that is to say, it is placed on a high platform, and some of the valuable tokens of wealth—a polished green stone blade, or a pair of arm shells, or a necklace of spondylus shell beads must be put before it as an offering.

It is very interesting to note that the *tauva'u* are believed to come from the Northern coast of Normanby Island, from the district of Du'a'u, and more especially from a place called Sewatupa. This is the very place where, according to Dobuan belief and myth, their sorcery originated. Thus, what to the local tribes of the originating place is ordinary sorcery, practised by men, becomes, when looked at from a great distance, and from an alien tribe, a non-human agency, endowed with such supernormal powers as changing of shape, invisibility, and a direct, infallible method of inflicting death.

The *tauva'u* sometimes have sexual intercourse with women; several present cases are on record, and such women who have a familar *tauva'u* become dangerous witches, though how they practise their witchcraft is not quite clear to the natives.

A much less dangerous being is the *tokway,* a wood sprite, living in trees and rocks, stealing crops from the field and from the yam houses, and inflicting slight ailments. Some men in the past have acquired the knowledge of how to do this from the *tokway,* and have handed it on to their descendants.

So we see that, except for the very light ailments which pass quickly and easily, all diseases are attributed to sorcery. Even accidents are not believed to happen without cause. That this is the case also with drowning, we shall learn more in detail, when we have to follow the Trobrianders in their dangerous sea trips. Natural death, caused by old age, is admittedly possible, but when I asked in several concrete cases, in which age was obviously the cause, why such and such a man died, I was always told that a *bwaga'u* was at the back of it. Only suicide and death in battle have a different place in the mind of the natives, and this is also confirmed by the belief that people killed in war, those that commit suicide, and those who are bewitched to death have, each class, their own way to the other world. . . .

. . . The Kula is a form of exchange, of extensive, intertribal character; it is carried on by communities inhabiting a wide ring of islands, which form a closed circuit. . . . Along this route, articles of two kinds, and these two kinds only, are constantly travelling in opposite directions. In the direction of the hands of the clock, moves constantly one of these kinds— long necklaces of red shell, called *soulava*. . . . In the opposite direction moves the other kind—bracelets of white shell called *mwali*. . . . Each of these articles, as it travels in its own direction on the closed circuit, meets on its way articles of the other class, and is constantly being exchanged for them. Every movement of the Kula articles, every detail of the transactions is fixed and regulated by a set of traditional rules and conventions, and some acts of the Kula are accompanied by an elaborate magical ritual and public ceremonies.

On every island and in every village, a more or less limited number of men take part in the Kula—that is to say, receive the goods, hold them for a short time, and then pass them on. Therefore every man who is in the Kula, periodically though not regularly, receives one or several *mwali* (arm shells), or a *soulava* (necklace of red shell discs), and then has to hand it on to one of his partners, from whom he receives the opposite commodity in exchange. Thus no man ever keeps any of the articles for any length of time in his possession. One transaction does not finish the Kula relationship, the rule being "once in the Kula, always in the Kula," and a partnership between two men is a permanent and lifelong affair. Again, any given *mwali* or *soulava* may always be found travelling and changing hands, and there is no question of its ever settling down, so that the principle "once in the Kula, always in the Kula" applies also to the valuables themselves.

The ceremonial exchange of the two articles is the main, the fundamental aspect of the Kula. But associated with it, and done under its cover, we find a great number of secondary activities and features. Thus, side by side with the ritual exchange of arm shells and necklaces, the natives carry on ordinary trade, bartering from one island to another a great number of utilities, often unprocurable in the district to which they are imported, and indispensable there. [*In view of what we have learned from other cultures, this ordinary trade might be considered primary.*] Further, there are other activities, preliminary to the Kula, or associated with it, such as building of seagoing canoes for the expeditions, certain big forms of mortuary ceremonies, and preparatory taboos.

The Kula is thus an extremely big and complex institution, both in its geographical extent, and in the manifoldness of its component pursuits. It welds together a considerable number of tribes, and it embraces a vast complex of activities, interconnected, and playing into one another, so as to form one organic whole.

Yet it must be remembered that what appears to us an extensive, complicated, and yet well ordered institution is the outcome of ever so many doings and pursuits, carried on by savages, who have no laws or aims or charters definitely laid down. They have no knowledge of the *total outline* of any of their social structure. They know their own motives, know the purpose of individual actions and the rules which apply to them, but how, out of these, the whole collective institution shapes, this is beyond their mental range. Not even the most intelligent native has any clear idea of the Kula as a big, organised social construction, still less of its sociological function and implications. If you were to ask him what the Kula is, he would answer by giving a few details, most likely by giving his personal experiences and subjective views on the Kula, but nothing approaching the definition just given here. Not even a partial coherent account could be obtained. For the integral picture does not exist in his mind; he is in it, and cannot see the whole from the outside. . . .

The Kula is not a surreptitious and precarious form of exchange. It is, quite on the contrary, rooted in myth, backed by traditional law, and surrounded with magical rites. All its main transactions are public and ceremonial, and carried out according to definite rule. It is not done on the spur of the moment, but happens periodically, at dates settled in advance, and it is carried on along definite trade routes, which must lead to fixed trysting places. Sociologically, though transacted between tribes differing in language, culture, and probably even in race, it is based on a fixed and permanent status, on a partnership which binds into couples some thousands of individuals. This partnership is a life-long relationship, it implies various mutual duties and privileges, and constitutes a type of intertribal relationship on an enormous scale. As to the economic mechanism of the transactions, this is based on a specific form of credit, which implies a high degree of mutual trust and commercial honour— and this refers also to the subsidiary, minor trade, which accompanies the Kula proper. Finally the Kula is not done under stress of any need, since its main aim is to exchange articles which are of no practical use.

From the concise definition of Kula given at the beginning of this chapter, we see that in its final essence, divested of all trappings and accessories, it is a very simple affair, which at first sight might even appear tame and unromantic. After all, it only consists of an exchange, interminably repeated, of two articles intended for ornamentation, but not even used for that to any extent. Yet this simple action—this passing from hand to hand of two meaningless and quite useless objects— has somehow succeeded in becoming the foundation of a big inter-tribal institution, in being associated with ever so many other activities. Myth, magic and tradition have built up around it definite ritual and ceremonial forms, have given it a halo of romance and value in the minds of the natives, have indeed created a passion in their hearts for this simple exchange. . . .

First of all, a few words must be said about the two principal objects of exchange, the arm shells (*mwali*) and the necklaces (*soulava*). The arm shells are obtained by breaking off the top and the narrow end of a big, cone-shaped shell (*Conus millepunctus*), and then polishing up the remaining ring.

These bracelets are highly coveted by all the Papuo-Melanesians of New Guinea, and they spread even into the pure Papuan district of the Gulf. . . .

The use of the small discs of red spondylus shell, out of which the *soulava* are made, is also of a very wide diffusion. There is a manufacturing centre of them in one of the villages in Port Moresby, and also in several places in Eastern New Guinea, notably in Rossell Island, and in the Trobriands. I have said *"use"* on purpose here, because these small beads, each of them a flat, round disc with a hole in the centre, coloured anything from muddy brown to carmine red, are employed in various ways for ornamentation. They are most generally used as part of earrings, made of rings of turtle shell, which are attached to the ear lobe, and from which hang a cluster of the shell discs. . . . We are more especially concerned with the very long necklaces, measuring from two to five metres, made of spondylus discs, of which there are two main varieties, one, much the finer, with a big shell pendant, the other made of bigger discs, and with a few cowrie shells or black banana seeds in the centre. . . .

The arm shells on the one hand, and the long spondylus shell strings on the other, the two main Kula articles, are primarily ornaments. As such, they are used with the most elaborate dancing dress only, and on very festive occasions such as big ceremonial dances, great feasts, and big gatherings, where several villages are represented. . . . Never could they be used as everyday ornaments, nor on occasions of minor importance, such as a small dance in the village, harvest gathering, a love-making expedition, when facial painting, floral decoration and smaller though not quite everyday ornaments are worn. . . . But even though usable and sometimes used, this is not the main function of these articles. Thus, a chief may have several shell strings in his possession, and a few arm shells. Supposing that a big dance is held in his or in a neighbouring village, he will not put on his ornaments himself if he goes to assist at it, unless he intends to dance and decorate himself, but any of his relatives, his children or his friends and even vassals, can have the use of them for the asking. If you go to a feast or a dance where there are a number of men wearing such ornaments, and ask anyone of them at random to whom it belongs, the chances are that more than half of them will answer that they themselves are not the owners, but that they had the articles lent to them. These objects are not owned in order to be used; the privilege of decorating oneself with them is not the real aim of possession.

Indeed—and this is more significant —by far the greater number of the arm shells, easily ninety percent, are of too small a size to be worn even by young boys and girls. A few are so big and valuable that they would not be worn at all, except once in a decade by a very important man on a very festive day. Though all the shell strings can be worn, some are again considered too valuable, and are cumbersome for frequent use, and would be worn on very exceptional occasions only.

This negative description leaves us with the questions: why, then, are these objects valued, what purpose do they serve? As it is always better to approach the unknown through the known, let us consider for a moment whether among ourselves we have not some type of objects which play a similar role and which are used and possessed in the same manner. When, after a six years' absence in the South Seas and Australia, I returned to Europe and did my first bit of sight-seeing in Edinburgh Castle, I was shown the Crown jewels. The keeper told many stories of how they were worn by this or that king or queen on such and such occasion, of how some of them had been taken over to London, to the great and just indignation of the whole Scottish nation, how they were restored, and how now everyone can be pleased, since they are safe under lock and key, and no one can touch them. As I was looking at them and thinking how ugly, useless, ungainly, even tawdry they were, I had the feeling that something similar had been told to me of late, and that I had seen many other objects of this sort, which made a similar impression on me.

And then arose before me the vision of a native village on coral soil, and a small, rickety platform temporarily erected under a pandanus thatch, surrounded by a number of brown, naked men, and one of them showing me long, thin red strings, and big, white, worn-out objects, clumsy to sight and greasy to touch. With reverence he also would name them, and tell their history, and by whom and when they were worn, and how they changed hands, and how their temporary possession was a great sign of the importance and glory of the village. The analogy between the European and the Trobriand *vaygu'a* (valuables) must be delimited with more precision. The Crown jewels, in fact, any heirlooms too valuable and too cumbersome to be worn, represent the same type as *vaygu'a* in that they are merely possessed for the sake of possession itself, and the ownership of them with the ensuing renown is the main source of their value. Also both heirlooms and *vaygu'a* are cherished because of the historical sentiment which surrounds them. However ugly, useless, and— according to current standards—valueless an object may be, if it has figured in historical scenes and passed through

the hands of historic persons, and is therefore an unfailing vehicle of important sentimental associations, it cannot but be precious to us. This historic sentimentalism, which indeed has a large share in our general interest in studies of past events, exists also in the South Seas. Every really good Kula article has its individual name, round each there is a sort of history and romance in the traditions of the natives. Crown jewels or heirlooms are insignia of rank and symbols of wealth respectively, and in olden days with us, and in New Guinea up till a few years ago, both rank and wealth went together. The main point of difference is that the Kula goods are only in possession for a time, whereas the European treasure must be permanently owned in order to have full value.

Taking a broader, ethnological view of the question, we may class the Kula valuables among the many "ceremonial" objects of wealth; enormous, carved and decorated weapons, stone implements, articles of domestic and industrial nature, too well decorated and too clumsy for use. . . . many so-called ceremonial objects are nothing but simply overgrown objects of use, which preciousness of material and amount of labour expended have transformed into reservoirs of condensed economic value. Again, others are used on festive occasions, but play no part whatever in rites and ceremonies, and serve for decoration only, and these might be called *objects of parade.* . . . Finally, a number of these articles function actually as instruments of a magical or religious rite, and belong to the intrinsic apparatus of a ceremony. . . .

The *vaygu'a*—the Kula valuables— in one of their aspects are overgrown objects of use. They are also, however, *ceremonial* objects in the narrow and correct sense of the word. . . .

The exchange of these two classes of

vaygu'a, of the arm shells and the necklaces, constitutes the main act of the Kula. This exchange is not done freely, right and left, as opportunity offers, and where the whim leads. It is subject indeed to strict limitations and regulations. One of these refers to the sociology of the exchange, and entails that Kula transactions can be done only between partners. A man who is in the Kula—for not everyone within its district is entitled to carry it on—has only a limited number of people with whom he does it. This partnership is entered upon in a definite manner, under fulfilment of certain formalities, and it constitutes a lifelong relationship. The numbers of partners a man has varies with his rank and importance. A commoner in the Trobriands would have a few partners only, whereas a chief would number hundreds of them. There is no special social mechanism to limit the partnership of some people and extend that of the others, but a man would naturally know to what number of partners he was entitled by his rank and position. And there would be always the example of his immediate ancestors to guide him. In other tribes, where the distinction of rank is not so pronounced, an old man of standing, or a headman of a hamlet or village, would also have hundreds of Kula associates, whereas a man of minor importance would have but few.

Two Kula partners have to *kula* with one another, and exchange other gifts incidentally; they behave as friends, and have a number of mutual duties and obligations, which vary with the distance between their villages and with their reciprocal status. An average man has a few partners near by, as a rule his relations-in-law or his friends, and with these partners, he is generally on very friendly terms. The Kula partnership is one of the special bonds which unite two men into one of the standing relations of mutual exchange of gifts and services so characteristic of these natives. Again, the average man will have one or two chiefs in his or in the neighbouring districts with whom he *kulas.* In such a case, he would be bound to assist and serve them in various ways, and to offer them the pick of his *vaygu'a* when he gets a fresh supply. On the other hand he would expect them to be specially liberal to him.

The overseas partner is, on the other hand, a host, patron and ally in a land of danger and insecurity. Nowadays, though the feeling of danger still persists, and natives never feel safe and comfortable in a strange district, this danger is rather felt as a magical one, and it is more the fear of foreign sorcery that besets them. In olden days, more tangible dangers were apprehended, and the partner was the main guarantee of safety. He also provides with food, gives presents, and his house, though never used to sleep in, is the place in which to foregather while in the village. Thus the Kula partnership provides every man within its ring with a few friends near at hand, and with some friendly allies in the far-away, dangerous, foreign districts. These are the only people with whom he can *kula,* but, of course, amongst all his partners, he is free to choose to which one he will offer which object.

Let us now try to cast a broad glance at the cumulative effects of the rules of partnership. We see that all around the ring of Kula there is a network of relationships, and that naturally the whole forms one interwoven fabric. Men living at hundreds of miles' sailing distance from one another are bound together by direct or intermediate partnership, exchange with each other, know of each other, and on certain occasions meet in a large intertribal gathering. . . . Objects given by one, in time reach some very distant indirect partner or other, and not only Kula objects, but various articles of domestic use and minor gifts. It is easy to see that in the long run, not only objects of material culture, but also customs, songs, art motives and general cultural influences travel along the Kula route. It is a vast, intertribal net of relationships, a big institution, consisting of thousands of men, all bound together by one common passion for Kula exchange, and secondarily, by many minor ties and interests.

Returning again to the personal aspect of the Kula, let us take a concrete example, that of *an average man* who lives, let us assume, in the village of Sinaketa, an important Kula centre in the Southern Trobriands. He has a few partners, near and far, but they again fall into categories, those who give him arm shells, and those who give him necklaces. For it is naturally an invariable rule of the Kula that arm shells and necklaces are never received from the same man, since they must travel in different directions. If one partner gives the arm shells, and I return to him a necklace, all future operations have to be of the same type. More than that, the nature of the operation between me, the man of Sinaketa, and my partner, is determined by our relative positions with regard to the points of the compass. Thus I, in Sinaketa, would receive from the North and East only arm shells; from the South and West, necklaces are given to me. If I have a near partner next door to me, if his abode is North or East of mine, he will always be giving me arm shells and receiving necklaces from me. If, at a later time he were to shift his residence within the village, the old relationship would obtain, but

if he became a member of another village community on the other side of me the relationship would be reversed. The partners in villages to the North of Sinaketa, in the district of Luba, Kulumata, or Kiriwina all supply me with arm shells. These I hand over to my partners in the South, and receive from them necklaces. The South in this case means the southern districts of Boyowa, as well as the Amphletts and Dobu.

Thus every man has to obey definite rules as to the geographical direction of his transactions. At any point in the Kula ring, if we imagine him turned towards the centre of the circle, he receives the arm shells with his left hand, and the necklaces with his right, and then hands them both on. In other words, he constantly passes the arm shells from left to right, and the necklaces from right to left.

Applying this rule of personal conduct to the whole Kula ring, we can see at once what the aggregate result is. The sum total of exchanges will not result in an aimless shifting of the two classes of article, in a fortuitous come and go of the arm shells and necklaces. Two continuous streams will constantly flow on, the one of necklaces following the hands of a clock, and the other, composed of the arm shells, in the opposite direction. . . .

. . . Also, they never stop. It seems almost incredible at first, but it is a fact, nevertheless, that no one ever keeps any of the Kula valuables for any length of time. Indeed, in the whole of the Trobriands there are perhaps only one or two specially fine arm shells and shell necklaces permanently owned as heirlooms, and these are set apart as a special class, and are once and for all out of the Kula. "Ownership," therefore, in Kula, is quite a special economic relation. A man who is in the Kula never keeps any article for longer than, say, a year or two. Even this exposes him to the reproach of being niggardly, and certain districts have the bad reputation of being "slow" and "hard" in the Kula. On the other hand, each man has an enormous number of articles passing through his hands during his life time, of which he enjoys a temporary possession, and which he keeps in trust for a time. This possession hardly ever makes him use the articles, and he remains under obligation soon again to hand them on to one of his partners. But the temporary ownership allows him to draw a great deal of renown, to exhibit his article, to tell how he obtained it, and to plan to whom he is going to give it. And all this forms one of the favourite subjects of tribal conversation and gossip, in which the feats and the glory in Kula of chiefs or commoners are constantly discussed and rediscussed. Thus every article moves in one direction only, never comes back, never permanently stops, and takes as a rule some two to ten years to make the round. . . .

The main principle underlying the regulations of actual exchange is that the Kula consists in the bestowing of a ceremonial gift, which has to be repaid by an equivalent counter-gift after a lapse of time, be it a few hours or even minutes, though sometimes as much as a year or more may elapse between payments. But it can never be exchanged from hand to hand, with the equivalence between the two objects discussed, bargained about and computed. The decorum of the Kula transaction is strictly kept, and highly valued. The natives sharply distinguish it from barter, which they practise extensively, of which they have a clear idea, and for which they have a settled term—in Kiriwinian: *gimwali.* Often, when criticising an incorrect, too hasty, or indecorous procedure of

Kula, they will say: "He conducts his Kula as if it were *gimwali.*"

The second very important principle is that the equivalence of the counter-gift is left to the giver, and it cannot be enforced by any kind of coercion. A partner who has received a Kula gift is expected to give back fair and full value, that is, to give as good an arm shell as the necklace he receives, or vice versa. Again, a very fine article must be replaced by one of equivalent value, and not by several minor ones, though intermediate gifts may be given to mark time before the real repayment takes place.

If the article given as counter-gift is not equivalent, the recipient will be disappointed and angry, but he has no direct means of redress, no means of coercing his partner, or of putting an end to the whole transaction. . . . Although, like every human being, the Kula native loves to possess and therefore desires to acquire and dreads to lose, the social code of rules, with regard to give and take by far overrides his natural acquisitive tendency.

This social code, such as we find it among the natives of the Kula is, however, far from weakening the natural desirability of possession; on the contrary, it lays down that to possess is to be great, and that wealth is the indispensable appanage of social rank and attribute of personal virtue. But the important point is that with them to possess is to give—and here the natives differ from us notably. A man who owns a thing is naturally expected to share it, to distribute it, to be its trustee and dispenser. And the higher the rank the greater the obligation. A chief will naturally be expected to give food to any stranger, visitor, even loiterer from another end of the village. He will be expected to share any of the betel nut or tobacco he has about him. So that a man of rank will have to hide away any surplus of these articles which he wants to preserve for his further use. In the Eastern end of New Guinea a type of large basket, with three layers, manufactured in the Trobriands, was specially popular among people of consequence, because one could hide away one's small treasures in the lower compartments. Thus the main symptom of being powerful is to be wealthy, and of wealth is to be generous. Meanness, indeed, is the most despised vice, and the only thing about which the natives have strong moral views, while generosity is the essence of goodness.

. . . *Noblesse oblige* is in reality the social norm regulating their conduct. This does not mean that people are always satisfied, and that there are no squabbles about the transactions, no resentments and even feuds. It is obvious that, however much a man may want to give a good equivalent for the object received, he may not be able to do so. And then, as there is always a keen competition to be the most generous giver, a man who has received less than he gave will not keep his grievance to himself, but will brag about his own generosity and compare it to his partner's meanness; the other resents it, and the quarrel is ready to break out. But it is very important to realise that there is no actual haggling, no tendency to do a man out of his share. The giver is quite as keen as the receiver that the gifts should be generous, though for different reasons. Then, of course, there is the important consideration that a man who is fair and generous in the Kula will attract a larger stream to himself than a mean one. . . .

Let us suppose that I, a Sinaketa man, am in possession of a pair of big arm shells. An overseas expedition from Dobu in the d'Entrecasteaux Archipelago, arrives at my village. I take my arm-shell pair and I offer it to my overseas partner, with some such words as "This is a *vaga* (opening gift) —in due time, thou returnest to me a big *soulava* (necklace) for it!" Next year, when I visit my partner's village, he either is in possession of an equivalent necklace, and this he gives to me as *yotile* (return gift), or he has not a necklace good enough to repay my last gift. In this case he will give me a small necklace—avowedly not equivalent to my gift—and he will give it to me as *basi* (intermediary gift). This means that the main gift has to be repaid on a future occasion, and the *basi* is given in token of good faith—but it, in turn, must be repaid by me in the meantime by a gift of small arm shells. The final gift, which will be given to me to clinch the whole transaction, would then be called *kudu* (clinching gift) in contrast to *basi*. . . .

Although haggling and bargaining are completely ruled out of the Kula, there are customary and regulated ways of bidding for a piece of *vaygu'a* known to be in the possession of one's partner. This is done by the offer of what we shall call solicitary gifts, of which there are several types. If I, an inhabitant of Sinaketa, happen to be in possession of a pair of arm shells more than usually good, the fame of it spreads, for it must be remembered that each one of the first-class arm shells and necklaces has a personal name and a history of its own, and as they circulate around the big ring of the Kula, they are all well known, and their appearance in a given district always creates a sensation. Now, all my partners—whether from overseas or from within the district—compete for the favour of receiving this particular article of mine, and those who are specially keen try to obtain it by giving me *pokala* (offerings) and *kaributu* (solicitary gifts). The former (*pokala*) consist as a rule of pigs, especially fine bananas, and valuable, large axe blades (called *beku*), or lime spoons of whale bone are given. . . .

I have enumerated the main rules of the Kula in a manner sufficient for a preliminary definition, and now a few words must be said about the associated activities and secondary aspects of the Kula. If we realise that at times the exchange has to take place between districts divided by dangerous seas, over which a great number of people have to travel by sail, and do so keeping to appointed dates, it becomes clear at once that considerable preparations are necessary to carry out the expedition. Many preliminary activities are intimately associated with the Kula. Such are, particularly, the building of canoes, preparation of the outfit, the provisioning of the expedition, the fixing of dates and social organisation of the enterprise. All these are subsidiary to the Kula, and as they are carried on in pursuit of it, and form one connected series, a description of the Kula must embrace an account of these preliminary activities. . . .

Another important pursuit inextricably bound up with the Kula, is that of the *secondary trade*. Voyaging to far-off countries, endowed with natural resources unknown in their own homes, the Kula sailors return each time richly laden with these, the spoils of their enterprise. Again, in order to be able to offer presents to his partner, every outward bound canoe carries a cargo of such things as are known to be most desirable in the overseas district. Some of this is given away in presents to the partners, but a good deal is carried in order to pay for the objects desired at home. In certain cases, the visiting natives exploit on their own account during the journey some of the natural resources overseas. For example, the Sinaketans dive for the spondylus in Sanaroa Lagoon, and the Dobuans fish in the Trobriands on a beach on the southern end of the island. The secondary trade is complicated still more by the fact that such big Kula centres as, for instance, Sinaketa, are not efficient in any of the industries of special value to the Dobuans. Thus, Sinaketans have to procure the necessary store of goods from the inland villages of Kuboma, and this they do on minor trading expeditions preliminary to the Kula. . . .

. . . Both the canoe-building and the ordinary trade have been spoken of as secondary or subsidiary to the Kula proper. This requires a comment. I do not, by thus subordinating the two things in importance to the Kula, mean to express a philosophical reflection or a personal opinion as to the relative value of these pursuits from the point of view of some social teleology. Indeed, it is clear that if we look at the acts from the outside, as comparative sociologists, and gauge their real utility, trade and canoe-building will appear to us as the really important achievements, whereas we shall regard the Kula only as an indirect stimulus, impelling the natives to sail and to trade. . . .

By studying the behaviour of the natives and all the customs in question, we see that the Kula is in all respects the main aim: the dates are fixed, the preliminaries settled, the expeditions arranged, the social organisation determined, not with regard to trade, but with regard to Kula. On an expedition, the big ceremonial feast, held at the start, refers to the Kula; the final ceremony of reckoning and counting the spoil refers to Kula, not to the objects of trade obtained. Finally, the magic, which is one of the main factors of all the procedure, refers only to the Kula, and this applies even to a part of the magic carried out over the canoe.

Some rites in the whole cycle are done for the sake of the canoe itself, and others for the sake of Kula. The construction of the canoes is always carried on directly in connection with a Kula expedition. . . .

Of course not only many of the surrounding tribes who know nothing of the Kula do build canoes and sail far and daringly on trading expeditions, but even within the Kula ring, in the Trobriands for instance, there are several villages who do not kula, yet have canoes and carry on energetic overseas trade. But where the Kula is practised, it governs all the other allied activities, and canoe building and trade are made subsidiary to it. And this is expressed both by the nature of the institutions and the working of all the arrangements on the one hand, and by the behaviour and explicit statements of the natives on the other.

The Kula—it becomes, I hope, more and more clear—is a big, complicated institution, insignificant though its nucleus might appear. To the natives, it represents one of the most vital interests in life, and as such it has a ceremonial character and is surrounded by magic. We can well imagine that articles of wealth might pass from hand to hand without ceremony or ritual, but in the Kula they never do. Even when at times only small parties in one or two canoes sail overseas and bring back *vaygu'a,* certain taboos are observed, and a customary course is taken in departing, in sailing, and in arriving; even the smallest expedition in one canoe is a tribal event of some importance, known and spoken of over the whole district. But the characteristic expedition is one in which a considerable number of canoes take part, organised in a certain manner, and forming one body. Feasts, distributions of food, and other public ceremonies are held, there is one leader and master of the expedition, and various rules are adhered to, in addition to the ordinary Kula taboos and observances.

The ceremonial nature of the Kula is strictly bound up with another of its aspects—magic. The belief in the efficiency of magic dominates the Kula, as it does ever so many other tribal activities of the natives. Magical rites must be performed over the sea-going canoe when it is built, in order to make it swift, steady and safe; also magic is done over a canoe to make it lucky in the Kula. Another system of magical rites is done in order to avert the dangers of sailing. The third system of magic connected with overseas expeditions is the *mwasila* or the Kula magic proper. This system consists in numerous rites and spells, all of which act directly on the mind (*nanola*) of one's partner, and make him soft, unsteady in mind, and eager to give Kula gifts. . . .

It is clear that an institution so closely associated with magical and ceremonial elements, as is the Kula, not only rests on a firm, traditional foundation, but also has its large store of legends. There is a rich mythology of the Kula, in which stories are told about far-off times when mythical ancestors sailed on distant and daring expeditions. Owing to their magical knowledge they were able to escape dangers, to conquer their enemies, to surmount obstacles, and by their feats they established many a precedent which is now closely followed by tribal custom. But their importance for their descendants lies mainly in the fact that they handed on their magic, and this made the Kula possible for the following generations. . . .

To pick this selection from Malinowski's most famous work into pieces, and to try to re-explain what he has made so abundantly clear, would be an act of anthropological sacrilege. I shall keep my remarks to a minimum, and use them only to show the relationship between the Trobriand Island culture and the rest of this book.

On page 309 he mentions the technique of bone pointing. This method of magical injury is also characteristic of Australians.

On page 307 we see that witches and other kinds of evil spirits are attributed to special localities, thus paralleling the regional specialization in technology.

On page 312 he uses the word "institution" in the older, nontechnical sense. Later in his career he used it in the same sense as in this book.

On pages 312–315, and again on page 319, he discusses the relationship between the ceremonial kula exchanges and the "undercover" trading that accompanied them. While he left the question open, as was wisest, it now seems likely from a study of comparative ethnography that the "undercover" trading was the vital activity, and the ceremonial exchange the means of making the former possible.

More trading went on, probably, in the Kula ring than among either Kurnai or Maidu. The Trobrianders with their gardening techniques produced, as Malinowski said, more than twice as much food as they needed. There was a surplus, and people specialized; those on rocky islets went in for manufacturing. The situation may be compared to that in the United States during the nineteenth century, when the New Englanders on their rocky, exhausted soil became specialists in manufacturing.

11

The Pygmies of the Ituri Forest

ANOTHER example of local specialization and intergroup relations is that of the African pygmies with their Negro hosts, as narrated by Patrick Putnam.*

THE FOREST ENVIRONMENT.

The Ituri forest is rolling country, so densely covered with trees that the relief of the landscape is invisible except from the air. It is a primary rain forest; that is, in most of the region it rains every day or every other day, averaging about one half of the days, from four to six in the afternoon—some 180 days a year. The annual rainfall is correspondingly great, about one and a half meters. The temperature is about 70° F. at night, and varies during the day from 75° to 80° F., depending upon whether it is sunny or cloudy. During January and February, the "dry" season, there are many overcast days; during the rest of the year it is either actually raining or else sunny, with quick changes. When the rain comes, it comes suddenly. It may be bright during the earlier part of the day, and then in the afternoon cloud up all at once in thunderheads. For a few minutes high winds rage through the trees, which tremble like grass in a breeze. Rotten branches and even huge trees crack and fall, crash-ing to the ground. The lightning flashes from the somber sky, and thunder rolls and re-echoes, followed by a pelting downpour. Then in an hour or two it will suddenly stop, sometimes for a brief period of sunshine before the dark of night.

The forest varies greatly in regard to underbrush. In some spots there is no undergrowth at all, and nothing but leaf mold between the boles of the trees; in others there is a wild tangle of bushes, reeds, and lianas. The densest thickets are found in small patches of secondary growth, where the Negroes have made clearings and then abandoned them. Most of the forest, however, is virgin growth, and unimpeded except for fallen tree trunks.

The forest provides game enough for the pygmies, and some to spare for their hosts. Many kinds of wild plants, huge trees, small shrubs, small plants, growing low on the forest floor, bear either edible fruits or medicinal leaves or bark. Many edible fungi are abundant.

The forest is also well watered; the

* Putnam has been living with the people of whom he spoke for nearly two decades. He dictated to me a somewhat longer story of pygmy life, which I have condensed to its present compass. He went over the copy carefully and made corrections. Not satisfied with it, he went back to learn more, but before he could report he died on December 12, 1953. This material has never before been published.

rolling hills are separated by perennial streams never more than a few miles apart. A pygmy can find water almost anywhere within a hundred yards.

NEGRO-PYGMY RELATIONS

This forest is inhabited by two kinds of people, Negroes and pygmies, who maintain an almost symbiotic relationship, based on trade. A Negro village may own approximately 100 square miles of forest territory. In this territory are the Negro village and the pygmy village. The former is permanent, in a clearing; the latter is temporary, under the forest trees. In maintaining their relationship, it is the pygmies' job to take in honey and meat, while the Negroes' obligation is to give them plantains. In addition, the pygmies may bring in a certain amount of wild baselli fruit in season, or roofing leaves, or rattan and fibers for net making; in return they may acquire ax blades, knives, and arrowheads from the Negroes.

There is no strict process of barter involved, and no accounting kept, other than through general observation. If the pygmies are stingy, their Negroes will hold back their bananas. If the Negroes are stingy, the pygmies will leave the territory and go to live with other pygmies serving other Negro hosts.

This relationship is interfamilial, between a pygmy family and a Negro family. It is a matter of close personal relations, inherited, on both sides, from father to son. These alliances may change from time to time, but when they do there are usually hard feelings; if a man's pygmy leaves him to serve another host it is a kind of divorce. In the old days, a frequent cause of inter-village warfare among the Negroes was the luring away of each other's pygmies.

Before the Belgians stopped inter-village and intertribal warfare, the most important single duty of the pygmy was to act as scout and intelligence agent in the forest. As soon as he became aware of a raiding party crossing the boundary of his host's territory he would hotfoot it to the village to give warning. This eternal vigilance on the part of the pygmy was probably of more value to his hosts than the meat that he brought in. Now that the need of this has ceased he is fulfilling only half of his contract; the Negro, who still provides plantains and manufactured objects, is still fulfilling all of his. Still both are satisfied.

Ordinarily, the pygmy keeps inside the territory of his Negro hosts. Individuals and small family groups may go outside to visit relatives in other bands, but this causes no disturbance because the visitors turn in their game to the hosts of the kinsmen whom they are visiting. This constant milling about evens up on the whole, and the number of pygmies in any band at any one time is about the same. There are occasions, however, when the hunters of a band may have a strong reason to pass beyond the landmarks which designate their hosts' territorial boundaries. If there is a lot of game just over the border and no pygmies there to catch it, the pygmies will tell their Negroes, who tell the Negroes owning that part of the forest. An agreement will be made between the two groups of Negroes, and the pygmies will be allowed to take the game, provided that they pay a part of it to the owners of the forest, and another part to their own hosts. This kind of economic treaty, therefore, brings the pygmies of a given band into contact with two groups of Negroes, and may initiate new relationships.

When the pygmy camp is close to the Negro village, some of the pygmies may come in every evening. They will leave a couple of old men to stay behind in the camp as guards, smoking hashish, and the rest will go into the village, usually around four o'clock in the afternoon, after the day's hunting is over. From then until dark a few pygmies are usually to be seen hanging about the women's quarters. If a white man arrives, however, they quickly disappear, through fear that he will confiscate their antelope, or any other game that they may have brought with them.

These mass visits are made particularly if it is going to be a moonlit night, and if wine drinking is going on. If there is a moon they will stay and dance; if not, they will come home at dark. The Negroes give them wine in a condescending way, and the pygmies put on what the Negroes consider to be wild, barbaric dances.

Sometimes the pygmy camp is as much as two days' journey from the village. In this case, the pygmies go in seldom, and browbeat their wives to make them go in to get plantains.

A visitor to a Negro village can nearly always see bunches of plantains lying around on the ground; they have been placed there for the pygmies, who pick them up and carry them home. There is no need for any special bargaining or designation; the pygmies know which bunches are for them.

Pygmy attitudes toward their Negroes.—The pygmies consider themselves inseparably attached to their hosts and think it their duty to provide them with meat. Although they feel that they are supposed to turn over all honey and elephant meat, in each case they eat all they can before taking it into the village. They never preserve or store any food. Their duty of feeding the Negroes meat is therefore regarded as somewhat of a nuisance. On the other hand, when the pygmy

wants something from a Negro, he wheedles and "begs" for it. He may thus "borrow" a mortar, a skin-headed drum for dancing, etc., and will not return it until the Negro comes after it or sends for it. He will not put any of these things under cover, or care for them; he leaves them out in the rain to mildew and rot. The owner has to see that his property is cared for, and this forms a subject on which the Negro can make fun of the pygmy.

The form of this relationship is therefore a grudging duty in the case of giving, and a wheedling begging in the case of receiving. These outer forms fail to reveal the inner feeling of loyalty and affection between the parties concerned, but rather symbolize the existing situation in which the Negro is at the top of the scale and the pygmy at the bottom.

Negro attitude toward their pygmies.—The Negroes distinguish four ranks or orders of living beings: people, pygmies, chimpanzees, and other animals. The pygmies are thus considered a species apart, neither human nor animal, but in between. The main point of distinction lies not in their size or physique, but in the fact that the pygmies do no cultivation.

The Negroes think of their pygmies as barbaric and uncultured, but at the same time they are often fond of them. A Negro may occasionally marry a pygmy woman, and the children are considered real children, complete human beings; they are brought up with the Negro's other children. The Negroes say that pygmy women are good in bed, cheap, and prolific, but that they are useless for women's work—cultivation and cooking. For a pygmy woman it is a great rise in the scale of living to marry a Negro as his second or third wife, despite the fact that pygmy wives are usually the butt of humor from the Negro wives. This is, however, a one-way process; no Negress could endure the pygmy way of living, and none of them ever marry pygmies.

The interplay between Negroes and pygmies may be illustrated by a number of examples in which they disagree on historical facts. The Negroes say that the pygmies once went naked, like animals. The pygmies hotly deny this, and assert that they always wore loin cloths. The Negroes admit that they themselves were once cannibals, but say that the pygmies ate more human flesh than they did. This too the pygmies deny; they claim that they never ate human flesh except when the Negroes gave it to them.

· · · ·

In addition to the exchange of food and, formerly, protection, which form the basis for Negro-pygmy interaction, there is another activity which helps to cement their relationship. The Negroes have a circumcision school, of the usual Negro variety. This school is held about once in four or five years. There is no specific interval; it is probable that they wait until there are enough boys ready to form a class of the right size. These boys are anywhere from nine to fourteen years of age. Now the pygmies associated with these Negroes may send their boys through this same school with the sons of their hosts. Thus, the pygmy boys are away from home several months, are in close association with the Negro boys, and are taught the same secrets that the Negro boys learn. At the end they are all circumcised together, and their parents come to the Negro village to dance and get drunk with the parents of the Negro boys.

The pygmies are thus age-graded like the Negroes. Each class has its own cheer, or song, as in American colleges. Each class also has its own name, such as "Hurricane" or "great army worm," depending on some event

which occurred during its period of isolation. This not only forms a strong bond between the pygmies and their hosts but it gives them a formal sequence of age grades in their own society. There are no special scarifications or other insignia for each class; it is a common experience to hear one person asking another, when strangers meet, "What class were you in? I am a Hurricane," and so forth, just like Harvard alumni asking each other what class they were in, and whom they knew, over a drink.

Pygmy Locomotion

The pygmies are very expert at getting about through the forest, and especially at moving swiftly through the thick undergrowth that a white man would have to chop down with a machete before he could enter. To a Negro, a white man trying to get through seems clumsy. To a pygmy a Negro seems clumsy. Schebesta observes that the small size of the pygmies makes them better adapted to locomotion in the forest than the larger Negroes and whites.[1]

The pygmies jump over fallen logs, and make their way using hands and feet—hands to toss dead branches and trunks aside. They can actually run through this tangle, and while so doing they sometimes pick up fallen logs and throw them so they will crash at a distance, to mislead pursuers, or game which they are stalking.

They are also very expert at climbing; the children practice this from babyhood. Their technique is far from simian, but a widely distributed method, similar in principle to that of a lumberjack. The climber cuts two

[1] Schebesta, P., *Revisiting My Pygmy Hosts*. London: Hutchinson & Co., 1936, pp. 78–79.

lengths of 20 feet or so each from some flexible liana, and passes the first around the tree trunk, which may be as much as six feet thick. Then he sets the second liana in place in the same manner, and passes the two under his shoulders. He sits parallel to the trunk, which he faces, and grips with his feet. While bracing against one liana, he moves the other upward, then braces on it while moving the other. In this way he can climb up the slick, limbless bole of the tree, to where the first limbs branch off, some hundred or more feet above the ground.

When he reaches the first branches, he takes off his lianas and walks along the limbs like a tightrope walker or structural steel worker, free of the limbs, with nothing to hold in his hands. When he has accomplished his mission he comes down again the way he went up.

PYGMY TECHNOLOGY

Basic tools.—The keynote to the simple and specialized pygmy technology is the fact that they do not have to make any of their basic tools, but instead obtain effective iron cutting tools from their Negro hosts. This eliminates much work and the need for much skill in toolmaking, and provides them with more efficient instruments than they could possibly make for themselves at a food-gathering level of technology.

When a pygmy needs an ax he will beg one from his Negro host. Perhaps the Negro will give him a whole ax, haft and all. The blade is a triangular piece of iron, made locally by Negro smiths, and set in a solid wooden handle, adzed out of a larger piece of wood. The handle has a hole which has been burned through it from side to side with a hot iron. Through this

hole goes the narrow end of the ax. This is essentially a Neolithic type of hafting.

Perhaps the Negro will give him only the ax head, without a haft. In this case the pygmy will cut down a thin sapling, or a tree branch, just the right thickness, and use it bark and all. He splits this with his knife, at one end. Then he wraps the split and the blade which he has thrust through it with twine or rattan. The pygmy will use the Negro-hafted ax on the ground, but if he is climbing a tree and needs an ax while up there, he will take along one of his own hafting by preference, because it is lighter.

Both men and women use these axes. The women also have knives of their own, of the same manufacture. These knives are about six inches long, leaf-bladed, double edged. The handle is simply a thick tang, twisted, and thus is all one piece with the blade. In some cases, however, small wooden handles are added. The women use these for many purposes—for peeling bananas, and preparing other foods for cooking; to cut monocotyledonous leaves for roofing, and to split the stem. In general, it is the all-purpose woman's tool.

The man's knife is larger and single edged, a kind of small machete, made in Germany. The Negroes obtain them from white men by trade and give them to the pygmies. I once tried giving them American machetes, of the kind prized in Central America, but they were too large and too heavy. The men use these machetes for cutting lianas, tree limbs, and so forth. For small woodwork, however, such as whittling an arrow shaft, they are more likely to use an arrowhead or spearhead, which is nearer the right size.

Axes and the two kinds of knives and arrowheads and spearheads are the only cutting tools the pygmies have or know how to use.

Also obtained from the Negroes are the cooking pots that all pygmy women own, essential for water storage and cooking. These pots are made by Negro women, and by relatively few Negro women at that; pottery making is a specialist occupation.

Fire.—The pygmies do not know how to make fire, nor do many of the Negroes with whom they are associated. Throughout all this countryside people keep fires going, and when one fire dies out the people will borrow it from each other. While on the march the pygmies carry glowing embers with them; they can keep a brand lighted for ten miles during a rainstorm. They do this by wrapping the burning ends in green leaves, and swinging it up and down; every two or three minutes they uncover it a bit and blow on it. At night these brands serve as torches. The Negroes have special wood which they use for torches but the pygmies do not. Their firewood is always fallen wood, and therefore always somewhat rotten and punky.

Houses.—When the pygmies have chosen a new camp, the women go out into the forest a little way to collect building materials. Each woman brings in a bundle of sticks about half an inch thick, and from three to six feet in length; she also brings a bundle of sarcophrynium leaves. She thrusts the ends of the sticks in the ground around in a circle about five feet in diameter. Then she gets inside the circle, and bends opposite pairs of sticks inward, and ties them together. She does this in the following manner: first she takes a stick in each hand, then she brings them together, then she holds the two with one hand, and wraps with the other.

This technique is not easy; it is much easier if two women work together, and in practice this is usually the case. The first woman, who is to live in the house, will hold the two sticks in her hands, and the second woman, with both hands free, will do the wrapping and tying. After they set up the first woman's house they will go to work on the second woman's. Once they have tied the uprights into a dome, they weave in horizontal pieces in the form of hoops, to complete the frame, leaving an opening as doorway.

Then the women take the sarcophrynium leaves which they have collected, and nick the stems with their knives. These leaves have no midribs; they are palmate like grape leaves. They slip the notch in each stem over a place on a cross hoop, and soon have the whole house completely shingled; this roof will be watertight in the rain, and will last in all likelihood as long as they need the house, which is only from two to three months. The whole house-building operation takes only two hours.

Basketry and cordage.—Each pygmy woman has a basket which she carries on her back when out collecting or when shifting camp. They plait these baskets themselves out of rattan and other fibers. The woman carries the basket on her back by means of a fiber tump line over her forehead. She will use a similar tump line to bring home her family's ration of plantains from the Negro village. There is a good reason for the use of the tump line here; in the forest it would be impossible to carry a head load very far without its being knocked off by a limb. The forest Negroes also use tump lines and back loads.

PYGMY ECONOMIC ACTIVITIES

Hunting is the principal occupation of the pygmies; it is their principal reason for being able to maintain their relationship with their Negro hosts.

Although between themselves the pygmies have little division of labor, in another sense they are all specialists in hunting, and the division of labor is between them and the Negroes. In this sense the pygmies form an ethnic caste, a genetically and occupationally segregated segment of a larger economic entity.

This does not mean that the Negro does no hunting. However, the pygmy spends all of his time hunting, the Negro only a portion of his. The pygmy depends largely on his ability to move noiselessly and swiftly about the forest, and to climb trees. The Negro depends on his greater patience and mechanical ingenuity, for he hunts largely by means of elaborate traps, deadfalls, pits, weighted spears dangled over elephant paths, and other deadly devices. The pygmy could never be induced to dig a pit; it is too much work, takes too long, and takes too much concentration and persistence. Nor do they ever use traps.

Throughout the pygmy country, the pygmies can be classified either as net hunters or non-net hunters, depending on whether they habitually practice big community hunts, driving animals into nets, or depend entirely on individual stalking as a means of securing game. They may also be classified by whether or not they use bows and arrows. In both net hunting and the use of the bow and arrow, the pygmies follow the lead of the Negroes among whom they live. Where the Negroes have nets, the pygmies have nets; where the Negroes have bows, the pygmies have bows. This is easily understood, since the Negroes make both the nets and the arrowheads. Presumably, the bowless pygmies are net hunters, for otherwise they could not live.

Whether the pygmies in a group are net hunters or bowmen or both makes a considerable difference in the rest of

their activities and in their social organization in particular, since the degree to which cooperation is required in hunting, and the numbers of people involved, are the principal factors in determining the composition of the band.

Net hunting.—The technique of net hunting can best be described by going through the chronological events of a single day. The details of where and how to hunt are decided during the usual evening conversation period the night before. The chief argument lies in the weather; if it is going to be dry it will be better for net hunting. Since it will sometimes rain for three days, then go two days without rain, it is a matter of some speculation and prediction whether or not it will rain on a given afternoon. In general the weather permits net hunting, for it usually does not begin to rain until 4:00 P.M., and by that time the pygmies often have enough game to make the day's work profitable. The season is also important, for during the dry season the fallen leaves crackling underfoot make such a noise that stalking is hard even for a tracker so expert as the pygmy. However, this condition is good for net hunting, since it is necessary that the game hear the hunters.

The men, women, and children start out early in the morning, and the women carry their babies on their backs. The men carry the nets. These are made of cordage, about the same width as tennis nets, but a little longer. Since the length of the net is functional in the hunting, the pygmies keep it fairly constant. As one end rots away they add onto the other end, until an old net may eventually be largely replaced by these additions. However, the pygmies prefer new nets made by the Negroes and, furthermore, there are rarely enough nets to go around. Hence they frequently beg their hosts for more.

When they have arrived at the right location, the men set up the nets in a line and stand by to tend them; the women spread out in a circle to beat. Often the pygmies will have dogs which they have borrowed from the Negroes, barkless dogs with wooden bells tied to their collars. Each woman cuts a lot of twigs and makes a little broom with them. She beats the bushes with it, and cries out, "Whoo, whoo, whoo, whoo!" over and over again. The young children, except for the babies which are being carried, are made to keep out of this.

When the women sight an animal and it heads for the nets, they change the tone of their baying; either they identify the kind of animal by this means or indicate that an animal in general is coming. When the animal rushes up to the net and entangles itself, the man who is tending that part of the net grabs the animal and kills it with his knife or spear. He will then beat his hand on his arm pit, and the others will come up to see what he has killed. Sometimes, however, the animal sees the net, or a man moves, and the animal leaps back into the line of women. Such an animal can well escape, for the women are not prepared to stop it. However, when a woman engaged in beating sights a slow animal, such as a turtle, pangolin, porcupine, or even a rat, she will dive for it and pop it into her basket which she carries on her back, and go on beating. This is merely incidental gathering; slow animals are women's game.

During the course of a single day a pygmy band may set up their nets, conduct a drive, take the nets down, and repeat the process as many as seven times, each time in a different place. If the clouds collect early, they will go home. If there are no clouds and they have a good bag of game, they will till go home, but if it is dry and they

have little game they will keep on until nearly dark.

There is a difference in value between net positions in a net hunt. The central position is best because it catches the most animals, and the flanks are the worst. The pygmies have a whole vocabulary to express the details of net hunting, including a whole group of verbs for net setting in various positions. There seems to be some rule about who sets his nets in which spot, but this has not been recorded.

If a big animal, like a buffalo, comes toward the nets, the men will try to get them down and let him rush through, for they do not want to foul and tear the nets or to encounter the dangerous animal. If the large animal does strike the net, however, it may delay him long enough for the nearest man to rush up and spear him.

Most of the animals they catch are no larger than a dog or goat; for example, a kuchinda is about that size. The hunter cuts its throat and carries it around his neck, with hind and front legs on opposite sides. The average day's bag is about half of an animal of this size per man. If they have caught an okapi, however, the hunter cuts it up on the spot, and they cut small lianas to tie up the pieces with. The women also will carry some of it in their baskets. Almost always the meat goes directly to the camp after a hunt, where it is divided. Only after this will the share of the Negroes be carried to their village.

Bow and arrow hunting.—In bow and arrow hunting, the pygmy relies not on his endurance but on his ability to move through the forest silently; that is his greatest skill and greatest asset. He can track an antelope to a thicket where it has lain down to sleep, and shoot it from five yards' distance before it wakes up. He shoots machine-gun style; he will pump five arrows in rapid sequence in the antelope's direction, and probably but one will hit him. The pygmy can do just as well by leaping on the animal barehanded, and either strangle it or kill it with a knife, and he often does this.

In his quiver the pygmy usually carries two kinds of arrows, the first with iron tips, which he generally uses on the larger, antelope-size, animals, and wooden-tipped ones which are poisoned, and which he uses for monkeys. He rarely shoots a monkey with an iron-tipped arrow, through fear of losing it. Each man makes his own poison as well as his own darts. The plants from which the poison is made are well known, and there is neither ritual nor mystery attached to the process. The vital plant is a strophanthus; they will mix other plants with it, but they know which one does the trick.

The strophanthus poison is a heart stimulant. Its action is not immediate. The monkey runs along a bit, grows weaker, and urinates. The pygmies watch for this, for the moment of urinating is the fatal one. If the monkey is out on a limb where there are no other branches, he will fall off; if he is within reach of a lateral branch or one rising upward, he will clutch it, and the hunter will be obliged to climb the tree if he wants the monkey. To do this he uses the technique described under pygmy locomotion. Since the monkeys are usually high in the trees and the pygmies are such poor marksmen, they undoubtedly miss more of them than they hit.

Elephant hunting.—Pygmy elephant hunting involves a technique that is wholly different from either of the above two. The pygmy elephant hunter is a specialist; not every pygmy has the courage to face an elephant and kill it, and not every man the skill. Whether or not pygmies ever killed elephants in the early days, the present form of elephant hunting is a recent development, the historical growth of which can be easily traced. It is also an important reason for Negro-pygmy relations.

The chief reason why the Negro hunts is to kill elephants. The elephants barge about in great herds, destroying the plantations which represent a great deal of labor in clearing the forest and planting the bananas, and which form the Negroes' whole capital, his whole means of livelihood. The elephants burst in, pushing down fences, eating some of the bananas by the bunch and trampling the rest. This dread calamity usually happens on moonless nights when it would be almost certain death to go out and attack the elephants. All the Negro can do is to let the elephants do their worst, and try to kill them later to prevent recurrence.

In the old days, when the Negroes had killed an elephant they did not know what to do with the tusks, other than make bark-cloth beaters from a few, and a number of other minor uses. The majority of the tusks were therefore stuck up around the Negroes' clearings as fences. Now when the Arab traders began coming in from Zanzibar, they were interested in commodities which were nonperishable and of concentrated value, and ivory filled these specifications best of all local goods. At first the Arabs bought the ivory from the Negroes for very low prices, since the Negroes were ignorant of its worth. Then when the Negroes began raising the prices to equally ridiculous heights, the Arabs raided them and seized it, and the Negroes began hiding it. Ivory is heavy, and the Arabs had to find bearers to carry it out to the coast. Hence they seized men and women and made them carry it, and when they arrived at the coast they sold their bearers as slaves, making a double profit. Slavery, therefore, was a by-product of these raids, and not the primary objective, which was to obtain ivory. When the white men came in, they said to the Negroes, "Why deal with these Arab slavers? Sell your ivory to us, and we will leave you alone." Thus, ivory became an important item to the Negroes, and the more they could get of it the better.

The pygmy could never, by himself, kill enough elephants to stop them from trampling his host's gardens. He could, however, kill enough to swell his host's supply of ivory and increase his host's capital. So a pygmy who was an elephant hunter became a special favorite of his Negro host and would get special gifts and favors in return for the ivory.

The pygmy elephant hunter uses a special spear. Its handle is three to four feet long; its blade is leaf-shaped, of thin iron, about eight inches long and four wide. It is Negro-forged, of soft iron; the pygmy hunter sharpens it on a stone, until it is razor sharp.

His technique of hunting is daring and simple, and takes as much skill as that of a Spanish matador. He tracks the elephant, which is not difficult, until he knows from the spoor that he is close to it. When he hears the elephant's bowels rumble, he goes along even more quietly, until he sees the elephant through the underbrush. He then approaches the elephant silently, up wind; he jabs his spear as far as he can into the elephant, gashing the belly just behind the ribs; then he pulls it right out again. The elephant at this point usually turns, and the pygmies say that if you as much as wink at this moment you are a dead pygmy.

The man stands stock still, so the elephant can't see him. Then he goes through a sequence of stab and jump and stand still, as many times as he can. Every time the elephant looks

away he stabs him, and every time the elephant turns he stands still. The elephant can run faster than a man, and the pygmy's only hope is to wound the animal so badly that it will be unable to catch him before he gets away.

Finally the elephant goes charging off with one or more wounds in his intestines. The hunter, with his spear in his hand, returns to the camp. Perhaps the other men will be there, but they may be out net hunting. In the latter case he waits until they have all assembled, and as soon as they are together he tells them his story. There is much excitement; men, women, and children crowd around him and inspect the spear. They may say, "Hmmm, only that much of the tip is bloody, probably he won't die. Let it go." But if the spear is bloody way down to such and such a point, then the elephant has a serious wound and they will follow him.

In the latter case the whole camp goes together. The women load on their babies and cooking pots, and their bunches of plantains. The men take their weapons, and they leave only an old man or two to watch the camp while they are away. They will follow the elephant two or three days, until he finally lies down and dies of peritonitis. Sometimes he has been dead for some time when they reach him, and he may be blown up like a balloon and rotten. Still they will eat him, for rotten meat, if thoroughly boiled, is edible.

When a group of pygmies reaches a blown-up elephant, a special ceremony takes place. A man other than the elephant hunter cuts a square of skin off the elephant's side. He cuts this up and puts pieces into the mouths of everyone. Then he cuts another layer, and passes this around, and another layer, until he comes down to a point where the body wall is very thin, and everyone has had a taste of the raw skin.

Then a small male child, squalling and screaming, is thrust on the elephant's side; he is told to bite, which he does, and the balloon bursts.

This ceremony is repugnant to the pygmies, as they do not like raw meat; it is especially repugnant to the child, who does not enjoy having the whole rotten insides of the elephant burst in his face.

The child is the youngest son of the man who killed the elephant. If the man has no suitable son, it may be his nephew; or, if he has several young sons and the youngest is too small, either to understand the order or to bite, it will be the next older son.

Now that the elephant has burst, the ceremony is over, and a free-for-all takes place; the men cut the sides open, pull out the entrails, and climb inside to hack away at the meat. Other men rush to the head and chop away the tusks. The women take the pieces of meat which their men hand to them, and boil them. As soon as they have cooked one chunk, they will start to boil another. Everyone eats as much of the boiled meat as he is able, and they spread out the rest on drying racks; when it has dried they will take it into the village to the Negroes, who keep it and eat it gradually, for the combination of boiling and drying serves as a means of preserving it, the only food preservation the pygmies practice, and then not for themselves. The tusks go to the special patron of the elephant hunter, and the patron sells them to the Greek or Hindu trader; the patron gives the pygmy a small share of what he receives.

Division of meat.—The need of giving some of the meat to their Negro hosts, and the knowledge that no one will starve as long as they can get bananas, makes the problem of meat division among the pygmies different than among food-gatherers who have a more direct and immediate dependence on hunting. The principles which the pygmies follow are: (1) The biological family is the least common denominator, the basic unit in sharing. No man would think of eating his meat without giving some to his wife and children. (2) The next unit in sharing is the family group. Any man who has acquired meat will share some of it with other biological families within his family group, but all the shares may not be equal or equivalent. (3) Each man who participates in a hunt is given a share commensurate with his degree of participation. Thus if men from several family groups combine in a hunt, the meat goes to them, and they share their portions within their family groups by single unit families.

For practical purposes, the chief distinction is between meat acquired by stalking and that acquired by net hunting. In the case of stalking, only one man, or more often two or three, will be involved, and these men may well belong to the same family group. With net hunting, however, the whole camp joins the hunt and the whole camp shares the bag.

When an animal is caught net hunting, a number of people have special rights. The man who owns a hunting dog which chased the animal gets the neck. Other special pieces go to the man in whose net it was caught. However, someone else may have borrowed the net and been tending it at the time, and the net tender thus gets a special piece. Then there are pieces for the men whose women bayed it in, and every degree of participation in the killing is recognized and suitably rewarded.

If they bring in five or six antelope there is enough meat for everyone to eat well that night. One family may get one cut of one animal, another cut of another, depending on what part they played in the capture of each. In any case, even if there is only one animal, everyone will get something to eat. This does not mean that all families eat equally well, however; some have more than others, some better cuts. There is both a reward for special luck and prowess, and a charitable mechanism for those who have shown neither. Sometimes the net hunters catch an okapi; in this case there is enough meat to feed the camp for a week, and everyone eats and eats well.

The meat is cut up by the man who killed the animal, or anyone who knows the rules. In any case there are always arguments. The man who makes a mistake is cried down; they all know the rules, or think that they know them. Government, as far as distribution of spoils is concerned, is by argument and common consent without specific leadership in any individual— the typical pygmy way of making decisions and ordering events.

In the case of the hunter who catches his animal all alone, without help of any kind, the carcass belongs to him alone. Theoretically, he and his family could eat it all up if he wished, but there is little chance that this would happen; he would not dare face public opinion. He would be labeled a mean man and would suffer for it in the end. It may happen however that he is behind in his gifts to his Negro host. In this case he will take the carcass uncut into the village, to avoid trouble from that quarter, and the other pygmies will not hold this against him, provided that there is other food to eat.

The division of spoils after an elephant hunt follows the same principle as it does among the Indians of Tierra del Fuego or Lower California when a whale washes ashore—regardless of who may be responsible there is a mountain of meat and a free lunch for all as long as it remains edible.

Gathering.—The gathering of fruits, nuts, and slow animals has a minor importance during most of the year, for the bulk of the pygmies' vegetable food derives from the crops of their Negroes. However, after the evening meal, while the men sit about the fires chatting, the women gather firewood and bring in, just before dusk, any mushrooms and slow game that they may encounter.

The dry season, in January and February, is the time of the ripening of certain fruits and seeds. At this time of the year the pygmies easily could live on the fruit borne by the wild forest trees. It is a period of seasonal abundance and feasting. The ibambi, a big luscious fruit that looks like a pineapple, is one of the most important of these fruits. It drops to the ground with a thud, and pygmies and chimpanzees alike will rush up when they hear it strike. The pygmies often tell stories of chimpanzees that get so full of ibambi that they can eat no more, but hide one in a crotch of a tree for future use; a pygmy sees this and steals it, and the chimpanzee gets a grudge against the pygmy and decides to annoy him in the future.

Next to the ibambi fruit in importance is the baselli nut. This is covered by a tough fibrous husk which can be opened only with a machete; hence, the chimpanzees do not rival the pygmies in this case.

Other gathered foods include termites, which come when the first heavy rains begin after the dry period; colonial caterpillars, which have a later season; and honey.

PYGMY INTERACTION

Evening talking time.—The pygmies seem to be a little less talkative than the Negroes, who are, in turn, more talkative than whites. In this regard—amount of interaction expressed in speech—the pygmies are about on a level with white men. There is little chance for extensive conversations during the daytime while out hunting, and hence the talking time is during the evening, when they have come home and are sitting in front of their huts, provided that they are not dancing.

At this talking time, each family sits around the entrance of its hut, using short butts of logs as seats. Dusk falls. They talk to each other across the circle, from hut to hut. Everyone can hear everyone else, so it is group interaction, even when one person is addressing one other specifically.

Their subjects of conversation are simple; they discuss what they have been doing that day, and in some cases they talk a little about what they plan to do tomorrow. Every now and then someone makes a joke about how a certain man was clumsy at handling his net during the day's hunt. Some people are quiet, others are noisier. Some men are clowns, habitually cracking jokes at the expense of others.

After bed time comes and the various families crawl into their huts to sleep, they get little uninterrupted rest, as they will keep chattering well into the night. Many of them will get up in the night, make water and have a smoke, and chat with others doing the same. There is almost always someone up, someone talking.

Dancing.—The pygmies will dance almost any night when the weather is clear, and if there is a full moon they will dance most of the night. Sometimes they stamp on the ground, or on a hollow log, but when they can beg or borrow a drum from the Negroes, they will beat on that.

Government.—There are no chiefs, councils, or any other formal governing bodies in a pygmy camp. In making any decisions concerning the whole camp, two factors are involved. The first of these is respect for older people.

A pygmy will always, in addressing a man of an older age group in any formal situation, call him "senior"; he will listen respectfully to an older man and will always obey any reasonable orders he may give. If a younger man shows disrespect, the other members of the camp will gang up on him and berate him. This respect for age, and for the opinions of wise old men, is the basis of pygmy government.

Secondly, while the opinions of most of the old men are respected, every man in the camp is entitled to state his own views on any subject. Thus, during the evening talking time, the pygmies will discuss whether to move camp, where to move it, and why; or whether to go net hunting, and where to hunt. The discussion has no leader and may go on for several evenings. Finally the men who are shouting out different opinions will come to an agreement and the decision will be acted upon.

In general it is the older and more experienced men who make the decision, but as some of the old men are considered eccentrics and freaks, little attention is paid to them. Rather, it is an oligarchy of the more respected among the old men, a body with no formal membership or specific composition. In their decisions the pungent remarks of the women also have a considerable influence.

PYGMY SOCIAL ORGANIZATION

Families and their extensions.— The smallest normal social unit in a pygmy camp is the individual biological family; that is, a man, his wife, and their children, if any. This group will occupy one hut together, and its personnel is normally fairly stable.

Each biological family belongs to a larger family group or extended family. All the families within a family group are closely related to each other through the male line. That is, each family group will consist of one or more closely related old men, and his or their male descendants and their families. It is these old men, from all the family groups in a camp, who together form the "ruling" age grade.

Ideally, a pygmy camp consists of a number of these family groups descended through the male line from a common ancestor, for whom they are named. Therefore, the basic pygmy camp is thus a classic gens, or, in looser terminology, a patrilineal clan.

The families and family groups are strictly exogamic, and the clan is also exogamic if all members live in the same camp. If, however, it is scattered, the exogamy is not too strictly enforced, although a pygmy will never marry anyone to whom he knows himself to be related, on either side.

The pygmy camp.—Although this is the formal, ideal situation, the composition of the camp is complicated by the presence of visitors from other camps who belong to different clans and can be married. So it can be seen that the clan and the camp are not, in practice, synonymous.

Pygmy camps are not all the same size; there is a minimum and a maximum number of people who can live together as a cohabitive group, owing to their needs of hunting, and so forth. Fifty huts is about the limit, with from twenty to forty the optimum, and twenty-five the average. Each hut contains one man, his wife, or wives, and a few children, so that one hundred and fifty might be an average number of pygmies, of both sexes and all ages, to a camp, with from twenty to forty active adult males.

Moving camp.—The pygmies live in any given camp for a month or two at a time. By that time they will have frightened most of the game out of the immediate neighborhood, so that they have to walk a long way to hunt and a long way back. Furthermore, since they relieve themselves at only a short distance from their huts, the whole camp will have become extremely malodorous by that time and uncomfortable even by pygmy standards, and a shift is doubly necessary.

When they have decided where to move, the women pack their carrying baskets with their pots and axes, and a small supply of ficus bark for the men to beat into cloth at their leisure. Whatever they own they will pile on their backs, along with their babies, the babies often mounting the rest of the load. The men will take only their weapons—their bows and arrows and elephant spears.

Once the women are loaded they will start out, and reach the new area at about noon. They begin wandering about looking for a good spot—a place near water where there is supposed to be game, and fruit. Game is the first consideration, then fruit, but a *sine qua non* is to be about fifty yards from drinking water. The next consideration is to have the camp on a moderate slope so it will not become a quagmire when it rains. Another consideration is the absence of dead branches or leaning trunks which might be blown down during the wind storm which precedes the afternoon rain.

When they have hit upon a suitable spot, the women build the huts in a circle with the doorways facing in. There is no orientation, nor are any spots preferred. There are no special huts for unmarried boys or girls, or widows; there are no ritual structures. There is simply one hut for each individual family. The relation of huts in the circle seems fortuitous, but it is dictated more than anything else by the friendship of women. Women are home most of the day; the men are out hunting. Women perform tasks that require no interaction, but they help each other for company. Friendship among the women generally takes the form of pairs, although subsidiary friendships may make larger groups. Hence the position of the huts, or rather the determination of who lives in which hut in what part of the circle, is determined purely on the intimacy of women in their daily work routines.

Once they are in this camp they will stay on another three months or so until the game is scarce, the fruit gone, the camp ringed by high refuse heaps and pungent with the smell of rotting food and human refuse. Or they will perhaps move on a little earlier if someone dies and is buried there. They do not count time; they simply respond to the practical needs of the moment, the way lower organisms respond automatically to changes in intensity of light. Moreover, they will never go back to exactly the same place. One reason for this may be the presence of funeral remains; but there may be other reasons. The pygmies do not say why, and probably do not know.

Intercamp visits.—For various reasons, individual pygmies and even whole families often visit neighboring camps. With exchange marriage it is necessary to know the people with whom an exchange is to be made. Thus, the need of finding wives makes it necessary to establish relationships between members of different camp units. Aside from marriage, other circumstances sometimes inspire these visits, as, for example, when an individual

man, or even several men, may feel picked on, or in other words are unable to adjust themselves to the other members of the group in which they live. They will go on extensive visits to kinfolk in other bands, and some may never return. In this case they will change their allegiance to new Negro hosts. Or they may have trouble with their Negroes and leave for this reason.

More frequently, however, a number of families will simply visit another camp, presumably because of the desire of women to spend some time with their parents, brothers, and other relatives. The camps are exogamous and the only chance a woman ordinarily has to see her own people is on such visits, during which the boys build up ties with their maternal uncles and cousins. These visits, again, serve to establish relationships leading to marriage. Visits of this kind usually do not last more than two or three months, or the ordinary life of a camp site, but they serve to keep the pygmy world in a state or circulation, and to break up the monotony of the limited sets of relations possible among pygmies in a single camp and between pygmies and their specific Negroes.

Marriage and divorce.—The usual form of pygmy marriage is monogamy. One reason for this is the scarcity of women—many prefer to become second wives of Negroes and live in the ease of the village, thus avoiding the hardships of forest food gathering. When a man does have two wives, one will live with him, while the other will live with her own kin, usually in a different camp, where he visits her on occasion. Actually, the economic incentive to polygyny is absent, for whatever work the second wife performs benefits her own kinfolk only.

Marriage takes place at or near puberty, and normally involves the technique of exchange. In its present form, this means that a man must offer his sister for marriage to his intended wife's brother. However, since all families do not contain an even number of boys and girls, this principle may be extended to the larger family group, and a young man may offer a cousin, or an older man a niece, as his exchange partner.

Divorce is common and as informal as marriage. Usually it is the woman who makes the initial decision: she simply packs up her belongings and moves out. She will take her children with her and will be considered a member of her own parents' kinship group until she should remarry. This principle is also followed in the case of a widowed woman. A divorced woman's sons will remain with her until they are old enough to go hunting, when they will rejoin their father.

Although the original pair in an exchange marriage may have been drawn to each other by mutual affection, the same is not always the case with the exchange partners, whose union may not be of long duration. The really unpleasant feature of exchange marriage is that if one union breaks up, the complementary marriage must also be dissolved; hence, if one couple cannot tolerate each other they will cause the separation of the other.

Because of the scarcity of women, a certain number of young men are forced to live out a painful bachelorhood for a number of years. Such bachelors usually, if not always, dally with girls whom they cannot marry because of kinship, or with other men's wives, and are a constant cause of trouble. However, if the family group of a boy's father fails to get him a wife, he may, in desperation, appeal to his mother's family group to provide one. If they do, he will go to live with his mother's people, although he is still technically a member of his father's

group and a stranger in the camp, if it is a different one.

PYGMY SYMBOLISM

Food tabus.—The pygmy recognizes certain animals as symbols of definite relationships or identifications, in connection with which recognition he observes special food tabus.

This principle is particularly involved in connection with the animals which represent the clan totems. Each clan has its own private totem animal, which is not, in most cases, actually considered an ancestor. Rather, it has acquired its position because, in the local mythology, an animal of the same species performed some special act of kindness which got one of the clan ancestors out of a perilous situation.

The animals which symbolize clans are always animals which are hunted by men; they are never slow-game animals, which women collect. Vegetable species are never used as totems. The totems are animals which may or may not be caught, about whose capture there is some element of chance, some possibility of crisis, and they are usually food animals, although leopards and chimpanzees, which are off the main dietary line, are totemic animals.

The pygmy will avoid eating the flesh of his own clan totem, but he can eat the flesh of totemic animals of any other clan. However, the pygmy recognizes seven species of antelope, and a dozen of small monkeys; and the clan totem will be, for instance, one species of antelope, rather than all antelopes. Therefore, these tabus do not cause anyone much discomfort, for no one species of these animals accounts for more than a small fraction of the total food supply, and each clan can eat six out of seven kinds of antelope, or eleven out of twelve kinds of monkeys.

Not only does the pygmy avoid eating the flesh of his totemic animal, but he cannot even eat out of any dish or container in which any of its flesh has been cooked; moreover, he avoids the animal itself when he sees it in the forest, and may even flee from it. Carrying the principle of avoidance even further, a pygmy whose totem animal is the chimpanzee will not even eat the berries that are that animal's favorite food.

The breach of any of these tabus is supposed to bring on illness or death, while their observance is, of course, an automatic mechanism to intensify the mutual relations of the members of the clan, who may be scattered through the forest in different bands. As the clan members become more and more distant from each other, as their frequency of relations falls below a certain level, the tabus will break down and the scattered members will take over the prohibitions of the people among whom they live and with whom they have in time come to identify themselves.

Besides the clan food tabus, there are sex tabus, condition tabus, and personal tabus. The sex tabus serve to symbolize the difference in activities between men and women. Women and children will eat frogs and toads, but men refuse to touch them. These amphibians probably symbolize water, and hence storms, and since it is the men who do the hunting they are the ones who are peculiarly vulnerable to storms.

The condition tabus are the same type as those described by A. R. Brown in *The Andaman Islanders*. A pygmy going through the puberty period, pregnancy, mourning, or any other crisis in the life cycle will abstain from certain foods, and the animals concerned are thus symbols of this critical situation. The personal tabus involve simply the refusal of an individual to eat certain foods. This may be due to a recognized allergy, to some unpleasant association, or to any one of a number of causes. The animals involved in these tabus include porcupines, snakes, and other slow game not found among the clan totems.

The animals of the forest, which symbolize clans, sexes, and individual and conditional idiosyncrasies, are very real people to the pygmies. In the old days, the mythical time, they could all talk and were on an even footing with men. Each species was symbolized by one individual, who was given an honorific name, as Mr. Turtle, Mr. Gray Antelope, or Mr. Chimpanzee. Mr. Turtle was a very wise and tricky individual, and the smallest antelope of all was King of the Beasts. The pygmies and their Negro hosts have an elaborate folklore about these animals and all their doings which might shed considerable light on their human relations.

Ritual symbols.—To the pygmies, water, rain, storm, thunder, lightning, snakes, and rainbows are all parts of a single symbolic configuration. The elements of this configuration, of course, represent the sudden rainstorms which arise without warning in the afternoons and sometimes, rarely, in the mornings as well. These may prevent hunting; flood huts; cause dead limbs to fall, crushing huts and killing people; or occasionally kill them by bolts of lightning. No other element in their life causes so much disturbance or upsets them so profoundly.

Both pygmies and Negroes believe in a *Nyama ya mai* (Swahili) or water animal, who lurks in streams and plays dangerous tricks on people. Sometimes he tips canoes over; sometimes he will grab the ankle of a woman fording a stream, so that she slips, and may even drown. If any serious mishap occurs in or in connection with the water, the people, will say, "It was the water animal that did it." Sometimes the water animal comes up out of his native element and assumes the form of a rainbow.

From time to time the Negroes and the pygmies find neolithic axes, which they say are "turds of lightning," excreta dropped in the process of the storm; when lightning splits a tree, one of these turds is always left.

The pygmies also believe in totemic spirits, which live in spirit places—in rock piles, hollow trees, and holes in the ground; classic *genii loci*. On their account, the pygmies refuse to go near certain rocky hills, on which there may be dense thickets. If a pygmy is out hunting with a white man, the white man may say, "Let us beat in there; there is game in that thicket." The pygmy will reply, "No Bwana, don't go in there; that hill is full of *sitana*." The word *sitana* is the local Swahili or Kingwana equivalent for the Arabic word *shaitan,* plural *shayatin.*

RITUAL ACTIVITIES

Weather magic.—One class of weather ritual involves the use of physical symbols taken from the context of situation—leaves, which wave violently and are blown down in a storm. Schebesta [2] describes a simple ceremony of this kind in an Efe camp. During the height of a storm the oldest man in the camp came out of his house and stood in front of it. He brought with him leaves and ashes. First he threw most of the ashes upward into the wind, then he smeared ashes on a leaf, rubbed some onto his own body, and threw the rest into the wind.

Other methods mentioned by Schebesta are the burning of certain leaves, especially those taken from a wild pepper plant, to stop storms; and the lighting of smoky fires in the forest, by the women in some camps, during the early or mid-day to keep the weather clear for hunting.[3] I have not witnessed these particular practices. My own experience with weather magic has been that on a number of occasions I was prevented from performing seemingly harmless actions. Once I started to pick a beautiful red hemanthus flower and was told, "Don't do that, master, or it will rain before we get back to camp." Again, I was about to drop a stone into a brook and was told the same thing. The pygmy attitude seemed to involve a simple cause and effect relationship between the human action and the weather. All the magic which I personally observed is designed to avoid making it rain.

Hunting magic.—Hunting magic is usually a simple business. During the division of meat, the elder who is cutting it cuts a small piece off the heart and tosses it into the forest, before he gives the heart, the hunter's portion, to the hunter. In some regions hunters rub ashes obtained from burning a certain leaf around their eyes, to make them see the game better.[4] Another trick is to take the leaves of a certain species, on which a certain kind of animal feeds, and drape them on the hunter's bow; he may also burn them and rub the ashes on his body.

Life cycle and rites of passage.— There appears to be no ritual recognition of the birth of a child. If a woman is out on the trail, and feels her time arriving, she will stop and bear her child, then go on. If she is in camp, which is usually the case, other women will help her. The women nurse their children a long while, well after they are able to walk and talk. There is a

[2] Schebesta, P., *Among Congo Pygmies.* London: Hutchinson & Co., 1933, p. 243.

[3] *Op. cit.,* p. 157.
[4] *Ibid.,* p. 157.

great deal of swapping children, fostering, and adoption. This takes place especially between sisters and between women who are friendly and work together. When a woman dies, her sister will normally take over her children, keeping the girls until they are ready for marriage. The boys join their father when they are old enough to hunt.

Among the pygmies living in my immediate neighborhood, there is no separate pygmy initiation ceremony. Girls are not publicly initiated at all, and as mentioned above, the boys go through the Negro bush school with the sons of their patrons. (See Negro-pygmy relations; p. 325.)

A marriage within the camp creates no disturbance in the relations of the group as a whole, and little between the individuals in particular, but an intercamp marriage does produce crises in the lives of those close to the principals, as well as of the principals themselves, for such a marriage requires ceremony.

Schebesta [5] describes one of the latter, in which the two groups of kin, complete with brides but not with grooms, met in the forest away from either camp. They set up their huts near each other, but in separate bivouacs, and feasted and danced *separately* for three days. Then the two groups came together and the elder men of each group brought the two brides face to face and gave them advice—to keep the camp full of food, to be polite and friendly, to be particularly thoughtful of old people and children, to live in peace and bear many offspring. After this excellent advice, each girl was led by the kinfolk of her new husband to the camp in which she was to live, and there she joined her new husband. She brought along with her a few girls of her own group to ease the strain of so

[5] *Ibid.*, pp. 134–135.

many new faces, and no doubt this in itself laid the groundwork for future matchmaking. For a month or so after marriage she would work for and with the other women of the camp, and then set up housekeeping on her own.

ILLNESS AND DEATH

For most of his bodily ills the pygmy can find a local remedy. Gastric disorders and diarrhea plague them rather frequently. For these the universal cure is an enema (enemas are even used to produce abortions). Any pygmy, apparently, can give an enema to any other pygmy, but as a rule it is the women who give them to their husbands, children, and female friends. The instrument is a long reed with a gourd gummed on one end; the operator thrusts the other end into the patient's rectum and holds up the gourd end. The gourd is filled with various vegetable decoctions used in solution; these include the *tebvo* liana for diarrhea and *gorogoro* bark for stomach upsets.

When a pygmy is suffering from some mysterious ailment which he and his fellows are unable to cure and which seems to be magical in nature, he will go to the village of his Negro hosts and beg the local witch doctor to cure him by sucking out "disease objects," by cupping with horns, or by the use of herbs.

The greatest single cause of mortality in the pygmy community is falling from a tree. When a pygmy falls from such a height, he has no real chance of survival, for there are seldom branches below him. The second most frequent cause of death is falling branches. As the pygmy camp is always constructed in the primary forest itself, never in a clearing, a branch falling in a windstorm may hit a house, killing four or five people at once.

After this come the various diseases which kill the pygmies. Pneumonia and dysentery are the greatest killers; infection is rare. Far less important than disease even is the action of hostile animals—elephants, buffalo, or leopards. Once in a while an old leopard, too old to catch antelope, will dare run the risk of sneaking into a pygmy camp at night. The pygmy houses have no doors, and the leopard may slink into a house and grab a pygmy. At the noise so created, other pygmies will wake up and attack the leopard with spears or firebrands. Sometimes the leopard wins completely and carries off his victim's body, to munch at leisure. Sometimes he drops the mangled corpse, and at other times the pygmy may survive. I have seen one pygmy woman who had most of her face bitten away by a leopard and who still lived. The pygmy resistance to wound infections is incredibly great, although they will die like flies from pneumonia.

Another occasional cause of death is burning. Pygmies are unusually restless during the sleeping hours of the night, and individuals get up frequently to relieve themselves. After doing so the pygmy seldom goes back to bed immediately. He usually sits in front of his hut for a while, in front of the fire. Here he will often light up his pipe and take a deep puff of tobacco, apparently to get the maximum effect of the nicotine in the least possible time. Sometimes this puff knocks him out; he faints, and falls forward into the fire.

Very often there are others up about the same business, who, when they hear the thud, will run over and pull the victim out of the fire, in which case he will survive with bad burn scars. Sometimes, however, no one hears him, and the burns are fatal.

When a pygmy dies, his kinsmen bury him near the camp. They get bananas or wine ready-made from their Negroes, and a regular bout of wine drinking begins. The members of the deceased's family cover themselves with white pipe clay, and weep and wail for several days. This noisy manifestation of grief is intermittent, and formally controlled. Sometimes they even put it off for two or three days until all the relatives who have been away visiting at other camps can be gathered in. Most of it is done by women, who will weep and wail for a while in concert, then rest together, then weep together again for another spell. Anyone who is really overcome with emotion weeps quietly by him or herself, alone and without interruption.

After a few days of this the whole group will break camp and move on to some other site, unless there are strong objections to leaving. In any case, they never return to the grave, and never decorate or touch it.

The foregoing selection is largely self-explanatory. The common notion that the pygmy of the forest leads a simple life is true only in a special sense. He has his band, his kinfolk elsewhere, his relationship with his hosts, his membership in an initiation grade. He has separate relationships with the members of his band, his clanmates outside, his hosts, and his classmates in the initiation school. Every pygmy is a specialist—at hunting—and some, the elephant hunters, are superspecialists. The key to all this is *trade* and an ethnic division of labor between pygmies and hosts.

One thing that struck me forcibly while I edited this material was the paucity of "religious" phenomena in pygmy culture. If you remember that ritual is always associated with *crises* and *change,* you will see that the reason is to be found in the lack of annual variation in the climate, and the paucity of critical situations. A thunderstorm, accidents in the water, and the excitement of an elephant hunt, all have their rituals.

The Ituri Pygmies are not the only ones in Africa. The Gabon Pygmies of West Africa have no hosts. They are at war with their neighbors, who recently moved in. As a result they are ruled by powerful chiefs, and have as specialists clairvoyants who can tell where elephants will be and how many hunters will kill, poison makers with the knowledge of a pharmacist, and an elite of elephant hunters. Their power structure is not loose and informal, as among their counterparts in the Ituri, but rigidly controlled.*

Other Pygmies, in the Kivu country, are organized unilaterally into clans, unlike the bilaterally structured Ituri Pygmies, and these clansmen serve rival Negro chiefs as fierce warriors.** On the shores of Lake Kivu still others form a caste of potters. Thus there are as many types of organization as there are groups among this extremely adaptable branch of mankind.

---

*R. P. Trilles, *Les Pygmées de la Forêt Equitoriale,* Paris: Bloud et Gay, 1912, Also *Anthropos* Vol. 3, No. 4. Excerpts from Trilles' work are given in translation in C. S. Coon's *The Hunting Peoples,* Boston, Atlantic-Little Brown, 1971.

**Peter Schumacher, *Expedition zu den zentralafrikanischen Kivu-Pygmäen,* Mémoires de l'Institut Royal Colonial Belge, I, 1949, and II, 1950.

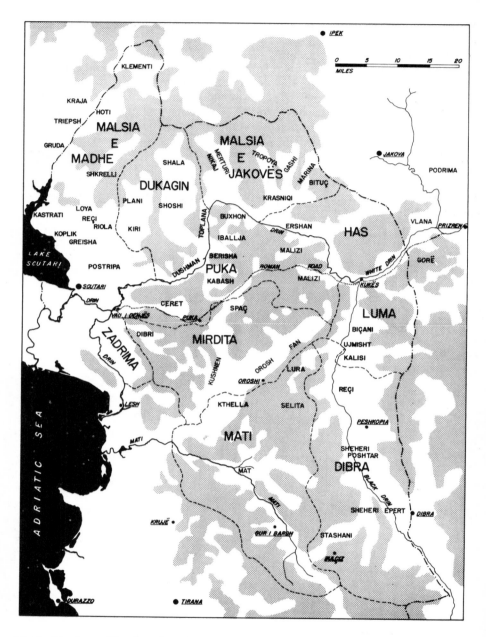

Fig. 1. Northern Albania—the tribal area. (Stippled area symbolizes mountain and forest, unoccupied except as seasonal pasture and source of timber.) Scale, 1: 250,000.

12

The Highland Ghegs*: Tribes and Feuding in Northern Albania

THE people who form the object of this study are the mountaineers who inhabit the Dinaric mountain chain on either side of the gorge cut by the river Drin on its way from the Serbian plain to the Adriatic. Most of their country lies inside the political boundaries of Albania, but parts of it have belonged to Yugoslavia for the past third of a century. They speak the northern of the 2 Albanian languages, or dialects,[1] Gheg. They are not, however, the only Gheg speakers. There are Lowland as well as Highland Ghegs. The present study concerns only the latter. The reason why they were specially chosen is that they still preserved, in 1929, a full tribal system of social organization, something very rare in Europe. This has one critical advantage: rules of preferential mating are definite, and are still observed. We know not only who marries whom, but we may also be sure that the same system has been going on for many generations.

*From The Mountains of Giants, by C. S. Coon, Cambridge, Mass.: Peabody Museum Papers Vol. 23 No. 3, 1950, by permission of the author and publisher.

[1]Gheg and Tosk in extreme dialectic forms are mutually incomprehensible. It would be hard to state definitely whether they are closely related languages or dialects of one language. Each has numerous local subdivisions. The official language of Albania is based on the southern Gheg dialect spoken in the city of Elbasan.

The Highland Ghegs who form the object of our investigation belonged to 10 tribes, shown on figure 1. These are Malsia e Madhe, Dukagin, Malsia e Jakovës, Has, Luma, Puka, Mirdita, Zadrima, Mati, and Dibra. Before 1913 all of the tribes, except Dukagin, which now touch Yugoslavia extended a certain distance into the present territory of that country. On parts of the northern border the overlap is an old one. Many of the Montenegrin gentes admit descent from Albanian families, and one finds every stage of linguistic and cultural assimilation between the 2 ethnic units. Just north of Scutari, however, several fully Albanian villages were handed over to Serbia after the Balkan War, and this caused both economic and political distress. Farther east, from Peia to Dibra, the boundary commission which laid out the border between the 2 countries at that time gave the Yugoslavs all of the strategic positions, and all of the market towns along the Serbo-Albanian border which served as an economic outlet for both peoples.

This ethnic border is far from clear-cut. Several whole tribes of Ghegs live on the Kossovo plain, along with villages of Serbs. The ancestors of these Lowland Ghegs migrated there in the time of the Turks, after the defeat of the Tzar Dushan. These displaced Ghegs are probably descended from the highland tribes, but it would take much work to establish their exact relationships. We were unable to measure more than a few of them, and therefore shall not consider them in this study.

The Lowland Ghegs of Albania, who equally eluded our calipers, occupy the country from the tribal regions eastward to the Adriatic and southward to the river Shkumbi, the traditional frontier between Ghegnia and Toskeria. Many of the Tosks are Greek Orthodox Christians. The Ghegs who are Christians are Roman Catholics. The majority of both divisions is Moslem. The most solidly Moslem part of Albania is the central region, in both Ghegnia and Toskeria, where the landscape is the least rugged. Both brands of Christianity lived through the Turkish regime most successfully in the mountains.

There are many Gypsies in other parts of Albania, where they ply their usual trades from metallurgy to prostitution, but in the Gheg mountains I heard of only two, both in the border tribe of Luma.

The country of the Highland Ghegs is entirely mountainous. Although on the map its length is 75 miles and its width 55, these dimensions fail to convey the vertical distance. The trails go up and down and all around, climbing, twisting and turning. In 1929 it took as long to go the length of the Gheg highlands by available means of travel as it did to cross the United States by rail. To an Albanian, Shala is as far from Dibra as, to an American, San Francisco is from Boston.

A concentrated jumble of snow-covered peaks, rising to 7000- and 8000-foot heights, the mountains of Ghegnia follow no simple system of parallel ranges and valleys, but instead form a knot through which the river Drin has cut a passage in its tumultuous journey from the plain of Kossovo to the Adriatic Sea. In the walls of the Drin gorge the traveler can see an impressive

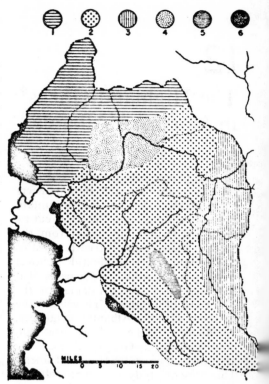

FIG. 2. Three main geological regions in Ghegnia. 1—*Mesozoic limestone;* 2—*Serpentine highland;* 3—*Metamorphosed Triassic and Upper Palaeozoic rocks;* 4—*Intense folding (Mesozoic-Eocene);* 5—*Tertiary basin;* 6—*Eocene flysch.* (Almagià, 1932, pp. 464-73, map on p. 467, "after Nowack.")

record of geological change—layer after layer of sedimentary rocks, twisted and upheaved like a slice of marble cake.

Figure 2 shows 3 main geological regions in Ghegnia. The first is the Mesozoic limestone mountains of Malsia e Madhe and parts of Dukagin and Malsia e Jakovës. This is a continuation of the bare rocky landscape so characteristic of Montenegro, which, north of Lake Scutari, reaches the sea in a succession of drowned valleys, the greatest of which is the Gulf of Kotor. Here the topsoil is thin, while alluvium is almost lacking in the stream beds. No trees crown the slopes, white in summer and winter alike from the alternate exposure of lime and snow. In the bend of the Drin the smaller area of intense folding is likewise mostly limestone, covering part of Dukagin, the Nikaj and Merturi sections of Malsia e Jakovës, and the Buxhon and Berisha *bairaks* (see Fig. 1) of Puka. In the country so far designated, most of which is north of the Drin, geological conditions resemble those found immediately north of the border.

The second zone is one of igneous rocks, composed mainly of serpentine and gabbro. This zone covers all of Mirdita, most of Zadrima, Mati, Puka, and Has, and parts of Dibra and Malsia e Jakovës. In this region limestone is so scarce that few people can afford to build stone houses, owing to the lack of mortar. From the dietary standpoint one must understand the importance of this contrast between the northern geological zone, where the water is permeated with lime, and the central, where it is lime-free. This takes on significance because all foods consumed are locally raised—the fodder, the grains, the milk, and the meat.

The third region is the eastern zone, including half of Has, all of Luma, and the greater part of Puka. This is composed of metamorphic Triassic and Upper Palaeozoic deposits, deeply eroded, with steep slopes and rich alluvial bottoms. From the dietary standpoint, it lies intermediate between the northern and the central regions.

Through these mountain masses, composed of different kinds of rocks laid down and upheaved at different periods, flow its 2 rivers and their tributaries. These are the Drin and the Mati. By studying them one can arrive most readily at a knowledge of the tribal geography of Ghegnia.

East of Kukës there are 2 Drins, White and Black. The White Drin carries off the water from the eastward slope of the Peia or Pesh region in Montenegro, then flows southward to the Albanian border, where it turns west. A short but swift confluent flows westward under the bridges and flour-mills of the city of Prizren. The Black Drin is the outlet for Lake Ochrida, south of Gheg territory. It flows northward in a nearly straight line through the Dibra valley, past the towns of Big Dibra and Little Dibra (Peshkopia). As it flows northward the valley grows narrow, and in places becomes a gorge, which opens out again before the river reaches Kukës.

At Kukës the 2 branches meet. From this point on, the slope of the river bed is great, and the water rushes down, foaming and leaping, through its canyon-like channel until it reaches the lowlands, where it divides into 2 channels. One flows into Lake Scutari, which in turn empties into the sea. The other goes directly into the Adriatic. Except for the last few miles of its passage, the Drin is too swift for navigation.

The other river, the Mati, flows into the sea a short distance south of Lesh. It drains the tribal lands of Mati, and most of Mirdita. It too is swift and unnavigable, and in winter and spring often impossible to ford.

These rivers and their watersheds form the usual boundaries between tribes. Dibra and Mati form the drainages of the Black Drin and Mati rivers, respectively; and the watershed between these rivers is their boundary. The White Drin, in Yugoslavia, is the boundary between Has and the lowland tribe of Podrima; in both countries it divides Has from Luma; and in Albania alone, the combined Drin divides Has from Puka, Malsia e Jakovës from Puka, Dukagin from Puka, and Malsia e Madhe from Puka and Zadrima. The northern branch of the Mati, the Fan, which is in turn divided into the Little

Fan and the Big Fan, drains Mirdita, except for the *bairak* of Spac, the northwestern finger of which forms part of the Drin system. With this same exception, the watershed between the Drin and the 2 Fans is the boundary between Puka and Mirdita. The continuation of the watershed between Mati and Dibra again separates, farther north, Mirdita from Luma. Mati and Mirdita, and Dibra and Luma east of the Black Drin, are parted by deep valleys, running laterally, cut on opposite sides of the river.

These rivers serve more often as tribal boundaries than as routes of travel. Their banks are so steep that the roads usually follow the crests and shoulders of the mountains, only dipping down into the valleys where it is necessary to cross them. All in all, they are barriers to travel and communication.

It is a rule long known to geographers that in the Mediterranean basin, lands lying on the western slopes of peripheral land masses receive more rain than those on the east.[2] The higher the mountains flanking the coast, the more the rain. Ghegnia and Montenegro have the heaviest rainfall of any Mediterranean countries. The Adriatic coast, from Lesh up to Dubrovnik, receives well over 60 inches of rain a year; and all of Ghegnia, back from the coast, gets between 60 and 40 inches, with the total decreasing to the east.

This is not all winter rain. It may rain any month of the year, and the summer rainfall totals anywhere from 4 to 8 inches, enough to permit the cultivation of maize by dry farming. This fact alone takes the Gheg highlands out of the Mediterranean climate area. The winter rain, which begins to fall in September, becomes snow at the higher altitudes. Only in the highest valleys and on the peaks does it last out the winter. Elsewhere a succession of snowfalls and thaws renders this region as unpleasant

[2]Semple, 1931, chap. 5.

as New England in early spring.

The temperature again prohibits the growth of many Mediterranean crops, such as the fig and olive, which soon disappear as one leaves the coast. All of the uplands receive severe winter frosts, and on the border of the Kossovo plain the climate becomes continental. The natural vegetation of the Gheg highlands has been preserved more completely than that of almost any other Mediterranean border country, thanks to the difficulty of travel and transportation. North of the Drin in the limestone area, the landscape is mostly bare, since the soil is too thin to support a forest. The igneous zone, however, is heavily forested, with oak succeeded by groves of enormous beech trees, some reaching 10 feet in diameter. At one point on the road between Puka and Kukës the road passes through such a forest, where the traveler used to see woodsmen hewing monoxylic table tops, for sale in Scutari, out of these giant trunks. Up beyond the level of beeches one meets pine, and these trees too are of great size, comparable to the forest, on similar soil, in the middle of Corsica.

While the peaks of Shala are forever white, those of Mal i Zi, the Black Mountain, to the south are forever dark with the coniferous cover. Only in a few places south of the Drin do the peaks emerge above the tree line. Over in the metamorphosed zone to the east one finds more beech and pine, and other broadleaf species such as elms and plane trees, while cypresses have been planted in Moslem cemeteries and mosque areas.

As might be expected the mountains and forests of this little-developed country still harbor a number of dangerous wild animals. The lion of Homeric times is gone, but the bear, the wolf, and the wild boar remain. Deer graze on the high mountain slopes, and in the forests, but the Ghegs will not kill them. The only wild animals of any economic importance are the various members of the weasel family, particularly martens, which a number of mountaineers trap for fur. Otherwise the fauna is a nuisance, since bears and wolves will steal sheep and kill cattle, and flocks need constant guarding by one or more men with rifles and a number of ferocious dogs.

It is in this environment, which must have changed but little since Roman and even earlier times, that the tribal Ghegs have survived until the present day, retaining a language and customs which carry them back to the Iron Age. The land forms, the climate, the geographical position away from main routes of travel and migration, all combine to make the mountains and forests of Ghegnia one of the most marginal and isolated regions of Europe. It is a true refuge area, comparable to the Caucasus and the western Himalayan reaches, the Appalachians, and the Ozarks.

Occupations and Technology: The Economics of An Isolated Society

While we were measuring Ghegs in their home territories, we added to anatomical data on each blank the subject's tribe, *bairak*, religion, occupation, and rank (if any). We then recorded how many wives the subject's father had wed, and how many children of either sex each wife had borne.

We measured 1102 persons. Of these, 1058 were tribesmen both of whose parents had come from the same tribe as the subject. Eleven resulted from intertribal marriages. Thirty-three others remain to be accounted for. Nine were sons of Has fathers and Podrima mothers, 4 were Podrima men. These 13 were living in Has tribal territory, on the Yugoslav side of the border. Podrima is one of the Albanian tribes situated on the plain of Kossovo, wholly in Yugoslav territory. No intermarriages were recorded between Podrima people and Has tribesmen from the Albanian side of the border.

The 20 others were outsiders in Albanian-controlled Gheg tribal territory. Sixteen came from the large market town of Big Dibra (Dibra e Madhe to the Albanians, Debar to the Serbs) in Yugoslavia, which contains a mixed population of Albanians, Serbs, and a few Turks. One was a Serbian-speaking Moslem from the alien *bairak* of Gorë which forms part of the tribe of Luma; his home lay also beyond the border. Another was an Albanian from the town of Jakova. Two others came from inside Ghegnia but outside the tribal territory—from Krujë and Elbasan, respectively.

These 20 men were all first-generation immigrants. There was no older generation like them. I measured none of their sons, and thus this particular immigration had had no effect on our series. All of them were specialists in some kind of technology. Through the study of the data on occupations given in our tabulations we can discover the exact situation of these people.

In our series of 1102 men, 36 occupations were listed. These may be grouped into 7 classes: extractive, processing, services, transport, trade, political, and religious. Their distribution among the 10 tribes and 44 "others" is as follows:[1]

Extractive: of the 930 men so listed, 926 were farmers, 3 shepherds, one a woodcutter. The woodcutter and one shepherd came from Luma, the other shepherd from Mirdita. Eighty-five per cent of all inhabitants of Ghegnia measured are farmers, 88 per cent of all tribesmen.

Processing: Twelve occupations are

[1]See Fig. 1 for full tribal names and locations.

	Total	Extr.	Proc.	Serv.	Trans.	Trade	Pol.	Rel.
MeM	105	101		1		2	1	
Duk	106	103					3	
MeJ	104	87		2	1	7	7	
Has	114	102	11					1
Lum	109	79		1		2	25	2
Puk	102	87		3		1	11	
Mir	101	89	4	1		1	6	
Zad	105	104					1	
Mat	104	80	2	2			20	
Dib	108	75	7		3	11	9	3
Others	44	23	7	2		7	4	1
	1102	930	31	12	4	31	87	7

listed under processing: charcoal burner, blacksmith, tinsmith, carpenter, saddler, hatter, tailor, shoemaker, butcher, baker, cook, and pastry cook.

The 2 charcoal burners, the smith, and the carpenter were Mirdites. Their occupations are mutually dependent. As a rule iron goods are imported, and distributed by merchants in the towns. Axe heads, sickles, billhooks, and other tools of familiar Iron Age shapes are produced by craftsmen in the larger centers, such as Scutari, for the mountain trade.

The other specialists fall into a different class. None were mountain men, except one cook and one baker, both natives of Mati, who worked in the new prefecture headquarters established at Bureli, within Mati territory, by King Zog. They were there because of the impact of the new central government on the mountain tribes. Neither of these men had long been professionals.

The tinsmith, the saddler, and the hatter were natives of Peshkopia, the principal town of Dibra. Of the 3 tailors in this town, one was a native, one had come from Big Dibra, and the third from Jakova. The butcher, one of the 2 bakers, and the cook measured in Peshkopia were Big Dibra men. The pastry cook worked in Kukës, in Luma. This leaves 11 bakers. These men all came from Gonaj and neighboring villages in Has, within walking distance of Prizren. Baking is their traditional hereditary occupation. They get their flour from the gristmills of Prizren and sell their bread in that city. Many of these Hasi bakers migrate to distant cities to work. Mr. Anthony Stevens, our guide, and an employee of the U.S. State Department, began life as one of these bakers; as a boy he went to Cincinnati to work in a bakery.

It can be seen that within Gheg tribal territory processing techniques are practised almost exclusively in the eastern borderlands. Peshkopia has grown rapidly because the international boundary commission of 1913 cut off the Dibra mountaineers from their natural market town of Big Dibra. Hence many of the Big Dibra men moved to Peshkopia, which is just inside Albania. In the same way Prizren was cut off from the Luma people, who build up Kukës; Jakova from the Malsia e Jakovës men, who also go to Kukës. On the western side no such disturbance has taken place. Scutari, Lesh, and Kruja now, as for centuries past, serve as market towns for the mountain people.

Services: Only 12 men are listed under "services." Two of these are innkeepers. One is a Puka man, host at Rrap, his native place. The other is an outsider, a Kruja man, whose inn is at Gur i Bardh in Mati. Kruja men specialize in innkeeping, and in the heyday of Ottoman power might be found all over the Turkish Empire, including Asia Minor. These *hanjis* marry in Kruja, and do not mix with the populations in the regions in which they do their business.

Three men were restaurant-keepers: one Koplik man, whose shop was presumably in Scutari, a Luma man, and a Malsia e Jakovës man, with shops in Kukës. The barber was a Malsia e Jakovës man, working in Kukës. Of the 2 waiters, one was a local man serving the gendarmes in their post at Puka, the other a Big Dibra man working in the hotel in Peshkopia, a new institution. Of the 3 listed as servants, all were local. One served the prefect and another the teacher in the new government center in Bureli. The third worked for a priest in Mirdita.

Of the 12 "services" listings, 9 can be accounted for as a result of recent political events.

Transport: Transportation in Gheg-nia in 1929 meant but one thing—the services of *kiragis,* those incredibly tough horse-drivers who would take you and your goods anywhere, and try to raise the price on the road, once you were at their mercy. Three out of 4 came from Dibra, and one from Malsia e Jakovës. As far as I know, all *kiragis,* like all *hanjis,* are Moslems.

Trade: All merchants in the mountain country are shopkeepers; there are no large or complex commercial institutions. Of the 31 shopkeepers measured, 18 were in Peshkopia. Of these 11 were locals, and 7 Big Dibra immigrants. Six shopkeepers were measured in Kukës, all Malsia e Jakovës men; 2 in Bicaj, a Luma village, were local. One Malsia e Jakovës man was measured in his own shop in Kolgecs, a local town. Thus 25 out of the 31 shopkeepers came from the eastern borderlands, from big towns or their neighborhood. The situation is the same as with the craftsmen whose goods they sell.

Four shopkeepers remain: 2 are from Malsia e Madhe, one with his shop in Scutari, the other at home. Of the other 2, one is a local in Puka, the other a local in Mirdita. The Mirdita man, who has the only shop in that tribe, claimed that his father was an Austrian officer who begat him during World War I. This would give him a maximum possible age of 14 years at the time of measuring. He was at least 30.

TECHNOLOGY, A REVIEW

From the foregoing study of the nonsomatological data collected in our series, and from what is generally known of the material culture of the Ghegs, we can make a brief summary, keeping in mind always our main purpose, to define the economic elements in the cultural situation within which the Ghegs live.

Cutting tools are of iron. They are made by blacksmiths in the market towns in which the Ghegs do their trading. In Scutari, for example, there is a whole quarter devoted to smiths, most if not all of whom are gypsies. With hammer and tongs, a small anvil, and a pair of foot-pump bellows they forge nearly all of the metal objects needed by the mountaineers in their farming, herding, transport, and household carpentry. They make small anvils, hammers, nails, axes, adzes, knives, ploughshares, shovels, hoes, toothed sickles, billhooks, beam ties, door hinges, horseshoes, horse hobbles, chains, bits, firetongs, andirons, tripods, lighting racks, and probably other articles which have escaped our attention.[2]

There is no smelting in the neighborhood of Ghegnia. The iron which the smiths use is all imported. Although city blacksmiths can make all of these implements out of trade iron, it is

[2]Haberlandt's, Nopcsa's, and mine. The best account of this is to be found in Haberlandt, 1917, p. 90.

unlikely that the rural smiths, like the one measured in Mirdita, do much more than horseshoeing. No one in Albania can make steel implements. Not only the material, but the finished implements themselves, must be imported, and hence they are expensive. That is why saws and augers are scarce in the mountains, where almost the only steel tools seen are files, useful for sharpening iron tools and for woodworking.

This explains the primitive nature of Gheg woodworking. Most wooden objects which require special tools or skills are bought in the market towns. Here 3 kinds of woodworking specialists carry on their crafts: the coopers, turners, and joiners. The coopers make tubs and buckets for kitchen use, including churns, butter firkins and casks for storing grain. The material of which these are made is pear wood. The turner cuts out on his lathe various parts for looms, to be set up later; bobbins, spools, reelers, winders, and spool frames. The joiners provide the mountaineers with solid, ornately decorated chests of pine wood, as well as cradles in which to carry their babies, of which more later.

The Gheg at home in his mountains is a jack-of-all trades. He may not be able to manufacture the special objects listed above, but he can adze out beams for his house, put together a new plough during the winter months when there is little work out of doors, or build one of his massive chairs. Professional carpenters are rare, although some men may show more skill in this than others.

In Ghegnia, as in most of the primitive world known to anthropologists, it is the custom not to let fires go out, for it is hard to start a new one. Sometimes a householder will walk several miles to borrow a glowing coal from a neighbor. In 1929 and 1930 most of the Ghegs were making fire with flint and steel or with old-fashioned dry-wick lighters. They did this slyly, and in my presence only when they could not borrow a match from me. King Zog had sold the match monopoly to the Swedish match trust, which had promptly set a price of 5 cents a box on penny matches. The king had at the same time prohibited the use of flint and steel or lighters. This left the mountaineers in an unenviable position—they could not afford matches nor legally start fires by other means. Outside the market towns, however, their illegal actions passed unnoticed.

North Albanian house types are usually divided, on the basis of ground plan, room arrangement, and architecture into four classes: simple one-roomed huts, usually employed in the summer only by shepherds on high mountain pastures; 2-roomed, one-storied houses, with one room for animals and the other for the family; the so-called veranda houses, with a wooden front porch and columns, reminiscent of the Homeric hall; and finally the *kulla* or defensible stronghold.

The 2-roomed house seems to be basic in the mountains, although historically the more complicated structures have made these edifices rare. The veranda house, although old in the Mediterranean, was apparently late to reach this refuge area, being spread with Islam. The *kulla,* or stronghold, is said to have come at the same time as the veranda house. Both reached Kastrati and Shala about 1850, being introduced by one man who had lived in Istanbul, Liho Čuni.

For building materials the Ghegs are strictly limited to local supplies, since transportation is so difficult. In the region designated on figure 2 as "serpentine highland," the stone is hard to cut, and unsuited for fine masonry except in the hands of experts. Furthermore, lime is found in few places only, and it is usually impossible to make mortar without many tedious trips with pack-horses or donkeys. In this region many of the houses are made of wood, with squared logs laid on each other and held in place by vertical or diagonal crosspieces. Others are made of wattle: vertical poles side by side, with flexible wands woven in and out between them. At times this wattling is bare, but usually it is covered with some sort of plaster or mud.

Where there is plenty of suitable stone and lime, these materials are used. The simpler, poorer houses are of dry masonry, but the majority are built with mortar. Roofing material varies from thatch to shakes, slate, and tile. Years ago thatch was much more commonly used than at present. The shift from wheat to maize as staple cereal deprived the farmers in many parts of Albania of roofing material.

The interiors of most houses are quite bare, with no carpets on the hewn plank floors, and little decoration on the walls. In the older houses a fireplace covers about 10 square feet of floor area, and the smoke finds its way out through the thatch or roof tiles. In so doing, it cures meats hung in a rack above the fire, particularly in Catholic houses where pork is preserved for the winter.

The introduction of the *kulla* brought with it some drastic architectural innovations. The *kulla* is a 3-storied square tower, built with one purpose in mind—defense. Nopcsa finds a high correlation between the incidence of *kullas* in different villages and *bairaks*, and that of death by violence. The lower floor of the *kulla* is for the shelter of animals. The second and third are for habitation. One door opens into the stable below, a second, up a flight of bare steps, to the living quarters.

With a multi-storied structure something had to be done about smoke. Hence fireplaces were built one above the other, and a high chimney ensured

draft. One of the principal troubles with the old-fashioned house was its lack of a toilet. The feuding Gheg, attending the needs of nature in a corn field of a frosty morning, made an excellent target to his enemies hiding in ambush, and the feudal code contained no sporting rules to outlaw this easy shot. The *kulla*-builders therefore constructed an overhanging enclosed balcony of masonry, to serve as "W.C." In the conflict between sanitation and safety, safety won. The drain hole is made crooked to prevent pot shots from below. Since there are few windows, and these are built more for gunplay than for light or ventilation, a strong draft usually rushes up the drain hole. Down below in a heap against the wall the refuse accumulates, and were it not for the healthy mountain climate and the hardihood of the mountaineers, epidemics would be commoner than they are.

Gheg houses have both a social and an economic implication. They are usually large, and accommodate an extended family and its animals. Serving for defense, they reflect the local independence of the families within them. In the *kullas,* women are placed on the second floor, men on top; or else the women will live in a nearby unfortified house, while the men take refuge in the *kulla*. This reflects the inviolability of women in the local feuding law.

Kulla-building requires the skill of professionals. All stones are squared, and carefully set in mortar. The fireplaces and chimneys must be properly aligned and made to draw. The great height of the walls requires scaffolding. Nopcsa[3] says that they are built by itinerant masons, and that in 1908 they cost between 440 and 660 crowns (110-165 dollars). I was told several times when I asked that the

[3]Nopcsa, 1925, p. 62.

kullas were built by masons from Dibra,[4] who also build them in Montenegro, Bosnia, and elsewhere in Yugoslavia. Exactly where in Dibra these masons come from I do not know. I have never seen one at work, nor did any appear in our series.

These houses, of whatever type, are heated by wood, which at the same time cooks the meals. In most of the region there is plenty of firewood, but in the northern limestone region it is scarce and must be sought afar. The mountaineers earn a little spare cash by carrying loads of firewood down to the market towns to sell.

In many houses in 1929 a primitive form of illumination was still employed. When it grew dark the host would lay a number of pine splinters in several iron racks, hanging from the roof, and light them. The oil in the wood would provide enough light to see by, but hardly enough for reading. In other houses, however, they used candles, and in still others oil lamps. Kerosene has been packed into this country in square 5-gallon tins for some time, and the tins themselves are as much sought after as their contents.

Gheg clothing has received even more attention than their housing. The costumes are picturesque, and make fine collections. They vary from tribe to tribe, *bairak* to *bairak,* and in some cases between villages. After six months of travel over the mountains I was able to tell where a man came from in many cases by the cut of his jacket, the color of his trousers, the shape of his cap, and particularly by the design on his stockings. If after 6 months a foreigner had reached this threshold of discrimination, a native mountaineer with good eyesight could identify a stranger as far as he could see him, just as easily as a modern boy can tell the make of a car or airplane at a glance. This habit of wearing one's insignia so conspicuously

[4]This is confirmed by Bishop Fan Noli.

has a very definite meaning. The man is proud of his family and native place, and defiant. His desire to be identified is greater than his fear of death. He does not go far from home unless his mission is a serious one.

The man's costume starts with a brimless felt cap, either conical or flat on top; often he wears a kerchief around it like a thin turban, or neckcloth. The upper part of his body is covered with a woolen jacket, with sleeves and some kind of collar, often sailor-fashion. As a rule he is shirtless. From waist to ankle he wears a pair of woolen breeches, usually skin-tight on the legs, and with a slight fullness in the seat in some regions which reflects the influence of the Turkish baggy pants. He goes without underdrawers. If wealthy, he may also wear an ornate sleeveless waistcoat. He usually sports some kind of wide cummerbund, or belt. His feet are shod in opingas, or rawhide buskins, the common primitive European footgear found not only in the Balkans but in Russia, Ireland, and other places where tradition is strong enough and shoes expensive enough to preserve this ancient homemade shoe type. In 1929 the poorer Ghegs were wearing pieces of automobile tire in place of opingas, and it gave one a start to see a fresh section of Goodyear or Michelin track on a mountain path 18 inches wide. At the same time the wealthier were wearing western manufactured shoes.

Both men and women wear stockings, knit by the women, which bear the family design as clearly as a Scottish tartan. I have seen many men, however, who had none. The women's dress varies from place to place, but is basically a combination of a full bell-like skirt, reminding one of a Cretan goddess's lower garment, surmounted by a full blouse or bodice. Add to that a headcloth or shawl, and much jewelry which is bought from silversmiths in the town, and the woman is clothed.

These costumes are undoubtedly ancient. Some of their elements may be traced back to the early Mediterranean, others to the central European Iron Age. However, the Ghegs themselves do not make all parts of them, but carry on the tradition by demand, like the Crow Indians for whom Stetson has, for decades, been manufacturing a special kind of hat.

The basic cloth is woven at home. The farmer gives his wife the necessary wool from his sheep, both white and black. She cards it with a homemade device, either a flick bow or a nail-studded card, and spins it. Her spinning kit consists of a distaff, a spindle, and a basket. Holding the distaff in one hand, she twists the wool with the other, and winds it onto the spindle in the basket. Whenever she has nothing else to do, or when she is walking along the trail, the Albanian housewife dutifully spins, and her spinning has soon become a reflex action, like knitting or bead-telling.

When she has enough yarn, she begins weaving. The Albanian loom is an ordinary European 2-beam affair, similar to those used in the Hebrides and the Kentucky mountains. It has a wooden frame, 2 beams or rollers between which the warps are stretched, a wooden batten, and a foot-operated heddle. The bobbin, within its shuttle, is hand-thrown. The men buy all of the delicate parts of this loom in the town, from turners. The rest of it they make at home. The loom is kept mounted only while a length of cloth is being woven. When not in use the loom is taken apart and piled in a corner with other household impedimenta.

Once the cloth has been woven, it must, if intended for masculine use, be fulled. This involves keeping it wet, working it about, and pounding it for several hours. The mountaineers employ an ingenious water-powered device for this purpose. Several writers have observed these mills; Nopcsa has drawn

one.[5] I saw several. The fulling mill consists of an open-air wooden structure powered by an overshot water wheel. A smaller stream of water runs through a trough to wet the cloth. The wheelshaft is studded with four wooden lugs or cogs, which lift up a heavy wooden hammer and let it drop, 4 times for each revolution. Two staggered sets of cogs and 2 hammers give the cloth a constant pounding as long as it is left there.

No one seems to know who invented these mills or who makes them. When you encounter them along a stream, they are usually unattended. Apparently the wife, having woven her cloth, turns it over to her husband, who takes it to the mill to be fulled. There is no professional fuller, and each mill seems to belong to the group of kinsmen or neighbors who use it.

The women make their own clothing, for the most part of unfulled cloth. They also crochet the stockings, and stitch the opingas, worn by both sexes. The men, however, carry the fulled and heavily felted cloth to the market town, to a tailor who then cuts it in the traditional design of his client's native place, and sews up the pieces and embroiders the finished garment.

A number of other specialists are involved in the production of men's clothing and equipment. A special craftsman provides the quantities of braid with which jacket and trousers are adorned. Hatters, equipped with wooden molds to suit every variation of tribal taste, shape the felt caps, conical or truncated, white or black, which all mountaineers wear. Leather-workers, who are traditionally Turks, make ornate belts for the men, as well as saddles, bags, and straps. Special shoemakers make footgear for those who can afford it, although most wear the opingas which their wives produce from local hides. Most of the shoe-

[5]Nopcsa, 1925, p. 134, fig. 99.

makers are Kruja men, and this is a Kruja specialty. At Kukës we saw zebra hides on display outside several shops. These had been sent all the way from South Africa for the manufacture of opingas.

As previously stated, wooden buckets are made by professional coopers in towns, and purchased by the mountain people, who use them in dairying and for food storage. Baskets, however, are local products; the country people often bring them to town for sale. Several villages near Scutari specialize in basket-making, and the women, who weave them, bring them to market along with embroidery. These include not only spinning baskets and hand-carrying baskets, but also large osier panniers used in transport—a man can carry one on his back, a horse, two. I believe that the panniers are made by men.

Other containers include copperwork and pottery. The coppersmiths in each town hammer out sheets of metal into round trays, which can be used for baking cheese dishes, pastry, etc., or for tea and coffee service. They also make kettles, water jugs, and wash-basins. All of these things are purchased by the mountaineers, who now and then acquire a European chamber-pot to use as a soup tureen, and a set of glass tumblers.

Three kinds of pottery find their way into the mountaineer's household. In the Catholic tribes, if not elsewhere, the women still make an Iron Age vessel, of simple profile, with handles, without slip, and decorated by incisions. It is hand-modeled, and fired in such a way as to give it a black surface. In the towns, professional male potters make a porous ware on the wheel. This is used for carrying and storing water. Regular modern glazed pottery is imported from Italy, and subsequently sold in the bazaars.

Food preservation and storage tech-

niques vary between Catholics and Moslems, owing to their differences in diet. The Catholics preserve much pork by salting and smoking. The men of each household will butcher as many fat pigs as the family needs or can spare, in the fall. They cut the belly fat into flitches and hang it over the fire. An especial delicacy is the *peshk*, or "fish," a long strip of lean back-bacon, smoke-cured, which they cut in slices and fry. Besides these whole pork pieces, they make sausages and cure them in the same way. The Moslems as a rule eat only fresh meat and live on mutton, whereas Catholics eat both mutton and pork.

Both store their cereals and legumes in tubs and bags in the house, and keep maize in special outdoor corncribs, elevated to protect them from rats. Very often a fierce dog will be seen and heard, chained under the crib. Both make butter from their cows' milk, and cheese from that of sheep and goats, although the use of the latter is much more common among the Moslems. Catholics, in country fit for grape-growing, make a potent red wine, which they resinate in Homeric fashion.

The Moslems, prohibited by the Koran from wine drinking, content themselves with distilled liquors. In every neighborhood one or more Moslem families will own a copper still, complete with boiler and cooling screw, which someone once bought in Scutari or another town. Neighbors borrow these stills from time to time, as American families used to borrow each other's ice-cream freezers. Much of the *raki*, or raisin brandy, so produced, is home distilled, but a certain amount is carried up from the towns. Green *mastica*, a vicious local variety of absinthe, is imported only. Both Catholics and Moslems smoke. While a few Moslems own *narghilehs*, most tobacco addicts smoke cigarettes. The economics of cigarette smoking is that as a rule each man grows his own tobacco, and sells what he does not consume. He has to buy cigarette paper, imported from France. He has to have some kind of a lighting device, which usually runs to expense, as previously explained. The social aspect of smoking is that it forms a ready means of polite interaction, for men give each other cigarettes, rolling and licking them for an honored guest.

Since the principal food of all the mountaineers, whatever their religion, is bread, usually a tough, unleavened cornbread which will keep for weeks and grow harder and harder instead of molding, one of their principal needs is some way to grind the grain. Most houses contain mortars and pestles, and many also contain hand querns, of Roman design, which the women operate. It is probable, but not certain, that all of the millstones come from the market, since suitable stone is found in few areas. A large part of the grain-milling, however, is done in small, water-driven mills, of which there are many. These mills, homemade except for the stones, are operated by vertical-shaft paddle wheels which are in effect primitive turbines. They save the expenditure of human muscular energy, and much time. In one place in Malsia e Jakovës, I saw another kind of mill, a pounding device which consisted of a trough-shaped log set on a pivot, and equipped with a heavy hammer at one end. Water flowed into this trough until enough had entered the lower end to tip the whole, and raise the hammer. Then when the water spilled out the hammer fell, and the cycle began again.

Although they utilize water power so cleverly and save so much effort, these two kinds of mills involve no specific division of labor. Some men may be more skillfull at setting them than others, but there are no professional mill-builders, and no millers. Like the fulling mills they belong to the families

that use them, and when not in use are unattended. In the cities, however, professional millers are to be found. Prizren, which has an ample supply of swift water running under the streets, is a milling town, and the traveler walking down the millers' street can hear the sharp ring of stone on stone for several hundred feet. These mills supply the needs of the bakers of Gonaj and Zum, and feed the citizens of Prizren. Bread from this region is of excellent quality and mountaineers coming to market often take a few loaves home.

The Ghegs eat one principal meal a day, late in the afternoon. In the morning a Moslem may take a small glass of *raki* for an eye-opener, and eat some bread and cheese; a Catholic will also break his fast. Both will munch a cold snack on the road or in the field for luncheon. But the time when the whole family gets together, when honored guests are entertained, comes when the day's work is over. Then the women cook the food, and the men squat around the communal table. In Moslem households the table is the only piece of furniture in evidence, aside from the omnipresent chests. Among the Catholics, each house usually contains one massive beechwood chair, made locally, which seats the head of the house or the guest of honor, and a number of low wooden stools.

Forks and other modern cutlery are usually absent. Mediaeval table manners are scrupulously observed, with all eating from the same dish, and with their fingers. Among the Moslems at least, the custom of passing a washbowl and jug of water with a towel before and after the meal is usual, as well as saying the Koranic grace, *bismillah*. At one meal which I attended at the house of Major Çen Eleze at Slatina, in Dibra, the table was at least 10 feet in diameter, the eaters numbered at least 15, with as many more waiting patiently for second table, and the dishes included a whole roast sheep, which the Major picked apart with his hands and distributed.

Professional cooks are found only in the towns and in new government stations. In Prizren and Scutari, many of these cooks are Turks and their dishes consist mostly of mutton with various kinds of vegetables. Personally I found this cuisine very tasty. They also make a fine *yughurt*. Pastry cooks form another special group, and concentrate on *baklava* and *kadaif*, the two honey desserts familiar to eaters in Greek restaurants in all countries. Although their products may be carried into the mountains, the pastry cooks themselves stay at home.

The mountaineers obtain almost all of their own food by farming and herding. Hunting provides little or none for most families, and the same is true of fishing. Along the Black Drin, just above Kukës, a few fish are sometimes caught, and welcomed in the kitchen. In Prizren, fresh river fish are sold in the market. But fish is an insignificant element in the Mountain Gheg diet. The same is true of wild vegetable products, shoots, berries, and the like, collected by women. Furthermore each family produces practically all of its own food, except for a little coffee and tea, and a bit of sugar and salt. Most families are too poor to afford these imported luxuries often. The significance of the absolute self-sufficiency of the Ghegs in their food supply is linked with local differences in geology, and must have a profound effect upon differences in physique attendant on diet.

Farming is a family affair. The man buys the iron implements which he needs in town, and makes the rest of wood. He breaks the soil with a spade, and ploughs it with oxen. As he ploughs each furrow, his wife walks behind him with a basket of seed, sowing it. Later the women will do the weeding, and the whole family comes out to reap. If the crop is wheat, they cut off each head of grain with a sickle and put the heads in a bag; if maize, they pick the ears and braid the husks for drying. They thresh small grains and beans with flails. When the tobacco leaves are ripe, the men cut them carefully and hang them on their verandas or the sides of their houses to cure. The Mountain Ghegs also grow much fruit on trees near their houses. The chief species are quinces, pears, and apples.

Women have charge of milking the cows and making butter, curds, and cheese. Small boys are usually employed as shepherds, and lead their flocks high on the mountains. In the summertime many Gheg families drive their cattle up to the Alpine meadows on the mountain passes, and keep them there weeks at a time while they make butter and cheese. While on these heights they live in small temporary houses. The people of Klementi, however, who live in high valleys, drive their flocks to the plain of Scutari every year for winter pasture.

Animal husbandry furnishes the Ghegs not only with much of their food, but also with a supply of energy, for they use oxen in ploughing, and horses for travel and the transport of goods. In the wintertime they keep their cows and horses indoors, while the pigs, in Catholic regions, have special sties. Late winter and early spring is the season when food is scarce. The corncrib may be empty, and only the seed corn hanging in bunches from the walls will remain untouched. The cows are dry, and the flitches of pork and bacon gone from the ceiling.

This is the time when the mountain people, their tempers more and more irritable, used to turn to raiding, and while some rustled each other's animals, others came down out of the mountains to steal cattle from the people on the plains. Mirdita raided Zadrima, and Mati raided the low country around Elbasan. This annual hunger was the result of a complete economic occupance of the land, coupled with an excess of births over deaths. Raiding brought in more food, but feuding caused more deaths. Between the two, plus a certain amount of emigration, the balance was reached.

Transportation in Ghegnia was, in 1929, as poor as anywhere in Europe. There were a certain number of roads over which people could walk, in some places ride animals, and in most, carry goods on animal back. In a few places the trails were too steep for animals, and men had to pack in goods by pannier. The principal road, which will be described later, goes from Scutari and Lesh by way of Vau i Denjës to Puka, then on to Kukës, and across the border to Prizren. This was an old Roman road, and has probably not changed much in a thousand years. At Kukës another road meets it, running south along the Black Drin to Peshkopia and outside Gheg country to Lake Ochrida and Korça. Parts of this road had been widened for vehicular traffic in 1929, but the wide pieces had not been connected.

Another trail goes from Tirana to Zall, thence to Gur i Bardh in Mati, through Klos, across the divide to Bulçiz in Dibra, and thence to Peshkopia. This is the principal route between the new capital and the important region to the northeast. Still another passes from Lesh to Bureli in Mati, following the banks of the Mati River. Bureli, now a prefect station, has grown important only with the Zog regime. From Bureli one can proceed to the northern Catholic country of Lura and Kthella, and thence down into Dibra, but the road is little traveled. North of the Drin a trail passes from Scutari to Shoshi over the Gur i Kutch, but in winter this is impassable. On the other side there is a road from Kukës across the Drin through the *bairaks* of Bituç, Gashi, and Krasniqi, past

Merturi, into Shoshi. In winter this can be passed by men but not animals. Hence in wintertime no animal traffic can enter either Shoshi, or Shala which lies to its north. Before the boundary was drawn between Albania and Yugoslavia the road from Tropoya, in Gashi (Malsia e Jakovës), to Jakova was much traveled; but now this is forbidden and the people of this tribe must go to market in Kukës.

As far as any considerable traffic is concerned, horseback and human back were, in 1929, the only methods of land transport available in Ghegnia. In a few of the flatter places, however, other means are used locally for short distances. In the country around Scutari just below the mountains, the farmers use carts, particularly in Zadrima. In Luma, on the flat land at the confluence of the Drins, and in Has on the other side, carts are likewise used, as well as ox-drawn summer sleds.

Crossing streams is not a simple matter in Ghegnia. Most of the crossings are fords, and very cold. I have seen men strip naked to swim across icy rivers in search of a place for animals to cross, and have waded up to my chin at night, with snow on either bank. When the streams are swollen, animals and men are not infrequently drowned. There is or was an old Turkish bridge across the White Drin, from Kukës to the northern bank. Several wooden bridges crossed the Black Drin in Dibra. On the road from Krasniqi to Shoshi, I have crossed a bridge which consisted of 2 poles, one to walk on, the other a little higher and to one side, to use as a rail.

In a few places, ferry boats are available, which operate by the principle of changing the mooring position of the cable after each crossing, so that the power of the stream will push the boat diagonally across to the other bank. There was one such at Kukës across the Black Drin, another at Bureli over the Mati. Other observers have witnessed Ghegs crossing these streams on inflated skins, but I have never seen it.

Navigation in Ghegnia is very limited. Although Nopcsa has a picture of a man in a boat at Merturi, I have seen it only on the lower course of the Drin, between Vau i Denjës and Scutari, where special boatmen ferry passengers to town in a few hours, to save the day's march over the road. These boats are long dugout canoes, usually double. The boatman propels them by sculling, like the gondoliers of Venice. The men who run the ferries, and these boatmen on the lower Drin, are without doubt specialists, as nearly fulltime as the traffic requires. Probably not more than a dozen men ply these trades. Much more numerous are the *kiragis,* the professional horse-drivers who may be seen on all of the roads in Moslem country, and in some Catholic tribes as well. The *kiragis* in our series were Dibra men, but others come from outside the tribal area, from such places as Elbasan and Tirana.

The *kiragi* is a hard-bitten man, disillusioned early in life by a close observation of human behavior under stress, since all travel in Ghegnia is difficult. He is a non-combatant, a man with no family ties in the regions in which he works, and not worth killing. Anyone who robs him too often will keep trade away and cut off the supply of needed imports. He will rent out anywhere from one to a half dozen horses, to go anywhere the road will take him, and the rate per day has to be argued over at length. He insists on taking grain for his horses at the customer's expense, and will refuse to go on if the grain is exhausted. All kinds of situations arise to produce arguments between *kiragi* and customer, such as the unexpectedly high price of grain in a certain place, inn charges, and the condition of the horses.

Besides carrying passengers and their goods, the *kiragi* will do errands; he will carry goods to market without their owners, sell them, and take his commission; then he will bring back a specified list of purchased objects. He must be reasonably honest or he will lose the traffic. At the same time the mountaineers who hire him are spared the risk of crossing hostile territory.

Kiragis are either in business for themselves or in partnership, or working on shares with an investing capitalist. Since Islam prohibits interest, the share system is the one employed. It is not big business, for the maximum number of persons involved will not exceed a half dozen, including the boys whom the *kiragi* takes with him to help with the horses. It is, however, one of the few ways in which the otherwise closed country of the Gheg mountaineers is systematically and constantly penetrated. In 1929 there must have been at least a hundred such professionals on the roads every day.

In Moslem country the principal roads are equipped, at appropriate distances, with inns. As with tourist cabins in the United States, it is best to start at daybreak or earlier, and get in well before sunset, for the inns are often full well before night. The usual inn consists of 3 rooms; a large stable, which occupies about three-fourths of the whole; a chamber with a low ceiling built into one corner of the building, some 14 feet wide by 30 or 40 feet long, with a fireplace at the far end; and a cubicle which serves as the *hanji's* (innkeeper's) private quarters, office, and store.

When you enter the inn, the *hanji* sees that you unload your animals, and assigns them space in the stable. He has straw there, and sometimes grain if you have not brought your own. Then he gives each guest a section of the floor, which is divided into 3 strips, the 2 on the sides being about 6 feet wide, and the center one, 2 feet. Guests sleep side by side on the lateral strips, with the center reserved as a passageway. The guests feed themselves with cooking privileges at the fireplace, while the host brews coffee for sale, and also dispenses *raki*. After his guests are in for the night he locks the door, and cannot ordinarily be persuaded to unlock it before morning, no matter how urgent the needs of the guests to go outside. This precaution is necessary owing to the frequency of violence.

Some of the *hanjis* are local men. Others come from Kruja, the home of innkeepers. All of them live as bachelors. This system, like the *kiragi* business, brings a certain number of outsiders into the country. All in all there are probably 12 to 18 *hans* in Ghegnia, in addition to the one European-style hotel at Peshkopia. The Catholics do not use this system; in their tribal areas guests are put up by important individuals through a system of reciprocal hospitality. Since local feuds are usually more prevalent in Catholic than in Moslem country, travel across the former is relatively light.

There remains only the question of trade, which has been partly covered. On the whole it may be said of the mountain Ghegs that they live by a regional, or geographic, and perhaps also ethnic, division of labor. The ordinary man is a farmer, who produces firewood, cereals, legumes, tobacco, wool, milk products, and sometimes wooden spoons. His wife produces cloth, crocheted stockings, embroidered scarfs, baskets, eggs, and a few other local products. These mountain products find their way to the market towns. Usually men and women come together; sometimes only the women make the trip, and sometimes the whole family stays at home, sending the goods by a *kiragi*.

The Ghegs are able to export these things because they produce a slight surplus of agricultural products. One reason for the surplus may be that they use a number of labor-saving devices, including fulling and mealing mills run by water power. This gives them more time for other pursuits, but does not increase their complexity of relations at home, since the mills are small and serve individual groups of related families.

On the other side of the picture lie the craftsmen and shopkeepers in the towns, some Albanian, others Turkish, others Serbian. These craftsmen live off the exports from the mountains and from the other agricultural regions around them, and supply the mountaineers with their needs, including firearms and ammunition, as well as the objects previously listed.

So far the picture is simple, mountaineers on one side of the fence, townsmen on the other. A mountaineer may become a townsman, but never the reverse. At several points, however, the security of the mountains is penetrated: by the itinerant masons who build *kullas,* by the *hanjis* and *kiragis* who handle traffic and care for travelers, and by the shopkeepers, who are themselves usually Ghegs, and who are found in the larger tribal villages, usually but one to a settlement. I can recall but one in Mirdita, none in Shoshi, while in the country villages of Dibra, Luma, and Puka, along the main roads, there were several. These men sold tea and sugar, needles and thread, cigarette papers, salt and pepper, a little candy, candles, kerosene, kerchiefs, and matches. They saved a trip to town for minor purchases.

With this balance of production and trade, the Ghegs barely succeed in making a living. If their average income could be accurately assessed, it would be one of the lowest in Europe. The ordinary farmer has just enough clothing to cover his family. In some cases I have seen brothers with one suit between them; one had to stay indoors while the other went out. This was in Merturi. The ordinary household has just enough food to get through the year, saving the next year's seed and selling a little in the town. Many houses are the scenes of tightened belts and near starvation every spring. Since there is no knowledge of contraception, many children are born. As ideas of sanitation are also lacking, many people die, and the population is always a little greater than the threshold of tolerance. Feuds, sudden death, and emigration are necessary safety valves. Another very recent one is enlistment in the gendarmerie.

The Family System: Who Marries Whom and Why[1]

TO THE anthropologist, selective marriage systems, such as cross-cousin and parallel-cousin, are run-of-the-mill phenomena. But the anthropologist is used to dealing primarily with non-European peoples, living far from centers of civilization. To the sociologist brought up on European and American subject matter it is an event to discover a "primitive" system in operation only 250 miles from Rome, in the 20th century.

As our study of material culture made clear, the Gheg family, like that of the early Israelites, or of the Chinese of any period, is an economic institution. One household, consisting of a man, his wife or wives, his sons, unmarried daughters, and son's children, lives in a single house or group of houses, and all ordinarily work together. The most complicated tasks which confront them require the co-operation of such a group, but no more, except in rare events when neighboring kinsmen may be called in. Isolation and political insecurity enhance the frequency and strength of the mutual relations of the family members. In some of the tribes, notably Dukagin, these households number up to 30 or 40 persons; the Arabic word *mehalla* (military camp) is used to designate them.

A sex division of labor clearly separates the work of the women from that of the men. Each needs the other. A houseful of widows and unmarried women would be unthinkable, as would a house occupied by men alone. The family must be a balanced unit. If a man dies his place must be filled if possible; if a woman fails to bear children another must be found who can. The family must continue, and since so many men are killed before they reach maturity, it must produce boys. The birth of girls is less important because they are not killed, and because they leave the family to get married.

For a number of very good reasons, it is considered desirable to obtain wives for one's sons from a distance. In the first place, if a boy were to marry a local girl, he might get in trouble with other local boys. Young men form attachments for the girls whom they see every day, and any feeling of rivalry in youth which was followed by such a marriage might continue the tension into manhood. The young men who live in one place must get along together as well as possible. Owing to economic pressure, all tensions run high, and tensions result in violence. Violence with one's immediate neighbors would be suicidal. Therefore it is best for fathers to arrange these matters well in advance, and to bring in new girls who have no local ties.

Then again, let us suppose that the marriage did not work well; that the bride was shy, disliked her husband, was slow to adjust herself to living with him, or resented her mother-in-law's

[1]The principal source of this chapter is my own records. However, I also made use of Miss M. E. Durham's publication of 1928, as well as material contained in a letter which she most kindly wrote me.

interference. If her parents lived close at hand, she could run home and complain to her mother. Soon her father and brothers would be making trouble for her husband and his family. Any wise person can see that it is much better to bring the bride from a distance, and then if any trouble arises between the two kins, they will be too far separated to cross each other's paths very often.

Once a family has formed the habit of getting its wives from another group in a distant area, that habit is likely to continue. A man will go to his wife's brother and say, "Haven't you a daughter for my son?" and the thing is easily arranged, providing that the earlier marriage has been successful. This requires less effort than breaking the ice with an entirely new group of people, but at the same time it preserves the necessary distance. Of course, if the man's wife's family has no daughters available for his son, he can try their

neighboring kinfolk, or some other family with which some of his cousins have worked out a similar arrangement. In this way 2 things are evened up; one does not give a girl away without some assurance of getting in return a wife for one's own son.

This system satisfies the universal principle which applies in all human mating, that *the ideal or normal choice of spouses shall be that which creates the least disturbance in the systems of relations of both parties concerned.* That a form of cross-cousin mating should have survived in the Gheg country is a natural consequence of the equal survival of an archaic technology in a rugged environment. The system fits the circumstances, as one might expect.

However, the Gheg father, if asked, would not give the answers detailed above as reasons for his choice of a bride for his son. He would voice a

Table 1: Numbers of Wives Married by Fathers of Subjects, and Numbers of Offspring

	MeM	Duk	MeJ	Has	Lum	Puk	Mir	Zad	Mat	Dib	Int	Total
One Wife, Moslems	40		54	72	76	50		9	69	74	3	450
Catholics	47	89	10	10		24	82	83	9		2	356
Total	87	89	64	82	76	74	82	92	78	74	5	803
Two Wives, Moslems ..	12		27	19	23	13		3	20	32	1	150
Catholics	5	16	5	3		12	16	7	1		3	68
Orthodox											1	1
Total	17	16	32	22	23	25	16	10	21	33	4	219
Three Wives, Moslems .			4	7	8	1		1	4			25
Catholics			2				1	1				4
Total			6	7	8	1	1	2	4			29
Four Wives, Moslems ..			1		2	1						4
Catholics		1					2					3
Total		1	1		2	1	2					7
Six Wives, Moslems ...			1						1			2
Total Fathers	104	106	104	111	109	101	101	104	104	107	9	1060
No. childless 1st wives ..		6	8	4	2	3	1	1	4	6		35
With daughters only ...	1	7	2			4	3	3	4	2	2	28
Total unsatisfactory 1st wives in plural marriages	1	13	10	4	2	7	4	4	8	8	2	63
No. boys born	400	317	332	366	394	325	300	298	271	365	31	3399
No. girls born	283	237	201	239	227	188	165	159	167	184	17	2067
Total children	683	554	533	605	621	513	465	457	438	549	48	5466
No. children per family .	6.6	5.2	5.1	5.8	5.7	5.1	4.5	4.4	4.2	5.1	5.3	5.2
Sex ratio of children ...	141	134	165	154	174	173	182	187	162	198	182	163

number of local rationalizations: that the son inherits body and soul from the father alone, the mother being merely a vehicle of reproduction; that it is dishonorable and unthinkable to marry any kin whatever. Since the mother's family is no relation, sons can continue to take their brides from it for generation after generation. The Law of Lek Dukagin, which the Gheg father would quote on such an occasion, has taken care of this subject once and forever.

The choice of a bride for his son is as much a political problem to a Gheg householder as it was to a 19th-century European king in the heyday of royalty. No mistakes must be made, and the preferences of the parties concerned are not considered important. Hence the fathers make the arrangements. A man normally pays 15 to 20 napoleons (60-80 dollars) for his son's wife. This is half the price of a new *kulla*. If the man has many sons, the youngest may not get a new wife, but have to content himself with a widow, who is cheaper. Also it may take some time to find a fiancée for each boy, and many young men wait until quite late in life for marriage.

The principal reason for this delay, aside from the price, is the peculiar birth and death rate figures for Ghegnia. Many more boys than girls are born. In some regions the boys outnumber the girls almost two to one (see table 1). However, as soon as a boy is big enough to carry a gun he may begin feuding, and stands a good chance of being killed. Then his marriage arrangements may be transferred to his brother, or cousin, and hence the young lady may marry someone quite different from her expectation.

The alert and provident father, ever on the lookout for daughters-in-law, may place a substantial part of his bride price on a baby girl, as soon as she is born. Or he may gamble on the sex of an unborn child. The baby girl may find herself, at the age of 14, married to a man of 40. Once she has been handed over to her new husband and the folk-rites performed, she is still on trial, and may be sent home if she fails to produce offspring within a reasonable time. Among the Catholics the church wedding is often delayed until after the birth of the first child. In this way the bride can be returned if found wanting, and the rule of Christian monogamy will not have been technically violated. Among the Moslems, where both polygyny and divorce are officially permitted, these subterfuges are not needed.

While the Gheg system of selecting mates may be well attuned to the exigencies of the environment, the economics, and the political life of the mountaineers, it permits little opportunity for personal adjustment between the husband and wife. Prince Jon Markajon of Mirdita summed this up when he said to me, gloomily, in the presence of his wife, "There is only one woman a man can trust—his mother." In the cases where cross-cousin marriage works out ideally, the boy and girl may have met before betrothal, or at least before marriage. The boy's mother, on a visit to her own kin, may take her youthful son with her, and he will have a chance to play with his maternal uncle's children. Then when the bride joins her husband in his father's house she will come directly under the supervision of her paternal aunt, a woman whom she has already seen, and who represents an extension of her own family in the strange household. Such an ideal arrangement still makes no provision for a selection of mates on the basis of personality adjustments. It merely makes the change from one household to the other a little easier than if the girl were a total stranger. Very often a girl's fiancé is killed and she has to marry one of his brothers, a cousin, or someone of an entirely different family, and there will be no familiar aunt to smooth things over, but instead a suspicious and exacting mother-in-law, with whom her only ties are through her husband.

It is no wonder that brides sometimes run away. If they come home their fathers usually return them. Not infrequently they elope and if they are lucky settle in some city, or distant countryside where the limb of Lek Dukagin's law is not long enough to reach them. Gheg epic poetry, which the traveler hears sung night after night in private houses, hans, and gendarmeries, dwells frequently on the theme of elopement. One hears at length about couple after couple, hopelessly in love, who break all of the rules, run away, and meet a tragic but inexorable fate. In the epics they seldom if ever make good their escape. In real life I believe that they sometimes succeed, and their elopements, successful or otherwise, help reduce the population of the mountains.

If a young woman is faced with a marriage which she cannot bring herself to consummate, and if she has enough strength of character to take the following step, she can avoid matrimony by becoming a "sworn virgin." She summons a meeting of the 12 elders of her community and in their presence swears perpetual chastity. By this means she not only gets out of her engagement, but also prevents a feud between her father's kin and those of her fiancé. At this point she becomes technically a man. She may or may not don masculine clothing. She will carry a gun, and fight like other men. She will plough and reap, and do all of the tasks of a man. If she breaks her oath, the elders will, in theory, burn her alive. It is doubtful if this punishment has been exacted on any such person within the last few generations.

As the reader can readily see, this custom has its economic aspects. The number of hands available for men's work is increased by two, that for women's work decreased by the same number. There is a second and less dramatic reason for a girl to swear virginity: if her father has no sons to help him with his work, or if his sons are killed. Then a daughter may step into the position of a son, and the situation is momentarily saved. However, since the pseudo-son will have no offspring, the line will become extinct with her death, and the property pass to the next of kin on the father's side. This custom is at variance with the usual one in comparable societies, in which the husband of the man's daughter comes to live with her parents, and is adopted as an heir. So strong is the belief in the continuity of the male line that this could not be done in Ghegnia.

On my travels I encountered only 2 sworn virgins. One wore men's clothes, and appeared to be either mentally defective or at least "queer." That also was her reputation. The second wore women's clothes. She was in her early twenties, and quite attractive. Since she spent the night with a junior member of my group of horse-drivers, I formed a poor opinion of the burning-alive theory. It is quite apparent that the practice of swearing virginity is not only often economic in motivation, but also a part of the whole business of local population control, along with the entire configuration of pride, insult, and feuding.

Two other mechanisms help maintain the personnel of the family at the optimum numerical working level, and to prevent the isolation of separate individuals or small, uneconomic groups. One is the levirate. Classically this means that when a man dies, his widow will be married to a surviving brother or next of kin if such a brother is lacking. In a country where the rate of death by violence reaches the level of 40 per cent of all male deaths in some localities, and where girls are married at 14 or 15, many are widowed.

Such a widow must be cared for by the men of her husband's family, since they have paid for her and she has joined their group. If there is a surviving brother who is single, obviously the expedient thing to do is to give her to him. She might even be given to a first cousin. However, the occasion sometimes arises in Ghegnia where the classical form of the levirate is indicated, and a brother, preferably an older brother, of the deceased, a man who is already married, takes the widow into his household. In Moslem communities this causes no ecclesiastical difficulty. In Catholic households it may bring about a conflict with the priest. In such a case the Law of Lek wins over the Law of Rome. Societal needs are stronger than religious taboos. The new husband may not be allowed a church marriage, and it is possible that he may not consummate the new union, but the woman enters his household, and he cares for her and her children.

The second mechanism is polygyny, in case the first wife fails to produce male offspring. This again is perfectly legal among Moslems and diametrically counter to Catholic rules. The priest will not allow the husband to divorce his wife who fails to give him sons. If she gives him daughters there is always hope that a son will follow, and the crisis may be delayed. But if after a suitable time there are no offspring whatever, he will need a new wife. He cannot divorce his old one, and he cannot legally marry his new one. Here again custom sometimes wins. I personally have visited only one household of Catholic Ghegs in which I knew that the master had 2 wives, and it was for this reason. It is little wonder, since Catholicism fits so imperfectly the economic needs of the Albanian family, that many of them went over to the much more satisfactory (in this respect) faith of Islam.

In designing this part of the measurement blanks we chose the subject's father rather than the man himself because we would thus be dealing with complete or nearly complete families. In every case we received specific answers; very few men, whose fathers had had 3 or 4 wives, could not remember how many children the oldest wife had had.

These statistics do not constitute a record of pregnancies. Children who died in infancy are probably not included. Female infanticide has not been reported in Ghegnia. Presumably all or most of the children grew to such an age that either they were still living in 1929-30, or were old enough at the time of death to have made an impression on their full or half brothers who were our subjects. Our figures tell how many wives each father had, but not how many at a time. It would be hard to get that information from a casual questioning done in public at the time of measuring. In 1929 polygyny was legally forbidden in Albania for Catholics and Moslems alike, and the Catholics had in addition the position of the church to keep them from revealing the polygyny of their parents in the presence of several dozen other people. One other obvious defect of our data is that we have no record of marriages in which no son was born, and no second wife taken. This circumstance, although rare, must have occurred. The reader may think, in view of the unusual sex ratio, 163 male to 100 female offspring, that Moslems failed to reveal the true number of girls born, but I do not believe that this was the case. The Catholics had the same sex ratio as the Moslems. Furthermore, if many more children had been born than were recorded, the reproductive systems of Gheg mothers would have been taxed beyond their capacities.

As table 1 reveals, 1060 Ghegs married 1375 women. Three-fourths of the men had but one wife each, the rest anywhere from 2 to 6. A third of all Moslems married more than once, compared to a sixth of Catholics. The greater plurality on the part of the Moslems reflects the greater fertility of the soil in the eastern tribes, which are almost wholly Moslem, and where a man can afford more wives and feed more children. The wholly Catholic tribes, Mirdita and Dukagin, are the poorest in Ghegnia. Where the Catholics and Moslems live together in about equal numbers, the Catholics marry as many wives as the Moslems. In fact, in Puka the Catholics had more. Religion, therefore, has little to do with the total number of wives a man marries, although it may have something to do with the number to whom he is married at one time.

Our statistics give us a little help in finding out why 256 Ghegs married more than one wife. In 82 cases, or 32 per cent, the first wife failed to provide her husband with an heir, although in 28 of these cases, or 11 per cent, she did produce one or more daughters. Since we do not know the date of birth of each child, we cannot be sure that some of the first wives who bore sons did not do so after a second wife had been taken, and the ratio of plural marriages concluded for this reason may be higher than our figures indicate. Some of our records reveal marriage after marriage without issue, until finally, the fourth or even the sixth wife bears a son. One can almost hear the gunfire and rejoicing.

Our intertribal mixtures, in 5 cases out of 9, were men whose fathers had taken more than one wife each. Of the 4 Has men whose mothers had come from Podrima, 3 had been reared in polygynous families. These figures strongly indicate a political motivation. The custom of taking plural wives from alien tribes in order to strengthen alliances is a widespread one, and goes back to the days of Solomon. Our figures are not suited to reveal the exact instance of this kind of exogamy.

These 2 reasons probably account for nearly a half of all plural marriages. The other half can easily have been caused by accommodations to untimely deaths. Upon the death of a man, the levirate might give one of his kinsmen a second wife. Upon the death of a woman, her husband would remarry, were he able. What with difficult deliveries, puerperal fever, and general exhaustion from having borne too many children in rapid succession, death must have taken many of the women listed in our series at an early age.

The figures on children show that 1060 fathers, through the agency of 1375 wives, produced 5466 offspring who lived long enough for our subjects to remember them. This yields an average of 5.2 children per family, of whom 3399, or 62 per cent, were boys. Thus the average Gheg householder had 3.2 boys to help work his farm. He had only 2.0 daughters to sell in marriage. This birth rate is so high that a considerable population pressure is created. It varies from 4.2 in Mati to 6.6 in Malsia e Madhe, with the largest families on either side of the mountains, the smallest in the middle. Even the smallest are too large for the landscape to feed without a change in methods of land utilization, a change which has not yet arrived.

In the country near Scutari, the city will take some of the excess. In the lands east of the Black Drin, migration onto the plain used to be possible, and habitual. Cvijič has shown[2] how, along the entire Dinaric chain, there has been for centuries a steady flow of population out of the mountains. In the center of the mountains, however, such emigration is not easy. Particularly in the old days when Catholics were not

[2]Cvijič, 1918.

welcome in Moslem territory, the mountain people had to stay at home. There is only one universal, immemorial method of disposing of excess population under these circumstances. That is the method found in the Rif, in the Caucasus, in the Kafir country of Afghanistan, and in many other places—feuding. If enough males are killed off, the population remains constant.

Males only are killed. A few statistics on deaths by violence are available.[3] During the period 1901-05 the ratios in a number of northern communities were Toplana, 39 per cent; Dushman, 23 per cent; Spaç, 32 per cent; Shala, 26 per cent; Orosh, 21 per cent; Nikaj, Shoshi, and Kačinari, 25 per cent each. Double these figures and one finds between 42 per cent and 64 per cent of males dying in internecine warfare. As if some natural mechanism were deliberately trying to compensate for this onesided loss, we find a sex ratio of 163 male births to every 100 females born.

Sex ratios of this magnitude have been found before in feuding countries, and in fact the ratio of male births has been shown to rise in our own country in time of war. The biological explanation[4] is that people living under conditions of warfare marry and produce children at an earlier age than they would in time of peace. Some mechanism upon which all biologists do not agree selects the sperm cells, or the fertilized eggs, in the mother's reproductive organs. That is why firstborn children tend preponderantly to be boys. It is the age of the mother that counts. In northern Albania, girls are married as soon as they come to sexual maturity and begin bearing children as soon as they are biologically able. There is no time of peace.

These statistics, though not complete,

help round out the picture drawn in the earlier chapters. All of these things fit together: the environment; the techniques of making a living on the specific kind of landscape; the division of labor between the sexes; the economic unity of the patriarchal household; its independence of similar households; the division of labor between mountain and town; the consequent absence of any need for a technological division of labor among the mountaineers; the difficulty and limitation of travel and transport; the struggle for life within an ever-increasing population; the consequent mechanisms of population control, consisting in some of the border tribes of a certain amount of emigration, but, by and large, taken care of by the time-honored technique of feuds and reciprocal murder, to which the whole system of marriage, and its biological compensations, are adjusted. They show, without question, the truth of the main point of this paper so far, that the Mountains of Giants form a genetic area peculiarly closed to outside influence.

We stated in our discourse on marriage that a boy might not marry a girl with whom he could trace any common patrilineal descent. That statement needs elucidation. Actually the Ghegs are divided up into a number of mutually exclusive gentes, called *fis*, based on traditions of common ancestry, complete with origin myths. The extent to which the myths are historically accurate probably depends on how far back the particular *fis* goes. Each *fis* is said to have been derived from a single man, usually someone who came into the country at one time or another, although a few are believed to have been descended from aborigines.

The most numerous and best known *fis* in Ghegnia is that of Dukagin. This includes the 3 *bairaks* of Orosh, Spaç and Kushnen, which constitute three-fifths of Mirdita, as well as Shoshi and

---

[3]Nopcsa, 1925. Data compiled by the Catholic clergy.
[4]Gates, 1946, vol. 2, pp. 872-73; Little, 1919, pp. 127-30.

Shala in the tribe which bears the Dukagin name. There are 2 origin myths, one told in Dukagin, the other in Mirdita.

According to the first legend, 3 brothers came from a place called Marina near Jakova. One carried a winnowing sieve (*shosh*) and became the ancestor of Shoshi. The other carried a saddle (*shal*) and sired Shala. The third carried nothing, said, "*Mir dit*" (Good day) and walked away. His descendants are the people of Mirdita. The Mirdita people tell a more detailed story. They list 5 brothers, Shosh and Shal as before, named for the objects they carried, and 3 others who settled Mirdita—Orosh, Spaç, and Kushnen. The meaning of these words is obscure.[5]

In Mirdita where these 3 brothers settled they found other people ahead of them, the ancestors of the inhabitants of the 2 remaining *bairaks* of Dibri and Fan. Dibri and Fan had several kinship lines each, hence each consists of a number of *fis*. Orosh, Spaç, and Kushnen *bairaks* form a single exogamic unit today. They take their wives from Dibri and Fan, from the Christian *bairaks* of Selita and Kthella in Mati, and they did from Lura before they fell in blood with them. They also marry Christian women from the 7 *bairaks* of Puka. No man from Orosh, Spaç, and Kushnen can marry any woman from these 3 *bairaks*, or from Shoshi or Shala.

Shoshi and Shala form an isolated geographical unit, with Shala at the high and Shoshi at the low end of an enclosed upland valley. It is not easy to enter or leave this area. Hence the

marriage restrictions between the two, if they ever existed, have disappeared, and Shoshi men regularly marry Shala women, and vice versa. The local rationalization is that over a hundred generations have passed since the time of the 2 ancestral brothers, long enough to remove any trace of consanguinity. By the same token they could theoretically marry their fellow *fis* members from Mirdita, except that the Mirdites would not agree. In any case the 2 tribes are so far apart, and so isolated, that the occasion would not arise. Shosh and Shala, like their brothers, found aborigines in their valley; with the descendants of these earlier residents they too can form convenient short-distance unions.

Merturi and Nikaj, the 2 Catholic *bairaks* of Malsia e Jakovës (the other Catholics, those of Krasniqi, migrated en masse some 30 or more years previously to Jakova) regularly intermarry, back and forth, like Shoshi and Shala. In general the larger exogamous units are found among Catholics, the smaller among Moslems. Most Moslems feel that 7 generations distance between kin is enough to permit marriage, which means that brides are usually taken from nearer home. North of the Drin, and in Mirdita, even when there are several intermarriageable *fis* in a single village, village exogamy is required. In the Moslem tribes to the south and east this is said to be unnecessary. In the town of Gur i Bardh, in Mati, we were told that village endogamy is usual. There can be little question that the Catholic system as practised in Mirdita, Dukagin, and Merturi-Nikaj is historically the older, and is the more closely associated with isolation and intense feuding.

In the next chapter we will go into detail on the number and locations of various *fis*. Here it is enough to state the principle, amply demonstrated by the evidence, that where there has been little

---

[5]The Mirdites claim that *spaç* meant "sickle," *kushnen*, "pitchfork." I did not learn what *orosh* was supposed to mean, nor can my Albanian friends in Boston identify it. *Orosh* may, however, be the same as Urosh, a Slavic name, borne by the son of the Tzar Dushan, who despoiled the lower Drin country at the end of the 14th century. It is obvious that these contemporary translations of the ancestral names are apocryphal.

travel and a minimum of immigration, one finds single kinship groups occupying wide areas, as in the cases just mentioned. Where there has been more travel and moving around and changing of domicile, one finds many little kinship units in a relatively small area. Thus in Puka, where the main highway passes, there are dozens of *fis*, of a few households each, and the same is true in the more traveled parts of Luma and Dibra, and in the neighborhood of Scutari.

The *fis*, as we have seen, is the basic unit of exogamy. Like all human institutions and aggregations it is a mobile unit, never completely static. It changes with local needs. We have seen how in Dukagin the local geographical requirements split a *fis*, and how in the relatively less warlike Moslem areas with a reduction in need for extended exogamy, the device of a 7-generation distance was innovated, while village exogamy disappeared. So far we are dealing with reductions in exogamy. However, there are instances in which the opposite occurs, and the incest group is extended. Two ritual mechanisms provide for this, blood brotherhood and godfatherhood.

When 2 men become close friends and allies, and find themselves in need of each other's assistance, particularly in feuds, their relationship becomes similar to that of brothers, which is an extremely close one. It is therefore considered necessary that they make this relationship legal, which they do by means of a simple ceremony. The 2 men prick their fingers with knives, and either lick each other's blood, or bleed mutually into a cup of *raki*, which both drink. Once this has been done they are one in blood, and their children cannot marry each other. The other rite, godfatherhood, has its motivation in exactly the same circumstances; but it is made to coincide with another rite of passage, that of the first haircut of a baby boy, the son of one of the participants. The father, child, and prospective godfather meet outdoors, in the presence of other kin. The godfather holds the boy in his lap, and snips off 4 locks of hair, if Christian, and 3, if Moslem. The difference lies in the refusal of the Moslem to make the sign of the cross. The godfather then burns the hair. A feast follows, during which the godfather gives the father a present of cash, the father reciprocating with a gift of fine clothing.

Both of these rites place the descendants of the 2 principals in an incest relationship. They do not, however, apply to collateral kin, for if *A* and *B* become blood brothers or godfathers, *A*'s brother's son can still wed *B*'s daughter, while *A*'s son cannot. This complicates the picture beyond this simple *fis* system and provides a number of special relationships to meet individual requirements. Needless to say, the local Catholic clergy frown on both these practices.

Politics and Feuding

T HE smallest political institution in tribal Gheg society is the household, the extended family living together, which is also an economic institution. The head of the household is the oldest male of the parental or grandparental generation, the patriarch. So strong is the feeling for age-grading in Albania that men will obey their fathers as faithfully at 40 and 50 as in their teens. Since all sons do not necessarily live with their fathers, but some may occupy separate houses, the institution of the household may thus be expanded spatially, although the relationships are maintained.

The household is a unit of warfare; when a man commits murder within his own tribe, his household suffers together. In seeking vengeance, a man can wipe out the blot on his family honor by killing the brother of his enemy; responsibility is held to be collective. If one member of a household kills another, which happens but very rarely,[1] nothing is done. The loss is that of the family.

The next unit is the village. It may be a compact group of houses, surrounded by its farmland and pasture; or it may consist of isolated homesteads, each in its own land. The latter is the more usual form. In either case, it has some central building, a mosque or a church; or it may merely have a flat place, usually shaded by an oak, where the elders meet. Each village is supposed to have 12 elders, whose office is partly hereditary, partly elective. Various families habitually furnish one man each to fill this position. The word for elder is *plak*, which Miss Durham traces back to the time of Strabo.[2] One of these elders is the *kryeplak*, literally, head elder. In one village in Has, when I measured the *kryeplak*, he told the recorder that he was "mayor" of the village. He calls the elders together when events arise that need their attention. These include the use of tribal lands, decisions whether or not to burn forest to make pasture, etc., although such matters usually involve several villages. The elders also convene as witnesses in oath-taking.

Above the village is the *bairak* (Turkish for banner, standard), a geographical area with some kind of natural unity, so that the people living in it habitually see more of each other than of those without. All of the village councils meet together for the *bairak* council, under the *bairaktar* (standard-bearer), or head of the *bairak*. His office is hereditary in certain families. King Zog's father was *bairaktar* of Mat, the principal *bairak*

of Mati; in Dibra Major Çen Eleze, who acted as host to our expedition, was one *bairaktar*, while Murat Kaloshi, his rival, was another. These men were great feudal leaders, maintaining large households of armed men, and dispensing lavish hospitality to all comers. Çen Eleze had sent two of his sons to the American Technical School in Tirana, where they learned modern agricultural methods as well as perfect English. These boys, huge fellows over 6 feet 3, were of great help to us when we visited Slatina.

The *bairaktar* can become an independent sovereign if he has a strong enough personality and if the tribal authority is weak, and that of the central government likewise. At other times he is under the authority of the head of the tribe, an official chosen from a ruling household, and bearing a different title in each tribe. In Mirdita he is called *Kapedan* (Captain); in Puka, *Shpij e Krye Ziut* (Black-Head House); in Malsia e Madhe, *Shpij e Madhe* (Big House), the exact equivalent of the ancient Egyptian *per āa*, or Pharaoh.

Fifty men, comprising 5 per cent of our metrical series, were office-holders in the Gheg tribal system. Eleven[3] were elders, 26 chief elders,[4] 8 *bairaktars*,[5] and 5 retainers of a tribal prince, Jon Markajon of Mirdita. Except for the chief elder of Karashegeç in Has, who was a baker, all of the elders, chief elders, and *bairaktars* were farmers. The baker was "mayor" of a village of bakers, outside the mountain area. All of these men were locals, born of local fathers and mothers taken from within the father's tribe. Preferences are thus shown for (a) agriculture as against

[1]Miss Durham gives one instance from Dukagin (Durham, 1928, pp. 69-70).

[2]Durham, 1928, p. 14.

[3]Four from Dukagin, 2 Puka, 4 Mirdita, 1 Zadrima.

[4]Nine from Malsia e Madhe, 1 Has, 4 Mirdita, 4 Zadrima, 3 Mati, and 1 Dibra.

[5]Three from Malsia e Madhe, 1 Malsia e Jakovës, 1 Puka, 1 Mirdita, 2 Dibra. All of these except the Mirdita man bore reserve titles.

handicrafts or trade, and (b) local as against outside descent.

Jon Markajon, the only tribal chief whom we met, and who entertained us very well at his capital in Orosh, would not allow us to measure him, although he summoned all of his subjects from nearby villages. The 5 retainers whom we measured in his house constituted his princely staff. Three of them were part-time farmers, and 2, full-time political employees. What their exact duties and titles were, we did not determine. The ancient tribal government of Ghegnia, if we may judge by the example of Mirdita, the one tribe in which it survived more or less intact until 1929, consisted of a graded hierarchy with three steps-elders and their chief, *bairaktars*, and tribal prince. Attached to the prince was his staff of special messengers, chamberlains, and guards.

The tribal government was in the hands of the prince and his council, which consisted of all of the elders of the tribe, with their chief elders, and the *bairaktars*. The heads of large and powerful households, even if they held no formal office, would be included. The council met in cases of murder within the tribe, of intertribal warfare, invasion, or other crises involving violence. It also met to decide on its own composition, i.e., to hear the petitions of neighboring *bairaks* to join it.

The strength of the prince as compared to that of the council depended on the former's personality. During the last 50 years, for example, Mirdita has been ruled by the following princes: Bib Doda, a great and powerful man who died about 1913; Preng Bib Doda, his son, who was killed shortly after in a blood feud; his cousin, Marka Gjoni, a weak character; his son, Jon Markajon, the incumbent in 1929, a man powerful enough to maintain the tribal system in defiance of the central government, to have his men exempted

from military service and taxation, and to exact from Ahmed Zog an annual stipend in return for which he would keep his men quiet.

Each tribe in Ghegnia is an aggregation of *bairaks*. In 1929 we found 13 *bairaks* in Malsia e Madhe, 6 in Dukagin, 7 in Malsia e Jakovës, 2 in Has, 5 in Luma, 7 in Puka, 5 in Mirdita, 1 in Zadrima, 4 in Mati, 4 in Dibra, making 54 in all. The names of these, as recorded on our measurement blanks, are:

Malsia e Madhe: Klementi, Gruda, Hoti, Kastrati, Koplik, Greisha, Shkrelli, Riola, Reçi, Loya, Postripa, Triepsh, and Kraja.
Dukagin: Shoshi, Shala, Kiri, Dushman, Pulati, Toplana.
Malsia e Jakovës: Krasniqi, Gashi, Bituç, Marina, Vunshaj, Merturi, Nakaj.
Has: Vlana, Ershan.
Luma: Biçani, Kalishi, Ujmisht, Dolovisht, Çaja (Gorë, a Serbian-speaking *bairak*, is sometimes also counted with Luma).
Puka: Kabash, Puka, Çeret, Mal i Zi, Berisha, Buxhon, Iballja.
Mirdita: Dibri, Fan, Orosh, Speç, Kushnen.
Zadrima: Zadrima.
Mati: Mat, Lura, Kthella, Selita.
Dibra: Reçi, Stashani, Sheheri Poshtar, Sheheri Epert.

This list cannot be wrong in the cases of Puka and Mirdita, for the members of these tribes use the names *shtat bairaket* and *pes bairaket*, meaning *seven bairaks* and *five bairaks*, to designate their tribes. In Luma, Malsia e Jakovës, and Malsia e Madhe the picture is complicated by the presence of the Yugoslav-Albanian border, which not only cuts through *bairaks*, but has caused wholesale migrations and flights within the lifetimes of the subjects measured. Dozens of *fis* of a few households each have shifted about, and it is hard to tell to which *bairak* each belonged at the time the series was measured.

Under the tribal system warfare was almost continuous. The underlying cause was of course population pressure. The overt causes were seduction, theft of women, elopement, cattle-stealing, and general raiding. It did not take much to give offense, particularly in the late winter, when food was scarce. Even a man who had almost enough to eat himself would be under severe tension, because of the general nervous strain of his kinsmen and dependents, and consequent maladjustment within the household.

A chance blow, a harsh word, even a play on words which is very easy in Shqip, or above all a cruel joke—these seemingly minor conflicts often led to gunplay and murder, with consequent feuding. I had several occasions to feel their Iron Age wit, so much like that of the Norse sagas. Once my host in Zadrima remarked, in front of many people, that I had the skinniest legs he had ever seen, and wondered how I could walk. The assembled company burst into Homeric roars. On another occasion, in a Puka *han*, I lifted my head suddenly and hit it a sound smack on a protruding nail, partially stunning myself in the process. This was the funniest thing in the world. Once again, when Farnsworth and I crawled into our sleeping bags for the night, the whole household laughed and laughed. When we asked what was the matter, they said, "Just think, if the house should catch on fire! You wouldn't be able to get out of those sacks, Ha! Ha! Ha!"

What happens when a man kills another of the same tribe can best be learned from the following quotation from Miss Durham.[6]

Murder may be the result of a quarrel or it may be a blood-feud, the cause of which is more or less remote. In either case the man who has taken blood flies at once to a safe place outside the tribe. [Miss Durham is using "tribe" in the restricted sense, as before.] Any house is bound to give him hospitality. In the case of a feud, he is regarded as a most unfortunate man who has but done his

duty. He at once proclaims his deed. The headmen of his tribe then meet and order his house to be burnt. Among the Dukagini the council has power also to destroy his crops, cut down his fruit trees, slaughter his beasts, and condemn the land to lie unworked for a term of years. An incredible amount of food-stuff is thus wasted. In this group not only the man who has taken blood, but all the males of his "house," are liable for blood, so they, too, have to fly. The "house" is the home maybe of a whole family community—forty people. But the law is carried out to the last letter. Such desolated spots have I seen. But "It is the Canon, so must be obeyed," was the answer to any remonstrance I made. The women and children may scatter and find shelter in other houses if they can; they usually do. A man can save his house if he can return to it and defend it three days successfully, so that the men sent by the council cannot set fire to it; I saw "a very brave man" in Berisha who had three times saved his house thus. Or a man can save his house by inviting the head of another mehala [household] to act as house lord and defend it with his own men. This might cause severe fighting. The council, to prevent this, then as a rule agrees to burn the house only and spare the property. The amount of property to be destroyed was always decided by the council ... In addition to the burning of the house, in all tribes a fine has to be paid ... in sheep or cattle ... to the Turkish Government. In the case of Maltsia e Madhe this was paid ... in Scutari .... punctually .... The Turkish Government had a certain hold on all the nearer tribes, for it could hold as hostage any member of a tribe which owed blood-gelt and came to market at Scutari. The outlying tribes of Dukagini by no means always either notified or paid for their murders.

Feuds being very weakening to a tribe, the headmen of the tribe or friends of the family would attempt to stop the feud. Blood-feuds of the Dukagini and Pulati tribes are settled in the mountains; those of Maltsia e Madhe were settled in Scutari before the representatives of those tribes [to the Turkish Government] who lived there.

The peace-making is preceded by the "gjaksur" (he who owes blood) sending some friends to the "zoti i gjakut" (lord of blood) to ask for "besa" (promise of truce). This may be granted and further prolonged, and during the truce the gjaksur and his relatives are safe. To end the feud ... twenty-four con-jurors are needed to swear the peace oath with the gjaksur. The plaintiff (lord of blood) has the right to name them. Or they may be named by the "bairaktar"[7] .... They examine the facts and decide if peace can be made and on what terms. If all twenty-four agree to take the peace

[6]Durham, 1928, pp. 66-68.

[7]Miss Durham translated *bairaktar* as "head of the tribe." This explains her confusion between tribes and *bairaks*.

oath with him he is then reckoned innocent, and he and his family do not owe any further blood, but pay blood gelt to the zoti i gjakut. This varied from about £25 to £50. . . .

Agreement having been come to, the whole party goes into the church (or mosque) before which the council has been held . . . and in the presence of the priest the gjaksur swears his innocence. He no longer owes blood. [After the others have all sworn] . . . the gjaksur and the zoti i gjakut frequently ratify the peace by swearing blood brotherhood. . . .

The oath being taken and the blood-gelt paid, the man is free to return to his burnt house and repair it. Being as a rule of solid stone, only the roof and woodwork need renewing. If he is a popular man, other members of the tribe help him both to pay the fine and start life again.[8]

Within the *bairak*, then, political mechanisms tended to reduce the frequency of murder by making it expensive. Murder between *bairaks* would likewise be discouraged if the central authority of the tribe were strong. Otherwise inter-*bairak* feuds could rage for decades before

[8]In this whole section I have used Miss Durham's spelling of local names, now obsolete. Also, I have left the definite article before *zoti i gjakut*, where it is grammatically superfluous.

peacemaking. Whole tribes could likewise be in blood with each other, or with single *bairaks*, just as Mirdita was in blood with Lura during the period in which we are interested.

A central political authority tended to strengthen the ties between tribal members, and with the numerous council meetings that were called, members of the more prominent families got about frequently within their tribal boundaries. This would give them opportunity to arrange marriages some distance from home. The blood feud, on the other hand, scattered them even more widely, and while most of the exiles returned home, some settled outside the mountains. Miss Durham discovered around Jakova, about 1912, small villages made up of people from Fan and other Mirdite *bairaks*, from Shala, Berisha, and other Gheg regions. Most of these exiles had probably left home involuntarily. The political framework of Gheg tribal society, particularly its warlike aspects, tends to promote emigration.

Ritual Life

FORTY-TWO per cent of our series was recorded as Catholic, and the rest, except for one man,[1] as Moslem. These figures reflect the approximate proportions of the 2 faiths in Ghegnia. Their territorial distribution is shown on figure 3. All of Mirdita, all of Dukagin, about half of Malsia e Madhe, most of Zadrima, and some *bairaks* of Mati, Puka, and Malsia e Jakovës are Catholic. Catholics occupy on the whole the least accessible areas, and those closest to Rome. Moslems occupy those nearest the direction of Istanbul, along the main roads, and in the vicinity of the larger towns.

While Islam is but 4 centuries old in Albania, Catholicism has been there at

[1]Both parents came from Dibra. He was Greek Orthodox, how or why I could not discover.

least 4 times as long. During the last 12 centuries many changes have taken place in the number and location of bishoprics and parishes, and in the number of communicants. At the time of our study, there was a bishop in Zadrima, to whom the parish priests of Mirdita reported; another took care of the territory north of the Drin. Some of the priests, like Father Krasnichi whom we visited in Mirdita, were native Albanians trained in Rome, others Austrians, Germans, or Italians. All were men of physical stamina and courage, for theirs was a difficult and rigorous assignment. Some were Franciscans. In Zadrima, near the bishop's residence, was a nunnery with about a dozen inhabitants.

Many of the Moslems of northern

Albania belong to an extremely heterodox brotherhood, that of the Bektashi. The tomb of the founder of the order lies in the inner recess of a long cave, really an ancient sandstone quarry, in the cliff outside the city of Cairo. His successor lives in a house at the entrance to the cave. The head of the order and all of his henchmen in

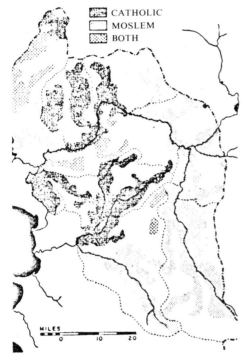

Fig. 3. Territorial distribution of religions.

residence are Albanians. The reason for this curious circumstance is that the Khedivial family of Egypt was originally Albanian, and they brought their spiritual chief, with the coffins of his predecessors, to Cairo with them. Although for two generations the royal family has abjured the Bektashi tenets and worshipped according to Hanafi rites, the shrine and its occupants remain. Young men who wish to become dervishes go, if they are able, to Cairo, and receive their instruction at

the central shrine. That is why many of the dervishes in Ghegnia spoke Arabic, and had some knowledge of other Moslem countries. Besides the village dervishes, the Bektashis have a number of monasteries, located in Has and Malsia e Jakovës. We measured the abbot of one of them, who was a Has man.

Despite its centuries in Ghegnia, Catholicism has failed to change many of the customs of the mountaineers, such as the *fis* system with cross-cousin marriage, trial marriage, the levirate, blood brotherhood, and the swearing of virginity. The reason is of course that the needs which these customs fill have not been eliminated. The Moslem faith permits them and thus has become more popular. Islam is deemed the more fashionable and more civilized religion. The people of the towns, rich men, army officers, and other sophisticates are usually Moslems. Most Catholics are poor. This attitude is of course a hold-over from the period of Turkish domination. Many Albanians admired the Turks. Many spoke Turkish by preference. I recall once riding along a lane in Zadrima with my interpreter, Mr. Frasheri, who reprimanded 2 old harvesters whom we passed for talking Turkish together. Bishop Fan Noli suggests that they may have been Turkish-speaking refugees from the towns of Prizren, Peia, or Podgoritza.

There is a certain dietary difference between Catholics and Moslems. The former eat pork, especially in the wintertime. The Moslems curl up their nostrils and gag at the smell of pork, and will not enter a room where it is cooking. In its place they use much mutton fat in their cooking. Catholics drink wine when they can get it; Moslems care for their alcoholic needs with *raki*. These differences are probably of no biological importance, as far as the growth and development of the individual are concerned, but they do serve to intensify the mutual antipathy of the 2 religious groups and inhibit a genetic interchange.

In Lura, in a population not exceeding a few hundred individuals, Catholics and Moslems intermarry. In a single household the father may be Catholic, the mother Moslem, and the children will choose their own religions. This is the only place in Ghegnia where this happens. Lura is in process of change from Catholicism to Islam. As the latter gains ground, mixed households are found. The government of Ahmed Zog made much of this isolated situation, urging other Albanians to follow the example of the Lurans in the interests of national unity.

Various stages in this process of shifting are found in different tribes and *bairaks*. In Merturi and Nikaj, the men adopt 2 sets of names, Moslem and Christian, and employ the former while traveling to avoid trouble. They get used to these names and in many cases use them at home. In Hoti, the *bairaktar* once led his men against the invading Serbs, with the help of the Turkish government. In gratitude for his brave and successful conduct the Turks granted him special privileges, and he went over, with his family, to Islam. The rest of the *bairak* is still mostly Catholic, but the tendency in such a case is for the others to follow the leader. In Lura, where mixed families are found, the Catholics have given up keeping pigs so as not to offend the Moslems, and celebrate Moslem festivals as well as Christian ones, to avoid trouble. Very rarely a Mirdite will marry a Moslem woman from Mati, but when he does she becomes Catholic.

When the Turks introduced Islam, all Ghegs were Catholics. Almost exclusively, the change has been in the Moslem direction. Hence we may assume that almost none of the present-day Catholics bear genetic elements brought in from outside the region by the Turks or their followers, while the same is not necessarily true of the Moslem Ghegs. *Bairak* by *bairak* and tribe by tribe, as conversion progressed, the line between the 2 religions has remained, by and large, a marital barrier. During the whole period of the Turkish rule, Catholics have furthermore been able to travel much less widely than Moslems, with resultant genetic implications.

In Albania one frequently hears the remark that "the Albanians are not very religious." This is usually said with pride, for the presence of 3 religions in so small a country is deemed a dangerous impediment to political unity. In one sense, the remark is quite true. Few Albanians are religious fanatics; few of them worry about their spiritual salvation. Most of the Catholics go to church with some regularity, and most of the Moslems keep Ramadan. However, their ancient way of life provides most of the ritual which they need to tide them over emotional crises, so that church and mosque are in many ways superfluous. A man's first loyalty is to his "blood," that is, his extended family. He spends much of his time, effort, and material goods keeping the family together and avenging any deed which has upset its internal stability. The very act of vengeance is a ritual, as is the constant repetition of the need for vengeance. The rites of blood brotherhood and godfatherhood are rituals performed by Catholic and Moslem alike.

Both Catholics and Moslems believe in a host of malevolent spirits which pay the mountains a seasonal visit in the springtime, and which can sometimes be kept at bay by the use of amulets. These evil spirits are of course the symbols of the general hunger, illness, and irritability which beset the mountaineers at this critical season. Catholics and Moslems alike attribute non-traumatic illnesses to spells cast by magicians, through the agency of hair and nail clippings. Wasting illnesses, such as consumption and cancer, may be attributed to vampires, sucking their victim's blood.

A vampire is said to be a human being, usually but not always a woman, who can change herself into an insect and fly into a room in which her victim is sleeping. As she fills with the blood, she has to leave now and then to spit it out. A person who finds such a gobbet of blood on the path is lucky; he can wrap it up and keep it as an amulet to protect him against vampires—and incidentally probably expose himself and his family to tuberculosis.

When people are hungry and ill, it is easy to suspect others of evil magic. The person named as a witch or vampire will of course be someone whose actions are eccentric or mysterious, who is a cause of disturbance in the community, and whose loss will not be greatly felt. If a child is suffering from malnutrition its parents may accuse some old woman, and drag her from her house. They will accuse her of having sucked blood from the child, and force her to spit in the child's mouth. Under protest she may spit merely in order to get away. If the child recovers, then the parents are sure she is a vampire; if the child dies she was innocent for her spittle did not cure it. People do not like being accused of witchcraft, or of having their aged grandmothers hauled off for trial; such actions, like the very suspicion itself, may result in bloodshed.

The Ghegs are great oath-swearers. Between blood feuds rivals will swear to keep the peace, on a stone in the presence of the elders. Even if they are persuaded to swear on the cross, they will not forego the stone, which is the symbol which gives their oath validity. They are also great believers in omens, and in divination. Men versed in this skill read the future by observing the sternal bones of fowl and the scapulae

of sheep. I have witnessed a performance of the latter. The bone has its special divisions, each of which has meaning. On the sheep's scapula, the joint socket is the house, and its depth or shallowness indicates whether the house will be empty or full of wealth. This can be used to predict success or failure of crops. The ridge on the blade shows whether or not flocks will multiply. Small holes on the blade are cradles, and the diviner can tell how close to the family, i.e., the "house," the birth will be by the distance from the socket. When you hold the blade up to the firelight or lamp, the shape and position of the marrow will tell where and when there will be fighting. Opaque white spots mean death, and their position indicates whether they will be within or without the household of the enquirer.

All of these rituals are concerned with the maintenance of equilibrium in Gheg society. Oaths give authority to agreements, and cannot be broken until a crisis arrives which is stronger than that which the oath-breaking will produce. By clever use of the divining bones, a knowledgeable man can evaluate the state of affairs in his neighborhood, and give warnings; he can also precipitate decisions from wavering allies, for if he is a diviner of reputation, his words will be believed. Very often what he predicts will come true.

Special ritual routines common to members of both official religions restore equilibrium after the crises of birth, marriage, and death. All of these rituals which reinforce their social habits are of much greater importance to the Ghegs than the rites of church or mosque, which are not as well adjusted to this particular form of society. Another such mechanism is traditional law, codified and memorized as the Law of Lek Dukagin, which expresses the mountain attitude toward marriage and the selection of wives, and toward the blood feud. It serves to crystallize forms of behavior and inhibit change in those who are trained from childhood to believe in its infallible authority.

Still another mechanism is that of art, expressed chiefly in singing to the *oud*, or *gusle*, as it is more familiarly known to outsiders. Singing hour after hour to the accompaniment of this one-stringed instrument, and sometimes throughout the night, warriors recount the deeds of their ancestors, and even of their contemporaries. By using traditional verse forms and a stereotyped vocabulary they can compose new epics as they sing, and recite old ones verbatim. Like illiterate bards elsewhere, they have prodigious memories. *Gusle*-singing stirs the mountaineer to action as surely as bagpipe music fires

the Highland Scot, thus rousing men to heroic deeds for which they may later pay dearly. It is a part of the whole complex of feuding, like that other and minor art form, the embroidered and crocheted decorations on the mountaineer's clothing by which he announces defiantly from the limit of eyesight his exact familial and political affiliation.

All of these cultural mechanisms belong to Moslems and Catholics without distinction. They make up by far the greater part of the emotional life of the people, and it is no wonder that Albanians say that they are not "religious." These customs are psychological means of reinforcing the habits of behavior by which the mountain people maintain their adjustment to their environment, and to each other.

Level Four

The Number of Institutions per Individual Increases, and Hierarchies Begin

13

The Mano of Liberia

ANOTHER American with many years of experience in Negro Africa was George Harley, director of the mission dispensary at Ganta, Liberia. About him I wrote, in 1941, the following: *

"He is a practitioner of tropical medicine who has had over twenty years of experience in West Africa, who has handled tens of thousands of cases, and who is known as a great healer to hundreds of thousands of natives throughout Liberia and neighboring countries. He speaks six African languages well. He understands the mental processes and cultural peculiarities of the native peoples with whom it has been his fortune to deal better than they understand themselves. He has the specialized knowledge of the black man, and the detached understanding of the exceptionally gifted white. He can think black or white, at will.

"Many whites have lived their lives in Negro Africa, and a number must have known as much about their black neighbors as Harley does. But very few have lived so exclusively with black men, have participated so completely in their culture, and at the same time have preserved their objective attitude, their critical faculty, and their power to write. Harley's rare accomplishment is his ability to live in and describe a second world, without removing his feet from that in which he was born and educated. In other words, he has perhaps gone further into the native consciousness than any other man who has not himself passed irretrievably over the line."

Dr. Harley's summary of Mano culture, in Chapter I of his book *Native African Medicine,* will serve as an introduction to the main business of this section.

In the transliterated Mano words used in this selection, a bold-face vowel is pronounced long and a light-face vowel is pronounced short. ε is short. The superior letter n (ⁿ) indicates that the preceding vowel is nasalized.

The present study . . . is based chiefly upon customs observed during ten years' residence among the Mah or Mano people of the northern tip of the central province of the Republic of Liberia, West Africa. This tribe numbers perhaps two hundred thousand people, half of whom live in the adjacent territory of French West Africa to the north.

The country which they inhabit is roughly the valley of the upper St. John River from its origin in the Nimba mountains to its junction with its second tributary, the Ya River which flows in from the east. South

* Reprinted by permission of the author and the publishers from Harley, George W., *Native African Medicine,* Harvard University Press, Cambridge, Mass., 1941.

and east of the Ya are the Geh and Gio tribes respectively, whose customs are very similar to those of the Mano. The country is hilly to mountainous, with an elevation of over one thousand feet in the valleys rising to two thousand feet in the hills to the north, where peaks reach a height of thirty-five hundred to four thousand feet.

Prior to the enforcement of law and order by the Liberian government a generation or so ago, the Manos were at constant warfare with the surrounding tribes, especially with the great Kpelle tribe to the west. There was also a perpetual state of petty cannibalistic warfare between clans within the tribe, a clan often consisting of no more than five or six towns. Time left from fighting was devoted to agriculture and hunting.

Their agriculture had reached a fairly settled state with land held communally by the chief as tribal patriarch. The main crops were rice and cassava, and a little cotton. Implements were limited to the cutlass and the hoe, both made of wrought iron smelted by the neighboring Kpelle people, but worked into shape by Mano blacksmiths who compared favorably in skill with any on the West Coast.

Their hunting was done with bow and arrow, aided by small smooth-haired dogs that made no sound when hunting, so that bells were tied to their necks to enable hunters to follow them. Bows were reinforced with collars of skin from the legs of antelope shot by the owner. Arrows, tipped with iron, were heavy and good only for short distances. Game was run down until so tired out that it took to the footpaths, where it was easily shot from ambush unless a hunter was fortunate enough to waylay it beforehand. Hunting of small game and birds was done with arrows of light bamboo splints, often poisoned. Fishing was limited to small streams and practiced almost entirely by women and children, instead of by men as is customary among the tribes living near the sea.

Fighting men also used bows and lighter iron-tipped arrows which were usually poisoned with strophanthus. The chiefs and leaders fought with short heavy spears, which were about one-third iron spearhead, one-third wooden shaft, and one-third iron tail piece. Head and tail pieces were both socketed; the head piece like a slender leaf with greatly exaggerated midrib, the tail piece like an elongated bird's tail.

Domestic animals were sheep, goats, cows, and chickens. These animals were a mark of wealth, and were not killed for food except for sacrifice to the spirits of the ancestors, to pay a fine for breaking some tribal law, or to celebrate some feast. All sacrifices were eaten.

There were clan totems, usually animals ordinarily used by other clans for food. Only cows, sheep, and chickens were universally eaten, These were used for sacrifices and feasts.

Marriage laws were flexible and allowed considerable variation, as was necessary in an essentially monogamous culture with polygyny as a mark of wealth. Extra wives were also captured in war.

Puberty rites were very highly developed and resembled those of the Melanesian peoples rather than the Bantu.

· · ·

The Manos recognized both patrilineal and matrilineal descent, but the most sacred inheritance passed to a man's sister's son.

Murder as we know it was practically unheard of, but poisoning was common enough, either personal, ritual, or public with a poison ordeal.

War captives were kept as slaves, and could be sold or eaten at will.

Those convicted by the poison ordeal, but not killed, were also slaves, to be sold outside the tribe. Freemen were divided into nobles and commoners. A temporary condition of serfdom was also in vogue, often for debt.

Fire was kept always burning. The art of making fire was apparently lost. Sacred fire for lighting the fire of the Poro and for burning farms came from the town where the Poro was supposed to have originated, in the Buzi country beyond the Kpelle country to the northwest.

The religion was based on ancestor worship, but beyond prayer by the common people at the graves of their fathers, it had degenerated into a system of frightfulness towards the women and children with a pseudopolitical organization among the men.

Food included everything edible, except for taboos. Clothing consisted of a loin cloth for commoners, and a robe for nobles. They slept on mats and covered themselves with a cloth of cotton homespun. Trade was chiefly in kola nuts, which were much in demand by the Mandingos to the north. This contact with a nominally Mohammedan tribe had brought in some foreign influence, but otherwise they were untouched by civilization.

Each family lived in a separate house, the typical round thatched hut with one door and no other opening. Huts were crowded close together, and the towns often surrounded by a palisade or high mud wall for defense.

Government was by chiefs, largely hereditary, but subject to approval by acclamation. The chief was, however, frequently a figurehead, as the real power was vested in the nobles meeting in secret in the sacred Poro grove.

The language was monosyllabic and spoken with three tones. There was no written record of any kind. They counted on their fingers, using the usual system of tens, hundreds and thousands. Their knowledge of astronomy was limited to the sun, moon, Venus, the Pleiades, the Milky Way and one or two constellations. Tops of mountains were sacred.

Man was supposed to have several souls—his shadow (*bi*), his dream soul (*zu*), his breath (*wu*), and his body soul that first stayed near the corpse but later left the body to go to God's town far away (*ge*). These souls were not very clearly distinguished. It seems, however, that his dream soul was most likely to get him into trouble or make trouble for others.

The soul which came finally to be worshipped as the ancestral spirit was most likely a combination of all the others, though it is spoken of as *ge*, the one which stays for a while at the grave, then goes far away to come back only when called by a sacrifice.

There is a great store of folk tales, riddles and parables.

This short account will serve as a background. . . . Except for the suppression of war, slavery, human sacrifice, and similar evils, and the assumption of political control by the Liberian government, the culture of these people remains today essentially unchanged.

Another of Dr. Harley's publications, *Notes on the Poro in Liberia,** sheds light on the mysterious business of the Mano initiation schools on which, indeed, the structure of society in this area, over and above the family level, seems to depend.

* Peabody Museum Papers, vol. 19, no. 2, Cambridge, Mass., 1941. By permission of the author.

In Dr. Bridges' account of the Yaghan we witnessed the apparent beginning of initiation schools, which served both as the mechanism for rites of passage and as a system of education. Both Spencer and Gillen and Howitt described these ceremonies in Australia, while Dixon showed how this kind of initiation fitted into the cycle of winter ceremonial among the Maidu.

In our selection from Malinowski, emphasis was placed on the kula system as a means of permitting regional specialization and trade; little was said about initiation schools. In some parts of Melanesia, however, particularly in the Banks Islands where there is no kula system, rituals and routines of gaining admission to various "secret societies" takes up much of the time and energy of the male population. These associations serve not only to keep in equilibrium a society in which there is much food to eat and little to do; they also furnish a mechanism for inter-village and inter-island exchange. The top men, the counterparts of thirty-second degree Masons, can go about anywhere, and visit each other in safety. A similar situation exists in the Liberia described by George Harley.

In Putnam's pygmy material it is mentioned that pygmies and their Negro hosts go through the same initiation school, but Putnam did not describe it. Putnam's specialty is the life of pygmies in their camps and hunting grounds. Initiation schools which place emphasis on secrecy are just as characteristic of Africa as of Melanesia. In both areas they serve the same purpose, as the following extract will show.

If George Harley's revelations of the details of the Poro initiation in Liberia cause you to catch your breath and ask, "Why suddenly this new note of horror?" please remember that this is a selective work, and that as we go up in the scale of cultural complexity we have to pick and choose more and more within each culture, and that in this case it is the initiation school that we are illustrating in most detail. Remember also that as human beings progress in technical efficiency, their ability to hurt one another increases. Think back over the past twenty years, and see if you can find any evidence of a diminution of cruelty. Which is worse, the fear of forming part of someone's supper, or that of being scorched by an atomic bomb?

Among those customs and institutions which belong to Africa as a whole, tribal initiation ceremonies are perhaps the most universal. Although these ceremonies vary in detail, the underlying principle is everywhere the same. No boy or young man is considered a member of the tribe until he has been initiated by suitable rites into the company of his elders. The adolescent must undergo certain ordeals to prove that he is ready and worthy to take on the responsibilities of citizenship—until then, he does not count. The boys who pass through this initiation together form an age group which acts as a social unit in after life, both in peace and war.

These initiatory rituals are conducted more or less in secret in a secluded part of the forest, though in some tribes the ceremonies are not only public, but even witnessed nowadays by the women. In the old days the usual custom was probably universal, viz. that boys were initiated in secret, so far as the women were concerned. Circumcision was part of the initiatory rite, and sexual continence was enforced during the period of segregation.

In many tribes a corresponding initiation ceremony was held for the girls, and the operation of clitoridectomy paralleled the circumcision of the boys. Both boys and girls were given sex instruction and prepared for the responsibilities of parenthood. They were also taught tribal lore and custom. This educational phase of tribal initiation is emphasized in some places more than others, and is especially prominent in West Africa, where this institution is commonly referred to as the bush school.

The idea of rebirth into a new life is clearly brought out at the end of the ritual. There is usually a ceremony more or less closely simulating death for the initiate as he enters the period of initiation, with a ceremony of rebirth as he returns to the community ready to face life on his own responsibility.

In addition to circumcision, there are in many tribes various mutilating operations frequently misunderstood by observers who describe them as peculiar modes of adornment of the skin, ears, nose, lips etc. They are usually more in the nature of tribal marks, easily so recognized when they take the form of tattooing, or scarification of geometrical designs upon the body. These marks may also denote a man's standing in the community or membership in a secret society.

Tribal initiation everywhere contains, along with the idea of instruction in tribal lore, a supposed contact with the ancestral spirits. The noise of the bull-roarer is everywhere supposed to be the voice of the ancestral spirits, and is used to intimidate the women, who are denied any direct contact with the spirit world.

In West Africa especially, the boys in the bush school are supposed to be in close contact with the spirits during the entire period of segregation, if not actually residing in the realm of the unseen. At any rate, they must not be seen by women. The discipline on this point is absolute in many tribes. It is the emphasis upon this point that makes the tribal initiation also a secret society.

In Liberia and adjacent countries the bush school has reached a very high stage of development, resembling in many important details the secret initiation schools of Melanesia and Australia more closely than those of Bantu Africa. Called by different names in different tribes, this complex organization in the extreme western part of Africa seems destined to be known to literature as the Poro, the term applied to it by the Mende of Sierra Leone.

The function and influence of the Poro does not stop after the puberty rites are performed and the class of boys is graduated. On the contrary it forms a very powerful and secret organ to control all its members, and this means all the adult male members of the tribe. The leaders of the society hold sway over the common men, impose laws upon them and keep them in check by the fear of the supernatural power with which they are believed to be endowed. This fear lies behind all chiefs and political leaders, behind all heads of families and men of standing. It has an enormous influence in regulating the social and economic life of the people.

So strong is this power that it is felt even outside tribal limits, and many details of the organization are intertribal, so that a man of high standing will be so recognized even in a distant tribe whose language he cannot speak. An elaborate secret language of signs has thus developed, which is said to be similar to that of freemasonry.

The religious significance of the Poro should be emphasized. Not only are the men supposed to meet the ancestral spirits in the sacred grove; but they conduct rites and sacrifices of a type suggesting the worship of high gods. Though these high gods do not form a pantheon as they do among the semi-Bantu of Nigeria, there is evidence that traces of them appear in the secret ritual within the Poro, perhaps visibly as masked figures. . . . The information concerning the secret ritual of the Poro is at present so scanty that little or nothing can be said about the high gods of the people where this organization is still strong.

Though the Poro was primarily a secret society initiation school, the upper degrees and inner circles included duties which controlled government, politics, war, and intertribal relations. It was possible for the peers to meet and decide certain things without the common men knowing anything about it. Yet they could not declare war without the consent of a similar body of women meeting in the sacred house of the Sande. A general war was theoretically impossible if either Poro or Sande was in session.

A man of standing in the bush when traveling in a strange country could enter the Poro school and be immediately received according to his rank. The one in charge would put him through his paces, degree after degree, until one of the two dropped out. The person out-ranked would "throw" his cow's tail (carried by all big men as a sort of badge of seniority) to the other. If the visitor was senior he returned the cow's tail handle first, making two times a slight motion in his host's direction, then the third time actually handing it to him. This should be done with the left hand.

The Poro may be thought of as an attempt to reduce the all-pervading spirit world to an organization in which man may participate. It was the mechanism by which man might contact the spirit world and interpret it to the people, where men became spirits. and

took on godhood. But since this spirit world was largely man-made, the Poro was a place where human ambitions used spirit powers for selfish ends. The final secret of the Poro was frightfulness. The all-highest knew enough to say simply: "I am what I am." In the meantime old age among both women and men enjoyed a comfortable respect, and each man had his place in the community.

Under the old regime the chief was not the central power of the tribe. He was useful for ordinary matters, but cases could be appealed to the tribunal of the Poro, which was final. When a masked "spirit" or a gɛ came to town the chief stood in the corner. Certain matters the chief had to refer to the Sande. The old men called (in Mano) *ki la mi* were beyond his jurisdiction. They could be tried only by their peers. They could not fight. They could not be insulted or made the object of physical violence. But there was usually one chief in the community who was also a peer. He was something of a king, and had power of life and death over his subjects provided he worked through the Poro, never against it.

Before initiation the boys were called *gbolo,* which means an image, shadow, or imitation. While in the Poro they were *bo gie,* or little spirits in the bush. After graduation they were *kwɛa,* or citizens. As *gbolo* they were not held legally responsible for their acts. Any lawsuit or complaint must be directed toward the father or uncle. The boy could own no property. If he did, it would do him no good, because once he was initiated all the past was null and void. If he had married a wife before then and took her again afterward he would have been killed. Consequently, if a boy inherited a wife from his father, she would have to be held in trust by his uncle until he was initiated. Any other wealth could be held by an uncle for him. He was allowed to transact petty business with other boys, but he was careful to collect all such debts before he went into the bush.

To him, as to the women, the officials of the Poro were known only as masked figures called gɛ's, and supposed to be spirits. These gɛ's spoke a foreign language in a rolling falsetto voice with a peculiar quality attained by speaking through a "blowing drum," or tube with holes at the sides covered with disks of membrane cut from the egg sacs of large spiders. The boy played with other boys, helped his mother on the farm, and ran errands for the chief and other men. He might go hunting with his father but he could never take part in any activity of the community as a whole. He was like a goat so far as the community was concerned, no matter how old he was.

There were three bushes or schools in the Mano tribes: (1) K'lɛ bo^n, or the circumcision school, which was of small importance if held separately. Graduation from this did not entitle him to any privilege, (2) Di da bo^n, the corresponding circumcision school for girls called Sande in other tribes, (3) Gɛ bo^n, the "devil bush," or Poro proper, where he was initiated into full manhood. Officials who wore masks and others who could not be seen but only heard by outsiders were called "devils" by the English-speaking Liberians from the time they first settled on the coast. It is better here to call them gɛ's, as they are called in Mano. Gɛ means spirit. They were supposed to be the spirits of the forest, or of the Poro. Poro means the earth, or the ground, and by association with Poro school, the forest camp in which the school was held.

It is impossible to discuss the gɛ without saying something about the ceremonial masks, which are frequently referred to as gɛ's, though the proper name for them in Mano is bai. They were neither gods nor devils, but a little of both. Yet it is not quite fair to call them demons and let it go at that, because they were primarily portrait masks of tribal heroes, especially those who had helped to establish the Poro. The founder of a Poro was a holy person. "He never died." His actual death was kept secret. His body was secretly disposed of, and in some cases embalmed by smoking and kept in the loft of the sacred house in town where no one but the keeper of the secrets ever went, unless it was the man who was to succeed the holy leader. He was prepared by fasting without water for four days, then admitted first to one house then another until he came finally into the sacred house. When the hand of the dead leader rested on his head, he seemed to feel his spirit enter into him. Then he went out disguised in the portrait mask of the dead leader and carried on his work. In this way an occasional mask became symbolically the dwelling place of the spirit of the ancestor whose portrait it was. . . . Other masks were caricatures, or faces half-animal, half-human. A few in time became conventionalized as ancestral gods; one, the god of the dance, was identified perhaps with the moon. . . . One with human breasts for horns became the god of childbirth and fertility. . . . The function of these various masks and their indwelling spirits will be understood from details to be given later. That they were greatly feared in themselves is shown by the death penalty meted out to anyone desecrating one, or exposing it to public gaze when properly worn with its accompanying complete disguise. This consisted of a shirt covering even the tips of the fingers, called gana; a raffia skirt touching the ground, called ga; and some sort of headdress, one form of which was a tall headpiece called *kpɛa*. The wearer was usually a *zo;* that is, a man who belonged to a family of men of special talents in spiritual matters, and consecrated to that work. His work will be described later in detail. There were also women *zo's* who worked in the girl's school or Sande. There were a few rare women who were consecrated as men, and went into the men's school, or Poro. Only one at a time reached official status, and as such was the consort of the *zo* who was the head of the Poro. She was called *wai*.

When the time came for the Poro, the town leaders might ask the proper officials to open a chapter in the community, but first the chief would sound out public opinion to be sure that they were ready, for it was a serious drain on the public wealth for the Poro to carry on its work for a period of three years or more. When the time was decided the chief called all the citizens to come home, no matter where they were. The men must be close to the home soil and help make everything go right. The people were in this way bound to their native soil. One did not leave home permanently unless exiled for witchcraft.

They usually waited until the chief's son was old enough so that he could be the leader of his age group, not only in the Poro, but afterward in other age groups. On graduation he would be leader of the young men or warriors organized into a subsidiary secret society called *Gaiyumbo;* later he would be chief; finally he would be a big man among the *ki la mi,* or peers. In the Poro there would be three classes: commoners; chiefs; and priests, or *zo's*.[1]

The information that has come to me from the Mano includes many details of the property and procedure of the various officials in the Poro. Let us look first at the whole thing the way the *zo* saw it. He was very near the center of everything, because he knew by hereditary right the inner workings of the Poro and its *gɛ's*. It was the duty of a *zo* to instruct his son privately in all these things before he went into the Poro. It was the right of the son to know all without learning it under the heavy discipline of the Poro school.

Among the *zo's* themselves were several grades. A big *zo nangma,* or *namu,* was head of each Poro chapter. The *zo zɛ gɛ . . .* was even higher, having power to kill a rival *zo* who was trying to make trouble for a *nangma*. There was a still higher *zo* who had the right to demand a fee from all other *zo's* for the privilege of sharpening their ceremonial razors on his sacred whetstone. This whetstone was an ancient celt, passed down from father to son. It could never be bought or sold, but its transfer to the son was solemnized by a human sacrifice—the oldest son of the recipient—killed in the house of the great *zo,* cooked by his ceremonial consort *wai,* and eaten by *zo* aristocrats assembled for the occasion, the father of the sacrificed boy partaking of the sacrament, with the others. This celt, called *lai,* was as sacred as heaven itself. (*Lai* means heaven, or sky.) Its keeper, called *da da lai* the messenger of the sky, was the big commander of all *zo* palaver. When any *zo* wanted to conduct a Poro session he had to sharpen his razor for the sacred scarifying operations on this stone, edge to edge, paying three cloths, plus one bucket of rice, plus one white chicken, plus ten white colas—a small

---

[1] The term *zo,* is roughly equivalent to our word "doctor," sometimes denoting one skilled in medicine, philosophy, or divinity, and sometimes—an honorary distinction.

The term *zo* also connotes something similar to the English word "lord," as *zo*-ship is hereditary.

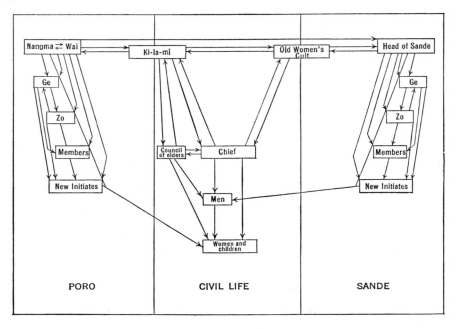

fee, in consideration of his being a *zo*. *Da da lai* could charge much more if he chose to do so. If the visiting *zo* nicked the edge of the celt, he paid one cow as fine for his carelessness. The one which I saw had evidently been worn down to less than half its original length by repeated sharpenings long, long ago. It seems probable that this celt was originally used for the operations now performed with the razor. If so, this use preceded the discovery of iron by these tribes.

When the keeper wanted to go on a journey he asked the celt about it by casting lots. This was done with the split halves of two cola nuts, saying to the celt: "They have called me. I want to go there. If you agree let the cola sit down." Then he threw the cola on the ground. If all pieces fell face down or all face up, it was well. If some were up and some down, he would not go. To make sure he did this three or four times, the best three out of four being the final decision.

If no cola was handy he could use four cowrie shells.

The celt had to pass on to some one else before the death of the keeper. He and his *wai* cooked and ate the sacred parts of the sacrifice—forehead, heart and larynx. The remainder of the body must be completely consumed by the other *zo*'s before leaving the house. During the ritual the "voice of *Gɛ*" was heard in the town so no one would venture into the quarters of the *zo*'s. The *gɛ* had many "voices," one of which was sweet music produced on a flutelike instrument.

The holder of the *lai* could also create other *zo*'s, and provide them with their fetishes and medicines and tricks of the profession. He could also superintend the carving of a mask for a *gɛ*, and make the sacred robe and skirt. Some of these powers he could pass on to the other *zo*'s, for suitable fees and sacrifices.

The greatest of these fetishes was *Dunuma,* for which the fee was the oldest son of the recipient sacrificed and eaten in the Poro. The symbols of *Dunuma* were a horn of medicine and a cone of black clay called *lai zo mba*. The holder was a law unto himself, and begged no man's pardon. With this power, however, came tremendous responsibilities, and the danger of poisoning at the hands of a jealous rival. He might call himself *Dunuma,* though never in public. The name itself was sacred and not to be uttered except when its power was to be used. He wore on occasion the mask of *Nangma,* or *gɛ nangma,* and was the grand master of the Poro chapter, which he conducted with the help of *Wai. Wai* could also have *Dunuma* on payment to him in like manner as he had paid, but her mask was different. It was also called *wai*. She could carry on in his absence as head of the Poro.

Dunuma even lorded it over the various *gɛ*'s. A waiting *gɛ* must apply to him for permission to dance in the town, presenting white cola to the *dunuma* mask and smearing a bit of the contents of the *dunuma* horn on his left heel, on his forehead and over his heart. One visiting *gɛ* failing to do this tripped while dancing, fell, and died. A "witch" can catch a *gɛ* only through the left heel.

Dunuma did not cut farm. All his needs were supplied by others. He went into the Poro only on special occasions, *Wai* carrying on for him in the meantime. His special duty there was to tell the members and initiates the laws which were to govern them. This happened after the scarification wounds of the initiates had practically healed. Wearing the mask of *nangma,* he walked in and said, *"Dunuma,"* at which everyone present bowed down to the ground resting their heads on folded arms, remaining so until he touched each in turn on the back with a bundle of sticks—his emblem of au-

thority. He then told them the laws of the Poro. All addressed him as *Dunuma*. Any initiate previously reported to him as troublesome or stupid was left prone as long as thought necessary. If a very bad boy he was intermittently flogged by *Wai;* rarely, by *Dunuma* himself, using a bundle of fine switches. The boy might even be left all day, and if he was a hopeless case, flogged to death. He then was consumed as a sacrifice to the discipline of the school. There were no graves in the Poro. Everything there was supposed to be in the sacred realm of the spirits who leave no graves behind them for others to ask questions about. There was also the idea that consecrated substance must meet a consecrated end, as in any sacrament. The mask of *dunuma* never appeared outside the Poro. If a quarrel was brewing, he would appear, say *"Dunuma,"* and leave them all face down to cool off.

To protect him from witch (poison) the big *zo* had a small tin of medicine of which he licked a little every day, probably itself a mixture of poisons to develop a tolerance. It was supposed to "catch" any person trying to bring "witch," throw him down, and make him confess. Then he would be killed and eaten. The big *zo* and *wai* ate the forehead, heart and larynx. The rest was eaten by the assembled Poro. Such protection was very necessary against other *zo*'s, jealous of his power. One might say: "This head *zo* has too good a reputation. It is about time something happened to spoil his good luck. I will see what I can do." Such rivalry and poisoning was not unusual. One big *zo* became so famous he was deified as the *zo* killer. . . . He had seventeen rivals to his credit before he himself became no more than a mask. This mask was so feared that a dog was supposed to fall dead on seeing it. An uninitiated person, especially a woman, would also "fall dead." When it was worn into town, a messenger gave warning. All women gathered children and dogs and scuttled inside the houses, kneeling and clapping their hands behind fastened doors. Even the initiated men crawled around at their duties on hands and knees. So one's deeds lived after him, and one's reputation was perpetuated.

Any *zo* could have poison. A big *zo* admitted publicly that he had it, a small *zo* dared not mention the fact. For this poison there was no known antidote. It was composed of crocodile gall (or python gall) mixed with the bark and leaves of two plants. A little smeared on the blade of a knife was enough—smeared on one side. The poisoner invited his rival to eat "meat" with him. This meant elephant meat, the proper food of *zo*'s. It could not be refused. The host then had only to remember which side of the knife had poison on it, use the knife to cut the meat, and give the victim the half from that side of the knife. *Zo*'s ate frequently together, one never knowing when the other might get the drop on him.

The popularity of a big *zo* depended largely on his skill with the scarifying razor. He might call other *zo*'s in to help him with the scarifications if there were a large number of boys, but he would ordinarily do the cutting himself. Big scars were a disgrace, both to the operator and to the initiate. Every man was proud of fine dainty marks. If the razor slipped and made a deep cut the operator must pay a fine of one cow and ten cloths. He could not go and get these things himself. He stayed in the Poro, himself a prisoner, with his foot in a stick until his family was notified by his superior or some other big *zo*. If the fine was not paid that same day, the prisoner forfeited his own life as the same sort

of a sacrifice that he had so often helped to eat. He was eaten by the other *zo*'s, not by the neophytes. He was a sacrifice to efficiency.

To avoid such a calamity the operating *zo* wore an iron ring around his arm, just above the elbow, "so all his muscles would be careful." To make the skin soft he rubbed it with the juice of a succulent plant. To help the boy sit still he rubbed his skin with the juice of one of the *urticaceae,* producing an itching like that of poison ivy. The boy didn't dare scratch. The cutting really felt good. The marks were cut with the help of two tiny hooks like fish hooks, or hawk's talons made of iron. With these hooks set close together in a suitable handle, the operator picked up two tiny bits of skin and sliced them both off at the same time, cutting with the edge of the razor against the points, lest points and razor should go too deep. If he was clumsy he was called the "old woman making pots," i.e. his marks were like those on a pot. If he was skillful, boys would be sent to him from adjacent towns, and his prosperity would be assured.

To aid in this popularity he had a fetish—a clay cone to which he prayed every new moon, sacrificing an egg or a chicken. If this was not convenient on the day the new moon was seen he must talk to it, spewing cold water on it from his mouth and saying: "I will owe you this month's sacrifice until next month" or "I will give you your part tomorrow." This cone, called *zang,* was supposed to be as intelligent as a person. In fact, it was supposed to turn into a person at night and go about saying good things about its owner. The ritual of sacrifice to this *zang* was quite elaborate.

He had also a bit of black magic with which to "tie" an enemy's name and so put a spell on him to cause bad luck, a certain sickness or even death. This fetish was a fearsome thing, not to be approached without due precaution. It could even turn on the owner if he did not wash the spell off of it after he was through. *Wai* also had something of the sort with which to tie her enemies.

All these properties the *zo* had to keep absolutely secret. The most sacred of them all were the two little hooks with which he lifted bits of skin. If he sold or revealed these he would be killed and eaten by all. Even his own son would partake, showing that the obligation in this respect was stronger than the clan tabus which forbade any eating of one's own family, though anyone else was good meat.

Any work he did in connection with fitting out a *gɛ* was also a high secret. The work must be done in a place as far away from his own village as practical, out in the forest. If anyone should stumble upon him while at work he must be sworn to secrecy. He usually made the outfit in pieces, each piece in a different place. When all was assembled, the *gɛ*-to-be was asked to pay as fee: "a white chicken," meaning a human sacrifice, to be eaten as usual except the heart, forehead and larynx. The larynx in this case was eaten by the *gɛ*-to-be so that his own voice might be fine and always disguised. He was given also the forehead to dry and keep so that he would not forget that he was a spirit—that his mask had the soul of the sacrifice to witness and tie him to the laws of the *gɛ*, especially the one that said he must die if he exposed himself to the public as a man with a mask. He must be merely a mask with a voice, acting in character, and always something more than human. The heart went to the *zo* who made the outfit. He had it dried and covered with leather by the blacksmith, and fitted with a cord so that it hung just over his own heart. One

zo would exchange courtesies with another by asking: "How many *zo*'s have come to you?" *Zo* means heart. He was sometimes vulgarly referred to as the "heart man."

Not every *zo* was a *zo* of the Poro. There were *zo*'s in every one of the professions: warrior *zo*'s, blacksmith *zo*'s, diviner *zo*'s, witch catching *zo*'s, herbalist *zo*'s, midwife *zo*'s and others. A *zo* in any organization was the one who knew all the secrets with power to pass them on to others.

A *zo* may or may not be a *gɛ*. That is a different matter. A *zo* may even defy a *gɛ* publicly if it had been so arranged previously. For a big chief to refuse to allow a *gɛ* to settle a palaver would add to the chief's prestige tremendously. I have heard of a warrior *zo*, who was also a big chief, who did just that. Yet people say that this same chief met his death by exposing the *gɛ*'s mask and property to profane eyes during a petty war.

Just what was a *zo*? He was first a member of the Poro. By heredity he knew many of its secrets from his father without being initiated. He was a sort of nobility. But a child, boy or girl, could become a *zo* if a diviner so decreed. Perhaps the child was sickly, or fretful. If the diviner said, "It is because he is a *zo* and has not been properly treated," the parents would hasten to the big *zo* and ask him to make for the child a *mæⁿ*, which is a small mask about two inches long, not to be worn on the face. Then they presented it to the child, saying: "We did not know you were a *zo*. Now that we know, we will be good to you." Such a child was supposed to have easy access to the spirit world. Perhaps he or she had a tendency to epilepsy or hysteria, or seemed to have some uncanny power of intuition. These were the ones who became *zo*'s. The diviner said: "the *mæⁿ* is behind him."

The *mæⁿ* was a small portrait of the owner. . . . No one else was supposed to see it. For a young child it was covered with cotton string wound on it. It was worn hung around the neck, until he was old enough to be told the mysteries of the *zo* and assume some of the responsibilities. If there was an uncle who was a *zo* he would be the one to instruct the boy, or an aunt the girl. The child then passed into the other family. If they did not make a *mæⁿ* for the child right away, they would be instructed, perhaps, to make three small *yinis* to hang on the child's neck. Or they might bring the fetish of the *zo* nearest in kin. This *zo* would take a chicken, show the child to the chicken, show the medicine to the child, and say: "This kind of medicine is your medicine. It was the medicine of our forefathers. We have asked the diviner about you. He says you are a *zo*. We know it now. You must get well. You will be a bigger *zo* than I am." Then they would kill the chicken, eat it with rice and palm oil, rub the *zo* fetish with some of the oil, and finally rub the child with some of the same oil.

The diviner might say of a girl, "She will be a man-*zo*." Then she would be sent to the men's bush school, never to the women's. She would be ritually a man. She would grow up to be *wai*, the consort of *nangma*, and the most interesting character in the Poro.

She alone of all women would have her *mæⁿ*. *Mæⁿ* was the mark of a man *zo*. The oath of a *zo* on the *mæⁿ* was more binding than life itself. It was spoken of as the mother of all masks, and therefore the mother of all *gɛ*'s. No woman was ever allowed to bear the name *mæⁿ*. There was a large one made for each chapter of the Poro. It lay on a mat at the entrance of the sacred grove where all who entered must swear on it that they had not had sexual intercourse the night before,

and so would not bring bad luck into the Poro. They must also swear that they brought no "witch" or poison. This big *mæⁿ* was the face of a woman, perhaps a relic of the earth mother idea, just as the Poro was "the earth itself."

Each *zo* carried his small personal *mæⁿ* in his pocket. He prayed to it every day if he did not forget. He *must not* forget to wash it and pray to it every new moon. The water must contain some of the bark of the tree called *gei*, beaten off the tree with a stone. A boy *zo* who dreamed of a *gɛ* or the Poro could rid himself of threatening trouble by so washing his *mæⁿ*. A big *zo* who was angry might cool off completely by so doing. He would talk to it and ask it for good luck and help. It was a nuisance, this *mæⁿ*, always demanding attention. But a *zo* must at least spit in its face and rub it against his forehead, then rub it between his hands and wish for luck. This was an acceptable substitute for washing it, except at new moon.

Just as no one was allowed to mourn the accidental or sacrificial death of anyone in the Poro, so no one was supposed to mourn a *zo*. The public was not even allowed to know he was dead if it was possible to keep it secret. They would finally say: "He has gone back into the water from which he came." No one ever saw the grave of a *zo*. The voice of the *gɛ* was heard, and all women went inside the houses. Then the *gɛ* and his companions took the body to the secret place in the forest, or disposed of it inside the sacred house in the *zo*'s quarters of the town. A big *zo* would be taken to the sacred grove far away where all really big men rest. There he would be placed in a sitting position between the prop roots of a cotton tree, itself called *gɛ* and greatly feared in its own right. There he would be covered with leaves, and closed in with a little fence of poles. No woman even went near this grove. Few men even knew of its existence except the great men of the tribe.

This lore of the *zo*'s was handed down to the boy *zo* when he was old enough to accept the responsibilities, but he must pay a fee to his uncle if he was not a *zo* by direct line. This fee was: a person for sacrifice in the Poro, and a cat with horns, and a ewe sheep with horns, and a sacred agrey bead, and a chimpanzee's tooth. Since a cat with horns was impossible, and a "woman" sheep with horns almost as rare, he had to make up the deficit with money or the equivalent in whatever he could get. The sacred bead might cost him another person, for the price of such a bead was a slave. A chimpanzee's tooth might also cause considerable trouble, as these animals were taboo and could not be killed. It was a real adventure to be a *zo* in the old days!

Wai was a woman, a *zo*, and ritually a man. She was not the only such woman in the Poro chapter. There were one or two others in training to succeed her if necessary. *Wai* should not be thought of as the wife of *nangma*, though she was that in a ritual way while in the Poro. They lived together in the same house in the sacred grove, but sexual relations were taboo. In fact she was ritually sexless, even though she had a perfectly good husband and children on the outside. Her husband was always a *zo*. Moreover, a "man-*zo*-woman" would be denied entrance to the Poro if she was pregnant, or if the girls' school was in session. It probably never happened that *wai* herself was pregnant since she was usually old enough to be practically sexless before she attained full ritual status as "*wai*."

She was not only consort to the big *zo*, but the cult mother in her own right. She had under her the quartermaster and cook, but hers was the duty of cooking the last ritual feast of graduation which will be described later. Hers was the hand that condemned a man to death for breaking the laws of secrecy and chastity. Hers was the hand that flogged the wayward boy lying prone before *dunuma*. If a Poro criminal tried to escape by running away, she simply "put his name in her *mæ*^{n}, and sent a messenger with the *mæ*^{n} to catch him. When he saw the *mæ*^{n} he knew there was no further chance of escape, and came back without protest. Brought before the assembled Poro he was confronted by *wai* wearing her mask. She struck him on the forehead with a small iron rod shaped like a hook at the end, but with an edge like a small axe. At this signal, the executioner cut his throat. (Because of this power a man-*zo*-woman is called *bo*^{n} *zɛ zo*, . . . "killer of the bush.") His family were forced to furnish salt, pepper, palm oil, greens and all the fixings for a feast—except meat—he was the meat. All the Poro ate. The family dare not mourn or refer in any way to his death. In fact his name was never mentioned again.

Wai could have *dunuma* fetishes which gave her further powers of a big *zo*. She had her substitute for the other fetishes of *Nangma*. Finally hers was the custody of the great *mæ*^{t} on which all men swear at the entrance of the sacred grove.

A caricature mask which was a grotesque face of a chimpanzee . . . had also an important place in the education of youth. A strong man wearing it played the part of a clown, sometimes in town, sometimes in the Poro. There was a lot of slapstick comedy and throwing around of heavy objects. If an onlooker got hurt or even killed, there was no protest. In the Poro this gɛ taught the boys good manners by always doing the wrong thing and doing everything exactly backward in an unforgettable barrage of clowning. Thereafter a favorite way of cursing a man was to call him a monkey. The word for monkey in ordinary language is *"wai,"* which heightens the humor of the performance.

It should now be possible to understand some of the inner workings of the Poro from notes more or less as they were taken down. They are not complete, nor are they as accurate as observations of an ·eye witness. They describe procedures no longer to be seen even by an initiate. They are subject to the inaccuracies of any outsider writing about a secret society.

When the year came for the opening of the bush school, the big *zo* called *wai* and said: "This is the year when we should make Poro." She answered: "Where is the chicken?" They got a white chicken and killed it. *Zo* said to the chicken: "This Poro is a cuƆtom of our ancestors. This year we will make Poro. Let us have good luck." *Zo* kept the left wing, *wai* the right, as mementos of the occasion. The chicken was cooked and eaten with boiled rice. It was taboo for either of them to touch the vessel with their fingers while eating. As they ate with their fingers this required no small amount of skill. Every grain of rice had to be eaten without touching the bowl. Penalty, another white chicken, and do it all over again. Incidentally the accident of touching the bowl meant that some rival *zo* would be making trouble for them. The chicken was killed by breaking its neck with the back of a blacksmith's hammer handle. No knife could be used. It was dismembered with the fingers. *Zo* and *wai* then discussed and fixed details of time and place.

All roads through the sacred forest were stopped, and signs of taboo set up. The entrance was curtained with long streamers of fresh raffia bud leaves hung on a fence of plantain stalks and cotton tree poles between two great cotton trees (*Bombax*). The outside of this fence was like a curtain of water falling over a dam, or a low waterfall. It was impossible to see through it. It was symbolical of falling rain, and the Poro itself was the earth —the "good old mother earth." In the center of the curtain it was possible to enter by stooping low and parting the curtain. This was the entrance of the Poro. No one entered by any other way.

Inside, the men built a house for *zo* and *wai*, huts for the other officials, and dividing fences for the three grades of initiates: commoners, chiefs, and those destined to be *zo*'s and *gɛ*'s. In some cases the boys built their own quarters after they entered.

When all was ready, a man wearing the mask *Zi kuⁿ gɛ* walked on the road crying out: "The *gɛ* will catch men today." The wearer of the mask impersonated the character of his mask, and felt that he was for the time being possessed with the spirit which dwells in the mask.[2] The name *gɛ* means spirit, but refers to the mask unless it is definitely stated that the man is not wearing his mask.

Tea blɪ si . . . stopped traffic on all roads leading to the Poro, and flogged people caught on the road after warning had been given. He had an assistant and interpreter with him. No *gɛ* talked the common language, but that of another tribe. This overlapping of languages may give a hint of the path of spread of the Poro.

[2] Hereafter, I shall use the name of the mask to indicate a man wearing it since that will convey better the fundamental Poro idea that it is the mask, not the man, which is doing the work.

Very early on the first morning *dɛ bu gɛ* . . . went first into the Poro grove, carrying the sacred razor and a fetish to ward off harm. The fetish, called *bua,* was a cow's horn filled with a brown mass with a chimpanzee's tooth stuck in the middle. Following him went the officials who were to do the work, carrying their property. This occurred long before daylight.

When the boys were ready, the chief's son went in first. He was called *bua,* after the fetish carried in first. He was to be the leader of his age group in the Poro and afterward. He was given the horn *bua,* for his badge of office, and was responsible for his group, making complaints to the proper official if anyone misbehaved.

At the entrance the boys went through a ceremonial "death." In the old days they were apparently run through with a spear and tossed over the curtain. Onlookers heard a thud as he was supposed to hit the ground inside, dead. Actually, the boy was protected by a chunk of plantain stalk tied on under his clothes. Into this the spear was thrust. A bladder of chicken's blood at the right spot was punctured and spilled to make it all very realistic to other boys and women who could not resist the desire to see their sons, perhaps for the last time. Inside the fence *sa yi gɛ* and two assistants, all masked, caught the boys in midair, and dropped a heavy dummy to complete the delusion. The boys were actually unharmed, and were quickly carried away into the deep forest which is the Poro grove.

T'to gɛ had medicine on which boys must swear secrecy. *T'to blι gɛ* . . . administered the oath not to tell a woman anything, not to see a woman, not to run away, The penalty was death. They were shown the *Kafu,* a tray containing toes and fingers of boys who had paid the penalty.

The making of the fire and fireplace was very important. The fire was kindled from a sacred fire kept eternally burning, and originally from the first of all Poro groves more than a hundred miles away. The hearth stones were gotten by *gɛlɛ wi gɛ* . . . who went to town and said: "I have come to get three stones to carry to the bush." Then with the blacksmith's big sacred two-handled sledge hammer he broke off three chunks from the anvil stone, or from any big stone near town. All people watched him. Then he showed the stones to the people and carried them off to the bush. There the big *zo* placed them with suitable ritual, putting "medicine" under each. They were to hold the cooking pot over the sacred fire.

On this hearth food was to be cooked, much of it sacrificial. In fact, a human sacrifice was necessary before any fire could be put there. A slave boy was brought.

Boⁿ kɛ tutu had medicine which he gave to the slave to make him blind and insensible to pain, for there must be no crying in the Poro. Then *boⁿ zɛ gɛ* . . . took his sacred razor and cut out the liver of the living victim. Then *siɛ kuⁿ gɛ* . . . kindled a fire which did not smoke, using specially prepared (magical) firewood, lit with sacred fire. *Boⁿ bulu kpa gɛ* was the cook who cooked the liver for all the big people of the Poro to eat. He must stir the pot with a stick of calamus vine. To have used any other stick for stirring human meat would have meant that he himself had to bring a human for another sacrifice.

Meanwhile the rest of the slave was being prepared for cooking to be eaten by the assembly. First bits of skin from the middle of the forehead, the abdomen, the palms of the hands and soles of the feet were taken by *bo kbo si* and incorporated in the fetish medicine of the big *zo nangma*. He also took the left second toe and the right thumb and little finger to add to the tray of *Kafu* medicine on which all boys were again sworn on pain of death never to tell about the things they had just seen. The blood of the sacrifice was sprinkled over the tray of medicine. Each boy ate one cola nut and one raw cassava root to seal the oath.

In the southern part of the tribal area *gɛa gɛ* went to town and sat all day and night until the people caught for him a small red-billed blue bird that makes a noise something like that of the *gɛ*'s shrill, rolling voice. This he carried to the big *zo* who cut its head off with the razor and cooked it with medicine. Another *gɛ* stirred the pot. All ate together.

White clay—the symbol of the spirit world—was mixed with the first food eaten by the boys to make them strong and less afraid. If a boy had to go a short way in the bush, he rubbed white clay all over his skin, and called out a warning to all who were not supposed to see him. This use of white clay was explained to him by *bɛlɛ kpo gɛ*, the white clay spirit. If any woman should happen to see him through no fault of her own, she would be told that she had seen a spirit, but she had better not say anything about it. She should have run away when she heard the warning.

If she deliberately refused to run away, she was caught and tied. Her relatives were notified and asked to bring a quantity of salt, four loads of rice, pepper, palm oil, beni seed, and a cow. Then the woman was killed anyhow, and all eaten in a great feast in the Poro. If the woman's people were wealthy or influential they could possibly save the woman's life by paying three more cows, but the woman could never speak again as long as she lived. She was given some kind of "medicine" which paralyzed the organs of speech,

or, more scientifically speaking, she was probably hypnotized. At any rate she never talked even one word to anyone. If she did she would have been killed, and she knew it. She could not even talk in her sleep!

She was made to eat some medicine out of a small iron mortar, which was then put upside down near the fire. Around it was put an iron ring. On top of this, each person present piled a stone. For one week this pile of stones stayed there. During this time the woman was in the Poro seeing everything, but was not initiated as a member. They showed her plenty. At the end of the week she went back to town, literally "dumb with fright."

The bull-roarer, *vu ni,* was used during the first part of the Poro merely to terrify the women. It was one of the voices of the spirits used especially at night when the high men of the Poro walked about without their masks. The men were quite frank to admit that it was merely a bit of frightfulness to keep the women under control.

Another voice of the spirit, *gɛ na,* was made with a set of whistles of pottery, three or four, each blown by a man. . . . The effect was amazingly sweet in the middle of the night when everything was quiet. A Poro official called out in a falsetto voice: "The spirit, the spirit is talking." This happened during the first part of the Poro when the boys were circumcised.

This circumcision was a minor rite among the Mano people. The cutting was done by a *zo* of special standing. The boy sat on a pole supported by two forked sticks, with his feet on a lower cross piece. The juice of a herb was rubbed on to deaden the pain, the foreskin pulled as far forward as possible and cut off with the razor while another man held the boy from behind. The wound was rubbed with strong, country lye soap. A boy was still an outsider even after being circumcised until the spirit had "eaten him," that is until he had been scarified with the special marks of the Poro.

The foreskins were saved, dried and turned over to the woman *zo* who was head of the girl's Sande school to be cooked at the proper time and eaten by all the girls to help heal their wounds. The clitorides and labiae minorae cut out in the Sande school were likewise saved and dried and given to the property man of the big *zo* of the Poro. When the boys were circumcised he had these parts ready. After a few days when the healing had begun these parts were cooked up in a fine soup called *teni,* and eaten by the boys to hasten their healing. This was one of the reasons that the Poro and Sande were never held at the same time, but alternately.

The operating *zo* had medicine prepared for him by *bo kbosi* from the soles of feet and the palms of hands of sacrifice victims mixed with herbs and charred. This medicine was supposed to prevent undue hemorrhage. The juice of a vine was also squeezed on the wound, and another leaf wilted in the fire was wrapped around it. This stayed on four days, then was removed and the boys allowed to go and sit in the water of a stream. As soon as the wounds were healed . . . training began.

Bo^n ku^n gɛ or *gɛ na,* went to town to catch boys who had not voluntarily entered the Poro, provided the consent of the parents had been given. This consent was seldom withheld unless there was some reason for waiting until the next session of the Poro some years later. The *gɛ* of course knew beforehand where the boy was hiding. He pretended to find him with the aid of a pointer made of the penis of the first sacrifice, which pointed to the house where the boy was hiding, and the door flew open!

Another official, who was really the quartermaster of the Poro, had power to catch any stranger on the road and force him to enter the organization.

Gblo zɛ gɛ . . . had the task of killing any boy who tried to peep into the mysteries from the outside. The culprit was caught, tied, made insensible by putting poison into his nose and eyes, and seated on the fire that would not smoke, specially prepared for the occasion. The toe, thumb, and little finger were added to the tray of *Kafu* medicine. After he was properly roasted, he was consumed by all the *zo*'s of the countryside called together for the occasion.

A similar fate awaited any boy who had previously ridiculed the Poro as nonsense, something he would "never join whatever happened," especially if he had cursed it or one of its officials. Another offence leading to death was to try to imitate the voices of the spirits.

The real initiation ceremony was that of scarring with the marks of the Poro, supposed by some to be the marks of the great crocodile spirit who had swallowed the boys and in whose belly they stayed during their sojourn in the bush as spirits. These marks were in two rows around the neck, down the chest where they branch into several double rows going around the sides of the chest to join in the back and go up to the neck again. The process of scarification has already been described as a duty of *gɛ nangma,* the big *zo*. When the scars had healed they said the spirit had eaten the boys. They were initiated, but not yet graduated, or as they say, the great spirit had eaten them, but they were to remain in his belly until his time came when he would give them rebirth, as men.

This process of scarification was not a simple matter. It was dangerous and sometimes fatal from hemorrhage or infection. To guard against hemorrhage, *to kuⁿ gε* was sent to town to collect a white chicken from each mother and promise to take good care of her boy. In the Poro they killed and ate all but a selected one which was fed a bit of the feast and consecrated with the prayer: "Let the blood go into the chicken, not fall on the ground." Excessive bleeding, supposed to be caused by witchcraft, would be prevented by the chicken. This fowl was watched with much concern so that no harm came to it. It was eaten with a ceremony of thanksgiving when all was safely over.

Yumbo so gε caught any blood that ran down from the wounds in a basin. It must not fall on the ground, which would be a sign to the spirits that another spirit was about to join them. This caught blood was cooked by *di a blι gε* and eaten by all men in the Poro, not by the boys.

If the boy was not reassured by all this and became unduly alarmed or hysterical, a few leaves of *fla lε* were squeezed into a moist ball and used to stop the bleeding. The boy was then forced to swallow the bloody mass of leaves. "His blood went into his belly." This caused much gas in his stomach, and he was naturally uncomfortable. It gave him something else to think about. He was the nervous type, and was said to have "big mouth in the presence of big people." The others made fun of him: *"zai bo lu has given him belly,"* (he is pregnant) but no one said he had swallowed his own blood. When the boy's father thought he had had enough discipline, he asked the *zo* people to stop it all. Then they took the bud shoots of *zu fιlι ko,* rubbed them between the hands, squeezed the juice into a gourd, added one egg and gave it to the boy. He drank that and his belly cooled off. All this was horse play; the bleeding was not enough to worry about.

If the bleeding was serious, that was another matter. They took a big pollard shoot of *lolo* and let the red sap drip on the wound. This mingled with the blood and hastened coagulation.

Kala kala gombo was the official who dressed the wounds until they were healed, using loops of bark to clean them and a brush of owl's feathers to apply palm-kernel oil. The boy was told to lie on first one side and then the other, then on his face, then on his back, so that the wounds would not make big sores.

Daⁿ ya boⁿ a . . . washed the wounds twice daily, at sunrise and sunset with hot water the first two days, then with cold. At noon he applied medicine called *ki a kpo.* In troublesome cases the *nyε gε* was called to squeeze other juices onto the wounds. He was the teacher of medicine as we know it—herbs, roots and poisons used as drugs.

If a boy was badly infected and got blood poisoning from it, *mi glι gε* (pl IV, d) called the boy to him, asked him if he was sick, sent him for firewood, and burned him alive. This sacrifice was not eaten, but the charred remains were powdered to make magic medicine to prevent any other boy from getting the same infection. It was a drastic but remarkably efficient control of an infection that might easily have become epidemic while each boy was going around with a hundred tiny wounds on his body.

When the wounds were first healed the scars were white. To hasten pigmentation the skin was rubbed with calcined *lolo* fruits powdered and mixed with palm-kernel oil.

But it was not all blood and terror in the Poro. *Daⁿ ya boⁿa* was the guardian of the boys. He treated their minor ills and regulated their daily habits. He received and himself tasted all food brought in from the outside. He could detect poison in the food and had the power to kill anyone bringing in poisoned food. He was especially watchful toward visiting *zo*'s who might want to spoil the reputation of the big *zo* in charge of the chapter.

The camp doctor, *nyε gε*, was also a good fellow, and was highly respected. He taught herbal remedies to those wanting to follow the medical profession. He was never seen outside the grove. His was the responsibility of the health of all concerned. He even had an assistant to give the boys enemas. This was frequently necessary toward the end of the session when all the boys had successfully passed their period of discipline, and were being deliberately fattened for the rebirth "graduation" entry into the town from which they had been absent for two or three years.

During this time the boys learned to build houses, to make their own farm and follow the trades of their choice. Just as in any other school, food was a big problem. They got some from their farm in the bush. Their mothers sent them as much as they could spare. This would have been enough for them, but their fathers and other men would drop in to visit and enjoy the bounty that was considered legitimate at the expense of whoever could pay. Various officials existed for no other purpose than to raid, beg, steal or commandeer food for the continuous feasting.

Five days after the opening *go gε* the "leopard *gε*" went to town, caught all the dogs he could see, took them back to the big *zo,* who killed them with his own hand. They were cooked and eaten by all. Next to human meat, dog meat was most sacred.

The "snake *gε*" was very quick tempered, and talked to no one outside the Poro. He gave all the big men of the town a mixture of herbs to attract

snakes and told them to bring two snakes apiece the next day. All the people hunted and killed snakes. They were taken to the Poro, cooked, and eaten.

The "bush hog *gε*" called a great hunt. After the kill had been taken to the town he appeared masked, and claimed all the credit. He took the liver and brisket for himself. At sunset he went back into the bush. The meat all went with him. He was the town's chief hunter in disguise.

The "greedy *gba dε gε*" . . . went about everywhere collecting and begging food for the boys in the Poro. "The shamer" went to the farms when they were cutting rice and called them names for being so selfish as not to give him any for his boys. He and his assistants went back loaded down. The "hawk *gε*" went into town and caught all the chickens he could see, aided by his "interpreter." Another *gε* was privileged to catch ducks. When anyone killed a great hornbill the *gε* of that bird came and demanded his share, or more likely imposed a fine of ten shillings for not calling him to the feast. Some were pure extortioners with little or no excuse for making people pay fines of one kind or another. The fruit-eating elephant came and demanded fruit of *lo*^{n}. The people gathered it, and he ate what he wanted, then carried a supply to the bush. A *gε* disguised as an old woman went about begging food. Long ago the Mandingoes were especially disliked by the hierarchy of devils in the Poro. One of them called himself *gba*^{n} *gε* "the dog" . . . and went out to catch Mandingoes to be cooked and eaten in frank cannibalism.

Inside the Poro there was a well-organized community. The boys learned by doing the things they would do in after life. One of the officials who had a tortoise shell for his medicine, containing fetish, was the police judge or magistrate. He was a sort of fact-finder who heard the evidence before presenting the summary to *wai*. She pronounced the sentence or imposed the fine. For instance, for fighting both must pay, regardless of guilt or "who hit first": one sheep, two cloths, one load of rice, palm oil, and salt. They were warned that the next time the fine would be heavy. Then all cooked and ate happily together, the cloths going to *wai* as "costs."

If a boy cursed another he was likely to be turned over to the official punisher, who made him kneel on a pile of cracked nut shells. He must stay there until sunset unless his people would ransom him for four anklets. Another *gɛ* was sent as messenger boy to tell the parents that their son was being so punished. They rushed the ransom back so that the boy could get up.

The warrior *gɛ* taught them war songs, and dances, and all the tactics of primitive combat. The age group preserved this lore when they got back to normal life in the organization known as *gɛ yumbo*, or the blood spirit, to be described later.

When a boy died a natural death in the Poro, he was cooked and eaten, all except his heart, which was saved to be eaten at the feast of purification at the end of the session. The skin from the forehead and abdomen was incorporated in the big *zo's* medicine.

At the end all the boys were washed or baptized by the big *zo* in a stream, or in medicated water with sacred leaves which he picked himself. Each one was given a new name, by which he was called for the rest of his life. They were then rubbed all over with white clay and went to the raffia curtain fence near the town. They could not yet see their folks, but all the townspeople came near the outside of the curtain and danced. They brought

cooked rice and animals which were cooked by *wai* in person inside the fence. On this occasion *wai* did not wear her mask, but if she had *dunuma* she rubbed some of it on each hip. This soup was made in many pots, sheep, goat, chicken and duck, so that all could eat and no one break his taboo. It was a day of great rejoicing. The boys went back and slept once more in the bush.

On or before this day all the parents were obliged to pay the *zo's* their fees of two cloths each. A bit of magic was supposed to guarantee payment. When the boys were scarified, a bit of blood on four blades of grass was saved by the big *zo,* and covered with cotton string. When the fee was paid he gave the packet to the father, who threw it into the water, and the boy got well. If not paid, the big *zo* hung the packet over the fire and the boy wasted away until he died. The *zo* gave the fathers who had paid, some magic medicine to protect him against "witch." This was appreciated because every man with a bit of property lived in constant fear of being poisoned for his wealth, and not without reason.

Finally, the boys came to town, smeared with white clay, and pretending to be new born by the *gɛ,* not knowing their own mothers or anyone else among their old associates. For one day they were given "the keys of the town." Those who had died in the Poro were not mourned. No one mentioned them, but on that day each bereaved mother found a broken pot at the door of her hut. Until then she did not know. She could not say anything about it, just carry on.

There were quite a number of *gɛ's* not definitely connected with the Poro school proper but with the fundamental idea of spirits returned from the other world by way of the sacred grove where the Poro was held. The Mano people speak of the spirit world as "up," but they never direct their prayers in that direction, rather to the remains in the grave, or to the spirit hovering near. It might seem on first thought that the lack of a logical arrangement of their spirits and gods in a heaven of some sort was due to its degradation by their spirit impersonation, so that the men's whole concern was to keep the women and children terrified and to use the higher knowledge of the inner circle of priests for selfish ends. This idea is not without foundation, but there is another explanation. It is simply that they had the corpse as their only tangible evidence of the deceased ancestor, whether in the grave, embalmed in the loft of a sacred house, or propped up between the buttress roots of a giant cotton tree in the forest. It was usually in the last-named place that the remains of great men and their spirits could be approached. So it follows that the important gɛ's were thought of as coming from the forest. The sacred house in the town was a kind of holy of holies. Here sacrifices were made as when the celt lai passed from father to son with the sacrifice of the grandson. Here a great ancestor priest might be kept embalmed. Here the masks were guarded by men in direct line of descent from the priest for whom they had been originally made. It was in this house that the priests were supposed to be buried, though in the case of a big man, his peers would take him away secretly into the forest at night and put him to rest at the foot of a great cotton tree, even if they had to tunnel through the floor of the house to the next house in order to escape the vigilance of fond relatives not supposed to know even that he was dead. He was supposed to be transferred without death to the realm of the spirits. Later on when it became necessary to tell where

the man was, they would announce his death, allow mourning by the relatives, and show them a recently disturbed area on the floor, saying that he had been buried there by his peers. Men of less importance were sometimes buried inside the house where death occurred. A big man seldom stayed in his own house if he was seriously sick, for fear that someone would take advantage of his illness to give him poison. He went to stay with some doctor, or in the sacred house where no one could see him but his peers. His actual death could therefore be kept secret for some time.

The story of one sacred house came to me in a peculiar way. Seven old masks and four smaller replicas were brought to me one night for sale. They had come from a sacred town at the far edge of the Mano country. Once a large town, it had only two huts left. Most of the people had died and the rest ran away from the curse that had settled on the town because the keepers of the masks had broken some sacred law. The blacksmith shop had caught fire, which was a sure sign of the wrath of the spirits. No one would live in the town except one old man who was the custodian of the masks, and his young son and daughter in the adjacent hut. The old man was too feeble to walk or see. The young man wanted to be free to his accursed masks. No other town would let the masks be transferred to its sacred house, lest they bring with them the curse of the broken laws. No woman would marry the young man because he was destined to care for the masks when his father died. No one dared get rid of the masks. Finally, after three days dickering with the one who was to bring them to me, the boy decided to overrule his old father's objections and sell them to me, curse and all. Then he called the people who had fled from the town to show them that the masks had all "run away."

They were all very old, and had not been used for many years. The oldest and most powerful was called go gɛ, . . . god spirit. It had been the first mask in that part of the country, brought with the original settlers from the east. It was spoken of as "He who has the town in his hand"; that is, the very earth on which the town was built. Another was the mi gli gɛ mentioned above as the one who burned the boy whose wounds had become infected. The four smaller ones were replicas of old ones that had been ruined by boring beetles and cockroaches, lest the spirit residing in the old mask have no place to rest. The other five were Poro officials whose function had been "forgotten" by the feeble old man, who had once worn one of them.

No one outside the family of keepers could go inside this house. The masks had been kept in the loft. When the house was first built all the gɛ's danced and "talked." Four humans had been sacrificed to solemnize the occasion. The town had been exempt from obligations to the tribe in time of war. Even when the tribe was brought under the rule of the government, the town had conveniently been exempt from taxes. It was the mother town of the Poro in that area.

One of the old gɛ's was the man spirit, gɛ go^n, who came to town perhaps once in two or three years. He called all the people together and blessed them. They gave him plenty of presents, or a piece of red cloth. When the people fought among themselves in town, he would come and stop them, telling them they had broken the law and must pay a sheep, a load of rice, and some money. The sheep and rice were cooked and eaten the same day by the town fathers. Gɛ go^n might speak from inside the sacred house, or walk in town with a red cloth over his head.

Lu bo bie . . . the gɛ that breaks big trees, was the elephant gɛ. This mask was kept in the sacred house and used when any person was spoiling the town laws, or refused to pay his debts. The matter had to be settled at once or the "elephant" would break down his house.

Gbana gɛ, the spirit of thunder, could even stop wars between two clans. The gɛ was immune to bullets or other weapons, When he walked between the fighters, they stopped. When he told them they were fighting foolishly, to go home, they did.

Some of these masked "spirits" now appear purely as entertainers. Whether they are old gɛ's whose original function is lost, or new creations purely for entertainment, it is impossible to say. One of these, *dia mi a ga* . . . is so fine a dancer and singer that no one will pass through a town while he is singing. A traveler will sit down to watch, and at the end of the day will say: "Oh, I started to go to that other town today."

Such a dancer will have an attendant with a broom to sweep down the raffia skirt. On the tip of the peaked headdress is a bit of magic medicine which is supposed to make the rain pass by when the clouds see this gɛ dancing. It will not rain that day.

Another dancer can make himself tall or short at will by some mechanism hidden under his skirt. But the most popular of all dancers is the one on stilts. He is "the dry leaf eater" so light and airy is his dancing. He is not really one of the Mano dancers, but from the Gio.

Fania is another gɛ not to be seen outside the Poro, but is said to be a dancer. Gɛ fwɩ fwɩ is a very clever little fellow, and his name is a byword for nimble fingers. Yo gɛ is a small-boy play devil, which is nothing more than a boy covered all over with dry plantain leaves tied on. He dances around for fun, collecting a small present occasionally from some benevolent father, in imitation of the real dancers. . . .

Concerning the Sande I know little in detail. It was an organization for the education of the girls. They were taken to the bush like the boys to live for a variable number of months in the camp prepared for them beforehand by the men of the tribe. While there, they were seen by no one except the big *zo* woman and her assistants. This head woman conferred with the big *zo* of the man's bush, for he was overlord of the Sande as well as the Poro. It was death to any other man who was so foolish as to trespass on their territory. Sexual intercourse was taboo, and if a Sande girl became involved with a man, he was killed in the old days. Later on he was merely required to pay to the Sande the equivalent of the bride price.

The girls were circumcised by cutting out the clitorides and the labiae minorae. They were taught all matters pertaining to sex, as well as the art of pleasing a husband. They learned to cook, take care of the household, sing and dance, the art of poisoning, and especially how to make simple herbal remedies for sickness. They were divided into three classes: the commoners, the chief's daughters, and the *zo*'s. The *zo*'s were especially trained in the use of herbal remedies and poisons. For this training the old women and *zo* women doing the work were paid at the end of the Sande. If a girl had been betrothed before entering, her future husband paid these fees. Her relatives could bring food, but had to leave it at a designated spot where it was picked up by the *zo* women. For misbehavior the girls were flogged.

The idea of death and rebirth does not seem to have been so clearly established in the Sande. But the girls were brought out of the bush by a masked official who was greatly feared. They were smeared with white clay as symbolic of the spirit world just as were the boys. They were taboo for a month after they came out. Then they were taken by their husbands, who gave a feast in honor of the occasion.

Except during "graduation" ceremonies, the Sande masks are seldom seen in public, and are very few in number when compared with the Poro masks.

During the time neither Poro nor Sande was in session, masked dancers appeared in public. Some of these were pure entertainers, who appeared on gala occasions to heighten the festivities, but they served also the function of keeping the population constantly aware of the ever-watchful spirit world. They were supposed to be spirits from the jungle. They were of three main types. One performed on stilts . . . and wore a heavy net veil instead of a mask, probably because he needed to see better than was possible when looking through the tiny slits serving as eye holes in the wooden masks. The second type of entertainer wore a rather beautiful mask with conventionalized features. . . . All of these danced in full costume, frequently with a tall headdress decorated with bells and surmounted with a tuft of feathers. Some of these also sang rather well and were accompanied by drums, rattles, and other musical instruments. The third type was the masked clown who frequently wore the burlesque chimpanzee mask, called *Wai.* . . .

Still others appeared in public to participate in public functions or execute justice as Poro officials.

The Poro *gɛ*'s were used in all important events: to stop village quarrels, or control fighting warriors; to catch, try, condemn, punish, or even execute social criminals; to intensify the holiday spirit of great occasions; to promote fertility of the fields and bountiful harvests; to cultivate public sentiment, regulate hygiene, build bridges and sacred houses; and to conduct and administer the Poro school which was all things to all men. In the olden days, among the Mano people at least, control of tribal affairs rested in the hands of a few privileged old men of high degree in the Poro who worked in secret and ruled by frightfulness. These old men were frequently the gɛ's themselves, wearing the masks and carrying out the decrees of custom. Although it is a question as to whether they wore the masks or the masks wore them—whether they acted the parts of the characters or whether the characters inspired movement for arm, leg, and tongue—the fact remains that these old men perpetuated the system, and profited by it. Only a very wealthy man of advanced years could pay the fees and hope to pass initiation into these higher degrees reserved for nobility.

These old men formed an inner society of patriarchs. They were the peers. They were called ki la mɪ because each carried with him always a skin on which to sit, preferably a striped or spotted skin. On any big question they went into the sacred grove to deliberate. Their decision was final. They had an organization among themselves and were sworn to obey their leader. They were men of peace, and settled all palavers by arbitration. They could not fight or be fought, nor could they be arrested or tried in the tribal court, but one could be tried by his equals. They were sacred even before death so that the transition from earthly to heavenly beings was an easy

one—so easy that their death was kept secret. When one of them died no one knew until a death mask had been made. Even then, his family could not mourn until a death fee of one pound sterling had been paid to the members. Sometimes they kept the death a secret and continued to collect cows from the family "to make soup for the sick man." This abuse of power was manifested in other things, and in many ways. All of the ki la mɪ were zo's and had secret burial attended to zo's only.

There was within this group another circle, the ki gbuo la mɪ, the big skin men who were the real royalty of the tribe. One of these men had a dignified poise about everything he did. Everyday affairs were executed with an air of being in a definitely circumscribed area of action with polite rules of conduct approaching ritual. The standing of such a man would be recognized in other tribes and other Poro systems, though the details of the Poro in a distant area might vary so much that the ordinary initiate would not be allowed even to see the least bit of the ritual. This higher brotherhood was very strong and closely knit.

In explanation of the diagram on page 352, it should be pointed out that the chief was the nominal center of civil life, but that the real power lay in the hands of the ki la mɪ, who could act through the council of elders or even depose a chief. Ordinarily the chief consulted the elders or the old women. Many of the more important elders were actually ki la mɪ. The position of the ki la mɪ was half civil, half Poro. This body was the court of final appeal when the Poro was not in session. Moreover certain cases could not even be tried by the chief, but had to be taken before the ki la mɪ assembled secretly, preferably in the Poro grove. A chief could not declare war without consent of both the *ki la mi* and the old women's cult. Ordinary women and children had nothing to say about public affairs.

When the Poro was in session, the men were entirely under Poro laws and influence. The entire organization exerted an influence of taboo and frightfulness upon the women and children. The power of the *Nangma* and *wai* was exerted either by relay down the line of officials or directly upon each group. The lesser officials as masked "devils" exerted the chief pressure upon the women and children, and constituted the only visible evidence of the workings of the Poro on the world outside. It is chiefly with this phase of the Poro that this paper deals. Much of the internal working of the Poro is still a mystery. In fact the organization shown in the diagram is partly conjectural. It is entirely possible that the Poro, like the organization of the Druids, had two doctrines, one for the initiated, one for the vulgar outsiders. In this paper it has been impossible to say much about the inner secrets, except as revealed by bits of information collected here and there during ten years of residence. The picture drawn here is a true one of the Poro's contact with the outside world and the means used to guarantee secrecy. The inner circles have scarcely been penetrated.

It is certain, however, that during the boy's stay in the sacred grove he learned tribal lore and the rules of polite conduct, as well as his trade or profession. He was equipped for life, but there were still many things he could not learn until he reached middle age and was admitted into a higher degree. The old men reached still higher levels, paying stiff fees with each step upward. The higher degrees were limited to certain families. In general, wisdom and science were reserved as a monopoly of the chosen few, and that monopoly was almost entirely hereditary.

I have said little about the initiations into higher degrees for the simple reason that I know little about them. There was, however, a system of postgraduate work in various fields. There were schools in "leaves," or the practice of medicine; "lightning," or prediction and control of rain, thunder, and lightning for personal ends; "rivers," or the demons of the waters and fertility; and finally "frightfulness," or the art of the innermost circles of the Poro itself.

The total effect of all this was ultraconservative. Private wealth was opposed by rival poisoning. Any individual inclined to be too progressive for the community as a whole, especially if his family standing did not allow it, was doomed eventually to destruction by some jealous rival, or even by common consent of the other men. From what I have seen of its workings in its more recent emasculated forms, I am willing to advance the hypothesis that the lack of progress of these West African tribes and similar people has been due in no small measure to their socialistic totality, pulling down and destroying the progressive individual, or sacrificing him deliberately to their conservative ideals. Inventive genius was not only suppressed, it was taboo in such a system. Even the abuse of privilege and power by the high and mighty ones was kept in check by the systematic use of poison by both men and women. To fight poison there was only a subtler poison; and frightfulness was overcome by a frightfulness more terrible still, until the all-highest could simply sit and say, "I am what I am."

You will recall that among the Kurnai the death of an important man, in his prime, from unknown causes, was always attributed to evil magic, and that a scapegoat was found and punished. Part of the rite of passage which the treatment of a scapegoat entails is always his trial. In Liberia the trial of a man accused of witchcraft can attract as much excitement as the trial of a handsome young man for the murder of a beautiful young woman in our own society. Legal machinery and ritual are hard to keep separate.

The following account, taken from Harley's work,* not only shows how such a rite serves its purpose but also reveals the details of the magic and shows how the specialists can obtain whichever outcome they wish.

.   .   .   .

The following information regarding the trial by *gli,* or sasswood (*Erythrophleum guineense*) was not obtained from a Mano man, but from a man formerly living in the Bassa country to the south. He was of a family of sasswood diviners. Since the ordeal was at one time practiced throughout Liberia, the account may be taken as representative, and practically first hand, though the practice has for some time been discontinued and forbidden by the government.

Anyone accused of being a witch and pleading not guilty could demand the right of trial by sasswood, but this could not be granted until a preliminary trial had been held to make sure that the evidence justified the taking of so serious a risk.

When an important person had died, the family of the deceased asked the diviner whom he believed to be the witch responsible for the death. The diviner, who was paid in advance, would not make the accusation at once but usually made an appointment for the next day, so that he might "get everything ready." In the meantime he found out all that he could about the circumstances. Any known personal enmity figured largely in the villages round about, and many whispered rumors that the diviner could collect by a few carefully placed spies. Divi-

nation of such importance was not to be made by the blind casting of lots.

The diviner knew beforehand whom he expected was to be caught by the divination. Of course he could not catch a guilty person when there was no guilt, when the deceased had died of disease and no witchcraft had been practiced, but he could be sure of catching a person who had the opportunity and the motive. It must also be someone to whom public opinion pointed as suspect.

Different diviners had different methods of catching the guilty person or pointing out a suspect. They were usually based on some device for answering "yes" or "no," and by many questions narrowing the possibilities down to a certain town, then to people in a certain quarter, members of a certain family, and finally to the individual.

When a person was so accused of witchcraft he was usually vehemently indignant and immediately demanded a trial by sasswood so that he might be cleared of the blame. Being innocent, he firmly believed that he would be acquitted. He went to the chief, usually arriving about the same time as the family of the deceased, who were equally sure that the man was guilty, and equally eager to see him executed by the sasswood in revenge for the death of their relative.

Each party paid the chief a fee as a

* *Native African Medicine.*

pledge of good faith, the fee of the winner to be returned when all was over. This preliminary trial by the chief did not attempt to establish guilt but merely to examine the facts and see if a sasswood trial was indicated.

Witnesses were called to show where the accused was at certain times and what he had been doing recently; whether or not he had certain medicines, and whether he had ever been seen near a poison tree or gathering medicines of a suspicious nature. He either defended himself or was defended by an informally appointed "lawyer."

If a case was found (and it usually was) the chief appointed four men to prepare and conduct the sasswood ordeal. They were publicly sworn on the oath medicine of the town to conduct a fair trial. The place and date of the sasswood ordeal was set and the preliminary trial was over. The place designated was always some other town than the residence of either plaintiff or defendant. The time was set far enough ahead for the spokesmen or "lawyers" to feel out public opinion for or against, for it was partly a matter of public opinion that determined the outcome of the whole thing. If it was pretty well understood that there was no chance for the accused, the trial followed rather promptly.

The prime concern of the four men was to see that the defendant did not escape or get medicine to enable him to vomit the sasswood. His lawyer stood bail for his appearance on the appointed day and used the time to look into the evidence to strengthen the defense.

The day before the actual ordeal, the prisoner was shut up in a house where he sat on leaves of the "leopard tongue" plant. Here he was closely watched by the four judges and the family of the deceased, to prevent his eating any medicine or going to the toilet. If he involuntarily soiled the leaves, it spoiled everything and a new trial was necessary.

Meanwhile a scaffold had been prepared on which the prisoner was to sit during the trial so that all could see him. It was placed at a crossroads near the town. A sasswood tree was selected nearby which was about six to eight inches in diameter. The bark of a bigger tree would be too strong and give the prisoner no chance at all.

About midnight the four sasswood men stood naked in the middle of the town and called four times if the prisoner were a man, three times if a woman. The spirit of the sasswood tree was supposed to answer with the voice of a night bird called *wona* (Bassa language). If the callers asked for confirmation of this answer, the second answer was like the voice of distant thunder.

Having received the answer from the tree, the four men took torches and a cutlass and went to the tree. Reaching it they took their positions on four sides of the tree: north, south, east, and west. The head man talked to the tree, telling it about the case in brief. "We are here. We came to call you to settle a dispute. You are a tree that never lies, a tree full of power. You give justice to all alike. If you agree that it is true that the accused" (calling his name) "is guilty of causing the death of the deceased" (calling his name also) "show it to us when this cutlass touches your body."

Then he made two parallel vertical cuts in the bark about two inches apart, cut across the bottom, and without touching the tree with his hand lifted the strip of bark with the cutlass beginning at the bottom and freeing a strip about a foot long. Then with a sudden twist of the cutlass he sent the strip flying away from the tree. If it fell with fresh side up it presaged innocence, if down, guilt. As it fell, the men cried: "Wonderful, you have power over all things." Then they knew how to prepare the bark. This was the heart of the trial, but did not absolutely determine the outcome. If the bark indicated innocence, the infusion would be made weak; if it showed guilt, the dose would be made stronger, but the accused still might possibly react either way to either dose; that is, he might vomit even the stronger dose and so be declared innocent, or he might be unable to vomit the weaker dose and so die—automatically executed by the poison which found him guilty by killing him.

Ordinarily, however, he would be expected to vomit the weak dose, or be killed by the strong one. Consequently, the falling of the bark would seem to have decided the whole matter, but it was not so simple as that. It merely told the men how much bark to take, and even that was open to human error for there was no way to weigh or measure the amount taken, or to assay its potency.

After an absence of an hour or so the men returned with the bark. Onlookers who knew could tell by the amount of bark what outcome to expect. The head man took a piece of bark about two inches square, roasted it over the fire and gave it to the prisoner to eat. He must finish it before dawn.

At dawn the four men beat up the bark, soaked it in a standard amount of water, strained it carefully and all was ready. A weak dose was light colored and foamy. A heavy dose was a dark orange color. The prisoner was not allowed to see the color of the dose in the pot, nor could he see much in the cup, for he drank from a big snail shell. The amount prepared was from twelve to sixteen cupfuls to be given in two doses if necessary, one at sunrise and one at noon.

At sunrise everybody was there, ready. The prisoner was brought and the trial began. The "lawyer" for the plaintiff recited the accusation, addressing the sasswood as though it were the jury, and calling on it to kill the prisoner. The "lawyer" for the defense protested the prisoner's innocence, asking the sasswood to allow the prisoner to vomit as soon as he had drunk the poison. The prisoner himself simply said: "I did not do it."

A nude virgin then gave the prisoner six cupfuls to drink, and he was told to climb up on the scaffold. Everybody watched to see what would happen. Meanwhile the "lawyers" vied with each other and argued back and forth. The prisoner's friends at first urged him to vomit, but if he could not and began to show that he was afraid, they begged him to say he was guilty and at least live, though in such a case he would have been deprived of tribal citizenship. But the victim with a clear conscience expected to vomit and kept on trying to do so.

If innocent the prisoner was supposed to vomit promptly. An old woman anxious to show her innocence once drank all twelve cupfuls at one time and vomited it immediately on climbing the scaffold. If something like this did not happen the onlookers would begin to speculate as to what was going on, and why.

Sometimes when the diviner found public opinion against him and feared that his reputation would suffer because he had accused an innocent person, he would bribe the sasswood men to fix the potion so that the prisoner would not be able to vomit. When the potion had been so "fixed," nothing happened. The victim sat there until noon, then was given six more cups to drink. If he still held out, his friends would urge him to plead guilty and have done with it, even if he was innocent. If he did so, they would rush him to the waterside, poke a stick with emetic leaves on it down his throat to make him vomit, then make him drink quantities of water and vomit again and again until they felt that he was safe. This seldom happened, however. If he was going to plead guilty at all, he usually did so soon after drinking the poison, and was saved by his friends from death, but not from exile.

Another speculation by the onlookers was that he or his people may have made medicine to enable his dream soul, *zu,* to leave his body as it does in sleep, and consequently the guilty part of him was not present. If this idea proved popular, it was suggested to the judges, who charged him with it. Then the prisoner would probably lose control and have a violent movement of the bowels. This was supposed to prove that he had strong medicine to protect him. He was considered to be as surely guilty as though he had really died. He had "spoiled the sasswood." He would say: "Take me down, the sasswood has caught me." Then they washed out his stomach and might possibly save him, as the bowel movement did not always mean that the sasswood was acting as a cathartic; —(he had been kept from going to toilet for the preceding 24 hours). The bowel movement might easily be nervous. At any rate such cases were sometimes saved, but they were exiled and sold into slavery.

In fatal cases, the action was often very prompt as though the prisoner had died from heart failure. Otherwise he would have a violent colic, begin to tremble and sweat profusely, his eyes got red, he even had convulsive movements of the stomach, visible to the watchers. He usually died of exhaustion before noon, and was thrown into the witch water.

Far from being the infallible and just "judge" that the people as a whole thought it to be, the sasswood ordeal offered several opportunities for trickery and manipulation. Public opinion could bring its force to bear upon the situation at three points. The diviner was careful not to accuse anyone whom the public would not uphold him in suspecting. The sasswood men were undoubtedly influenced, and their head man who cut off the first piece of bark could conceivably throw it so as to control its fall. The amount of bark taken and its maturity were also variables which might subconsciously be influenced by public opinion working through the sympathies of the sasswood men. Finally, a sympathetic audience might affect the prisoner himself by reassuring him in case the actual effects of the poison were just about evenly balanced. Certainly an unsympathetic audience could augment his fear, which would result in a spastic contraction of the stomach as in any strong emotion. The effect of strong emotion in stopping all gastric function is well known. The sasswood men themselves were also open to bribery within certain limits, either by the diviner who was afraid he had caught the wrong man, or by either one of the contestants for justice.

The small square of roasted bark given the prisoner to eat in the middle of the night offered another opportunity for trickery. Its maturity might affect the outcome, or it might even be a different kind of bark, easily substituted in the darkness, which would tend to neutralize the effect of the sasswood, or augment it. On the one hand it might be an emetic; on the other hand it might be a violent cathartic. If this piece of bark offered no chance for the friends of the prisoner to help him, there was left the possibility of evading the guards and giving the prisoner something to help him vomit.

There was also the opportunity to prepare the accused for the ordeal during the few days that elapsed between the preliminary trial and the ordeal. Whether he fasted or ate heavily might have some effect. His emotional equilibrium could be made more stable by procuring medicines supposed to enable him to vomit, and there were several of these. One called *Nao'ra* (Bassa language) was especially prepared for this purpose. A little of it was eaten daily. He might even practice vomiting, though there is no evidence to suggest that this was done.

When all was conducted fairly the ordeal cup was of such a strength that it could be vomited or act as a cathartic, in which case enough might be absorbed to cause death. Therefore catharsis without death was believed to indicate guilt. It seems likely that the old woman, who drank the whole potful at once with a clear conscience and promptly vomited it, has given us the secret of acquittal. She drank rapidly what was undoubtedly an overdose of a strong poison diluted with enough water to distend the stomach to its full capacity. Vomiting under such circumstances is almost inevitable. But a smaller dose of the same poison drunk reluctantly and slowly by someone already "paralyzed with fear" would as inevitably be fatal. It was most likely a guilty conscience that gained for sasswood its African-wide reputation of being able to catch the guilty person without fail.

Sasswood is undoubtedly a violent poison, even the sawdust from the dry wood causing a dangerous constriction of the throat and air passages. Because of its qualities, the growing tree is thought to have a soul almost human, and superhuman in certain respects. For conducting an ordeal the four men were paid by the losing party a fee equivalent to the value of a slave. Consequently, if the prisoner was found innocent, the family of the deceased lost the value of another person in addition to the deceased.

If the accused was found to be guilty, as indicated by his death, his family was likewise decreased by two, one principal and one slave or an equivalent value. If he was believed to be guilty but lived, he himself was sold, and the value turned over to the sasswood men. All this was in addition to the fees of the diviner and the "costs" of the chief's preliminary trial.

Because the diviner was interested in upholding his reputation by obtaining convictions, and because the potion was a violent poison, killing the prisoner in doubtful cases, it is not likely that a very large percentage were acquitted by the ordeal, in spite of the fact that most of them were innocent and should have had a clear conscience.

There was always believed to be the shadow in the background, however, of the dream soul, *zu*, which might have been out at night doing things of which the person was not aware. This was more likely if the man had a strong personality. Such a man would surround himself with protective medicines, and most likely have a horn of medicine to make him vomit. Every day he would lick a little off the end of his finger or a porcupine quill. . . .

The outcome of the sasswood ordeal was never questioned. It was too highly religious to be challenged. One might challenge the fairness of other ordeals, but never the sasswood. This points not only to the great antiquity of the practice but possibly to an essential fairness of the method when properly carried out and to the belief of the natives in its infallibility in convicting one who knew he was guilty.

The student has every right to ask at this point, what was the need of so much ritual, and particularly of such an elaborate organization as the Poro? The answer requires more information than has already been given. In the first place, the Poro and the Liberian government were two conflicting political institutions. Before the government achieved control in Mano country, the Poro ruled. When the government came in, the Poro lost ground.

Aside from taxation, the principal interest of the government is to preserve law and order, so that people can move about freely. If they can move about freely, they can trade. While the Poro was in power, it permitted traders to go from one village to another, and even, to a lesser extent, to circulate between tribes. This was particularly important since one of the chief commodities of commerce was human livestock. People sold other people, to be eaten, and to serve as slaves. Any ordinary man found outside his own small locality would inevitably be seized, but a big Poro man would be immune.

Human flesh was not the only commodity sold. No iron was smelted in Mano country, and every scrap of iron, to be used for hoes, cutlasses, knives, and other purposes, came in from the Kpelle country. On the other hand, there was a big demand for cola nuts over the French border. The following quotation from the new monograph of Dr. George Schwab * gives a picture of trade before and after government control arrived.

. . . .

Before it was possible for traders to go into the interior, trade with the coast was conducted as follows: At the coast a native bought an article from a trader. This he sold to someone in the next clan toward the interior. The buyer sold it to someone in the clan beyond his own, and thus the article passed to the hinterland until it finally found a buyer who did not let it go farther. The matter was simple: in each transaction the seller augmented the price as much as he could. The buyer, who was very seldom able to pay either in cash or kind, bought and resold on credit. This continued, the article passing toward the interior from one buyer to another, until it finally came into the hands of one who could and did pay. Whatever was obtained for it—usually goats, sheep, fowls, or cattle, if a big sale had been made—then made the reverse journey via each creditor and finally reached the coast. There the original seller "cashed" the payment, and after taking his profit, sent the rest on to the next buyer, and so on, until what was left—little enough—got to the last seller on credit. The time required to liquidate such a transaction was considerable. Everyone in the chain knew the whole story, from one end to the other and back again. The system depended upon mutual realization of profits at each step in the game.

Captain D'Ollone [1901] has left a record of the beginning of the cola trade among a tribe he called the Gons or Ngueres. Part of these are indicated on his map as living in what seems to be the region occupied by the Gio. He indicates the supposed habitat of a clan which he named Dɛos. They were to the west of the route traversed by him and his party and may possibly be meant for the Gio proper, who called themselves Dɛ.

He met two itinerant Mandingo

* Schwab, George, *The Rain Forest People of Liberia*. Peabody Museum Papers, vol. 30, Cambridge, Mass., 1947. Reprinted by permission of the author.

traders at the town of Diaro Bondo, paramount chief of the Gon clan which he called the Hounés, living near the Cavally, not very far from Tapi Town. These two Mandingos, he learned, had been permitted to enter that region because of an arrangement between the chief of the Hounés and Badia Galao, a Sudanese chief who had fled with his people in 1892 to escape the raiding hosts led by one of the infamous Samory's lieutenants. Badia and his people settled at Ngo, a town of the Gons, located at the foot of the Nimba Mountain mass, just over the present Liberian frontier, in what is now French Guinea. He kept in communication with the Sudan. From there his traders brought salt, cloth, cattle, and captives, which they exchanged with the forest peoples of those regions for cola nuts. It appears that the prospect of buying slave captives was the chief reason for the freedom of movement permitted the traders, as the Gons were *"des anthropophages pratiquant et passionnés"*—a characteristic of the Gio. Although they had cattle and other domestic animals in abundance they preferred human flesh. The slave captives were bought for cola nuts. Those not eaten were traded with other tribes until they finally reached the slaving ships on the coast

Before reaching the country of the Gons, D'Ollone passed through that of a small tribe he calls the Kopo's, living north of the Tiᵉⁿ. Remarking on the abundance of cola trees in that region, he cites Binger as stating that there existed a secret society in the Sudan whose object was the transportation of cola nuts from all the forest region to the Sudan "to prevent this mystery of the forest from becoming known." Traveling on from this region he found near each village a circular place cut out of the forest and evidently used as a meeting place, possibly as a market.

He says, "We found bales of cola nuts, well packed as though for a long journey, with marks painted on them, perhaps those of their owners or of the consignee." We have remarked somewhat at length on this, because we found considerable cola trading at the Mano markets when we were there, though the season for these nuts was about over in the north.

MARKETS

While trade has long been carried on in most parts of the country in the manner described above, and more recently by traders, markets have recently been introduced in Gio and in Tiᵉⁿ at the instigation of Government officials. In the other parts of the southeast none had been established up to the time of our leaving. In Gbundɛ, Loma, northern Kpɛllɛ, and Mano, where the market has long been an institution, it has come in through Mandingo influence. Some of the market places give indications of having been established for a considerable time. . . . The market was always a neutral ground where even enemies might meet without concern for their safety and where the carrying of anything which might be used as a weapon was absolutely prohibited. . . .

The market place is usually a shady spot between two towns or just outside a town. That at Tapi Town was held in sheds without sides, built around three sides of an open court. We found the best and largest markets at the big towns near Government posts.

In the north, especially among the Loma and Mano, we saw well-developed and well-attended markets with produce in plenty. The gathering was apparently of social importance.

In Gbundɛ, Loma, and Mano, the name for market, *lo, do,* has become the accepted term for "week." Days derive their names from the different markets.

On market days, before the market is opened for trade, any babies who are brought for the first time are "initiated to market" by touching them to the ground—girls three times, boys four times. (Mano.) We saw this done at Sakripie. Each time the baby came in contact with the ground onlookers chorused, *"Hou."*

Everyone must wait until the signal is given before beginning to buy and sell. After most of the people have gathered, which is sometimes as late as noon, the chief, through the town crier, makes known any new laws of the elders, any announcements of his own, or anything that may be of general interest to the people.

The lowering of a string stretched between two trees, followed by handclapping from the market men and women, is the signal for buying and selling to begin at Pandamai, Zorzor, and Sakripie. In Mano and Gio the town or market crier, waving his cow's tail to include all present, may simply announce the opening. All respond by clapping hands and shouting, *"A o."* A Mano market seen at Zuluyi was typical of all the larger ones, except that this was a more important occasion than usual, being the first appearance of the paramount chief after a trip to Monrovia. On this account the opening seems to have been unusually formal.

The people begin straggling in about the middle of the morning. The market place gradually assumes an air of festivity. People are seated in groups: on blankets, on coiled cloths that have been used as head pads, on wooden stools, on the roots of trees, on the bare ground. Their wares are scattered around them. Walking in and out of the groups, or self-consciously standing near their own, are girls and young women in holiday attire. One has a streak of yellow clay down the middle of her forehead, a streak over the eyelids to the temples, and a black streak from the nose down across the middle of the chin. Another is streaked with white clay around the eyes, looking from a distance as if she wore spectacles. There is one girl adorned with a necklace of leopard's teeth and one lion's tooth, bought dearly from a Sudanese peddler; she has marks on her abdomen. There are women wearing the attractive blue-and-white native cloths fastened around the loins or chest, men in simple native shirts, and Mandingo traders in long, flowing robes.[1]

A Mandingo man blows a whistle for an order. An old man appears carrying a cow's tail. To the front of his blue-and-white striped robe of native cloth are fastened his old man's cap and two medicine horns ornamented with bunches of cowrie shells. He also wears a necklace of large crystal and blue beads. He greets us with three snaps of his fingers, looks over the various groups, greets friends among them, and disappears for a moment.

When he returns he calls, "All sit down. Don't fear white man. Today any people come [all may come]."

The crowd waits; becomes impatient. At last the paramount chief and his party arrive. The people must always wait for the dignitary, whether District Commissioner, paramount chief, or speaker.

The crier announces, "Paramount chief comes. Quiet! Quiet!"

Two iron folding chairs brought from Monrovia stand ready. The young lads who have been resting their

[1] The Mandingos began coming to Mano markets about 1920, trading first at the old market at Busi, near French territory. They exchanged cloth, salt, and tobacco from the Sudan for cola and produce.

legs on the backs of the chairs rise to attention. The paramount chief and speaker sit down. The mustached paramount chief has on a white helmet, a wide blue-and-white striped robe of country cloth, European trousers under it, and shoes. He carries an umbrella. The paramount chief is scarcely seated when he arises, the speaker with him to interpret for him. The speaker takes the cow's tail from the old crier and proceeds to interpret the words of the paramount chief for us.

"Hello! Thank you! New Secretary [of the Interior] make town clean. I come from Monrovia. I see my town good. People say at Monrovia, Mano country no good, no people stay in town. I come and see all people in town. I see market good. I thank you. People have cola, sit down in one place. Why I come and no see plenty Mandingo people? Mano plenty."

A Mandingo arises here and says, "If Mandingo people buy cola there is no way to pass for [to] French side."

The chief continues, "Mandingo people must buy what people bring to market. If they no buy, Mano people no come. People must come at twelve o'clock. [It was then five.] Make no palaver at market. After market go home, cut farm, so we have rice for market. Must not leave fire in house when go to farm; must leave water there so town no catch fire. They tell me at Monrovia when I come back I find no people in Mano. I find many people. I thank you."

The speaker, switching the tail around toward all, now calls to each group, "Market begin now! *Ai! ai ai!* Market is open!" A chorus of shouting assent arises, and again the air is filled with the bargaining voices and the sound of the rattling calabashes and pans. . . .

The following is a list of things we saw at the market. *Brought by the natives*: cows' skins and hoofs; fresh cow meat; chickens; eggs; dried fish and antelope meat; dried termites, caterpillars, and grasshoppers; snails (*Achatina*); rice; guinea corn; Kaffir corn; beni-seed; taro; cassava roots, both fresh and dried; plantains; lima beans, white and red; greens; onions; toasted flat seeds of *Cucumeropsis edulis;* small red tomatoes; native eggplant; pumpkins; sweet potatoes; shelled corn; red peppers; black pepper; dried okra; dried mushrooms; peanuts; bananas; pineapples; papayas; limes; wild mango kernels; palm oil; palm nuts; cola nuts; nuts of the tree *Coula edulis;* native cloth; native cotton yarn; horns for snuff; calabashes of all sizes; rice fanners; leaves of the *bo* tree (*Mitragyne stipulosa*), for lining the braided palm-leaf *kinja's* in which cola nuts are carried; vine toothbrushes; clay pots; etc. *Brought by the traders*: enamel basins, iron for axe heads, cutlasses, pocket knives, key rings, mirrors, perfume, tin combs, beads, aluminum bracelets, small lengths of half-inch bar aluminum for making jewelry, galvanized iron buckets, iron pots, matches, fish hooks, tobacco, snuff, cigarettes, shirts, shorts, cheap cotton cloth, calico dresses, soap, indigo leaves for dyeing cotton, salt, old felt hats, and kerosene. . . .

Regarding trade and prices in the old days, D'Ollone says:

"These people have a passion for commerce and make of it their constant occupation.

"This commerce revolves around four principal articles: women, cattle, guns, captives; these last reserved for the very rich. All have their fixed price with slight variations caused by the state of the object itself.

"Here is the tariff of the forest:

"A head of cattle is worth three

guns, a 10-lb. keg of powder, two fathoms of cloth.

"A male captive: four guns, a keg of powder, four fathoms of cloth, a hat, a machete, a cooking-pot, twenty gun-flints, four heads of tobacco.

"A female captive: three guns, three fathoms of cloth, a machete, ten gun-flints, three heads of tobacco.

"A sheep or goat: one gun or a 20-lb. keg of powder."

．　．　．　．

Markets such as one finds in Liberia are common in Africa. One sees them also in India and China, and among the more highly organized agricultural peoples of the New World, such as the Maya, Aztecs, Inca, and Aymara. In Europe also they were the principal means of exchange before the rise of the market towns during the late Middle Ages. Cattle fairs and other markets held on special days are still kept up in England and on the continent.

As everyone living in modern world society knows, tools are basic to civilization, and more basic than tools even are the ferrous metals—iron and steel—from which tools are made. Iron ore and coal are the two primary ingredients of the metal-producing industry. Iron ore and coal are brought together and smelted in quantity in only a few areas of the world, of which Pittsburgh, Birmingham, Düsseldorf, Mulhouse, Stalingrad, are centers. World trade centers about the steel industry, and political institutions rise and fall with it.

Among "primitive" peoples the same principle is true, the difference being merely one of degree. The Mano, like the inhabitants of Cambridge, Mass., and New Haven, Conn., smelt no iron ore. All their metal has to be brought in from outside. In Massachusetts and Connecticut federal, state, and local laws, enforced by appropriate officials, permit the free passage of raw and processed metal goods, as of other commodities. In Liberia, before the government took matters in hand, the trade in iron was kept open by the mechanism of the Poro, in which the blacksmiths, who traded and processed the metal, were important men and allowed a greater freedom of circulation than ordinary persons.

There is another way in which the same result can be obtained. In North Africa, among the Berbers living in the mountains, where the only law is that of local clans constantly feuding with one another, the blacksmiths form a debased caste, and can circulate freely, for no one will touch them. They travel from their mountain smithies to the large cities, where they buy raw metal originally produced in Europe or America. They take this metal home, make up the hoes, plowshares, sickles, etc., that their patrons need, and sell them in their shops or in the local weekly markets, in which people meet under truce to trade.

The blacksmiths in North Africa are Negroes, or of partially Negroid descent. They are strangers, foreigners, with their own kin scattered through the tribes, and a few centers, as at Targuist in the Rif, where they have their homes. They farm themselves out to live and work in clans and villages, much as Chinese laundrymen do in American cities. They are untouchable, and the system works, just as the opposite one does in Liberia.

14

The Complicated Lives of Desert Nomads: The Ruwalla Bedawin

W E ARE now beginning to deal with a level of civilization characterized by a multiplicity of simple institutions, overlapping in each geographical area, in which the average individual is some kind of specialist served by other specialists. One place in which an environmentally extreme form of this situation may be studied is the desert of Northern Arabia.

Deserts are poor places for the development of complex civilizations. The scarcity of water keeps the population down no matter what technical devices people use. The irregularity of the rainfall furthermore keeps the few people whom the land can support in a state of instability, for what was a good camping place last year cannot be counted on to support life twelve months later.

Desert dwellers who have only their legs to move about with must spend most of their time afoot and have little chance to develop large or stable groups. One possession, however, transforms the desert from a last-stop-before-Hell refuge into a profitable working place for those who are bold enough to take advantage of it. That possession is the camel.

Men on camels can ride from well to well and from pasture to pasture. They can drink milk and at times eat meat. They have a staple product to trade with the settled peoples in the agricultural lands—the increase of their herds. Being mobile in a land where the unreliability of the rainfall is notorious, they have to fight for their water and pasturage during dry years. And they need trade goods. This need is met by a further elaboration of the system which we have seen in North Africa—the immunity of craftsmen and traders.

The great authority on the Arabian Bedawin, Alois Musil, wrote several great books, from one of which, *Manners and Customs of the Rwala Bedouins,** I have taken the following extracts.

The student may appreciate, before finishing this passage, a few words of warning about the spelling of Arabic words. Colonel T. E. Lawrence summed up the problem neatly: "Arabic names won't go into English, exactly, for their consonants are not the same as ours, and their vowels, like ours, vary from district to district. There are some 'scientific systems' of transliteration, helpful to people who know enough Arabic not to need helping, but a wash-out for the world. I spell my names anyhow, to show what rot the systems are." †

* The American Geographical Society of New York, 1928. Reprinted by permission.
† From *Seven Pillars of Wisdom* by T. E. Lawrence, copyright, 1926, 1935 by Doubleday & Company, Inc., p. 25. By permission.

Musil spelled his Arabic words in accordance with a special system, which is confusing to English-speaking readers. It was designed for a Czech audience. I have taken the liberty to recast his spellings.

Most consonants (and it is consonants that make the difference in Arabic) which are spelt with ordinary characters are pronounced as in English, with the following exceptions. R is trilled. Kh is similar to ch in the Scottish *loch*. Gh is a voiced guttural fricative, similar to a French r, but not identical. It is not a uvular trill, but is activated lower down the throat. The letters reproduced in boldface represent palatalized sounds. In technical works these are represented by a dot under the letter. One more remains, the 'ain, an unvoiced guttural, the companion to the gh. It is represented by a raised hook, '. If you listen to Arabs talking behind closed doors, the distinctive sound that you notice most is this 'ain. It is also found in Hebrew, and has gone over into Yiddish.

· · · ·

The Rwala divide human beings into *hazar,* or those who dwell in permanent houses, and *'arab,* or those who dwell in movable tents. Arab, therefore, is the name given throughout the desert to the inhabitants of a black tent only. . . .

The dwellers in houses . . . are divided into *karawne* (the individual is known as *karawani*), or those who never leave their permanent dwelling, and *ra'w* (or *ra'iyye*), or those who change from their permanent dwellings during the rainy season to movable tents. After the sowing of crops in the autumn, the *ra'w* or *ra'iyye* leave their villages and with their flocks of goats and sheep make their way into the steppe, where they dwell both in black goat's-hair tents and in gray tents of cotton fabric. At the end of April and in May, when the harvest is near, they return from the steppe to their houses.

The Arabs consist of Bedouins and *shwaya* (or *shuyan*). The *shwaya* have two things black, black tents of goat's hair and flocks of black goats and sheep. These flocks do not permit them to go into the interior of the desert. . . . They are limited to the territory where there is abundance of water and where annuals grow every year. They encamp on the edge of the

desert and . . . acknowledge the supremacy of various Bedouins, to whom they pay a tax for protection. . . . The Bedouins are Arabs who breed camels exclusively, or at least in the main, and for ten months dwell in the interior of the desert. . . . At the end of June they go to the edge of the desert . . . dwell among the settlers until the middle of August or the beginning of September, provide themselves with grain, clothing, and weapons, and then return to the desert again.

. . . The Rwala are recognized by all tribes as being true and pure Bedouins. They . . . belong to the large group of tribes called 'Aneze, which is scattered almost throughout the peninsula and is divided into a southern and a northern branch. The southern 'Aneze comprise the tribes from which are descended the Ab-al-Kheyl, Ibn Sabbah, Ibn Sa'ud, and various clans of the **K**ahatan and Muntifek. The northern 'Aneze are the **Z**ana Muslim and **Z**ana Bishr. The latter includes the Sba'a, Fed'an, and 'Amarat. The former include the Weld 'Ali and Rwala, who are also known as the Al[1]

---

[1] *Al*, plural *Awil*, means a group of Kin, family, and must not be confused with the definite article *al*.

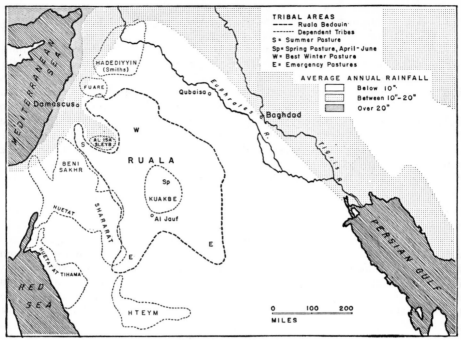

The Ruwala Bedawin (after Raswan).

Jlas. All the tribes and all the clans of the 'Aneze, in the opinion of the Rwala, have a common father and therefore are their *beni al-'amm,* their paternal cousins.

Only blood relationship on the father's side bestows the right of *ibn al-'amm.* It is common to hear such a remark as: "His ancestor was not, at a remote period, our relation on the father's side; how could he now be our paternal cousin? . . ."

. . . .

According to the Rwala, their tribe is known as *kabilet . . . ar-rwala. . . .* The clan and sometimes the kin are denoted by the word *al. . . .*

The *ahl* (for which we shall use the word "kin," in a technical sense) is a group fixed in relation to the individual only, a man's kin differing from the kins of his father or son (although all three kins in this case would include many individuals in common). A

man's kin comprises his descendants to the third generation—that is, his sons, grandsons, and great-grandsons. It also includes his ascendants to the third generation—that is, his father, grandfather, and great-grandfather— and the descendants of these ascendants to the third generation from each. Descent is reckoned through male lines only. Second cousins are the most remote collaterals that may belong to one's kin.

An easy way of determining whether X belongs to the same kin as Y is to count from X up to the common ancestor of both X and Y and thence to count down to Y. Provided not more than five individuals are thus counted between X and Y and provided, also, that the common ancestor is not separated from either X or Y by more than three generations, X and Y will belong to the same kin. . . .

The *ahl* of a Rweyli protects him

from injustice and suffers for his guilt. The representative of his blood relationship is likewise known as *ahl*. This representative, that is, the *ahl* in the narrower sense of the word, is usually either the father, the uncle, or the elder brother. . . .

.   .   .   .

The rank of chief is hereditary in a definite house, *al*. It is usual to recognize as chief that member who is most suitable by reason of his mental and physical qualities, nor need he be the oldest in the ruling house. Among the clans and tribes ruling houses persist as such until they die out, although their power may have become extremely weak and many families may have deserted them. A head chief or prince to whom the other chiefs have submitted either of their own free will or under compulsion and who represents a whole tribe or group of tribes is overthrown more frequently than an ordinary chief, and his rank passes to another kin. This most frequently happens if the hereditary head chief is not distinguished by warlike ability. He then directs the external affairs of his tribe as *sheykh al-bab,* while affairs of war are left to a man renowned for his courage and prudence even though he may be descended from a different kin. Such a leader is known as *sheykh ash-shadad* or *sheykh al-harb*. If he succeeds in overcoming the enemy and concluding a favorable peace, several clans become attached to him. They obey him in peace, and there ensue wars in which the hereditary head chief generally succumbs and his house acknowledges the supremacy of the previous military commander, who then becomes *sheykh al-bab* as well.

.   .   .   .

The Rwala give the name of *sheykh* and also *shuyukh* to their head chief or prince. . . .

The head chief an-Nuri ibn Sha'lan

declares war and concludes peace. Under the Turkish regime he provided surety for the taxes which the Government demanded from the Rwala during the annual stay in an-Nukra. In 1907 he paid £T 3500 ($15,750), in 1908 only £T 2000 ($9000), because many clans of the Kwakbe tribe migrated to Irak. An-Nuri used to increase the tax by one half and allot it among the different chiefs, who in turn would likewise increase it and collect from the owners of separate tents their allotments according to the number of their camels. After a certain time an-Nuri or his son would ride out with his slaves to the different chiefs and collect the tax. Those who escaped and did not pay the tax were punished, when caught, with the loss of one camel. The collected tax was punctually conveyed by the prince to the Government, the prince retaining the half by which he had increased it. From this amount he made allotments to members of the ruling house and some chiefs; thus the following amounts were distributed: to Khaled ibn Sattam £T 150 ($675); to 'Adhub ibn Mejwel £T 20 ($90); to Fahad ibn Mashhur £T 50 ($225).

He himself retained at least £T 150 ($675), and in addition to this he sold annually three or four horses and twenty to thirty camels.

For each of his 30 to 35 horses the prince buys 5 loads of barley at £T 1 ($4.50) per load; for his guests, slaves, and family, 40 loads of flour at 40 *mejidiyyat* ($36) per load, 20 loads of wheat at 15 *mejidiyyat* ($13.50), 7 loads of *burghul* at £T 2½ ($11.25), 3 loads of rice at £T 4 ($18), 1½ loads of coffee at 100 *mejidiyyat* ($90), 2 loads of sugar at £T 5 ($25), butter at £T 55 ($247.50); at least 100 rams or sheep for food at 3 *mejidiyyat* ($2.70) each; five camels for food at £T 10 ($45) each; clothing and coverlets for his family and slaves and for gifts cost

£T 130 ($585). He has 80 rifles, and every year he requires at least 6000 rounds of ammunition at the equivalent of 10 to 12 cents for each round. The repair of the tents and the upkeep of the tent materials and ropes cost annually £T 50 ($225). He must send gifts to the chiefs from time to time and feed an average of twenty people daily.

.   .   .   .

A weaker tribe has to acknowledge the supremacy of a stronger one and pay it a special tax, which is known as *khuwa*. The Rwala collect the *khuwa* from all the Hteym as well as from the inhabitants of various villages. . . . Every settlement and every tributary tribe has among the Rwala its brother, *akh* (or *khawi*), to whom it pays annually about 25 *mejidiyyat*. The *akh* is bound to restore to the settlement all the property which his fellow tribesmen have stolen from it. The basis of *khuwa* is *kuwa,* force. Those who are strong compel the numerous settlements to raise *khuwa* for them. Those who have no *akh* must rely only on the drawn sword. . . . Those who receive the *khuwa* must protect those who give it to them, or, as the Rwala say: "He who eats a young goat must protect its mother. . . ."

.   .   .   .

To marriage the Rweyli is led by mutual inclination or love. A boy of twelve has a liking for a girl of the same age, and it is generally recognized; no one objects. It is said: "Love comes from Allah. . . ." The boy calls on his beloved in her tent, talks with her there, helps with the work, and the parents recollect the time of their first love. An older boy may join his sweetheart where and whenever he wishes to. He helps her water the camels, draw the water, strike and pitch the tent; he attends her on the march, and pays her a visit in

the evening. Usually they meet in a tent that is either vacant or little visited. The Shararat women whose husbands are serving as herdsmen or who are widowed gladly lend their small tents . . . for the lovers' meetings. There in the cold seasons of the year they sit all night by the fire, parting only when the morning star makes its appearance. . . .

.   .   .   .

In the choice of a wife the Rweyli is considerably limited. He must not marry the divorced wife of his father nor her daughter, not even if she was begotten by another man. He is not allowed to marry the divorced wife of his son or his son's widow, the mother of his wife, the daughter of his brother or sister. Neither may he marry his foster sister. No member of the Ibn Sha'lan kin will take to wife a daughter of the **H**wetat or Beni 'Atiyye tribes nor allow his daughters to marry any of them. Neither the **H**wetat nor Beni 'Atiyye are by birth equal to the Ibn Sha'lan, because they paid, as late as the first half of the nineteenth century, a tax for protection, *khwa,* to the despised Shararat tribe and camped with them as their . . . protected neighbors.

No Rweyli dares marry a member of the **S**leyb, al-**H**awazem, al-**F**heyjat, Shararat, or 'Azem tribes. All these are also called Hteym. They have their chiefs and their social organization, they live in tents and breed camels just like the other Bedouins, and yet they are not held in esteem. The reason is that they pay a tax for protection, *khwa;* that they are neither able to protect themselves nor gain full independence. Being thus compelled to buy the protection of the more vigorous tribes, they are not allowed to enter into blood relationship with their protectors. . . .

A Rweyli cannot marry the daughter of a blacksmith . . . or other mechanic who camps with the Rwala or lives in their settlements. . . .

Marriages with slaves are also forbidden. A man marrying a slave would be killed by his kin, *ahl*. No one dares defile the blood of his kin.

Moreover, there are inequalities even among the free Arab tribes. All those belonging to the 'Aneze group consider themselves aristocrats, hold the other tribes in contempt, and dislike forming matrimonial bonds with them. . . .

The children of parents descended from the respectable old 'Aneze families are the best. Yet even here the bridegroom is not entirely free in choosing a wife, for according to the ancient custom every girl is to wed the nearest young relative whom it is permissible to marry, *ibn al-'amm*. This is, generally, a son of her father's cousin; should this cousin have no sons or if the grandfather had no brothers, the girl falls to the nearest kinsman descended from the great-grandfather's brother. The *ibn al-'amm* occasionally claims the girl exclusively for himself, but even if he does not, the girl cannot marry without his consent, for it is said: "No one but the nearest kinsman can tie or untie her. . . ." Only when her father wants to marry again, and gives her in exchange for his new wife . . . is the *ibn al-'amm's* claim null and void. On the other hand, if the girl refuses to be wedded to her *ibn al-'amm,* he may kill her without becoming liable for compensation.

If the *ibn al-'amm* knows that the girl will not hear of him, being already in love with someone else, he forbids the marriage and the girl grows old.

If the father of the girl claimed by her *ibn al-'amm* dies and the girl loves another, she goes immediately after the father's death to the relative who claims her exclusively for himself, called in this case *hajjir,* and asks: "My father has passed away; I want thee to release my neck; I want thee to release me in return for my father, who has passed away. . . ." The *hajjir* is expected to take pity on her and allow her freely to choose a husband for herself, but nobody can compel him to do so.

In case of his refusal there is nothing left for the girl but to elope. She flees with her youth to some distant tribe; there they put themselves under the protection of a powerful chief. . . . They can then marry and live as man and wife in the same tent but are always threatened with the revenge of the *ibn al-'amm*. An elopement is punished in the same way as murder, and the thirst for revenge must be satisfied.

. . . .

If the *ibn al-'amm* kills the man who has eloped with the girl, he pays only half of the blood money, as the eloper was himself the cause of his own death.

. . . .

The wedding, as a rule, takes place immediately after the wooing. In the morning someone—even a slave—kills before the bridegroom's tent a she-camel, as a . . . wedding sacrifice. Neither of the betrothed needs to be present. Towards evening a small round tent . . . is pitched by the women near by and the bridal bed made there. Among the poorer people a corner of their inhabited tent is partitioned off for the young couple. Two or three of the bridegroom's female relatives go to the bride to bring her towards sunset to the prepared tent. A little later the bridegroom also enters, after which the tent is closed altogether. . . .

There are no special wedding ceremonies. Part of the meat from the slaughtered she-camel is distributed among the members of the bride's kin and acquaintances, the rest is served for supper in the bridegroom's tent. Nobody is invited, nobody brings any wedding presents. There is no party, no dancing; neither the girls nor women sing or shout with joy. Often even the relatives of either the bridegroom or the bride do not even know that there is going to be or has been a wedding. . . .

. . . . .

The Rwala usually have only one woman in a tent, seldom two, and very rarely three. A young Rweyli almost always marries a girl whom he loves, and remains faithful to his young wife till the sixth or seventh month of her pregnancy. Then his love cools and in many cases he begins to look for another girl or divorced woman whom he also marries, unless he is setting out on a raid. If the latter is of several weeks' duration and he comes back exhausted, he desires no new marriage and waits for his wife's confinement. If she bears a boy, the young father is so happy he clings to her again and banishes the thought of all others from his mind. If the wife behaves with sense, keeps the tent in order, can cook cleanly, is not strongheaded and quarrelsome, the husband often remains faithful to her all his life.

. . . . .

When a man has two wives, each cooks for him a day in turn, and on that day he usually eats and sleeps with her. Such is the woman's right . . . which nobody is allowed to violate. . . . Even when he does not love his wife, the man should devote himself to her on the nights belonging to her. He need not have sexual intercourse with her, but neither must he with the woman he loves. In such cases he usually sleeps in the men's compartment, or lying down at his wife's head he says: "Tonight I wish for nothing . . ." and the woman dares not say a word. Sometimes the women haggle among themselves: "Let me have the man tonight!" "What wilt thou give me for

it?" If they come to an agreement, the woman who has the right of sleeping with the man that night . . . says to him: "I grant thee furlough, now go to thy wife over there! . . ." But should the man infringe the right of one of his wives and spend several nights with the other, the deceived woman may rage as much as she will, but it will not do her any good, especially if her husband has paid to her kin the price asked for her. If a near relative of the woman dies, the man may and even should have intercourse with her for several nights, to comfort her in this way at least. . . .

The rôle of the woman is to bear and bring up children, to prepare the meals, to sew, and to pitch, strike, and load the tents . . . also to load up the entire outfit of the tent, to collect the camel's hair and weave from it the bags and various saddle ornaments . . . to procure water . . . to gather fuel . . . to go out to buy wheat and barley . . . and to supply the mare with fresh [fodder].

The man who loves his wife helps her in all these labors. He never lets her pitch, strike, or load up the tent alone, but along with his herdsman, servants, and sons always aids her. The camels carrying the supplies are guarded on the march by a servant or slave, the master or his son once in a while coming to see whether any of the pack camels needs help. Hauling water from a distant well is likewise usually the work of the son, servant, or herdsman; the master himself in this case drives out the herd to the pasture. A careful husband often loads two or three camels with fuel . . . all this to save his beloved wife labor. Even the grass and hay is brought in by the sons and servants.

On the other hand, a man not on good terms with his wife lets her do all the work herself, urging her on to greater speed all the time. When the whole camp is on the move, the man saddles both his mare and camel, lights a fire near his tent, makes coffee for himself, and watches his wife with the servant or daughter strike and load the tent, furniture, and supplies. When this is done, he attaches the mare by the rein to the camel, mounts the latter, and rides forward to the head of the moving camp where he joins the warriors . . . not troubling in the least about his pack camels. . . .

. . . . .

The husband cannot be compelled to divorce his wife; there are no reasons which would either require or prevent it. . . . If he wants to divorce her he can do so without telling her the reason, even should she beg him on her knees to keep her. Often he does not know the reason himself, for he has none. He simply takes a notion to divorce her and he does so, even though he may regret it soon afterwards. This is done most frequently by the younger chiefs who for political reasons are obliged to advance themselves by marrying the daughters of other chiefs. After six months or . . . one year they divorce their young wives, regardless of whether they have borne them children or are pregnant, and marry another girl or woman, so that they never have more than one wife in the tents.

According to common opinion, a man should divorce his wife as soon as the one becomes disagreeable to the other. As the proverb has it: "Reproach a herdsman or a wife with nothing; if thou hast occasion to reproach them frequently, thou hadst better dismiss them. . . ." When divorcing a woman the man says to her: "Go away! See, now thou art divorced and may attach thyself to another man! . . ." Or he says: "Thou art free altogether. Thy saddle cover is spread over thee! . . ." This means

that in the same way as a saddled mare may be ridden by any one, any man may marry a divorced, and thus perfectly free, woman. . . .

The divorced woman may be remarried three times by her former husband. . . .

No quarreling, words of abuse, or lamentations of married couples are ever heard in the Rwala camps. A man ought never to be seen beating his wife and vice versa, as by doing so they would disgrace . . . themselves and their respective kins for all time. . . . This is the reason why a man never quarrels aloud with his wife, although he may often and thoroughly beat her . . . being careful, however, that nobody shall see him. . . .

Mishref ibn Kurdi once beat his young wife, a daughter of Prince an-Nuri, for more than an hour not only over her back but over the head as well, so that it was swollen for ten days. On complaining to her father, the only satisfaction she received was that she would get still more if she did not behave herself. She was known to torment Mishref in a hundred ways, while he repaid her with sound beatings. For no sooner was she born, than Mishref, her second cousin, claimed her for his future wife. When she grew up she could not bear the sight of her bridegroom-to-be, but the more she scoffed at him, the more he insisted on marrying her. Prince an-Nuri himself and his son Nawwaf also begged Mishref to give the girl her freedom, but, appealing to his privilege as her nearest relative whom it is permissible for her to marry, *ibn al-'amm,* he maintained that he would not do so before she had become his wife. Finally Nawwaf himself advised her to consent, comforting her with the hope that Mishref would free her immediately after the wedding. Then she answered: "I shall not disregard the counsel my father and my brother give me nor act against their advice. . . ." On the wedding night she escaped from the round tent . . . and would not allow Mishref to come near her. After becoming Mishref's wife she admitted that she was in love with Mamduh ibn Sattam and resolved to remain a virgin until she could marry him. Mishref, who loved her greatly and was now suffering not only from jealousy but also from the sneers of his friends, gave vent to his anger by beating her and swearing that he would never give her back her freedom.

.   .   .   .

A married woman . . . has plenty of opportunity to make the acquaintance of other men. . . .

Of her love for another man no secret is made by a woman, and soon it is said publicly: "So-and-so's wife is in love with So-and-so. . . ." If this comes to the husband's ears and he is a man of a magnanimous disposition, he releases her without raising objections and asks no compensation, although he is entitled to the return of the dowry he has given for her. A man of this kind is wont to say: "She is a free daughter of a free tribe. Allah made her love another man, so I will not hinder or make a slave of her." It is only the base men . . . who take advantage of their wives' love to benefit themselves, asking five and even ten times as much as they themselves had paid. . . . If his wife's lover cannot meet the demand and her kin will not help, the lover can only elope with her. Then they seek refuge either with the Shammar between the middle Euphrates and the Tigris, or with the Lheyb in the vicinity of Aleppo, or, perhaps, with the Sirhan and Beni Sakhr on the southwest border of the Hawran. . . .

.   .   .   .

In every Rwala camp there lives a

member of another tribe who has left his kin for some reason and who, for a time at least, desires to make his home in a different territory. Such a stranger generally comes to an agreement with some Rweyli that they will be neighbors, *kusara* (sing., *kasir*), and as such will protect each other. . . .

The Rweyli protects his *kasir* against the Rwala and the *kasir* does the same for the Rweyli against his own people. A *kasir*, a guest, *zeyf*, and a traveling companion, *khawi*, all of whom enjoy special privileges, are not subject to the ordinary regulations of the tribe. . . . Their stick has as much force as another Bedouin's saber. . . . The *kasir* is treated as a man possessed of power . . . and justice is always done to him. . . . Even in cases where a Rweyli comes in conflict with a neighbor from elsewhere, the latter's Rweyli neighbor obtains, by force if necessary, a fair decision for him. . . .

When a Rweyli has a claim against a *kasir,* he may not make this demand himself, but must put it in the hands of the stranger's Rweyli *kasir.* . . .

.   .   .   .

When a Rwala camp is attacked by the enemy and among other things the stranger *kasir's* camels or mare are captured, it is the duty of his *kasir* to return to his stranger neighbor all that was stolen from him out of the booty taken by the Rwala in their next successful raid. . . .

In the same way the native neighbor is protected by the stranger *kasir* against the latter's own tribe. Only when both tribes declare war on each other, in the course of which the stranger's property is captured, is the native *kasir* absolved from helping him, unless he has made a prior agreement to do so. . . .

When a member of a hostile tribe is hired by a Rweyli to herd his camels and the herd entrusted to his care is attacked by his tribesmen, he is allowed by the raiders to keep for the Rweyli three she-camels, one for riding and two for milking. . . .

In almost every camp there lives a wandering merchant called a Kubeysi (pl., Kubeysat), although he does not always hail from the settlement of al-Kubeysa, near Hit on the right bank of the middle Euphrates. He comes with one or two camels laden with his goods, quarters himself as a guest with a Bedouin, pitches beside the black tent of his host his round white tent . . . and begins to sell cheap kerchiefs, men's shirts, material for women's shirts, shoes, and numerous other articles of clothing . . . and also tobacco, coffee . . . cardamom, and some drugs. He pays the owner of the tent where he boards with cloth enough to make one suit. The chief gets nothing at all.

Few Bedouins buy for cash, but nearly all buy on credit, paying 25 percent interest in five months. . . .

. . . Both the debt and interest must be paid at the time when camel markets are held, namely in July or August, when the Bedouins camping in the tilled country sell their camels. . . . Every debtor brings his bondsman, who declares in the presence of the creditor that so much is owed and that the principal together with the interest . . . will be paid at a certain stated date. Should the Kubeysi in the meantime die, his host . . . collects the amounts due to him and hands them over to his heirs. Debts contracted with the Kubeysat, the Bedouins pay regularly enough, mainly because they fear that otherwise no merchants would come to them.

When the Rwala camp in a settled region, some of the big merchants send messages to the prince to inquire whether he will allow them to come to his camp with goods to sell. If the messengers receive the prince's assurance that he will take them under his protection . . . the wholesaler loses no time in dispatching his employees to the camp, and before long from fifty to seventy white tents . . . will be seen in the prince's camp. In these everything is sold that the Bedouin's heart desires. For each of these tents one new pack saddle . . . and one *rotol* (2.56 kilograms) of green coffee are delivered to the prince as his due. Their stay in the camp terminates about the middle of August, for at the end of that month the Rwala usually return to the inner desert.

In the settled territory many merchants take camels in exchange for their wares, thus enabling the Bedouins to provide themselves with everything they need or desire. . . .

. . . . .

Slaves are owned not only by the chiefs but by ordinary Bedouins as well. Adult slaves cannot be bought any longer; small Negro children, however, are still brought from Nejd and offered for sale. . . . No Negro is a chattel . . . of his master, for he may not be sold or killed and is free to choose another master. As a rule, however, the slaves remain with the same family all the time. . . . Every married slave has his own tent, camels, and weapons, all this being given to him by his master, to whom he must return everything, should he wish to leave him. Even the slave's clothing is furnished by the master. The slaves in the household of a prince or great chief live entirely carefree. If the supplies are not well guarded by their master's mother or wife, they help themselves at their pleasure, cooking, roasting, and frying in their tents without a thought as to whether anything is left for the prince or chief. Then when the supplies are gone, they merely say: "We are hungry," and the master must replenish his larder anew.

If the chief entertains visitors, the slaves eat up all that is left over, so that the chief has to go to bed hungry.

Work is shunned by the slaves whenever possible. If the master himself does not see that it is done, they remain leaning peacefully against their camel saddles, smoking their master's tobacco and drinking his coffee. Their chief work is watering the camels. . . . The slaves load and unload supplies and lead the laden camels. They also help the women with the unloading, loading, transporting, and pitching of the tent, but only when afraid of the master. However, if they know him to be on bad terms with his women, they at once take his side and will not move a finger to do anything for the women. They work voluntarily only when they expect to gain something by doing so. When important guests arrive, the complaisance and affability of the slaves is boundless. But should the guest fail to tip them well on his departure, they will not deign to notice him when he comes again. They are very eager to share in the raids, loot, of course, being their main object. All the horses captured by the slave must be delivered to his master, who, however, is obliged to give the slave a camel for every horse. One half of the captured camels go to the master, the others are the slaves' share.

The little sons of the chiefs are brought up by the slaves; they make friends with the slaves' sons, and everything that they do is on the advice of the slaves and with their assistance. The slave is frequently the confidant of the first love of his master's son, negotiates with the girl's kin, protects his wife and children in a rebellion or hostile invasion, and is often the real guardian of his master's orphans, whom he also assists to regain their power and property. When the master's daughter marries into another tribe, as a rule she is accompanied thither by a reliable slave.

．　．　．　．

Among themselves the slaves have kin, *ahl,* like the Bedouins. They form marital ties without paying any heed to their master, only the consent of their own kin being necessary in this case. The master has no right to choose a wife for his slave or to take her away from him. Killing and murder they avenge not only among themselves, but on the free Bedouins as well. . . .

Yet, no matter how powerful, a slave can never marry the daughter of even the poorest Bedouin; and, on the other hand, the least of the herdsmen would not think of marrying a slave's daughter. . . . Only the sons and daughters of white blacksmiths, *sunna',* enter into blood relations with slaves. If a black slave marries a white girl, the daughter of a *sane',* and their son also marries a daughter of a *sane'* again, the third and fourth generations are quite white, and yet they do not become free, *horr,* but always remain slaves, *'abid.* In the settlements—especially in the cultivated regions—the origin of such whites is sometimes forgotten, but never among the Bedouins of the desert.

．　．　．　．

As the Rwala are occupied almost exclusively in camel breeding, it is only in exchange for camels that they can get grain, clothing, arms, saddles, and other necessities of life. The camels they sell either in the inner desert or in the settled territory, nearly always to the same wholesale merchants who live in the larger towns on the borders of Arabia as well as in Egypt and India. The most prominent among these is the Ibn Bassam family, from the settlement of Bassam in al-Kasim. Its members own large business houses at Basra, Bombay, Taif, Cairo, and Damascus. They export camels from

Arabia, they act as agents for the importing of coffee, spices, and rice, not only by ship or railroad but also by pack camels, and they supply the Bedouins with arms. There is no large settlement in inner Arabia where an agent of Ibn Bassam does not reside.

The Al Salem family also is now engaged almost exclusively in the buying and selling of camels. These merchants hail from ad-Der'iyye but live at Baghdad and Damascus. Members of this family once helped the Wahhabite princes of the Ibn Sa'ud family with money, and even now they have many friends in Nejd.

The third firm engaged in trading in camels—also in clothing—is the Al 'Isa family. They reside at Damascus and trade chiefly with the 'Aneze and Hwetat tribes.

The wholesale dealers hardly ever visit inner Arabia. They have their middlemen to whom they furnish money for dealings on their behalf. All these middlemen or agents are natives of al-Kasim and are called 'Akeyl, whether they belong to the tribe of that name or not. An 'Akeyli agent gets money from the wholesale dealer to buy camels from a certain tribe. He drives the animals which he has bought to Egypt or Basra or Kuweit where he sells them. . . .

Such an 'Akeyli agent hires assistants, usually his countrymen from al-Kasim, provides himself with light white tents, coffee, rice, and often also arms both for sale and exchange, and rides with letters of recommendation to the prince or chief of the tribe from which he means to buy. Having delivered the letters and gifts sent to those dignitaries by the wholesale dealer, he puts up his tents either in the prince's camp or, if permitted, in the camp of some chief. The chief of the camp where the trader has put up his tents

is also his host . . . in so far as he protects him as his guest but does not board him. The Bedouins now bring their camels to his white tents . . . and as a rule sell them for cash. Only when the agent has brought arms and ammunition from Kuweit or al-'Aker for sale, will they exchange their animals for these articles. On the sale of every camel the prince or the chief gets one-half or one *mejidiyye* ($0.45 or 0.90). The purchased animal is then branded with the 'Akeyli mark and left to graze in the herd with the others. For his herdsmen the 'Akeyli hires youths from the tribe where he is buying at the time. Many herdsmen accompany the agent's herds as far as Egypt and on their return tell of the wonderful things they have seen or learned on their trip. If the 'Akeyli buys camels in the inner desert, he remains with the purchased herds for many weeks, or even months, with the same tribe, waiting until it moves to the settled territory, generally toward the end of June. . . . On reaching the border of the desert, the 'Akeyli proceeds to the nearest large town where camel markets are held. . . .

The herds belonging to the 'Akeyl may be captured by strange raiders, just as the herds of members of the tribe with whom he happens to be migrating, and for that reason the 'Akeyl have in every large clan their brother, *akh,* to whom they pay . . . from four to five Turkish pounds ($18 to 22.50), one good riding camel, and two or three good cloaks annually. This brother is obliged to restore to them every camel stolen by a member of his clan. . . . If the Rwala bring home from one of their raids camels bearing the 'Akeyl brand and there is no 'Akeyli camping with them, the *akh* drives these camels into his own herd and waits till some 'Akeyli comes to claim them. Thus a brother's eye cares for the 'Akeyl even during their absence. . . .

In the opinion of the Rwala, Allah created with the first Bedouin also the first smith, *sane'* (pl. *sunna'*). Every camp and every settlement of inner Arabia has its blacksmith who works for the whole clan or for the whole oasis. Often the same blacksmith family has camped with the same clan from time immemorial and yet cannot be adopted by it, for the *sunna'* remain strangers forever. Among themselves the blacksmiths form kins of their own, and the blacksmiths of the Rwala are relatives, *beni al-'amm,* of all the blacksmiths in Arabia. They live in almost the same way as the Bedouins or settlers and are subject to claims of vengeance among themselves; but they never make war or take part in raids, even as allies of the Bedouins. During an attack on the camp where their tents stand they go on with their work unconcernedly, defending neither themselves nor their neighbors, for they have their brother, *akh,* in every tribe whose duty it is to return to them anything of which a member of that tribe has robbed them. Among the Rwala a member of the Al Mijwel kin is the brother of the *sunna'*. If a Bedouin does any wrong to a blacksmith, the latter complains to Ibn Mijwel, who must put matters right. When the raiders bring along, besides other booty, camels bearing the *sunna'* brand, their brother takes them all into his herd and sends word to the blacksmith of the raided tribe: "Your camels are held by me." They then come, pick out their animals, and return home with them. But if camels branded with the mark of the brother's tribe are found among those of the *sunna'*, he returns them to his tribesmen. For his trouble the brother keeps every fifth animal as well as such as are not claimed by the owner blacksmith.

The *sane'* not only shoes horses but repairs rifles, daggers, etc., and often makes new rifles, fine sabers, and spears, for there are many good artisans in his craft. For shoeing a horse he will make no charge. His reward is a two-year old she-camel . . . for every horse captured and all the horse saddles brought home from the raids, which he then sells for his own profit. When the Bedouins procure supplies of grain in the tilled territory for their stay in the inner desert, the blacksmith demands one *mejidiyye* ($0.90) on each horse in order to buy his provisions. Whoever slaughters a camel must give the blacksmith all its entrails and the shins of its hind legs.

No Bedouin, not even a member of despised tribes like the Shararat, Sleyb, Hawazem, etc., would marry the daughter of a blacksmith nor let his daughter marry him. For the *sane'*, although white, is not independent, is not *horr*.

.   .   .   .

The people whom Musil calls Sleyb are also called Sulubba (both are plurals of Slubbi). The renowned head of the Transjordan army, Brigadier General J. B. Glubb (Glubb Pasha)* has written a brief but very informative article about them, which follows.

* *The Sulubba and Other Ignoble Tribes of Southwestern Asia,* General Series in Anthropology, Number 10, George Banta Publishing Co., Menasha, Wis., 1943. Reprinted by permission of the author and the publishers.

The Sulubba are to be found in an area extending roughly from Damascus to Mosul in the north, down to Jauf, east of the Nefud, Hail, Persian Gulf, the Euphrates, the Tigris above Baghdad, and Mosul.

They are scarcely ever found in Trans-Jordan west of the Wadi Sirhan; I believe that they do not exist in the Hejaz or in the western half of Arabia. This distribution might reinforce the legend of their origin from Hasa Province on the Persian Gulf, from which they might well have emigrated north to the more fertile lands in Syria or Iraq, but would have been unlikely to have emigrated to the Hejaz, which is less fertile than the Hasa itself.

The Sulubba have long been regarded by the Beduins as a subject race. Many of them work as tinkers for the Beduin tribes and perform other menial duties. They have never taken part in the wars and feuds, which have occupied the greater part of the Beduins' lives for centuries. A Sulubbi, like a woman, was a creature with whom it was too inferior to fight. The Sulubba maintained a strict neutrality in raids, and, for fear of being beaten, told all raiders what they knew of the nature of the country and the movements of their enemies.

Until about 1930, the Sulubba paid regular tribute to all the Beduin sheikhs for protection. This did not, however, safeguard them from continual petty pilfering, beatings and insults. Beduin travelers or raiders invariably called at Sulubba tents if they could find them, and demanded food and hospitality. The Beduin, who is normally a model of sedateness and reserved decorum among strangers, exhibited the worst aspects of his character in a Sulubba camp. He shouted, bullied, cursed, and swaggered in a manner sometimes shameful. He demanded the best food, cursed his host, complained of everything, ate all he could and then demand more food to take with him as supplies for his journey. The Salubba cowered and whined. Long oppression has indeed made them very low class. The ingratiating whine in which they address the Beduin as "Ya Amaimi," "Oh, my little uncle," makes one ashamed of human nature!

Prostitution is reputed to be widespread among the women. Whether or not this statement is too sweeping, there can be little doubt that most of them have a very low standard of morals, and are frequently sought by Beduins for immoral purposes. This traffic can scarcely be unknown to their husbands and brothers, but they seem too debased to protest. While there is a good deal of immorality among the Beduins themselves, such offences are kept strictly secret, and any woman creating a scandal is likely to be murdered. Only the Sulubba seem to be shameless in this respect.

The Sulubba are par excellence the children of the desert. Every Sulubbi is nicknamed by the Beduins "Abu al Khala" or "Father of the empty spaces." If the Beduin, compared to the townsmen, is a hardy traveler at home in the great desert, he is but a pampered tenderfoot compared to the Sulubba. Often in summer, when the great Beduin camps move to the Euphrates, or on to the main groups of wells around which cluster tented towns of hundreds of families, odd Sulubba families will remain far out in the desert, drinking from some tiny water hole in a lonely ravine known only to the Sulubba themselves. There they will live almost the lives of wild animals, with only a few sheep or donkeys, hunting gazelle and often dressing in their skins.

The Sulubbi alone knows the wild animal life of the desert intimately. As a gazelle hunter, his skill is incredible, and many live very largely on gazelle meat and dress in their skins. The Beduins often employ the Sulubba as guides in the desert or consult them regarding routes, grazing, or camping grounds.

Apart from hunting gazelle, and menial work for the Beduins, the Sulubba also live by grazing and breeding animals. Some of them are prosperous and own large flocks of sheep. They have a few camels, but their most distinctive possessions are the white asses. Probably the Sulubba originally bred asses rather than camels for riding purposes, because if they had any good camels the Beduins were likely to covet them. But since no Beduin would stoop to ride an ass, the Sulubba were left in undisputed possession. Some of these animals have marvelously swift paces, and are almost as capable of resisting thirst as is the camel.

During the last ten years, the desert belonging to Iraq, Syria, and Trans-Jordan has been brought under Government control. As a result the Beduins are no longer able to bully the Sulubba quite as unrestrainedly as before and the latter are learning to complain to the police when they are beaten or abused.

In 1919–22, the recrudescence of Wahhabism in central Arabia produced a tremendous outburst of religious enthusiasm and fanaticism. The Beduin manifested his enthusiasm by declaring that all Moslems were equal before God, and hence that the Sulubba were equal to "free men," i.e., Beduins. Ibn Saud, anxious to increase his fighting men, backed this idea (in fact he may have originated it), and raised fighting forces from the Sulubba and gave them war banners. The Sulubba took part in a number of warlike operations, and it is said that, in the massacres which usually followed a Wahhabi victory at this time, the Sulubba were the most cruel and bloodthirsty.

The outbreak of fanaticism, however, died down from 1925 to 1929, and it is believed that these Nejd Sulubba have again fallen back to their original condition.

In order to escape unwelcome Beduin guests, the Sulubba live in tiny tents, many of them scarcely larger than a blanket. They show great skill in pitching these tents in the beds of ravines or behind rocks so as to be invisible to passers-by. The more important Beduin sheikhs take pride in pitching a large tent in a prominent place, which conveys not only defiance of enemies but a distant welcome to guests. According to Beduin interpretation the Sulubba reveals his baseness by concealing his camp from both strangers and guests.

•   •   •   •

Returning to Musil's account:

Among the Bedouins there are persons, both male and female, who know and see hidden things and are able to heal the sick. . . . They maintain that they inherit their supernatural qualities, their *islam,* from their forefathers and that, therefore, the ability to heal the sick, discover what is hidden, fore-tell the future, etc., is confined to certain families. . . .

The seer maintains that he communicates with an angel . . . who announces to him the will of Allah. . . . Besides the angel the seer's ancestors also appear to him in the night between Thursday and Friday, instructing him how to behave. Yet neither the angel nor the ancestors ever appear without a thorough preparation on the part of the seer.

Every seer has his disciples . . . who are taught all the external performances necessary to display if the [angel] is to appear. They come to the seer on Thursday night, accompany him on his visits to the sick and on raids, and join him whenever he commands them. One part of their duty is to carry little drums and other musical instruments. . . . If the sorceror wants to call the spokesman-angel to him, he beckons to the disciples to play, while he himself squats with his head bent down. After a while he begins to move, stands up, stretches out his hands, jumps about, contorts his body, and puts his hands, feet, and even his head close to the fire, clapping his hands. . . . When his enthusiasm reaches its climax, either Allah's spokesman or some of the seer's ancestors appear on the scene. After the climax has subsided, the seer, greatly exhausted, complains that he can do nothing. The Bedouins, however, who cannot be made to believe that this ecstasy is a mere preparation for the angel's appearance, deride the sorcerer, imitate his gestures, and call him one possessed and a juggler. Especially those of the new sorcerers whose ancestors were not known as seers are the target of their ridicule when trying to establish themselves. . . . However, by perseverance, patience, and courage a sorcerer-to-be in a few years will gain recognition not only from the Bedouins but from the hereditary sorcerers as well. The advance of such a sorcerer's son in his father's calling is, as a matter of course, much easier and speedier.

.   .   .   .

At the time when this was written (1909) the following persons were recognized as true seers: men: Mnahi ibn Dabbagh, Rannam ibn Jel'ud, Sayyah ibn Jleydan, Za'al ibn 'Awwad; women: 'Eshba bint Hmezi, Batha bint 'Awwad, and Dleyyil bint Mazi.

A sorcerer can give information whether and for how long it is going to rain; whether a wife will bear a boy or a girl; whether the young produced by the mare or camel will be a male or a female; whether a raid will succeed, etc.

War expeditions on a large scale are always accompanied by a sorcerer who instructs the commander in anything he may undertake. The latter asks the sorcerer's advice only on occasions when he is at a loss what to do. Then the seer stimulates himself with music and works himself into an ecstasy, which helps him hear the angel speak and proclaim the will of Allah.

Very often a sorcerer is summoned to the bedside of a person who is seriously ill. He comes either with all or a few of his disciples and settles down in the tent as a regular guest. During the day, but especially in the evening, he orders his disciples to play, while he squats by the fire with his head wrapped up and his face in his hands, listening to the music. After a while he begins to contort the upper part of his body, jumps up, seizes a small drum, beats it wildly, circles around the fire, and, dancing around the patient, raps him with the drum on the head and legs; then, throwing the drum aside, he lies above the patient, supporting himself by the feet and hands, breathes into his mouth and nostrils, kneels down, rubs the patient on the breast, stomach, and back, jumps up, dances around, and, then, lying on him again, mumbles unintelligible words. Sometimes he cures the sick person by this process; sometimes the patient dies.

Sulhan's little son, Fejer, six years

old, fell ill. Greatly troubled, the father entreated a sorcerer to cure his child. The seer soon appeared with his wife, and the first thing they did was to lay the boy's head south and his feet north. The woman began to play, while the sorcerer bent down to the fire, waiting for the *islam* to take hold of him. Then he jumped up, danced, lay on the boy, covering him with his body, breathed on his cheeks, and made curious grimaces, . . . the woman beating a little drum all this time and dancing around them. The boy recovered.

．　　．　　．　　．

There are people living among the Bedouins, both men and women, who in some inexplicable way are able to tell of hidden things, whether of the past, present, or future. One of their ways is to prophesy from the position of twenty-three objects cast about promiscuously. These objects are: seven round white pebbles . . . one small piece of ambergris; one fragment of broken glass . . . one small piece of a burned brick . . . one fragment of a broken glass armlet . . . five small white sea shells . . . one small piece of sea shell . . . four date stones . . . one small piece of a glass ring such as is worn by mares on their necks . . . and one smooth silver ring. . . . The soothsayer, who keeps all these twenty-three objects in a leather pouch, shakes them out on the palm of his hand, throws them down on the carpet, and then begins to prophesy from their relative positions.

Bleyhan related to me: "My little brother, Ji'an, went on a raid and did not return for a long time. My heart was sick with longing for him. . . . So I went to a Hazmiyye (woman of the Hawazem tribe) soothsayer . . . and gave her a little tobacco. . . . She said:

'What brings thee here, O youth? . . . Dost thou need something. . . ?'

'I seek a lost camel and want thee to give me the sign. . . .' Taking out from a bag . . . the pouch with those twenty-three things, she shook them out on her right palm, which she first lifted and then lowered again, threw them . . . broadcast on the carpet, glanced over them, and then exclaimed:

'O youth, thou seekest not a she-camel. . . . Thou art troubled about a raider; it is for him thy heart is aching. But be it known to thee that today his heart is calmer than thine. . . . He will return to thee merry and unwounded. . . .'

'If he returns thus thou shalt get a dress or silk kerchief . . .' said I and left, somewhat relieved. And, true enough, five days after this Ji'an came back well and bringing four captured she-camels. Then I gave the soothsayer that silk kerchief."

．　　．　　．　　．

Slight disputes and quarrels between members of the same tribe are settled by friendly intercession. . . .

More serious differences are settled among the Rwala by the hereditary native judge, *'arefa* (pl., *'awaref*). Judicial dignity is hereditary in certain kins and passes as a rule from father to son. If the latter lacks the necessary intelligence . . . the litigants turn to his uncle . . . or to some other member of his kin. Furthermore, every chief may pass sentence, but may not interfere in any way with the jurisdiction of the hereditary judges; he must submit when the contending parties appeal from his verdict to the hereditary judge. When acting as a judge, a chief is never called *'arefa,* not being recognized as such. When a chief adjudicates disputes he does so because he wields power which it is not always possible to resist and because he can support his judgment or his will by force.

. . . .

A lawsuit . . . may be decided either by witnesses or by black oaths. . . . An oath is black because it disgraces a man, blackens his countenance or his honour, implying that his mere word is not believed. Besides, the swearer is always in danger of God's anger, as he can never explain things as they really happened.

Generally two witnesses are required in court. . . . Only a man of good repute . . . who is no babbler . . . and never contradicts his story . . . will be admitted as a witness. . . . An eyewitness . . . should be honest . . . must not hate him whose case depends on him, must not yearn for a reward for his testimony, and must be known for his veracity. . . . Every witness is entitled to compensation for coming to testify. . . . As a rule an eyewitness will not ask for it; but if he says: "I want the price of my tongue . . ." then two of his kin have to declare him to be a trustworthy witness . . . which means that he is not a hired witness. . . .

. . . .

One who knows a fact only from hearsay cannot give valid testimony, for he has seen nothing himself but has only heard it from others, and mouths will always chatter. Knowledge of this kind . . . has no validity even when supported by five men. . . .

In the absence of trustworthy eyewitnesses the judge calls on the party which has entered a denial to swear. As in the opinion of the Bedouins every court process defiles and every oath disgraces . . . the oath is universally avoided, and a man is angry with one who urges him to swear. The simplest words of an oath are:

"I swear by Allah and eight camels laden with grain that I did not say.

. . ." Thus he calls on Allah to punish him and to do him an injury equal to the loss of eight loads of grain which he has bought in the settled territory; he would then die of hunger in the desert.

. . . .

In serious disputes the judge requires the *msabba'* oath, so called from seven lines drawn with a saber on the ground. The judge first draws a circle with a saber, then its diameter; this he intersects with five vertical lines, inviting the witness to step inside and facing south to swear: "A false oath is the ruin of the descendants, for he who [swears falsely] is insatiable in his desire [of gain] and does not fear his Lord; thus and so happened. . . ."

Scarcely is the oath finished when the witness jumps out of the circle and, full of rage, runs at his opponent, who has made him swear. The people present at the trial have to surround and hold him till he calms down.

. . . .

Protection granted by a man against his tribesmen or allies to a person regardless whether present or not is called a countenance, *wajh*. Before the countenance of some Rweyli it is possible to travel through the whole Rwala territory without fear of an attack or of violence. Before the countenance of Prince an-Nuri one may cross not only the Rwala territory but also that of all other tribes which acknowledge his sovereignty. It is said of the prince that he resembles a long branch to which smaller twigs are attached.

Whoever wishes to travel through the territory of a powerful chief goes first to him with the following request: "I desire to ride through the pastures of thy tribe, so grant me the protection of thy countenance." If the chief answers: "Undertake thy journey in peace!

Behold, I give thee my countenance . . ." he may start as tranquilly as if accompanied by the chief himself.

. . . .

If the traveler distrusts some tribe, he tries to hire as comrade either a member or an ally of the tribe, that he may then ride before his face. A companion protecting the traveler from both his fellow tribesmen and allies is called a *khawi*. To travel with a *khawi* is always easier than to travel before a chief's countenance, because a *khawi* can be seen and heard, whereas the protection of a chief, often living at a great distance, must be first proved, which not only takes some time but in most cases is difficult. For this reason the chief usually gives the traveler in addition to his protection one of his slaves or servants to act as companion.

. . . .

One single face protects against all members of the Zana Muslim; the same applies to the Zana Bishr and also to all the 'Amarat, the other two great division of the 'Aneze. As a result, three *ikhwan* * suffice for protection against all the 'Aneze from Aleppo to the Nefud and from the Sirhan depression to the river Tigris.

. . . .

The members of the Shararat tribe, which has no head chief who can dictate to all the clans . . . are not secure even against their own fellow tribesmen. Then it pays to be very exact in inquiring whether the *khawi* can protect against the whole of his clan or merely against a few kins. A Sharari *khawi,* too, keeps his engagement for one day only. Should the traveler fail to renew the agreement with him, his *khawi* may himself rob him on the next day or make common cause with the robbers.

. . . .

A chief who is commonly spoken of
* Plural of *khawi*—Ed.

as a *saheb al-marjala* stands in high esteem among the Rwala. Such a one has a brave, strong heart . . . knows how to wrestle with the greatest danger . . . has a broad outlook . . . thinks of the future . . . and never acts hastily. . . . He who is merely a daring fighter, *saheb al-farsa,* is not fit to be either a chief or a leader in time of war. He, too, has a strong heart but lacks calm consideration . . . therefore he throws himself into danger recklessly, unmindful of victory or death. . . .

But the most popular among the chiefs is the *saheb al-mruwwa.* He is kind . . . truthful . . . disregards trifles . . . and knows no distinction between great and small. Of such the proverb says: "A wolf does not suffer hunger with him, neither do his sheep perish. . . ."

A generous man is universally esteemed, as is often visited by guests who then carry his fame far and wide. . . .

Ash-shima is among the most prominent qualities of a famous man. It is but rarely found, and the man possessing it excels all others in the same way as the head projects above the body. He who has *ash-shima* will not always insist on his right, gladly yielding to one weaker than himself and sometimes giving up his claim to a thing which clearly belongs to him. . . .

. . . .

The report of a death or murder causes a stir not only in the camp but throughout the clan and even the whole tribe. The nearest female relatives of the dead person tear away the buckles holding their shirts under the neck, scratch their faces with their fingernails, besmear themselves with ashes and sand, cut off their braids above the temples, and run out of the camp either south or north into the desert, where they cry three times: "Ah, woe is me!

O thou father of mine . . . !" Or: "Ah, woe is me! O thou little brother of mine . . . !" The white kerchief they wear on their heads for at least a month. . . .

The men of the whole camp run out to the dead body, examine the wounds, and discuss the manner of death. Those who are not his kin on the father's side . . . return to the camp, watch their tents, send out the news to the pasturing grounds and the nearest camps, and take care that neither they nor their herds come between the avengers and the culprits.

The guilt rests on the whole kin, *ahl,* of the murderer; vengeance also becomes the duty of the whole kin of the dead man.

The whole kin is bound to mutual protection, both aggressive and defensive. . . . The more distant relatives, i.e., those who are in the fourth and later generations from the ancestor common to themselves and the culprit, generally offer the avengers a two-year-old camel . . . and are left in peace.

The avengers are called violators . . . or those who carry on blood feud in defense of the culprits . . . while the culprits are spoken of as the blood-stained. . . . The avenger proper is generally the nearest healthy adult male relative of the murdered man; the first culprit is the murderer himself; should he die a natural death in the meantime, his next of kin is considered the culprit. However, for the first three days after the murder nobody pays the least attention either to the avenger or to the perpetrator. These three days are called the seething of the blood . . . or the anger . . . fury . . . or madness. . . . The avengers ride out on horseback and camels to seek the guilty ones and their herds. If they meet a little boy, an adult, or even an old man of the culprit's kin,

they kill him; if they meet their mares or herds, they cut their arteries below the knees of the forelegs . . . but must not drive them away captive.

No one of the perpetrators must defend himself, for then he would be deserted by his whole clan and even by the whole tribe. The defense is to be left to others. Therefore the culprits proceed with all haste possible to one of the more powerful chiefs to ask his protection. The first one to reach him cries:

"Behold, we ask Allah and thee to protect the hair of our heads from So-and-so, as well as the herds on our borders. . . ."

The chief answers: "Welcome to us! May Allah save your lives! Ye are saved. Your pursuer has already halted. . . ."

The protector then calls his slaves, servants, and his whole kin, hastens to the tents and herds of the guilty kin, loads the tents and everything that is in them on camels, carries them away, and drives the herds between his own tents. To the avenger he calls out:

"Behold, your blood shedder has put himself, according to ancient custom, under our protection; so beware . . . !"

The avengers then inquire: "Wilt thou let them stay with thee a short while only or for several days?"

"Beware, I tell you, and guard your hands from committing violence!"

"We know well, tribesman, that thy protection is powerful, yet thou are not a protector of little girls . . . therefore wilt not protect culprits forever. . . ."

"How many days' truce will you grant me?"

"We will grant thee four [twelve, at the most] days."

During the truce the chief loads the guilty men's tents and accompanies them and their herds to another chief.

Should the avengers refuse to allow the culprits to go with their protector to another tribe, their fellow-tribesmen will intercede in his behalf and compel them to abandon their vengeance altogether. For they have blackened the face of the protector and exposed themselves in turn to his vengeance.

In the desert there are chiefs, the descendants of famous kins, whose protection is universally known and respected, or, as the saying goes, whose face insures a safe journey. . . . Such are especially Ibn Ghubeyn of the Fed'an tribe, Ibn Jandal of the Rwala, and Ibn Tayyar of the Weld 'Ali. These send only a slave or servant with their protégé, whereas others accompany their protégés in person. The protector leads the culprits to some chief who is camping in the direction in which they are fleeing and hands them over to him with the words:

"Behold, these shedders of blood. I protected them from So-and-so, and now, hear me, I put them under thy protection. My duty will now be thy duty."

The new protector answers: "May Allah keep both thee and them alive! They are saved, and their pursuer will return without achieving his object!"

From here they are conducted by the chief himself to another protector and emerge at length from the desert either among the Lheyb, who dwell north of the al-Hass and Shbekh mountains, or among the Shammar al-Jarba, who camp between the middle Euphrates and the Tigris, or, finally, among the Sirhan and Beni Sakhr on the southwestern borders of the Hawran. The camps of the tribes here named are univerally recognized as places of refuge, where the culprits are tolerably safe. . . .

After some time the chief of the camp where the culprits have found refuge sends to the chief of the avengers this message:

"Your fellow tribesmen . . . dwell among us. Accept the blood price. . . ."

If the blood price is refused by the avengers, the guilty parties can only remain abroad. . . . But if the avengers say: "We will accept the blood price," the chief asks them to name their sureties of peace, or arbitrators . . . while the culprits name their sureties for the payment. . . . Then both parties agree on the chief before whom they will meet to settle the matter. When the culprits with their tents and herds, accompanied by their sureties for payment, arrive there, they send word to the avengers. . . .

"Here we are with our surety. Make haste to come here too; we wish to pay you the blood price. . . ."

The avenger proper then sets forth with his surety of peace to the chief with whom the guilty party is camping, and in his tent the chief asks the avenger in the presence of all:

"What dost thou ask from thy fellow tribesman?"

"I want this or that mare."

The surety rises, brings the mare, and, handing her over to the avenger, says: "Thy fellow tribesman gives thee this mare."

The next question is: "What else dost thou ask of thy fellow tribesman?"

"I ask fifty she-camels; a complete armament of a rider—that is, a rifle, a saber, a dagger, a camel saddlebag, a hunting falcon, and a greyhound bitch. . . ." If the culprits object, pleading their inability to pay so much, the chief threatens to have them escorted to the camp where they sought refuge. . . . This makes the guilty party declare their willingness in these words:

"We came here to agree to pay the blood price and will fetch every animal demanded. . . ."

One third of the blood price is paid by them at once, the rest as soon as possible. . . .

.   .   .   .

No chief or surety must ask or accept compensation for aiding those who carry on the blood feud in defense of the culprit, for that would stain his honor. His sole reward is the public acknowledgement that he has been instrumental in doing good . . . and preventing fresh shedding of blood. The guilty party show their gratitude to their protector in various ways. They like best of all to raise a white flag over the tent of the culprit proper, where they leave it for several days and ride around the camp shouting:

"May Allah whiten So-and-so's face! May he exalt his name both in this world and hereafter!"

The returning culprits are welcomed by their fellow tribesmen with equestrian mock battles, merry feasting, and cries of joy. . . . For do not they return who might have been lost forever?

The blood price of a man . . . from a related tribe is one mare, fifty she-camels, and a complete rider's outfit. For the blood of a woman no more than twenty-five she-camels is paid, because a woman is never valued as highly as a man. . . . The compensation for a man from an alien tribe is only seven camels.

.   .   .   .

The Rwala are ever at war with one tribe or another. Without war a Rweyli could not live. War gives him an opportunity of displaying his cunning, endurance, and courage. He neither loves the shedding of blood, nor craves booty, but is allured by danger and delights in the predatory art. The booty itself he will give away without thinking much about it—even to the wife of the very man he has just robbed. Some tribes, not always entirely strangers, hate each other cordially. Between them peace is never of long duration. Despite the greatest efforts of the chiefs to prevent war, their people continue to attack and destroy one another. With the tribes settled along the desert borders and fully subject to the Government, peace is never concluded. If the Government, which is supposed to protect them, is weak, the Rwala despoil them whenever they are so inclined. The more distant the pastures of two tribes are, the longer will the war between them last.

The causes of war are, as a rule, petty thefts and the capturing of stray animals. The individual tribesmen begin to accuse each other of harbouring stolen she-camels. . . . Then they call on their chiefs for help. Couriers ride from tribe to tribe with verbal and written messages. Evidently both tribes desire war. Finally the chief of one tribe sends to the chief of the other a letter worded somewhat as follows:

"To the well-born, highly honored brother, Chief So-and-so! May Allah preserve his good name! Amen. Extending our greetings and entreating Allah's mercy and blessing for you, we announce to you that your Arabs are harassing our people and robbing them of their property continually without any effort on your part to put a stop to it. From this we judge that it happens with your assent. We now demand that you return without delay the stolen camels. If you refuse, you are, behold! hereby deprived of your fair name . . . and our face shall remain blank to you. You must not accuse us and blacken our face. This much for you to know, and greetings, Your brother, X Y."

Should the other chief be averse to war, he will write back: "Both thine and my people rob each other mutually.

. . . If thou desirest war with us . . .
return our fair name to us. . . . We
do not intend to fight with you and
shall not return your integrity to you.
Let us know whether ye are our friends
. . . or enemy. . . ."

.   .   .   .

The chief of any tribe may declare
war. If several tribes ally themselves
under one prince, they do not thereby
renounce their right of declaring war
independently. . . .

As soon as war has been declared
raids, both large and small, begin and
often a regular battle, *manakh,* is also
fought. If the hostile tribes camp
somewhere near, a few men start out
for robbery on foot. . . . If the camps
are at some distance, they ride on
camels. . . . When more than twenty
men on camels . . . or on horses and
camels . . . gather, then it is a raid.
. . . Every expedition of this kind
has a leader . . . who need not always
be a chief of a tribe, as every tribe can
have its own military leader or war
commanders . . . if the chief is not
possessed of sufficient military ability,
or is ailing, or too old. Sometimes the
chief's son or one of his relatives is entrusted with the command. But any
Bedouin conspicuous for his prudence
and bravery in time of war may be
promoted from leader of the men on
foot to leader of mounted men and may
even be recognized as the commander-
in-chief. The chief generally tries to
gain his favor, marries his daughter to
him, and adopts him into his kin, but
likewise may bring about his death on
finding that the commander does not
wish him well. For a leader who rises
in such a manner usually deposes the
reigning kin and becomes chief himself. Therefore the members of the
reigning kin are very careful when
choosing a chief and recognize only the
most distinguished of their kin. This
is also the reason why the dignity of a

chief does not pass from father to son
as a matter of course.

.   .   .   .

. . . On the whole, both small and
large expeditions are made preferably
in the time of abundance . . . when
edible plants, good pasture, and plenty
of water may be found anywhere.
This is the time when the inner desert
swarms with raiders of every description.

.   .   .   .

Old men and small boys must not go
on a raid. They are left at home to
guard the camp. However, a boy of
twelve is old enough to join the raiders
and may properly do so, especially in
the . . . season when neither thirst
nor hunger threatens. In the hot
months mainly men between 16 and 40
take part. They do not like to be accompanied by a young husband . . .
in the first year of his married life.
This time . . . is not very favorable
to important ventures, therefore it is
better that the young husband should
stay at home. . . .

.   .   .   .

On the day agreed on they depart in
smaller or larger groups either for the
commander's tent or the appointed
place of rendezvous. A guide familiar
with the watering places . . . is always taken and, whenever possible, a
member of the tribe to be attacked as
well. This is usually an elderly herdsman who has hired himself out with
them; he is sent for by the commander at the last moment before setting
out.

The commander is also accompanied
on the raid by a seer or sorcerer . . .
to whom Allah sends dreams in his
sleep of a certain significance. . . . He
is asked by the commander: "O So-
and-so, didst thou have a dream of
such-and-such a significance. . . ?"
It is a favorable omen, for instance, if
he has dreamed of a mare or a she-

camel; if he has kissed a girl, put on a new dress, or eaten dates—all these presage a rich capture of camels. If he has eaten meat in his dream, it means that tents will be captured, together with the kettles in which the meat is boiled. . . . Of unfavorable significance . . . is a dream in which the sleeping seer sees a wounded, a naked, or a snake-bitten man; or one in which he has his front teeth knocked out; or in which he falls down a well . . . or is fettered, or holds gold in his hand, or goes blind. But if he puts on a red jacket in his dreams, then the commander's blood is sure to flow.

The commander takes care not to meet before his tent any member of the 'Orzan (Misfortunates) kin of the Kwakbe, of the Fleta (Surprised) of the Rwala, of the Bdur (Oppressed) of the Eshaje'a, or of the Kshush (Chased Away) of the 'Abdella, for the names of these kins prove that they possess qualities very unfavorable to any large undertaking. . . .

In every raid there is a commander or leader. In smaller ones there is only one, in the larger there may be more. . . .

If the raiding party is made up of various tribes or clans, each of them has its own wholly independent leader. Only when the commander-in-chief also participates will he command in person and thus become . . . the one who gives orders when to rest and when to march. . . .

The commander also decides whether the booty is to be divided . . . or whether every one has to seize it on his own account. . . .

If the commanders of a raid agree to share the booty obtained by all . . . they begin by counting the participants. If one of the leaders has many and another only a few men with him, the latter is given more, so as to equalize the strength of all the troops. The booty is divided equally into as many parts as there are leaders; these take their share and apportion the rest among their men. Demanding a head rope from each man, the leader lays these ropes over his left arm and, walking among the captured animals, hangs one rope after another around their necks. Every one then takes the she-camel with his head rope. . . . The manner of getting booty and of its division should always be agreed on before the raid, to prevent trouble afterwards.

When all the men taking part in a raid assemble, the leader informs them whither they are bound. After midnight two or three men on horseback are ordered to ride ahead in order to examine the country through which the expedition has to pass as far as their next night's rest. They are called 'ayn (pl., 'uyun) ["eyes"]. . . .

. . . . .

If no report comes in from the 'uyun, the commander rides without stopping to the night quarters, where the 'uyun always wait for him. But should the commander see a troop of riders who on coming closer are found to be enemies, there ensues a fight the result of which decides whether the raiders shall return or go on with their venture. . . .

. . . . .

When the 'uyun report that the enemy is close by, at a command from the leader six or eight men mount three or four camels and go to examine the situation. These are called sabr. . . . Concealing their camels in a gully, they find out in the daytime how many camps there are in the neighborhood and where the camels are grazing; at night they try to count the tents and horses in the camp. If they succeed in capturing one of the enemy, they bring him to the leader, who makes him tell, by kindness or, if necessary, by threats, all he wants to know. Otherwise he must depend merely on the report . . . brought by the *sabr*.

Having learned the strength of the enemy and the location of their pastures, the leader examines the camels of his own party. The exhausted or slow animals are separated from the hardy and fast ones. The former . . . are then laden with all the baggage of the raiders and sent back to the previous night's quarters where they are to wait. The rest of the camels are then mounted each by two men armed with rifles. . . . Each horse is mounted by a man carrying a revolver or pistol and, when possible, a spear. The leader rides on horseback in front. Near the camp they conceal themselves. The cavalry prepare for the attack . . . while those on camels wait quietly for whatever may happen.

The attack is timed either for sunrise . . . when the left forelegs of the resting camels are being unfettered, or for the *zaha,* i.e. when the herds start for the pasture. . . .

The order to attack is given by the leader with the words: "Gain success, O ye looters . . . !" and by a gesture of his hand to the cavalry to advance. For their part they shout: "O Allah, by Allah himself!" or: "O Allah, thy will be done . . . !" and throw themselves on the herds without paying attention to the herdsmen. Every one tries to reach an animal with his spear, calling at the same time on his comrades to witness that it was he who captured it; he then drives it before him to a second and third, which he also makes his own. A long spear is very useful in this kind of work. . . .

The captured herds are driven by the cavalry to the leader, who waits for them with the camel riders. There the cavalry divides. One half, armed with spears, drives the booty to the last

quarters, the others, armed with revolvers, pistols, and rifles conceals itself in some suitable spot between the leader and the camp of the enemy. . . .

Both the reserve and the leader with the camel riders . . . wait for the counterattack . . . which the enemy usually makes in order to rescue the captured animals and to drive the raiders back. . . .

. . . it is only on rare occasions that the enemy can be taken wholly by surprise, because the chief of every camp follows the rule of sending out riders on camels . . . to observe the country on all sides. They usually start before sunrise, ascend the highest hillocks, survey the neighborhood in all directions, and do not return till after sunset. Should the pastures be more than twenty kilometers from the camp, the herds are accompanied by a troop of cavalry . . . who stay with them all day and also return only after sunset. Besides this, on all the highest elevations at different points around the pastures and between them and the camp, sentinels lie hidden behind piles of stones. These keep a sharp outlook for anything suspicious that may appear on the horizon. If something unusual is noticed by one of the mounted pickets . . . he ties his kerchief to the muzzle of his rifle, waves it in the direction of whatever has aroused his suspicion, and shouts at the top of his voice: "At their backs, O riders, an attack threatens you! . . ."

This shout is repeated and the direction indicated by the next sentinel, so that the whole camp is put on its guard in a few minutes. . . .

. . . .

If the attackers learn that there is in the camp to be assailed a fighter feared for his bravery, they prepare to destroy him. The evening before the attack the leader takes a cup of black coffee in his hand and says:

"This cup is filled with the blood of So-and-so. Who will drink it?"

If one of the men present takes the cup and drinks the coffee with the words "I am drinking the blood of So-and-so," he is obliged to meet the aforesaid hero in a duel. . . .

. . . . .

It is a fact that there are still many who drink the blood of the stricken enemy. 'Awda abu Tayeh shouted: "O Allah, give Da'san to me that I may drink his blood!" Da'san al-Hemsh was a brave Sharari warrior. Meeting him in a battle, 'Awda abu Tayeh with a well-aimed bullet swept him from the saddle, jumped down on him, and, putting his mouth to the wound, drank his blood. Then he cut open his breast, tore out the still beating heart, and ate it.

. . . . .

The fight called *manakh,* as distinguished from the *ghazw* or raid for booty, is very different. When a stronger tribe wants to possess itself of the territory of a weaker or to increase its fame . . . it moves all its herds and tents into the territory occupied by the latter . . . and finally encamps near the main camp of the enemy. The tents form as a rule two long rows, behind which the herds graze; in front of them, within rifle shot, stands the tent of the leader and a few others belonging to his retinue. In these few tents there is nothing except the utensils for making black coffee, meat being prepared in the tents behind. All the mares stand saddled by these war tents . . . while the riding camels lie fettered between the other tents. The men on foot are posted right and left of the war tents. Before the attack, the men on foot sometimes hide by the war tents. The cavalry attempts to drive the enemy to them and within rifle shot. Before the attack the tribal emblem Abu-d-Dhur is fastened to a camel which walks in the midst of the bravest youths on horseback. These warriors are accompanied by the prettiest women and girls of the camp, who, with their bosoms bared and hair loosened, keep shouting:

"He who runs away today shall never receive anything from us. . . ." Their inspiring high-pitched cries . . . are heard for a great distance. In order to raise the courage and steadiness of his warriors the chief orders the 'Atfa, a fancy litter, to be placed on a she-camel and the handsomest of the girls to take her place in it. Throwing off her kerchief the maiden loosens her hair, unfastens the string holding together the dress under the throat, and seats herself in the litter. Her female companions, likewise, mount she-camels and shouting *zagharit* hasten to join the melée in order to encourage their relatives and friends. If it is impossible to withstand the superior strength of the enemy, they call out to the girl on the 'Atfa to conceal herself, as the capture of the 'Atfa by the enemy would mean the greatest disgrace for both the reigning kin and the whole tribe. Thereupon the girl on the 'Atfa drives her animal to her father's tent, makes it kneel here, and either jumps off, unbuckles the litter, and pulls it inside the tent, or flees with it from the camp.

. . . . .

The Rwala have no flag of their own. They go on raids without any special device; but when waging war, whether of aggression or defense, that endangers the whole tribe, they take with them a special kind of a litter, called Abu-d-Dhur or al-Markab. This is perhaps the old decorated litter 'Atfa designed originally for the prettiest girl, who used to lead the tribe to the decisive battle. But there is nobody now who can remember that a girl ever sat in it. The Markab litter . . . is constructed of stout poles. . . . All the poles are wrapped round with ostrich feathers; to the upper poles are tied 12 short pegs . . . with plumes of bent ostrich feathers. . . . To be loaded, the Markab is placed in the litter . . . and this is tied to a camel with ropes. . . .

The Rwala believe that the litter is called Abu-d-Dhur, Father of Indefinite Periods of Time, because it is inherited from generation to generation, from age to age . . . and that it will last forever. Al-Markab forms the visible token of princely power, and therefore this litter remains in the prince's tent all the time, in the part of the tent reserved for the women; here it is guarded, day and night, both by the prince himself and by his slaves, against everybody and especially against the prince's nearest kinsmen. . . .

.   .   .   .

When the Rwala engage in a war of al-manakh . . . during which they move all their herds and tents into an enemy's territory, the camel carrying the Abu-d-Dhur walks at the head of the whole tribe, surrounded by warriors who follow every movement of the animal with the closest attention. They believe that Allah gives signs by means of the Abu-d-Dhur, from which the outcome of the fight can be foretold. Sometimes, in a dead calm, the ostrich feathers adorning the Abu-d-Dhur begin to flutter. At other times the litter leans to the right or left, but suddenly straightens itself, remains quietly upright, and then rocks a few times from side to side. All this, the Rwala think, happens by the power of Allah . . . who sends them help . . . from al-Markab, where He is believed to seat himself for a while. The waving of the feathers and the straightening of the Abu-d-Dhur are signs that Allah has touched it with his power.

After each victory a camel is killed before the Abu-d-Dhur in honor of Allah. This is also done every year, even if the Rwala have had no war to which the Abu-d-Dhur had to be taken.

If any reader believed that the life of the camel nomad was a simple affair of feeding his animals and moving them from pasture to pasture, he should by now be disabused. I can only compare the desert to the sea. Mariners put out on it, but they must some time come to shore. They may be like the cod fishermen on the Grand Banks, who stay out for months at a time, while supply ships bring them their food and take away their catch. Or they may be like pirates, supplying themselves by force from the stores of more timid victims.

For the student to whom this comes as new material, a few remarks may help tie it in with the rest of the world.

Page 381. The ra'w (ra'iyye) are what geographers call transhumants, people who live part of the year by farming, and part by pastoralism. Transhumants take their women and children out to the pastures with them and thus again differ from village people, who send their herds to the mountains or steppes with a few herdsmen. Transhumants may also be found in North Africa, the Iranian Plateau, and the Turkestans. Wherever people (non-machine-age) with agriculture and domestic animals live on the edge of a desert or seasonally dry steppe, transhumance is the most profitable means of livelihood.

The Shwaya are people just beyond the agricultural zone, where the rainfall is too scarce for crops. Still there is enough grass for sheep. Sheep cannot be moved rapidly, and the Shawiya cannot live where the annual rainfall reliability is not great. Their lack of mobility makes them easy prey for the Bedawin.

The Beni Sa'ud is the tribe of 'Abd el 'Aziz Ibn Sa'ud, founding king of Saudi Arabia.

Page 382. The *ahl* or kin is not a clan or gens because it is not a mutually exclusive unit. A given individual may be in *ahl* with several persons who are not in *ahl* with each other.

Page 383. The Bedawin pay the government taxes when they have to, and the less mobile tribes pay the Bedawin tribute, for protection against other nomads. Political power, in the form of military ability, is a negotiable commodity, like grain or cloth. The camel gives the Bedawin their mobility. The instability of the desert climate makes it necessary for them, in time of need, to take what they can from those who have plenty. From the point of view of the sedentary farmers or shepherds, it is better to pay one tribe of Bedawin a fixed sum each year for protection than to be at the mercy of any raiding tribe. The protecting tribe must in turn see to it that its protégés are able to produce the food that both need. The situation has many parallels elsewhere.

Pages 388–394. Seven different kinds of strangers may be found in a Bedawin camp—kusara, **K**ubeisis, slaves, Akeyl, smiths, and sloubbis. Each stranger has his own family affiliation elsewhere, his own institution; thus one camp may contain individuals from eight or more overlapping institutions. Since except for the kusara (guests) all are different kinds of specialists, this represents a considerable division of labor. The fact that the smiths cannot be touched in a raid insures the vital supply of tools and weapons. By the integration of all these different kinds of people, in combination with seasonal migrations and intertribal warfare, the Bedawin maintain a delicate adjustment with their otherwise difficult environment.

The Abu-d-Dhur, or sacred litter of the Rwala, is a symbol of the freedom and unity of the entire tribe. It may be compared directly to the Ark of the Covenant of the Old Testament, and to the sacred bundles of the Omaha Indians, now permanently deposited in the Peabody Museum at Harvard.

While the camel made the desert habitable, another possession has brought with it the end of the nomadic life. That is the automobile. Armed men in American cars can shoot down warriors on horse and camel, and thus people from tne settled countries can compete politically with those on the desert. Furthermore, trucks carry goods, in Egypt and Iraq, once borne by Arabian camels. The bottom has fallen out of the camel market. Ibn Saud pacified the nomads in his domain and spent large amounts of the money he has taken in from the pilgrimage, oil royalties and other revenues on irrigation projects, using artesian water. Some of the nomads have settled down. The life depicted by Musil was a going concern at the beginning of this century, and even to the time of World War I, but now it is passing into history.

Level Five

Hierarchies and Compound Institutions

15

The Vikings Abroad and at Home

To COMPARE the camel to a ship is far from original. Still the comparison is valid. We have dealt with the camel. Now for the ship, and the people who sail it. In Chapter 6 we saw how the skill of the Trobriand people at navigation made it possible for them to trade between islands and develop local specialization in manufacturing. The Polynesians were far more skillful and sailed over thousands of miles of the Pacific. They too traded. However, in the days before gunpowder and Columbus, the greatest volume of shipping existed, for millenia, in two other bodies of water—the Indian Ocean and the Mediterranean Sea.

In the Indian Ocean the alternation of monsoons blows ships before the wind in a great arc, from Malaysia and Southern India along the coast of Arabia, thence up the Persian Gulf or over to East Africa. When more archaeological work has been done we will probably know more about the extent of this traffic and be able to identify the sailors. In the Mediterranean, the Minoans were sailing from headland to headland, and even to the Atlantic gateways. The Phoenicians, who moved from the Persian Gulf to Syria about 1400 B.C., took most of this trade away from the Minoans, and went out into the Atlantic, even sailing around Africa. Greeks competed with and largely succeeded the Phoenicians.

Some of these sailors, of what particular nationality we do not know, skirted Portugal and Spain, and sailed between Ireland and Wales, to round the top of Scotland and cross the North Sea. They probably arrived in Scandinavia between 2200 and 1800 B.C. From that time on the Scandinavians were interested in shipbuilding, on the Mediterranean model. At the period of the breakup of the Roman Empire, Vikings entered the Mediterranean. Others rowed up the rivers emptying into the Baltic, skidded their ships over the snow to the headwaters of the rivers entering the Black Sea, and thus approached the great mart of Byzantium from the north. Still others portaged into the Volga, to reap the rich overland trade from India and China.

Furs from the north, silks from the east, metals and jewelry from the south, slaves from everywhere—these were the precious goods in which they traded. Few people realized, however, the importance of their river traffic until the discovery of the manuscript of Ibn Fadhlan, an Arab missionary en route from Baghdad to Kazan, via Bokhara, in 922 A.D. He had been sent by his Caliph, at the request of the Khan of the Bolgars at Kazan, to convert those Tartars to Islam. On the way up the Volga, the zealous Muslim encountered a settlement of Scandinavian merchants, whose manners and customs made a deep impression on him.

I submit his eyewitness account,* the earliest known contemporary text describing in detail the Varangians, as historians call the Scandinavian traders in early Russia. Ibn Fadhlan calls them Rusiya. From this word came the name of Russia. The Russian nation was founded less than a century before this encounter by another group of Northmen under Rurik, at Kiev. By 988 A.D. these various companies of merchants had been united under the power of the Kiev princes and converted to Christianity.

Page 80.—He says, I have seen the Rusiya when they came hither on their trading voyages and had encamped by the river Atil. I have never seen people with a more developed bodily stature than they. They are tall as date palms, blond and ruddy so that they do not need to wear either a qurtaq nor a kaftan; rather the men among them wear a garment (*kisa*) which only covers the half of his body and leaves one of his hands free.

[*The garments of the Vikings were not as well adapted for the cold weather as those of the Eskimo. They did not have to be.*]

Page 81.—Each one of them has an axe, a sword and a knife with him and all of these whom we have mentioned never let themselves be separated from their weapons. Their swords are broad-bladed, provided with rills and of the Frankish type.

Each one of them has from the edge of his nails to the neck figures and trees and other things tattooed in dark green.

Page 82.—Each of their women has fastened upon the two breasts a brassière (*huqqa*) of iron, silver, copper or gold, in weight and value according to the wealth of her husband. Each brassière has a ring (*halqa*) to which a knife is likewise fixed and is dependent upon the breast. Around the neck the women wear rings of gold and silver. For the man, if he possesses ten thousand dirhems, has a neck ring made for his wife; if he has twenty thousand in his possession, then he has two neck rings made for her. And so his wife receives another neck ring with the addition of each ten thousand dirhems. Accordingly it often happens that there are a number of neck rings upon the neck of one of them. The most highly prized ornaments are considered by them the green glass beads (*lit.* coral) made out of clay which are found in the ships. They bargain for these beads and buy a bead for a dirhem apiece and string them into necklaces for their women.

[*This is a very early mention of faience trade beads. In such remote places as the Congo and the interior of Borneo, one finds very old beads treasured by the natives. Experts can trace some to China, others to the eastern Mediterranean in antiquity, others to Venice. They are prime "tracers" of cultural diffusion. The Northmen were diffusing them at the time of Ibn Fadhlan's visit.*]

Page 83.—They (the Rus) are the dirtiest creatures of God. They have no shame in voiding their bowels and bladder nor do they wash themselves when polluted by emission of semen nor do they lave their hands after eating. They are, then, like asses who have gone astray. They come from their own country, moor their barks on the strand of the Atil, which is a great river, and build on its bank great houses

* Blake, Robert, and Frye, Richard, *Observations on the Manners and Customs of the Northmen Encamped on the Volga*, Βυξαντίνα καὶ μεταβυξαντίνα, New York, 1947, Fasc. 2. in press. By permission of the authors.

out of wood. In a house like this ten or twenty people, more or less, live together. Each of them has a resting bench whereon he sits and with them are the fair maidens (slave girls) who are destined for sale to the merchants and they may have intercourse with their maiden while their comrades look on. At times a crowd of them come together and do such things, the ones in the presence of the others. It also happens that a merchant who comes into the house to buy a girl off one of them finds him in the very act of having intercourse with her and he (the Rus) will not let her be until he has fulfilled his intention.

Page 84.—As a matter of duty they wash daily their faces and heads in a manner so dirty and so unclean as could possibly be imagined. Thus it is carried out. The girl brings each morning early a large vessel with water and gives the vessel to her master and he washes in it his hands and face and the hair of his head; he washes it and combs it with a comb into the bucket, then blows his nose and spits into the bucket. He holds nothing impure back but rather lets it go into the water. After he has done what is needful, the girl takes the same vessel to the one who is nearest and he does just as his neighbor had done. She carries the vessel from one to another until all in the house have had a turn at it and each of them has blown his nose, spat into, and washed his face and hair, in the vessel.

[*The "dirtiness" of the Northmen which shocked the delicate Arab reflects a difference of custom. Even today Arabs think us unclean for bathing in tubs, and thus re-using polluted water. They insist on having water poured over them, shower-bath fashion. The "immodesty" of the Northmen in reference to solitary bodily functions has survived into our own culture; I*

have heard Arabs complain about Christians for the same reason. As for their sexual immodesty, remember that the girls were foreigners and the Northmen were far from home. No mention is made of this practice in the saga literature, possibly because it came down to us through a Christian filter, but more likely because the saga characters had mothers and wives in residence.]

Page 85.—When their barks come to this anchorage each one of them goes ashore with bread, meat, onion, milk and nabid (probably beer) and betakes himself to a tall wooden pole set upright that has a face like to a man: around it are small images and behind these are long, tall poles driven into the earth. And he (the Rus) comes to the great image and prostrates himself before it; then he says, "O my Lord, I have come from a far country and have with me so many slave girls and so many sable pelts," until he has enumerated all the goods which he has brought for sale and then continues: "To Thee have I brought this gift." Then he lays down what he had brought before the wooden *image* and continues: "I wish that Thou shouldst provide me with a merchant who has many dinars and dirhems and who should buy from me at the price I desire and will raise no objection to me to aught I may say." Then he departs. If he has difficulties in his trading and the days of his stay become extended, then he makes a second and a third gift. Should difficulties again arise over what he hopes to attain, he then brings a gift to all these little figures, and begs them to intercede and says: "These are the wives, daughters and sons of our Lord," and so he continues to approach each image one after the other and to beg them and implore them to intercede and prays before them in abasement. His dealings often go on more easily and he sells everything he has brought with them; then he says, "My Lord has fulfilled my desire. I must repay it Him." He gathers a number of sheep and oxen, slaughters them, gives away a part of the meat as alms and brings the remainder and casts it before that great wooden image and before the little wooden images which stand around it, and hangs the heads of the cattle or those of the sheep on the poles which are erected in the earth. In the night the dogs come and devour all, and he who has made this sacrifice says, "Verily, my Lord is content with me and he has eaten up my gift."

[*This account of the worship of idols by the Northmen may be the only detailed, contemporary, eyewitness account of the heathen Scandinavian ritual in existence. Like other specialists in trade, they had gods which helped them in this enterprise.*]

Page 86.—If one of them falls ill, they erect a tent for him at a distance from themselves and leave them there. They put beside him a little bread and water, do not approach him and also do not speak to him. Indeed what is still more, they do not visit him at all during all the days of his illness even if he is weak or if he is a slave. When he has recovered and gets up, they come back to him. If, however, he dies, they cremate him. If he is a slave, they let him be and then the dogs and the carrion fowl devour him. If they catch a thief or a robber, they lead him to a stout tree, throw a trusty rope around his neck and hang him to the tree, and he remains hanging until with the wind and rain he falls to pieces.

[*The Northmen isolated the sick in small huts outside the camp. This is an old practice common among American Indians and also found in the Caucasus tribes of modern times. It is due, of course, to an ignorance of the cause of illness and a fear of contagion, magical or otherwise.*]

Page 87.—They told me that they carry out many ceremonies when their chiefs die, the least whereof is the cremation, and it interested me to find out more about it. Finally, the news was brought me that a prominent man among them had died. They laid him in a grave and covered it with a roof over it for ten days until they were through with the cutting out and sewing together of his garments. Thus it is: if the deceased is a poor man, they make for him a small bark, put him in it and burn the bark; if he is a rich man, they gather his possessions together and divide them in three parts: one third remains for his family; with the second third they cut garments out for him, and with the third part they brew nabid (beer) for themselves which they drink on the day when his slave girl kills herself and is cremated with her master. They drink the nabid to insensibility day and night. It often happens that one of them dies with his beaker in his hand. When a high chief dies, his family says to his slave girls and servants, "Which one of you wishes to die with him?" Then one of them answers, "I." When he has said this, he is bound. He can in no way be allowed to withdraw his word. If he wishes it, it is not permitted. For the most part, this self-sacrifice is made by the maidens.

Page 88.—When the above-mentioned man had died, his relatives said to his maidens, "Who will die with him?" Thereupon one of them answered, "I." Then the relations of the deceased charged two maidens to watch her and to go with her wherever she went. Indeed they even washed her feet with their own hands. The relatives of the deceased then began to occupy themselves with the preparations for the funeral ceremonies, to have the garments cut out for him and to prepare whatever else was necessary. The maiden meanwhile drank all day long and sang joyfully and enjoyed herself in view of the future.

Page 89.—When the day had come on which he and the maiden should be cremated, I put in an appearance at the river where his bark lay. I saw that this had already been hauled up on land. There were four props set up for the ship, of birch and other wood, and around the bark had been built a large structure like a large ship-gantry of wood. Then they hauled the ship further up until it was placed inside this structure. The people then began to move hither and thither and to speak words that I did not understand, while he (the deceased) was still lying in his grave, out of which they had not yet taken him. Then they brought a resting bench, placed it on the ship and covered it with drapes of Byzantine brocade and also with pillows of Byzantine brocade. Thereupon an old woman came, whom they call the angel of death and spread the drapes mentioned over the resting bench. She had had the oversight over the sewing of the garments of the deceased and their completion. This old woman kills the girl. I saw that she was an old giantess, fat and grim to behold. When they came to his grave, they removed the earth from the timbers and raised the timbers, drew him forth in the same garment in which he had died and I saw how he had turned black from the cold earth. I also noted that they had put in his grave nabid (beer), fruits and a kind of mandolin (tanbura). They now took all these out of the grave. Naught had changed in the deceased apart from the color of his skin. They then dressed him in stockings, trousers, boots, a quartaq and kaftan of brocade with gold buttons, put a cap of brocade and sable pelts

upon him and carried him into the tent which had been erected on the bark. Here they placed him upon the drapes, propped him up with cushions, brought nabid, fruits and flowers and laid these beside him. They also brought bread, meat and onions and strewed them before him. Then they brought a dog, cleft it in two halves and laid it in the ship. Thereupon they brought all his weapons and laid them by his side. Then they took two horses, drove them until they sweated, then cleft both of them in twain with a sword and laid their flesh in the bark. Then they brought two cows, cut them in twain likewise and laid them in the ship. Then they brought a cock and a hen, killed them and threw both into the ship. The maiden who wished to be put to death went hither and thither and went into each one of their tents, and the head of each tent had intercourse with her saying: "Say to thy lord, I have done this out of love of thee."

Page 90.—On Friday in the afternoon they brought the maiden to a structure which they had erected rather like a door frame. She put both her feet on the palms of the men and was lifted up onto this door frame and said her say. Then they let her down again. Thereupon they put her up a second time. She repeated what she had done the first time, and then they let her down and let her go up a third time, and again she did as she had done on the first two occasions. Then they gave her a hen. She cut off its head and cast it away. They took the hen and laid it in the bark. Thereupon I asked the interpreter what her actions meant. He said, "When they raised her up the first time, she said, 'Behold! I see my father and my mother'; the second time she said, 'There I see all my deceased relatives sitting'; the third time she said, 'There I behold my lord sitting in paradise and paradise is fair and green and around him are men and servitors. He calls me. Bring me to him.' " Now they led her to the ship; she took off the two armlets which she wore and gave them to the old woman, whom they called the angel of death and who was to kill her. Then the slave girl took off both anklets which she had and gave them to the two maidens who had waited on her and who were the daughters of the old woman known as the angel of death. Then the people lifted her onto the ship but did not yet let her go into the tent. Hereupon came the men with shields and staves and gave her a beaker of beer, whereupon she sang and drank it off. The interpreter said to me, "With this she is bidding goodbye to her friends." Then she was given another beaker. She took it and sang for a long time while the old woman was urging her to drink the vessel off and to go into the tent where her lord lay. Then I saw how disturbed she was. She wished to go into the tent but put her head between the tent and the side of the ship. Then the old woman took her by the head, made her go into the tent and also entered with her. Then the men began to beat their shields with the staves so that her shrieks would not be heard and the other maidens terrified. Then six men went into the tent and all had intercourse with the maiden. Then they placed her beside her dead lord, two men seized her by the feet and two by the hands. Then the old woman whom they call the angel of death placed a rope in which a bight had been made and gave it to two of the men to pull at the two ends. Then the old woman came to her with a broad-bladed dagger and began to jab it into her ribs and pull it out again and the two men strangled her with the rope until she was dead.

Page 91.—After they had laid the maiden they had killed beside her master, wood for kindling the fire was prepared. The closest relative of the deceased approached and took a piece of wood, kindled it and then walked backwards to the vessel, keeping his face turned to the spectators, holding the burning brand in one hand and placing his other upon his anus. He was naked and walked backwards until he had reached the vessel and set fire to the wood that had been prepared beneath the vessel. Then the people came with kindling and other fire wood, each having a brand burning at the end and laid this stick in the pile of wood. Fire then spread through the wood and spread to the kindling, the ship, the tent the man, the maiden and everything that was in the ship. A strong and violent wind sprang up through which the flames were fanned and its burning greatly enhanced.

Page 92.—A man of the Rusiya was standing beside me and I heard him talking to the interpreter and I asked what the Rus had said to him. The interpreter answered that he said, "They, the Arab communities are stupid." So I asked, "Why?" He said, "You go and cast into the earth the people whom you both love and honor most among men. Then the earth, creeping things and worms devour them. We however let them burn for an instant and accordingly he enters into Paradise at once in that very hour," and he burst out into immoderate laughter. He said, "His Lord sent the wind for love of him so that he might be snatched away in the course of an hour." In fact, an hour had not passed by when ship, wood, maiden and lord had turned to ashes and to dust of ashes. Then they built on the place of the ship that they had hauled up out of the stream something like to a rounded mound. In the middle of this they erected a great beam of birchwood and wrote upon it the name of the man and the name of the King of the Rus, whereupon they departed.

[*This is probably the only eyewitness account of a ship burial in existence. One is reminded of the account, in Book IV, chapters 71–73 of Herodotus, of the burial of a Scythian king which also took place on the shores of the Volga. Predynastic Sumerians and Egyptians, the Mongols of the time of Genghis Khan, the Natchez Indians of Louisiana, and the people of Benin, in West Africa, fifty years ago, all sacrificed human beings at the funerals of their important dead. In India widows of important men were burned on their husbands' pyres until modern times. Under certain conditions, when a society has developed a hierarchy in which a single individual becomes so powerful that his death shatters the equilibrium of his associates, the funeral rites must also be impressive, if a restoration is to take place. No element in a ritual can be more laden with emotional content than human sacrifice.*]

As to the king before he died, Ibn Fadhlan added the following:*

It is the custom among the Northmen that with the king in his hall there shall be four hundred of the most valiant and trustworthy of his companions, who stand ready to die with him or to offer their life for his. Each of them has a girl to wait upon him—to wash his head, and to prepare food and drink; and besides her, he has another who serves as his concubine. These four hundred sit below the king's high seat, which is large, and adorned with precious stones. Accompanying him on his high seat are forty girls, destined for his bed, whom he causes to sit near him. Now and again he will proceed to enjoy one of them in the presence of the above mentioned nobles of his following. The king does not descend from his high seat, and is therefore obliged, when he needs to relieve himself, to make use of a vessel. If he wishes to ride, his horse is led up to his high seat, and he mounts from there; when he is ready to alight, he rides his horse up so close that he can step immediately from it to his throne. He has a lieutenant, who leads his armies, wars with his enemies, and represents him to his subjects.

The Northmen described by Ibn Fadhlan belonged to a culture ancestral to our own, and physically they were part of the genetic pool which produced the ancestors of many Americans. It is a healthy exercise to read the impression of a cultured Arab, who came from what was probably the highest civilization of his time, on the subject of our crude and hearty forebears.

Within a century after Ibn Fadhlan, other Northmen were compiling accounts of their own, the Sagas and Eddas. These also provide a wealth of eyewitness material. Just as some of the Scandinavians went eastwards over the rivers to the trading centers of the east, so others raided and traded along the coasts of western Europe and the British Isles. Still others, seeking refuge from enforced conversion to Christianity, settled Iceland. It is from the last group that most of the literary material emanates. With all, however, the cultural details were much the same. In order to illustrate these I quote from a manuscript by Charles Harding III,* who in turn draws on saga and edda material. The comments which interlard the quotations are Doctor Harding's unless italicized.

*Translated by Albert Stanburrough Cook, in Journal of English and Germanic Philology, Vol. 22, 1923, pp. 54-63.

* The Social Anthropology of Early Iceland. Unpublished manuscript. By permission.

As regards to status it may be said that in Iceland there were roughly speaking three classes. The more or less classical description and the mythical origin of these is told in *Rigsthula* in *The Poetic Edda,* wherein the god (Heimdall) wanders abroad in the world under the name of Rig and sleeps with three women, the resulting offspring being the ancestors of the three classes. The thralls are described as being short, dark, gnarled and ugly, doing unskilled labor; the karls "ruddy of face, and flashing his eyes," ploughing and building houses; the jarl

Blond was his hair, and bright his cheeks,
Grim as a snake's were his glowing eyes,

and he spent his time practicing the use of weapons.

The thralls mentioned in the sagas and *The Landnamabok* are usually Irish or Scotch. Thralls were bought and sold, the average price being about a mark of silver and half, wergeld for them the same (equal to half that of a free man). They did the manual labor around the house, in the barns and in the fields. A rich man might have female thralls or (ambatts) for concubines. In *The Laxdale Saga* there is an excellent account of the purchase of a female thrall.

Gilli asked what he and his companions wished to buy. Hoskuld said he should like to buy some bondswoman, "if you have one to sell." Gilli answers: "There, you mean to give me trouble by this, in asking for things you don't expect me to have in stock; but it is not sure that that follows." Hoskuld then saw that right across the booth there was drawn a curtain; and Gilli then lifted the curtain, and Hoskuld saw that there were twelve women seated behind the curtain. So Gilli said that Hoskuld should come on and have a look, if he would care to buy any of these women. Hoskuld did so. They sat all together across the booth. Hoskuld looks carefully at these women. He saw a woman sitting out by the skirt of the tent, and she was very ill-clad. Hoskuld thought, as far as he could see, this woman was fair to look upon. Then said Hoskuld, "What is the price of that woman if I should wish to buy her?" Gilli replied, "Three silver pieces is what you must weigh me out for her." "It seems to me," said Hoskuld, "that you charge very highly for this bondswoman, for that is the price of three (such)." Then Gilli said, "You speak truly, for I value her worth more than the others. Choose any of the other eleven, and pay one mark of silver for her, this one being left in my possession." Hoskuld said, "I must first see how much silver there is in the purse I have on my belt," and he asked Gilli to take the scales while he searched the purse. Gilli then said, "On my side there shall be no guile in this matter; for, as to the ways of this woman, there is a great draw-back which I wish, Hoskuld, that you know before we strike this bargain." Hoskuld asked what it was. Gilli replied, "The woman is dumb. I have tried in many ways to get her to talk, but have never got a word out of her, and I feel quite sure that this woman knows not how to speak." Then, said Hoskuld, "Bring out the scales, and let me see how much the purse I have got here may weigh." Gilli did so, and now they weigh the silver, and there were just three marks weighed. Then said Hoskuld, "Now the matter stands so that we can close our bargain. You take the money for yourself, and I will take the woman. I take it that you have behaved honestly in this affair, for, to be sure, you had no mind to deceive me herein." Hoskuld then went home to his booth. That same night Hoskuld went into bed with her. The next morning when men got dressed, spake Hoskuld, "The clothes Gilli the Rich gave you do not appear to be very grand, though it is true that to him it is more to dress twelve women than it is to me to dress only one." After that Hoskuld opened a chest, and took out some fine women's clothes and gave them to her; and it was the saying of every one that she looked very well when she was dressed. . . .[1]

In general thralls, as they appear in the sagas, are stupid or surly. Little mention is made of them. However in *The Landnamabok* there are several accounts of revolts of thralls, evidently due to harsh treatment.

But in the spring he wished to sow. He had one ox only, and he made his thralls drag the plough. But when Heor-leif and his men were in the hall, Duf-thac made a plan that the thralls should slay the ox, and say that a bear of the wood had slain it, and then that they should fall upon Heor-leif and his men as they were seeking the bear. And they did so, and told their tale to Heor-leif. And as they went forth to seek the bear, and were scattered through the shaw, the thralls slew every one his man, and murdered them every one. Then they ran away with the women and the stock and the boat. The thralls went out to the islands which they could see in the sea to the southwest, and there they dwelt for some little while. . . .[2]

House carls were free men who lived with and worked for wealthier men. They were craftsmen, warriors and farmers.

The term bondi is applied to any free man owning his own land. He may be rich, poor, have thralls and carls, or not. He is distinguished from the carls simply by owning land.

The upper classes or chieftains were the wealthy landowners. They were known as "Godar" as they owned and kept the temples. Their office was known as "godord." Also in early times they conducted the local things. They enlisted the support of the neighboring bondi for upkeep for the temple and support in the things as their thing-

men. The position of Godi (the godord) and the temple or hut were inherited by all the sons, but only one of the sons functioned in this office. Godords could be bought. In *The Saga of Hrafnkel Freysgodi* we have an excellent description of such a man.

. . . When Hrafnkel had taken land at Manor, he made a great sacrifice, and had a great temple built. Hrafnkel loved no other god more than Frey, and to him he gave the half of all his best treasures. Hrafnkel settled all the valley, and gave men land, but wished to be their master all the same, and took the godord over them, on which account his name was lengthened and he was called Freysgodi, and was a very overbearing but talented man. He forced under him the men of Glacierdale as thingmen. Hrafnkel was gentle and blithe with his own men, but harsh and stubborn towards those of Glacierdale, and men got no fair play from him. Hrafnkel took part in many single combats, and paid wergeld to no man, so that no one got any redress from him whatever he did.[3]

There was considerable division of labor along sex lines. Men built houses, fished, tilled the fields, tended the herds and in the winter made furniture, boats and tools.

Skallagrim was a very hard-working man. He had always many men with him, and had fetched many of the provisions and means of subsistence, for at first they had but few cattle in comparison with what was needed for so many. His cattle found their own food during the winter in the forests. He was a great shipwright, and there was no want of drift-timber west of Myrar. He had a boer built at Alptanes, and had another household there; his men went out fishing, seal-catching, and egg-gathering from there, as there was a quantity of these things; he

---

[1] Press, Muriel A. C. (trans.), *The Laxdale Saga*. J. M. Dent and Co., London, 1899.
[2] Vigfusson, Gudbrand and F. York Powell, *Origines Islandicae*, vol. I, Oxford University Press, London, 1905.

[3] Jones, Gwyn (translator), *Four Icelandic Sagas*. American Scandinavian Foundation, N. Y. Princeton University Press, Princeton, N. J., 1935.

also had drift-timber brought in. Many whales were there then, and they could shoot as many as they wanted, for the creatures were not used to men. He had a third boer near the sea, in the western part of Myrar, where it was still easier to procure drift-wood; there he had grain grown and called the farm Akrar. Some outlying islands there were called Hvalseyjar, because whales were found on them. Skallagrim also had his men up at the salmon rivers to fish, and placed Odd Einbui at Gljufra to take care of the catch; he lived at Einbuabrekkur, and Einbuanes is named from him. . . . When the cattle of Skallagrim grew numerous they all went up on the mountains in the summer. He found that those cattle which went up on the heaths became much larger and fatter, and that the sheep kept themselves during the winter in mountain valleys if they were not taken down so he had a farm made up at the mountain, and had a household there where his sheep were taken care of. Gris took care of that farm, and Grisartunga is named from him.[4]

[Many of the men also went on long sea voyages for the purpose of trading.]
Thorlaf Cimbe took his passage that summer with merchants that lay in Stream-frith, and he was in a berth with the mates. It was then the custom of merchants not to have a meatswain or cook, but the messmates cast lots among them to find who should do the cooking day by day. All messmates were bound to have drink in common, and a butt stood against the mast which the drink was in, and a lid over the butt, but some of the drink was in casks or beakers, and thence the butt was filled as it was drunk out. But when they were all ready bound for sea, there came a man to the pier-rock where the booth was. This man was big of growth, and had a burden on his back; there seemed to them something strange about him. He asked for the captain, and was shown his booth. He put down his

bag hard by the booth-door, and then went into the booth. He asked if the captain would give him a berth to sea. They asked him his name, but he gave his name as Arnbeorn the son of Asbeorn from Comb, saying he wished to go abroad to seek Beorn his brother that had been abroad some winters, and of whom there had been no news ever since he went to Denmark. The Eastmen [Swedes—Ed.] said that the cargo was all stowed, and that they could not break bulk again. He said that he had no more outfit than could lie on deck. And because they thought the voyage was urgent upon him they received him, but he had no messmate, and berthed forward on deck. In his bag there were three hundred wadmal [standard lengths of coarse woolen cloth—Ed.] and twelve merchantable rugs and his provender. Arnbeorn was a good help, and ready to lend a hand, and the merchants liked him well. They got a smooth voyage and made Haurdland, and came ashore at an outlying reef. They cooked their meat ashore. It fell to Thorlaf Cimbe to cook, and he had to cook porridge. Arnbeorn was ashore, and he was making porridge for himself; he had the mess-kettle which Thorlaf was to use afterwards. Thorlaf went ashore then, and he asked Arnbeorn to give him the kettle, but he had not yet done stirring his porridge, and was still stirring it in the kettle, and Thorlaf stood by him. Then the Eastmen called from the ship to Thorlaf to get their food ready, saying that Thorlaf was a regular Icelander in his laziness. Then Thorlaf lost his temper, and took the kettle and poured out (Arnbeorn's) porridge, and then turned away with the kettle. Arnbeorn was left there with the porridge-spurtle in his hand, and he struck at Thorlaf with it and hit him on the neck. It was not a heavy blow, but inasmuch as the porridge was hot, Thorlaf was scalded on the neck. He said, "The Eastmen must not laugh at us, that we are two Icelanders here and have to be pulled apart like two *fighting* dogs, but it shall be remembered when we are back in Iceland." Arnbeorn made no answer. They lay there a few nights before they got a

[4] (Egil's Saga, c. 29.) Du Chaillu, Paul B., *The Viking Age*, 2 vols., Charles Scribner's Sons, N. Y., 1890, p. 528.

fair wind for the shore, and there they unloaded the ship. Thorlaf took up guest-quarters there, but Arnbeorn took a berth with certain traders east to Wick, and thence to Denmark to seek his brother Beorn.[5]

Thorolf had a large seagoing ship; in every way it was most carefully built, and painted nearly all over above the water-line; it had a sail with blue and red stripes, and all the rigging was very elaborate. This he made ready, and or-dered his men-servants to go with it; he had put on board dried fish, skins, tallow, gray fur and other furs, which he had from the mountains; all this was of much value. He sent it westward to England to buy cloth (woollen) and other goods he needed. They went southward along the coast, and then out to sea; when they arrived in England they found a good market, loaded the ship with wheat and honey, wine and cloth, and returned in the autumn with fair winds" (Egil's Saga).[6]

Women sewed, spun, wove, made cheese, butter, beer, prepared food, tended the small children. They took no part in the things or the games of the men. At feasts women filled the bowls of the guests. Priestesses are mentioned.

Age made some difference. A boy could not become a godi until of age.

It was the law at that time that when the heirs were minors the Thingman who was thought the fittest should keep the godiship (until they were of age).[7]

Children are seldom encountered in the sagas. A woman in childbirth was cared for by her housemaids and neigh-bor's wives.

Housemaids and neighbouring women shall be at the *bedjourney* of every woman until the child is born, and not leave it be-fore they have laid it to the breast of the mother. . . . No woman shall have her

child at the breast longer than three fasts, but shall have it until the third one. If her husband says that she must take her child from the breast and his wife has such power that she will not obey his words, she is liable to pay three marks of her own property. If he does not heed it any more than she, then they are each to pay three marks of their property.[8]

After birth children were sprinkled with water and given a name. This occurred even in pagan times, though it may have been an aspect of Christianity which diffused into the north before Christianity as a whole arrived. When a child cut his first tooth he was given a tooth-present.

Asta, Gudbrand's daughter, bore a boy who was named Olaf when he was water-sprinkled by Hrani. It was said by some that Gudbrand would not let him be raised on account of the hatred he had against his father (Harald Graenski), until Hrani told him that he had seen light over the house in which the child was born. Gud-brand himself went to look at it. Then the boy was taken and brought up with great love. Hrani gave him a belt and a knife as tooth-fee, and when he grew up he gave him a ring and a sword.[9]

In general it would seem the boys went with their fathers when old enough and the girls stayed with their mothers. Thus they learned their roles in the society.

Family relationship may be easily de-termined in the sagas, as long genealo-gies are given. Kinship is of great im-portance in the sagas, especially in feuds and legal contests. Marriage joined two families together, but the marriage contract was largely an eco-nomic contract. There were no reli-gious or ceremonial bonds and it was in some cases a very brittle affair. Other sorts of relations such as foster or

---

[5] Vigfusson & Powell II, *Eyrbyggia Saga*, pp. 119–20.

[6] Du Chaillu II, p. 209.

[7] (Vatnsdaela, c. 41, 42.) Du Chaillu I., p. 528.

[8] (Borgarthing Law, 3.) Du Chaillu II, p. 36.

[9] (St. Olaf's Saga, vol. iv; Fornmanna Sogur.) Du Chaillu II, p. 37.

blood-brotherhood were used to strengthen the ties between the two families.

With regard to geographical distribution it may be simply said that to some degree the interaction between people is more frequent the nearer they live together. The more people there are in an area the greater number of relationships and interactions there are. This is often important and must be considered. Also customs and laws varied slightly from district to district, but the basic pattern was the same.

There is one other factor to consider. This is the periodicity of events. By this I mean such things as feasts, thing meetings, and sacrifices, which occurred on set calendric dates, and also such broader reoccurrences as the change of occupation with the season, the summer being the time for farming and fishing and trading, winter for manufacturing and playing games. By knowing these periodicities one can tell what a man will be doing at certain times, not his actions in detail, of course, but their general pattern.

Laws of a country provide a formalized and ideal pattern of behavior and it is therefore important to consider the legal set-up.

In the earliest period the godords and the associated things were owned and conducted by the chieftains, who had built the temples and had thus become godar. These were the nuclei of the political organization. The godi was his own priest and others had to pay for the privilege of worshipping in the temple. Within his own district the godi represented the law. He presided over thing meetings. The other men, his dependents of the district, supported him and he was supposed to look after their interests or they would put themselves under the protection of another chief. The early things were simply courts for the settlement of legal cases. With an increasing population it became necessary to find a means to settle disputes between the thingmen of different godar. So in the *Saga of the Men of Keelness* and the *Eyrbyggia Saga* we find accounts of several godar conducting things together. This development led to the establishment of an Althing for the whole of the island.

In 927 Ulfljoti of Lon was sent to Norway to study the law of the Gulathing and the result of his report was the establishment of the Althing at Thingvollr. The local things still looked after local matters. All power, even in the Althing, was still in the hands of the godar. In 965 the local organization was changed. Iceland was divided into four quarters, each of which was divided into three districts, except the Northlanders' Quarter where there were four, and the thingmen were obliged to seek justice in their own districts at the local Spring or Varthing, which took the place of the courts held by the Godar. The number of godar was limited to thirty-nine, three to a district, and it would seem that the bondi got some control over them. The quarters had higher quarter-things. Changes were made also in the Althing.

In Icelandic law the emphasis was laid on going through the proper procedure accurately. It was the letter of the law, not the spirit, that counted. A slip in a single detail might lose a case. The support of a powerful man was necessary, for often the sheer force of his authority or the number of his followers would turn the tide. Once a case was won the victor had to enforce the decree of the court himself. If he were a man of small means and few followers, he could do nothing without the support of a more powerful man. There is an excellent example of this in *The Saga of Hrafnkel Freysgodi.* Sam, an uninfluential bondi, took suit against a powerful godi, Hrafnkel. He was fortunate enough to get the support of three very influential brothers who had many friends and followers, and so won his case.

They stayed there till the judges fared out. Then Sam called up his men and went to the Hill of Laws. The court was then set there. Sam went boldly to the court, forwith began naming witnesses, and carried on his case according to the true law of the land against Hrafnkel Godi, without a slip and with goodly pleading. With that, along came the sons of Thjostar with a great band of men. All the men from the west country gave them aid, and it was clear that the sons of Thjostar were popular men. Sam carried on the case in court until Hrafnkel was called on for the defence, unless that man was there present who wished to bring forward a defence in law. The applause was great at Sam's case, and it was a question whether anyone would wish to bring forward a legal defence for Hrafnkel. Men hastened to Hrafnkel's booth and told him what was afoot. He stirred himself quickly, called up his men, and went to the court, reckoning that there would be little defence there. He had it in mind to put an end to the bringing of lawsuits against him by petty folk, and meant to wreck the court for Sam and drive him from his case. But of this there was now no chance. There was such a press in front of him that Hrafnkel could get nowhere near, and he was crowded away by sheer force, so that he could not hear their case against him, and was therefore unable to bring forward a legal defence for himself. But Sam carried his suit the full length of the law, until Hrafnkel was outlawed at this Thing.[10]

The central theme of all sagas is the feud. The feud was a family affair and followed kinship lines both of blood and marriage. If a man were killed his

[10] Jones, Gwyn (translator). *Four Icelandic Sagas.* American Scandinavian Foundation, N. Y. Princeton University Press, Princeton, N. J., 1935. P. 50

near relatives tried to kill his killer. If they could not kill him, one of his relatives did just as well. It was a matter of honor to avenge one's relatives and friends, and men felt disgraced if they were unable to do so. Furthermore they lost prestige as their thingmen and retainers relied upon them for their protection. If the chieftain could not avenge himself, he could do little for others. All insults, wounds and damage to property were avenged. Not only was there a question of honor and prestige, but there was also a real feeling of loss that demanded satisfaction. Thus a man's brother might avenge. Later his sons would grow up and they too would feel the obligation to avenge him. So the feud spread.

To a considerable degree the taking up of cases of the thing was an extension of the feud. The thing exercised no executive function and the party winning the case had to enforce the sentence. Conflicts would then start again.

In a society pervaded by the feud a man who had neither family nor supporters or was not the supporter of another and more powerful man had a difficult time. But there was a very strong tendency for men to group together. The family formed the most natural group and a large family was fairly safe and could exert considerable influence by extending or withholding its support. The family group was extended by marriage and by the institution of fostering. A ceremony of blood-brotherhood was performed to bind two or more men together. Then they were obliged to avenge one another.

Less wealthy men and small landholders put themselves under the godar for protection, and in turn supported him.

In general little enough is told of berserks. They seem to have no land

and no families, except that sometimes two berserks are brothers. They wander about in groups or singly with a band of followers. They demand women or property from those they encounter. They are described as being very strong and easily angered almost to a state of frenzy. Often they took service under Scandinavian kings or nobles who kept body guards of fighting men. The only explanation for them that I can arrive at is that possibly they were men of rank who had lost their land or younger sons who, having no land, wandered about taking what they could get. In many cases they were little better than robbers. Finally berserks were outlawed.

At Yule came Grettir to a bonder who was called Einar, he was a rich man, and was married and had one daughter of marriageable age, who was called Gyrid; she was a fair woman, and was deemed a right good match; Einar bade Grettir abide with him through Yule, and that proffer he took.

Then it was the wont far and wide in Norway that woodmen and misdoers would break out of the woods and challenge men for their women, or they took away men's goods with violence, whereas they had not much help of men.

Now it so befell there, that one day in Yule there came to Einar the bonder many ill-doers together, and he was called Snoekoll who was the head of them, and a great bearserk he was. He challenged goodman Einar to give up his daughter, or to defend her, if he thought himself man enough thereto; but the bonder was then past his youth, and was no man for fighting: he deemed he had a great trouble on his hands, and asked Grettir, in a whisper, what rede he would give thereto: "Since thou art called a famous man." Grettir bade him say yea to those things alone, which he thought of no shame to him.

The bearserk sat on his horse, and had a helm on his head, but the cheek-pieces were not made fast; he had an iron-rimmed shield before him, and went on in the most monstrous wise.

Now he said to the bonder, "Make one or other choice speedily, or what counsel is that big churl giving thee who stands there before thee; is it not so that he will play with me?"

Grettir said, "We are about equal herein, the bonder and I, for neither of us is skilled in arms."

Snoekoll said, "Ye will both of you be somewhat afraid to deal with me, if I grow wroth."

"That is known when it is tried," said Grettir.

Now the bearserk saw that there was some edging out of the matter going on, and he began to roar aloud, and hit the rim of his shield, and thrust it up into his mouth, and gaped over the corner of the shield, and went on very madly. Grettir took a sweep along over the field, and when he came alongside of the bearserk's horse, sent up his foot under the tail of the shield so hard, that the shield went up into the mouth of him, and his throat was riven asunder, and his jaws fell down on his breast. Then he wrought so that, all in one rush, he caught hold of the helmet with his left hand, and swept the Viking off his horse; and with the other hand drew the short-sword that he was girt withal, and drove it at his neck, so that off the head flew. But when Snoekoll's fellows saw that, they fled, each his own way, and Grettir had no mind to follow, for he saw there was no heart in them.

The bonder thanked him well for his work and many other men too; and that deed was deemed to have been wrought both swiftly and hardily.[11]

[*All challenges were not met in so informal a fashion. If Grettir had waited, he might have had to fight the berserk in a holmgang.*]

The holmgang provided the legal means for the berserks to make their demands. The holmgang was a very formalized duel which was legal until about 1006. There were many laws

[11] Eiriker Magnusson and William Morris, *The Story of Grettir the Strong* (trans.), Longmans, Green & Co., London, 1909, Ch. XL, pp. 122–124.

concerning it. A man who had thought himself wronged or a man who wished another's property was the challenger. They met with followers on the island (holm) on the proper day and the laws of the holmgang were read. The hide on which the fight was to take place was measured out and pegged down. The man who had been challenged struck the first blow. The victor always won property of some sort. If the stakes had not been decided beforehand, the victor could demand a ransom if his opponent was only wounded, if killed he took all his possessions.[12]

. . . .

This was the holmgang law: that the cloak should be 10 feet from one end to the other, with loops in the corners, and in these should be put down pegs, having a head at the upper end; these were called *tjosnur*. The one who made the preparations must go toward the pegs, hold his ear-lobes, and stand with his feet apart, seeing the sky between them, using the formulary which was afterwards used at the sacrifice called *Tjosnublot* (peg sacrifice). Three squares, each one foot wide, must be marked around the cloak. Outside the squares must be placed four poles, called *hoslur* (hazel poles); it was called a *hazeled field* when it was prepared thus.

Each man must have three shields, and when these were made useless he must stand upon the cloak, even if he had walked out of it before, and thereafter defend himself with his weapons.

He who had been challenged was to strike first. If one was wounded so that blood came upon the cloak he was not obliged to fight any longer. If either stepped with one of his feet outside the hazel poles, it was held he had retreated; and if he stepped outside with both, he was held to have fled. One man was to hold the shield before each of the combatants. The one who had received most wounds was to pay a *holmlausn* (i.e., indemnity for being released from the fight) three marks of silver.[13] [*And the*

[12] Vigfusson and Powell, I., pp. 320–321.
[13] Du Chaillu I, pp. 564–5.

winner had to kill an ox as peg (tiosno)-*sacrifice to feed the assembled retainers and spectators.*]

The Tiosno-sacrifice.—There was led forth a steer, great and old. It was called the Beast of Sacrifice. He shall strike it that had the victory. There was sometimes one beast; sometimes each that went on the holm would lead forth his own.[14] [*Here is an account of a specific holmgang.*] One winter there came to Vors (Voss) Thorstein, a kinsman of the brothers Ivar and Hreidar (with whom the Icelander Eyulf was stopping), who owned a farm in Uppland. He told his troubles, which was that a Berserk, Asgaut by name, had challenged him to *holmganga* because he had refused to give his sister to him; he asked them to follow him with many men to the *holmganga*. They did not like to refuse, and went with thirty men to Upplond and to the place where the meeting was to be. They asked their men if any one wanted to win a wife by *holmganga* against Asgaut; but, although they thought the woman fair, no one was ready to do this. The brothers asked Eyulf to hold the shield before Thorstein. Eyulf said he had done that for no one, not even for himself. "I shall not be happy if he is slain on my hands (i.e., while I hold the shield before him); there seems to me no fame in this. If the man is killed, shall we then go home, leaving matters thus, or get a second and a third champion? Our disgrace will increase the more, the more men of ours fall; and little honour will there be on our journey if we go back with Thorstein unavenged, if he falls. Rather ask of me to go into *holmganga* against the Berserk; that is helping one's friend, but the other I will not assist in." They thanked him, but, nevertheless, thought he risked too much. He added: "It seems to me as if none of us would go back if he is not avenged, and that it would be worse to fight against the Berserk if your kinsman is first slain." Thereupon he advanced, and Ivar offered to hold the shield before him. Eyulf said: "That is a generous offer; but I can best

[14] Egil's Saga, ch. 68. (Vigfusson and Powell, I., pp. 320–21).

take care of it, and the old saying true is, 'One's own hand is most faithful' "; then he went to the place of the *holmganga*. The Berserk said: "Will this fool fight against me?" Eyulf replied: "Is it not that thou are afraid to fight against me? It may be that thou are of such a cowardly disposition as to fear a large man, and braggest before a small one." He answered, "That is not true; but I will pronounce for the laws of *holmganga*. Six marks will absolve me from the *holm* if I get wounded." Eyulf added, "I do not think it due to observe the laws towards thee when thou puttest a value on thyself, for in our own land (Eyulf was an Icelander) such a value as thou settest on thyself would be thought a thrall's value." Eyulf had to strike the first blow, and his sword struck the lower part of the shield and cut off it and the foot of the Berserk. Eyulf got great fame from this deed, and thereupon went home with the brothers. Much property was offered to him, but he said he had not done this for the sake of property nor for the woman, but rather from friendship towards the brothers [15]

[*Among the Vikings, as elsewhere, the line between warfare and games was a thin one.*]

That summer there was a great horse-fight at Langafit below Reykir, whither a great many people came together. Atli of Bjarg had a good stallion of Keingala's race; grey with a dark stripe down his back. Both father and son valued the horse highly. The two brothers Kormak and Thorgils in Mel had a very mettlesome brown stallion, and they arranged to match it against that of Atli from Bjarg. Many other excellent stallions were brought. Odd the Needy-Skald, Kormak's kinsman, had the charge of their horse on the day. He had grown into a strong man and had a high opinion of himself; he was surly and reckless. Grettir asked Atli who should have charge of his stallion.

"That is not so clear to me," said Atli.

"Would you like me to back him?"

"Then you must keep very cool, kinsman," he said. "We have men to deal with who are rather overbearing."

"Let them pay for their bluster," he said, "if they cannot control it."

The stallions were led out and the mares tethered together in the front on the bank of the river. There was a large pool just beyond the bank. The horses fought vigorously and there was excellent sport. Odd managed his horse pluckily and Grettir gave way before him, holding the tail of his horse with one hand and with the other the stick with which he pricked it on. Odd stood in the front by his horse, and pretended not to notice it. The horses then came near the river. Then Odd thrust with his pointed stick at Grettir and caught him in the shoulder-blade which Grettir was turning towards him. He struck pretty hard, and the flesh swelled up, but Grettir was little hurt. At the same moment the horses reared. Grettir ducked beneath the flank of his horse and drove his stick into Odd's side with such violence that three of his ribs were broken and Odd fell into the pool with his horse and all the mares that were tethered there by the bank. Some people swam out and rescued them. There was great excitement about it. Kormak's men on one side and those of Bjarg on the other seized their arms, but the men of Hrutfirding and Vatnsnes came between them and parted them. They all went home in great wrath, but kept quiet for a time. Atli said very little, but Grettir rather swaggered and said that they should meet again if he had his way.[16]

Ball games formed another diversion. They were played after sacrifices and feasts and during the winter when large numbers of men were together and had little to do. A chief or godi and his thingmen played another and his men. The games were rough and men were often injured or killed. There seem to have been at least two

---

[15] (Vigaglum's Saga, c. 4.) Du Chaillu I, pp. 569–70.

[16] Hight, G. A. (translator), *The Saga of Grettir the Strong*, Everyman's Library, J. M. Dent and Sons, London; E. P. Dutton and Co., N. Y., 1913, pp. 78–80.

sorts of ball games. In one bats were used; in another there was just a ball. Once the king (Hring) had a game called *soppleik;* it was played with eagerness and they tried Bosi in it; but he played roughly, and one of the king's men had his hand put out of joint. The next day he broke the thigh-bone of a man, and the third day two men attacked him, while many were harassing him; he knocked out the eye of one with the ball, and he knocked down another man and broke his neck (Herraud and Bosi's Saga, c. 3).[17]

[*Ritual furnished another mechanism for keeping people occupied.*]

The godar built and ran the temples (called hofs) and the godord and hof were inherited from father to son. Thus the chief god of a family, the god for whom the hof was built was also inherited.

And the summer in which Thor-stan was twenty-five years old, Thora bare a man-child, and he was named Grim when he was sprinkled with water. Thor-stan dedicated this boy to Thor, and declared that he should be a temple priest, and called him Thor-grim.[18]

There was a ceremony gone through when a man took up a godord after his father had died, or after he had acquired one by purchase.

Hoskuld said: "Let us redden ourselves in the blood of the godi according to ancient custom." He killed a ram, reddened his hands with its blood, and declared Arnstein's godiship to be his. . . . (Ljosvetninga Saga, c. 4.)[19]

All the thingmen and supporters of the godi paid temple toll to worship in the hof. The godi could have maintained half of the costs and made up the rest from the tolls.

There were priestesses as well as priests in Iceland. They were closely bound up with the cult of Frey. This leads Olsen to say,

We may now consider that we have found the clue to the following general note: In the ancient Scandinavian worship of the gods priestesses held a regular place only in the cult of Frey, the god of all growth and nature. We may imagine that when a godi in charge of a temple of Frey was looking round for a wife, he preferred to select her from a circle of women initiated into the mysteries of Frey worship, and, therefore, pleasing in the eyes of the god. And when the godi of Frey died, important advantages of a material order necessarily offered themselves to the man who married the widow, the priestess of Frey.[20]

There he let build a temple, and a mighty house it was. There was a door in the sidewall and nearer to one end thereof. Within the door stood the pillars of the high seat, and nails were therein; they were called the Gods' Nails. There within was there a great frith-place. But off the inmost house there was another house, of that fashion whereof now is the choir of a church, and there stood a stall in the midst of the floor in the fashion of an altar, and thereon lay a ring without a join that weighed twenty ounces, and on that must men swear all oaths; and that ring must the chief have on his arm at all man-motes. On the stall should also stand the blood bowl, and therein the blood rod was, like unto a sprinkler, and therewith should be sprinkled from the bowl which is called "Hlaut," which was that kind of blood which flowed when those beasts were smitten who were sacrificed to the Gods. But round about the stall were the Gods arrayed in the Holy Place. To that temple must all men pay toll, and be bound to follow the temple-priest in all farings even as are now the thingmen of chiefs. But the chief must uphold the temple at his own charges, so that it should not go to waste, and hold therein feasts of sacrifice.[21]

[17] Du Chaillu II, p. 375.
[18] Vigfusson and Powell.
[19] Du Chaillu I, p. 526.

[20] Olsen, Magnus, *Farms and Fanes of Ancient Norway.* Instituttet for Sammenlignende Kulturforskning, Oslo, 1928, p. 291.

[21] Morris, William (translator), *The Story of the Ere-Dwellers.* Vol. II of the Saga Library, London, 1892. *The Eyrbyggia Saga.*

There is still to be seen the doom-ring wherein men were doomed to sacrifice. In this ring stand Thunder's stone, on which the men that were to be sacrificed were broken; and there is still to be seen the blood-stain on the stone. This moot-stead was a most hallowed place, albeit men were not forbidden to do their business there on the grass as they would.[22] Sigurd, the Jarl of Lade, was a great sacrificer and so had been Hacon his father. Sigurd the Jarl upheld all the blood offerings for Trondlaw on the king's behalf. It was an old custom, when they made an offering, for all the bonders to come to the temple and bring their eatables which they would need as long as the offering lasted. At that offering all men should have ale. There they also slew all kind of cattle and horses, and all the blood which flowed from them was called *laut,* the bowls in which the blood stood were called laut-bowls and *laut-teinar,* which were made like a sprinkler, with all this they should stain the stalls red and likewise all the men; the flesh was cooked as meat for the guest feast.

There should be fires in the midst of the temple floor and thereover should hang kettles; they should carry bowls to the fire and he who was making the offering and was chief should bless the bowl and all the flesh, but he should first bless Odin's bowl (which should be drunk for the king's victory and power) and afterwards the bowls of Niord and Frey for good seasons and peace. It was usual to drink last Bragi's bowl; they also drank bowls for their howe-laid [*A howe in this sense is a communal burial mound*] kinsmen and that was called *minni.* Sigurd the Jarl was very generous; he did work which was much spoken of, in that he made a great feast at Lade and alone bore all the cost of it. About this Kormak Agmundson says in Sigurd's drapa:

No man bore cup
Or basket with him
To the jarl's feast
(The gods betrayed Tjassi)
Who would not with joy
Go to the blood offering
Which the generous prince gave.
(The king fought for gold). . . .[23]

As this material amply illustrates, good seagoing ships gave the Scandinavians of the Viking Age a means of transportation which could carry them anywhere from the Caspian Sea to Sicily, North Africa, and Byzantium. It gave them the ability to raid any settlements lying near the sea which were not too strongly defended against their type of commando raid. Trading and raiding made these Northmen rich. At home, they lived by agriculture and fishing, in a three-class system—noblemen, craftsmen and workers, and agricultural serfs. Their political organization varied from place to place and time to time, but for the most part they were able to build up small kingdoms and in Iceland they established the world's oldest democratic parliament, the Althing, which still meets.

The student can examine this material from many points of view. Institutionally, it can be shown that the Northmen had a considerable division of labor with many kinds of specialists, and a great deal of trade; that while the religious institutions were still simple, the political was becoming compound, and the class system provided a mechanism for the division of labor. The student of law will find some evidence useful to him, as will the person interested in pre-Christian Germanic paganism. These documents were written down after the conversion of the Northmen to Christianity. World travel and trade, contact with peoples who had long been subject to Christianity and to secure legal systems, opened their eyes to the wastefulness of such customs as the holmgang, and the

[22] Vigfussion & Powell, p. 265.

[23] Sturlason, Snorre (Erling Monsen, translator), *Heimskringla or the Lives of the Norse Kings.* W. Heffer and Sons, Ltd., Cambridge, 1932, pp. 86–90.

inadequacy of their heathen worship in a more complex society. The Norse culture, which lasted until less than a thousand years ago, was a faithful replica in all essentials of the old Indo-European system, with its three classes and its Olympian household of gods. Its survival to so late a date gives the historian much comparative material with which to reconstruct events known to him only through archaeology and occasional fragments of classical literature.

The student probably noted (p. 425) that the Northmen spent their time feasting at the turn of the season, from fall to winter, and played many games "during winter when the nights were long and the days short, and large numbers of men were together and had little to do." As with the Maidu, most work was done in the summer, and the winter was a time for entertainment. Kormak, mentioned in the account of the horse fight, was either an Irishman or the descendant of one. The Norse brought many Irish to Iceland.

In the account of the sacrifice we see boys dedicated to special gods in childhood, and priests conducting sacrifices for entire neighborhoods. The men who participated in the sacrifices paid the priest, and he in turn had to provide the upkeep of the temple. He received property and expended it. Men "did business" at the place of sacrifice, in Iceland as elsewhere. (Cf. Trobriands, Maidu, Kurnai.) Men swore oaths at holy places, on the theory that a falsehood stated under such circumstances would bring down the wrath of the god. We see this in many countries; Arabia is an outstanding example. The details of the sacrifice are very similar to those still practiced in the nineteenth century by the Mordvins, Cheremisses, and other Finnish minority peoples in the Upper Volga country in Russia. Remember that while pagan Europeans, Semitic peoples, and other Old World peoples made a specialty of sacrificing animals, they did this for a good reason. In the first place they *had* domestic animals. In the second, in the days before modern meat packing and cold storage, when an animal was killed it had to be eaten at once. It takes a large number of persons, ordinarily more than a single household, to eat an ox or a horse. Hence economically it was most practical to kill such an animal in sacrifice and serve its flesh to the communicants. What the god received was the blood, sprinkled on the worshippers and on the walls. Our English word "to bless" originally meant "to sprinkle with blood."

The selections quoted above are but a small sample of Icelandic literature. Any student who wishes to pursue this subject further will find many translations available in any college library.

16

Tenochtitlan, The City of Sacrifices

WHILE the Northmen held the initiative at sea during the late Middle Ages, by the time of the Renaissance it had passed to the Spaniards and Portuguese. Sailing in galleons equipped with cannon, they crossed the Atlantic and Pacific oceans and conquered the most powerful of the American Indian nations, the Aztec city-state, and the Inca Empire. The conquistadores who accompanied Cortez to Mexico left particularly excellent records which show us that the Aztecs had reached a level of civilization fully equal in complexity to that of the European and Asiatic peoples with whom we have already dealt.

Their home, the Valley of Mexico, was ideally located for such keen traders as the Aztecs were. Located at 19° North Latitude, at an elevation of 7500 feet, it formed the narrow southern end of the Mexican plateau, strategically situated so that it was within easy reach of the coastal strips to either side and the tropical forest region to the south. While enjoying a fine, healthy, semi-arid climate, with summer rains suitable for maize cultivation, the Aztecs were within easy reach of the rich woods, gums, cacao, tropical feathers, and other products obtained from lower altitudes. Furthermore, their valley was filled with lakes. These provided fish, an important food in a country without domestic animals other than turkeys and dogs. The lakes were also essential for transportation. Lacking beasts of burden, the Indians of the Valley of Mexico could move their produce from village to market by boat. Mexico City itself was an American Venice.

Another great advantage of this site was the presence of great deposits of obsidian, that natural volcanic glass from which the Aztecs knapped the finest silicious cutting tools ever made. Tenochtitlan, as Mexico City was called, was not only the Venice of America, but its Sheffield. These blades were much in demand and constituted a high-priced, highly portable commodity for the Aztec merchants to take with them on their expeditions.

So great was the wealth of this small nation, and so great the quantity of materials traded, that many kinds of specialists arose in it. Goldsmiths and silversmiths worked in the metals brought from the south. Featherworkers, jade workers, turquoise mosaic workers, and carpenters turned out ornamental objects used mostly by the nobility. Different villages, different clans, specialized in different products. The Aztec markets were equal to any the Spaniards had seen at home.

For a fresh description of these marvels, we may turn to the account of Bernal Diaz,* who entered Tenochtitlan with Cortez.

*Bernal Diaz del Castillo, *The True History of the Conquest of Mexico (1568)*, translated by Maurice Keatinge. J. Wright, London, 1800.

MEXICO, NOV. 8TH, 1519. DESCRIP-
TION OF THAT COURT AND CITY.
TRANSACTIONS AND OCCUR-
RENCES THERE.

On the next day we set out, accompanied as on the former one, and proceeded by the grand causeway, which
is eight yards wide, and runs in a
straight line to the city of Mexico. It
was crowded with people, as were all
the towers, temples, and causeways, in
every part of the lake, attracted by
curiosity to behold men, and animals,
such as never had been before seen in
these countries. . . .

When we arrived at a place where a
small causeway turns off, which goes
to the city of Cuyoacan, we were met
by a great number of the lords of the
court in their richest dresses, sent as
they said before the great Montezuma,
to bid us welcome. After waiting there
some time, the nephew of Montezuma
and other noblemen went back to meet
their monarch, who approached, carried in a most magnificent litter, which
was supported by his principal nobility.
When we came near certain towers
which are almost close to the city,
Montezuma who was then there quitted
his litter, and was borne in the arms of
the princes of Tezcuco, Iztapalapa, Ta-
cuba, and Cuyoacan, under a canopy of
the richest materials, ornamented with
green feathers, gold, and precious
stones that hung in the manner of
fringe; he was most richly dressed and
adorned, and wore buskins of pure
gold ornamented with jewels. [*Montezuma was carried on a litter. This is
the most sumptuous means of carrying
people by land known in regions devoid of large domestic animals capable
of being ridden or of hauling vehicles.
The Inca in Peru rode in a litter; so
did the Great Sun among the Natchez
Indians. Litters were also known in
the Old World. but chariots, riding*

*horses, and elephants were more im-
pressive.*] The princes who supported
him were dressed in rich habits, different from those in which they came
to meet us, and others who preceded the
monarch spread mantles on the ground,
lest his feet should touch it. All who
attended him, except the four princes,
kept their eyes fixed upon the earth, not
daring to look him in the face.

When Cortes was told that the great
Montezuma approached, he dismounted
from his horse, and advanced towards
him with much respect; Montezuma
bid him welcome, and Cortes replied
with a compliment, and it appeared to
me, that he offered to yield the right
hand to Montezuma, who declined it,
and put Cortes on his right. Our general then produced a collar of those
artificial jewels called margajitas,
which are of various colours, set in
gold, and threw it upon the neck of
Montezuma; after which, he advanced
to embrace him, but the lords who surrounded the monarch, taking him by
the arm, prevented him, it appearing to
them not sufficiently respectful. [*Cortez was not allowed to touch Montezuma. The sacredness of the king's
person is a common enough feature.
It was carried to an extreme in Hawaii.
It simply serves to symbolize his great
importance as head of a hierarchy. In
Chapple's terms, he originates all the
action. In Frazerian terms, the king is
full of* mana.] Cortes then said, that
he rejoiced in having seen so great a
monarch, and that he was highly honored by his coming out to meet him,
as well as by the many other marks of
his favor. To this Montezuma made
a gracious reply, and gave orders to the
princes of Tezcuco and Cuyoacan to
attend us to our quarters. Attended by
his nobility, he then returned to the
city, all the people standing close to
the walls, without daring to lift up
their eyes, and thus we passed, without

obstruction from the crowd. Who could count the multitude of men, women, and children, which thronged the streets, the canals, and terraces on the tops of the houses, on that day! . . . .

Our lodgings were provided in the buildings which had been inhabited by the father of Montezuma; here the monarch had the temples of his gods, and a secret treasure of gold and valuables, which he had derived from his father Axayaca. We were lodged here, because being considered as Teules, they thought we were in our proper place amongst their idols. [*The Aztecs apparently thought at first that the Spaniards were gods. To a Christian of that period, any god other than Jehovah was a devil, or teule.*] Be it how it may however, here they brought us to lodge in large apartments, a raised platform being assigned for our general, and mats for each of us, with little canopies over them, such as are used in that country. The whole of this palace was very light, airy, clean, and pleasant, the entry being through a great court. Montezuma here led Cortes by the hand to the apartment destined for him, and taking a large collar of gold, placed it round the general's neck. Cortes declared his gratitude for these favors, and Montezuma said, "Malintzin, here you and your friends are at home; now repose yourselves." With these words he departed. We were allotted to our quarters by companies, our artillery was posted in a convenient place, and all was arranged in such a manner as to be prepared for any contingency; a very sumptuous entertainment was provided for us, which we sat down to with great satisfaction, and here ends the true and full account of our adventurous and magnanimous entry into Mexico, on the eighth day of November, in the year of our Lord 1519. Glory be to Jesus Christ for all! . . . .

The great Montezuma was at this time aged about forty years, of good stature, well proportioned, and thin: his complexion was much fairer than that of the Indians; he wore his hair short, just covering his ears, with very little beard, well arranged, thin, and black. His face was rather long, with a pleasant countenance, and good eyes; gravity and good humour were blended together when he spoke. He was very delicate and clean in his person, bathing himself every evening. He had a number of mistresses, of the first families, and two princesses his lawful wives; when he visited them, it was with such secrecy, that none could know it except his own servants. He was clear of all suspicion of unnatural vices. The clothes which he wore one day, he did not put on for four days after. He had two hundred of his nobility as a guard, in apartments adjoining his own. Of these, certain persons only, could speak to him, and when they went to wait upon him they took off their rich mantles, and put on others of less ornament, but clean. They entered his apartment barefooted, their eyes fixed on the ground, and making three inclinations of the body as they approached him. In addressing the king they said, "Lord, my lord, great lord." When they had finished he dismissed them with a few words, and they retired, with their faces towards him, and their eyes fixed upon the ground. I also observed, that when great men came from a distance about business, they entered his palace barefooted, and in a plain habit; and also, they did not enter the gate directly, but took a circuit in going towards it.

[*The courtiers donned humble garments to approach Montezuma, and retired from his presence walking backward, their faces still toward him. These customs simply symbolize again the high position of Montezuma in the hierarchy. They can be duplicated in oriental courts in the Old World, and in Mediaeval European courts. The similarity is not due to diffusion, but to the development of similar situations in two mutually sealed-off halves of the world.*]

His cooks had upwards of thirty different ways of dressing meats, and they had earthen vessels so contrived as to keep them always hot. For the table of Montezuma himself, above three hundred dishes were dressed, and for his guards, above a thousand. Before dinner, Montezuma would sometimes go out and inspect the preparations, and his officers would point out to him which were the best, and explained of what birds and flesh they were composed; and of those he would eat. But this was more for amusement than any thing else. It is said that at times the flesh of young children was dressed for him; but the ordinary meats were, domestic fowls, pheasants, geese, partridges, quails, venison, Indian hogs, pigeons, hares, and rabbits, with many other animals and birds peculiar to the country. This is certain; that after Cortes had spoken to him relative to the dressing human flesh, it was not practised in his palace. At his meals, in the cold weather, a number of torches of the bark of a wood which makes no smoke and has an aromatic smell, were lighted, and that they should not throw too much heat, screens, ornamented with gold, and painted with figures of idols, were placed before them. Montezuma was seated on a low throne, or chair, at a table proportioned to the height of his seat. The table was covered with white cloths and napkins, and four beautiful women presented him with water for his hands, in vessels which they call Xicales, with other vessels under them like plates, to catch the water; they also presented him with towels. Then, two other women brought small cakes of bread, and when the king began to eat, a large screen of wood, gilt, was placed before him, so that people should not during that time see him. The women having retired to a little distance, four ancient lords stood by the throne, to whom Montezuma from time to time spoke or addressed questions, and as a mark of particular favor, gave to each of them a plate of that which he was eating. I was told that these old lords, who were his near relations, were also counsellors and judges. The plates which Montezuma presented to them, they received with high respect, eating what was in them without taking their eyes off the ground. He was served on earthenware of Cholula, red and black. While the king was at table, no one of his guards, or in the vicinity of his apartment, dared for their lives make any noise. Fruit of all the kinds that the country produced was laid before him; he eat very little, but from time to time, a liquor prepared from cocoa, and of a stimulative, or corroborative quality, as we were told, was presented to him in golden cups. We could not at that time see if he drank it or not, but I observed a number of jars, about fifty, brought in, filled with foaming chocolate, of which he took some, which the women presented to him. At different intervals during the time of dinner, there entered certain Indians, humpbacked, very deformed, and ugly, who played tricks of buffoonery, and others who they said were jesters. There was also a company of singers and dancers, who afforded Montezuma much entertainment. To these he ordered the vases of chocolate to be distributed. The four female attendants then took away the cloths, and again with much respect presented him with water to wash his hands, during which time Montezuma conversed with the four old noblemen formerly mentioned, after which they took their leave with many ceremonies. One thing I forgot, and no wonder, to mention in its place, and that is, that during the time Montezuma was at dinner, two very beautiful women were busily employed making small cakes with eggs and other things mixed therein. These were delicately white, and when made they presented them to him on plates covered with napkins. Also another kind of bread was brought to him in long loaves, and plates of cakes resembling wafers. After he had dined, they presented to him three little canes highly ornamented, containing liquid amber, mixed with an herb they call tobacco; and when he had sufficiently viewed and heard the singers, dancers, and buffoons, he took a little of the smoke of one of these canes, and then laid himself down to sleep; and thus his principal meal concluded. After this was over, all his guards and domestics sat down to dinner, and as near as I could judge, above a thousand plates of those eatables that I have mentioned were laid before them, with vessels of foaming chocolate, and fruit in an immense quantity. For his women and various inferior servants, his establishment was of a prodigious expense; and we were astonished, amidst such a profusion, at the vast regularity that prevailed. His major domo was at this time a prince named Tapiea; he kept the accounts of Montezuma's rents, in books which occupied an entire house. [*A special official kept household accounts in books which occupied an entire house. This is something new in our progress from simple to complex. The business of government, and of provisioning an elaborate household, required accounts, and a crude kind of writing was developed to accommodate it. In Peru, they used knotted strings, called* quipus, *for the same purpose.*] Montezuma had two buildings filled

with every kind of arms, richly ornamented with gold and jewels, such as shields large and small, clubs like two-handed swords, and lances much larger than ours, with blades six feet in length, so strong that if they fix in a shield they do not break, and sharp enough to use as razors. There was also an immense quantity of bows and arrows, and darts, together with slings, and shields which roll up into a small compass, and in action are let fall and thereby cover the whole body. He had also much defensive armour of quilted cotton ornamented with feathers in different devices, and casques for the head, made of wood and bone, with plumes of feathers, and many other articles too tedious to mention.

[*Also an innovation was this government armory, to supply all warriors with uniform equipment of standard quality. In the cultures we have been studying so far, each man owned and carried his own weapons.*]

In this palace was a most magnificent aviary, which contained every description of birds that continent afforded, namely, royal eagles, and a smaller species, with many other birds, down to the smallest parroquets, of beautiful colours. It was here that the ornaments of green feathers were fabricated. The feathers were taken from birds which are of the size of our pyes in Spain, and which they call here Quetzales, and other birds, whose plumage is of five different colours, green, red, white, yellow, and blue. The name of this species of bird I do not know. Here was also an immensity of parrots, and certain geese of fine plumage, and a species which resembled geese. All these bred here, and were stripped of their feathers every year at the proper season. Here was a large pond of clear running water, where were a number of great birds, entirely red, with very long legs; there are some like them in the Island of Cuba, which they call Ipiris. There was also a species which lives entirely in the water.

[*The zoo is again a novelty. One finds them in such Old World civilizations as ancient Sumeria, modern Yemen, and other states on about the same level of complexity.*]

We likewise saw another great building, which was a temple, and which contained those which were called the valiant or fighting gods, and here were many kinds of furious beasts, tygers, and lions of two species, one of which resembles a wolf, called here Adive. Also foxes, and other smaller animals, but all carnivorous. Most of these were bred in the place, being fed with game, fowls, dogs, and as I have heard the bodies of Indians who were sacrificed, the manner of which as I have been informed is this. They open the body of the victim while living, with large knives of stone; they take out his heart, and blood, which they offer to their gods, and then they cut off the limbs, and the head, upon which they feast, giving the body to be devoured by the wild beasts, and the skulls they hang up in their temples. In this accursed place were many vipers, and poisonous serpents which have in their tails somewhat that sounds like castanets; these are the most dangerous of all, and were kept in vessels filled with feathers, where they reared their young, and were fed with the flesh of human beings, and dogs; and I have been assured, that after our expulsion from Mexico, all these animals lived for many days upon the bodies of our comrades who were killed on that occasion. These beasts and horrid reptiles were retained to keep company with their infernal gods, and when these animals yelled and hissed, the palace seemed like hell itself.

[*The Aztecs sacrificed human vic-*

tims while the Vikings, Arabs, and other Old World peoples who did much sacrificing more commonly used large animals like sheep, goats, pigs, and cattle. The Aztecs had nothing else to sacrifice larger or more impressive than a dog or turkey.]

The place where the artists principally resided was named Escapuzalco, and was at the distance of about a league from the city. [*The special sections of the town for artisans reminds one of the artisans' quarters in oriental cities, from Morocco to China. It is natural for urban craftsmen to group together.*] Here were the shops and manufactories of all their gold and silver smiths, whose works in these metals, and in jewellery, when they were brought to Spain, surprised our ablest artists. Their painters we may also judge of by what we now see, for there are three Indians in Mexico, who are named, Marcos de Aquino, Juan de la Cruz, and Crespillo, who, if they had lived with Apelles in ancient times, or were compared with Michael Angelo or Berruguete in modern times, would not be held inferior to them. Their fine manufactures of cotton and feathers, were principally brought from the province of Costitlan. The women of the family of the great Montezuma also, of all ranks, were extremely ingenious in these works, and constantly employed; as was a certain description of females who lived together in the manner of nuns.

One part of the city was entirely occupied by Montezuma's dancers, of different kinds, some of whom bore a stick on their feet, others flew in the air, and some danced like those in Italy called by us Matachines. He had also a number of carpenters and handicraft men constantly in his employ. His gardens, which were of great extent, were irrigated by canals of running water, and shaded with every variety of trees. In them were baths of cut stone, pavilions for feasting or retirement, and theatres for shows, and for the dancers and singers; all which were kept in the most exact order, by a number of labourers constantly employed.

When we had been four days in Mexico, Cortes wished to take a view of the city, and in consequence sent to request the permission of his Majesty. Accordingly, Aguilar, Donna Marina, [*Donna Marina was an Indian woman from the coast who served Cortez as interpreter.*] and a little page of our general's called Orteguilla, who already understood something of the language, went to the palace for that purpose. Montezuma was pleased immediately to accede, but being apprehensive that we might offer some insult to his temple, he determined to go thither in person, which he accordingly did, in the same form, and with the same retinue, as when he first came out to meet us, but that he was on this occasion preceded by two lords bearing sceptres in their hands, which they carried on high, as a signal of the king's approach. Montezuma, in his litter, with a small rod in his hand, one half of which was gold, and the other half wood, and which he bore elevated like a rod of justice, for such it was, approached the temple, and there quitted his litter and mounted the steps, attended by a number of priests, and offering incense, with many ceremonies, to his war gods. [*The Aztecs burnt copal, a resinous gum, for incense, just as the Old World peoples burnt frankincense and myrrh, comparable gums.*] Cortes at the head of his cavalry, and the principal part of our soldiers under arms, marched to the grand square, attended by many noblemen of the court. When we arrived there, we were astonished at the crowds of people, and the regularity which prevailed, as well as at the vast quantities of merchandise, which those who attended us were assiduous in pointing out. Each kind had its particular place, which was distinguished by a sign. The articles consisted of gold, silver, jewels, feathers, mantles, chocolate, skins dressed and undressed, sandals, and other manufactures of the roots and fibres of nequen, and great numbers of male and female slaves, some of whom were fastened by the neck, in collars, to long poles. The meat market was stocked with fowls, game, and dogs. Vegetables, fruits, articles of food ready dressed, salt, bread, honey, and sweet pastry made in various ways, were also sold here. Other places in the square were appointed to the sale of earthenware, wooden household furniture such as tables and benches, firewood, paper, sweet canes filled with tobacco mixed with liquid amber, copper axes and working tools, and wooden vessels highly painted. Numbers of women sold fish, and little loaves made of a certain mud which they find in the lake, and which resembles cheese. The makers of stone blades were busily employed shaping them out of the rough material, and the merchants who dealt in gold, had the metal in grains as it came from the mines, in transparent tubes, so that they could be reckoned, and the gold was valued at so many mantles, or so many xiquipils of cocoa, according to the size of the quills. The entire square was inclosed in piazzas, under which great quantities of grain were stored, and where were also shops for various kinds of goods. I must apologize for adding, that boat loads of human ordure were on the borders of the adjoining canals, for the purpose of tanning leather, which they said could not be done without it. Some may laugh at this, but I assert the fact is as I have stated it, and moreover, upon all the public roads, places for passengers to resort to, were built of canes, and thatched with straw or grass, in order to collect this material.

The courts of justice, where three judges sat, occupied a part of the square, their under officers being in the market, inspecting the merchandise.

[*It was natural to hold the court of justice in the market, because that was where the most people came together. The same is true in Morocco and many other Old World countries.*]

From the square we proceeded to the great temple, but before we entered it we made a circuit through a number of large courts, the smallest of which appeared to me to contain more ground than the great square of Salamanca, with double inclosures built of lime and stone, and the courts paved with large white cut stone, very clean; or where not paved, they were plastered and polished. When we approached the gate of the great temple, to which the ascent was by a hundred and fourteen steps, and before we had mounted one of them, Montezuma sent down to us six priests, and two of his noblemen, to carry Cortes up, as they had done their sovereign, which he politely declined. When we had ascended to the summit of the temple, we observed on the platform as we passed, the large stones whereon were placed the victims who were to be sacrificed. Here was a great figure which resembled a dragon, and much blood fresh spilt. Montezuma came out from an adoratory in which his accursed idols were placed, attended by two priests, and addressing himself to Cortes, expressed his apprehension that he was fatigued; to which Cortes replied, that fatigue was unknown to us.

Montezuma then took him by the hand, and pointed out to him the different parts of the city, and its vicinity, all of which were commanded from that place. Here we had a clear prospect of the three causeways by which Mexico communicated with the land, and of the aqueduct of Chapultepeque, which supplied the city with the finest water. We were struck with the numbers of canoes, passing to and from the main land, loaded with provisions and merchandise, and we could now perceive that in this great city, and all the others of that neighbourhood which were built in the water, the houses stood separate from each other, communicating only by small drawbridges, and by boats, and that they were built with terraced tops. We observed also the temples and adoratories of the adjacent cities, built in the form of towers and fortresses, and others on the causeway, all whitewashed, and wonderfully brilliant. The noise and bustle of the market-place below us could be heard almost a league off, and those who had been at Rome and at Constantinople said, that for convenience, regularity, and population, they had never seen the like. Cortes now proposed to Fra. Bartholome to apply to Montezuma for permission to construct our church here, to which the father for the present objected, thinking it ill-timed. Cortes then addressing himself to Montezuma, requested that he would do him the favour to shew us his gods. Montezuma having first consulted his priests, led us into a tower where was a kind of saloon. Here were two altars highly adorned, with richly wrought timbers on the roof, and over the altars, gigantic figures resembling very fat men. The one on the right was Huitzilopochtli their war god, with a great face and terrible eyes; this figure was entirely covered with gold and jewels, and his body bound with golden serpents; in his right hand he held a bow, and in his left a bundle of arrows. The little idol which stood by him represented his page, and bore a lance and target richly ornamented with gold and jewels. The great idol had round his neck the figures of human heads and hearts, made of pure gold and silver, ornamented with precious stones of a blue colour. Before the idol was a pan of incense, with three hearts of human victims which were there burning, mixed with copal. The whole of that apartment, both walls and floor, was stained with human blood in such quantity as to give a very offensive smell. On the left was the other great figure, with a countenance like a bear, and great shining eyes, of the polished substance whereof their mirrors are made. [*The mirrors were of obsidian.*] The body of this idol was also covered with jewels. These two deities, it was said, were brothers; the name of this last was Tezcatepuca, and he was the god of the infernal regions. He presided, according to their notions, over the souls of men. His body was covered with figures representing little devils with tails of serpents, and the walls and pavement of this temple were so besmeared with blood that they stunk worse than all the slaughterhouses of Castille. An offering lay before him of five human hearts. In the summit of the temple, and in a recess the timber of which was most highly ornamented, we saw a figure half human and the other half resembling an alligator, inlaid with jewels, and partly covered with a mantle. This idol was said to contain the germ, and origin of all created things, and was the god of harvest, and fruits. The walls and altars were bestained like the rest, and so offensive, that we thought we could never get out soon enough.

In this place they had a drum of most enormous size, the head of which was made of the skins of large serpents: this instrument when struck resounded with a noise that could be heard to the distance of two leagues, and so doleful that it deserved to be named to music of the infernal regions; and with their horrible sounding horns and trumpets, their great knives for sacrifice, their human victims, and their blood besprinkled altars, I devoted them, and all their wickedness to God's vengeance, and thought that the time would never arrive, that I should escape from this scene of human butchery, horrible smells, and more detestable sights.

Cortes, half in jest, addressing himself to Montezuma, expressed his wonder how so wise a prince could worship such absurd and wicked powers; and proposed to him to place on the summit of that tower a cross, and in these adoratories the image of the holy Virgin, and he assured him that he should then be soon convinced of the vanity and deception of his idols. Montezuma shewed marks of displeasure at these expressions, saying, that he would not have admitted us into the temple, had he thought that we would have insulted their gods, who were kind to them, who gave them health and seasonable rains, good harvests, fine weather, victories and whatever else they desired, and whom they were in duty, and in gratitude, bound to worship. Cortes dropped the discourse, observing that it was time for us to go; and Montezuma assenting, said, it was necessary for him to remain, to expiate by sacrifice the sin which he had committed, in admitting us there. Cortes then took leave, and thus we concluded our visit to the great temple of Mexico, descending the steps with much pain to our invalids.

[*The discussion about building a church on the temple mound represents one of the most clear-cut cases known to history of a violent conflict between symbolic configurations. See Appendix, Sec. 7.*]

I will now proceed to relate other

matters, in which, if I am not so correct as I ought to be, let it be remembered that my situation was that of a soldier, who was obliged to be more attentive to the orders of his officers, than to the objects of curiosity around him. The ground whereon his temple stood, was as much as six of the largest buildings of this country occupy. From the base it diminshed to the summit, whereon was a tower, in which the idols were placed, and from the middle of ascent, to the top, were five concavities, like barbicans, but without parapets. However there are many paintings of temples in the possession of the conquerors, one whereof I have, and those who have seen them will easily form an idea of the outside of this temple. I have heard that at the time they laid the foundations of it, the natives of all that country made offerings of their gold, silver, and jewels, of the seeds of the earth, and of prisoners, all of which were buried in the foundations of the building. The inquisitive reader will naturally ask, how I came to know any thing of this, which happened upwards of a thousand years ago. I will inform him. When we got possession of this great city, and [decided] that it was to be built upon a new plan, it was determined to place the church of St. Jago on the ground where this temple stood; and in sinking the foundations, we found great quantities of gold, silver, and other valuables, and a Mexican who obtained part of the same ground, discovered more treasure, about which there was a law-suit in support of his Majesty's right, the result of which I am ignorant of. The account was also confirmed by Guatimotzin who was then alive, and who said that the transaction was recorded in their ancient historical paintings. The church which now stands here is called St. Jago el Taltelulco. This temple I have

before observed, was surrounded by courts as large as the square of Salamanca, inside of a double inclosure of lime and stone. At a little distance from it stood a tower, a true hell or habitation for demons, with a mouth resembling that of an enormous monster, wide open, and ready as it were to devour those who entered. At the door stood frightful idols; by it was a place for sacrifice, and within, boilers, and pots full of water, to dress the flesh of the victims, which was eaten by the priests. The idols were like serpents and devils, and before them were tables and knives for sacrifice, the place being covered with the blood which was spilt on those occasions. The furniture was like that of a butcher's stall, and I never gave this accursed building any name except that of hell. Having passed this, we saw great piles of wood, and a reservoir of water, supplied by a pipe from the great aqueduct; and crossing a court, we came to another temple, wherein were the tombs of the Mexican nobility; it was begrimed with soot and blood. Next to this was another, full of skeletons, and piles of bones, each kept apart, but regularly arranged. In each temple were idols, and each had also its particular priests, who wore long vestments of black, somewhat between the dress of the dominicans and our canons; their long hair was clotted together, and their ears lacerated in honor of their gods.

At a certain distance from the buildings of which I have last spoken were others, the idols of which were, as they said, the advocates, or superintendent deities of human marriages, and all round the great court were many houses, which were not very lofty, and wherein resided the priests, and others who had charge of the idols. Here was also a great reservoir of water, supplied with pipes, exclusively for the service of the two idols Huitzilopochtli and Tezcatepuca, and hard by, a large building, where were a number of the young Mexican women, who resided there as in a nunnery, until they were married. They worshipped two female deities, who presided over marriages, and to them they offered sacrifices, in order to obtain good husbands. I have been thus diffuse in my description of this great temple, because it was the most considerable of that city, amongst the many sumptuous building of that kind which it contained. The temple of Cholula however was higher than this, having a hundred and twenty steps; it was also held in great veneration, and was built on a plan different from that of Mexico. The temple at Tezcuco was very large, having a hundred and seventeen steps. All these were of different structure, but agreed in having a number of outer courts, and a double inclosure. One ridiculous circumstance is, that each province had its own peculiar gods, who were supposed to have no concern with any other, so that the idols were innumerable in this country. Having fatigued ourselves with the examination of these scenes, so new to us, we retired to our quarters. . . .

If you can lay your hands on a copy of Bernal Diaz's book, I am sure that many of you will want to read the narrative chapters, about the fighting on the causeway, the Noche Triste, the ransom of Montezuma, and the rest.

Few American anthropologists, trained in their profession at our universities, who joined the American army during the last war, could have given more detailed, objective descriptions of cities which they entered in the course of military operations. Bernal Diaz was a gifted and an objective observer. His descriptions of the palaces and temples and markets remain unsurpassed. His glimpse into Montezuma's life is also very informative. It is interesting to read one of the world's first accounts of the use of tobacco and chocolate. Montezuma's own statement to Cortez about the relationship between gods and men could not be clearer. Still, Bernal Diaz was not in a position to know everything. There were details of the organization of the Aztec state which only came out later, after a much longer period of contact between Spanish and Indians.

He did not know at that time, apparently, that the command was split between Montezuma, who was the war chief, and the Snake Woman, a man who served as civilian leader, and whose duties included such details of civil administration as the collection of tribute and taxes. Montezuma as war chief was thus also foreign minister, and he was the one who lived in pomp and ceremony, because external rather than internal affairs were the chief concern of the Aztecs at that time.

In the city itself were twenty *calpullec* (plural of *calpulli*) which may be translated either as "clans" or "wards," since they partook of the nature of both. The *calpulli* was in turn composed of families. Each *calpulli* owned agricultural land in common, which its members worked together. They had their own council of elders, special god, priests, school, judges, and two leaders, a military chief, who led them as a company of militia in war, and a civil chief who had charge of the disposal of their common property.

These *calpullec* were grouped in four "quarters" of five each. Each quarter had its special temple, armory, and boys' school, its own war chief, who was entitled to wear his hair tied in a red leather fillet, as was the supreme war chief,

Montezuma. Indeed, it was from the group of quarter war chiefs that the supreme chief was always selected, within a limited number of families. The supreme command of the government rested in a council which included the supreme war leader, the Snake Woman, one representative from each of the *calpullec,* and the head priests. This council had the power to select the new leader, and to depose him if it saw fit.

The Aztecs administered justice through five different kinds of courts: (1) the council of clan elders for minor offences within the *calpulli;* (2) the quarter court, which met every day with a presiding judge, two assistant judges, and three bailiffs; (3) the court of appeals, held in the palace of Montezuma, in secret session—here were tried cases appealed from the lower courts, and new cases involving nobles; (4) the supreme court for nobles, presided over by the Snake Woman, with a jury of thirteen elders. The proceedings were recorded in picture writing. (5) Military courts, for treason and cowardice, severe as all military courts are. If the soldier were found guilty of either offence, he would be put to death, but if of treason, his family would be enslaved as well.

The nobility was made up of men who had distinguished themselves in battles, and they wore special ornaments, just as our heroes wear ribbons. The government gave them landed estates, outside the city territory, and the farmers who lived on the land had to work for them. These estates could be inherited. Other warriors were stationed in conquered territories, and given lands and workmen. They preserved the *Pax Aztecica* in outlying parts. Slaves were the kin of traitors, or persons who through failures at gambling or other reverses found it necessary to mortgage their services. A distinction was made between slaves of this kind and slaves taken captive in war, who could be sacrificed.

THE ritual practices of the Aztecs were most completely recorded by Fray Bernardino de Sahagun, whose book * consists of Aztec picture writing with notes and commentaries in Spanish. It is an extremely valuable document. This is a long book, from which a short extract is offered here.

. . . Now we come to Tlaculteutl, the goddess of carnal matters, who had three different names. First, Tlaculteutl, which means goddess of carnality. The second name was Ixcuina; they called her this because they said there were four sisters; the first born or oldest was Tiacapan; the second was the youngest and they called her Teicu, the third was the middle one, called Tlaco; the fourth was the youngest of all Xucotzin. All these four sisters were the goddesses of carnality; in these names all women are included who are fit for the carnal act. The third name of the goddess is Tlaclquani, which means eater of filthy things. This signifies that, according to their sayings, all such carnal men and women confessed their

* *A History of Ancient Mexico,* translated by Fanny R. Bandelier, Fisk University Press, Nashville, Tenn., 1932. Reprinted by permission of the publishers.

sins to these goddesses, no matter how uncouth and filthy they might have been, and they were forgiven. It is also said that this goddess or these goddesses had the power to produce lust; that they could provoke carnal intercourse and favored illicit love affairs, and that after such sins had been committed, they also held the power of pardoning and cleansing them of the sin, forgiving them if they confessed them to their Sátrapas (priests), who were the soothsayers who kept the books of divination and of the fate of the newly born, of witchcraft and prognostication as well as of ancient traditions, which were transmitted from mouth to mouth from the ancients down to them.

[*Do not forget that Sahagun was a medieval Roman Catholic priest and that to him sexual relations were carnal and unclean. Although the Aztecs undoubtedly had confession, it is doubtful if their concept of sin was identical with that of contemporary Christians.*]

When a penitent was ready for confession, he would at once go in search of one of these priests or divines to whom they were wont to confess, saying to him: "Sir, I want to go to god almighty who is the protector of all . . . for I wanted to speak in secret of my sins." Hearing this, the Sátrapa would answer: "Be very welcome, my son, for what you say you wish to do is for your salvation and advantage." After saying this he would at once consult his book of divination which was called Tonalamatl, in order to find out by this book what day would be the most opportune for such a deed. As soon as he had found the propitious day, he would say: "Come on such and such a day, for on that day the sign is favorable to do this successfully." When the appointed day had come for the penitent to return he would buy a new mat (petate), white incense

which they call copalli, and wood for the fire, over which the copalli was to be burned. If the penitent was a prominent man or invested with some official dignity, the priest would go to his house to confess him (or by chance the penitent man even being a prominent person might choose to go to the house of the priest). Upon arrival (wherever it might be), the place where the new mat was to be spread was very well swept and the confessor seated himself on the mat; the fire was lighted and he, the Sátrapa, threw the incense into it, and addressed himself to the fire, saying to it: "I wish to inform you, oh, lord, who are the father and the mother of all the gods and who are the most ancient god, that there has come today one of your vassals, this your servant, who comes here weeping in deep sorrow; he comes with great suffering; by all this it is clear that he has erred, that he stumbled and met with and found some of the obscenity of sin even with serious crime worthy of death, and he is very sad about it and downcast. Our very merciful lord who are our protector and supporter, accept the penitence and listen to the anguish of your servant and vassal." This prayer finished, the priest then turned to the penitent and spoke to him as follows: "Son, you have come into the presence of god, the helper and supporter of all; you came to tell him your inward shame and rottenness, to disclose unto him the secrets of your hearts; be careful not to lead a riotous life nor to throw yourself headlong into it, nor get lost by lying in the presence of our lord. Rid yourself and throw out all your shame and disgrace in the presence of our lord, whose name is Yoallichectla, that is to say, Tezcatlipoca. It is a fact that you are before him (in his presence), although you are not worthy to see him; and even if he doesn't speak to you, because he is invisible and not palpable, mind how you come before him, with what kind of a heart; do not fear to declare your secrets in his presence, tell him your life, tell your (good) deeds in the same way you confessed your excesses and offenses, pour out your evil deeds in his presence, tell them all sorrowfully to our lord god, who is the protector of all, and who holds his arms open and is ready to embrace you and to carry you. See to it that you do not omit anything out of shame or cowardice!" When the penitent had heard all this, he took the oath to tell the truth —in their own way of taking an oath, which is touching the earth with the hand and licking off whatever had stuck to it. He then threw copal into the fire, which was another way of taking an oath. Then he seated himself opposite the priest and, considering him (in this instance), as god's representative, he began his confession, saying: "Oh, lord, who accepts and helps everyone, listen to my baseness and rottenness. In your presence I disclose myself. I throw out all my shameful acts as many as I have committed, for, to be sure, none of the wickedness I am guilty of is hidden from you, because all things are apparent and clear to you." After this he at once began to tell his sins in the order he had committed them, with entire calm and distinctness, like a person who recites a poem or legend, very slowly and well enunciated, or like one who goes on a very straight road without deviating to one side or the other. After having thus confessed everything he had done, the priest spoke to him and said, "My son, you have spoken before our lord god, telling him of all your wicked acts; now also in his name I shall tell you what you are obliged to do. When the goddesses called Civapipilti come down to earth, or when the feast to the goddesses of

carnality whose name is Yxtuiname, is celebrated, you are to fast for four days, punishing your stomach and your mouth, and on the very day of the feast of Yxtuiname, in the morning or at daybreak, you are to make the proper penitence as suits your sins, and that is to pass through your tongue from one side to the other some twigs of what they call teucalcacatl or tlacotl, and if you should wish to do more than that, pass them through the ears, one or the other. This you must do as a penitence and atonement for your sins; it is not to be as a merit, but as a penitence for your evil deeds. You are to pierce first your tongue in the middle with a maguey thorn and through that same hole you will pass the twigs, passing each one in front of your face and, as you pull them out of the tongue, throw them behind you toward your back. If you should wish to unite (tie) all of them, you may attach one to the other, be there four hundred or eight hundred, in short, just as many as you wish to pass through your tongue; doing this, all the wickedness and filth you committed will be forgiven you." [*Sacrifice by passing thorns or thread through the tongue, ears, etc., was a form of blood sacrifice common in Middle America. Perhaps if they had had more adequate domestic animals this self-immolation might have been avoided.*] If the penitent has not committed neither very many nor serious sins, the priest to whom he confesses tells him, "My son, you are to fast; tire your stomach by hunger and your mouth by thirst, eating only once a day at noon and repeating this for four days," or he might tell some penitent to go and offer papers at the accustomed places and make images and to cover these images—as many and fashioned as his devotion would command—with these papers and go through the devotional ceremony of singing and dancing, as is customary in their presence. Or he might say: "You offended god by getting drunk, so you must appease the god of wine, called Totochti, and when you go to comply with your penance you are to go at night, naked with only a paper in front and one at the back to cover your privy parts; when you are ready to return after your prayers are offered, you are to throw the papers that had covered your front and back at the feet of the gods that are there."

Once his confession made and after having received the penance he was to make, the penitent would go home and try never again to incur in the same sins he had just confessed, because it was said that if these same sins were repeated then there was no more absolution.

Confessions of great sins, such as adultery, were only made by old men, and this for the simple reason to escape wordly punishment meted out for such sins; to escape from being condemned to death, which was either having their head crushed or ground to powder between two stones. It must be said that the priests who heard confessions were utterly discreet, never disclosing what they had learned in confession; this was because they considered that it was not they personally who had heard these confessions, but their god, who was the only one before whom sin was revealed, hence it was not supposed that any human heard them, nor had they been told to human ears, only to god (in his representative). . . .

It is supposed that Yiacatecutli, god of merchants, was the one who started trading among those people, and that for this reason the guild of the merchants adopted him as their god and honored him in different ways, one being to offer him paper with which they covered his statues wherever they

found them. [*The merchants had their own god, whom they considered a historical person. They believed that he started their profession. This belief is comparable to that in Alchera heroes by the Australian aborigines. Whether or not we follow a "historical" school, we must admit that most peoples of the world use history, however inaccurate or mythological, as a pattern on which to fashion their rules of behavior. The god Yiacatecutli may well be compared with St. Christopher.*] They also venerated the cane (stick) with which they walked, which was a solid cane called utatl (also otate). They have still another kind of cane or walking stick made of a solid light black cane without a knot, and which looks like reed such as is used in Spain.[1] All merchants used that kind of canes on the road. When they reached the place where they were to spend the night, they would gather all their canes and tie them into one bundle, which they then stuck at the head of the sleeping place or camp. They would sprinkle blood in front of this bundle, which blood they obtained by bleeding their own ears, tongue, arms or legs. Then they offered incense by building a fire and burning copal in front of this bundle of sticks, which they considered as the image of the god Yiacatecutli, and by this means they asked him to protect them from all danger. These merchants traveled over the whole land, bartering, trading, buying in some place and selling in another what they had purchased. They also travel through towns, along the seashore, and in the interior. There isn't a place they do not pry into and visit, here buying, there selling; it is neither too hot for them in this place nor too cold in that one. They don't shun a road because it is too rough nor too difficult to search for whatever is there, either pretty or

[1] The well known Malacca cane.

valuable or advantageous to buy and sell again. These traders suffer great hardships and are exceedingly daring; they go anywhere, even if it should be an enemy's domain and they are very sly in their deals with strangers, in learning their languages, as well as in their tactics, attaining through kindness what they want, thus gaining their confidence. They find out where the feathers (plumes) and the precious stones can be had, or the gold; there they purchase them and take them to where they are worth a great deal. They also know where to go to find exquisite and valuable skins of beasts, and where to resell them at high prices. Likewise do they deal in precious cups of many different kinds and material adorned with diverse painted figures, and which are used in all the different districts; some of these cups have covers made of tortoise shell and spoons of the same to stir the cocoa; there are cups with covers painted in different colors and figures, made to resemble a leaf of the "vinarbol" [2] and with various kinds of beautiful sticks with which they stirred their cocoa. If they are forced to enter an enemy's realm, they first learn the language of these people; they adopt their mode of dress so they might not be taken for strangers, but for people of that same country. [*Here we see cloak-and-dagger work in an obsidian setting—commercial intelligence in enemy territory.*] It often happened that the enemy recognized them, capturing and killing them. If one or two or more were able to escape, they were wont to notify the chief or principal lord of the province, as, for instance, Mocteccuzuma or any of his predecessors, bringing him as an offering some of the treasures of those countries, making a present of these things in remuneration of their sufferings,

and in order to be honored by their people and considered courageous. They would give him an amber bib, which is a large, transparent, yellow stone which hangs from the lower lip as a sign that he was brave and noble, too; this bib was highly valued.

Whenever these traders or merchants left for such a voyage to foreign lands they took leave of their relatives amid great ceremonies, in accordance with ancient rites. They remained absent many years, and when they returned they brought back great riches (many treasures). In order to display what they had and to give an account of the countries they had visited and the things they had seen, soon upon their return they would invite all the traders (merchants), especially the principal ones, as well as the chieftains of the town, and arranged a great festivity for them. These festivities they called "washing of feet." The guests did great honor to the cane (walking-stick) with which the traveler had gone and come back; considered it the image of Yiacatecutli, god of the merchants, who had favored them to travel the roads and brought them back safely. [*The life of a merchant was critical, both for the nation and for his family. Hence all the ceremony attending his departure and his return.*] In order to do due honor to the cane they placed it in one of the temples they had in the different quarters of the town, and which they call calpulli, which means church of the district or parish. In the calpulli to which this particular trader belonged, he put the cane in an honored place, and when the dinner was served to his guests, he first placed food, flowers, and acayietl (small tube containing incense of oderiferous herbs which was burned in front of the stick); and even afterwards, after the invitation was over, each time the trader was about to eat he first placed food and all the other

[2] Probably a name for the grape-vine.

things in front of the stick (cane), which he now kept in his own home, in the private oratory thereof. All these traders, after returning from one of their voyages, as they now were wealthy, would buy male and female slaves, whom they offered to their god on his feast, this generally being Yiacatecutli, who had five brothers and one sister, all being held as deities, and according to the size of their devotion, they would sacrifice slaves to each one of them separately on his personal feast, or to all together, or to the sister alone. One of the brothers was called Chiconquiavitl, the other Xomocuil, the next Nacxitl, another Cochimetl, the fifth Yacapitzaoac; the sister's name was Chalmecacioatl. To each one of these or to one or the other they offered one or more slaves, sacrificing (killing) them in front of these gods, dressed in the insignia of the respective one as if he were his image. There was a regular fair in a town (village) called Azcapotzalco, at two leagues from Mexico where slaves, men and women, were sold. There those who wanted any went to select among a great number of them, for they were very careful that the slave, male or female, should be without blemish of body and free of disease of any kind. After having purchased these slaves, men or women, they were very well treated; they bathed them in hot water, gave them well to eat and drink and in abundance, so that these slaves grew fat, for they were to be eaten and offered to their god. They also feasted them, making them dance and sing at times on the flat roofs of their houses or on the public square; there they sang all songs they knew until they became tired of singing. They did in no way fear or mind the sort of death awaiting them.

These slaves were killed at the feast called panquetzalistli, and all the time before that feast they were treated to everything, as we have said.

If among these slaves there was a man who appeared to have fair judgment, was quick and intelligent in serving and perhaps could sing well, or if there was a woman among them who was willing and able to prepare food and drink, could embroider or weave, the chiefs or prominent people would buy them for their own service in their homes, and thus these escaped from being sacrificed.

The image of this god represents an Indian who travels with his cane; the face was spotted black and white; in his hair he wore two tassels of the fine feathers (plumes) called quetzalli; these plumes were tied in the center of the head where the hair was gathered like a sheaf at the top (of head). His ears were of gold; he wore a blue mantle, and over the blue was thrown a black net so that the blue shone through the meshes of the net. The mantle had a fringe all around with flowers woven into it. Around the ankles he wore yellow leather straps from which hung diminutive sea-shells. His feet were clad in sandals gracefully made and very elaborate. His shield was yellow with a light blue spot in the center quite plain, without any ornamentation; in his right hand he held a cane such as traders (travelers) carry on the road. . . .

The first month of the year was called among the Mexicans Atlacahualco, and elsewhere Quavitleloa. This month began on the second day of the month of February, when we celebrate the Purification of our Lady (the Virgin). On this first day of the month they celebrated a festival in honor (according to some) of the gods Tlaloc, whom they considered as the gods of rain. But, according to others, it was in honor of their sister Chalchiutlicue, the goddess of the water; still others pretended it was in honor of the great priest or god of the winds, Quetzalcoatly, so we may safely say that this feast was probably held in honor of all of them. This month, like all the others, which in all are eighteen, counted twenty days.

CALENDAR
Atlacahualco or Quavitleloa

In this month they killed many children; they sacrificed them in many places on the top of mountains, tearing out their hearts in honor of the gods of rain, so that they might grant them abundant rain.

They adorned the children thus to be sacrificed with many ornaments and carried them on their shoulders in litters. These were adorned with plumes and flowers and they played musical instruments, sang and danced in front of them.

If the children who were to be killed cried a great deal and shed many tears they were glad of it, for they took it as a prognostication of a great deal of rain for that year. [*They sacrificed children for rain. Children weep, rain falls. QED.*]

They also killed a great many prisoners in that month in honor of the same gods of water. First they stabbed them with knives, fighting them as they were tied on to a stone which looked like a millstone, from which they routed them by means of knife-thrusts. They then took them to the temple called Yopico, where their hearts were torn out.

When these slaves were to be killed, their owners, who had captured them, danced, magnificently dressed (with plumes on the head) ahead of them, demonstrating their courage. This happened on all the days of this month. . . .

The second month was called Tlacaxipeoaliztli. On the first day of this month they celebrated a festival in honor of the god Totec, who is also called Xippe, when they killed and flayed a number of slaves and captives.

Tlacaxipeoalistli

The captives were killed by scalping them, taking the scalp off the top of the head, which was kept by their owners as a relic. The ceremony was performed in the calpul in front of the fire.

When the masters of these captives took their slaves to the temple where they were to be killed, they dragged them by the hair. As they pulled them up the steps of the Cú, some of these captives would faint, so their owners had to drag them by the hair as far as the block where they were to die.

As soon as they had dragged them to the block, which was a stone three spans (3 palmost—24 inches) high, more or less, by almost two in width, they threw them down on their back, five men holding them, two by the feet, two by the arms, and one by the head. Then at once the priest, who was to kill him, would come and strike him a blow on the chest with both hands, holding a flint knife shaped like the iron of an anchor, cutting a hole. Into this hole he would thrust one hand and tear out the heart, which he then offered to the sun: later he put it into a bowl or jar.

After thus having torn their hearts out, and after pouring their blood into a jicara (bowl made of a gourd), which was given to the master of the dead slave, the body was thrown down the temple steps. From there it was taken by certain old men called Quaquaquilti, who carried it to their calpul (or chapel), cut it to pieces, and distributed them to be eaten. [*The consumption of human flesh is commonly found in two circumstances: (1) when there is much starch food and little protein, as here and among the Mano; (2) when there is little food at all, as among the Central Eskimo and western Australians.*]

Before cutting them up they would flay the bodies of the captives; others would dress in their skins and fight sham battles with other men.

After the above, they would kill other captives, fighting again with them while they were tied around the waist with a rope which ran through the hole in the center of a stone like a millstone. The rope was so long that the man could walk around the stone on all sides. He was given his weapons to fight with; four men, armed with sword and shield, would now come to fight with him until they slew him. . . .

The fifth month was Toxcatl, and on its first day they celebrated a big feast in honor of the god Titlacaoa, known by one other name as Tezcatlipoca, and whom they held to be the god of gods. In his honor they killed on the day of his festival a chosen young man without a blemish on his body and who had been kept in all the delights of life for a whole year, being instructed to play musical instruments, to sing and speak (recite).

Toxcatl

This was the principal festival of all. It was like Easter, and came very close to the Christian Easter, perhaps a few days later. The youth, educated as told above, was very well grown and chosen from among many. He wore his hair long, as far down as his waist.

When they killed the youth whom they had maintained for a whole year for this purpose, they at once chose another one who, before being sacrificed one year hence, went through the whole town very well dressed, with flowers in his hand, and accompanied by certain personalities (probably prominent people). He would bow graciously to all whom he met, and they all knew he was the image of Tezcatlipoca and prostrated themselves before him, worshipping him wherever they met him. Twenty days previous to the festival they gave this youth (who was to die)

four maidens, well prepared and educated for this purpose. During these twenty days he had carnal intercourse with these maidens. His clothes were changed when they first brought them to him; they cut his hair as for a captain, and gave him some other luxuries of dress. [*The reader is invited to compare the treatment of prospective sacrificial victims with that of the young lady who volunteered to die with her lord in the excerpt from Ibn Fadhlan.*]

Five days before he was to die they gave festivities for him, banquets held in cool and gay places, and many chieftains and prominent people accompanied him. On the day of the festival when he was to die they took him to a Cú or oratory, which they called Tlacuchcalco. Before reaching it, at a place called Tlapituoaian, the women (maidens) stepped aside and left him. As he got to the place where he was to be killed, he mounted the steps (staircase) by himself and on each one of these he broke one of the flutes which he had played during the year. Once at the top they threw him down onto the block and tore his heart out, then brought his body down on their hands (arms); down at the foot they cut the head from the trunk and impaled it on a pole called Tzonpantli. Many other ceremonies were celebrated during this festival. . . .

The ninth sign was called Cecoatl. They said it was quite lucky and prosperous, and those born in its first house (on its first day) were to be happy and prosperous. They considered it to be lucky, or propitious to attain wealth, also that it would bring good luck in warfare. In the case of women (born that day) they would be honest and become wealthy, but, as already stated, if they were careless about doing penance, and if they did not accept the advice of their elders, they would lose their good fortune, would be lazy and sleepy, unfortunate, miserable, and altogether unhappy. To merchants this sign was very favorable, and they were great devotees of it. They always awaited this sign to come around again before leaving home to go on their long journeys to remote provinces to make their barters and purchase their merchandise. Before departing, and with their packs already made, they would invite old merchants and their relatives to a feast, telling them to which provinces they intended to go and what they meant to do there, and this was done principally to gain fame among merchants, and to let them know that while they were absent from home they were earning their livelihood in different provinces. . . .

After the meal was over and when the one who had offered the feast was ready to leave for the journey, more particularly when this was his first trip, every one of the old merchants made a speech, encouraging him to face all the hardships he would meet. The first (to speak) would address him as follows: "My son, you have assembled here all of us who are your fathers (elders) and merchants like yourself, and it is therefore well that we should advise you and play the part of elders that must encourage and advise you now. I, the first one to speak, wish to give you my opinion as I would to a son. You are about to depart for faraway lands and to leave your village, relatives and friends, your comfort and rest, to travel over long roads, mountains, valleys and deserts. Exert yourself, my son, for there is no reason why you should end you life here (at home), nor that you should die without having accomplished something worthwhile to gain honor as we, your elders, wish you to gain and, therefore, though with tears, we pray that thus it may be, and that your efforts may crown our good wishes. Your fore-

bears in these hardships have toiled on the road and have attained the honors accorded them as valiant men attain them in war. Through these toils they obtained from our lord the wealth they left. You must be courageous to stand the hardships that await you, such as hunger, thirst, fatigue and lack of provisions; you will have to eat your bread hard, your tamales mouldy, and drink turbid and bad-tasting water; you will reach swollen rivers with freshets that make a frightful noise and cannot be waded, and which therefore will detain you for several days, suffering from hunger and thirst. Beware, my son, not to lose heart on account of all this, nor forsake the work already started, for by so doing you would offend us who are your elders. Over the same road went our forebears, risking their lives a good many times, but being courageous, they became honored and wealthy. Finally, my poor young man, if our lord grants you some luck, it is best for you to first suffer hardships and poverty, almost intolerable fatigues such as are experienced by all who wander from town to town, from village to village. These fatigues are excessive with copious sweats, great colds or extreme heat. You will travel covered with dust, the mecapal [3] will press hard around your head, you will wipe perspiration from your brow with both hands, your hardships may increase when you are compelled to sleep in a corner or behind the door of strange houses, where you will stand with bowed head and ashamed; there will be times when from hunger your stomach will feel as if glued to your ribs, when you will travel from village to village reasoning in your mind, worried and doubtful about the sale of your ware

[3] Mecapal is the leather band with rope attached and worn across the forehead by porters to carry loads. It is still used throughout Mexico.

which perchance may not sell at all, so that it will cause you sadness and tears. Ere you amass any wealth or good luck, you will have to suffer to the utmost, you will be distraught and downhearted and, moreover, you will many times find yourself forced to spend the night in some deep ravine, a cave, or under a protruding rock or close to a large boulder. We know not whether, perchance, our lord might kill you at any one of these places, and thus, perhaps, you may never come again back to your country; who knows? It is wisest that you should travel along these roads, devoutly invoking god and doing penance, and at the same time meekly attending your elders by humble service, such as carrying water for them, sweeping, etc. Beware not to get discouraged; beware not to turn your back to what you commenced to do; and beware not to think of all the (good) things you left behind; continue and persevere on your way and accept its hardships. Perchance it may please our lord to let you return wealthy so that we, your elders, and your relatives may see you again; mind and accept the advice we, who are your parents, give you herewith as a good support that will encourage and inspire you to go on. Very beloved son, be of good cheer and go with god; we your elders give you godspeed that you may carry your deal through, leaving behind your relatives, etc."

In this manner the old merchants encouraged and harangued the young men who departed for the first time in the company of other dealers; they told them of the suffering and difficulties they would face, in villages as well as in deserts, while they were engaged in their trade. . . .

Even to young men who were about to leave on trading expeditions having had experience on roads and their hardships from previous trips, those old merchants gave a short allocution at the time of departure, speaking about as follows: "Young man here before me, you are not a child any more, for you have already had experience on the road and know its hardships and the dangers this trade presents when traveling from village to village, bartering. You have been over the roads and have visited the towns you now intend to see again. Perchance your life may come to an end in one of those towns or on one of those trips, but always remember, wheresoever this might happen to you, the counsels and the tears of your elders are with you, since we love you like a son and we hope to deserve the pleasure of your safe return, of seeing you here once more in good health and prosperity. Thus, my son, take heart and go with god, for well we know that on your journey you will find hardships, because the road in itself is rough and troublesome. Beware not to leave behind those who accompany you, do not forsake them nor stray away from them, but rather consider them and treat them like younger brothers; teach them what to do upon reaching the stopping places, make them gather grass and make seats that the older ones of your company might rest. We have already admonished all such of your companions who have not yet gone to trade, and hence do not know the roads; you all are now to travel together, and it is therefore not necessary to talk any longer. We have told you in few words, my son, what your duty will be; go therefore, in peace, exert yourself in attending to your business."

After the old men had thus spoken, the youth answered briefly as follows: "I consider it a great favor, honored sirs, that you should have granted me this consolation, for I am not worthy of it. You have acted like parents, as if I had been engendered by you, in thus giving me your advice. You have uttered golden words from the treasure in your hearts more precious than gold, precious stones or rich plumes, and as such I receive and honour them. Never shall I forget such beautiful expressions; in my heart and soul shall I enclose them forever. What I now entreat you is that in my absence you will see to it that there is always someone in my house to sweep and "light the fire," for there remains my father, or mother, or sister, or my aunt (as the case may be), and I entreat you to so favour and protect them that no one may injure them. And if it should please our lord to end my life on this journey, I beg the same favour of you, and with this (assurance) I depart comforted."

After this speech all those present began to weep, men as well as women, taking leave from the one who departed, and after his departure they all commenced to eat and drink. . . .

After the trader had taken leave of his relatives or those of his own household, father, mother, wife, or children, all these left behind only washed their heads or faces every eighty days, which meant that they did penance for their son, husband or father who was absent. And, although they washed their bodies during this period, they never washed their heads until the return of the absent one. If by chance he died over there (on the road), it was the old merchants who were informed first, and they went to announce his death at his house, that they might mourn him and celebrate his exequies, as was their custom. In such a case all the relatives of the deceased went to visit and to console his widow or parents and, four days after the funeral rites, they washed their faces and soaped their heads (hair), saying that this took away the sadness (sorrow). If, perchance, that merchant was killed by his enemies, as soon as those of his household were informed of this, they made his statue (effigy) of torches (candlewood) tied together and adorned it with the apparel they would have put on the body had he died at home. This consisted mostly of different kinds of paper with which they were wont to adorn the bodies of their dead. They offered other papers before this statue and carried it to the Calpulco (community house), that is, the church of his district, and there it remained one day, and they mourned him there. At midnight they carried the statue into the court of the temple and burned it in a certain place of that court which they called Quauhcicalco or Tezompantitlan. If the trader had died on the road from some disease or other, they made a similar statue, but they burnt it in the court of his own house at sunset. . . . [*Here as in China, they burned paper at funerals; symbols of symbols.*]

Three main points appear from this quotation of Sahagun:

1. The Aztec gods exactly fitted the routine of life of the people who worshipped them, symbolizing the most critical moments or events. Huitzilopochtli, the war god, symbolized their most spectacular occupation. The Aztecs fought wars to get captives for sacrifice, to keep the trade routes open, and to preserve the equilibrium of their own tightly organized and highly complicated society during the slack work season. The Tlalocs, or rain gods, symbolized the summer rains essential for the ripening of their chief food source, maize. The maize goddesses represented the various stages of maturation of the plant, while the Flayed God Xipé represented the removal of the husk. Quetzalcoatl represented

he artisans and technicians, each of whom had a separate god of their own. Procreation, drunkenness, etc., were all equally symbolized.

2. The measurement of time had become of great importance to a people as highly organized as the Aztecs. First of all they had to know when to plant. Then it was essential for merchants to know how long they had been gone, and what seasons they would strike in different places. With an elaborate sequence of rituals which kept people emotionally unified all the year, a calendar was necessary. With the development (or borrowing) of a calendar, the role of the diviner entered—some days were magically favorable and others unfavorable for specific undertakings, and astrologers plied their trade, as they do in our own civilization today—with one difference; among the Aztecs apparently everyone believed them. You will find the same dependence on the calendar for prediction in the Babylonian civilization, the auguries of ancient Rome, and modern astrology.

3. The fact is that the Aztec state consisted of a number of interlocking institutions, some of which were internally complex. These included in one sense the *calpullec* quarters, and state as a whole; in another the special professions and the traders, and in still another the various grades of priests and warriors, each with its clientele. These institutions were characterized by a high degree of internal strength, as manifested by their possession of separate gods. The worship of the national gods, Huitzilopochtli, the Tlalocs, and others, helped to unify the whole. The Aztec nation was an expanding state. Like the British in the early nineteenth century, it was establishing outposts of Empire and assuming the white (here the red) man's burden. It needed much pomp and fanfare, and it had it.

17

India, from an Early Chinese Manuscript

Returning to the Old World, and keeping within the north latitude range of Mexico, our closest counterpart to Tenochtitlon in cultural complexity would be northern India, and particularly the Indo-Gangetic plain. Today it is overpopulated, deforested and almost insufferably hot in summer, reaching a daily mean temperature of 94° F in May. But in the early centuries of our era it still bore a forest cover, heaviest in Bihar, the state where the Central Indian hills reach closest to the jungly Terai of Nepal. There and then the climate was relatively temperate, and people lived a happier and heartier life than is possible today.

One of the few available sources on this felicitous period, antedating the influences of the Arabs, Persians, Moghuls, and Europeans, was the diary of a Chinese Buddhist pilgrim, Huien Tsiang* (A.D. 600-664), whose path led him to Benaras, in Bihar.

1. NAMES OF INDIA

[*This section is the attempt of the author to adapt names from a polysyllabic, inflectional language to his own tonal monosyllabic Chinese, lacking the consonants B, D, R, X, and Z. His purpose was probably to relate what he is about to describe to something already familiar to his readers, just as I have tried to do.*]

On examination, we find that the names of India (T'ien-chu)† are various and perplexing as to their authority. It was anciently called Shin-tu, also Hien-tau; but now, according to the right pronunciation, it is called In-tu. The people of In-tu call their country by different names according to their district. Each country has diverse customs. Aiming at a general name which is the best sounding, we will call the country In-tu. In Chinese this name signifies the Moon. The moon has many names, of which this is one. For as it is said that all living things ceaselessly revolve in the wheel (of transmigration) through the long night of ignorance, without a guiding star, their case is like (the world), the sun gone down; as then the torch affords its connecting light, though there be the shining of the stars, how different from the bright (cool) moon; just so the bright connected light of holy men and sages, guiding the world as the shining of the moon, have made this country eminent, and so it is called In-tu.

*Huien Tsiang, *Buddhist Records of the Western World*, translated by Samuel Beal, vol., I. Trübner & Co., London, 1884. Book II and Book V.
† Parentheses are the translator's.

484

The families of India are divided into castes, the Brâhmans particularly (are noted) on account of their purity and nobility. Tradition has so hallowed the name of this tribe that there is no question as to difference of place, but the people generally speak of India as the country of the Brâhmans (Po-lo-men).

2. EXTENT OF INDIA, CLIMATE, &C.

The countries embraced under this term of India are generally spoken of as the five Indies. In circuit this country is about 90,000 li; on three sides it is bordered by the great sea; on the north it is backed by the Snowy Mountains. The north part is broad, the southern part is narrow. Its shape is like the half-moon. The entire land is divided into seventy countries or so. The seasons are particularly hot; the land is well watered and humid. The north is a continuation of mountains and hills, the ground being dry and salt. On the east there are valleys and plains, which being well watered and cultivated, are fruitful and productive. The southern district is wooded and herbaceous; the western parts are stony and barren. Such is the general account of this country.

3. MEASURES OF LENGTH

To give a brief account of matters. In point of measurements, there is first of all the *yôjana* (*yu-shen-na*); this from the time of the holy kings of old has been regarded as a day's march for an army. The old accounts say it is equal to 40 *li;* according to the common reckoning in India it is 30 *li,* but in the sacred books (of Buddha) the *yôjana* is only 16 *li.*

In the subdivision of distances, a *yôjana* is equal to eight *krôsas* (*keu-lu-she*) ; a *krôsa* is the distance that the lowing of a cow can be heard ; a *krôsa* is divided into 500 bows (*dhanus*) ; a bow is divided into four cubits (*hastas*) ; a cubit is divided into 24 fingers (*angulis*) ; a finger is divided into seven barley-corns (*yavas*) ; and so on to a louse (*yûka*), a nit (*likshâ*), a dust grain, a cow's hair, a sheep's hair, a hare's down, copper-water, and so on for seven divisions, till we come to a small grain of dust; this is divided sevenfold till we come to an excessively small grain of dust (*anu*) ; this cannot be divided further without arriving at nothingness, and so it is called the infinitely small (*paramânu*).

[*His smallest units of linear space and of time are too small to be measured by any device known in either India or China at that time. One* kshana = .0133 *seconds. Whether or not his informants were having fun with the learned pilgrim, this passage shows the interest of these peoples in exact measurement. As with our inches, feet, yards, furlongs, and miles, the Hindus had an irregular system based on concrete or material phenomena, such as a cow low and a bowshot, partly duodecimal (4, 8, 24), with seven, a magical number, used for the fabulous micro-units. His units of time, 5, 6, 30, 60, 120, follow the abstract Babylonian system, as do ours.*]

4. ASTRONOMY, THE CALENDAR, &C.

Although the revolution of the *Yin* and *Yang* principles and the successive mansions of the sun and moon be called by names different from ours, yet the seasons are the same ; the names of the months are derived from the position (of the moon in respect) of the asterisms.

[Yin *and* Yang *are the Chinese male and female principles. The female principle is dark and evil, the male light and good. They refer of course to the alternation of winter and summer. This dualism permeates Chinese philosophy, as it does that of the Iranian peoples. It was carried over into Christianity, without the sex linkage.*]

The shortest portion of time is called a *t'sa-na* (*kshana*) ; 120 *kshanas* make a *ta-t'sa-na* (*takshana*) ; 60 of these make a *la-fo* (*lava*) ; 30 of these make a *mau-hu-li-to* (*muhûrta*) ; five of these make "a period of time" (*kâla*) ; six of these make a day and night (*ahôrâtra*), but commonly the day and night are divided into eight *kâlas*.

The period from the new moon till full moon is called the white division (*Sukla-paksha*) of the month ; the period from the full moon till the disappearance (of the light) is called the dark portion (*Krĭshna-paksha*). The dark portion comprises fourteen or fifteen days, because the month is sometimes long and sometimes short. The preceding dark portion and the following light portion together form a month ; six months form a "march" (*hing,s.ayana*). The sun when it moves within (the equator) is said to be on its northward march ; when it moves without (the equator) it is on its southern march. These two periods form a year (*vatsara*).

The year, again, is divided into six seasons. From the 16th day of the 1st month till the 15th day of the 3d month is the season of gradual heat ; from the 16th day of the 3d month till the 15th day of the 5th month is called the season of full heat ; from the 16th day of the 5th month till the 15th day of the 7th month is called the rainy season ; from the 16th day of the 7th month till the 15th day of the 9th month is called the season of growth (vegetation) ; from the 16th day of the 9th month to the 15th day of the 11th month is called the season of gradual cold ; from the 16th day of the 11th month to the 15th day of the 1st month is called the season of great (full) cold.

According to the holy doctrine of Tathâgata [*one of the names of the Buddha*], the year is divided into three seasons. From the 16th day of the 1st month till the 15th day of the 5th month is called the hot season ; from the 16th day of the 5th month till the 15th day of the 9th month is called the wet season ; and from the 16th day of the 9th month to the 15th day of the 1st month is called the cold season. Again, there are four seasons, called spring, summer, autumn, winter. . . . In old times in India the priestly fraternity, relying on the holy teaching of Buddha, has a double resting-time (during the rains), viz., either the former three months or the latter three months ; these periods were either from the 16th day of the 5th month to the 15th day of the 8th month, or from the 16th day of the 6th month to the 15th day of the 9th month.

Translators of the *Sûtras* (*king*) and the *Vinaya* (*liu*) belonging to former generations employed the terms *Tso-hia* and *Tso-la-hia* to signify the rest during the rainy season ; but this was because the ignorant (common) people of the frontier countries did not understand the right sounds of the language of the middle country (India), or that they translated before they comprehended the local phrases : this was the cause of error. And for the same reason occur the mistakes about the time of Tathâgata's conception, birth, departure from his home, enlightenment, and *Nirvâna,* which we shall notice in the subsequent records.

5. Towns and Buildings

The towns and villages have inner gates ; the walls are wide and high ; the streets and lanes are tortuous, and the roads winding. The thoroughfares are dirty and the stalls arranged on both sides of the road with appropriate signs. Butchers, fishers, dancers, executioners, and scavengers, and so on, have their abodes without the city. In coming and going these persons are bound to keep on the left side òf the road till they arrive at their homes. Their houses are surrounded by low walls, and form the suburbs. The earth being soft and muddy, the walls of the towns are mostly built of brick or tiles. The towers on the walls are constructed of wood or bamboo; the houses have balconies and belvederes, which are made of wood, with a coating of lime or mortar, and covered with tiles. The different buildings have the same form as those in China: rushes, or dry branches, or tiles, or boards are used for covering them. The walls are covered with lime and mud, mixed with cow's dung for purity [*the cow being sacred*]. At different seasons they scatter flowers about. Such are some of their different customs.

The *sanghârâmas* are constructed with extraordinary skill. A three-storied tower is erected at each of the four angles. The beams and the projecting heads are carved with great skill in different shapes. The doors, windows, and the low walls are painted profusely; the monks' cells are ornamental on the inside and plain on the outside. In the very middle of the building is the hall, high and wide. There are various storeyed chambers and turrets of different height and shape, without any fixed rule. The doors open towards the east; the royal throne also faces the east.

[*This description would fit any oriental town. The* sangharamas *werp monasteries.*]

6. Seats, Clothing, &c.

When they sit or rest they all use mats; the royal family and the great personages and assistant officers use mats variously ornamented, but in size they are the same. The throne of the reigning sovereign is large and high, and much adorned with precious gems: it is called the Lion-throne (*simhâsana*). It is covered with extremely fine drapery; the footstool is adorned with gems. The nobility use beautifully painted and enriched seats, according to their taste.

7. Dress, Habits, &c.

Their clothing is not cut or fashioned; they mostly affect fresh-white garments; they esteem little those of mixed colour or ornamented. The men wind their garments round their middle, then gather them under the armpits, and let them fall down across the body, hanging to the right. The robes of the women fall down to the ground; they completely cover their shoulders. They wear a little knot of hair on their crowns, and let the rest of their hair fall loose. Some of the men cut off their moustaches, and have other odd customs. On their heads the people wear caps (crowns), with flower wreaths and jewelled necklets. Their garments are made of *Kiau-she-ye* (*kauśêya*) and of cotton. [*Cotton was old in India.*] *Kiau-she-ye* is the product of the wild silkworm. They have garments also of *Ts'o-mo* (*kshauma*), which is a sort of hemp; garments also made of *Kien-po-lo* (*kambala*) which is woven from fine goat-hair; garments also made from *Ho-la-li* (*karâla*). This stuff is made from the fine hair of a wild animal: it is seldom this can be woven, and therefore the stuff is very valuable, and it is regarded as fine clothing.

In North India, where the air is cold, they wear short and close-fitting garments, like the Hu people. The dress and ornaments worn by non-believers are varied and mixed. Some wear peacocks' feathers; some wear as ornaments necklaces made of skull bones (the *Kapâla-dhârinas*) ; some have no clothing, but go naked (*Nirgranthas*) ; some wear leaf or bark garments ; some pull out their hair and cut off their moustaches ; others have bushy whiskers and their hair braided on the top of their heads. The costume is not uniform, and the colour, whether red or white, not constant.

The Shamans (*Śramanas*) have only three kinds of robes, viz., the *Sang-kio-ki*, the *Ni-fo-si-na*. The cut of the three robes is not the same, but depends on the school. Some have wide or narrow borders, others have small or large flaps. The *Sang-kio-ki* covers the left shoulder and conceals the two armpits. It is worn open on the left and closed on the right. It is cut longer than the waist. The *Ni-fo-si-na* has neither girdle nor tassels. When putting it on, it is plaited in folds and worn round the loins with a cord fastening. The schools differ as to the colour of this garment : both yellow and red are used.

[*The variety of costumes in India is still great, reflecting the extensive division of labor on caste and ethnic lines. Contrast it with the uniformity of costume on an American street, and explain.*]

The Kshattriyas and the Brâhmans are cleanly and wholesome in their dress, and they live in a homely and frugal way. The king of the country and the great ministers wear garments and ornament themselves with bracelets and necklaces.

There are rich merchants who deal exclusively in gold trinkets, and so on. They mostly go barefooted; few wear sandals. They stain their teeth red or black; they bind up their hair and pierce their ears; they ornament their noses, and have large eyes. Such is their appearance.

8. CLEANLINESS, ABLUTIONS, &c.

They are very particular in their personal cleanliness, and allow no remissness in this particular. All wash themselves before eating; they never use that which has been left over (from a former meal) ; they do not pass the dishes. Wooden and stone vessels, when used, must be destroyed; vessels of gold, silver, copper, or iron after each meal must be rubbed and polished. After eating they cleanse their teeth with a willow stick, and wash their hands and mouth. [*In ablutions the Indians outdo even the Arabs.*]

Until these ablutions are finished they do not touch one another. Every time they perform the functions of nature they wash their bodies and use perfumes of sandal-wood or turmeric.

When the king washes they strike the drums and sing hymns to the sound of musical instruments. Before offering their religious services and petitions, they wash and bathe themselves.

9. WRITING, LANGUAGE, BOOKS, THE VEDAS, STUDY

The letters of their alphabet were arranged by Brahmâdêva, and their forms have been handed down from the first till now. They are forty-seven in number, and are combined so as to form words according to the object, and according to circumstances (of time or place) : there are other forms (inflexions) used. This alphabet has spread in different directions and formed diverse branches, according to circumstances ; therefore there have been slight modifications in the sounds of the words (spoken language) ; but in its great features there has been no change. Middle India preserves the original character of the language in its integrity. Here the pronunciation is soft and agreeable, and like the language of the Dêvas. The pronunciation of the words is clear and pure, and fit as a model for all men. The people of the frontiers have contracted several erroneous modes of pronunciation; for according to the licentious habits of the people, so also will be the corrupt nature of their language.

With respect to the records of events, each province has its own official for preserving them in writing. The records of these events in their full character is called Ni-lo-pi-ch'a (Nîlapita, blue deposit). In these records are mentioned good and evil events, with calamities and fortunate occurrences.

[*For the first time in this book we see writing on a full scale with a competent alphabet, used to record events. This technique, an extension of language, created a special class or caste of clerks and secretaries. In this chapter one should note the length of time spent in education and the importance attached to it. In India there was much to learn. In Chapter 10 we shall see that the rewards for scholarship were great, as in China.*]

To educate and encourage the young, they are first taught (led) to study the book of twelve chapters (*Siddhavastu*).

After arriving at the age of seven years and upwards, the young are instructed in the five *Vidyâs, Sâstras* of great importance. The first is called the elucidation of sounds (*Sabdavidyâ*). This treatise explains and illustrates the agreement (concordance) of words, and it provides an index for derivatives.

The second *vidyâ* is called *Kiau-ming* (*Silpasthânavidyâ*); it treats of the arts, mechanics, explains the principles of the *Yin* and *Yang* and the calendar.

The third is called the medicinal treatise (*Chikitsâvidyâ*); it embraces formulae for protection, secret charms (the use of) medicinal stones, acupuncture, and mugwort.

The fourth *vidyâ* is called the *Hêtu-vidyâ* (science of causes); its name is derived from the character of the work, which relates to the determination of the true and false, and reduces to their last terms the definition of right and wrong.

The fifth *vidyâ* is called the science of "the interior" (*Adhyâtmavidyâ*); it relates to the five vehicles, their causes and consequences, and the subtle influences of these.

The Brâhmans study the four *Vêda Sâstras*. The first is called *Shau* (longevity); it relates to the preservation of life and the regulation of the natural condition. The second is called *Sse* (sacrifice); it relates to the (rules of) sacrifice and prayer. The third is called *Ping* (peace or regulation); it relates to decorum, casting of lots, military affairs, and army regulations. The fourth is called *Shu* (secret mysteries); it relates to various branches of science, incantations, medicine.

The teachers (of these works) must themselves have closely studied the deep and secret principles they contain, and penetrated to their remotest meaning. They then explain their general sense, and guide their pupils in understanding the words which are difficult. They urge them on and skilfully conduct them. They add lustre to their poor knowledge, and stimulate the desponding. If they find that their pupils are satisfied with their acquirements, and so wish to escape to attend to their worldly duties, then they use means to keep them in their power. When they have finished their education, and have attained thirty years of age, then their character is formed and their knowledge ripe. When they have secured an occupation they first of all thank their master for his attention. There are some, deeply versed in antiquity, who devote themselves to elegant studies, and live apart from the world, and retain the simplicity of their character. These rise above mundane presents, and are as insensible to renown as to the contempt of the world. Their name having spread afar, the rulers appreciate them highly, but are unable to draw them to the court. The chief of the country honours them on account of their (mental) gifts, and the people exalt their fame and render them universal homage. This is the reason of their devoting themselves to their studies with ardour and resolution, without any sense of fatigue. They search for wisdom, relying on their own resources. Although they are possessed of large wealth, yet they will wander here and there to seek their subsistence. There are others who, whilst attaching value to letters, will yet without shame consume their fortunes in wandering about for pleasure, neglecting their duties. They squander their substance in costly food and clothing. Having no virtuous principle, and no desire to study, they are brought to disgrace, and their infamy is widely circulated.

So, according to the class they belong to, all gain knowledge of the doctrine of Tathâgata; but, as the time is distant since the holy one lived, his doctrine is presented in a changed form, and so it is understood, rightly or not, according to the intelligence of those who inquire into it.

10. BUDDHIST SCHOOLS, BOOKS, DISCUSSIONS, DISCIPLINE

The different schools are constantly at variance, and their contending utterances rise like the angry waves of the sea. The different sects have their separate masters, and in various directions aim at one end. [*Whether Buddhist or Hindu, the Indians are always divided into many schools and sects.*]

There are eighteen schools, each claiming pre-eminence. The partisans of the Great and Little Vehicle are con-

tent to dwell apart. There are some who give themselves up to quiet contemplation, and devote themselves, whether walking or standing still or sitting down, to the acquirement of wisdom and insight; others, on the contrary, differ from these in raising noisy contentions about their faith. According to their fraternity, they are governed by distinctive rules and regulations, which we need not name.

The *Vinaya (liu)*, discourses (*lun*), sûtras (*king*), are equally Buddhist books. He who can entirely explain one class of these books is exempted from the control of the *karmadâna*. If he can explain two classes, he receives in addition the equipments of an upper seat (room); he who can explain three classes has allotted to him different servants to attend to and obey him; he who can explain four classes has "pure men" (*upâsakas*) allotted to him as attendants; he who can explain five classes of books is then allowed an elephant carriage; he who can explain six classes of books is allowed a surrounding escort. When a man's renown has reached to a high distinction, then at different times he convokes an assembly for discussion. He judges of the superior or inferior talent of those who take part in it; he distinguishes their good or bad points; he praises the clever and reproves the faulty; if one of the assembly distinguishes himself by defined language, subtle investigation, deep penetration, and severe logic, then he is mounted on an elephant covered with precious ornaments, and conducted by a numerous suite to the gates of the convent.

If, on the contrary, one of the members breaks down in his argument, or uses poor and inelegant phrases, or if he violates a rule in logic and adapts his words accordingly, they proceed to disfigure his face with red and white, and cover his body with dirt and dust, and then carry him off to some deserted spot or leave him in a ditch. Thus they distinguish between the meritorious and the worthless, between the wise and the foolish.

The pursuit of pleasure belongs to a worldly life, to follow knowledge to a religious life; to return to a worldly life from one of religion is considered blameworthy. If one breaks the rules of discipline, the transgressor is publicly reproved: for a slight fault a reprimand is given or a temporary banishment (*enforced silence*); for a grave fault expulsion is enforced. Those who are thus expelled for life go out to seek some dwelling-place, or, finding no place of refuge, wander about the roads; sometimes they go back to their old occupation (resume lay life).

11. CASTES—MARRIAGE

With respect to the division of families, there are four classifications. The first is called the Brâhman (*Po-lo-men*), men of pure conduct. They guard themselves in religion, live purely, and observe the most correct principles. The second is called Kshattriya (*T'sa-ti-li*), the royal caste. For ages they have been the governing class: they apply themselves to virtue (humanity) and kindness. The third is called Vaiśyas (*fei-she-li*), the merchant class: they engage in commercial exchange, and they follow profit at home and abroad. The fourth is called Sûdra (*Shu-t'o-lo*), the agricultural class: they labour in ploughing and tillage. In these four classes purity and impurity of caste assigns to every one his place. When they marry they rise or fall in position according to their new relationship. They do not allow promiscuous marriages between relations. A woman once married can never take another husband. Besides these there are other classes of many kinds that intermarry according to their

several callings. It would be difficult to speak of these in detail.

[*The four main groups of caste divisions still obtain. However, they are divided into a myriad of special castes and subcastes, as the next selection will make clear. Caste is of course a mechanism for maintaining the* status quo *in a society characterized by a complex division of labor, with high technical skill but simple utilization of energy, and with little technological change.*]

12. ROYAL FAMILY, TROOPS, WEAPONS

The succession of kings is confined to the Kshattriya (*T'sa-li*) caste, who by usurpation and bloodshed have from time to time raised themselves to power. Although a distinct caste, they are regarded as honourable (or lords).

The chief soldiers of the country are selected from the bravest of the people, and as the sons follow the profession of their fathers, they soon acquire a knowledge of the art of war. These dwell in garrison around the palace (during peace), but when on an expedition they march in front of an advanced guard. There are four divisions of the army, viz.—(1) the infantry, (2) the cavalry, (3) the chariots, (4) the elephants. The elephants are covered with strong armour, and their tusks are provided with sharp spurs. A leader in a car gives the command, whilst two attendants on the right and left drive his chariot, which is drawn by four horses abreast. The general of the soldiers remains in his chariot; he is surrounded by a file of guards, who keep close to the wheels.

The cavalry spread themselves in front to resist an attack, and in case of defeat they carry orders hither and thither. The infantry by their quick movements contribute to the defence. These men are chosen for their courage and strength. They carry a long spear, and a great shield; sometimes they hold a sword or sabre, and advance to the front with impetuosity. All their weapons of war are sharp and pointed. Some of them are these—spears, shields, bows, arrows, swords, sabres, battle-axes, lances, halberds, long javelins, and various kinds of slings. All these they have used for ages.

[*Note the complexity of the army, with infantry, cavalry, a chariot brigade, and an elephant corps. The possession of large and tractable domestic animals made this division possible. Contrast this with the Aztec army— they were limited by the necessity of fighting on foot, and of making cutting edges of obsidian.*]

13. MANNERS, ADMINISTRATION OF LAW, ORDEALS

With respect to the ordinary people, although they are naturally lightminded, yet they are upright and honourable. In money matters they are without craft, and in administering justice they are considerate. They dread the retribution of another state of existence, and make light of the things of the present world. They are not deceitful or treacherous in their conduct, and are faithful to their oaths and promises. In their rules of government there is remarkable rectitude, whilst in their behaviour there is much gentleness and sweetness. With respect to criminals or rebels, these are few in number, and only occasionally troublesome. When the laws are broken or the power of the ruler violated, then the matter is clearly sifted and the offenders imprisoned. There is no infliction of corporal punishment; they are simply left to live or die, and are not counted among men. When the rules of propriety or justice are violated, or when a man fails in fidelity or filial piety, then they cut his nose or his ears off, or his hands or feet, or expel him from the country or drive him out into the desert wilds. For other faults, except these, a small payment of money will redeem the punishment. In the investigation of criminal cases there is no use of rod or staff to obtain proofs (of guilt). In questioning an accused person, if he replies with frankness the punishment is proportioned accordingly; but if the accused obstinately denies his fault, or in despite of it attempts to excuse himself, then in searching out the truth to the bottom, when it is necessary to pass sentence, there are four kinds of ordeal used— (1) by water, (2) by fire, (3) by weighing, (4) by poison.

When the ordeal is by water, then the accused is placed in a sack connected with a stone vessel and thrown into deep water. They then judge of his innocence (truth) or guilt in this way—if the man sinks and the stone floats he is guilty; but if the man floats and the stone sinks then he is pronounced innocent.

Secondly, by fire. They heat a plate of iron and make the accused sit on it, and again place his feet on it, and apply it to the palms of his hands; moreover, he is made to pass his tongue over it; if no scars result, he is innocent; if there are scars, his guilt is proved. In case of weak or timid persons who cannot endure such ordeal, they take a flower-bud and cast it towards the fire; if it opens, he is innocent; if the flower is burnt, he is guilty.

Ordeal by weight is this: A man and a stone are placed in a balance evenly, then they judge according to lightness or weight. If the accused is innocent, then the man weighs down the stone, which rises in the balance; if he is guilty, the man rises, and the stone falls.

Ordeal by poison is this: They take a ram and make an incision in its right thigh, then mixing all sorts of poison with a portion of the food of the accused man, they place it in the incision made in the thigh (*of the animal*); if the man is guilty, then the poison takes effect and the creature dies; if ·he is innocent, then the poison has no effect, and he survives.

By these four methods of trial the way of crime is stopped.

[*These ordeals, like the sasswood trial in Chapter 12, are acceptable only to people ignorant of the cause-and-effect relationships between physical phenomena. They lasted through the Middle Ages in Europe.*]

14. FORMS OF POLITENESS

There are nine methods of showing outward respect—(1) by selecting words of a soothing character in making requests; (2) by bowing the head to show respect; (3) by raising the hands and bowing; (4) by joining the hands and bowing low; (5) by bending the knee; (6) by a prostration; (7) by a prostration on hands and knees; (8) by touching the ground with the five circles; (9) by stretching the five parts of the body on the ground.

Of these nine methods the most respectful is to make one prostration on the ground and then to kneel and laud the virtues of the one addressed. When at a distance it is usual to bow low; when near, then it is customary to kiss the feet and rub the ankles (of the person addressed).

Whenever orders are received at the hands of a superior, the person lifts the skirts of his robes and makes a prostration. The superior or honourable person who is thus reverenced must speak gently (to the inferior), either touching his head or patting his back, and addressing him with good words of direction or advice to show his affection.

When a Śramana, or one who has entered on the religious life, has been

thus respectfully addressed, he simply replies by expressing a good wish (vow).

Not only do they prostrate themselves to show reverence, but they also turn round towards the thing reverenced in many ways, sometimes with one turn, sometimes with three: if from some long-cherished feeling there is a call for marked reverence, then according to the desire of the person.

15. MEDICINES, FUNERAL CUSTOMS, &c.

Every one who falls sick fasts for seven days. During this interval many recover, but if the sickness lasts they take medicine. The character of these medicines is different, and their names also. The doctors differ in their modes of examination and treatment.

When a person dies, those who attend the funeral raise lamentable cries and weep together. They rend their garments and loosen their hair; they strike their heads and beat their breasts. There are no regulations as to dress for mourning, nor any fixed time for observing it.

There are three methods of paying the last tribute to the dead: (1) by cremation—wood being made into a pyre, the body is burnt; (2) by water—the body is thrown into deep flowing water and abandoned; (3) by desertion —the body is cast into some forest-wild, to be devoured by beasts.

When the king dies, his successor is first appointed, that he may preside at the funeral rites and fix the different points of precedence. Whilst living they give (their rulers) titles according to their character (virtue); when dead there are no posthumous titles.

In a house where there has been a death there is no eating allowed; but after the funeral they resume their usual (habits). There are no anniversaries (of the death) observed.

Those who have attended a death they consider unclean; they all bathe outside the town and then enter their houses.

The old and infirm who come near to death, and those entangled in a severe sickness, who fear to linger to the end of their days, and through disgust wish to escape the troubles of life, or those who desire release from the trifling affairs of the world and its concerns (the concerns of life), these, after receiving a farewell meal at the hands of their relatives or friends, they place, amid the sounds of music, on a boat which they propel into the midst of the Ganges, where such persons drown themselves. They think thus to secure a birth among the Dêvas [*deities*]. Rarely one of these may be seen not yet dead on the borders (of the river).

The priests are not allowed to lament or cry for the dead; when a father or mother of a priest dies they recite their prayers, recounting (pledging) their obligations to them; reflecting on the past, they carefully attend to them now dead. They expect by this to increase the mysterious character of their religious merit.

16. CIVIL ADMINISTRATION, REVENUES, &C.

As the administration of the government is founded on benign principles, the executive is simple. The families are not entered on registers, and the people are not subject to forced labour (conscription). The private demesnes of the crown are divided into four principal parts; the first is for carrying out the affairs of state and providing sacrificial offerings; the second is for providing subsidies for the ministers and chief officers of state; the third is for rewarding men of distinguished ability; and the fourth is for charity to religious bodies, whereby the field of merit is cultivated (planted). In this way the taxes on the people are light,

and the personal service required of them is moderate. Each one keeps his own worldly goods in peace, and all till the ground for their subsistence. These who cultivate the royal estates pay a sixth part of the produce as tribute. The merchants who engage in commerce come and go in carrying out their transactions. The river passages and the road barriers are open on payment of a small toll. When the public works require it, labour is exacted but paid for. The payment is in strict proportion to the work done.

The military guard the frontiers, or go out to punish the refractory. They also mount guard at night round the palace. The soldiers are levied according to the requirements of the service; they are promised certain payments and are publicly enrolled. The governors, ministers, magistrates, and officials have each a portion of land consigned to them for their personal support.

[*The government is moderately complicated. However, in all of the Indian states, today as then, most of the people live in villages which are self-governing and only loosely associated with the central governments of the cities.*]

17. PLANTS AND TREES, AGRICULTURE, FOOD, DRINK, COOKERY

The climate and the quality of the soil being different according to situation, the produce of the land is various in its character. The flowers and plants, the fruits and trees are of different kinds, and . . . it would be difficult to enumerate all the kinds of fruit; we have briefly named those most esteemed by the people. As for the date . . . the chestnut . . . the loquat . . . and the persimmon . . . they are not known. The pear . . . the wild plum . . . the peach . . . the apricot . . . the grape . . . &c., these all have been brought from the country of

Kaśmir, and are found growing on every side. Pomegranates and sweet oranges are grown everywhere.

In cultivating the land, those whose duty it is sow and reap, plough and harrow (weed), and plant according to the season; and after their labour they rest awhile. Among the products of the ground, rice and corn are most plentiful. With respect to edible herbs and plants, we may name ginger and mustard, melons and pumpkins, the *Heun-to* (Kandu?) plant, and others. Onions and garlic are little grown; and few persons eat them; if any one uses them for food, they are expelled beyond the walls of the town. The most usual food is milk, butter, cream, soft sugar, sugar-candy, the oil of the mustard-seed, and all sorts of cakes made of corn are used as food. Fish, mutton, gazelle, and deer they eat generally fresh, sometimes salted; they are forbidden to eat the flesh of the ox, the ass, the elephant, the horse, the pig, the dog, the fox, the wolf, the lion, the monkey, and all the hairy kind. Those who eat them are despised and scorned, and are universally reprobated; they live outside the walls, and are seldom seen among men.

With respect to the different kinds of wine and liquors, there are various sorts. The juice of the grape and sugar-cane, these are used by the Kshattriyas as drink; the Vaiśyas use strong fermented drinks; the Śramans and Brâhmans drink a sort of syrup made from the grape or sugar-cane, but not of the nature of fermented wine.

The mixed classes and base-born differ in no way (as to food or drink) from the rest, except in respect of the vessels they use, which are very different both as to value and material. There is no lack of suitable things for household use. Although they have saucepans and stewpans, yet they do not know the steamer used for cooking rice. They have many vessels made of dried clay; they seldom use red copper vessels: they eat from one vessel, mixing all sorts of condiments together, which they take up with their fingers. They have no spoons or cups, and in short no sort of chopstick. When sick, however, they use copper drinking cups.

18. COMMERCIAL TRANSACTIONS

Gold and silver, *teuo-shih* (native copper), white jade, fire pearls, are the natural products of the country; there are besides these abundance of rare gems and various kinds of precious stones of different names, which are collected from the islands of the sea. These they exchange for other goods; and in fact they always barter in their commercial transactions, for they have no gold or silver coins, pearl shells, or little pearls.

In Huien Tsiang's day the predominant faith of India was Buddhism, which has since been replaced by a re-emergence of Hinduism, while large minorities have adopted Islam, Sikhism, and Jainism. Despite this change those of you who are familiar with India today will find little difference between what he describes and what you have seen with your own eyes, especially in the villages, where technology is archaic, and the local council is to a considerable extent autonomous.

Level Six

One Complex Political Institution

18

The Athenian Democracy

YOU must all have been exposed, in primary or secondary school, to some kind of classical education. Although Greek and Latin are not taught as widely as they were a quarter of a century ago, still some of you must have read classical works in the original tongues, even in Greek. The rest of you have all no doubt studied ancient history and know something about the Athenian empire during its most prosperous period, the fifth century B.C. But I doubt that many of you could sit down and write out a detailed table of organization of the Athenian state. Neither ancient history nor the Greek language is taught that way. In fact, only one ancient document gives a complete picture of the Athenian govern·ment—Aristotle's Athenian Constitution. Like so many of Aristotle's works, this was originally presented in the form of lectures, orally, and was written down by his students, just as you write out lecture notes. This work of Aristotle was lost until a few decades ago, and most textbooks on ancient history were written in ingorance of it.

The Greeks enjoyed the benefits of a Mediterranean climate. With winter cereals, olive yards, and summer fruits grown under irrigation, the 35,000 citizens of Athens and their dependents were able to raise part of the food and other supplies which they needed; the rest came from abroad. The Athenian mariners brought home wheat from the shores of the Black Sea, oil and dried figs from Asia Minor, timber from the rainy forest of Eastern Georgia, and metal from many regions. For all of these imports, something had to be sent out in trade. The Athenians were fine craftsmen, bold sailors, and shrewd businessmen. They manufactured pottery which is still famous. The Attic vases which you see on museum shelves were meant not as works of art, but as containers for liquids, particularly wine. This wine was drunk far afield, by bearded Scythians on the Volga, by mustached Kelts in Gaul, and by people everywhere that the Greek ships could reach.

Besides pottery and wine, they manufactured and sold fine metal goods, particularly jewelry. For the barbarian trade they made up heavy gold vessels, designed in styles calculated to suit the purchasers, and many kinds of personal adornments such as brooches, plaques, chains, and armlets. We all know of the skill of their architects and sculptors. In every kind of hand work—everything to which artistic talent could be turned—the Athenians were pre-eminent.

Three factors made possible the developmnt of a special kind of political organization in Athens: skilled workmanship, easy transportation by sea to all points of the Mediterranean and Black Sea, and highly organized trade. Let us compare them for a moment with the Aztecs. The latter could transport goods by water for a few miles only, around the shores of a series of lakes; the Athenians had the benefit of the world's largest inland sea. The natural limits of Athenian expansion were much greater.

With a wide market for her goods, the chief problem of the Athenian merchants was to produce enough to meet the demand. Although highly skilled, the Greek workmen had no way of utilizing the energy of wind or water; the potter turned his wheel with his own foot, the miller ground grain with the force of human muscle, the woman drawing water had to haul it out of the well herself. Animals were of some use, but the feed problem was critical. In Mediterranean lands the grass dries in the summer, and grain is human food as well. A horse eats more than a man. The answer was, of course, cheap labor. The Athenians imported large numbers of slaves and also let in many free foreigners, who had no civil rights. Hence the Athenian democracy of which so much has been said was a democracy of one portion of the population only—of the free citizens. Bearing this in mind, we can proceed with Aristotle.*

XLII. The present form of the constitution is as follows. Citizenship belongs to persons of citizen parentage on both sides, and they are registered on the rolls of their demes at the age of eighteen. At the time of their registration the members of the deme make decision about them by vote on oath, first whether they are shown to have reached the lawful age, and if they are held not to be of age they go back again to the boys, and secondly whether the candidate is a freeman and of legitimate birth; after this, if the vote as to free status goes against him, he appeals to the jury-court, and the demesmen elect five men from among themselves to plead against him, and if it is decided that he has no claim to be registered, the state sells him, but if he wins, it is compulsory for the demesmen to register him. After this the Council revises the list of persons that have been registered, and if anyone is found to be under eighteen years of age, it fines the demesmen that registered him. And when the cadets have been passed by this revision, their fathers hold meetings by tribes and after taking oath

elect three members of the tribe of more than forty years of age, whom they think to be the best and most suitable to supervise the cadets, and from them the people elects by show of hands one of each tribe as disciplinary officer, and elects from the other citizens a marshal over them all. These take the cadets in a body, and after first making a circuit of the temples then go to Peiraeus, and some of them garrison Munichia,[1] others the Point.[2] And the People also elects two athletic trainers and instructors for them, to teach them their drill as heavy-armed soldiers, and the use of the bow, the javelin and the sling. It also grants the disciplinary officers one drachma a head for rations, and the cadets four obols a head; and each disciplinary officer takes the pay of those of his own tribe and buys provisions for all in common (for they mess together by tribes), and looks after everything else. They go on with this mode of life for the first year; in

[1] A hill above the sea south of the city commanding Peiraeus and the two other harbours.

[2] The southern promontory of Peiraeus.

* Reprinted by permission of the publishers from Aristotle, *The Athenian Constitution*, H. Rackham (translator), Loeb Classical Library. Cambridge, Mass.: Harvard University Press, 1935.

the following year an assembly is held in the theatre, and the cadets give a display of drill before the people, and receive a shield and spear from the state; and they then serve on patrols in the country and are quartered at the guard-posts. Their service on patrol goes on for two years; the uniform is a mantle; they are exempt from all taxes; and they are not allowed to be sued nor to sue at law, in order that they may have no pretext for absenting themselves, except in cases concerning estate, marriage of an heiress, and any priesthood that one of them may have inherited. When the two years are up, they now are members of the general body of citizens.

XLIII. Such, then, are the regulations about the registration of the citizens and about the cadets. All the officials concerned with the regular administration are appointed by lot, except a Treasurer of Military Funds, the Controllers of the Spectacle Fund, and the Superintendent of Wells; these officers are elected by show of hands, and their term of office runs from one Panathenaic Festival to the next.[3] All military officers also are elected by show of hands.

The Council is elected by lot, and has five hundred members, fifty from each tribe. The Presidency is filled by each tribe in turn, in an order settled by lot, each of the first four selected holding the office for thirty-six days and each of the latter six for thirty-five days; for their year is divided into lunar months.[4] Those of them serving as Presidents first dine together in the Round-house,[5] receiving a sum of money from the state, and then convene meetings of the Council and the People, the Council indeed meeting on every day excepting holidays, but the People four times in each presidency. And the Presidents put up written notice of the business to be dealt with by the Council, and of each day's agenda, and of the place of meeting. They also put up written notice of the meetings of the Assembly: one [6] sovereign meeting, at which the business is to vote the confirmation of the magistrates in office if they are thought to govern well, and to deal with matters of food supply and the defence of the country; and on this day informations have to be laid by those who wish, and the inventories of estates being confiscated read, and the lists of suits about inheritance and heiresses, so that all may have cognizance of any vacancy in an estate that occurs. In the sixth presidency in addition to the business specified they take a vote on the desirability of holding an ostracism, and on preliminary informations against persons charged as malicious informers, citizens and resident aliens, up to the number of not more than three cases of either class, and charges of failure to perform a service promised to the People. Another meeting is given to petitions, at which anyone who wishes, after placing a suppliant-branch,[7] may speak to the People about any matter he may wish whether public or private. The two other meetings deal with all other business, at which the laws enact that three cases of sacred matters are to be dealt with, three audiences for heralds and embassies, and three cases of secular matters. And sometimes they do business without a preliminary vote being taken. Also the Presidents give a first audience to heralds and to ambassa-

---

[3] I.e. in every four years; the Great Panathenaic Festival, as also the Pythian, was held in the third Olympian year.

[4] Alternate months of 29 and 30 days make a year of 354 days, as does 36×4+35×6.

[5] At the N.E. of the Areopagus, near the Council-chamber.

[6] One in each presidential term of office.

[7] An olive-branch wreathed with wool was carried by the suppliant and placed on the altar in the assembly.

dors, and to the Presidents dispatches are delivered by their bearers.

XLIV. The Presidents have a single Head elected by lot; he holds office for a day and a night, and may not hold office longer, nor serve a second time. He is keeper of the keys of the temples in which the money and documents of the state are lodged, and of the state seal, and he is required to stay in the Round-house, and so is whichever Third of the Presidential Boards he orders. And whenever the Presidents call a meeting of the Council or of the People, this official selects by lot nine Chairmen, one from each tribe except the tribe presiding, and again from these a single Head, and he hands over the list of agenda to them; and after receiving it they superintend procedure, bring forward the business to be dealt with, act as tellers, direct all the other business and have power to dismiss the meeting. A man cannot become Head more than once a year, but he can be Chairman once in each presidency.

They also conduct elections of Generals, and Cavalry Commanders and the other military officers in the Assembly, in whatever manner seems good to the People; and these elections are held by the first board of Presidents, after the sixth Presidency,[8] in whose term of office favourable weather-omens may occur. These matters also require a preliminary resolution of the Council.

XLV. The Council formerly had sovereign power to pass sentences of fine, imprisonment and death. But once it had brought Lysimachus to the public executioner, when, as he already sat awaiting death, Eumelides of the deme Alopecē rescued him, saying that no citizen ought to die without sentence by a jury; and when a trial was held in a jury-court Lysimachus got off, and he got the nickname of "the man from the drum-stick";[9] and the People deprived the Council of the power to sentence to death and imprisonment and to impose fines, and made a law that all verdicts of guilty and penalties passed by the Council must be brought before the jury-court by the Legislators, and that any vote of the jurymen should be sovereign.

Trials of officials are held in most cases by the Council, particularly those of the officials who handle funds; but the verdict of the Council is not sovereign, but subject to appeal to the jury-court. Private persons also have the right to lay an information of illegal procedure against any official they may wish; but in these cases also there is an appeal to the People if the Council passes a verdict of guilty.

The Council also checks the qualifications of the Councillors who are to hold office for the following year, and of the Nine Archons. And formerly it had sovereign power to reject them as disqualified, but now they have an appeal to the jury-court.

In these matters therefore the Council is not sovereign, but it prepares resolutions for the People, and the People cannot pass any measures that have not been prepared by the Council and published in writing in advance by the Presidents; for the proposer who carries such a measure is *ipso facto* liable to penalty by indictment for illegal procedure.

XLVI. The Council also inspects triremes after construction, and their rigging, and the naval sheds, and has new triremes or quadriremes, whichever the People votes for, built and rigged, and naval sheds built; but naval

[8] I.e. the Presidents holding the seventh or a later term of office, see xliii. 2. Rain, thunder, etc., were bad omens, but the regulation had a practical value for the open-air meetings in the Pnyx.

[9] I.e. the man who escaped the bastinado.

architects are elected by the People. If the outgoing Council does not hand over these works completed to the new Council, the members cannot draw their honorarium, which is payable when the next Council is in office. For the building of triremes it elects ten of its own members as Naval Constructors. It also inspects all public buildings, and if it finds any commissioner in default it reports him to the People, and if it gets a verdict of guilty hands him over to a jury-court.

XLVII. The Council also shares in the administration of the other offices in most affairs. First there are the ten Treasurers of Athena, elected one from a tribe by lot, from the Five-hundred-bushel class, according to the law of Solon (which is still in force), and the one on whom the lot falls holds office even though he is quite a poor man. They take over the custody of the statue of Athena and the Victories [10] and the other monuments and the funds in the presence of the Council.

Then there are the ten Vendors, elected by lot one from a tribe. They farm out all public contracts and sell the mines and the taxes, with the cooperation of the Treasurer of Military Funds and those elected to superintend the Spectacle Fund, in the presence of the Council, and ratify the purchase for the person for whom the Council votes, and the mines sold and the workings that have been sold for three years and the concessions sold for . . .[11] years. And the estates of persons banished by the Areopagus and of the others they sell at a meeting of the Council, but the sale is ratified by the Nine Archons. And they draw up and furnish to the Council a list written on whitened tab-

lets [12] of the taxes sold for a year, showing the purchaser and the price that he is paying. And they draw up ten separate lists of those who have to pay in each presidency, and separate lists of those who have to pay three times in the year, making a list for each date of payment, and a separate list of those who have to pay in the ninth presidency. They also draw up a list of the farms and houses written off [13] and sold in the jury-court; for these sales are also conducted by these officials. Payment must be made for purchases of houses within five years, and for farms within ten; and they make these payments in the ninth presidency. Also the King-archon introduces the letting of domains, having made a list of them on whitened tablets. These also are let for ten years, and the rent is paid in the ninth presidency; hence in that presidency a very large revenue comes in. The tablets written up with the list of payments are brought before the Council, but are in the keeping of the official clerk; and whenever a payment of money is made, he takes down from the pillars and hands over to the receivers just these tablets showing the persons whose money is to be paid on that day and wiped off the record, but the other tablets are stored away separately in order that they may not be wiped off before payment is made.

XLVIII. There are ten Receivers elected by lot, one from each tribe; these take over the tablets and wipe off [14] the sums paid in the presence of the Council in the Council-chamber, and give the tablets back again to the official clerk; and anybody that has defaulted in a payment is entered on

---

[10] Golden figures, kept in the Parthenon; probably there had been ten, but eight were melted down for coinage towards the end of the Peloponnesian War.

[11] The number half erased may be 10 or 3.

[12] Wooden boards coated with chalk, on which notices were scratched; they could be easily rubbed off, cf. xlviii.

[13] I.e. registered as confiscated.

[14] See note 12.

them, and has to pay double the amount of his arrears or go to prison; and the legal authority to impose this fine and imprisonment is the Council. On the first day, therefore, they receive the payments and apportion them among the magistrates, and on the second day they introduce the apportionment, written on a wooden tablet, and recount it in the Council-chamber, and bring forward in the Council any case in which somebody knows of anyone, either an official or a private person, having committed a wrong in relation to the apportionment, and put resolutions to the vote in case anyone is found to have committed any wrong.

The Council also elect by lot ten of their own body as Accountants, to keep the accounts of the officials for each presidency. Also they elect by lot Auditors, one for each tribe, and two Assessors for each Auditor, who are required to sit at the tribal meetings according to the hero after whom each tribe is named,[15] and if anyone wishes to prefer a charge, of either a private or a public nature, against any magistrate who has rendered his accounts before the jury-court, within three days from the day on which he rendered his accounts, he writes on a tablet his own name and that of the defendant, and the offence of which he accuses him, adding whatever fine he thinks suitable, and gives it to the Auditor; and the Auditor takes it and reads it, and if he considers the charge proved, he hands it over, if a private case, to those jurymen in the villages who introduced this tribe, and if a public suit, he marks it to the Legislators. And the Legislators, if they receive it, introduce this audit again before the jury-court, and the verdict of the jurymen holds good.

XLIX. The Council also inspects the Knights' chargers, and if anybody having a good horse keeps it in bad condition, it fines him the cost of the feed, and horses that cannot keep up with the squadron or will not stay in line but jib it brands on the jaw with the sign of a wheel, and a horse so treated has failed to pass the inspection. It also inspects the mounted skirmishers, to see which it considers fit for skirmishing duty, and any that it votes to reject are thereby deposed from that rank. It also inspects the foot-soldiers that fight in the ranks of the cavalry, and anyone it votes against is thereby stopped from drawing his pay. The Knights' roll is made by the ten Roll-keepers elected by the People; and they pass on the names of all whom they enroll to the Cavalry Commanders and Tribe Commanders, and these take over the roll and bring it into the Council, and opening the tablet on which the names of the Knights have been inscribed, they delete those among the persons previously entered who claim on oath exemption from cavalry service on the ground of bodily incapacity, and summon those enrolled, and grant discharge to anyone who claims exemption on oath on the ground of bodily incapacity for cavalry service or lack of means, and as to those who do not claim exemption the Councillors decide by vote whether they are fit for cavalry service or not; and if they vote for them as fit they enter them on the tablet, but if not, these also they dismiss.

At one time the Council used also to judge the patterns for the Robe,[16] but now this is done by the jury-court selected by lot, because the Council was thought to show favouritism in its decision. And the Council has joint supervision with the Steward of the

Army Funds over the construction of the Victories and over the prizes for the Panathenaic Games.

The Council also inspects the Incapables; for there is a law enacting that persons possessing less than 3 minae [17] and incapacitated by bodily infirmity from doing any work are to be inspected by the Council, which is to give them a grant for food at the public expense at the rate of 2 obols [18] a day each. And there is a Treasurer for these persons, elected by lot.

The Council also shares in the administration of virtually the greatest number of the duties of the other offices.

L. These then are the matters administered by the Council. Also ten men are elected by lot as Restorers of Temples, who draw 30 minae from the Receivers and repair the temples that most require it; and ten City Controllers, five of whom hold office in Peiraeus and five in the city; it is they who supervise the flute-girls and harp-girls and lyre-girls to prevent their receiving fees of more than two drachmas, and if several persons want to take the same girl these officials cast lots between them and hire her out to the winner. And they keep watch to prevent any scavenger from depositing ordure within a mile and a quarter of the wall; and they prevent the construction of buildings encroaching on and balconies overhanging the roads, of overhead conduits with an overflow into the road, and of windows opening outward on to the road; and they remove for burial the bodies of persons who die on the roads, having public slaves for this service.

LI. Also Market-controllers are elected by lot, five for Peiraeus and five for the city. To these the laws assign

the superintendence of all merchandise, to prevent the sale of adulterated and spurious articles.

Also ten Controllers of Measures are appointed by lot, five for the city and five for Peiraeus, who superintend all measures and weights, in order that sellers may use just ones.

Also there used to be ten Corn-wardens elected by lot, five for Peiraeus and five for the city, but now there are twenty for the city and fifteen for Peiraeus. Their duties are first to see that unground corn in the market is on sale at a fair price, and next that millers sell barley-meal at a price corresponding with that of barley, and baker-women loaves at a price corresponding with that of wheat, and weighing the amount fixed by the officials—for the law orders that these shall fix the weights.

They elect by lot ten Port-superintendents, whose duty is to superintend the harbour-markets and to compel the traders to bring to the city two-thirds of the sea-borne corn that reaches the corn-market.

LII. They also appoint the Eleven, officers chosen by lot to superintend the persons in the prison, and to punish with death people arrested as thieves and kidnappers and footpads that confess their guilt, but if they deny the charge to bring them before the Jury-court, and if they are acquitted discharge them, but if not then to execute them; and to bring before the Jury-court lists of farms and houses declared to be public property and to hand over to the Vendors those that it is decided to confiscate; and to bring in informations—for these too are brought in by the Eleven, though the Legislators also bring in some informations.

They also elect by lot five men as Introducers, who introduce the cases to be tried within a month, each official those of two tribes. These cases in-

[17] 1 mina = £4, 100 drachmae = 1 mina, 6 obols = 1 drachma.

[18] Say threepence.

clude prosecutions for non-payment of dowry due, actions for the recovery of loans borrowed at a drachma interest,[19] and of capital borrowed from one party by another wishing to do business in the market; and also actions about outrage, friendly-society business, partnerships, slaves, draft animals, naval command,[20] and bank cases. These officials, therefore, bring into court and decide these suits within a month; but the Receivers[21] decide suits brought by tax-farmers or against them, having power to deal summarily with suits up to ten francs but bringing the others into the Jury-court within a month.

LIII. They also elect by lot forty persons,[22] four from each tribe, who are the court before which the other suits are brought; formerly they were thirty and went on circuit trying cases in each parish, but since the oligarchy of the Thirty their number has been raised to forty. They have summary jurisdiction in claims not exceeding ten drachmas, but suits above that value they pass on to the Arbitrators. These take over the cases, and if they are unable to effect a compromise, they give judgement, and if both parties are satisfied with their judgement and abide by it, that ends the suit. But if one of the two parties appeals to the Jury-court, they put the witnesses' evidence and the challenges and the laws concerned into deed-boxes, those of the prosecutor and those of the defendant separately, and seal them up, and attach to them a copy of the Arbitrator's verdict written on a tablet, and hand them over to the four judges taking the cases of the defendant's tribe. When these have received them they bring them before the Jury-court, claims within 1000 drachmas before a court of two hundred and one jurymen, and claims above that before one of four hundred and one. The litigants are not permitted to put in laws or challenges or evidence other than those passed on by the Arbitrator, that have been put into the deed-boxes. Persons fifty-nine years of age may serve as Arbitrators, as appears from the regulations for the Archons and Name-heroes; for the Heroes giving their names to the Tribes are ten in number and those of the years of military age forty-two,[23] and the cadets used formerly when being enrolled to be inscribed on whitened tablets, and above them the Archon[24] in whose term of office they were enrolled and the Name-hero of those that had been Arbitrators the year before, but now they are inscribed on a copper pillar and this is set up in front of the Council-chamber at the side of the list of Name-heroes. The Forty take the last one of the Name-heroes and distribute the arbitration-cases among those of his year and assign by lot the cases that each is to arbitrate upon; and it is compulsory for each of them to complete the arbitration of the cases allotted to him, for the law enacts the disfranchisement of anybody who does not become Arbitrator when of the proper age, unless he happens to hold some office in that year or to be abroad, these being the

[19] A drachma a mina a month = 12 per cent per annum.

[20] I.e. particularly an action to recover expenses, brought by the captain of a trireme against his successor who had failed to relieve him when his year of office was over.

[21] See xlviii.

[22] Perhaps the Greek should be altered to give "the Forty."

[23] Of the 100 Attic heroes, 10 gave their names to the Tribes, and of the remaining 90, 42 names were affixed to the successive years of active citizenship, military service being from the age of 18 to 59, and those in their sixtieth year serving as *diaetetae*. As each year expired, the Name-hero of the men now passing the age of 60 was transferred to those now just 18.

[24] I.e. the senior of the Nine Archons, called Ἐπώνυμος because his name dated the year.

only grounds of exemption. Anybody unjustly dealt with by the Arbitrator may indict him before the Arbitrators, and the laws prescribe the penalty of disfranchisement for an Arbitrator found guilty; but the Arbitrators also have an appeal. The Name-heroes also are employed to regulate military service; when soldiers of a certain age are being sent on an expedition, a notice is posted stating the years that they are to serve, indicated by the Archon and Name-hero of the earliest and latest.

LIV. They also elect by lot the following officials: five Highway-constructors, whose duty is to repair the roads, with workmen who are public slaves; and ten Auditors and ten Assessors with them, to whom all retiring officials have to render account. For these are the only magistrates who audit the returns of officials liable to account and bring the audits before the Jury-court. And if an official is proved by them to have committed peculation, the Jury convict him of peculation, and the fine is ten times the amount of which he is found guilty; and if they show that a man has taken bribes and the Jury convict, they assess the value of the bribes and in this case also the fine is ten times the amount; but if they find him guilty of maladministration, they assess the damage, and the fine paid is that amount only, provided that it is paid before the ninth presidency; otherwise it is doubled. But a fine of ten times the amount is not doubled.

They also appoint by lot the officer called Clerk for the Presidency, who is responsible for documents, is keeper of the decrees that are passed and supervises the transcription of all other documents, and who attends the sittings of the Council. Formerly this officer was elected by show of hands, and the most distinguished and trustworthy men used to be elected, for this officer's name is inscribed on the monumental slabs above records of alliances and appointments to consulships [25] and grants of citizenship; but now it has been made an office elected by lot. They also elect by lot another officer to superintend the laws, who attends the sittings of the Council, and he also has copies made of all the laws. The People also elect by show of hands a clerk to read documents to the Assembly and to the Council; he has no duties except as reader.

The People also elects by lot the ten sacrificial officers entitled Superintendents of Expiations, who offer the sacrifices prescribed by oracle, and for business requiring omens to be taken watch for good omens in co-operation with the soothsayers. It also elects by lot ten others called the Yearly Sacrificial Officers, who perform certain sacrifices and administer all the four-yearly [26] festivals except the Panathenaic Festival. One of the four-yearly festivals is the Mission to Delos (and there is also a six-yearly [27] festival there), a second is the Brauronia, a third the Heraclea, and a fourth the Eleusinia; a fifth is the Panathenaic, which is not held in the same year as any of the others mentioned. There has now been added the Festival of Hephaestus, instituted in the archonship of Cephisophon.

They also elect by lot an archon for Salamis and a demarch for Peiraeus, who hold the Festivals of Dionysus [28] in each of those places and appoint Choir-leaders; at Salamis the name of the archon is recorded in an inscription.

[25] An honourable office assigned to a citizen of another state who represented Athenian interests there.

[26] I.e. taking place once in every four or six years: in Greek this is called "five-yearly," "seven-yearly."

[27] Both the text and the facts are most uncertain.

[28] τὰ Διονύσια τὰ κατ' ἀγρούς.

LV. These offices, then, are elected by lot and have authority over all the matters stated. As to the officials designated the Nine Archons, the mode of their appointment that was originally in force has been stated before; [29] but now the six Lawgivers and their clerk are elected by lot, and also the Archon, [30] King and War-lord, from each tribe in turn. The qualifications of these are first checked in the Council of Five Hundred, except the Clerk, but he is checked only in a Jury-court, as are the other officials (for all of them, both those elected by lot and those elected by show of hands, have their qualifications checked before they hold office), while the Nine Archons are checked in the Council and also again in a Jury-court. Formerly any official not passed by the Council did not hold office, but now there is an appeal to the Jury-court, and with this rests the final decision as to qualification. The questions put in examining qualifications are, first, "Who is your father and to what deme does he belong, and who is your father's father, and who your mother, and who her father and what his deme?" then whether he has a Family Apollo and Homestead Zeus, [31] and where these shrines are; then whether he has family tombs and where they are; then whether he treats his parents well, and whether he pays his taxes, and whether he has done his military service. And after putting these questions the officer says, "Call your witnesses to these statements." And when he has produced his witnesses, the officer further asks, "Does anybody wish to bring a charge against this man?" And if any accuser is forthcoming, he is given a hearing and the man on trial an opportunity of defence, and then the official puts the question to a show of hands in the Council or to a vote by ballot in the Jury-court; but if nobody wishes to bring a charge against him, he puts the vote at once; formerly one person used to throw in his ballot-pebble, but now all are compelled to vote one way or the other about them, in order that if anyone being a rascal has got rid of his accusers, [32] it may rest with the jurymen to disqualify him. And when the matter has been checked in this way, they go to the stone on which are the victims cut up for sacrifice (the one on which Arbitrators also take oath before they issue their decisions, and persons summoned as witnesses swear that they have no evidence to give), and mounting on this stone they swear that they will govern justly and according to the laws, and will not take presents on account of their office, and that if they should take anything they will set up a golden statue. After taking oath they go from the stone to the Acropolis and take the same oath again there, and after that they enter on their office.

LVI. The Archon, the King and the War-lord also take two assessors each, chosen by themselves, and the qualifications of these are checked in the Jury-court before they hold office, and they are called to account when they retire from office.

Immediately on coming into office the Archon first makes proclamation that all men shall hold until the end of his office those possessions and powers that they held before his entry into office. Then he appoints three Chorus-leaders for the tragedies, the wealthiest men among all the Athenians; and formerly he used also to appoint five for the comedies, but these are now returned by the Tribes. Afterwards he receives the Chorus-leaders nominated by the Tribes for the men's and boys' competitions and the comedies at the Dionysia and for men and boys at the

[29] Chaps. iii, viii, xxii, xxvi.
[30] I.e. the Archon Eponymus, see note 25.
[31] The gods of the Athenian's home.
[32] I.e. has bribed them to let him off.

Thargelia [33] (for the Dionysia one for each tribe, for the Thargelia one for two tribes, which take turns to supply them), and deals with their claims for substitution by exchange of property,[34] and brings forward their claims to exemption on the ground of having performed that public service before, or of being exempt because of having performed another service and the period of exemption not having expired, or of not being of the right age (for a man serving as Chorus-leader for the boys must be over forty). He also appoints Chorus-leaders for Delos and a Procession-leader for the thirty-oared vessel that carries the youths.[35] He supervises processions, the one celebrated in honour of Asclepius when initiates keep a watch-night, and the one at the Great Dionysia, in which he acts jointly with the Supervisors; these were formerly ten men elected by show of hands by the People, and they found the expenses of the procession out of their own pockets, but now they are elected by lot, one from each tribe, and given 100 minae for equipment; and he also supervises the procession of Thargelia, and the one in honour of Zeus the Saviour. This official also administers the competition of the Dionysia and of the Thargelia. These, then, are the festivals that he supervises. Criminal and civil law-suits are instituted before him, and after a preliminary trial he brings them in before the Jury-court: actions for ill-usage of parents (in which anybody who wishes may act as prosecutor without liability to penalty); for ill-usage of orphans (which lie against their guardians); for ill-usage of an heiress (which lie against the guardians or the relations that they live with); for injury to an orphan's estate (these also lie against the guardians); prosecutions for insanity, when one man accuses another of wasting his property when insane; actions for the appointment of liquidators, when a man is unwilling for property to be administered in partnership; actions for the institution of guardianship; actions for deciding rival claims to guardianship; actions for the production of goods or documents; actions for enrolment as trustee; claims to estates and to heiresses. He also supervises orphans and heiresses and women professing to be with child after the husband's death, and he has absolute power to fine offenders against them or to bring them before the Jury-court. He grants leases of houses belonging to orphans and heiresses until they are fourteen years of age, and receives the rents, and he exacts maintenance for children from guardians who fail to supply it.

LVII. These are the matters superintended by the Archon. But the King superintends, first, the mysteries, in co-operation with Superintendents elected by show of hands by the People, two from the whole body of the citizens, one from the Eumolpidae and one from the Heralds.[36] Next the Dionysia in Lenaeon;[37] this festival consists of a procession and a competition, the former conducted by the King and the Superintendents jointly, the latter organized by the King. He also holds all the Torch-race Competitions;

[33] A festival in May, at which there were competitions of cyclic choruses and a procession.

[34] A citizen appointed to one of these expensive public offices could challenge another as better able to afford it, and the man challenged could only escape undertaking the office by exchanging estates with the challenger.

[35] For the festival at Delos see liv. 7; boys' choruses went from Athens.

[36] The Eumolpidae and Kerykes were two ancient priestly families at Athens.

[37] Held at the Limnae, S.E. of the Acropolis, at the end of January. The seventh Attic month, Gamelion (January–February) was in old Ionic called Lenaeon.

also he is the director of practically all the ancestral sacrifices. He holds the court that tries charges of impiety and disputed claims to hereditary priest-hoods. He adjudicates between clans and between priests in all disputed claims to privileges. Before him are also brought all murder cases, and proclamations of exclusion from customary rites are made by him. Trials for deliberate murder and wounding are held in the Areopagus, and for causing death by poison, and for arson; for these only are tried by the Council, whereas involuntary homicide and plotting to murder, and murder of a slave or resident alien or foreigner, come before the court at the Palladium;[38] and one who admits homicide but declares it to have been legal (for instance when he has killed a man taken in adultery), or who in war has killed a fellow-citizen in ignorance, or in an athletic contest, is tried at the Delphinium; but if, when a man has taken refuge in exile after an offence that admits of satisfaction, he is charged with homicide or wounding, he is tried at the Precinct of Phreatus,[39] and delivers his defence from a ship anchored near the shore. Commissioners appointed by lot try these cases, except those that are held on the Areopagus; the cases are introduced by the King, and the court sits within the sacred precinct in the open air, and when the King is acting in a case he takes off his crown. The accused man all the rest of the time is debarred from sacred places and is even forbidden by law from setting foot in the market-place, but at the trial he enters the precinct and makes his defence. When the King does not know

who committed the act, he institutes proceedings against "the guilty man," and the King and Tribal Kings try the case, as also prosecutions of inanimate objects and animals for homicide.

LVIII. The War-lord offers sacrifices to Artemis the Huntress and to Enyalius,[40] and arranges the funeral games in honour of those who have fallen in war, and makes memorial offerings to Harmodius and Aristogeiton. Only private law-suits are brought before him in which resident aliens, ordinary and privileged, and foreign consuls are concerned; he has to take the list of cases and divide it into ten portions and assign one portion by lot to each tribe, and to assign the jurymen for each tribe to the Arbitrators. He himself brings forward cases in which resident aliens are concerned, on charges of acting without their protectors[41] or of lacking a protector, and as to estates and heiresses; and all other actions that in the case of citizens are brought in by the Archon, in the case of resident aliens are introduced by the War-lord.

LIX. The Lawgivers are responsible, first, for preparing lists of the days on which the jury-courts are to sit, and then for giving them to the officers, for these follow the arrangements that the Lawgivers assign. Moreover it is they who bring before the People indictments, and bring in all votes of removal from office, preliminary informations sent on by the Assembly, impeachments for illegal procedure, proceedings against inexpedient legislation, a suit against a President or a Superintendent, and audits imposed on Generals. Also they hear indictments for which a

---

[38] This shrine and the Delphinium were probably S.E. of the Acropolis.

[39] Near the harbour of Zea; doubtless the eponymous hero was fictitious, the place being really named from a well, φρέαρ. If the defendant had landed he would have been arrested for his former offence.

[40] A form of Ares.

[41] A *metoikos* (other than the *isoteleis,* who for taxation and military service ranked with citizens) had to be enrolled under a citizen, whose sanction was necessary for his actions if important.

fee is paid, on charges of alien birth, alien corruption (that is, if a person charged with alien birth secures his acquittal by bribery), malicious information, bribery, false entry of public debts, personation of a witness, conspiracy, non-registration, adultery. They also introduce [42] the tests of qualification for all offices, and claims to citizenship rejected by vote of the deme, and verdicts of guilty passed on from the Council.[43] They also introduce private actions in commercial and mining cases, and actions against slaves for slandering a freeman. And they assign the public and the private jury-courts by lot among the magistrates. They ratify contracts with other states, and bring into court suits arising under those contracts, and prosecutions for false witness instituted by the Areopagus.

All the Nine Archons with the Law-givers' Clerk, making ten, elect by lot the jurymen, each electing those of his own tribe.

LX. These are the functions of the Nine Archons. They also elect by lot ten men as Stewards of the Games, one from each tribe, who when passed as qualified hold office for four years, and administer the procession of the Panathenaic Festival, and the contest in music, the gymnastic contest and the horse-race, and have the Robe [44] made, and in conjunction with the Council have the vases [45] made, and assign the olive-oil to the competitors. The oil is procured from the sacred trees; and the Archon levies it from the owners of the farms in which the trees are, three quarters of a pint from each trunk. Formerly the state used to sell the fruit, and anybody who dug up or cut down a sacred olive-tree was tried by the Council of Areopagus, and if found guilty punished with death; but ever since the olive-oil has been provided as rent by the owner of the farm, though the law still stands, the trial has gone out; and the state's claim to the oil is calculated on the estate and not on the number of trees.[46] So the Archon collects the tribute of oil accruing in his year, and passes it on to the Treasurers at the Acropolis, and he is not allowed to go up to the Areopagus before he has handed the full quantity over to the Treasurers. These have it in their keeping in the Acropolis always, except that at the Panathenaic Festival they dole it out to the Directors of the Games and these to the victorious competitors. For the prizes are for the victors in music silver money and gold vessels, for those in manly beauty shields, and for those in the gymnastic contest and the horse-race olive-oil.

LXI. They also elect by show of hands all the military officers—ten Generals, formerly one from each tribe, but now from all the citizens together, and the vote decides the assignment of duties to these—one being appointed to the heavy infantry, who commands them on foreign expeditions; one to the country, who guards it and commands in any war that takes place in it; two to Peiraeus, one of them to Munychia and the other to the Point, who superintend the protection of the population of Peiraeus; one to the Symmories,[47] who enrols the Captains of triremes and carries out their exchanges and introduces their claims for exemption; and the others they dis-

[42] I.e. before the bodies that checked these qualifications, see lv.

[43] See xliv.

[44] See xlix.

[45] In athletic contests the prize was a vase of oil and a garland of foliage from the sacred olive-trees.

[46] I.e. the amount per tree stated above is only approximately calculated.

[47] The 20 companies in which the 1200 richest citizens were enrolled for payment of the εἰσφορά or property-tax levied to meet emergency expenses of war.

patch on expeditions as occasion arises. A confirmatory vote is taken in each presidency upon the satisfactoriness of their administration; and if this vote goes against any officer he is tried in the jury-court, and if convicted, the penalty or fine to be imposed on him is assessed, but if he is acquitted he resumes office. When in command of a force they have power to punish breach of discipline with imprisonment, exile, or the infliction of a fine; but a fine is not usual.

They also elect by show of hands ten Regimental Commanders, one of each tribe; these lead their fellow-tribesmen and appoint company-commanders.

They also elect by show of hands two Cavalry Commanders from the whole body of citizens; these lead the Knights, each commanding a division consisting of five tribes, and their powers are the same as those of the Generals over the heavy infantry. The Cavalry Commanders' election also is submitted to a confirmatory vote.

They also elect by show of hands ten Tribal Commanders, one for each tribe, to lead the cavalry as the Regimental Commanders lead the heavy infantry.

They also elect by show of hands a Cavalry Commander for Lemnos, to take control of the cavalry in that island.

They also elect by show of hands a Treasurer of the Paralus,[48] and at the present day a Treasurer of the ship of Ammon.

LXII. The officials elected by lot were formerly those elected from the whole tribe together with the Nine Archons and those now elected in the temple of Theseus who used to be divided among the demes; but since the demes began to sell their offices, the latter also are elected by lot from the whole tribe, excepting members of the Council and Guards;[49] these they entrust to the demes.

Payment for public duties is as follows: first, the People draw a drachma for ordinary meetings of the Assembly, and a drachma and a half for a sovereign meeting;[50] second, the Jury-courts half a drachma; third, the Council five obols; and those acting as president have an additional obol for food. Also the Nine Archons get four obols each for food, and have to keep a herald and a flute-player as well; and the archon for Salamis gets a drachma a day. Games-directors dine in the Prytaneum in the month of Hecatombaeon, during the Panathenaic Festival, from the fourth of the month onward. Amphictyons for Delos get a drachma a day from Delos. All the officials sent to Samos, Scyros, Lemnos or Imbros also get money for food.

The military offices may be held repeatedly, but none of the others, except that a man may become a member of the Council twice.

LXIII. The Jury-courts are elected by lot by the Nine Archons by tribes, and the Clerk of the Lawgivers from the tenth tribe. The courts have ten entrances, one for each tribe, twenty rooms, two for each tribe, in which courts are allotted to jurors, a hundred small boxes, ten for each tribe,[51] and

---

[48] One of the state triremes used for embassies, etc. The other, the Salaminia, was superseded by the one named after Zeus Ammon, specially used to convey missions to Cyrene on the way to the shrine of Zeus Ammon.

[49] Possibly the guards of the docks, mentioned at xxiv.

[50] See xliii.

[51] The dicasts in each tribe are distributed over all the 10 divisions into which all the dicasts are divided. In each tribe all the tickets (πινάκια) bearing the names of the dicasts in the division A are placed in the first κιβώτιον; those of division B in the second, and so on for all the 10 divisions. According to the number of dicasts required, an equal number of tickets is drawn by lot from each of the 100 κιβώτια. Each ticket

other boxes into which the tickets of the jurymen drawn by lot are thrown, and two urns. Staves are placed at each entrance, as many as there are jurymen, and acorns to the same number as the staves are thrown into the urn, and on the acorns are written the letters of the alphabet, starting with the eleventh, *lambda,* as many as the courts that are going to be filled. Right to sit on juries belongs to all those over thirty years old who are not in debt to the Treasury or disfranchised. If any unqualified person sits on a jury, information is laid against him and he is brought before the jury-court, and if convicted the jurymen assess against him whatever punishment or fine he is thought to deserve; and if given a money fine, he has to go to prison until he has paid both the former debt, for which the information was laid, and whatever additional sum has been imposed on him as a fine by the court. Each juryman has one box-wood ticket, with his own name and that of his father and deme written on it, and one letter of the alphabet as far as *kappa;* for the jurymen of each tribe are divided into ten sections, approximately an equal number under each letter.

As soon as the Lawgiver has drawn by lot the letters to be assigned to the courts, the attendant immediately takes them and affixes to each court its allotted letter.

. . . .

LXIV. The ten boxes lie in front of the entrance for each tribe. They have inscribed on them the letters as far as *kappa.* When the jurymen have thrown their tickets into the box on which is inscribed the same letter of the alphabet as is on the ticket itself, the attendant shakes them thoroughly and the Lawgiver draws one ticket from each box. This attendant is called the Affixer, and he affixes the tickets taken from the box to the ledged frame on which is the same letter that is on the box. This attendant is chosen by lot, in order that the same person may not always affix the tickets and cheat. There are five ledged frames in each of the balloting-rooms. When he has thrown in the dice, the Archon casts lots for the tribe for each balloting-room; they are dice of copper, black and white. As many white ones are thrown in as jurymen are required to be selected, one white die for each five tickets, and the black dice correspondingly. As he draws out the dice the herald calls those on whom the lot has fallen. Also the Affixer is there corresponding to the number. The man called obeys and draws an acorn from the urn and, holding it out with the inscription upward, shows it first to the superintending Archon; when the Archon has seen it, he throws the man's ticket into the box that has the same letter written on it as the one on the acorn, in order that he may go into whatever court he is allotted to and not into whatever court he chooses and in order that it may not be possible to collect into a court whatever jurymen a person wishes. The Archon has by him as many boxes as courts are going to be filled, each lettered with whichever is the letter assigned by lot to each court.

LXV. And the man himself having again shown it to the attendant then goes inside the barrier, and the attendant gives him a staff of the same colour as the court bearing the same letter as the one on the acorn, in order that it

---

so drawn has a court assigned to it by lot; and the tickets are now all placed in the second set of 10 κιβώτια, all tickets assigned to dicasts of any special court being placed in the κιβώτιον which bears the letter corresponding to that court. The names of all the dicasts selected to serve are thus distributed over the several courts that are to sit on the day in question (Sandys). See further ch. lxiv.

may be necessary for him to go into the court to which he has been assigned by lot; for if he goes into another, he is detected by the colour of his staff, for each of the courts has a colour painted on the lintel of its entrance. He takes the staff and goes to the court of the same colour as his staff and having the same letter as is on the acorn. And when he has come into it he receives a token publicly from the person appointed by lot to this office. Then with the acorn and the staff they take their seats in the court, when they have thus entered. And to those to whom the lot does not fall the Affixers give back their tickets. And the public attendants from each tribe hand over the boxes, one to each court, in which are those names of the tribe that are in each of the courts. And they hand them over to the persons appointed by lot to restore the tickets to the jurymen in each court by number, in order that according to these when they examine them they may assign the pay.

LXVI. When all the courts are full, two ballot-boxes are placed in the first of the courts, and copper dice with the colours of the courts painted on them, and other dice with the names of the offices written on them. And two of the Lawgivers are chosen by lot, and throw the two sets of dice in separately, one throwing in the coloured dice into one ballot-box and the other the names of the offices into the other. And to whichever of the offices the lot falls first, it is proclaimed by the herald that this will use the first court allotted. . . .

(*Of chapters lxvi. 2-lxviii. 2 (MS. pp. 33, 34) only fragments remain, variously put together and supplemented by editors.*)

LXVIII. . . . [a copper token marked with a] 3 (for on giving this up he gets three obols), so that they all may vote; for nobody can get a token if he does not vote. And there are two jars placed in the court, one of copper and one of wood, separate so that a man may not secretly throw in pebbles undetected, into which the jurymen put their votes, the copper jar to count and the wooden jar for pebbles not used, the copper jar having a lid with a hole in it only large enough to take just the pebble alone, so that the same man may not throw in two. And when the jury are about to give their verdict, the herald first asks whether the litigants wish to challenge the evidence of the witnesses; for they are not allowed to challenge it after the voting has begun. Then he proclaims again, "The pebble with the hole through it is a vote for the first speaker, and the whole pebble one for the second speaker." And the juryman when taking the pebbles out of the lamp-stand presses the pebble against the lamp-stand and does not let the parties to the action see either the perforated pebble or the whole one, and throws the one that he wishes to count into the copper vessel and the one that he discards into the wooden one.

LXIX. And when all have voted, the attendants take the vessel that is to count and empty it out on to a reckoning-board with as many holes in it as there are pebbles, in order that they may be set out visibly and be easy to count, and that the perforated and the whole ones may be clearly seen by the litigants. And those assigned by lot to count the voting-pebbles count them out on to the reckoning-board, in two sets, one the whole ones and the other those perforated. And the herald proclaims the number of votes, the perforated pebbles being for the prosecutor, and the whole ones for the defendant; and whichever gets the larger number wins the suit, but if the votes are equal, the defendant wins. Then again they assess the damages, if this has to be done, voting in the same way, giving up their ticket and receiving back a staff; as to assessment of damages each party is allowed to speak during three pints of water. And when they have completed their legal duties as jurymen, they take their pay in the division to which each was assigned by lot. . . .

Aristotle's treatise falls into three main divisions: (1) Citizenship and military training, Chapter 42; (2) How officials are chosen, Chapters 43–55; (3) The duties of the officials, Chapters 56–69.

In Chapter 42 it is made clear that citizenship was a privilege which could be obtained by birth alone. There were no naturalization laws, as in our country. The three years of military service between the ages of 18 and 21 may be compared to the puberty schools of more simply organized peoples whom we have already studied. Isolation, instruction as members of a class, and a certain amount of danger and privation would do much to prepare the young men for the responsibilities of government shortly to be assumed. Like the Aztecs, the Athenians provided arms and uniforms, while pay and rations came from the tribes, the Greek counterparts of the *calpullec*.

In Chapters 42 through 55 certain themes stand out. One is the equality of the citizens in their responsibility and capacity for all but the more critical details of government. Signs were posted. This means that all could read. Many of the officers were chosen by lot. This was calculated to give everyone a chance and to eliminate prejudice and ambition. To us, a choice by lot means that we leave a selection to chance alone. To the ancient peoples, lots were the expression of divine will. That is why lots were carried in the Ark of the Covenant, in the Old Testament. To what extent the Athenians considered the lots divine, and how much they knew about probability, I do not know. In our own society we use lots only in selecting jurors and men for the draft. In offices where men of specific ability and training were needed, they could not trust to chance, but voted for nominees by a show of hands.

There were many officials, and they held office for four years only. Thus through rotation many citizens were in positions of authority during their lifetimes. The three head officials were the Archon, King, and War Lord. Each had charge of some of the numerous public ceremonies that marked the changes in the seasons and activities. The Archon was responsible for civil justice, the King for criminal cases, and the War Lord for foreign affairs. The Archon was trustee for the estates of women and children, the King had charge of the priests and their offices, while the War Lord cared for the resident aliens. Thus each of the three had ritual, legal, and executive duties.

A close watch was kept over the regulation of standards of weight and measurement, over markets, over the coinage, over public works and particularly highways and streets; much care was taken to control prices and prevent inflation through competitive bidding. Rich men were given positions that required a large outlay of money. Accountants, auditors, and assessors saw to it that the books were in order. The army, the merchant marine, the priesthood, all departments of public life were the concern of everyone.

The people ruled. All of this machinery of government was carried on without benefit of printing presses, typewriters, telephones, or automobiles, and even without an adequate notation system for mathematics. There seem to have been no hereditary occupations, other than the priesthood; no castes and virtually no classes within the citizen body. The average wealth must have been considerable, and many men could spend their time in education and in letters. The state consisted of one large political institution within which was a maze of interlocking familial, economic, religious, and other smaller institutions, all well integrated through the high level of general education and the excellent means of communication in a geographically small area, in a population small enough so that everyone could know everyone else who was of any importance. The Athenian state was in this sense a miniature of an ideal modern one.

From our twentieth-century point of view there was, however, one serious flaw—the presence of a slave population which was not allowed to enjoy the privileges of self-expression or the responsibilities of participation in the government. Slaves are people too, and they cannot be kept at the bottom of the hierarchy indefinitely. The Athenian state was really one half of a symbiotic organization of which the slaves and the foreigners formed the other.

19

The Technical Skills of the Romans

THE student must not form the impression that Athenian civilization was unique, or that it grew in a vacuum. All of the peoples of the Mediterranean practiced the same kind of agriculture, pastured the same species of domestic animals, cooked their food in more or less the same way, and wore similar clothing. Many of them sailed ships. Cultural diffusion had played a vital part in the formation of the power of Athens, for many of the slaves were skilled craftsmen from across the Aegean and from the coasts of Palestine and Syria. Later on, when the Romans extended their political domain to form the Empire, the knowledge and skills and manpower of the whole Mediterranean region were pooled. The following selections from Neuberger's careful and detailed study of *The Technical Arts and Sciences of the Ancients* * are offered to you here to lay a foundation for the study of the human relations of that much discussed period.

. . . The technical science of antiquity differs from that of the present chiefly in having, by methods much simpler than those which would now be available, achieved results which are in some ways so remarkable that they have not since been surpassed. In making full use of steam and electricity and of the other sources of power which have become known to us in the course of time our technical science has developed more broadly, whereas on the other hand that of the ancients certainly penetrated more deeply. The much more limited knowledge of that time was exploited to the utmost. Simple means were used for hundreds or even thousands of years without in many cases being essentially improved, but so ingeniously and efficiently as often to astonish us.

. . . What has been accomplished technically by the ancients is in many instances so surprising and extraordinary that one often hears the opinion that the ancients must have possessed knowledge that has since become lost to us; they must have been familiar with properties, particularly of a physical nature, of which we have not the faintest idea. In some cases this opinion is not to be entirely ignored, but no cogent proof of its correctness has ever been adduced. . . . The astronomical, mathematical, and physical knowledge then available was exploited to the fullest extent. It was applied practically in every way possible at that time. It may be that the knowledge of some particular substance or plant which the ancients used for a special technical purpose, such as for painting or em-

* From Albert Neuberger, *The Technical Arts and Sciences of the Ancients,* Translated by Henry L. Brose. By permission of The Macmillan Company, publishers, 1930.

balming, has not been handed down to posterity; nevertheless we are fairly well informed generally about the extent and details of their knowledge. It is not then this knowledge itself that excites our admiration so much as the systematic and deliberate manner in which they applied it; with a comparatively meagre equipment they often accomplished as much as—indeed, sometimes even more than—we who have at our disposal such wide knowledge in the most diverse fields. Among the factors utilized to the utmost was human labour and the time element, to which little value was attached at that period. . . .

If the technical scientist nowadays occupies the position to which his general education, knowledge, and achievements entitle him, we must not forget that it has been won only after a hard and prolonged struggle, and that even now there are representatives of other branches of knowledge who deny him full standing. In antiquity, however, the technical expert was a much sought after person who enjoyed the greatest respect. It may even be conjectured that among some races there were certain relationships between such experts and the priests, who held supreme rank. The form of some ancient constructions still bears witness to the high honour in which the technical worker was held in antiquity. In the ancient Roman Empire, indeed, there was hardly a bridge that was not crowned by a sort of triumphal arch in honour of the builder. The mightiest rulers of the world drew the technical scientist into their service and in some cases gave him a particularly high position. Very often, too, provision was made for the special training of expert workers. Technical officers were appointed for the State as well as for the towns, and some armies had even a special corps for engineers. . . .

[MINING]

. . . almost all ancient people sank and worked their mines according to the same principles . . . in consequence of the growth of trade and commerce technical science was communicated from people to people. We thus find in the Indian and Chinese mines very much the same conditions as later in the Phoenician and Egyptian mines, and still later in those of the Greeks, Romans, Celts, Gauls, Britons and others. The treasures that were being sought and the ores that were being separated out differ more or less in the various countries, but the manner of their extraction was much the same in all.

The miner of ancient times was nearly always either a slave or a criminal. This explains why the means used remained almost unchanged for thousands of years. The purpose of machines is to economize labour or time. It was not considered necessary to make the work easier for the slave, whose hard lot inspired no sympathy, although it kept him to the end of his days buried in the gloomy depths of the earth, suffering all sorts of torments and privations. There was mostly a superabundance of slaves. After campaigns there were usually so many that great numbers of them were massacred. So there was no dearth of labour. Time was as yet but little valued. And so it happened that in almost all the mines of the ancients only the simplest means were adopted. In the copper mines of Rio Tinto and Tharsis in the Spanish province of Huelva, which were worked by the Romans and the Carthaginians, the method of working was so simple that the slaves in the mines had to scratch off with their fingers the clay which covered the ore. The clay which is found nowadays in ancient mines still bears the impress of thousands of fingers; if we examine them we make a curious observation, viz., that on account of the nature of the work the thumb is very highly developed, as in the case of certain artisans even at the present time. Usually, however, the ancients used hammers and wedges, and probably also bones and horns.

. . . the . . . work . . . was done sometimes in a standing, sometimes in a sitting, sometimes in a lying posture . . . the mines were illuminated by amphorae suspended from the roof, although the more usual method of lighting was by lamps placed in small stone cavities. Further, boys collected the mineral in baskets provided with a handle, which were then tied up and passed up to other boys, who likewise passed them up or else carried them away . . . in order to descend into the mines either steps were hewn out of the stone (perhaps ladders were used) or wooden blocks were let into the stone.

The tunnels constructed in the rock by these simple means are often of astonishing length. It has been computed and confirmed by observing the marks of wedges that in even relatively soft stone the progress made amounted to about half an inch in twenty-four hours: in hard stone it was not more than 25 or 30 feet per year. This low efficiency was compensated to some extent by making the tunnels very low, by working only along the seams of the ore and by avoiding as far as possible the removal of unnecessary stone. Consequently, the galleries and tunnels were so narrow that a slave could squeeze himself through only with great difficulty. In many mines, in particular those of the Egyptians, Greeks and Romans, children were employed, so that as little stone as possible would have to be removed. Although the slaves must have become weakened by their sojourn in the mines and by the unhealthy posture during work, as well as through sickness—in lead mines particularly through lead-poisoning—they must often have used very heavy tools. Hammers have been found which weighed between 20 and 26 pounds.

At the same time there were no precautions against accidents. The galleries were not propped up and therefore often collapsed, burying workmen beneath them. In ancient mines many skeletons have been found of slaves who had lost their lives in this way while at work. Nor were attempts made to replenish the supply of air or to take other steps for preserving health. When the air in the mines became so hot and foul that breathing was rendered impossible the place was abandoned and an attack was made at some other point. These conditions must have become still more trying wherever, in addition to the mallet and chisel, the only other means of detaching the stone was applied, namely fire. The mineral-bearing stone was heated and water was then poured over it. There was no outlet for the resulting smoke and vapors. This method of constructing tunnels and galleries is described by Pliny somewhat as follows: "Tunnels are bored in the mountains and are carefully explored. These tunnels are called 'arrugiae,' little ways or little streets. They often collapse and bury many workers. When hard minerals occur one seeks to blast them with fire and vinegar. As the resulting steam and smoke often fill the tunnels, the workmen prefer to split the rock into pieces of 150 pounds or more, and for this purpose they use iron wedges and hammers. These pieces are removed from the galleries that have been hewn out, so that an open cavern is formed. So many of these caverns or hollows are made adjacent to each other in the mountain that finally they collapse with a loud noise, and so the mineral in the interior becomes exposed. Often the eagerly sought gold vein fails to appear, and the long sustained and arduous work which had often cost many human lives has been in vain."

[GRAIN MILLING]

. . . The hand-mill consisted of two stones, of which the lower was fixed while the other was rotated on it. Originally the upper stone was probably always lifted off when fresh grain had to be added. Later, however, the upper stone had a hole in the centre while the lower had a projection which passed through this hole. Between this pivot and the hole enough space remained for adding grain when necessary. A grip was added to the upper stone to enable it to be turned more easily, and the lower one was provided with a rim which was to prevent the grain from falling out. When ground the grain was run off through leads into a receiver underneath. . . . In order to spread the grains entering at the central hole over the whole space between the two mill-stones, the latter had small grooves running out radially, between which further grooves were inserted inclined at acute angles to them. These grooves also increase the friction and in this way aid the crushing of the grain. There followed as a logical development of the hand-mill those typical Roman mills which have been handed down to us through excavations at Pompeii, and are represented in pictures and so forth. The earliest confirmation of the use in Rome of these mills, which Varro and Pliny report were invented in the town Volsinii (Bolsena), is given in the second century B.C. The improvement, made in order to grind more rapidly, was prob-ably attained by attaching two grips to the upper mill-stone so that two people could grind simultaneously; they presumably did this by passing the grips from one to the other in rotation, but in the earlier stages they still used only their hands. The whole weight of their bodies could be applied only when larger mills were used, which consisted of a conical base of stone on which the milling-stone rotated; the upper stone was, of course, hollowed out so as to fit over the cone. As the entrance funnel was fixed immediately above, the mill-stone assumed the form of two bells placed with their necks end to end and so the mill-stone presented the aspect of an hour-glass. In order to be able to rotate it two pivots were inserted at the outside of the junction of the necks radially, that is horizontally, so that rotating levers could be applied in the hollows of the pivots. In the case of large mills worked by animals these levers were riveted, or else strengthened by a scaffolding which passed over the whole entrance funnel as a sort of protective covering. The heavy grinding-stone was not allowed to rest directly on the base stone as it could not then be rotated, nor could the grain have glided between the two. For this reason the base stone had an iron pivot on which the grinding-stone rested in such a way that a small space remained between them, which was particularly narrow at one point owing to the slight convexity of the grinding stone. Connection between the mill-stone and the pivot of the base stone was made by a disc placed inside the mill-stone at the narrowest point and having five holes. . . . The pivot passed through the large central hole (socket), while the other four holes allowed the grain to pass through into the mill. By lengthening the central pivot or, in the case of larger mills, by extending the beam, which supported the framework of the entrance funnel, coarser flour could be obtained. As already mentioned, the mills were turned either by animals, usually asses or mules, or by slaves and criminals (not by free men). . . .

Later, the water-mill appeared, which Vitruvius describes (X, 5, 2) somewhat as follows: "The water-mills are driven in the same way (that is, by means of the under-shot wheel). These mills are similar in all other respects except that they have a toothed wheel . . . at the end of the shaft. Working in this toothed wheel is another . . . at right angles to it and having at its upper end a double swallow-tail . . . which is plugged into the mill-stone. Thus the mill-stones . . . are rotated owing to the horizontal wheel being made to turn by the motion transmitted by the teeth of the vertical wheel attached to the shaft (the paddle-wheel). The mill-hopper . . . placed above the mill-stones feeds the grain into the latter, where it becomes ground up." It is remarkable that this ancient Roman mill with the low-lying under-shot wheel as described by Vitruvius is still in use at the present time in some localities. It also serves as an example of how long some technical constructions last before they are superseded. Such regions also contain other relics which indicate that they once belonged to the Roman Empire. For instance, the author found an example of this mill in the furthermost parts of Val di Gardena, where a dialect derived from Latin is still spoken. A peculiar feature of these mills is that the under-shot wheel described by Vitruvius was always used even when the conditions were such that much greater efficiency would have been obtained by the use of an over-shot or middle-shot wheel. . . .

In place of the water-wheel a pulley was often used. . . . In the sixth century A.D. the floating-mill came into use; its invention was due to the cir-cumstance that Vitiges, King of the Goths, had the water-channels blocked up when he besieged Rome in the year A.D. 536. The animals which had turned the mills had to be slaughtered on account of the shortage of water, and the slaves were required for purposes of defense; so Belisarius had the mills mounted on ships that were afloat on the Tiber. Technically the floating-mill had the advantage of working independently of the level of the water. The undershot wheel thus always obtained its supply of water. Hence its chief disadvantage, which often required special dams or weirs to be constructed, was eliminated.

[BAKING]

. . . In the endeavour to economize . . . labour mechanical kneaders were developed, about the construction of which we have information from discoveries at Pompeii. They consist of a kneading trough of circular cross-section, carrying a wooden shaft pointing vertically upwards. It is provided with wings that reach almost as far as the inner walls of the kneading-trough. In order to scrape off the dough that collects between the wings, horizontal rigid rods pass through the sides of the trough into the interior. They were fixed in such a position that when the shaft rotated they came to lie between the wings, so that the dough remained hanging on the rods and then fell down of its own weight. As is shown in old reliefs the kneading-machine was turned either by human beings or by animals. To enable the machine to be turned the vertical shaft was furnished with a horizontal beam. . . .

The dough was salted and leavened before being kneaded. For leavening, the Romans used a mixture of sun-dried bran and fermenting must, which could be kept for a whole year. In Pliny's time, just as now, leaven was kept over from one day to the next (Pliny, XVIII, 104). Pliny (XVIII, 68) is also acquainted with yeast, which he calls "condensed foam," which forms when beer ferments. He does not mention whether it was used by the Romans for making bread, but merely states that the Gauls and the Spaniards used it in place of leaven for baking bread. . . .

[Oil Extraction]

In order to extract . . . [olive] oil, the fruits were picked when they had attained the right degree of ripeness, or rather of unripeness. In antiquity the unripe fruits were also used in order to obtain an oil of particularly good quality and pleasant taste and smell, both for nutritional and medicinal purposes. . . . They were then put into the oil mills, in which they were first crushed, in order to release them from the kernels. . . . For this purpose, a mill was used, which appears to have been built similarly to that used for grinding corn. Supported on a lower fixed stone was a second stone which had a hole bored through the centre, to allow it to rotate on a vertical pivot. Other mills were also in use, which consisted of a stone tub in which there were vertically-placed stones which could rotate; and these represent the arrangement which modern technical sciences calls edge-rollers or vertical mills. When they first appeared is doubtful. They were used by the Romans and were known by the name *trapetum*. . . .

Many of these vertical mills also had special devices in the form of interior parts which could be attached to the pivot in order to raise or lower the stone. The fastening of the horizontal axle and the shape of the pivot were

subject to small alterations, so that we find differences in these parts of the *trapeta* that have been found and described. The whole machine had to be so arranged that the crushing-stones exerted only a gentle pressure. The skin and the pulp alone were to be crushed, while the kernels were to remain whole; oil was not yet to flow out. That is why exact dimensions still exist for each individual part, large as well as small. The dimensions of such vertical mills are carefully recorded by Cato (*de agric.*, 20–22: 136, 6–7); and he described the adjustment of the crushing-stones down to the smallest detail. . . .

The substance, which came out of the mill, and consisted of crushed olives, was sorted out, in order to remove the kernels. This was followed by the pressing out of the kernel-less fruits. Very different devices were employed for this purpose. Originally they were probably placed in a kind of basket, and pressed out by placing stones on the basket. The oil ran out between the wickerwork of the basket, and was collected in a vessel placed below. Later, the method was made more perfect. The substance—or the wickerwork containing it—was placed between wooden boards, and several such layers were placed on a framework.

A long lever beam was then fixed above, which was weighted in front with large stones, fastened by means of cords. By climbing up on the lever beams and jerking with the weight of the body, the effect was intensified. The oil ran out into the lower frame, and from here probably along grooves, into a large gutter, the opening of which lay above a collecting vessel. . . . The press-beam was weighted with stones, and was pulled down by jerking with the weight of the body. Later still, the screw was introduced. There arose a new type of oil press, in which the board resting on the olives was pressed against its base by means of a screw. . . .

[REFRIGERATION]

The Greeks and the Romans, particularly the latter, constructed their snow-cellars in accordance with important technical rules. They were large pits which were covered with grass, chaff, or (according to Seneca) with earth, manure, or branches of trees; so the protection against heat was effected by the correct choice of non-conducting substances. Moreover, the snow was tightly pressed together before being introduced into the pits. As snow becomes ice under pressure, it is not improbable that artificial ice was at that time made by this process. The snow had often to be fetched from far away; perhaps pressure was used to economize space and so to facilitate transport. No further details are known to us.

Plutarch enters into a detailed discussion about the protection furnished by chaff against the melting of the snow; and from his reflections it is easily inferred that the snow was also wrapped in thick cloths in order to keep it longer. Moreover, the method of preserving just described, was used, according to Athenaeus, by Alexander the Great. Snow was added directly to beverages. The water resulting from it when it melted was used for the same purpose, after it had been run through cloths or sieves in order to purify it. As mentioned by Pliny (XXXI, 21), the drinking of strongly cooled beverages produced illnesses of very different kinds. When this circumstance became known, the beverages were cooled from without, by placing the vessels in snow —an invention which is attributed to the Emperor Nero; so that we have to regard Nero as the discoverer of the champagne-cooler! Galen reports that Nero had also made the observation that water which had been previously heated cooled more rapidly than ordinary water. This observation, which, by the way, had already been mentioned by Aristotle (*Meteorologica,* I, 12), is correct. Ordinary water contains air and carbon dioxide, which retard cooling. Boiling the water drives off both of these gases. . . .

[OTHER MEANS OF FOOD PRESERVATION]

The fact that cold was used in antiquity for purposes of preserving is clear from various data—above all, from ancient Roman cookery books, in which it is advised to cover certain dishes, especially prawns, with snow. As these are particularly prone to decay, and as the snow can hardly have been regarded as a delicacy, we can interpret this only as a method of preserving. Other methods of preserving food-stuffs consisted in drying them in the air, in smoking them, in salting them, and in excluding the air. The latter was performed chiefly by placing the food-stuffs in oil. Besides this, however, the food was also placed in vinegar, in salt, and in salt water. Salting seems to have been used universally. . . .

Preserved fish from ancient Egyptian times have remained unimpaired up to the present day. The method of preserving was certainly a little complicated. In the case of the ancient Egyptians, the particular fish used was one that resembled a perch and was regarded as sacred, the *Lates Niloticus.* Great quantities of this fish were found in a sandy desert stretching east of the town Esna; they have also been found in excavated tombs. The fish were wrapped round with linen strips, and were then placed into water of the Egyptian lakes, which contain much soda, and were left in contact with the water for some time. (The researches of French savants prove that sodium was present in some form; whether this sodium arises from the use of soda or of ordinary salt seems doubtful. . . .) The fish were then packed into a mixture of sand and clay, and once again placed in brine. In some cases they still look nowadays as if they had just come out of the water. The skin is shiny and has colour, and in the eyes one can still clearly discern the iris. This method of preserving is a process in which pickling, excluding the air (clay), as well as drying, aided by the exceptional dryness of the Egyptian climate, probably acted in concert to produce this result.

[CERAMICS]

In examining Greek vases, which represent the zenith of ancient Hellenic ceramic art, two aspects must be sharply differentiated; the artistic and the technical point of view. Although these vases are perfect in artistic respects, they are just the contrary from the technical of view. . . . An endless number of publications have appeared about them, but they discuss the Greek vases almost in all cases only from the archaeological and artistic point of view. The technical aspect received less attention. Only recently, more attention has been paid to the ancient Greek ceramic art by the technical scientist. It was then discovered, as already indicated above, that the technical processes were by no means perfect. Above all, no very high temperature was reached, and consequently the clay remained too porous for many purposes. It did not frit together suf-

ficiently densely, and the glaze was not first applied in order to embellish it, but rather it served the necessary purpose of making the vessel water-tight, to make it impenetrable—which it would not perhaps be otherwise. Out of this necessity there then grew a virtue; the glaze, and also the painting under it, were developed to a high degree of artistic excellence. In general, Greek vases are black, brown or red, and are more or less polished. At the end of the third century B.C. a glaze appeared on them. They are often so porous that we can understand that the glaze was necessary, for even if water —as in the Egyptian gullah—might have kept very fresh in many of these vessels, they were probably quite inappropriate for other purposes. The potter's wheel was used in the earliest times. . . . In all cases the potter's wheel is turned by hand. . . .

The ceramic art of the Romans was in many ways influenced by that of the Greeks. On the whole it does not differ much at first in its essentials; and indeed a common main stream runs through the ceramic art of the whole of antiquity. . . . Later on, in Roman ceramic art, just as in that of other peoples, particular methods developed, of which some did not even originate on the Italian peninsula. As an example of this, we may quote the barbotine process, which was practised in the Gallic and Rhenish provinces of the Roman Empire, and which was not known in Rome and in Italy. It has been discovered only recently that it was also known in Egypt and Asia Minor. It consists of washing the clay till it is very fine and then, by stirring it with water, forming a thin barbotine. This is then filled into a funnel provided with a fine orifice from which it escapes in a thin stream on to the earthenware vessels to be decorated. In this way, raised ornaments appear on the earthenware vessels. We see that this is the same process as that nowadays still used by confectioners in order to decorate their pastry with inscriptions and figures. Whereas, originally, simple ornaments such as circles and lines were applied, later, really magnificent show-pieces were made by the barbotine process, which exhibited entire hunting scenes and the like.

A further peculiarity of Roman ceramic art was the almost complete absence of glaze. The firing process is thus technically better than that of the Greeks. . . .

Roman ceramic art worked itself out most characteristically, however, in that species of earthenware which is called *terra sigillata* on account of its similarity with impresses of seals carrying relief, or else on account of its being decorated with raised figures (*sigilla*). . . . The *terra sigillata* represented the finer types of earthenware that existed in ancient Roman times. We find vessels or fragments of *terra sigillata* wherever the Romans penetrated. They are sometimes of light, sometimes of dark red, simple in form, or of noble contour, smooth or ornamented. But all of them exhibit a beautiful velvety matt finish. It is this finish which constitutes their real beauty. . . .

[THE TEXTILE INDUSTRY]

. . . the milling of textiles was supposed to have been invented by a certain Nikias in Megara. The purpose of milling is to unite closely the comparatively loose fibres of the woven material, so that cloth is produced from them. The process brought about by milling is felting. This converts the texture into cloth . . . the woven materials are sometimes beaten, as well as trodden on, and milled by hand.

We must regard this process as differing from that of washing only in the length of time required, and in the energy expended. When washing alone was done, one worked for only a short time, and with less expenditure of work; in the case of milling, more power was used, and the process was continued until its aim—the production of felt—was achieved. The apparatus used for both purposes was probably fairly similar; it consisted of troughs or pits situated in the vicinity of flowing water. The material was trodden on . . . while soda was added . . . or else decomposed urine, or clayey substances, which easily combined with fat. There was even a fuller's earth, known as "Kimolian," because obtained from the island of Kimolos, one of the Cyclades in the Aegean Sea. Such earth was also brought to Greece and Rome from Samos and other places. The methods and the means were probably the same among most peoples of antiquity, namely, when the material had been sufficiently milled, it was subjected to washing and beating, which completed the process of felting. . . . As is still done nowadays, the felted material then had its surface dressed, for which purpose thistles were used, fixed in appropriate instruments with handles. . . .

In the textile industry these thistles are now called fuller's thistles or teazles. They were mounted in a framework and brushed up and down over the stretched cloths. The prickles of the hedgehog were used for the same purpose, perhaps also metal combs, provided with sharp teeth, or brushes. The wood fibres scratched off in this way were carefully collected and were a favourite means of stuffing cushions.

The production of pieces of cloth by the succession of individual processes described above was a trade that was practised on a large scale by the Romans; its importance and special peculiarities made it necessary to adapt buildings to its purposes. In this way, factories for milling cloth arose, in part after the manner of our present day factories, as regards their technical equipment. The milling factory [*Fullonica (in Pompeii) in the Street of Mercury consists of thirty-six separate rooms or areas. Eight of these are made up of four separate shops, each with a back room; these shops, which faced the street, had nothing to do with the factory itself. There were special rooms for beating, treading, dyeing, and drying the cloth, each with its special equipment in the way of troughs, tables, etc. Some of the rooms were living quarters, while one contained a bakery, presumably to feed the workers.*]

[OF TIME AND ENERGY]

Many of the technical achievements of antiquity excite the greatest admiration in us on account of their massiveness, of the colossal conceptions embodied in them, and of the splendid manner in which they have been executed. This admiration is still further increased when we realize that all these achievements were accomplished with comparatively simple machines, with contrivances which throughout result from exploiting a few easily recognizable physical laws. "Work" is the product of "time" by "power." We can understand how these achievements were possible in spite of the simple machines used, if we bear in mind that there was an abundance of both time and power available at that period. Time was of practically no account; in order to produce a definite piece of work, any amount of time could be used. There was likewise no lack of power: the existence of slavery provided more than enough labour, and it could be used to the fullest extent. In view of this profusion of power and time, machines could well be of a simple kind. . . .

[THE SCREW]

The inclined plane acquired particular importance by being used in the form of the screw, which is supposed to have been invented by Archimedes while travelling in Egypt. But it is to be assumed that it had long been in use in that country, namely for pump-work in mines ("Egyptian or Archimedes" screw). The method of making it is described in Vitruvius (X, 6). From this description we see that the screw or worm was made of wood, and served at first exclusively for drawing water. It was in the shape of a long worm . . . whose grooves were enclosed in an envelope . . . bound by hoops and covered with tar. The lower part of the worm, which ran obliquely and was fixed in scaffolding and driven by means of a treadle, dipped into water; by continual turning the liquid was raised. Later, the screw was used for the single-screw olive-presses, and in the double-screw cloth-presses and so forth. In other mechanical constructions, it was also used in the form of the "endless screw" . . . in fibulae we find little screws of gold; iron screws do not seem to have been used by the ancients, as they have never been found. . . .

[THE WHEEL]

There were very many different kinds of Roman vehicles. Some were drawn by two horses, others by three or four, which were always harnessed side by side (*bigae, trigae, quadrigae*). The drag-chain (*plaustrum*) was also known. It was wound through the back-wheel and chained to the body of the vehicle so as to prevent the rotation of the wheel. The usual method was to wind the chain round the felly between two spokes. The felly was not always cut out in a curved shape, but was bent artificially after the fibres of the wood had been softened in hot water. The process seems to date from very early Grecian times; at least we may infer this from the following passage in Homer (*Iliad,* IV, 486): "This (the poplar) hath a wainwright felled with gleaming steel, to bend him a felloe for a goodly chariot." . . . The wheel also gave rise to one of the most important of the simple machines, namely the toothed wheel. If the teeth of two such catch in each other, the wheels always rotate in opposite directions. It has not been possible to ascertain when this contrivance first came into use. Nor do we know whether Aristotle is referring to toothed wheels . . . when he talks in his book on "Mechanical Problems" of "tools that set many circles in motion simultaneously by means of a single circle, like those votive offerings in the temples which consist of bronze or iron wheels, arranged as follows. When the wheel AB is turned forwards, while in contact with CD, the latter moves backwards, and, at the same time, for the same reason, EF revolves in the original direction, and so forth if there are still further wheels." There are many reasons for believing that this refers to toothed wheels.

Vitruvius, on the other hand, often mentions the toothed wheel; and Heron of Alexandria applies it elegantly in an appliance like the modern taximeter which served the purpose of measuring the distance covered. In this hodometer . . . a pin attached to the axle of the wheel . . . catches in the radial pegs, and turns them when the axle rotates. This rotation is transmitted by means of endless screws and further toothed wheels to the indicator . . . carrying a small hand. . . .

Very important forms of application of the wheel were the capstan and the tread-wheel. The capstan is mentioned by Vitruvius, who is well aware of the difference between the capstan (or whim, *ergata*) and the windlass (*cula*). The first of these two kinds has its axle placed vertically; in the second the axle lies horizontally. The capstan was chiefly used in Roman mills, where it was worked either by man-power or by animals, particularly asses. . . .

The tread-wheel served for pumping water, for moving loads, and also for erecting columns and similar objects. In the amphitheatre of Capua there is a relief still extant which represents a tread-wheel in which two naked youths are shown running. The motion of the wheel causes a rope to wind up on a pulley suspended from a framework of beams. A heavy column is fastened to one end of the rope. . . .

To exploit the pressure of water the water-wheel was used, but it was known only in the under-shot form. In Roman times it was used both on land and on ships. The frequent assertion that over-shot water-wheels were also used for technical purposes is not corroborated by trustworthy evidence. One important form in which the under-shot wheel was universally used in antiquity was the Persian wheel or noria. Vitruvius (X, 5, 1) writes as follows about it:

Wheels are used in rivers in the same fashion as has been described above. Around them boards are attached and these being struck by the rush of the stream move forward and force the wheel to turn, and in this fashion they draw up the water in buckets and carry it to the top without workmen to tread the wheel. Thus, being turned by the flow of the stream, the wheels furnish what is necessary for the purpose in hand.

Water-mills are turned in the same fashion.

For the rest, the under-shot water-wheel has survived up to the present day in many Alpine valleys, whose civilization dates back to Roman times even in places where the middle- or over-shot wheel would have been equally suitable on technical grounds.

[PUMPS]

. . . An . . . important application (of gas-pressure) is the force-pump, . . . invented by Ktesibios, of which several descriptions have been handed down to us. We will quote that of Vitruvius (X, 7), which seems to be the best:

It is made of bronze, and has at the bottom a pair of cylinders . . . set a little way apart, and there is a Y-shaped pipe . . . connected with both . . . and joining them to a vessel . . . which is between the cylinders. In this vessel are valves . . . accurately fitting over the upper vents of the pipes, which stop up the vent-holes and keep what has been forced by pressure into the vessel from going down again.

Over the vessel a cowl . . . is adjusted, like an inverted funnel, and fastened to the vessel by means of a wedge thrust through a staple, to prevent it from being lifted off by the pressure of the water that is forced in. On top of this a pipe is jointed, called the trumpet, which stands up vertically. Valves are inserted in the cylinders, beneath the lower vents . . . of the pipes, and over the openings . . . which are in the bottoms of the cylinders.

Pistons . . . smoothly turned, rubbed with oil, and inserted from above into the cylinders work with their rods . . . and levers upon the air and water in the cylinders, and, as the valves stop up the openings, force and drive the water, by repeated pressure and expansion, through

the vents of the pipes into the vessel, from which the cowl receives the inflated currents, and sends them up through the pipe at the top; and so the water can be supplied for a fountain from a reservoir at a lower level.

There were no hoses to the pump. The architect Apollodorus, who lived in the reign of Trajan, sought to overcome this defect by using the intestines of oxen for hoses. To one end of them was attached a reservoir made of skins sewn together and filled with water. The water was expelled by pressing together these *siphones,* as they were called. Fire-men's work was carried out in Rome by the *siphonarii.*

In the ruins of Castrum Novum a pump was found which in the main agrees with the above description, except that the two pipes are not oblique but run horizontally into the air-chamber; this chamber is weakly constructed, being of one piece with the cowl, whereas Vitruvius prescribes two pieces. . . .

[FIRE MAKING]

Wood of the laurel was employed by the Greeks and Romans for a very long time for the purpose of ignition. A large piece of soft wood was taken, preferably ivy or clematis, in which several holes were bored. In one of these holes a rod of hard wood was placed which was provided with a handle of hemispherical form similar to that of the bores used in the same way. One hand was placed upon the handle and this hard pointed end of the rod was pressed into the soft piece of wood. Then it was rotated quickly by a bow and bowstring till the easily inflammable material, the "tinder," placed in the hollow space, took fire. For tinder such things as charred canvas, wood-dust, dry grass, dried mushrooms, leaves and so forth were used. . . . Besides these fire-appliances, others were also known to the ancients. In Greece and Rome steel and tinder were used in combination with not only ordinary flint but also pyrites, and other kinds of suitable stone. The "steel" was either a longish piece of steel, a nail, a key, or another piece of the same stone (Pliny, XXXVI, 138). Furthermore, fire was made with the help of concave mirrors composed of bronze and covered with silver-foil, which were already known in 640 B.C., and lenses were made of rock-crystal or glass, as has been proved by Layard's discovery in the palace of Assur-nazir-pal at Nineveh. Aristophanes (450–385 B.C.) says in his comedy *The Clouds* (767) that a burning lens, such as Strepsiades uses in order to rid himself of a debt of five talents by melting a wax tablet, is also used for lighting fires. If the sacred flame went out in Rome it was ignited again, according to Plutarch, by means of bronze or silver concave mirrors or burning lenses. Pliny (XXXVII, 28) and Isidore (XVI, 13, 1) mention that the latter were sometimes made of rock crystal. . . .

[LIGHTHOUSES]

The assumption that beacons were used for assisting navigation in very ancient times seems quite natural, as the idea of indicating in this way the place of landing to sailors overtaken by darkness would very readily suggest itself. In the course of time these watch towers grew higher and more magnificent. Some of them became world-renowned, such as the lighthouse which was built at Alexandria (299–280 B.C.) at the cost of 800 talents, equivalent to £180,000; it was constructed of white marble and had several stories, on the terraces of which people could easily walk about (Pliny, XXXVI, 12, 83; *et al.* . . . .). Accord-

ing to Hennig's thorough investigations, the lighthouse of Alexandria served first of all as a day-signal for navigation, and it was not till after A.D. 41 and before A.D. 65 that the Romans turned it into a lighthouse.

The same author regards the lighthouse of Ostis, dating from A.D. 42, as the oldest genuine lighthouse in the world. There are, however, only scant records in existence about the lighting-equipment of these old lighthouses. But in all probability it consisted mostly of open fires burning in the air without a lantern. For instance, the Jewish author Josephus (A.D. 37–95) (Βίος. VI, 105) says that on the lighthouse of Alexandria an open wood-fire was kept alight by specially appointed watchmen. According to the same report of Josephus this fire could be seen at a distance of 300 stadia (about 36 miles). The picture of such a fire showing the harbour of Ostia and its lighthouse, constructed by the Emperor Claudius, near the mouth of the Tiber at Ostia, is still preserved in a relief. A high open flame is seen burning on the top landing of the tower, built in several stories with terraces. Probably the fuel was of wood mixed or saturated with tar, resin or asphalt. The lighting power, however, of such open fires, whose light was collected neither by reflectors nor by lenses, can hardly have been as great as Josephus indicates above. Such luminosity can only be attained by modern methods, and even then only by intense sources of light; and at the distance stated by Josephus it is not the source itself that can be seen but only the reflection of the flashes.

·   ·   ·   ·

[CENTRAL HEATING]

However important a role the fireplace played in human life, it had one great disadvantage: it was immovable.

When it was needed for purposes other than cooking food, such as for heating a room, it failed when the habitation consisted of more than one room. For this reason it was replaced by a new device which no longer served the double purpose of heating and cooking, but was used for cooking alone. This new article of furniture was the coal-pan or brazier. In antiquity it was widely used as a heating apparatus in many different forms: indeed, it was sometimes an object of great artistic merit. It has, however, the same disadvantage as the hearth: it allows parts of the waste-products of combustion to escape into the rooms, even if there are chimneys specially built for them . . . it has been shown by Krell's thorough investigations that rooms of a considerable size can be heated with comparatively small braziers. Krell writes as follows: "The brazier found in the tepidarium of the baths in the forum of Pompeii, standing in the place were it was originally used, has a heating surface of 7 ft. 8 in. by 2 ft. 8 in. It is quite sufficient even at the lowest winter temperature to heat a large church with a seating accommodation for over two thousand people, such as the Church of S. Egidius in Nuremburg." Exhaustive researches have also been carried out as to whether the atmosphere of the rooms become polluted by the use of ancient braziers to a degree injurious to human health. The result may be briefly summarized as follows: The only gas produced in moderately warmed rooms is carbon dioxide. Carbon monoxide only develops at high temperatures, and the quantity increases with the rise in temperature . . . the present author, while engaged in research on the history of poisoning by carbon monoxide, has been able to collect numerous reports of ancient authors themselves about the dangers of using such braziers owing to the pos-

sibility of their causing asphyxia. Among the ancient reports worth mentioning are those of Lucretius (96–55 B.C.), Galen (A.D. 131–200), Erasistratos (about A.D. 300) and of the Emperor Julian the Apostate, who reigned from A.D. 361 to 363. It has been shown that, on the whole, ancient braziers could be regarded as harmless if the layer of [char]coal burned on them did not exceed a thickness of 6 in., and if the temperature was kept low. Considering the great popularity of these braziers the conclusion may be drawn that the ancients well knew how to manage them, that is, how to regulate the depth of [char]coal and the temperature. On the other hand, it must be concluded that the manifold accounts of poisoning by coal gas due to the use of braziers prove how dangerous they were when handled incorrectly.

. . . .

Fixed stoves were unknown to the ancients, but they turned the coal-pan into a kind of portable stove by closing in the fire on all sides. A stove of this description found at Pompeii consists of a metal cylinder with a stove hole and stands on three legs shaped like a lion's paws. . . . A little over halfway up the metal cylinder there are two apertures masked with lion's heads. They admit the supply of air necessary for maintaining the fire inside. Since the upper part of the stove contains a copper [kettle] it is obvious that the apparatus was used both for ordinary heating and for boiling water. . . .

. . . .

The system of central heating had been met with only among the Romans, and the oldest form of it is undoubtedly the method of heating by hypocausts, whose inventor is said to have been C. Sergius Orata. . . . The hypocaust consists of a hollow space below the floor of the room to be heated, and in most cases extends the whole length and breadth of the room above. The floor lies some 3 feet above the ground and is supported by brick pillars whose upper parts widen to a kind of capital. These capitals consist of projecting tiles the uppermost of which sometimes touch the corresponding tiles of the adjacent pillars. These tiles carry the actual floor. . . . The fire-chamber lies outside the building and communicates with the above hollow space through a channel which corresponds to the flue or snore-hole in modern industrial establishments for heating. In front of the fire-chamber there is a kind of roofless ante-room also sunk into the ground and reached by a few steps.

From this open room, called the *praefurnium,* the fire is kindled and kept up in the fire-chamber, and the daily supply of fuel is piled up here. . . . The smoke and fumes, passing through the hollow space under the floor, eventually escape through pipes in the sides.

In many cases the walls of a room also contain hollow spaces, which form as it were a continuation of the empty space below the floor. Hollow tiles (*tubuli*) of square cross-section were used for this purpose up to a height of 5 ft. above the floor or as high as the roof, in which case they provide an outlet for the smoke. . . . Instead of these, other tiles were sometimes used provided with bosses (*tegular mammatae*) and fixed to the walls with iron clamps. Occasionally an opening closed with a plate is found in the floor. Through it the hot air contained in the hypocaust was allowed to enter the room after the flue had been closed and the fire had gone out. . . .

.   .   .   .

[CITY PLANNING]

The Roman method of building towns was partly based on ancient tra-

ditions, and partly influenced by the example of Hippodamos, and again they were determined by the fact that some towns arose out of former Roman fortifications, the castra or camps. The ancient tradition is chiefly ancient in the choice of the site. The preference was given to hills or the junction of two valleys forming a promontory upon which the town was built. . . .

But the group of streets customary in Roman camps is also found in other kinds of towns, and may therefor be regarded as the criterion of the Roman town. As a rule both the town and the camp have two main thoroughfares crossing at right angles in the centre and dividing the settlement into four quarters. One of these main streets was the high-street proper, the *via principalis.* The gates standing at its ends were called the *porta principalis dextra* and the *porta principalis sinistra.* The *via decumania* or simply the *decumanus,* the main street cutting the *via principalis* at right angles, ended in the *porta decumana* and at the other end in a gate called in camps the *porta praetoria.* The main streets were usually marked out according to the four cardinal points, but not with particular accuracy, the direction in which the sun rose and set being ascertained only approximately. For the rest, certain superstitions caused the system to appear turned round in the course of time, so that the North-south street, the *via principalis,* often became the West-east street. Moreover, strategic considerations led to the *porta praetoria* being turned towards the enemy. Details of this kind vary in the different cases, but on the whole, the ground-plan of a Roman town is a quadrilateral, mostly an oblong, crossed perpendicularly by two intersecting streets.

.   .   .   .

. . . "When the regal period drew to a close Rome still looked like a country town of to-day in spite of its great extent, which was marked out by the course of the Servian wall. Agricultural work and cattle-rearing were still done in the interior of the city. The houses were built almost entirely of wood and clay, and covered with a thatched roof. People walked in clouds of dust on the unpaved roads when it was summer, and in filth when it was winter.

The defects in the later design of the city were attributed by the ancients to the fact that the reconstruction after the burning by the Gauls in 390 B.C. was carried out roughly and without a plan. The quarters were laid out irregularly, the streets were narrow and crooked, and in many places the houses stood crowded together. Tiled roofs came into use very slowly, shingles being used for a covering as late as the war with the King Pyrrhus (284 B.C.), a fact which bears witness to Italy's former wealth in forests, which was ruthlessly squandered at a later time when the houses in Rome were time and again burnt down and rebuilt many stories high of timber framework. The paving of streets was started much later. At the same time the city little by little changed its rural aspect. For example, before the year 310 B.C. the wooden stalls of the butchers in the Forum gave way to the banking premises of the money-lenders; but the general progress towards beauty took place so slowly and sporadically that even in 174 B.C. a party hostile to Rome at the court of King Philip of Macedonia found cause to scoff at the ugly appearance of Italy's capital which excelled neither in public buildings nor in private residences. Really handsome houses had only begun to be erected a short time previously.*

In spite of the fact that most magnificent and palatial buildings were constructed in Rome from the time of Sulla, the general course of the streets remained unaltered, and even Augustus, who undertook the architectural reorganization of the Roman capital, was

* Friedländer; *Darstellung aus der Sittengeschichte Roms,* Leipzig, 1888–1890.

unable to remove this defect. The disadvantages of such an arrangement of streets were clearly recognized. In the reign of Tiberius people complained that the houses were so high and the spaces between them so narrow that there was no protection against fire and it was impossible to escape in any direction in case a house collapsed. The Neronian fire of A.D. 64 owed its vast extent entirely to these shortcomings. Even later on, after the burnt-out quarters had been rebuilt and the lower parts of the houses had been made of fire-proof material such as Alban and Gabinian stone, *peperino* and *sperone,* the original drawbacks of irregular growth continued and made themselves felt in an unheard-of increase in the value of the land. As a consequence of this, people were compelled to extend their houses by adding to their height, as is the case in large cities today. According to the account of Juvenal, there were windows in Rome at such a height that objects down below in the streets were seen as though through a mist; and Pliny thought that no other city in the world could compare in size with Rome if the height of her houses was taken into consideration as well as her area and circumference. That her houses were higher than those of an average large modern city is shown in a comparative list by Friedländer. "Whereas the building regulations of Berlin of the year 1860 allow facades only 40 ft. in height on streets of the same width, and higher ones only on streets which are proportionately wider, the by-laws of Vienna fix the maximum height at 50 ft., or allow four stories, and those of Paris at 70 ft. on roads of the same width, the Emperor Augustus decreed that the front of the houses in Rome should not exceed a height of 70 Roman (about 67 English) *feet i.e.,* six or seven stories, while Trajan is alleged to have limited them to 60 (58) *feet, i.e.,* five or six stories. But these decrees could hardly have been observed strictly and did not affect the rear part of the houses, which undoubtedly often surpassed the height prescribed for the fronts. Martial writes of a poor wretch who had to ascend 200 steps to reach his bedroom. Conditions were aggravated by the fact that the maximum height was allowed on any street regardless of its width. In this respect Rome was far behind any modern city. In Berlin the average width of the streets comes out at 73 ft., whereas it was only 17 to 21 ft. for the Roman main roads; this is less than the narrowest width (26 ft.) allowed in the Paris regulations of to-day, for which façades not exceeding 40 ft. are permitted. A road even as lively and busy as the Vicus Tuscus, owing to its shops, was only 15 ft. from side to side of its pavement, and the Vicua Iugarius only 18 ft. . . ."

· · · ·

[Domestic Architecture]

In Greece houses stood alone, whereas in Italy they had *parietes communes* —that is, they were built together. Owing to the rain which collected in the partitions and damaged the woodwork, every house had to provide its own arrangement to drain off the rainwater. This caused people to set up a kind of funnel on the roof through which the rain-water entered the house, where it was collected in a special basin. This arrangement, indeed, gave the Roman house, which is derived from the Etruscans, its characteristic form, whereas in the Greek house the central court is not roofed at all. The central hall, the *atrium,* round which are grouped the various rooms, was completely covered by a roof with a funnel-shaped aperture (the *compluvium*) through which the rain-water flowed into the atrium, where it was collected in a basin, the *impluvium;* it was then generally passed into a cistern for domestic use. Like the court of the Greek house, the atrium is surrounded by rooms, the most important of which is the master's room, the *tablinum,* adjacent to the atrium. . . . The entrance door (*ianua*) opposite to the tablinum leads the visitor into a corridor adjacent to the atrium. The *parietes communes* were very convenient for the laying out of streets, and since the latter were favourite resorts for business transactions, shops were built at a very early date on both sides of the street-entrance and of the corridor behind. As a rule they were not connected with the interior of the house in any other way and were accessible only from the street. In the atrium, behind the impluvium, stood the hearth (*focus*), which gave its name to the hall, because it filled the whole room with smoke and made it black. The Latin *ater* means black or dark . . .

Influenced by all sorts of models, the most important of which were Greek, the original form of Roman house developed into a new type in the course of time—which was a combination of the Italian and Greek dwelling. Properly speaking the new type consisted of two houses—a Roman one in front containing the compluvium, atrium, and tablinum, with a corridor shortened by bringing the street door further inside. By this process a narrow exterior entrance hall, a *vestibulum,* was created. At the back this Roman house led into a Greek one characterized by the peristyle court, with its surrounding columns. Since here, as in Greece, two houses were combined into one, it was quite natural that this house, like the ancient Greek, should be divided into men's apartments and women's apartments. The latter were contained in the Greek part, that having a peristyle. Both houses were encircled by a common wall with only a few small windows. Inside rooms received their light from the court. As in the Greek house, the outer world was effectually cut off by the wall; the privacy was undisturbed by the presence of the shops —in many cases, however, there were none. . . .

. . . . .

By degrees this type of Roman house —the most original form of which frequently possessed a small garden adjacent to the tablinum—underwent many changes, which were chiefly due to the increasing luxury, to the want of space in the cities . . . and the consequent rise in the price of land. How the last-mentioned process reacted on the further extension of Rome has been graphically described by Friedländer, who bases his remarks partly on Seneca: "The contractors not only economized the building land by putting up as many stories as possible, but more so by narrowing and decreasing the rooms of individual dwellings to the utmost limit, reducing, at the same time, the cost of building to a minimum." But this method also increased the danger of fires.

The walls of these flats were piled on top of each other and consisted of wood or wood and brick; being very thin, they afforded no protection from heat or cold. A favourite pattern for walls was so-called net work, *opus reticulatum*. . . . Speculative jerry-builders favoured the handsome design for the sake of appearance. The result was often a lack of stability of the structure, as walls built in this form cracked very easily.

Friedländer continues:

"A part of our fears," say Seneca, "are our roofs; people flee from the halls of large palaces, adorned with paintings, as soon as they hear a creaking." A large number of tenement houses were in a dilapidated state, the most necessary repairs being neglected or done insufficiently. If a landlord "had strengthened the tottering walls by a support and covered over an old chink, he would assure his tenants that they might sleep safely, although a collapse was imminent." The collapsing of houses and the prevalence of fires were two of the evils characteristic of Rome even during the last years of the Republic.

. . . . .

. . . The ground-plan of the Roman house thus changed more and more. Yet its original features were still to be recognized in the luxurious residences of a later period. . . .

But it was completely lost sight of when the Romans began to equip the large villas in the neighbourhood of the greater cities with more and more magnificence. Pliny the Younger says of his two villas that one was provided with an open swimming-bath and that a sojourn there was made pleasant by large rooms with two windows, gardens, and fountains. But such a villa was nothing compared with the gigantic and palatial buildings that arose during the time of the Caesars, to which the ruins of Hadrian's villa near Tivoli still bear witness today. This was no longer a house but a multitude of buildings scattered over an extensive stretch of land. . . . It was no longer planned according to a definite technical tradition but entirely adapted to the special features of the ground and the caprice of the builder.

. . . . .

If we enter into the technical details of the interior of Roman houses we are struck by the smallness of the individual rooms as compared with those of modern times. The house of Pansa at Pompeii is 110 ft. wide and 20 ft. deep. . . . A modern builder would perhaps fit 15 to 20 rooms into this space. But Pansa's house contains no fewer than 60 chambers. The same applies to almost any Roman house. Even in Hadrian's vast and luxuriously equipped villa the guest-chambers are nothing more than small and rather dark rooms. . . .

.   .   .   .

[THEATRES]

The ancient theatres were extremely large, some holding as many as 20,000 people. The acoustics of these buildings was therefore a matter of great importance. Not only did the builders endeavour to make a theatre a satisfactory resonance chamber as a whole, they also placed special bronze vessels, called *echeia* . . . in recesses; these were intended to magnify the sound. Moreover, the masks of the actors were shaped in such a way as to strengthen the sound. The point had been frequently raised how it was that these masks, which were after all a hindrance to the actors, continued in use for such a long time instead of being replaced by natural facial expression. If we consider the colossal size and the openness of the ancient theatres it is obvious that great demands were made on the human voice. No actor would have been able to shout through a leading part and sustain a tone which could be heard all over the theatre. It was soon discovered that the opened mouth of a mask could easily be formed into a sort of speaking-tube. The mouths of all ancient stage-masks are shaped in a most peculiar fashion. Following a suggestion by Castex, replicas of such masks were made for special acoustic experiments in which both actors and singers with voices of different pitches, that is, basses, sopranos, and others, participated. A number of spectators were also engaged in order that the action of these masks should be thoroughly tested in every direction. The very first experiments with masks revealed

that to the hearers the intensity of the human voice appeared strikingly increased. Words spoken in a low voice without a mask were found to be unintelligible to the audience, but when a mask was applied the words were easily understood in all parts without the speaker increasing his efforts. Further, the voice became more distinct. This result was considerably more marked in the case of tones of higher pitch. The tone was neither blurred nor did it acquire a nasal quality through the mask. The peculiar formation of its mouth caused the sound to be conveyed with increased intensity not only towards the front but also towards the sides of the auditorium. The actor at once felt in his voice a sensation of increased carrying power. He found the simple face-masks to be acoustically superior to the animal masks which covered the whole head and which caused a buzzing sensation. The result of these experiments all point to the conclusion that the actors of antiquity were well aware of the advantages gained by the use of the mask.

.   .   .   .

[THE WATER SUPPLY]

Roman aqueducts were also often based on the pressure system, although it was avoided wherever possible owing to the difficulty of constructing them and keeping them watertight. When a single sloping conduit was sufficient, it was adopted. Among other pressure aqueducts constructed by the Romans there is that at Alatri near Rome. Wherever the Romans took footing, one of their first cares was to provide for a good water-supply. They were well aware of the advantages of spring-water. When this was not available they followed the advice of Vegetius (*de re milit* IV, 10), "*Si natura (fontes) non praestat, effodiendi sunt putei aquarumque haustus funibus extrahen-*

di." (If nature supplies no springs, wells must be dug out and the water must be drawn up by means of ropes.)

. . . With the exception of pressure-mains, which as already mentioned, were avoided wherever possible, all other details of water-supply reached an unusually high standard among the Romans of the ancient Empire. This development is not surprising when we consider the partiality of the Romans to water, of which they made prodigal use. The ancient Roman aqueducts daily supplied about one million cubic metres of water, that is, about 120 gallons of water per head of the population. Even nowadays Rome still holds first place in the matter of water-supply, a fact which it owes not least to the existence of the ancient Roman aqueducts. Nowhere else in the world is there such a superabundance of water, nowhere are there so many wells, fountains, water-jets, etc. Although a large proportion of these fountains was designed by artists of the Renaissance and rococo periods, the foundation of all this beauty, the vast quantity of water available, is due to ancient Rome, which provided this lavish supply, and has so vast a wealth of fountains, *jets d'eau,* baths and other such means of spending it. And every provincial Roman town was a miniature Rome. So that wherever Roman civilization has penetrated, we find the remains of their highly developed water-systems— above all, the characteristic aqueducts, which are of such imposing size.

Like other ancient systems, those of the Roman had no main-pipe leading from the principal reservoir to the town; rather, the water flowed from the source partly along conduits which were often of considerable length and partly over aqueducts to the water-tower (*castellum*) which represents our main reservoir. . . . The interior of the water-tower was usually divided

into four compartments, namely, into the tank proper and three subsidiary tanks connected with the main tank by pipes. One of these smaller tanks served to supply the baths with which it communicated. The second subsidiary tank supplied the private houses, while the third received the overflow from the first two, which was conducted into the public fountains and water-jets.

The second tank, which supplied the private houses, was not connected with them by a main pipe and branch pipes. Instead, the water was first led into a sort of minor water-tower situated near the houses to be supplied. From this tower it flowed into a cistern, from which it was finally conducted into the individual houses. In the case of more extensive systems this method was of course correspondingly repeated: the aqueduct supplied not one but several main water-towers. From the latter it was again passed on to several private cisterns in various parts of the town, and so forth. The chief disadvantage of this system is that it necessitates the use of very long pipe-lines; for a special subsidiary pipe must be laid from the minor water-towers to each house, and these minor towers have each again to be connected with the main tower. Consequently much of the water runs away unused, and the amount of water required for the system is very much greater than is effectively used; further, it is difficult to control the working. Nevertheless modern Rome has retained many of its water-systems (Aqua Marcia) in this ancient form.

To provide the towns with the necessary water, the Romans spared no effort. At the beginning they, like other peoples, constructed their water-systems underground. Later, however, in Rome as well as in other places, they fetched their water from such great distances that difficulties opposed themselves to the underground construction of the pipes. Moreover, our way of overcoming differences of level by means of water-pressure was avoided by them as much as possible. They preferred to have recourse to the most costly and most laborious artificial constructions in the form of tunnels and aqueducts. In this way the surroundings of many ancient Roman towns, above all of Rome itself, assumed the characteristic appearance due to the presence of these aqueducts. The Campagna, the wide plain surrounding Rome, is traversed in all directions by the gigantic arches of these aqueducts, of which some still nowadays conduct water from distant hills as in ancient times. The Aqua Marcia, which is the third of the fourteen water-systems constructed in the course of time for supplying Rome, connects the capital city with the source 33 miles away. The total length of the system amounts to no less than 57 miles, and there are nearly 7 miles of aqueducts. As the sources are situated 1,056 ft. above sea-level, whereas Rome is only 180 ft., the course could have been made much shorter in view of the gradient of 876 ft. in 33 miles. Instead of doing this, however, the Romans followed all the irregularities of the ground and even passed round hills and spurs, so that the actual length of pipe became extended to the extraordinary distance of 57 miles. . . .

.   .   .   .

Within the towns the water was conducted in subterranean channels. It is noteworthy that in the ancient Roman water-systems a sort of pressure-reducer occurs, which, in places where there was a steep gradient and consequently a high pressure in the channel, reduced the pressure to within practical limits. Such a device has been found, for example, at Pompeii. It consisted of two pillars with an open container at the same level. The water was conducted up a pipe in the one pillar into the container and then passed on through the other. Its pressure was then only that due to the height of the pillar and the width of the second pipe. The pressure due to the original gradient was thus eliminated.

To conduct the water further to the wells and houses pipes of clay or lead were used. Stone pipes are also found, but they are rare. The lead tubes were simply made from sheet-lead, bent round a core. . . .

.   .   .   .

In the streets water was drawn from the public fountains, in the houses either also from fountains that were constantly running or from tapping-cocks. . . .

The water used in the houses had to be paid for. The mouth of the pipe was therefore often closed by means of a stopcock or tap . . . so that the amount of water used could be regulated to prevent waste. The water used was paid for in Rome in terms of a definite unit, the "Quinarius." The quinarius (called after the silver coin of the same name) corresponded to the quantity of water that flowed per unit of time through a vertical pipe slightly less than 1 ft. long and about 1⅕ in. wide, when there was a column of water at rest 30 ft. 1 in. above its inlet. In 24 hours this yielded a quantity of water amounting to, roughly, 92 gallons. . . .

.   .   .   .

[ROADS]

Striking improvements manifest themselves when we come to consider Roman roads. They represent the highest stage of development in road-making. The Romans were compelled to have good roads, as it was only by constructing and preserving them that the Roman Empire could exist and endure. Rome's extensive trade made greater demands on the laying down of the network of roads than was the case with other peoples. It was necessary to be ready at any moment to transfer soldiers—sometimes mighty armies—to frontiers that were often far distant. So Roman rule spread and the system of roads developed simultaneously. A special class of craftsman, the road-builder, came into being; numerous workmen were enlisted into the service of building and maintaining roads. At first it was the legions themselves who did this, since work had to be found for them, too much leisure tending to produce dissatisfaction and mutiny. Further, slaves and conquered people had to lend their aid when a military road was to be built. These vassal peoples were well aware of the value of roads for upholding Roman rule; they knew that they could be permanently freed from the Roman yoke only when the roads had been destroyed. When the Roman Empire fell to pieces, this was, therefore, the first act of many peoples in order to hinder armies from advancing anew. Nevertheless numerous old Roman roads have been preserved to the present day—the best proof of their excellent construction and the high stage of development reached in Roman road-building.

There was, indeed, ample scope for development in the course of centuries. The total length of the roads built by the Romans is estimated at over 47,000 miles, a distance approximately equal to twice the circumference of the earth. The roads constituted a network of lines resembling those of our modern railways: the shortest route was aimed at, no matter what obstacles were in the way. Rocks were cleared away, tunnels were dug through hills, embankments were thrown up, swamps were drained, and the road itself was built as if to last for ever. Matschoso says expressively that Roman roads resembled walls that had been laid on their sides.

This advanced technique of road-building started from simple beginnings. In the Roman Empire, as elsewhere, simple connecting ways were first made, which were gradually improved until finally a smooth high-road resulted. But even the original simple roads seem to have been constructed with a view to their lasting for ever. Even nowadays we find, for example, in the Grand-Duchy of Oldenburg, ancient Roman timber-roads, that is, roads made only of logs or planks, which have outlasted centuries. . . . The planks consist partly of oak and partly of fir-wood, and are mostly shaped. They have the form of boards with wedge-shaped cross-section. . . . The planks lay either close to each other or overlapped a little, so that the thin edge of each plank was under the thick edge of the next. In soft swampy ground longitudinal beams were fixed under the planks. Each plank had a triangular or rectangular hole at each end through which a plug was inserted in order to keep the structure rigid. The unevennesses that resulted from the wedge-shape of the planks was filled in with sand or earth. . . .

.   .   .   .   .

We are probably not wrong in assuming that these timber-roads, laid down as late as in the period of the Roman Empire, are one of the oldest forms of Roman road-construction: for in the vicinity of Rome there were numerous swamps that had to be traversed. Until better methods were devised, the timber roads were probably also laid down there.

Later, a better road was constructed, starting from Rome and passing in particular through the Pontine marshes, which lead in a straight line to

Cumae; this is the 'via Domitiana,' of which the poet Statius (A.D. 45–96) gives a detailed description (*Silvae,* IV, 3, 40). According to his account two parallel furrows (*sulci*) were first dug, which marked the limits of the road and were also to receive and conduct away the water that drained off it. The earth between the two trenches was next removed so that a wide trench resulted, which was to receive the bedding. A row of large kerb-stones (*umbones*) was placed along the sides of this trench to mark its boundary and to keep in the bedding. To fix them firmly in marshy ground strong wooden stakes were rammed in at their sides. The bedding was then covered with large flag-stones over which further layers of stone were placed. Care was taken to make the road convex upwards. The actual surface consisted of a layer of smaller stones which was stamped down and filled in with sand or gravel. In this way a smooth surface was obtained from which, in consequence of the convexity, the rainwater could drain off on either side into the trenches or gutters.

.   .   .   .

Nor is the quality of the surface always the same. In general it consists of small stones stamped down and mixed with sand. In many cases, however, the roads are paved, different kinds of material being used for this purpose. We find ordinary paving-stones with not even the top surface smoothed (for example, at Septimer) and we also find well-paved roads constructed with the utmost care (Via Appia). . . .

The width of the roads varied greatly. Whereas the Via Iulia and some others were only 6½ ft. wide, the Via Appia, as well as the Roman road to the Saalburg and many others, was 14 ft. wide. Again, others were 23 ft. wide, and even more. Many roads,

however, had not even the whole of their surface paved. In particular, the Alpine roads were often paved over a strip only 5 ft. wide, whereas the road itself had a width of nearly 7 ft., and in some places even 10 ft.

The roads also varied greatly in their aspect. Many were quite plain, others exhibited important decorative features, in particular, those that started from the great towns. The latter had sculptured sepulchral monuments for miles along the road on both sides. Frequently these high-roads had footpaths running alongside which were often raised and separated from the road proper by a low kerb of stones. Besides this, stones were laid down to make it easier to mount horses and to load and unload beasts of burden. Often there were seats. There were always milestones, mostly in the form of round columns which stated the distance exactly and also other facts such as the name of the emperor under whose direction the road was built . . .

In building roads it was often found necessary to make a passage through rocks. The Romans were undaunted by this task and so we find numerous Roman roads consisting in part of cuttings and tunnels, for example that at the Iron Gate (*Eiserner Tor*) which runs along the Danube and was built by Tiberius. It was completed as late as A.D. 103 by Trajan. . . .

.   .   .   .

[BRIDGES]

Of the ancient Greek bridges there are comparatively very few remnants left and these give us no idea of what stage of progress the Greeks had reached in the building of their best bridges. On the other hand, the Romans showed themselves to be masters in this art. At first they used wooden bridges. The oldest Roman bridge, the *"pons sublicius,"* built in the year 625

B.C., was of wood, and is supposed to have been loosely jointed, as has been asserted by various investigators, because the use of iron was prohibited by religious prescriptions at that time. Later these rules were no longer closely observed, and bridges were built in great number with planks fastened by iron clamps.

The old wooden bridges, however, soon gave place to stone bridges. . . . The arch was built up over a scaffolding, the stones were connected together by iron clamps fastened in by means of molten lead. . . . The mortar, when used, either consisted of mixtures of lava and limemortar or else hydraulic mortar was used. The town of Amalfi at the entrance of the valley of Molini has an old bridge that dates back probably to the fifth century A.D.; in it natural pozzolona was used as a cement. The bridge is still extant and has lasted through nearly 1,500 years in spite of the absence of iron clamps.

Its span is 23 ft., its width 5 ft., and its height above the river-bed about 10 ft. It is evident that the Romans used in their bridge-construction all the means practised in the other branches of building.

Ancient Roman bridges often exhibit astonishingly high vaulted arches, which artificially raised the roadway. Consequently ramps were necessary to lead up to them. If we enquire into the reason for this peculiar construction we again recognize that the Romans did not know how to span over large distances; the piers therefore considerably narrowed the free passage of the stream, so that at high water a considerable rise in level had to be expected. What was taken in width had to be made up in height in order to prevent dangerous accumulation of water. Consequently the bridge was built as high as possible, and the openings of the arches were also extended upwards as far as possible. . . .

Neuberger's researches give us a detailed picture of the amazing heights reached by the scientists, artisans, and craftsmen of the period of the Roman Empire. They had begun to use the power of natural forces in the form of water wheels, but did not proceed further. Slave labor was the principal source of energy. Slaves were human beings. They fitted into the social structure, as coal, oil, and atomic energy do not. The social structure was built to accommodate the presence of this human energy, and to substitute some other force for it would have shattered the equilibrium of imperial society. Coal, oil, and atomic energy have shaken social equilibria just as much, but their effects have been indirect and hence not anticipated.

The Romans developed to the limit the techniques of transportation known to them. They built large ships to carry grain from North Africa and Egypt, but the sails were no better than those of earlier ships. They multiplied the number of banks of oarsmen on galleys to the limit of efficiency. They built the best possible roads along natural corridors of travel and set up systems of garrisons and inns; even so, there was a natural limit to the geographical extent of their conquests, just as there was to that of the Aztecs, and of the Athenians.

20

Imperial Rome

ROME contained no Aristotle. No one bothered to write out the table of organization of the imperial government or, if he did, the record has not been preserved. Having troubled my colleagues in the classics department in vain, I turn to what seems to be still the best presentation of the subject, extracts from Gibbon's *Decline and Fall of the Roman Empire*.* Being the last selection in the book, it forms a suitable companion piece to the first, that of Carpenter.

In the second century of the Christian Aera, the empire of Rome comprehended the fairest part of the earth, and the most civilized portion of mankind. The frontiers of that extensive monarchy were guarded by ancient renown and disciplined valour. The gentle, but powerful, influence of laws and manners had gradually cemented the union of the provinces. Their peaceful inhabitants enjoyed and abused the advantages of wealth and luxury. The image of a free constitution was preserved with decent reverence. The Roman senate appeared to possess the sovereign authority, and devolved on the emperors all the executive powers of government. . . .

The principal conquests of the Romans were achieved under the republic; and the emperors, for the most part, were satisfied with preserving those dominions which had been acquired by the policy of the senate, the active emulation of the consuls, and the martial enthusiasm of the people. The seven first centuries were filled with a rapid succession of triumphs; but it was re-

served for Augustus to relinquish the ambitious design of subduing the whole earth, and to introduce a spirit of moderation into the public councils. Inclined to peace by his temper and situation, it was easy for him to discover that Rome, in her present exalted situation, had much less to hope than to fear from the chance of arms; and that, in the prosecution of remote wars, the undertaking became every day more difficult, the event more doubtful, and the possession more precarious and less beneficial. . . .

His generals, in the early part of his reign, attempted the reduction of Aethiopia and Arabia Felix. They marched near a thousand miles to the south of the tropic; but the heat of the climate soon repelled the invaders and protected the unwarlike natives of those sequestered regions. The northern countries of Europe scarcely deserved the expense and labour of conquest. . . . On the death of that emperor his testament was publicly read in the senate. He bequeathed, as a valuable legacy to his successors, the advice of

* J. B. Bury, ed., London; Methuen & Co., 1900.

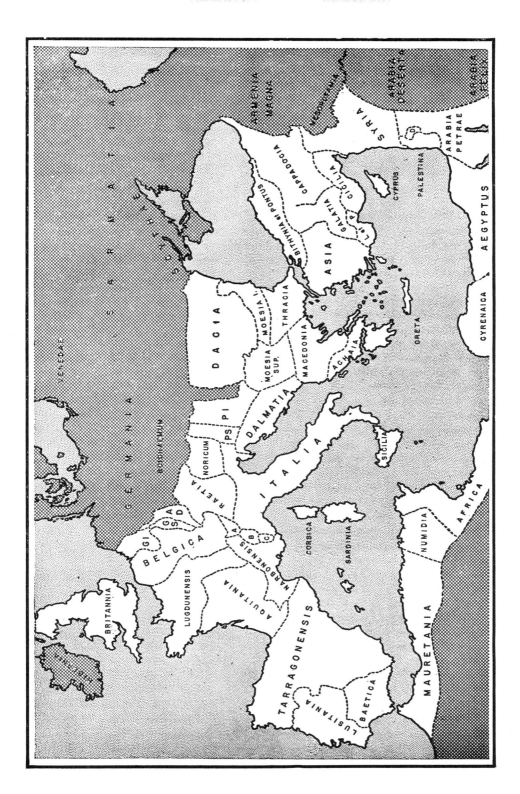

confining the empire within those limits which nature seemed to have placed as its permanent bulwarks and boundaries; on the west the Atlantic ocean; the Rhine and Danube on the north; the Euphrates on the east; and towards the south the sandy deserts of Arabia and Africa.

. . . .

The only accession which the Roman empire received during the first century of the Christian aera was the province of Britain. . . .

In the purer ages of the commonwealth, the use of arms was reserved for those ranks of citizens who had a country to love, a property to defend, and some share in enacting those laws which it was their interest, as well as duty, to maintain. But in proportion as the public freedom was lost in extent of conquest, war was gradually improved into an art, and degraded into a trade. The legions themselves, even at the time when they were recruited in the most distant provinces, were supported to consist of Roman citizens. That distinction was generally considered either as a legal qualification or as a proper recompense for the soldier; but a more serious regard was paid to the essential merit of age, strength, and military stature. In all levies, a just preference was given to the climates of the north over those of the south; the race of men born to the exercise of arms was sought for in the country rather than in cities, and it was very reasonably presumed that the hardy occupations of smiths, carpenters, and huntsmen would supply more vigour and resolution than the sedentary trades which are employed in the service of luxury. After every qualification of property had been laid aside, the armies of the Roman emperors were still commanded, for the most part, by officers of a liberal birth and education; but the common soldiers, like the merce-

nary troops of modern Europe, were drawn from the meanest, and very frequently from the most profligate, of mankind.

. . . On his [the common soldier's] first entrance into the service, an oath was administered to him with every circumstance of solemnity. He promised never to desert his standard, to submit his own will to the commands of his leaders, and to sacrifice his life for the safety of the emperor and the empire. The attachment of the Roman troops to their standards was inspired by the united influence of religion and of honour. The golden eagle, which glittered in the front of the legion, was the object of their fondest devotion; nor was it esteemed less impious than it was ignominious, to abandon that sacred ensign in the hour of danger. These motives, which derived their strength from the imagination, were enforced by fears and hopes of a more substantial kind. Regular pay, occasional donatives, and a stated recompense, after the appointed term of service, alleviated the hardships of the military life, whilst, on the other hand, it was impossible for cowardice or disobedience to escape the severest punishment. The centurions were authorized to chastise with blows, the generals had a right to punish with death; and it was an inflexible maxim of Roman discipline, that a good soldier should dread his officers far more than the enemy. . . .

The recruits and young soldiers were constantly trained, both in the morning and in the evening, nor was age or knowledge allowed to excuse the veterans from the daily repetition of what they had completely learnt. Large sheds were erected in the winter-quarters of the troops, that their useful labours might not receive any interruption from the most tempestuous weather; and it was carefully observed, that the arms destined to this imitation of war should be of double the weight which was required in real action. . . . The soldiers were diligently instructed to march, to run, to leap, to swim, to carry heavy burdens, to handle every species of arms that was used either for offence or for defence, either in distant engagement or in closer onset; to form a variety of evolutions; and to move to the sound of flutes in the Pyrrhic or martial dance. . . .

The constitution of the Imperial legion may be described in a few words. The heavy armed infantry, which composed its principal strength, was divided into ten cohorts, and fifty-five companies, under the orders of a correspondent number of tribunes and centurions. The first cohort, which always claimed the post of honour and the custody of the eagle, was formed of eleven hundred and five soldiers, the most approved for valour and fidelity. The remaining nine cohorts consisted each of five hundred and fifty-five; and the whole body of legionary infantry amounted to six thousand one hundred men. Their arms were uniform, and admirably adapted to the nature of their service; an open helmet, with a lofty crest; a breast-plate, or coat of mail; greaves on their legs, and an ample buckler on their left arm. The buckler was of an oblong and concave figure, four feet in length, and two and a half in breadth, framed of a light wood, covered with a bull's hide, and strongly guarded with plates of brass. Besides a lighter spear, the legionary soldier grasped in his right hand the formidable *pilum,* a ponderous javelin, whose utmost length was about six feet, and which was terminated by a massy triangular point of steel of eighteen inches. This instrument was indeed much inferior to our modern fire-arms; since it was exhausted by a single discharge, at the distance of only ten or twelve paces. Yet, when it was launched by a firm and skilful hand, there was not any cavalry that durst venture within its reach, nor any shield or corslet that could sustain the impetuosity of its weight. As soon as the Roman had darted his *pilum,* he drew his sword, and rushed forwards to close with the enemy. It was a short well-tempered Spanish blade, that carried a double edge, and was alike suited to the purpose of striking or of pushing; but the soldier was always instructed to prefer the latter use of his weapon, as his own body remained less exposed, whilst he inflicted a more dangerous wound on his adversary. The legion was usually drawn up eight deep; and the regular distance of three feet was left between the files as well as ranks. A body of troops, habituated to preserve this open order, in a long front and a rapid charge, found themselves prepared to execute every disposition which the circumstances of war, or the skill of their leader, might suggest. The soldier possessed a free space for his arms and motions, and sufficient intervals were allowed, through which seasonable reinforcements might be introduced to the relief of the exhausted combatants. . . .

The cavalry, without which the force of the legion would have remained imperfect, was divided into ten troops or squadrons; the first, as the companion of the first cohort, consisted of an hundred and thirty-two men; whilst each of the other nine amounted only to sixty-six. The entire establishment formed a regiment, if we may use the modern expression, of seven hundred and twenty-six horse, naturally connected with its respective legion, but occasionally separated to act in the line, and to compose a part of the wings of the army. The cavalry of the emperors was no longer composed, like that of the ancient republic, of the noblest youths of Rome and Italy, who, by performing their military service on horseback, prepared themselves for the offices of senator and consul; and solicited, by deeds of valour, the future suffrages of their countrymen. Since the alteration of manners and government, the most wealthy of the equestrian order were engaged in the administration of justice, and of the revenue; and whenever they embraced the profession of arms, they were immediately intrusted with a troop of horse, or a cohort of foot. Trajan and Hadrian formed their cavalry from the same provinces, and the same class of their subjects, which recruited the ranks of the legion. The horses were bred, for the most part, in Spain or Cappadocia. The Roman troopers despised the complete armour with which the cavalry of the East was encumbered. *Their* more useful arms consisted in a helmet, an oblong shield, light boots, and a coat of mail. A javelin, and a long broad sword, were their principal weapons of offence. The use of lances and of iron maces they seemed to have borrowed from the barbarians.

The safety and honour of the empire was principally intrusted to the legions, but the policy of Rome condescended to adopt every useful instrument of war. Considerable levies were regularly made among the provincials, who had not yet deserved the honourable distinction of Romans. Many dependent princes and communities, dispersed round the frontiers, were permitted, for a while, to hold their freedom and security by the tenure of military service. Even select troops of hostile barbarians were frequently compelled or persuaded to consume their dangerous valour in remote climates, and for the benefit of the state. All these were included under the general name of auxiliaries; and howsoever they might vary according to the difference of times and circumstances, their numbers were seldom much inferior to those of the legions themselves. Among the auxiliaries, the bravest and most faithful bands were placed under the command of praefects and centurions, and severely trained in the arts of Roman discipline; but the far greater part re· tained those arms, to which the naturf of their country, or their early habits of life, more peculiarly adapted them. By this institution, each legion, to whom a certain proportion of auxiliaries was allotted, contained within itself every species of lighter troops, and of missile weapons; and was capable of encountering every nation with the advantages of its respective arms and discipline. Nor was the legion destitute of what, in modern language, would be styled a train of artillery. It consisted in ten military engines of the largest, and fifty-five of a smaller size; but all of which, either in an oblique or horizontal manner, discharged stones and darts with irresistible violence.

The camp of a Roman legion presented the appearance of a fortified city. As soon as the space was marked out, the pioneers carefully levelled the ground, and removed every impediment that might interrupt its perfect regularity. Its form was an exact quadrangle; and we may calculate, that a square of about seven hundred yards was sufficient for the encampment of twenty thousand Romans; though a similar number of our own troops would expose to the enemy a front of more than treble that extent. In the midst of the camp, the praetorium, or general's quarters, rose above the others; the cavalry, the infantry, and the auxiliaries occupied their respective stations; the streets were broad and perfectly straight, and a vacant space of two hundred feet was left on all sides, between the tents and the rampart. The rampart itself was usually twelve feet high, armed with a line of strong and intricate palisades, and defended by a ditch of twelve feet in depth as well as in breadth. This important labour was performed by the hands of the legionaries themselves; to whom the use of the spade and the pick-axe was no less familiar than that of the sword or *pilum*. Active valour may often be the present of nature; but such patient diligence can be the fruit only of habit and discipline.

Whenever the trumpet gave the signal of departure, the camp was almost instantly broken up, and the troops fell into their ranks without delay or confusion. Besides their arms, which the legionaries scarcely considered as an encumbrance, they were laden with their kitchen furniture, the instruments of fortification, and the provision of many days. Under this weight, which would oppress the delicacy of a modern soldier, they were trained by a regular step to advance, in about six hours, near twenty miles. On the appearance of an enemy, they threw aside their baggage, and, by easy and rapid evolutions, converted their column of march into an order of battle. The slingers and archers skirmished in the front; the auxiliaries formed the first line, and were seconded or sustained by the strength of the legions; the cavalry covered the flanks, and the military engines were placed in the rear.

. . . We may compute . . . that the legion, which was itself a body of six thousand eight hundred and thirty-one Romans, might, with its attendant auxiliaries, amount to about twelve thousand five hundred men. The peace establishment of Hadrian and his successors was composed of no less than thirty of these formidable brigades; and most probably formed a standing force of three hundred and seventy-five thousand men. Instead of being confined within the walls of fortified cities, which the Romans considered as the refuge of weakness or pusillanimity, the legions were encamped on the banks of the great rivers, and along the frontiers of the barbarians. As their stations, for the most part, remained fixed and permanent, we may venture to describe the distribution of the troops. Three legions were sufficient for Britain. The principal strength lay upon the Rhine and Danube, and consisted of sixteen legions, in the following proportions: two in the Lower, and three in the Upper Germany; one in Rhaetia, one in Noricum, four in Pannonia, three in Maesia, and two in Dacia. The defence of the Euphrates was intrusted to eight legions, six of whom were planted in Syria, and the other two in Cappadocia. With regard to Egypt, Africa and Spain, as they were far removed from any important scene of war, a single legion maintained the domestic tranquillity of each of those great provinces. Even Italy was not left destitute of a military force. Above twenty thousand chosen soldiers, distinguished by the titles of City Cohorts and Praetorian Guards, watched over the safety of the monarch and the capital. . . .

The navy maintained by the emperors might seem inadequate to their greatness; but it was fully sufficient for every useful purpose of government. . . . To the Romans the ocean remained an object of terror rather than of curiosity; the whole extent of the Mediterranean, after the destruction of Carthage and the extirpation of the pirates, was included within their provinces. The policy of the emperors was directed only to preserve the peaceful dominion of that sea, and to protect the commerce of their subjects. With these moderate views, Augustus stationed two permanent fleets in the most convenient ports of Italy, the one at

Ravenna, on the Adriatic, the other at Misenum, in the bay of Naples. Experience seems at length to have convinced the ancients that, as soon as their galleys exceeded two, or at the most three ranks of oars, they were suited rather for vain pomp than for real service. Augustus himself, in the victory of Actium, had seen the superiority of his own light frigates (they were called Liburnians) over the lofty but unwieldy castles of his rival. Of these Liburnians he composed the two fleets of Ravenna and Misenum, destined to command, the one the eastern, the other the western division of the Mediterranean; and to each of the squadrons he attached a body of several thousand marines. Besides these two ports, which may be considered as the principal seats of the Roman navy, a very considerable force was stationed at Frejus, on the coast of Provence, and the Euxine was guarded by forty ships, and three thousand soldiers. To all these we add the fleet which preserved the communication between Gaul and Britain, and a great number of vessels constantly maintained on the Rhine and Danube, to harass the country, or to intercept the passage of the barbarians. If we review this general state of the Imperial forces, of the cavalry as well as infantry, of the legions, the auxiliaries, the guards, and the navy, the most liberal computation will not allow us to fix the entire establishment by sea and by land at more than four hundred and fifty thousand men. . . .

.   .   .   .   .

Till the privileges of Romans had been progressively extended to all the inhabitants of the empire, an important distinction was preserved between Italy and the provinces. The former was esteemed the centre of public unity, and the firm basis of the constitution. Italy claimed the birth, or at least the residence, of the emperors and the sen-

ate. The estates of the Italians were exempt from taxes, their persons from the arbitrary jurisdiction of governors. Their municipal corporations, formed after the perfect model of the capital, were intrusted, under the immediate eye of the supreme power, with the execution of the laws. From the foot of the Alps to the extremity of Calabria, all the natives of Italy were born citizens of Rome. Their partial distinctions were obliterated, and they insensibly coalesced into one great nation, united by language, manners, and civil institutions, and equal to the weight of a powerful empire. . . .

The provinces of the empire . . . were destitute of any public force of constitutional freedom. In Etruria, in Greece, and in Gaul, it was the first care of the senate to dissolve those dangerous confederacies which taught mankind that, as the Roman arms prevailed by division, they might be resisted by union. Those princes whom the ostentation of gratitude or generosity permitted for a while to hold a precarious sceptre were dismissed from their thrones, as soon as they had performed their appointed task of fashioning to the yoke the vanquished nations. The free states and cities which had embraced the cause of Rome were rewarded with a nominal alliance, and insensibly sunk into real servitude. The public authority was everywhere exercised by the ministers of the senate and of the emperors, and that authority was absolute and without control. But the same salutary maxims of government, which had secured the peace and obedience of Italy, were extended to the most distant conquests. A nation of Romans was gradually formed in the provinces, by the double expedient of introducing colonies, and of admitting the most faithful and deserving of the provincials to the freedom of Rome. "Wheresoever the Roman conquers, he inhabits," is a very just observation of Seneca, confirmed by history and experience. The natives of Italy, allured by pleasure or by interest, hastened to enjoy the advantages of victory; and we may remark that, about forty years after the reduction of Asia, eighty thousand Romans were massacred in one day by the cruel orders of Mithridates. These voluntary exiles were engaged for the most part in the occupations of commerce, agriculture, and the farm of the revenue. But after the legions were rendered permanent by the emperors, the provinces were peopled by a race of soldiers; and the veterans, whether they received the reward of their service in land or in money, usually settled with their families in the country where they had honourably spent their youth. Throughout the empire, but more particularly in the western parts, the most fertile districts and the most convenient situations were reserved for the establishment of colonies; some of which were of a civil and others of a military nature. In their manners and internal policy, the colonies formed a perfect representation of their great parent; and [as] they were soon endeared to the natives by the ties of friendship and alliance, they effectually diffused a reverence for the Roman name, and a desire which was seldom disappointed of sharing, in due time, its honours and advantages.[1] The municipal cities insensibly equalled the rank and splendour of the colonies; and in the reign of Hadrian it was disputed which was the preferable condition, of those societies which had issued from, or those which had been received into, the bosom of Rome. . . . Those of the provincials who were permitted to bear arms in the legions; those who exercised any civil employment; all, in a word, who performed any public service, or displayed any personal talents, were rewarded with a present, whose value was continually diminished by the increasing liberality of the emperors. Yet even in the age of the Antonines, when the freedom of the city had been bestowed on the greater number of their subjects, it was still accompanied with very solid advantages. The bulk of the people acquired, with that title, the benefit of the Roman laws, particularly in the interesting articles of marriage, testaments, and inheritances; and the road of fortune was open to those whose pretensions were seconded by favour or merit. The grandsons of the Gauls who had besieged Julius Caesar in Alesia commanded legions, governed provinces, and were admitted into the senate of Rome. Their ambition, instead of disturbing the tranquillity of the state, was intimately connected with its safety and greatness.

So sensible were the Romans of the influence of language over national manners, that is was their most serious care to extend, with the progress of their arms, the use of the Latin tongue. . . . The language of Virgil and Cicero, though with some inevitable mixture of corruption, was so universally adopted in Africa, Spain, Gaul, Britain, and Pannonia, that the faint traces of the Punic or Celtic idioms were preserved only in the mountains, or among the peasants. Education and study insensibly inspired the natives of those countries with the sentiments of Romans; and Italy gave fashions, as well as laws, to her Latin provincials. . . . The situation of the Greeks was very different from that of the barbarians. . . . They had too much taste to relinquish their language, and too much vanity to adopt any foreign institutions.

[1] Twenty-five colonies were settled in Spain . . . and nine in Britain, of which London, Colchester, Lincoln, Chester, Gloucester, and Bath, still remain considerable cities. . . .

. . . Nor was the influence of the Grecian language and sentiments confined to the narrow limits of that once celebrated country. Their empire, by the progress of colonies and conquest, had been diffused from the Hadriatic to the Euphrates and the Nile. Asia was covered with Greek cities, and the long reign of the Macedonian kings had introduced a silent revolution into Syria and Egypt. In their pompous courts those princes united the elegance of Athens with the luxury of the East, and the example of the court was imitated, at an humble distance, by the higher ranks of their subjects. Such was the general division of the Roman empire into the Latin and Greek languages. . . .

It is a just though trite observation, that victorious Rome was herself subdued by the arts of Greece. . . . Whilst they acknowledged the charms of the Greek, they asserted the dignity of the Latin tongue, and the exclusive use of the latter was inflexibly maintained in the administration of civil as well as military government. The two languages exercised at the same time their separate jurisdiction throughout the empire: the former, as the natural idiom of science; the latter, as the legal dialect of public transactions. Those who united letters with business were equally conversant with both; and it was almost impossible, in any province, to find a Roman subject, of a liberal education, who was at once a stranger to the Greek and to the Latin language.

.   .   .   .

. . . there still remained, in the centre of every province and of every family, an unhappy condition of men who endured the weight, without sharing the benefits, of society. In the free states of antiquity the domestic slaves were exposed to the wanton rigour of despotism. The perfect settlement of the Roman empire was preceded by ages of violence and rapine. The slaves consisted, for the most part, of barbarian captives, taken in thousands by the chance of war, purchased at a vile price, accustomed to a life of independence, and impatient to break and to revenge their fetters . . . when the principal nations of Europe, Asia, and Africa were united under the laws of one sovereign, the source of foreign supplies flowed with much less abundance, and the Romans were reduced to the milder but more tedious method of propagation. In their numerous families, and particularly in their country estates, they encouraged the marriage of their slaves. . . .

Hope, the best comfort of our imperfect condition, was not denied to the Roman slave; and, if he had any opportunity of making himself either useful or agreeable, he might very naturally expect that the diligence and fidelity of a few years would be rewarded with the inestimable gift of freedom. . . . It was a maxim of ancient jurisprudence, that a slave had not any country of his own; he acquired with his liberty an admission into the political society of which his patron was a member. The consequences of this maxim would have prostituted the privileges of the Roman city to a mean and promiscuous multitude. Some seasonable exceptions were therefore provided; and the honourable distinction was confined to such slaves only as, for just causes, and with the approbation of the magistrate, should receive a solemn and legal manumission. Even these chosen freedmen obtained no more than the private rights of citizens, and were rigourously excluded from civil or military honours. Whatever might be the merit or fortune of their sons, *they* likewise were esteemed unworthy of a seat in the senate; nor were the traces of a servile origin allowed to be completely obliterated till the third or fourth generation. . . .

Without interpreting, in their utmost strictness, the liberal appellations of legions and myriads,[2] we may venture to pronounce that the proportion of slaves, who were valued as property, was more considerable than that of servants, who can be computed only as an expense. The youths of a promising genius were instructed in the arts and sciences, and their price was ascertained by the degree of their skill and talents.[3] Almost every profession, either liberal[4] or mechanical, might be found in the household of an opulent senator. . . . It was more for the interest of the merchant or manufacturer to purchase than to hire his workmen; and in the country slaves were employed as the cheapest and most laborious instruments of agriculture. To confirm the general observation, and to display the multitude of slaves, we might allege a variety of particular instances. It was discovered, on a very melancholy occasion, that four hundred slaves were maintained in a single palace of Rome. The same number of four hundred belonged to an estate, which an African widow, . . resigned to her son, whilst she reserved for herself a much larger share of her property. A freedman, under the reign of Augustus, though his fortune had suffered great losses in the civil wars, left behind him three thousand six hundred yoke of oxen, two hundred and fifty thousand head of smaller cattle, and,

what was almost included in the description of cattle, four thousand one hundred and sixteen slaves.

The number of subjects who acknowledged the laws of Rome, of citizens, of provincials, and of slaves, cannot now be fixed with such a degree of accuracy as the importance of the object would deserve. . . .[5]

Among the innumerable monuments of architecture constructed by the Romans, how many have escaped the notice of history, how few have resisted the ravages of time and barbarism! And yet even the majestic ruins that are still scattered over Italy and the provinces would be sufficient to prove that those countries were once the seat of a polite and powerful empire. Their greatness alone, or their beauty, might deserve our attention; but they are rendered more interesting by two important circumstances, which connect the agreeable history of the arts with the more useful history of human manners. Many of those works were erected at private expense, and almost all were intended for public benefit.

It is natural to suppose that the greatest number, as well as the most considerable of the Roman edifices, were raised by the emperors, who possessed so unbounded a command both of men and money. Augustus was accustomed to boast that he had found his capital of brick, and that he had left it of marble. . . .[6]

[2] See Pliny (*Hist. Natur.* I xxxiii.) and Athenaeus (*Deipnosophist,* I vi. p. 272). The latter boldly asserts that he knew very many . . . Romans who possessed, not for use, but ostentation, ten and even twenty thousand slaves.

[3] A learned slave sold for many hundred pounds sterling; Atticus always bred and taught them himself. Cornel. Nepos in Vit. c. 13.

[4] Many of the Roman physicians were slaves. . . .

[5] . . . Merivale reckons the entire population under Augustus, "including both sexes, all ages and every class of inhabitants," at eighty-five millions, of which forty fall to the European, forty-five to the Asiatic provinces. . . .

[6] . . . Augustus built in Rome the temple and forum of Mars the Avenger; the Temple of Jupiter Tonans in the capitol; that of Apollo Palatine, with public libraries; the portico and basilica of Caius and Lucius; the porticoes of Livia and Octavia, and the theatre of Marcellus. The example of the sovereign was imitated by his ministers and

. . . These monuments of architecture, the property of the Roman people, were adorned with the most beautiful productions of Grecian painting and sculpture; and in the temple of Peace a very curious library was open to the curiosity of the learned. At a small distance from thence was situated the Forum of Trajan. It was surrounded with a lofty portico in the form of a quadrangle, into which four triumphal arches opened a noble and spacious entrance: in the centre arose a column of marble, whose height of one hundred and ten feet denoted the elevation of the hill that had been cut away. This column, which still subsists in its ancient beauty, exhibited an exact representation of the Dacian victories of its founder. The veteran soldier contemplated the story of his own campaigns, and, by an easy illusion of national vanity, the peaceful citizen associated himself to the honours of the triumph. All the other quarters of the capital, and all the provinces of the empire, were embellished by the same liberal spirit of public magnificence, and were filled with amphitheatres, theatres, temples, porticos, triumphal arches, baths and aqueducts, all variously conducive to the health, the devotion, and the pleasures of the meanest citizen. . . .

Ancient Italy is said to have contained eleven hundred and ninety-seven cities. . . . The spirit of improvement had passed the Alps, and been felt even in the woods of Britain, which were gradually cleared away to open a free space for convenient and elegant habitations. York was the seat of government; London was already enriched by commerce; and Bath was celebrated for the salutary effects of its medicinal waters. Gaul could boast of her generals; and his friend Agrippa left behind him the immortal monument of the Pantheon.

twelve hundred cities; and, though, in the northern parts, many of them, without excepting Paris itself, were little more than the rude and imperfect townships of a rising people, the southern provinces imitated the wealth and elegance of Italy. . . . Spain [could boast of] three hundred and sixty cities. . . . Three hundred African cities had once acknowledged the authority of Carthage, nor is it likely that their numbers diminished under the administration of the emperors: Carthage itself rose with new splendour from its ashes. . . . Under the reign of the Caesars, the proper Asia alone contained five hundred populous cities. . . . The capitals of Syria and Egypt held a still superior rank in the empire: Antioch and Alexandria looked down with disdain on a crowd of dependent cities, and yielded with reluctance to the majesty of Rome itself.

All these cities were connected with each other, and with the capital, by the public highways, which, issuing from the Forum of Rome, traversed Italy, pervaded the provinces, and were terminated only by the frontiers of the empire. If we carefully trace the distance from the wall of Antoninus to Rome, and from thence to Jerusalem, it will be found that the great chain of communication, from the north-west to the south-east point of the empire, was drawn out to the length of four thousand and eighty Roman miles. . . .[7]

[7] The following Itinerary may serve to convey some idea of the direction of the road, and of the distance between the principal towns. I. From the wall of Antoninus to York, 222 Roman miles. II. London 227. III. Rhutupiae or Sandwich 67. IV. The navigation to Boulogne 45. V. Rheims 174. VI. Lyons 330. VII. Milan 324. VIII. Rome 426. IX. Brundusium 360. X. The navigation to Dyrrachium 40. XI. Byzantium 711. XII. Ancyra 283. XIII. Tarsus 301. XIV. Antioch 141. XV. Tyre 252. XVI. Jerusalem 168. In all 4080 Roman, or 3740 English miles. . . .

They united the subjects of the most distant provinces by an easy and familiar intercourse; but their primary object has been to facilitate the marches of the legions; nor was any country considered as completely subdued, till it had been rendered, in all its parts, pervious to the arms and authority of the conqueror. The advantage of receiving the earliest intelligence, and of conveying their orders with celerity, induced the emperors to establish, throughout their extensive domains, the regular institution of posts. Houses were everywhere erected at the distance only of five or six miles; each of them was constantly provided with forty horses, and, by the help of these relays, it was easy to travel an hundred miles in a day along the Roman roads. The use of the posts was allowed to those who claimed it by an Imperial mandate; but, though originally intended for the public service, it was sometimes indulged to the business or conveniency of private citizens. Nor was the communication of the Roman empire less free and open by sea than it was by land. The provinces surrounded and enclosed the Mediterranean; and Italy, in the shape of an immense promontory, advanced into the midst of that great lake. The coasts of Italy are, in general, destitute of safe harbours; but human industry had corrected the deficiencies of nature; and the artificial port of Ostia, in particular, situated at the mouth of the Tiber, and formed by the Emperor Claudius, was an useful monument of Roman greatness. From this port, which was only sixteen miles from the capital, a favourable breeze frequently carried vessels in seven days to the columns of Hercules, and in nine or ten to Alexandria in Egypt.

. . . Under the protection of an established government, the productions of happier climates and the industry of more civilized nations were gradually introduced into the western countries of Europe; and the natives were encouraged, by an open and profitable commerce, to multiply the former as well as to improve the latter. . . . 1. Almost all the flowers, the herbs, and the fruits that grow in our European gardens are of foreign extraction, which, in many cases, is betrayed even by their names: the apple was a native of Italy, and, when the Romans had tasted the richer flavour of the apricot, the peach, the pomegranate, the citron, and the orange, they contented themselves with applying to all these new fruits the common denomination of apple, discriminating them from each other by the additional epithet of their country. 2. In the time of Homer, the vine grew wild in the island of Sicily and most probably in the adjacent continent; but it was not improved by the skill, nor did it afford a liquor grateful to the taste, of the savage inhabitants. A thousand years afterwards, Italy could boast that, of the fourscore most generous and celebrated wines, more than two-thirds were produced from her soil. The blessing was soon communicated to the Narbonnese province of Gaul; but so intense was the cold to the north of the Cevennes, that, in the time of Strabo, it was thought impossible to ripen the grapes in those parts of Gaul. This difficulty, however, was gradually vanquished; and there is some reason to believe that the vineyards of Burgundy are as old as the age of the Antonines. 3. The olive, in the western world, followed the progress of peace, of which it was considered as the symbol. Two centuries after the foundation of Rome, both Italy and Africa were strangers to that useful plant; it was naturalized in those countries; and at length carried into the heart of Spain and Gaul. The timid errors of the ancients that it required a certain degree of heat, and could only flourish in the neighbourhood of the sea, were insensibly exploded by industry and experience. 4. The cultivation of flax was transported from Egypt to Gaul, and enriched the whole country, however it might impoverish the particular lands on which it was sown. 5. The use of artificial grasses became familiar to the farmers both of Italy and the provinces, particularly the Lucerne, which derived its name and origin from Media. The assured supply of wholesome and plentiful food for the cattle during winter multiplied the number of the flocks and herds, which in their turn contributed to the fertility of the soil. To all these improvements may be added an assiduous attention to mines and fisheries. . . .

The most remote countries of the ancient world were ransacked to supply the pomp and delicacy of Rome. The forest of Scythia afforded some valuable furs. Amber was brought over land from the shores of the Baltic to the Danube; and the barbarians were astonished at the price which they received in exchange for so useless a commodity. There was a considerable demand for Babylonian carpets, and other manufactures of the East; but the most important and unpopular branch of foreign trade was carried on with Arabia and India. Every year, about the time of the summer solstice, a fleet of an hundred and twenty vessels sailed from Myos-hormos, a port of Egypt, on the Red Sea. By the periodical assistance of the monsoons, they traversed the ocean in about forty days. The coast of Malabar, or the island of Ceylon, was the usual term of their navigation, and it was in those markets that the merchants from the more remote countries of Asia expected their arrival. The return of the fleet of Egypt was fixed to the months

of December or January; and as soon as their rich cargo had been transported on the backs of camels from the Red Sea to the Nile, and had descended that river as far as Alexandria, it was poured, without delay, into the capital of the empire. The objects of oriental traffic were splendid and trifling: silk, a pound of which was esteemed not inferior in value to a pound of gold; precious stones, among which the pearl claimed the first rank after the diamond; and a variety of aromatics, that were consumed in religious worship and the pomp of funerals. The labour and risk of the voyage was rewarded with almost incredible profit; but the profit was made upon Roman subjects, and a few individuals were enriched at the expense of the Public. As the natives of Arabia and India were contented with the productions and manufactures of their own country, silver, on the side of the Romans, was the principal, if not the only, instrument of commerce. It was a complaint worthy of the gravity of the senate, that, in the purchase of female ornaments, the wealth of the state was irrecoverably given away to foreign and hostile nations. The annual loss is computed, by a writer of an inquisitive but censorious temper, at upwards of eight hundred thousand pounds sterling. . . .

.   .   .   .

Every barrier of the Roman constitution had been levelled by the vast ambition of the dictator; every fence had been extirpated by the cruel hand of the triumvir. After the victory of Actium, the fate of the Roman world depended on the will of Octavianus, surnamed Caesar by his uncle's adoption, and afterwards Augustus, by the flattery of the senate. The conqueror was at the head of forty-four veteran legions, conscious of their own strength and of the weakness of the constitution, habituated during twenty years' civil war to every act of blood and violence, and passionately devoted to the house of Caesar, from whence alone they had received and expected the most lavish rewards. The provinces long oppressed by the ministers of the republic, sighed for the government of a single person, who would be the master, not the accomplice, of those petty tyrants. The people of Rome, viewing with a secret pleasure the humiliation of the aristocracy, demanded only bread and public shows, and were supplied with both by the liberal hand of Augustus. The rich and polite Italians, who had almost universally embraced the philosophy of Epicurus, enjoyed the present blessings of ease and tranquillity, and suffered not the pleasing dream to be interrupted by the memory of their old tumultuous freedom. With its power, the senate had lost its dignity; many of the most noble families were extinct. The republicans of spirit and ability had perished in the field of battle, or in the proscription. The door of the assembly had been designedly left open for a mixed multitude of more than a thousand persons, who reflected disgrace upon their rank, instead of deriving honour from it.

The reformation of the senate, was one of the first steps in which Augustus laid aside the tyrant, and professed himself the father of his country. He was elected censor; and, in concert with his faithful Agrippa, he examined the list of the senators, expelled a few members, whose vices or whose obstinacy required a public example, persuaded near two hundred to prevent the shame of an expulsion by a voluntary retreat, raised the qualification of a senator to about ten thousand pounds, created a sufficient number of patrician families, and accepted for himself the honourable title of Prince of the Senate, which had always been bestowed by the censors on the citizen the most eminent for his honours and services. But, whilst he thus restored the dignity, he destroyed the independence of the senate. . . .

. . . . .

Without any violation of the principles of the constitution, the general of the Roman armies might receive and exercise an authority almost despotic over the soldiers, the enemies, and the subjects of the republic. With regard to the soldiers, the jealousy of freedom had, even from the earliest ages of Rome, given way to the hopes of conquest, and a just sense of military discipline. The dictator, or consul, had a right to command the service of the Roman youth, and to punish an obstinate or cowardly disobedience by the most severe and ignominious penalties, by striking the offender out of the list of citizens, by confiscating his property, and by selling his person into slavery. The most sacred rights of freedom, confirmed by the Porcian and Sempronian laws, were suspended by the military engagement. In his camp the general exercised an absolute power of life and death; his jurisdiction was not confined by any forms of trial or rules of proceeding, and the execution of the sentence was immediate and without appeal. The choice of the enemies of Rome was regularly decided by the legislative authority. The most important resolutions of peace and war were seriously debated in the senate, and solemnly ratified by the people. But when the arms of the legions were carried to a great distance from Italy, the generals assumed the liberty of directing them against whatever people, and in whatever manner, they judged most advantageous for the public service. It was from the success, not from the justice, of their enterprises, that they expected the honours of a triumph. In the use of victory, especially after they were no longer controlled by the commissioners of the senate, they exercised the most unbounded despotism. When Pompey commanded in the East, he rewarded his soldiers and allies, dethroned princes, divided kingdoms, founded colonies, and distributed the treasures of Mithridates. On his return to Rome he obtained, by a single act of the senate and people, the universal ratification of all his proceedings. Such was the power over the soldiers, and over the enemies of Rome, which was either granted to, or assumed by, the generals of the republic. They were, at the same time, the governors, or rather monarchs, of the conquered provinces, united the civil with the military character, administered justice as well as the finances, and exercised both the executive and legislative power of the state.

From what has been already observed in the first chapter of this work, some notion may be formed of the armies and provinces thus intrusted to the ruling hand of Augustus. But, as it was impossible that he could personally command the legions of so many distant frontiers, he was indulged by the senate, as Pompey had already been, in the permission of devolving the execution of his great office on a sufficient number of lieutenants. In rank and authority these officers seemed not inferior to the ancient proconsuls; but their station was dependent and precarious. They received and held their commissions at the will of a superior, to whose *auspicious* influence the merit of their action was legally attributed. They were the representatives of the emperor. The emperor alone was the general of the republic, and his jurisdiction, civil as well as military, extended over all the conquests of Rome. It was some satisfaction, however, to the senate that he always delegated his power to the members of their body. The imperial lieutenants were of con-

sular or praetorian dignity; the legions were commanded by senators, and the praefecture of Egypt was the only important trust committed to a Roman knight.

Within six days after Augustus had been compelled to accept so very liberal a grant, he resolved to gratify the pride of the senate by an easy sacrifice. He represented to them that they had enlarged his powers, even beyond that degree which might be required by the melancholy condition of the times. They had not permitted him to refuse the laborious command of the armies and the frontiers; but he must insist on being allowed to restore the more peaceful and secure provinces to the mild administration of the civil magistrate. In the division of the provinces Augustus provided for his own power and for the dignity of the republic. The proconsuls of the senate, particularly those of Asia, Greece, and Africa, enjoyed a more honourable character than the lieutenants of the emperor, who commanded in Gaul or Syria. The former were attended by lictors, the latter by soldiers. A law was passed that, wherever the emperor was present, his extraordinary commission should supersede the ordinary jurisdiction of the governor; a custom was introduced, that the new conquests belonged to the imperial portion; and it was soon discovered that the authority of the *Prince,* the favourite epithet of Augustus, was the same in every part of the empire.

In return for this imaginary concession, Augustus obtained an important privilege, which rendered him master of Rome and Italy. By a dangerous exception to the ancient maxims, he was authorized to preserve his military command, supported by a numerous body of guards, even in time of peace, and in the heart of the capital. His command, indeed, was confined to those citizens who were engaged in the service by the military oath; but such was the propensity of the Romans to servitude, that the oath was voluntarily taken by the magistrates, the senators, and the equestrian order, till the homage of flattery was insensibly converted into an annual and solemn protestation of fidelity.

Although Augustus considered a military force as the firmest foundation, he wisely rejected it as a very odious instrument, of government. It was more agreeable to his temper, as well as to his policy, to reign under the venerable names of ancient magistracy, and artfully to collect in his own person all the scattered rays of civil jurisdiction. With this view, he permitted the senate to confer upon him, for his life, the powers of the consular and tribunitian offices, which were, in the same manner, continued to all his successors. The consuls had succeeded to the kings of Rome, and represented the dignity of the state. They superintended the ceremonies of religion, levied and commanded the legions, gave audience to foreign ambassadors, and presided in the assemblies both of the senate and people. The general control of the finances was intrusted to their care; and, though they seldom had leisure to administer justice in person, they were considered as the supreme guardians of law, equity, and the public peace. Such was their ordinary jurisdiction; but, whenever the senate empowered the first magistrate to consult the safety of the commonwealth, he was raised by that degree above the laws, and exercised, in the defence of liberty, a temporary despotism. The character of the tribunes was, in every respect, different from that of the consuls. The appearance of the former was modest and humble; but their persons were sacred and inviolable. Their force was suited rather for opposition than for action. They were instituted to defend the oppressed, to pardon offences, to arraign the enemies of the people, and, when they judged it necessary, to stop, by a single word, the whole machine of government. As long as the republic subsisted, the dangerous influence which either the consul or the tribune might derive from their respective jurisdiction was diminished by several important restrictions. Their authority expired with the year in which they were elected; the former office was divided between two, the latter among ten persons; and, as both in their private and public interest they were adverse to each other, their mutual conflicts contributed, for the most part, to strengthen rather than to destroy the balance of the constitution. But when the consular and tribunitian powers were united, when they were vested for life in a single person, when the general of the army was, at the same time, the minister of the senate and the representative of the Roman people, it was impossible to resist the exercise, nor was it easy to define the limits, of his imperial prerogative.

To these accumulated honours the policy of Augustus soon added the splendid as well as important dignities of supreme pontiff, and of censor. By the former he acquired the management of the religion, and by the latter a legal inspection over the manners and fortunes, of the Roman people. If so many distinct and independent powers did not exactly unite with each other, the complaisance of the senate was prepared to supply every deficiency by the most ample and extraordinary concessions. The emperors, as the first ministers of the republic, were exempted from the obligation and penalty of many inconvenient laws: they were authorized to convoke the senate, to make several motions in the same day, to recommend candidates for the honours of the state, to enlarge the bounds of the city, to employ the revenue at their discretion, to declare peace and war, to ratify treaties; and by a most comprehensive clause, they were empowered to execute whatsoever they should judge advantageous to the empire, and agreeable to the majesty of things private or public, human or divine.

When all the various powers of executive government were committed to the *Imperial magistrate,* the ordinary magistrates of the commonwealth languished in obscurity, without vigour, and almost without business. The names and forms of the ancient administration were preserved by Augustus with the most anxious care. The usual number of consuls, praetors, and tribunes were annually invested with their respective ensigns of office, and continued to discharge some of their least important functions. Those honours still attracted the vain ambition of the Romans; and the emperors themselves, though invested for life with the powers of the consulship, frequently aspired to the title of that annual dignity, which they condescended to share with the most illustrious of their fellow-citizens. In the election of these magistrates, the people, during the reign of Augustus, were permitted to expose all the inconveniences of a wild democracy. That artful prince, instead of discovering the least symptom of impatience, humbly solicited their suffrages for himself or his friends, and scrupulously practised all the duties of an ordinary candidate. But we may venture to ascribe to his councils the first measure of the succeeding reign, by which the elections were transferred to the senate. The assemblies of the people were for ever abolished, and the emperors were delivered from a dangerous multitude, who, without restoring liberty, might have disturbed, and perhaps endangered, the established government.

By declaring themselves the protectors of the people, Marius and Caesar had subverted the constitution of their country. But as soon as the senate had been humbled and disarmed, such an assembly, consisting of five or six hundred persons, was found a much more tractable and useful instrument of dominion. It was on the dignity of the senate that Augustus and his successors founded their new empire; and they affected, on every occasion, to adopt the language and principles of Patricians. In the administration of their own powers, they frequently consulted the great national council, and *seemed* to refer to its decision the most important concerns of peace and war. Rome, Italy, and the internal provinces were subject to the immediate jurisdiction of the senate. With regard to civil objects, it was the supreme court of appeal; with regard to criminal matters, a tribunal, constituted for the trial of all offences that were committed by men in any public station, or that affected the peace and majesty of the Roman people. The exercise of the judicial power became the most frequent and serious occupation of the senate; and the important causes that were pleaded before them afforded a last refuge to the spirit of ancient eloquence. As a council of state, and as a court of justice, the senate possessed very considerable prerogatives; but in its legislative capacity, in which it was supposed virtually to represent the people, the rights of sovereignty were acknowledged to reside in that assembly. Every power was derived from their authority, every law was ratified by their sanction. Their regular meetings were held on three stated days in every month, the Calends, the Nones, and the Ides. The debates were conducted with decent freedom; and the emperors themselves, who gloried in the name of senators, sat, voted, and divided with their equals.

To resume, in a few words, the system of the Imperial government, as it was instituted by Augustus, . . . it may be defined an absolute monarchy disguised by the forms of a commonwealth. The masters of the Roman world surrounded their throne with darkness, concealed their irresistible strength, and humbly professed themselves the accountable ministers of the senate, whose supreme decrees they dictated and obeyed.

The face of the court corresponded with the forms of the administration. The emperors, if we except those tyrants whose capricious folly violated every law of nature and decency, disdained that pomp and ceremony which might offend their countrymen, but could add nothing to their real power. In all the offices of life, they affected to confound themselves with their subjects, and maintained with them an equal intercourse of visits and entertainments. Their habit, their palace, their table, were suited only to the rank of an opulent senator. Their family, however numerous or splendid, was composed entirely of their domestic slaves and freedmen. Augustus or Trajan would have blushed at employing the meanest of the Romans in those menial offices which, in the household and bedchamber of a limited monarch, are so eagerly solicited by the proudest nobles of Britain.

The deification of the emperors . . . was easily transferred from the kings to the governors of Asia; and the Roman magistrates were adored as provincial deities, with the pomp of altars and temples, of festivals and sacrifices. It was natural that the emperors should not refuse what the proconsuls had accepted . . .

. . . .

In elective monarchies, the vacancy of the throne is a moment big with danger and mischief. The Roman emperors, desirous to spare the legions that interval of suspense, and the temptation of an irregular choice, invested their designed successor with so large a share of present power, as should enable him, after their decease, to assume the remainder without suffering the empire to perceive the change of masters. Thus Augustus, after all his fairer prospects had been snatched from him by untimely deaths, rested his last hopes on Tiberius, obtained for his adopted son the censorial and tribunitian powers, and dictated a law, by which the future prince was invested with an authority equal to his own over the provinces and the armies. . . .

. . . .

If a man were called to fix the period in the history of the world during which the condition of the human race was most happy and prosperous, he would, without hesitation, name that which elapsed from the death of Domitian to the accession of Commodus. The vast extent of the Roman empire was governed by absolute power, under the guidance of virtue and wisdom. The armies were restrained by the firm but gentle hand of four successive emperors, whose characters and authority commanded involuntary respect. The forms of the civil administration were carefully preserved by Nerva, Trajan, Hadrian, and the Antonines, who delighted in the image of liberty, and were pleased with considering themselves as the accountable ministers of the laws. Such princes deserved the honour of restoring the republic, had the Romans of their days been capable of enjoying a rational freedom.

The labours of these monarchs were over-paid by the immense reward that inseparably waited on their success; by the honest pride of virtue, and by the exquisite delight of beholding the general happiness of which they were the authors. A just but melancholy reflection embittered, however, the noblest of human enjoyments. They must often have recollected the instability of a happiness which depended on the character of a single man. The fatal moment was perhaps approaching, when some licentious youth, or some jealous tyrant, would abuse, to the destruction, that absolute power which they had exerted for the benefit of their people. The ideal restraints of the senate and the laws might serve to display the virtues, they could never correct the vices, of the emperor. The military force was a blind and irresistible instrument of oppression; and the corruption of Roman manners would always supply flatterers eager to applaud, and ministers prepared to serve, the fear or the avarice, the lust or the cruelty, of their masters.

These gloomy apprehensions had been already justified by the experience of the Romans. The annals of the emperors exhibit a strong and various picture of human nature, which we should vainly seek among the mixed and doubtful characters of modern history. In the conduct of those monarchs we may trace the utmost lines of vice and virtue; the most exalted perfection and the meanest degeneracy of our own species. The golden age of Trajan and the Antonines had been preceded by an age of iron. It is almost superfluous to enumerate the unworthy successors of Augustus. Their unparalleled vices, and the splendid theatre on which they were acted, have saved them from oblivion. The dark unrelenting Tiberius, the furious Caligula, the stupid Claudius, the profligate and cruel Nero, the beastly Vitellius, and the timid inhuman Domitian, are condemned to everlasting infamy. During fourscore

years (excepting only the short and doubtful respite of Vespasian's reign), Rome groaned beneath an unremitting tyranny, which exterminated the ancient families of the republic, and was fatal to almost every virtue and every talent that arose in that unhappy period.

Under the reign of these monsters the slavery of the Romans was accompanied with two peculiar circumstances, the one occasioned by their former liberty, the other by their extensive conquests, which rendered their condition more wretched than that of the victims of tyranny in any other age or country. From these causes were derived, 1. The exquisite sensibility of the sufferers; and 2. The impossibility of escaping from the hand of the oppressor.

. . . the empire of the Romans filled the world, and, when that empire fell into the hands of a single person, the world became a safe and dreary prison for his enemies. The slave of Imperial despotism, whether he was condemned to drag his gilded chain in Rome and the senate, or to wear out a life of exile on the barren rock of Seriphus, or the frozen banks of the Danube, accepted his fate in silent despair. To resist was fatal, and it was impossible to fly. On every side he was encompassed with a vast extent of sea and land, which he could never hope to traverse without being discovered, seized, and restored to his irritated master. Beyond the frontiers, his anxious view could discover nothing, except the ocean, inhospitable deserts, hostile tribes of barbarians, of fierce manners and unknown language, or dependent kings, who would gladly purchase the emperor's protection by the sacrifice of an obnoxious fugitive. "Wherever you are," said Cicero to the exiled Marcellus, "remember that you are equally within the power of the conqueror."

Gibbon was not an eyewitness, but he had read every available document on the organization of the Roman Empire. Even so, we are not too clear about who did what to whom, where, when, why, and in what fashion. His six-volume work is subjective from start to finish. He wanted to know why Rome "fell." In his day the information which he needed was not available. He did not know that literate civilization had begun some two and a half millenia before Rome in the valleys of Mesopotamia and Egypt, that Crete had possessed a brilliant maritime civilization long before Greece, and that the general march of civilization was moving westward and northward, just as the center of population of the United States has been shifting westward for many years.

His reference on p. 540 to the "unwarlike" Ethiopians and Yemenites is evidence of his ignorance of these peoples. Had the Romans reached them, the legions would have met some brisk resistance. From the geographical standpoint it is interesting that the northern boundary of the Roman Empire follows more or less the 32° F. winter isotherm; that is why Britain was habitable by Romans while Scythia was not, although the latter, attainable by sea, was actually more accessible.

With his eighteenth-century horror of democracy, Gibbon considered the granting of Roman citizenship to outsiders a cause of decadence. The citizenship of Rome was easier to get than that of Athens. From the long-range view, it is hard to see that either state survived the longer because of its attitude toward citizenship.

The Roman Army described by Gibbon was the largest and best disciplined standing army which had existed until its time. However, owing to the lag in technological advancement due to the slave system, the army was no better equipped than were its barbarian enemies, except in siege engines. Its real superiority lay in organization, discipline, and uniformity of equipment. The Roman soldiers were full-time specialists, drilled to the state in which obedience to an order was a conditioned reflex. This army included work corps, to level the ground, dig ditches, etc., called by Gibbon "pioneers," a term still used by the British army. One legion with its auxiliaries, including all kinds of troops and specialists, amounted to 12,500 men, almost exactly the size of a modern streamlined division. The total Roman armed forces, including army and navy, came to about 450,000 men, small by modern standards, but adequate to police an empire of 85,000,000 people. There was thus one soldier or sailor to less than every 200 civilians. The branch of the army known as the Praetorian Guard was a corps of legionaries recruited from outside Italy. They were the private army of the emperor, and owed allegiance to him alone, like the Senegalese fighting for the French in North Africa. With the Praetorian Guard as the sole military force in the capital, the emperor was able to enforce his ideas. At the same time the Praetorian Guard was able to choose the emperor. One is reminded of Hitler's SS during the last war.

The Roman empire was a huge superstate. It was a complex political institution with all sorts of sub-institutions, but it was not as well integrated as the Athenian state described by Aristotle. If it had been, that would have been a strange circumstance. In the first place, the lines of communication were far too extended. Only by the most efficient use of the existing system of transport and communication could the central government keep in touch with the outlying provinces. That is why it was more efficient to have two capitals, at Rome and at Byzantium. The division into the Eastern and Western empires was merely a reflection of the failure of the Romans to invent new techniques of transport and communication. If they had suddenly acquired jeeps and planes, no such split would have been needed.

Many reasons have been put forward to explain the gradual political deterioration of the Roman Empire. Simkhovitch very practically lays much of it to the exhaustion of the soil and the need to bring more and more food from greater and greater distances.* Another reason, which is probably even more valid, lies in the insistence of the Romans on using slave labor, which inhibited the adoption of devices for the utilization of natural power. Certainly inventive genius was not lacking in the empire. Short-sighted politicians were more interested in the maintenance of equilibrium than in the development of techniques which would permit its re-establishment on a new and higher level. We have similar problems to cope with; petroleum pipe lines have been abandoned because they interfered with the much less efficient shipment of gasoline by tanker from Texas to New York. The British held up the development of motor vehicles for nearly a century to prevent competition with the horse-drawn coach lines.

The early Christians saw the fallacy in slave labor, and admitted all human beings into the brotherhood of Christ. It took them a long time to make these ideas popular. The torch of civilization passed to Byzantium and Alexandria, to the Arabs, who also believed in human brotherhood, to Italy once more, and Spain, to a liberated western Europe, to England, and America. Much has been written about the progress of civilization from one center to another, and much more remains to be said, but this is not the place for it. I have tried to lead you through the maze of increasing complexity in human institutions, from the level of an ape to that of an imperial Roman.

We have covered six arbitrarily determined stages or levels of institutional complexity. All of them exist in one place or another at the present day. Each one of them had to be attained for the first time somewhere. At the "dawn of history," 3000 B.C., the sixth stage had already been reached in Egypt and Mesopotamia.

The sixth stage involved a high development of the political institution. Economic institutions were stalemated for millenia, for a simple reason—goods were still being made by hand. This meant that in most parts of the world people still made most of their tools, containers, and garments locally. Processed articles brought from centers of industry fell mostly into two classes: metal for tools, and luxury objects.

Two inventions or diffusions broke the 4500-year log jam. These were cannon mounted on ships and the mariner's compass. The Portuguese, Spanish, and Italians developed and used these during the fifteenth century. The stimulus was the closing of the trade route to the Indies by the Turks. Ships armed with cannon had to be designed so as to permit broadsides without capsizing. Sails had to be improved. Columbus discovered America; Magellan circumnavigated the globe. The world was one, in the most rudimentary sense, for the first time.

So great was the potential trade which resulted from the opening up of the Americas, the Indies, and China to Europeans that constant pressure was exerted on the craftsmen to produce more and more goods. Power machinery, instead of

* Simkhovitch, V. G., "Rome's Fall Reconsidered," in *Toward the Understanding of Jesus.* New York, The Macmillan Co. 1937.

throwing people out of work and disturbing equilibrium, actually made work far easier, and restored equilibrium on a new level. With the use of power machinery, the division of labor in industry increased. Complex economic institutions arose for the first time in history with the formation of the East India Companies. With the discovery that coke could replace charcoal for smelting and the resulting abundance of iron and steel for machinery, processing institutions also grew complex.

The slave labor of the Romans was replaced by the factory labor of the early Industrial Revolution. The disturbances caused by the exploitation of cheap labor during the nineteenth century are not over yet, but seem to be on the way out. The use of newly discovered sources of energy is gradually releasing Americans and Europeans from too much monotonous and solitary work. But the time has not yet come when we can sit back and censure the Romans for their inhumanity to slaves. We too have exploited the labor of millions of people in Asia, Oceania, and Africa; we have denied the opportunities of education and self-government to the yellow and brown and black people, who have been kept at menial tasks for generations. As long as these people are denied their heritage as full-fledged human beings, our chances of survival will be no greater than those of the Romans. No world can survive "half slave and half free."

Index

563